CW00602916

501

GREAT PLACES TO STAY

501
GREAT PLACES TO STAY

Bounty Books

Publisher: Polly Manguel

Editorial & Design Manager: Emma Hill

Designer: Ron Callow/Design 23

Production Manager: Neil Randles

Production Controller: Allison Gonsalves

First published in Great Britain in 2012 by Bounty Books,
a division of Octopus Publishing Group Limited,
Endeavour House,
189 Shaftesbury Avenue,
London WC2H 8JY
www.octopusbooks.co.uk

An Hachette UK Company
www.hachette.co.uk

A CIP catalogue record is available from the British Library

ISBN: 978-0-753723-09-8

Printed and bound in China

Please note: We now know that political situations arise very quickly and a city or country that was quite safe a short time ago can suddenly become a 'no-go' area. Please check with the relevant authorities before booking tickets and travelling if you think there could be a problem.

The seasons given in this book relate to the relevant hemisphere. Be sure to check that you visit at the correct time.

All efforts have been made to trace the copyright holders prior to publication, but this has not always been possible. If notified, the publisher would be pleased to rectify any errors or omissions at the earliest opportunity.

Key to Cost:

Budget up to $100
Reasonable $100-250
Expensive $250-600
Astronomical $600+

These figures tend to be for one, so it's worth pointing out that
a) two sharing will generally be cheaper than the indicated cost level
b) there are almost always deals to be done that can reduce the indicated cost level (on line or direct with the venue).

Contents

Introduction

In 1873, When Jules Verne wrote the adventure travel book *Around the World in 80 Days*, the gripping tale of Phileas Fogg's dramatic global circumnavigation captured the public's imagination. It was then barely two generations since the vast majority of people had horizons limited by the round-trip distance that could be walked in a day. But, with the help of burgeoning railway networks and increasingly reliable international travel, the Victorians quickly came to appreciate one of life's great truths – travelling as widely as possible to stay at interesting places whilst exploring the world and its wonders is one of the most exciting and rewarding activities known to humankind.

The ability to relax in interesting and sometimes exotic locations was once the exclusive province of rich (and often rather idle) travellers. The leisurely Grand Tour was a cultural 'must' for Europe's upper classes, who would stay in fine apartments or luxury hotels where their every whim could be (and was) catered for. But times have changed, and growing prosperity means that tourism has become a major cornerstone of the global economy, enjoyed each year by countless millions of get-up-and-go people. A huge variety of stimulating places to stay can be found almost everywhere in the world, catering for every budget and taste, and if there's a problem in selecting that dream destination it's that today's enquiring traveller is spoilt for choice.

That's where this book comes in. It features a wonderful selection of appealing places to stay. How about an underwater bedroom where the fish are looking in at you, or a treehouse you share with forest birds? An old bullring in Mexico or traditional *riad* in Morocco? A magical safari camp in the Galapagos or vintage railway carriage in the English countryside? A five-star hotel in one of the world's great capitals or mud hut in northern India? An island paradise in the sunny Pacific or ice hotel inside the Arctic Circle? An eco-resort on Easter Island or *ger* in the Gobi Desert? A haunted hotel in New Mexico or castle in Ireland? A New England colonial inn or 15th-century manor house in the English countryside? A Victorian steamship in Peru or cave in Spain? A Napoleonic fortress in France or windmill in Greece? A paper house in Japan or working cattle station in the Australian outback? A *tipi* in the Canadian wilderness or jungle lodge in South America? A (grounded) jumbo jet or old gaol complete with cells?

They're all to be found in these pages, along with a whole lot more that is bound to stimulate the imagination. Of course, you don't have to restrict yourself to the actual venues described, for these can equally well serve as a pointer to the sort of dream holiday accommodation that's out there, just waiting to be discovered and enjoyed. And remember that tourism not only brings prosperity to established destinations, but also helps to bring economic activity to undeveloped corners of the globe with nothing to declare but their unspoilt natural assets. Hand-in-hand with that goes growing awareness that it's vital to conserve the very things that attract visitors in the first place. This has led to the rise of sustainable tourism that leaves the lightest possible human footprint on the environment, using as few unrenewable resources as possible. Many of the places featured in this book reflect this accelerating trend, offering impeccable 'green' credentials that will appeal mightily to the increasing band of eco-travellers.

But perhaps the last words should be reserved for those who think they've stayed in every sort of accommodation that's out there and still want more. Those words are 'watch this space'. For the restless human spirit is always seeking new frontiers, and before very much longer any list of exciting places to stay will have to include a pressurized cabin beyond the final frontier, as commercial space trips move from drawing board to launch pad. In the meantime, exploring the myriad of fascinating possibilities in our wonderful world with a little help from *501 Great Places to Stay* will lead mere terrestrials to some of the most rewarding destinations to be found . . . anywhere and everywhere on this planet!

AMERICAS
& THE
CARIBBEAN

Hôtel de Glace

Looking for something completely different? Read on! Since 2001, just a few minutes from downtown Quebec City, a truly extraordinary structure has arisen every December. This is the Hôtel de Glace, North America's first ice hotel, offering an interesting opportunity to sleep on a bed of solid ice, in a building made of solid ice where glasses in the bar are made of . . . solid ice. Located in a beautiful setting at the foot of Mount Tourbillion, the ice hotel gives adventurous guests an opportunity to spend a warm and cosy night in a magical winter castle.

The hotel offers four levels of luxury. In ascending order these are: the Northern Discovery Package, the Adventure Package, the Romantic Getaway Package and Ultimate Getaway Package. Accommodation ranges from intimate regular rooms up to individually themed suites with fireplaces and private spas. And those ice beds aren't quite as daunting as they may sound, for each comes with a conventional mattress and a warm-as-toast nordic sleeping bag. Better still, each package includes a room and meals at a nearby hotel of conventional construction, where luggage may be left and hot showers blissfully taken. All guests also receive a full briefing to ensure that they know everything they need to know to avoid frostbite and enjoy a comfortable stay.

If you can't afford to stay the night at the Hôtel de Glace (or suffer from an afraid-of-freezing-to-death-in-an-ice-bed phobia), it's possible to join the many like-minded wimps who simply turn up to have a look at this dazzling creation. And any couple wanting to tie the knot in one of the world's most unusual venues need look no further than the hotel's vaulted ice chapel – a white wedding absolutely guaranteed.

WHERE:
On the outskirts of Quebec City
COST:
Expensive (but those who book well in advance, including families, can obtain good discounts)
BEST TIME OF YEAR:
The hotel only opens from January to March (after which it simply melts away).
DON'T MISS:
A fascinating afternoon guided tour of this beautiful but ephemeral work of art; the Nordic Area's hot tubs and sauna under the burning winter stars; a whizz down the hotel's grand ice slide
THINGS TO DO:
Simply chilling out is good. But there are rewarding activities nearby from alpine skiing, snowmobiling and dog sledding through to the thrilling Duferrin Terrace blue-ice slide and skating at Place d'Youville in downtown Quebec City. If the timing's right (late February to early March), join the Quebecois for the biggest winter carnival in the world, featuring a talking snowman called Bonhomme who inhabits the Snow Palace and presides over horse-drawn sleigh rides, a canoe race across the partly frozen St Lawrence River, dog-sled races, parades and the International Snow Sculpture Event.
YOU SHOULD KNOW:
The Hôtel de Glace is made of 15,000 tons of snow and 500,000 tons of ice. The walls are up to four feet thick and this amazing structure is completely redesigned and rebuilt each year to reflect a different theme. And it has a comforting steel frame to ensure that guests aren't buried in an unexpected avalanche.

Bic Camping

WHERE:
Bic National Park, Quebec (campground access is via the Rivière-du-Sud-Ouest entrance off Route 132 between Saint-Fabien and Bic)
COST:
Budget
BEST TIME OF YEAR:
Any time, depending on chosen recreational activities (July, August and September are the warmest)
DON'T MISS:
The large population of seals basking close to shore when the sun's out; abundant birdlife, including migratory species in season
THINGS TO DO:
Hiking, biking, kayaking (summer); skiing, snowboarding, tubing, snowshoeing (winter)
YOU SHOULD KNOW:
There is a small park admission fee. Visitors to the park can take advantage of an extensive programme of discovery activities, varying with the seasons but including guided tours, wildlife observation, theatre, informative lectures, as well as evening activities.

Bic National Park is on the banks of the St Lawrence River's mighty estuary and it's a great place for those who like travelling light and living the simple life. The park's natural attributes are breathtaking, including capes and bays, coves and islands, woods and meadows, mountain and foreshore. Numerous outlooks offer stunning views.

The park has affordable facilities for campers, with an assortment of possibilities available at the Rioux and La Coulée campgrounds. There are over 40 camping sites with water and electricity, a further five with water only, more than 125 unserviced pitches and (for the back-to-nature brigade) nine tent platforms for primitive camping. In the ready-to-camp category there is also choice as the park has 20 Huttopia tents, eight yurts, seven trailer tents and, in winter when the park turns into that proverbial winter wonderland, igloos.

With its temperate climate, Quebec Maritime has four distinct seasons, each bringing a dramatic transformation to the landscape, and the services and recreational choices in Bic National Park also change with the seasons. Despite the stunning location and ability to get away from it all, the park does have useful facilities for visitors, so even primitive camping is possible without too much pre-planning. There's a convenience store and nature boutique, laundromat, bicycle rental for explorers of dramatic mountain-bike trails, a boat ramp, children's playground, play area with sports equipment, picnic tables and fire pits. If that all sounds a bit like a conventional camping experience, don't be fooled. It takes but a few moments to leave all that behind and simply vanish into the Great Outdoors.

Hi-Ottawa Jail Hostel

WHERE:
Nicholas Street, Ottawa, Ontario
COST:
Budget
BEST TIME OF YEAR:
April to September
DON'T MISS:
The daily tour of the top floor, once the jail's Death Row and now maintained pretty much in its original state
THINGS TO DO:
Local sightseeing – the hostel is within easy walking distance of Parliament Hill, Byward Market and all Ottawa's major downtown attractions
YOU SHOULD KNOW:
The hostel offers entertaining activities every day, ranging from all-the-wings-you-can-eat football evenings on Mondays to dance parties on Friday nights.

The impressive stone-built Ottowa Jail has been around since 1862, when the embryonic city still had something of the wild frontier town about it, and continued to incarcerate local miscreants until 1972. Thereafter, the only inmates have been those who can't resist the lure of a night in jail – albeit with the benefit of sure and certain knowledge that it's possible to play their get-out-of-jail card and walk free the following morning.

In truth, conditions are rather less draconian than those experienced by jailbirds in times past, when hundreds of men, woman and children were forced to use overcrowded small cells designed for single occupation, or only slightly larger shared cells. Nowadays, with over one hundred 'rooms' on offer, it's not only possible to opt for a single, twin or shared cell but also to choose more conventional shared or private hotel-style accommodation if you want to feel a cut above the other inmates. But times have certainly changed – even the lowliest incarceree in the smallest cell is permitted a reading light, not to mention wifi.

Even so, inmates should be on their best behaviour – the jail's original gallows are intact and remain fully functional (but don't worry too much, they were last used in 1946 to dispatch the murderer of a policeman), although it does give the establishment's slogan – 'a great place to hang out' – a slightly sinister ring. It would be criminal simply to describe this place as an affordable hostel in the heart of Ottawa, because it really does offer a unique stopover experience (especially if one of the well-documented ghosts of anguished former inmates, said to haunt the corridors and former cells, shows up).

Wild Exodus Glamorous Camping

If you're drawn by the siren call of the wild but not all that keen on basic camping, the solution is obvious. Go glamping (or, to give this up-and-coming option its full title, glamorous camping). Sadly this does not involve sharing a tent with a movie star, but rather signing up for a true wilderness trip with an outfit like Wild Exodus Glamorous Camping, based at Timmins in Ontario's rugged northeast. These are people who can make it all happen for you, offering a selection of custom trips that are more like old-fashioned luxury safaris than mere camping expeditions.

Glampers not only get all the satisfaction of cuddling Mother Nature, but also enjoy exceptional accommodation, meals and comfort. Naturally there's no wearying humping of essential survival gear into the remote backwoods. Everything is taken care of, including the Gucci luggage. A typical seven-day all-inclusive package with Wild Exodus will take you deep into the pristine boreal forest of Ontario's Wilderness Region, guided by experts. These trips can involve general exploration or a specific focus such as outdoor adventure, nature appreciation or local heritage. It's also possible to book special family trips.

After a day spent on the water or hiking through the forest, the evening brings a sumptuous meal cooked by chefs, followed by a leisurely nightcap in the camp lounge. Later, a queen-sized bed with crisp linen awaits in a large prospector tent equipped with electric lighting, heating and an indoor toilet. Should you have by then forgotten that you are actually camping, as you head for bed you will certainly be reminded by the sight of a brilliant starscape, sounds of the wild and the freshest air God ever made.

WHERE:
Starting from Timmins, Ontario
COST:
Reasonable (seven-day trip, nightly charge)
BEST TIME OF YEAR:
The season runs from May to November (winter activities include snowmobiling, dog sledding and ice fishing).
DON'T MISS:
Before or after your glamping trip – the opportunity to take the fascinating Timmins Underground Gold Mine Tour
THINGS TO DO:
Canoeing; fishing; boreal forest hiking; bird- and wildlife-watching; learning survival techniques
YOU SHOULD KNOW:
Those super-glampers who prefer not to bend their backs over a canoe paddle in order to reach the remote camp by water and the sweat of their brows can, of course, choose to fly in by floatplane. And for those adventurers who don't even like walking, Wild Exodus Glamorous Camping does ATV expeditions.

Killarney Lodge

WHERE:
The Lodge is on Highway 60 at the Lake of Two Rivers, just over 32 km (20 mi) inside the park, entering from the West Gate, and about the same distance from the East Gate.

COST:
Reasonable (although prime cabins with the best views are expensive in peak season)

BEST TIME OF YEAR:
The lodge is open from mid May to early October.

DON'T MISS:
Jet skis – there aren't any to disturb this tranquil place; feeding the ducks, ducklings and friendly chipmunks that take food from your hand

THINGS TO DO:
Relaxing; canoeing; wildlife-watching (moose sightings are commonplace, red squirrels race around the tall pine trees); visiting nearby Algonquin Park Visitor Centre, the Logging Museum and stunning Art Centre

YOU SHOULD KNOW:
That eerie wailing cry during the day or (more scarily) at dusk that causes you to shiver isn't the nearest wolf pack winding up for action – it's the haunting cry of a loon (once heard, never forgotten). Despite Algonquin's vast wilderness area, Killarney Lodge is not that far from the busy main road that bisects the park.

Don't be fooled – despite the name, Killarney Lodge is not to be found in the Emerald Isle, instead occupying a stunning lakeside setting in rugged Algonquin Park. This is Ontario's greatest wilderness, covering over 7,700 sq km (2,970 sq mi) of unspoilt forests, lakes and wild rivers. And right in the centre of the park, on a private peninsula jutting from the shore of the scenic Lake of Two Rivers, you'll find Killarney Lodge.

The lodge itself is a 75-year-old building, surrounded by wonderful flower gardens and specimen trees. It's traditionally constructed from logs and serves as a focal point for select waterside cabins also made of logs or pine, fitted out and furnished in rustic style, widely spaced to give a sense of privacy. Each overlooks the water, each has its own canoe and, because people come here for peace and quiet, cabins do not have televisions, radios or telephones (but do have necessary comforts like showers and heating for chilly nights). There is a choice based on size (one-bed, two-bed and duplex) and position (shoreline or main lake views). There is also a three-bedroom family cottage.

Three meals a day are included, while complimentary hot and cold drinks, fruit and cookies are available in the lodge 24/7, and in the evenings guests often congregate around the log stove in the lounge to swap stories of the day's doings. It's hard to avoid relaxing completely (which is one of the main attractions) but anyone determined to get up and go will not be sorry they made the effort. Algonquin Park with its spectacular scenery, diverse flora and fauna and great hiking trails is a magical place for nature lovers.

Flora Bora Forest Lodging

Yurts were once reserved for nomadic herdsmen in Central Asia (who use them still), but these sustainable portable dwellings have now become popular with tourists keen to ensure that their travels have the least possible impact on the natural world. The Flora Bora Forest Lodging (the forest in question being Saskatchewan's awesome boreal forest) certainly meets that sustainable objective, offering comfortable yurts in a stunning wooded setting all year round . . . without leaving a heavy permanent footprint.

The yurts are surrounded by dense forest and the site has a small lake. This is an ideal place to escape from the hustle and bustle of everyday life, consume food grown in the organic gardens and commune with nature. But eco-friendly doesn't have to equate with primitive. The Flora Bora Forest Lodging is indeed run with the best environmental principles in mind, but their application isn't fanatical. So the yurts seem more like homes-from-home rather than the sort of temporary hide-covered shelter a nomad on the steppes would recognize. The principles of simple circular construction using a wooden frame remain the same, but these westernized versions have insulated fabric covers and are topped with a clear dome that allows sunlight in by day and encourages stargazing. Each one is beautifully fitted with a fully equipped kitchen, bathroom (flush toilet) and queen-size bed, with a private deck outside. Each has a different theme and comes stocked with everything needed for a relaxing stay. Welcome to nomadic life North-American style!

Still, don't expect to find a TV, mobile phone reception or wifi. The whole point of a secluded forest retreat is escape from the relentless electronic intrusions of modern life, and the ability to do so in a stunning natural setting is what makes Flora Bora Forest Lodging special.

WHERE:
Off Scenic Route 263 north of Prince Albert, Saskatchewan
COST:
Reasonable
BEST TIME OF YEAR:
Any (but avoid November through March unless winter wonderlands are your thing)
DON'T MISS:
A trip to nearby Emma and Christopher Lakes for great scenery and excellent beaches
THINGS TO DO:
Get up close and personal with the unspoilt landscape and have a go at boating, canoeing, hiking, biking the trails, wildlife-watching (especially birds) – or just loaf on the beach.
YOU SHOULD KNOW:
There is a minimum two-night-stay requirement at Flora Bora Forest Lodging. Rates are significantly reduced in low season (mid September to mid May). All yurts are non-smoking, while candles and incense-burning are not allowed and pyromaniacs are banned.

Fairmont Chateau Lake Louise

WHERE:
Lake Louise, Banff National Park, Alberta
COST:
Expensive (astronomical for those choosing super-exclusive Fairmont Gold Packages)
BEST TIME OF YEAR:
Any time
DON'T MISS:
Some of the world's most scenic drives, such as the Icefields and Bow Valley Parkways; a heli-tour of Banff National Park's rugged scenery; horse-drawn sleigh rides in winter
THINGS TO DO:
Mountaineering, downhill skiing, cross-country skiing, snowmobiling, ice skating (winter); mountain climbing, wilderness hiking, horseback riding, canoeing, rafting
YOU SHOULD KNOW:
The first European to see Lake Louise (subsequently named in honour of Queen Victoria's fourth daughter) was an employee of the Canadian Pacific Railway, who found it in 1882 with the help of local Stoney Indians and was enchanted by its incomparable setting. In 1890 the shrewd railway company constructed 'A hotel for the outdoor adventurer and alpinist'. It was a single-storey log cabin with two small bedrooms. The wilderness experience proved so popular that the cabin evolved into a grand hotel within a couple of decades.

Do you enjoy listening to the call of the wild? Then begin with a two-hour drive from Calgary through stunning scenery along the Trans-Canada highway, before reaching journey's end – the Fairmont Chateau Lake Louise, in the heart of rugged Banff National Park. Standing within a UNESCO World Heritage Site, the progressive Fairmont takes pride in demonstrating that responsible environmental stewardship and a resort hotel can coexist in perfect harmony.

Occupying a truly awesome location overlooking the bowl of Lake Louise, with its glacier and steep wooded banks, Chateau Lake Louise used to be a highly fashionable summer-only resort adored by the rich and famous. The Prince of Wales (later King Edward VIII) visited in 1912 and Hollywood discovered the place in the 1920s, with several films being shot hereabouts and countless movie stars mixing with royalty and the socialites who have frequented this alluring place over the years. However, with the help of Austrian and Swiss guides, the area also attracted mountaineers and skiers, and in the late 1970s Chateau Lake Louise started opening all year round, even as Banff National Park began to develop into the world-class winter sports destination that it is today.

This is an opportunity not only to enjoy the comforts of a luxurious resort hotel in an incomparable setting, but also to sample the wide selection of stimulating outdoor activities on offer in the pristine national park. For visiting families, there are also organized children's activities. And at the end of a rewarding day in the open air, guests can unwind with some fine dining or relaxing in the intimate wine bar. There's a spa, too, to sooth those tired but happy bones (or simply pamper stay-at-home guests). Unforgettable!

Sundance Lodges

WHERE:
Off the Trans-Canada Highway between Banff and Calgary in Kananaskis Country Alberta
COST:
Budget
BEST TIME OF YEAR:
Sundance Lodges opens only from late May to mid September.
DON'T MISS:
A tranquil walk along the banks of the Kananaskis River for great mountain views (watch out for migrating bald eagles in late spring and early autumn); a visit to the adjacent Beaver Ponds recreation area
THINGS TO DO:
Hiking, fishing, volleyball, soccer or badminton around the site; close by it's possible to enjoy mountain biking, horseback riding, canoeing and kayaking, whitewater rafting and rock climbing; shop in nearby Kananaskis Village for crafts, collectibles, clothes, posters and souvenirs
YOU SHOULD KNOW:
Food must always be securely stored in a locked vehicle and all garbage placed in one of the bear-proof bins. This is bear country, but they're truly wild black bears that have never bothered campers at Sundance Lodges (so don't tempt them to start!). Water is available at three wells and must be carried back to individual sites. There is no electricity on any of the sites. This is not the place for noisy teenagers (or late-night revellers) – there is a mandatory quiet time from 22.30 to 08.00.

Adventurous travellers who feel the need to escape the rat race, however briefly, should ensure that Sundance Lodges in Canada's Rocky Mountains is on their itinerary. There simply couldn't be a more relaxing place to be at one with Mother Nature in all her majesty. This riverside destination offers the simplest – and most rewarding – of outdoor living within the spectacular Kananaskis government recreation area west of Calgary.

It's possible to book Sioux canvas *tipis* that are brightly painted with authentic designs. Each has its own wooded site, surrounded by forest. Large *tipis* easily sleep four, while smaller ones are ideal for couples. Each has a fire pit with grill for cooking, together with a picnic table at which to eat those satisfying self-cooked meals. For people who prefer rustic home comforts, trapper's tents with their wooden floors, foam mattresses and small heaters are a shrewd choice. They, too, are on secluded individual sites with a fire pit. There are also facilities for those who bring their own camping equipment, or travel in style in a home-on-wheels RV.

Visitors must carry in everything they need, although essentials like firewood, ice and emergency supplies are available at the Sundance Trading Post. But savvy campers should bring their own logs, warm clothing (nights can be chilly), an emergency tarpaulin, warm bedding, cooking equipment, cooler, food, flashlight, outside lantern, an axe and matches. However, if anything is overlooked or forgotten, many of these items can actually be rented upon arrival. There are washrooms and showers in the Trading Post and no site is very far from an outdoor toilet.

This is wild camping at its best, in a simply stunning location.

King Pacific Lodge

The words 'luxurious' and 'ecotourism' don't always sit comfortably in the same sentence, but certainly have a pleasing ring when combined in the slogan 'King Pacific Lodge provides the ultimate in luxury adventure travel and ecotourism vacations from its location in the heart of the Great Bear Rainforest'. And this is no hollow boast by a hyped-up PR man, for this splendidly isolated lodge on the north coast of British Columbia has consistently been voted top of Canada's 'Best Resort' list by satisfied ecotravellers.

Accessible only by floatplane, this may not be (no, definitely *isn't*) for budget travellers, but those able to afford the exclusive wilderness lodge will enjoy a unique experience that cannot be duplicated anywhere else on the planet. They will also help to sustain 8.5 million hectares (21 million acres) of pristine temperate rainforest, safeguarding it for future generations and the indigenous Gitga'at people who have lived there for thousands of years.

The lodge is at Princess Royal Island, an uninhabited wilderness frequented by many species of animals and birds. The island has a fjord-like coastline and the surrounding rainforest is one of the world's unspoilt ecological treasures, where ancient cedars and Sitka spruce tower above an untrodden floor covered with moss, maidenhair fern and salmon berry.

And at the end of a day spent enjoying another open-air adventure, there's nothing better than eating on the open deck watching a spectacular sunset, or relaxing in a club chair beside a roaring log fire in the Great Room, enjoying good company and contented conversation before retiring to bed, tired but happy. Oh, it's worth mentioning that the lodge isn't actually a lodge, but a three-storey floating platform that's towed into position at the start of each season, leaving no permanent footprint on this idyllic spot.

WHERE:
British Columbia, some 90 km (56 mi) south of Prince Rupert, off the southern tip of the Alaska panhandle

COST:
Astronomical (then some, with helicopter excursions, bear viewing, spa services, various other goodies, gratuities, tax and conservation charge all extra)

BEST TIME OF YEAR:
The short season is from June to September only.

DON'T MISS:
The chance to see a super-rare spirit (or Kermode) bear, a striking white subspecies of the black bear with a total world population of fewer than a thousand, all found only in this part of British Columbia (other wildlife to be spotted includes grizzly and black bears, white-tailed deer, sea lions, wolves, otters and eagles)

THINGS TO DO:
World-class fly fishing for trout and salmon; heli-hikes; whale-watching; wilderness-hiking; kayaking

YOU SHOULD KNOW:
The Lodge has kids' clubs so that parents can relax and enter into the activities on offer. Explorers is for under tens and offers a range of stimulating indoor activities. Adventurers is for under 17s and features outdoor challenges such as rainforest trekking and assisting with conservation work. During the season temperatures range from 17°C to 25°C (62°F to 77°F) in the day to 10°C to 17°C (50°F to 62°F) at night.

Tipi Camp Nature Retreat

WHERE:
Kootenay Lake, British Columbia (near Nelson, departing from Grey Creek)
COST:
Reasonable
BEST TIME OF YEAR:
Open from June to September
DON'T MISS:
On the way in to Tipi Camp (or on the way back out), be sure to call in on the Artisans of Crawford Bay, just north of the boat dock. There you will see blacksmiths, broom makers, potters, artists, weavers, copper enameler, glass-blowers, jewellers and wizard makers at work and learn about the various crafts.
THINGS TO DO:
Pondering the meaning of life; relaxing; swimming; canoeing; hiking along the forested lake shore; striking inland on a network of trails
YOU SHOULD KNOW:
The camp is a pet-, alcohol- and drug-free zone, while cigarette smokers must always use designated areas. Hollywood actor Peter Duryea (son of Dan) was joint-founder of the Guiding Hands Recreational Society.

For people who really like to get away from it all (no roads, no mobile phones, no email, no satellite dishes), the remote Tipi Camp Nature Retreat on British Columbia's Kootenay Lake comes as a breath of the freshest air it's possible to breathe on the planet. Tipi Camp was established by the Guiding Hands Recreational Society in the 1980s. The aim is to educate the public about natural values and the benefits of healthy outdoor recreation in our stressed modern society, also to promote the importance of environmental protection and sustainable rural communities. To that end, informative workshops, interactive experiences and summer camps for youngsters are run.

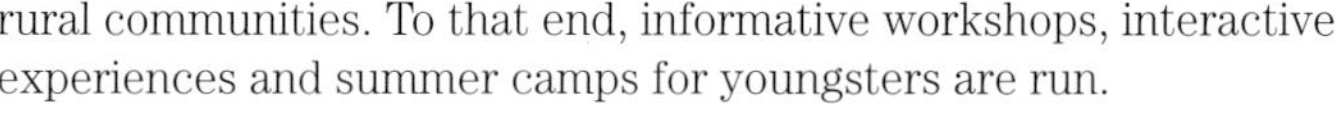

But if you take all those objectives as read anyway, don't worry – you'll be supporting the society's aims simply by visiting, and can enjoy Tipi Camp's ultimate wilderness chill-out experience in the company of like-minded green pioneers. Family Nature Weekends are very popular and start with a boat trip to the camp, which is located on the secluded shores of Kootenay Lake's rocky Pilot Peninsula with stunning views of the ruggedly beautiful Selkirk and Purcell Mountains.

The camp features large waterside *tipis* that can sleep seven or eight. A bigger tent with a floor can be reserved for yoga retreats and other group activities. There are also primitive shelters for guests who want to spend the night communing with nature, while sites for those who prefer to do their own thing by bringing personal tents are also available. The camp has hot and cold outdoor showers as well as state-of-the-art composting toilets. There is a large outdoor kitchen where committed staff serve hearty vegetarian meals (included within the price), and this really is a place where it's easy to feel connected to nature, allowing earth's natural rhythms to soothe away the cares of modern living.

Free Spirit Sphere

Tree houses are just for kids, right? Not these ones! Free Spirit Spheres are for over 16s only, and offer a truly unusual way of spending a night (or two) high in the trees of Vancouver Island's rainforest. Suspended by a web of ropes, the spheres move with the motion of the canopy above, ever so gently rocking the grown-up occupants to sleep.

This is not an experience for travellers who like to be pampered, but rather one for those who love being in the wild. There are three hand-crafted spheres to choose from – Eve, Eryn and Melody. Eve, made from cedar strips, is really for singles (or couples who love being really snug) and a stay might be described as 'basic sphereing' (although she does have electricity and speakers for plug-in music players). Erin is a Sitka spruce sphere, nearly twice the size of Eve, and she sleeps three (two in a double, one in a loft bed). She has five windows, is electrically heated and also has a sound system. Melody is the same size as Eryn but made of bright-yellow fibreglass with not-quite-all-but-some mod cons (heating, a small sink, crockery, work stations and a fold-down bed. She is the sphere of choice for those who want a longer stay or creative studio space.

The spheres are reached by spiral staircases and short bridges. There are composting toilets at ground level, although more traditional facilities are found on the other side of the site's central pond. These include two washrooms, two showers, a sauna and a covered deck with barbecue and picnicking resources for those who want to self-cater rather than eat out.

WHERE:
Near Qualicum Beach (north of Parksville), Vancouver Island, British Columbia
COST:
Budget (couple, per person); reasonable (single)
BEST TIME OF YEAR:
Any time
DON'T MISS:
The view from the sphere's windows on a moonlit night, engendering a wonderful sense of peace and harmony with nature
THINGS TO DO:
Taking in the local natural wonders – Horne Lake Caves, Mount Washington and the Georgia Strait
YOU SHOULD KNOW:
While normal motion is minimal, sudden movement within a sphere will lead it to rock quite violently. Breakfast is not provided.

Four Seasons Hotel

WHERE:
57 East 57th Street, New York City
COST:
Astronomical (but hey, if you have to ask you can't afford!)
BEST TIME OF YEAR:
Any time (the city never sleeps)
DON'T MISS:
Complimentary goodies – use of the spa and fitness room, morning coffee in the lobby for early starters, free newspaper; agonizing over the tempting menu in L'Atelier de Joël Robuchon while sipping the driest of vodka martinis (shaken, not stirred?) and watching everyone who's someone pass by
THINGS TO DO:
For starters (although there's so much more to see and do) the Four Seasons is close to the city's most exclusive shops and famous New York sights such as Times Square, UN Headquarters, the Rockefeller Centre and Grand Central Station
YOU SHOULD KNOW:
The Four Seasons Group operates hotels and resorts all over the world but doesn't actually own any of them. Although centrally involved in the planning, design and control of each property, the group runs them to the highest standard on behalf of the funding investor in return for a slice of the take.

What's in a name? Well, if the name happens to be 'Four Seasons', it means cutting-edge style, incomparable service and luxurious accommodation. And if that name also happens to include 'New York', a memorable stay in a great hotel in one of the world's greatest cities is absolutely assured. Set in the heart of Manhattan, between Madison and Park Avenues, this splendid building was designed by world-famous architect I M Pei and features over 350 five-star rooms and suites, some with terraces and views over Central Park and that iconic high-rise skyline.

All are discreetly but lavishly equipped with the finest furniture, wood panelling, desks, leather chairs, refrigerated bars, cable TVs, CD/DVD players, wifi, air conditioning and marble bathrooms with glass shower stalls, deep tubs and changing areas. Plus, of course, the vital in-room safes in which to stash the pile of cash and bearer bonds required to pay the bill. Although the Four Seasons is of particular appeal to business people, private guests also quietly revel in the levels of service expected by and given to America's serious movers and shakers.

Needless to say, the renowned food more than matches the high standard of the accommodation. The Four Seasons is a popular hang-out for representatives of the great and the good bent on enjoying intimate fine dining, and more casual cuisine is available day and night in the extraordinary Garden, with its four 6-m (20-ft) acacia trees all the way from Africa. This is the place to brunch 'n' lunch before sampling the huge selection of taster plates accompanied by appropriate fine wines (offered by the glass) served each evening. And when you finally get home, broke but happy, you can dine out on the bragging rights for months.

Plaza Hotel

One of only two New York hotels to have achieved National Historic Landmark status, the Plaza is one of the world's great lifestyle destinations. This imposing 20-storey structure dating from 1907 rises to a height of 76 m (250 ft) and occupies the west side of Manhattan's Grand Army Plaza (hence the name), overlooking Fifth Avenue and Central Park South. This striking building has architectural flourishes reminiscent of a grand French *château*, including steep gables and a corner turret. After an honourable century of good service to New York's (and international) glitterati, the hotel closed for three years in 2005 for substantial renovations that included the creation of a number of high-end apartments worth megabucks (one sold for $50 million, keep the change).

But the hotel itself – now duly restored to its original splendour after the trifling outlay of $450 million – retained over 280 luxurious guest rooms and 100 sumptuous suites for the delectation of discerning (and self-indulgent) patrons who expect (and get) the ultimate in comfort and traditional white-glove service. But the building's timeless elegance has been subtly married with the latest technology, so visitors will find that in-room systems cater for their every electronic need. Think marble, crystal and gilt meet wifi and you'll get the picture (with a little help, if you need it, from the butler assigned to every floor).

Naturally, this is a place that offers exceptional opportunities to wine, dine and be seen in fabulous surroundings such as the Champagne Bar, Oak Room & Oak Bar, Palm Court and the Rose Club. The grandeur and opulence of this five-star establishment is legendary, and the Plaza Hotel should definitely be on everyone's stay-there-before-I-die wish list. Some even go as far as saying that the Plaza Hotel is New York, and it's not hard to see why.

WHERE:
Fifth Avenue at 59th Street, New York City

COST:
Astronomical (but there are deals to be done)

BEST TIME OF YEAR:
Any time, remembering only that winters can be raw and the city swelters in high summer

DON'T MISS:
A legendary New York institution – afternoon tea in the Plaza's famous Palm Court (served from 13.00 to 17.00 daily); drooling over designer shops in the Plaza's underground shopping mall; the guided Plaza tour, if only to see the hotel's spectacular Ballroom and Terrace Room

THINGS TO DO:
Exploring Central Park; hitting the shops on Fifth Avenue

YOU SHOULD KNOW:
The Beatles stayed at the Plaza Hotel in 1964 on their way to conquering the USA. Donald Trump owned the place for seven years but paid too much and took a massive loss when he sold it in 1995.

Waldorf-Astoria Hotel

WHERE:
301 Park Avenue, New York City
COST:
Expensive (Waldorf-Astoria); Astronomical (Waldorf Towers); online deals available
BEST TIME OF YEAR:
January to December
DON'T MISS:
New York, New York
THINGS TO DO:
Exploring the hotel, which is as good as any Art Deco museum; dipping a toe or 10 in the fabulous Guerlain Spa; eating at one of four gourmet restaurants in the Waldorf-Astoria or simply loafing in one of the three elegant lounges to see and be seen
YOU SHOULD KNOW:
The original Waldorf-Astoria hotel stood on the site now occupied by the Empire State Building on Fifth Avenue. The hotel has its own platform at Grand Central Station, particularly handy for famous former guests such as President Franklin D Roosevelt (who used the lift capable of accommodating his limo).

If there's one place in New York that says 'You've arrived' it's surely the Waldorf-Astoria Hotel. This is one of only two National Historic Landmark hotels in the city (along with the nearby Plaza), and both establishments aspire to the title of 'New York's finest traditional hotel'. Those who win lotteries or run multinational companies might come up with an answer by staying at each for a week and comparing notes, but for most mortals wanting to visit the city in superior style it's a case of either/or.

The Waldorf-Astoria (actually branded for some arcane reason as the Waldorf=Astoria) is the result of an historic amalgamation of two hotels (yes, the Waldorf and the Astoria) once owned by rival members of the fabulously wealthy Astor clan. Naturally, nothing but the best was good enough – a tradition maintained to this day. By way of example, the Waldorf-Astoria was the first hotel to offer room service, also transforming the whole industry by becoming an important social centre rather than a mere traveller's rest and (shock, horror!) admitting *unaccompanied women*.

Times may have changed but the level of luxurious service offered within this classic Art Deco structure on Park Avenue remains the same. From the moment visitors step into the stunning lobby and spot the signature clock, it's apparent that a memorable stay looms. But wait, there's more! The upper floors of the building are devoted to the Waldorf Towers, an exclusive enclave featuring opulent residential-style suites beloved of the rich and famous where levels of service are even more dedicated. So, downstairs to be part of the New York social scene, or upstairs to mingle with royalty, movie stars and billionaires? Tough choice!

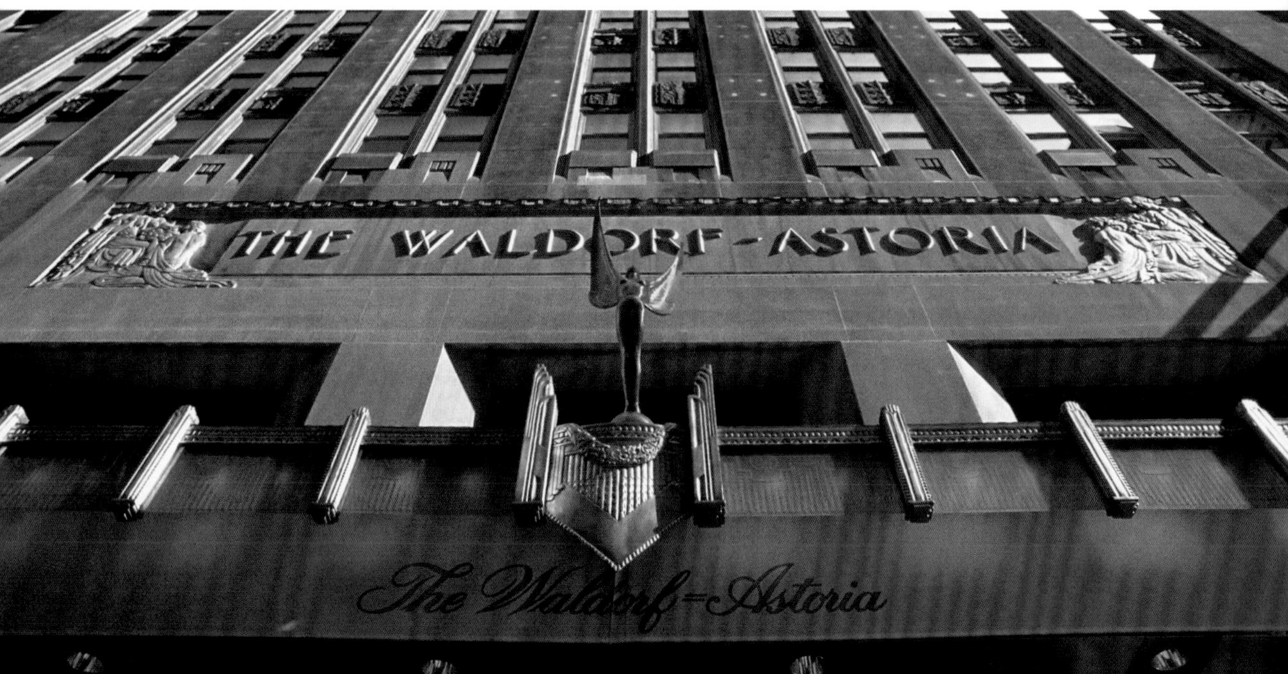

Aloft Brooklyn

New York has plenty of classy hotels, ranging from the exceptional to really good, but most subscribe to the view that visitors favour timeless elegance and a traditional approach to service and hospitality. But now for something completely different: for one, it's not in high-rise Manhattan but in trendy Brooklyn, for two it's funky rather than frumpy, for three the whole joint deliberately fizzes with life. Aloft Brooklyn is part of the fast-growing chain that appeals both to a younger set and hip oldies who prefer action and excitement to being served (however well).

That's not to say Aloft offers poor service – quite the reverse, because the staff are always attentive and helpful – but the whole atmosphere is rather more relaxed and informal than that of Manhattan's grand hotels, inspired by the clean and simple 'loft' design look that New York made famous. The rooms (and suites) at Aloft all have sleek bathrooms, crisp modern furnishings, beds to die for and Aloft's one-stop connectivity centre that plays and recharges just about everything electronic known to personkind. The rooms also have a work station and a built-in safe.

The rooftop Brooklyn Terrace with its all-round outlook is a great place to enjoy a drink or three, set to the music of a DJ or live band. The w xyz bar also offers music and live happenings, served with everything from champagne cocktails to a cold beer (plus tasty appetizers and free snacks). Or hit re:fuel, the hotel's innovative self-service facility dispensing one-stop goodie-food and drinks 24/7. Get the idea? Going Aloft really is a whole new energizing travel experience that breaks the mould!

WHERE:
Duffield Street, Brooklyn, New York City
COST:
Reasonable
BEST TIME OF YEAR:
Any time
DON'T MISS:
A brisk workout in the open-all-hours gym; a game of pool; enjoying the lively company of like-minded visitors in the spacious lounge (or simply finding a quiet corner to unwind after sallying forth to do New York)
THINGS TO DO:
Visit the hip shops on Brooklyn Heights, Carroll Gardens and Cobble Hill; ride the Subway to Manhattan (it's only three stops) or do it the hard but scenic way by walking across Brooklyn Bridge; explore Prospect Park; take the tasty but waist-expanding Slice of Brooklyn Pizza Tour.
YOU SHOULD KNOW:
There is hotel-wide high-speed internet access. The Camp Aloft programme for youngsters aged up to 12 offers special bedding, kid-friendly food, treats and fun activities that are guaranteed to keep youngsters amused while their parents chill.

Beekman Arms

WHERE:
Route 9 (the former Albany Post Road), Rhinebeck, New York
COST:
Reasonable (and the inn also offers great value-for-money budget off-season packages)
BEST TIME OF YEAR:
Any time (but May through September are the warmest months and winters can turn nasty)
DON'T MISS:
The Antique Market, a multi-dealer emporium behind the Beekman Arms in a traditional red barn
THINGS TO DO:
Visit the estates of some of America's famous names, all within easy reach of Rhinebeck in the National Historic Landmark District – including those of the Vanderbilts, President Franklin D Roosevelt and Samuel Morse (of Code fame); see weekend flying displays by World War I aircraft at Old Rhinebeck Aerodrome; tour the famous Culinary Institute of America.
YOU SHOULD KNOW:
Two-night stays are the minimum at weekends during high season (May to October). Frequent visitor Franklin D Roosevelt ended every one of his political campaigns for governor and president (four times) by addressing his supporters from the front porch of the Beekman Arms.

America's oldest continuously operated inn may be found in the centre of the Hudson Valley's long-established Rhinebeck Village. The Beekman Arms dates back to 1766 but would-be guests at this fine old inn should be aware that some accommodation is not within the historic building, but rather in more modern detached cottages that lack the same ambience. But providing you lodge at the inn itself, it will not be hard to understand why the place was voted 'One of the 12 most romantic inns in New York'. Despite additions and renovations over the years, the original structure of oak beams and broad plank floors remains largely untouched. And local residents, travellers and guests still enjoy good food, drink and lively conversation – as they have since the 18th century.

Although its pleasantly old-fashioned atmosphere is part of the attraction, the Beekman Arms has been tastefully modernized within to ensure that all the guest rooms have a private bath, TV, telephone, free internet access . . . and a genteel decanter of sherry. The restaurant has bags of character, with its beamed Colonial Tap Room featuring an open fireplace and old-fashioned bar. Luncheon and dinner are served daily and Sunday brunch is something of an institution. Diners may choose between several different locations, including a garden room.

Accommodation is also available at the Beekman Arms' sister inn, Rhinebeck's intimate colonial bed-and-breakfast Delamater Inn. Designed by Alexander Jackson Davis, one of America's first recognized architects, this fabulous old building is one of the USA's finest remaining examples of American Carpenter Gothic style. Either/or, you won't be disappointed.

Mohonk Mountain House

When hearing the words 'New York' many people think of nothing but that vibrant city and its famous landmarks. But in truth the state that also bears the name has some of the finest scenery in the entire US of A. Rather proving the point, just 145 km (90 mi) from New York City in the Hudson Valley is a destination that could be in another world. On the rocky shores of picturesque Mohonk Lake, surrounded by vast tracts of pristine forest, is the last thing anyone would expect to find in a wonderful backcountry setting like this – a fairytale castle.

The dream of two Victorian twin brothers who first saw this spectacular mountain-top location in 1869, the Mohonk Mountain House grew from a small inn to the grand resort hotel that stands today – still run by the founding Smiley family, still attracting those who appreciate a relaxing sojourn surrounded by nature's bounty. This astonishing edifice with its eclectic mix of architectural styles is set in fabulous gardens and seemingly stretches for ever along the lake shore – although actually it's 'only' around 200 m (660 ft) long. The hotel has 600 Victorian-themed rooms and guest cottages with open fires, offering every comfort couples or families could wish for. For those who have more in mind than simple unwinding and the recharging of batteries, there are activities galore to fill the days.

The old-fashioned ambience of Mohonk Mountain House extends to the grand dining room, where wholesome modern American cuisine features seasonal, local produce. To help work up a good appetite, those stimulating outdoor activities beckon, while the stay-at-homes can hit the indoor heated swimming pool and fitness centre. And after dinner there's nightly entertainment. America personified, folks!

WHERE:
Mountain Rest Road, New Paltz, New York

COST:
Astronomical (but overnight rates include meals and most resort activities, and deals can be done)

BEST TIME OF YEAR:
Any time, with something different to see and do in each season

DON'T MISS:
A not-so-brief encounter with treatments at the resort's award-winning spa, full-service salon, solarium, steam room, sauna and outdoor heated mineral pool; the spectacular leaf show in autumn

THINGS TO DO:
Carriage rides, swimming, golf, lawn games, tennis, trail hiking and horseback riding, mountain biking, rock climbing (spring, summer and autumn); snow tubing, ice skating, cross-country skiing, snowshoeing (winter)

YOU SHOULD KNOW:
Mohonk Mountain House specializes in themed programmes designed to inform and entertain, featuring subjects as diverse as culinary excellence, performing arts, yoga, meditation, dance and nature appreciation. The resort also offers special activities for young ones and teens, plus a keep-them-busy junior nature programme.

Thayers Inn

WHERE:
Main Street, Littleton, New Hampshire
COST:
Budget to reasonable, depending on season and accommodation chosen
BEST TIME OF YEAR:
Any time
DON'T MISS:
The inn's Pollyanna Room, a tribute to classic children's-book author Eleanor Hodgman Porter, who was born in Littleton; the 1843 room, a re-creation of exactly what a visitor would have experienced in the year the inn opened for business; great views over Littleton from the roof-top cupola
THINGS TO DO:
Visit Chutters on Main Street, which makes the *Guinness Book of World Records* for possessing the world's longest candy counter. Tour the working Littleton Grist Mill, established in 1798.
YOU SHOULD KNOW:
Winter visitors might be attracted by the fact that the inn is just 15 minutes' drive from Cannon Mountain Ski Area. The inn offers various winter-sports packages, including cross-country and downhill skiing.

Many fine 19th-century inns survive in the USA, all proudly proclaiming their early origins. But behind those historic facades things are sometimes not as they appear, with successive waves of modernization over many years often resulting in public spaces and guest rooms that bear little resemblance to the originals. But upon entering Thayers Inn in Littleton, New Hampshire, it is apparent that *this* historic inn is rather different and . . . genuinely historic.

Littleton, in the scenic White Mountains, is a town that prides itself on representing the very best of traditional small-town America and was described by author Bill Bryson as 'the friendliest little place I had ever seen'. It has thriving eateries and shops, markets and a movie theatre, also plenty of historic sites. And Thayers Inn certainly contributes to the traditional atmosphere. Built in 1843 as a railway hotel, it boasts a classic appearance complete with bold portico and crowning cupola. Inside, nostalgia rules. The staircases are original and creak, the floors tend to slope a little, and the 40 guest rooms (while naturally enjoying all necessary mod cons) have a decidedly old-fashioned feel to them.

The balcony and back porch allow guests to chill out and watch the world go by, while those up for a fine-dining experience head for Bailiwicks Martini Bar and Restaurant in the inn's basement (it's popular, so book in advance). A good pampering is also on the cards – it's not always a case of all our yesteryears at Thayers Inn, because the decidedly 21st-century Fresh Salon and Day Spa caters to every beauty and relaxation need.

Equinox Resort and Spa

The Equinox has a long and distinguished history. A hostelry has been standing here since the 1760s – before Independence it was an American revolutionaries' drinking hole and later Abraham Lincoln's family took vacations here.

Over the years this grand old hotel has undergone several name changes and architectural transformations. The rambling main building is a glorious period hotchpotch with colonial trappings of shuttered windows and colonnade. It stands on the village green in the picturesque little town of Manchester, overlooked by the towering 1,160-m (3,800-ft) peak of Equinox Mountain, one of the highest mountains in Vermont. The hotel grounds seem to go on forever – you can wander around 525 ha (1,300 ac) of formal gardens and wild countryside. Hiking and cycling trails lead into the mountains and the Equinox is renowned for its superb golf course.

Inside, the hotel exudes New England elegance and charm. It has a wonderfully solid, old-fashioned atmosphere with cosy lounge corners where open log fires invite you to draw up an armchair. Or you can relax beside the fire pit on the hotel patio and admire the dramatic view of Mount Equinox, even loll in the outdoor hot tub under a night sky of twinkling stars.

The hotel facilities are superb. All sorts of outdoor activities are laid on, including archery, off-road driving and even falconry. The 25 m (82 ft) indoor swimming pool is large for a private pool, the spa treatment rooms are spotlessly clean, and there is an airy yoga and Pilates studio.

Manchester village's picture-postcard clapboard houses, antique shops, museums, studios and galleries are all just a short stroll away. The combination of history and verdant New England countryside is simply unbeatable.

WHERE:
Manchester, Vermont

COST:
Expensive, but lots of special deals to make a stay here more affordable

BEST TIME OF YEAR:
October to see the glorious New England fall foliage; December to February for winter-sports enthusiasts

DON'T MISS:
The Skyline Drive – a scenic drive to the top of Equinox Mountain; the historic Hildene Estate, summer home of President Abraham Lincoln's son; trying your hand at glass-blowing at the Manchester Hot Glass Studio; experiencing a falconry lesson

THINGS TO DO:
Golf; archery; tennis; fly fishing; canoeing; horse riding; hiking; cycling; off-road driving; skiing and winter sports; yoga; shopping; visiting museums and galleries

YOU SHOULD KNOW:
There is a variety of accommodation, including self-catering, in a choice of annexed buildings, one of which was formerly the home of Abraham Lincoln's granddaughter. It is listed as a US National Historic Place and four US presidents have stayed here. Vermont's ski resorts are within easy reach.

OMNI PARKER

Omni-Parker House Hotel

If ever a hotel could be described as an institution, then it's the Omni-Parker House in Boston. This great establishment dates back to the mid 19th century and pioneered many features now considered to be an essential part of best hotel practice. It has long served as a gathering place for this patrician city's great and not-always-quite-so-great citizens and visitors (John Wilkes Booth stayed at the hotel a week before he assassinated President Abraham Lincoln), also attracting many a literary giant, several presidents and numerous movie stars.

This is America's oldest continuously operating hotel. Self-made man Harvey Parker opened his ornate five-storey dream in 1855, after arriving in Boston from Maine with just one dollar in his pocket 25 years earlier. The building was constructed of brick and stone, faced in gleaming white marble, and the interior was lavishly appointed. And from sculpted bronze entrance doors to any one of this luxury hotel's 550 rooms, historic charm married to modern convenience has remained the order of the day. Those rooms range from affordable singles right up to the spectacular Harvey Parker Suite, named in honour of the hotel's founder. Each enjoys a full range of in-room facilities, including desks and wifi, plush robes and extra bedding, iron and ironing board, climate control and cable TV.

Old Harvey would have been delighted that traditional service remains a cornerstone of the guest experience, and especially pleased that the then-revolutionary fine dining he introduced in the mid 19th century flourishes to this day, with Parker's Restaurant a byword for superior Boston cuisine. There simply couldn't be a better place to dine (and stay) for anyone who wants to be in tune with this historic city.

WHERE:
School Street, Boston, Massachusetts
COST:
Budget (for a coyly named Petite Single) to reasonable (varying by season and availability, with good deals available in advance)
BEST TIME OF YEAR:
Any time (but sightseeing in winter is likely to result in a red nose and chilled fingers)
DON'T MISS:
Local specialties invented in the hotel's kitchens – Boston Cream Pie, the Parker House Roll and Boston Scrod (a delectable fish dish)
THINGS TO DO:
Walk the famous Freedom Trail – a red-brick path through downtown Boston connecting 16 important historic sites. The hotel is on the trail, which involves a 4-km (2.5-mi) walk from Boston Common to Bunker Hill Monument in Charlestown. The city's other important trail to tramp is the Black Heritage Trail, linking antebellum structures and historic sites connected with the early anti-slavery movement, including the African Meeting House.
YOU SHOULD KNOW:
Writer Charles Dickens made the Omni-Parker House Hotel his home base when touring America, giving his first American reading of *A Christmas Carol* to the hotel's renowned Saturday Club – a regular monthly meeting place for prominent writers and intellectuals. The thrifty Dickens wrote home announcing that 'the cost of living is enormous, but happily we can afford it'.

Concord's Colonial Inn

WHERE:
Monument Square, Concord, Massachusetts
COST:
Reasonable
BEST TIME OF YEAR:
Any time (although from December to February the weather can be harsh and many choose October and November for the spectacular autumn foliage)
DON'T MISS:
Eating at the inn's Village Forge Tavern and restaurant, for fine all-American and local New England cuisine
THINGS TO DO:
Check out the Ralph Waldo Emerson House and Concord Museum (local history). Stroll to The Minute Man National Historical Park and Minute Man Monument (don't miss Daniel Chester French's well-known Minute Man Statue of 1875). Hike the 8-km (5-mi) Battle Road Trail between Lexington and Concord, a restored colonial landscape approximating to the path of running skirmishes between British troops and Colonial militia in 1775.
YOU SHOULD KNOW:
Paul Revere's famous 'Midnight Ride' to warn colonists of approaching British troops ended on the road from Lexington to Concord when he was detained by a British patrol, but a companion escaped and raised the alarm in Concord. A monument marks the spot and his headlong gallop is re-enacted every year.

Concord in Middlesex County, Massachusetts, is generally agreed to be one of the most beautiful towns in New England. The USA's modern history may not go back all that far, but Concord's been around for most of it and the town has played an important part in significant events that shaped the nation. It has also produced eminent citizens such as poet Ralph Waldo Emerson, writer Nathaniel Hawthorne and Louisa May Alcott, author of *Little Women*.

Monument Square is the town's common and at the heart of this historic community; Concord's Colonial Inn overlooks the square. The original structure dates back to 1716, and in 1775 one of its outbuildings was used to store arms and provisions for those opposing British rule. The British sent troops to seize the weapons, the partisan Minutemen faced them at the town's North Bridge . . . and the first battle of the American War of Independence began (the Minutemen won).

Nowadays Concord's Colonial Inn is a satisfying blend of old and new, offering every modern convenience along with a traditional atmosphere. The well-appointed guest rooms in the original inn are all different and many have wonderful period details. A 1970s extension and nearby guest cottages add to the options for families, groups and those wanting to linger awhile. Every room has a bath, air conditioning, free wifi, phone with voice mail, cable TV, iron and ironing board, hair dryer and coffee maker. It all adds up to living history, gift-wrapped in a relaxing opportunity to enjoy a stay in this archetypal American small town and explore its significant historic monuments.

The Liberty Hotel

Riddle – how is it possible to stay in a historic Boston hotel that's practically brand new? The answer lies in the tongue-in-cheek name of the city's unusual Liberty Hotel, for this imposing building, designed to the latest penal principles and built in 1851, used to be Charles Street Jail. A cruciform stone structure that is regarded as a near-perfect example of Boston Granite Style, the hotel stands at the foot of historic Beacon Hill, not far from the harbour of Tea Party fame. And lest visitors should fear that such an institution might be gloomy within, it should be noted that it was constructed with windows that were claimed to let in four times more light than any jail then standing.

This has helped make the 21st-century hotel conversion particularly successful, for while the fabric of this marvellous Victorian landmark has been preserved (and indeed enhanced, with the addition of a new cupola that was in the original plans but never built for cost reasons), the jail's soaring atrium forms an awesome centrepiece and reception area, and guest rooms are light, airy and deliciously modern. In stark contrast to the experience of former 'visitors', the Liberty takes pride in ensuring that nothing is too much trouble when it comes to ensuring that today's guests enjoy the smoothest of stays. The rooms have every facility and the views from many of them over Boston and the water are simply stunning. There are five splendid drinking and dining options within the hotel, while the secluded inner courtyard has become a tranquil landscaped area.

Many hotels are unique, but it has to be said that some are more unique than others – and this is definitely one of them. Staying at the Liberty Hotel is an experience unlike anything to be found anywhere on the planet.

WHERE:
Charles Street, Boston, Massachusetts
COST:
Reasonable
BEST TIME OF YEAR:
Those wishing to explore Boston's many historic areas and famous sights should avoid mid winter
DON'T MISS:
The detailed Charles Street Jail Tour, showcasing preserved features and offering fascinating information on interesting former inmates (ask at Reception)

THINGS TO DO:
A reconditioning session at the hotel's 24/7 fitness centre, or guided jogging with the running concierge (really, but only in season!); a whirl round Old Boston on one of the hotel's bicycles; a meal in Clink, the hotel restaurant lined with original jail cells
YOU SHOULD KNOW:
The hotel offers all sorts of special themed packages throughout the year, such as a Museum of Fine Arts Package, Winter Wonderland Package, the Guilty Pleasures Romantic Package . . . and more.

The Aviary

How about spending a night at the ever-so-refined Wheatleigh Country House Hotel in the Berkshire Mountains, for around $700? Or perhaps you'd prefer to pay over $2,000 to stay in the garden? If you opt for the latter you won't be roughing it, because you'll be spreading your wings in The Aviary, almost certainly the most luxurious treehouse ever contemplated by mankind. This is very definitely not your typical creaky back-yard timber construct, but rather a luxurious suite over two floors, complete with spiral staircase and private covered terrace. And before you ask, this extraordinary place was once . . . a rich man's aviary.

The garden in question is actually the Wheatleigh's lush parkland, surrounding this grand 19th-century mansion house with more than a dash of Florentine architectural refinement that sits atop its green knoll and now serves as a classic country-house hotel. The Aviary is one of its most luxurious suites – a loft-style complex that comes complete with stunning views of lake and mountains, downstairs living room, limestone en-suite bathroom with antique bath and shower area, plus a full entertainment system. The circular stairs are encased in glass and lead to the privacy of an upper-floor bedroom floating amid the tree tops.

The Wheatleigh's central facilities are there to enhance the experience. The place really does have the elegance and style of a grand country house, suitably complemented by modern enhancements such as a heated pool. As you would expect, the level of personal service and the hotel's fine cuisine are exceptional, and after getting home you get to casually mention to your friends that you've stayed in the world's best treehouse.

WHERE:
Hawthorne Road, Lenox, Massachusetts
COST:
Astronomical
BEST TIME OF YEAR:
May to September for the best of the weather, October and November to see the spectacular New England autumn leaves
DON'T MISS:
Beautiful Tiffany stained glass and an impressive art collection in the main building; eating at a balcony table in summer; a hot-air balloon ride over the surrounding mountain scenery
THINGS TO DO:
If you must stray from the leisurely comforts of the hotel, the concierge can arrange diverting activities such as golf, horse riding, biking, fishing or winter skiing.
YOU SHOULD KNOW:
Casual dress seems inappropriate when eating in the rather grand formal dining room, but it's possible to loosen up a bit if choosing the former library. Take a good sweater – evenings can be chilly in the Berkshires, even in summer.

Winvian Resort

And now for something (almost) completely different. The Winvian Resort in Connecticut's fabled Litchfield Hills might have been made for those who dream of a totally relaxed break, freed from the stresses and strains of everyday life . . . and actually that's precisely who it *was* created for. Extraordinary getaways are the speciality of this unusual resort, located in the idyllic and unspoilt northwest corner of Connecticut.

Winvian is an extensive green enclave adjoining the much larger White Memorial Foundation – a unique non-profit-making organization devoted to conservation that oversees a wildlife sanctuary extending to around 1,600 ha (4,000 ac) of fields, water and woodlands. A stay at Winvian means going back to nature, with a satisfying twist. That twist is the tempting choice of romantic hideaways tucked away in stunning locations around the estate. These are very special cottages, all different, each designed to appeal to the eye. With 20 on offer, the hard part is choosing which one.

Architects have been given the chance to let their imaginations run free and, as a result, each cottage has fantastic character. This can be illustrated by the amazing Helicopter – a meticulously restored 1968 Sikorsky Sea King Pelican HH3F converted to luxurious accommodation, complete with wood-burning stove. Others are equally whimsical or more traditional in appearance, ranging from Artist – a 1920s bungalow complete with studio – through to Woodlands with its own waterfall and sinks crafted from solid wood. Along the way are evocatively named alternatives such as Beaver Lodge, King Arthur's Court, Golf, Greenhouse, Log Cabin, Secret Society and Treehouse. You simply have to smile – and the longer you stay, the broader that smile becomes. This truly is a place that can boast 'once experienced, never forgotten'.

WHERE:
Alain White Road, Morris, Connecticut

COST:
It's expensive going on astronomical, depending on season, time of the week and chosen cottage. But it's a get-away-from-it-all treat that couples will find is well worth paying for. For a party of four or a family the *per capita* rate for a cottage can swiftly descend towards the reasonable.

BEST TIME OF YEAR:
This is a country retreat for all seasons.

DON'T MISS:
A workout at the Winvian Playground (actually a fitness area equipped with pretty much everything needed for any routine from yoga and Pilates through mild exercise to advanced physical torture – with or without the assistance of a personal trainer)

THINGS TO DO:
Any or all of the many outdoor activities offered as part of the Winvian experience – badminton, canoeing, croquet, hiking, kayaking, leisure and mountain biking, tennis and *bocce*, volleyball and wiffle ball; a visit to the nearby White Memorial Conservation Centre's Nature Museum (and the shop full of tempting hand-crafted pieces from local artisans)

YOU SHOULD KNOW:
Fully inclusive rates are available, or guests who prefer to self-cater or go *à la carte* can do so (and save plenty). Anyone who doubts that Winvian is special should know that the resort has featured on US TV's Travel Channel in *Extreme Mind Blowing Hotels*, a show that focuses on the country's most unusual and interesting places to stay.

Mayhurst Inn

WHERE:
Mayhurst Lane, Orange, Virginia
COST:
Reasonable
BEST TIME OF YEAR:
Any time (the inn's *Dining Diversions and Day Trips* advice offers a comprehensive list of places to visit, things to do, local events and dining options, whatever the season)
DON'T MISS:
The spot where 18,000 Confederate troops encamped during the winter of 1863–64 (General Ambrose Powell Hill commanded them from his tent on Mayhurst's front lawn, although his wife preferred life as a house guest); a tour of the house with it's wonderful original four-storey staircase climb up to the rooftop cupola from whence General 'Stonewall' Jackson once surveyed his army (spot the original Civil War Graffiti scratched into the glass).

If it wasn't for the fact that you'll seriously want to stay on for a while longer, a night at the Mayhurst Inn in Central Virginia would be to die and go to heaven for. This is a place where you can chill for America, while imagining (and indeed experiencing much of) the atmosphere and gracious living of an elegant antebellum plantation house. The old-fashioned pace of life in the slow lane is instantly relaxing and the whole place oozes Southern charm personified.

This exuberant Italianate gem was built in 1859 by one Colonel John Willis, but he and his family had little time to enjoy their new home, or the wealth generated by his large plantation with its 50 slaves. He lost the place to a Northern carpetbagger after the Civil War and died in poverty. But the house he left behind is an impressive legacy, now immaculately restored and surrounded by 15 ha (37 ac) of manicured lawns, gardens, trees and meadows. Easy living was once a way of life here, but 21st-century visitors also

expect (and get) every modern comfort. So the eight beautifully decorated guest rooms are all air-conditioned with a private spa bath and come with a hairdryer, complimentary chocolates, bottled water, quality toiletries, luxury linens and high-speed wifi . . . plus a thoroughly traditional fireplace.

Many guests choose simply to enjoy the unique Mayhurst experience but, for those who like action, the inn arranges all sorts of imaginative vacation packages with themes like adventure, golf, winery tours, Civil War history, fall foliage and winter escape. They'll even arrange a hot-air balloon flight, taking off from the lawn. Better make that booking for at least a week!

THINGS TO DO:
Fishing (in the grounds); horseback riding; hiking; visiting a choice of former presidential homes (Montpelier, Monticello and Ashlawn); touring one or more of six nearby Civil War battlefields

YOU SHOULD KNOW:
Well-behaved children are welcome (as are pets, by appointment). Mayhurst is listed on the National Registry of Historic Places and is also a Virginia Historic Landmark, listed for historic and architectural merit.

The Inn at Narrow Passage

This is Civil War country and there was room at the inn for General 'Stonewall' Jackson's headquarters in 1862 during the hard-fought Valley campaign. Long before that the place was a colonial outpost, built in 1740 as the great drive westwards gathered pace, to succour and shelter pioneers from marauding Indians fighting to defend their homeland. This colourful history is easy to imagine at today's Inn at Narrow Passage, originally named for its strategic location at a point where the Great Wagon Road was wide enough for but a single wagon. Happily, the modern equivalent (the Old Valley Turnpike, aka Route 11) is rather wider.

Beautifully restored with that proud American pedigree in mind, this welcoming bed-and-breakfast inn is located between the Blue Ridge Mountains and the Alleghenies, alongside Narrow Passage Creek and the rolling Shenandoah River. Although close to Woodstock, the wonderful country setting makes for a relaxing stay, with hands-on owners ensuring that traditional personal service is king. There is a choice of 12 guest rooms, delightful common areas and extensive grounds. The oldest rooms have pine floors and are cleverly decorated to remind visitors of colonial times, while rooms in the later additions are finished in similar style but have the advantage of porches that offer great views across the lawn to the river and mountains beyond. All feature charming woodwork and antique furniture.

Those who argue that the USA is a tad short on gen-u-ine heritage should stop here awhile, for the surrounding area not only has many splendid old colonial buildings, but also Civil War battle sites such as Cedar Creek and New Market, plus historic plantations including Belle Grove. And the full-of-character Inn at Narrow Passage provides a perfect base from which to explore the historic Shenandoah Valley's many attractions.

WHERE:
Chapman Landing Road, Edinburg, Virginia

COST:
Reasonable

BEST TIME OF YEAR:
Any time (mint juleps in summer, sensational treescapes in autumn, log fires in winter)

DON'T MISS:
A refreshing glass of local wine produced by Shenandoah or North Mountain Vineyards; antique shops in the nearby towns of Woodstock and Edinburg; a visit to the awesome Luray and/or Shenandoah Caverns

THINGS TO DO:
Fishing; hiking in the National Forest; horse riding ditto; rafting or tubing down the river (bring your own kit and the inn will convey you up stream to float back in style); a morning or evening hot-air balloon flight over the Shenandoah Valley

YOU SHOULD KNOW:
Don't expect to hear Julie Andrews in full voice, but in summer the hills do indeed come alive with the sound of music. The popular Shenandoah Valley Music Festival presents weekend events ranging from blue grass to concerts by the ever-popular Fairfax Symphony Orchestra.

The Greenbrier Resort

WHERE:
West Main Street, White Sulphur Springs, West Virginia
COST:
Expensive up to stratospheric (for the seven-bedroom Presidential Suite)
BEST TIME OF YEAR:
Any time, depending on your choice of indoor/outdoor recreational activities (winters are cold, summers hot and humid)
DON'T MISS:
Take a tour of the formerly secret Bunker, a covert relocation centre completed in the early 1960s under cover of a major extension of Greenbrier, intended to house the US Congress in the event of nuclear war and kept fully stocked and ready for use until after the Soviet Union imploded in 1989.
THINGS TO DO:
Gamble at the resort's tasteful casino; luxuriate in the choice of super-spa treatments.
YOU SHOULD KNOW:
A mere 26 current and former presidents have stayed at the place, and Greenbrier's grand re-opening after World War II was attended by the likes of the Duke and Duchess of Windsor, Bing Crosby and various Kennedys. Subsequent guests included Prince Rainier and Princess Grace of Monaco.

There's nothing like a bit of seemly modesty and that's certainly the policy of West Virginia's Greenbrier Resort in the wondrous Allegheny Mountains, which mentions in passing that it's 'the finest luxury resort in the world'. No misunderstanding there, then. So what justifies this sweeping claim? Well, the Greenbrier (subtitled 'America's Resort') does has everything it takes for a memorable stay, and then some. An awesome white hotel building with classical portico (a National Historic Landmark) sits at the centre of a 2,600 ha (6,500 ac) wooded estate, dotted with cottages for those who prefer total privacy. There is accommodation to suit every (expensive) taste, right up to exclusive Windsor Club level where you can 'live like royalty'.

Actually (whisper it if you dare) the resort's superior status was tarnished by bankruptcy in 2009, but new owners are putting everything into restoring this iconic slice of Americana to its five-star glory days, with such success that today's visitors would never guess that times were recently hard. The whole place grew up around a popular 19th-century spa where wealthy visitors took the waters, and sulphur springs still bubble up into the white-columned spring house that's the resort's long-standing symbol.

But Greenbrier now offers far more than healing waters and impeccable service, with a range of amenities and recreational possibilities that cater for every taste. A huge selection of leisure pursuits and outdoor adventures is available on the vast estate. The resort also offers special opportunities ranging from golf packages on a historic course through outdoor adventures to ballroom dancing weekends. Children are catered for with a range of facilities and it's hard to find anything that Greenbrier doesn't offer, indoors or out.

The Homestead

It sounds very down-home American: a humble frontier dwelling where a pioneer family lives a simple life based on hard work and self-reliance. But this particular Homestead is different. It certainly dates from the right period and has authentic credentials, having grown from a few early cabins built around hot springs in Virginia's Allegheny Mountains, although that's where the similarity ends. For in 1766 a military colleague of George Washington established the homestead that would eventually develop into one of the USA's oldest resorts and spas – and one of its most famous.

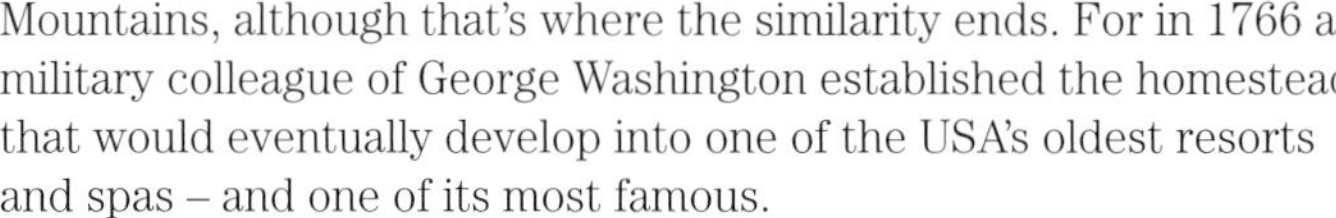

This Homestead is a palatial building which was constructed after a destructive fire in 1901, when the place had been flourishing as a renowned spa for over half a century. Throughout the 20th century The Homestead prospered as a destination for America's elite and, after a major refurbishment in the 1990s, now offers its guests the ultimate luxury resort spa experience. It has nearly 500 rooms and suites that provide a super-comfortable night's sleep, punctuating days spent exploring the Homestead's exceptional recreational facilities and its breathtaking surroundings. Families are welcome.

The house speciality is tailored packages. Typical examples include an activities package (everything and anything from archery though canoeing to horseback riding, mountain biking and sporting clay-pigeon shooting), spa package (choice of super-pampered spa sessions) and a winter activities package (ice skating, skiing, horseback riding, skeet shooting and more). All that rewarding activity in clean mountain air works up a keen appetite. The Homestead is famed for fine food, never more impressively served than in the grand dining room with nightly ballroom dancing. But there are plenty of less formal options – a grill offering seasonal local fare, casual lunch spots and various bars.

WHERE:
Sam Snead Highway, Hot Springs, Virginia

COST:
Reasonable to expensive (but many activities are included, except at the basic bed-and-breakfast rate)

BEST TIME OF YEAR:
Appropriate outdoor action is available all year round, depending on the season.

DON'T MISS:
The Homestead's Mews is an exceptional falconry centre where you can learn about this traditional form of hunting using trained birds of prey, including falcons, hawks and owls.

THINGS TO DO:
A round of golf on a historic course (with the USA's oldest first tee still in use); the off-road dune-buggy adventure; a back-in-time carriage ride; the spectacular gorge hike; a lively paintball session; the fascinating Homestead history tour; fly fishing (with or without instruction)

YOU SHOULD KNOW:
The list of current and future presidents who have patronized the spa is lengthy, starting with a young George Washington's appearances at the original homestead in the mid 1750s through to President Bill Clinton's visit in 2000.

WHERE:
Broad Street, Charleston, South Carolina
COST:
Reasonable to expensive depending on season and level of accommodation chosen
BEST TIME OF YEAR:
Any time (but expect occasional hurricanes and regular rainstorms from June to September)
DON'T MISS:
Breakfast served in the ballroom or the inn's pleasant courtyard; afternoon tea in the piazza overlooking historic Broad Street, one of the city's most impressive thoroughfares
THINGS TO DO:
Leisurely exploration of Old Charleston, and/or a horse-drawn carriage tour; a ferry ride to Fort Sumter, scene of the first shot fired in the American Civil War; a trip to one of the area's fascinating plantations for an atmospheric glimpse of a vanished past – Boone Hall and Magnolia Plantations, Drayton Hall and Middleton Place are all splendid; a keep-trim workout arranged by the inn at a nearby health club
YOU SHOULD KNOW:
Up to two children under 13 years of age can stay free of charge, using existing beds, while a relatively modest extra charge is levied for older children or a second adult using existing beds. Despite its historic credentials, the inn has wifi that may be used free of charge and offers every modern facility. Photo identification and a credit card are required at check-in. Off-street car parking is available.

John Rutledge House Inn

In 1670 English colonists arrived at the Charles Towne Landing to establish the first European settlement in the Carolinas. Less than a century later, Charleston was a thriving port and South Carolina had grown rich through trade and cotton produced by surrounding plantations. One of its most prominent citizens was one John Rutledge, a successful lawyer from a large local family. In 1763 he built a magnificent town house for his new bride and later played a major role in repulsing the British, becoming one of 55 signatories to the US Constitution, much of which he drafted, and serving on the US Supreme Court.

That imposing house still bears his name and has become America's most historic inn, offering elegant accommodation within the house and converted coach houses. Visitors to today's John Rutledge House Inn are following in eminent footsteps. George Washington is known to have dropped by, while President Taft stayed over in the early 1900s. The place was remodelled several times after Rutledge sold it towards the end of the 18th century, but always in the finest taste using the best craftsmen. Following careful restoration it is now the very epitome of a grand Southern residence, filled with wonderful antiques and exquisite period detail.

Guests will not only savour the ambiance of this unique inn, but also enjoy the friendly welcome and warm hospitality for which the American South is justly famous. With bed, breakfast and afternoon tea all part of the service, guests can eat dinner at one of Charleston's famous restaurants, after spending the day exploring this historic city's charming antebellum districts for a true flavour of the Old South.

Jekyll Island Club Hotel

If you'd been here a century ago, you would have been a member of one of the world's most exclusive clubs, rubbing shoulders with America's wealthiest elite – multi-millionaires with names like Morgan, Rockefeller, Astor, Pulitzer and Vanderbilt, all arriving at Georgia's Jekyll Island on ever-more-impressive yachts to escape the northern winter, hell-bent on outdoing fellow club members in the status stakes. But the Great Depression saw membership slump, and World War II finally finished this historic institution. In 1947 Georgia purchased Jekyll Island, which was thus transformed from private paradise to public state park.

But the superbly appointed Victorian clubhouse with its iconic tower remained, along with summer cottages (for which read holiday mansions) built by those swashbuckling entrepreneurs of an earlier age. Today, the Jekyll Island Club Hotel occupies that clubhouse, along with two of the millionaire mansions, all beautifully refurbished in keeping with their original character. It's a wonderful opportunity for guests to spend time in this historic resort, with its immaculate grounds and stunning views, in a close-to-the-beach setting.

Despite respecting tradition, this is nonetheless a 21st-century resort hotel offering every modern comfort and extensive facilities. With over 130 rooms, there's something to suit everyone, from singletons to families. And service levels would have pleased those mighty moguls of old, with a choice of eateries and watering holes, heated pool, fitness room, in-room massages, croquet lawn, putting green, private beach pavilion and much more besides. Doing nothing here equates with pampered pleasure, but most visitors will want to get out and about to sample the sights and activities that make this idyllic island such a special place (with the helpful concierge standing by to make any necessary arrangements).

WHERE:
Riverview Drive, Jekyll Island, Georgia
COST:
Reasonable (regular double rooms) to moderately expensive (suites)
BEST TIME OF YEAR:
Any time (June to August can be very hot, but sea breezes make outdoor life pretty comfortable)
DON'T MISS:
Dine in the club's Grand Dining Room with its fabulous leaded art glass and classical details, where influential members once enjoyed fine food and the best wines as they discussed matters that would shape the future of the USA – or swapped the latest society gossip.
THINGS TO DO:
Anything and everything a superior seaside holiday can offer, from carriage rides through horseback riding and canoeing to dolphin cruises and deep-sea fishing is available. There's lots to explore (including the National Historic Landmark District and oak woods) and lots to see (such as a fine art gallery and the turtle centre), not to mention mile after mile of beautiful beaches. Not for nothing was Jekyll Island the favourite playground of the great and the not-always-so-good of yesteryear!
YOU SHOULD KNOW:
Children aged 17 and younger can occupy the same room as their parents free of charge, using existing bed arrangements. Photo identification and a credit card are required at check-in. If you happen to arrive in your own plane, the hotel has a private airstrip.

Jules Undersea Lodge

WHERE:
Key Largo, Florida
COST:
Expensive
BEST TIME OF YEAR:
Any time, but perhaps safest to avoid the hurricane season (June to November) – or at least the height of it, August to October
DON'T MISS:
Marine Lab, an underwater research laboratory in the Emerald Lagoon
THINGS TO DO:
Scuba diving; underwater filming; watching marine life

Jules Lodge must be the world's most unlikely hotel. Named after the science-fiction writer Jules Verne, author of *Twenty Thousand Leagues Under the Sea*, the lodge is in fact a refurbished marine research capsule, once used for monitoring the coastal waters off Puerto Rico. It is now securely anchored 9 m (30 ft) down in the Emerald Lagoon at the 'diving capital of the world', Key Largo.

This is the only hotel in the world where guests literally dive through the front door. You wade through a tangle of mangroves and plunge into the lagoon, diving down more than 6 m (20 ft) to find the entrance. You swim through a secret opening in the belly of the capsule into an enclosed pool, from where you miraculously surface into the lodge's wet room. Hatchways lead from the wet room to bedrooms on one side and living quarters on the other.

The air-conditioned accommodation is snug without being at

all claustrophobic. There are two comfortable double bedrooms, the wet room has the luxury of a hot shower, and the living area has extra fold-away beds, a fully equipped kitchenette, hi-tech entertainment centre, and communication lines to the outside world. Gourmet meals can be ordered and there is even a pizza service – delivered to you in a waterproof container by your undersea waiter.

Both bedrooms and living area have enormous porthole windows, more than a metre (3.3 ft) in diameter. The lagoon is an exotic undersea garden of sponges and anemones, a nursery habitat for parrot and angel fish, snappers and barracuda. You will soon find yourself in a trance, gazing at the hypnotic view – an underwater movie in the making.

YOU SHOULD KNOW:
Jules Lodge is the only undersea hotel (and one of only two underwater hotels) in the world. The capsule helps the underwater environment, oxygenating the water and acting as an artificial reef for marine life. Although prior scuba-diving experience is not essential, novice divers should try to have one or two lessons beforehand to get the most out of their stay; no children under the age of ten.

The Floating Inn

There are so many places to stay on the tourist islands of Florida Keys that it's hard to choose between them. But if you're looking for somewhere cheap, clean and comfortable yet with a bit of offbeat charm then you can't beat The Floating Inn.

This unpretentious little four-roomed hotel is a custom built houseboat with a faintly ramshackle, bohemian air about it. It is well away from the beaten track, moored in a private cove on the Largo Sound – pure Humphrey Bogart territory. The double-decker houseboat floats in a metre (3.3 ft) of water beside its own little beach. It is surprisingly stable and most of the time you would scarcely know you were afloat, but for the sound of rippling water lapping against the boat. When the wind is up, you'll be soothed to sleep as the houseboat gently sways to the rhythm of the waves. There are breathtaking ocean views from the upper deck and each of the spotlessly clean air-conditioned rooms is self-contained with its own private entrance and porch, kitchenette and bathroom.

The hospitable couple who own The Floating Inn don't live on board, so you never feel they're breathing down your neck, but they're only a stone's throw away and will immediately run to your aid if you need help with anything. They seem to take real pride in their service and go out of their way to make their guests feel comfortable and at ease.

If you're looking for luxury and maid service this is definitely not the place for you. But if you want to hang out somewhere a bit different in a completely relaxed atmosphere, then The Floating Inn is a terrific deal.

WHERE:
Key Largo, Florida
COST:
Budget
BEST TIME OF YEAR:
December to May; avoid the height of the hurricane season between August and October
DON'T MISS:
A glass-bottomed boat ride at John Pennekamp State Park to see the living coral reef
THINGS TO DO:
Snorkelling; scuba diving; fishing; kayaking; sailing; jet-skiing; paragliding; cycling; lazing on the beach
YOU SHOULD KNOW:
Rooms are equipped with satellite TV and internet access; breakfast is not provided, but there's a great little local diner only a step away; you will need insect repellent – mosquitoes thrive in the subtropical climate of Largo Sound.

Little Palm Island Resort

The remote islands of the Lower Florida Keys, once the haunt of artists, smugglers and ne'er do wells, have become increasingly popular as a hangout for celebrities and the super-rich. And Little Palm Island is the most exclusive hideaway of them all, as remote as it gets, a tiny 2 ha (5 ac) coral islet accessible only by boat or by seaplane.

The accommodation is in 30 picturesque, thatched-roof cottages scattered round the island. The spacious, airy rooms are luxuriously furnished, with private porches and outdoor showers. There are never more than 60 guests at a time, so the island never feels at all crowded. You can wander along paths of crushed sea-shells through a miniature subtropical paradise with views of the ocean all around you in complete solitude and tranquillity, your only companions being the cute little 'Bambi' deer that roam wild here.

Your days can be spent lolling in a hammock under the swaying palm trees and swimming in the heated freshwater pool. In the evenings you can sit beside the fire pit, sipping a cocktail and watching spectacular ocean sunsets. If you want a bit more activity, all the facilities for scuba diving, sea trips and kayaking are laid on, while a state-of-the-art spa and fitness centre offers all sorts of exotic body treatments. The dining room on the ocean front serves an exotic fusion menu of Cuban, French and Asian creations, and the kitchen is only too willing to provide a customized personal service for you to picnic anywhere on the island.

Little Palm Island is not only an idyllic respite from urban stress but also the ultimate in romantic adventures.

WHERE:
Off Little Torch Key, Lower Keys, Florida
COST:
Astronomical
BEST TIME OF YEAR:
December to May; avoid the hurricane season of August to October
DON'T MISS:
Soaking in a lemongrass-scented *ofuro* (Japanese wooden tub) in the spa; diving or snorkelling at Looe Key National Marine Sanctuary, one of the best diving spots in the Keys; a seaplane tour of the Dry Tortugas, the islets at the tip of Florida Keys
THINGS TO DO:
Scuba diving; snorkelling; fishing; kayaking; boating; sea trips
YOU SHOULD KNOW:
Guests must be aged at least 16. There's no TV or telephone and no ocean swimming from the shore.

The Grand Hotel

Leave the vehicle behind for this one, which is not a suggestion but an order. That's because the family-owned (very) Grand Hotel is situated on Mackinac Island in Lake Huron, where automobiles are not allowed. Open since 1887, it soon became a get-away-from-it-all haven for the well-heeled visitors who arrived by train and then lake steamer from North America's developing cities. Since then, this all-American flag-waver has kept pace with modern innovations and now offers every facility that's expected of a top-drawer hotel in the 21st century, while maintaining traditional standards behind a facade with an awesome covered balcony promenade, ablaze with colourful geraniums and overlooking the water, that's pure 19th-century perfection.

That timeless look is complemented by the island's tranquillity and serene natural beauty, where guests are perforce reminded of a forgotten era when afternoon tea on an immaculate lawn might be followed by a stately evening dance to Strauss waltzes, and a horse-drawn carriage was the only way to travel locally. There are over 500 horses on the island still, helping the many summer visitors to get around, although walking and taking to two wheels are equally good (if rather more energetic) ways of exploring this small but charming island. Highlights include garden tours and a visit to historic Fort Mackinac, now a museum in the grounds of Mackinac Island State Park.

That said, some guests may choose to wander no further than the hotel's beautiful grounds, content to go back to the future with the help of luxurious possibilities such as the salon and spa, fitness centre, tennis, croquet and evening concerts, not to mention three exceptional meals that divide up the day perfectly. A stay at the Grand Hotel really does recall a bygone era of elegance and comfort, combined with every modern luxury.

WHERE:
Mackinac Island, Michigan

COST:
Expensive to astronomical, depending on choice of accommodation (full board is included and children under the age of 11 stay free with their parents)

BEST TIME OF YEAR:
The season runs from late April into October.

DON'T MISS:
The hotel's ever-popular signature dessert, Grand Pecan Balls

THINGS TO DO:
Play a round on the hotel's 18-hole golf course, The Jewel (and browse happily in the pro shop). Plunge into the pool where legendary Hollywood swimming star Esther Williams was filmed in the movie *This Time for Keeps* back in 1947. Splash some cash in the hotel's tempting boutique stores.

YOU SHOULD KNOW:
No tipping is expected within the hotel, but there are hefty percentage add-ons of various sorts to basic room rates. In 1895 Mark Twain gave a lecture at the Grand Hotel (admission $1).

WHERE:
Corner of South Broadway and Main Street, Lebanon, Ohio
COST:
Reasonable
BEST TIME OF YEAR:
Any time, although winters can be hard
DON'T MISS:
Dining at the nationally famed Golden Lamb restaurant
THINGS TO DO:
Visit the Warren County Historical Museum, one of the USA's most outstanding county museums; tour Glendower State Memorial, a splendid mansion built in the Greek Revival style popular in 1840s Ohio, full of splendid Victorian furnishings (and you might even find Civil War re-enactors going at it hammer and tongs in the grounds).
YOU SHOULD KNOW:
The simple rooms at the inn are named after famous guests, from Charles Dickens to President George W Bush. Rooms are furnished with antiques and all have private bath, television, air conditioning and telephone. They are all on upper floors and the building has no elevator. Every bedroom and dining room is non-smoking.

Golden Lamb

Ohio was on the pioneer road westwards, and in the early 19th century that road was travelled by an assortment of characters, ranging from hopeful settlers to ne'er-do-wells. In 1803, Jonas Seaman strode back to his two-storey log house in the developing town of Lebanon bearing a $4 licence to keep 'a house of public entertainment', and the fascinating commercial life of The Golden Lamb had begun.

The inn he opened became a major meeting place for locals and travellers alike, as both a place of public entertainment permitted by Seaman's licence – including readings, plays, musical occasions, animal acts and freak shows – and a haven for those movers and shakers busy transforming Lebanon in particular and Ohio in general from frontier territory to developing modern state. As the 19th century unfolded, the place became a stopping-off point famed for its good food and warm hospitality and notable visitors over time have included no fewer than 12 presidents of the United States.

In 1820 the log tavern was replaced by a fine brick structure which, with additions later in the century, is pretty much the impressive building that awaits guests arriving to stay at this grand old hostelry today. But bricks alone, however characterful, do not by themselves make for a memorable stay. That is ensured by the fact that – inspired by the drama and romance that has centred on The Golden Lamb since it all began back in 1803 – this is an establishment that cherishes all that's best in the American way of life and is determined to ensure that guests can experience fine food, old-fashioned gracious living and traditional tavern life in the historic setting of downtown Lebanon.

Buxton Inn

In November 1805, the founders of Granville arrived in covered wagons drawn by oxen, pursuing the dream of an ideal community modelled on those in their native New England. From a few log cabins the settlement grew steadily. Denison University was founded in 1831 and the following year Granville was formally incorporated as a village. By 1832, the Buxton Inn (then simply 'The Tavern') had been operating for 20 years, beginning its unbroken run as Ohio's oldest inn using the original building.

In those early years it not only served the needs of villagers, but also operated as Granville's first post office and a stopover for stagecoaches hurrying between Columbus and Newark. In 1865, the place was purchased by Major Horton Buxton and his wife. He gave it his name and the Buxtons were amiable hosts for over 35 years. After further changes of ownership the by-then-dilapidated inn was rescued and refurbished in the 1970s, becoming a romantic complex of immaculately restored historic buildings redolent of America's pioneering days.

When visiting the Buxton Inn, today's visitors are following in the footsteps of generations of townsfolk, countless travellers and famous people. These include three presidents of the USA, one of whom – dashing General and later short-lived President William H Harrison – rode his horse up the courtyard steps and into the inn's ballroom where a party was taking place. It is that sense of enduring history that makes this place so special. Its rooms are furnished with antiques and the period atmosphere is carefully maintained. A warm welcome is assured, with a choice of dining areas suitable for everything from a candlelit dinner to a family party.

WHERE:
East Broadway Street, Granville, Ohio
COST:
Budget (with up to four people allowed per room for a modest surcharge)
BEST TIME OF YEAR:
Any time, but be prepared to be snowed in during January or February and to simmer gently in June, July and August
DON'T MISS:
The original cellar where stagecoach drivers were housed, with its rough-hewn beams, big fireplace used for cooking and stone walls; a leisurely stroll in the wonderful gardens with their cascading fountains
THINGS TO DO:
Simply enjoy the wonderful ambiance; explore Granville's Historic District with its New England-style houses and gardens; check out the local antiques establishments; visit the Robbins Hunter Museum at Avery Downer House, one of the finest residential examples of American Greek Revival architecture, built in 1842 and now a museum housing American decorative arts.
YOU SHOULD KNOW:
For guests finding difficulty in unwinding, the Buxton Inn has a fully qualified in-house hypnotherapist.

French Lick Resort

WHERE:
French Lick, Indiana
COST:
Reasonable
BEST TIME OF YEAR:
Any time (the hotels offer some seriously appealing winter packages)
DON'T MISS:
The extraordinary domed atrium of the West Baden Springs Hotel, a true engineering marvel of its day, described upon its completion in 1902 as the 'Eighth Wonder of the World'
THINGS TO DO:
Gambling; golf; horse riding at the resort's stables; carriage rides; hiking or biking in the nearby Hoosier National Forest; swimming (indoors and out)
YOU SHOULD KNOW:
Indiana law permitted only water-based gambling, so when the casino was first established it was designed as a riverboat floating on a small pond. As soon as the rule was eased, the pond was filled in and the rest (including those 1,300 slot machines) is history. The resort stages special events to occupy and entertain younger children and teens. Regular concerts by headline acts take place at the resort and there's musical entertainment every Saturday.

Welcome to oddly named but vibrant French Lick Resort. Claimed to be 'the Midwest's premier resort, spa and golf destination', the complex boasts two luxury hotels (the West Baden Springs and French Lick Springs), together offering just about everything a comfort-hungry vacationer could hope to find in the Midwest in general and Indiana in particular. Centrally located within easy(ish) reach of cities such as Chicago, Cleveland, Detroit, St Louis, Cincinnati, Nashville and Indianapolis, French Lick is a former French trading post from colonial times that really grew up after 200+ years when the French Lick Resort Casino opened in 2006.

This took advantage of the fact that French Springs and environs already had those two old-established Victorian hotels, built to cater for spa trade attracted by the (alleged) healing properties of the town's bubbling sulphur springs. The French Lick Springs Hotel and West Baden Springs Hotel were both destroyed by fire and rebuilt in the early 1900s. These two fine spa hotels then established an enviable reputation for looking after guests, attracting the rich and famous – including future four-term President Franklin D Roosevelt, who announced his candidacy at the French Lick Springs Hotel in 1931. Both places declined during the Great Depression and revived big-time only when the new casino came to town.

Now, as essential parts of the all-embracing French Lick Resort, these grand old hotels (both listed on the National Register of Historic Places) have regained their former stature, and provide excellent accommodation and gracious living for all who stay, whether or not they head for the nearby gaming tables. Indeed, many guests simply come for the sophisticated reminder of an elegant bygone era. Choose from the recreational opportunities (three golf courses, including one PGA Championship 18-holer) and/or luxuriate in some seriously decadent self-indulgence (spa treatments have advanced more than somewhat since sulphurous days).

The American Club

How times – and societies – change. Once a haven providing food and shelter for newly arrived immigrants working for the all-powerful local Kohler Company in the aftermath of World War I, the American Club in central Wisconsin has morphed over time into a five-star resort hotel that offers the promise of a memorable stay, especially for tweedy folk who know their mashie niblick from a fairway wood, or perhaps nowadays the subtle difference between Ping and Titleist.

Yup, this is a renowned golf resort, offering can't-wait-to-tee-off access to the Blackwolf Run and nearby Whistling Run course complexes. The latter, on the shores of Lake Michigan, replicates British links courses right down to the flock of insouciant black-faced sheep. But if thrashing round championship golf courses in the gigantic footprints of golfing greats isn't your thing, a visit to the American Club can still be a thoroughly satisfying experience for couples or families (special activities offered for kids).

The whole ambiance is luxurious, with deluxe rooms and suites featuring traditional decor and all mod cons. Those who prefer the contemporary look can opt for the Carriage House, which has the added benefit of being right next to the Kohler Waters Spa (shameless pampering a speciality). While golfers are on course for glory those left behind can explore the quaint village of Kohler, do their own thing at the health and fitness centre, head for the spa or browse through more than 25 specialist shops. And when conquering (or not) heroes return from the 19th hole, it'll be time to sample some exceptional cuisine. Actually, the whole point of a resort hotel is to offer a complete experience, so there's really no need to look around for outside activities.

WHERE:
Highland Drive, Kohler, Wisconsin
COST:
Reasonable and on upwards, depending on season, accommodation and package chosen
BEST TIME OF YEAR:
Any time (whatever the season, there's always a choice of activities indoors and out)
DON'T MISS:
The Sports Core Health & Racquet Club for tennis, swimming or the whirlpool beside an open fireplace; the self-guided garden tour; a little gentle pedal-boating or canoeing
THINGS TO DO:
Golf, private golf lessons, more golf, fishing, clay-pigeon shooting, carriage rides, horseback riding and birdwatching in summer; ice fishing, game shooting, skating, cross-country skiing, sledding and snowshoeing in winter
YOU SHOULD KNOW:
The American Club is still owned by the Kohler Company (manufacturer of plumbing products to the wider world), which created a community named after itself in 1912 as a model village to house employees after moving to a greenfield site. So it's a safe bet that the en-suite bathrooms at the American Club are top-notch!

WHERE:
East Wisconsin Avenue, Milwaukee, Wisconsin
COST:
Reasonable
BEST TIME OF YEAR:
April to June, September (winters are cold, windy and snowy while summers are hot and humid)
DON'T MISS:
The hotel's impressive Victorian art collection; a super lake view from the Blu wine bar on the 23rd floor
THINGS TO DO:
A stroll along the Milwaukee Riverwalk with its art displays, cafés and bars, then a river-taxi ride from one of the embarkation points along the way; the Milwaukee Art Museum with its extraordinary $100-million 'wing'; a spectacular rooftop sculpture garden at the Milwaukee School of Engineering's Grohmann's Museum, itself worth a visit; the Pabst mansion, former home of a brewing magnate, for superb Victorian interiors
YOU SHOULD KNOW:
Milwaukee used to be the brewing capital of the USA, but now only one major brewery remains – although the city still has a noticeably generous number of watering holes.

The Pfister Hotel

Grand elegance + historic tradition + gracious service + impeccable style + downtown Milwaukee = (what else?) the Pfister Hotel. Standing four square just three blocks from Lake Michigan, this has been a city landmark since its million-dollar construction in 1893 and it has been a leading example of America's golden age of Victorian hotel-building ever since. It was advanced for its time, with innovations like climate control throughout, but was overtaken by time and completely renovated and upgraded with the addition of a striking circular tower in the 1960s, to create today's refined pleasure-to-stay-at establishment.

Over 300 guest rooms and suites are furnished and equipped to combine old-world charm with every facility, including voicemail and high-speed internet access, and they all have sweeping views over lake or city. The hotel's commitment to providing top-notch service may be gauged by touches like the 24/7 room service that will efficiently deal with requests large and small. And for those in need of serious relaxation, Milwaukee's only private spa can be found on the first floor of the Pfister, offering trendily described WELLness services in the WELL

Spa. There's also a tempting choice of eateries and bars within the hotel.

Despite its inexorable decline as an industrial powerhouse, Milwaukee is busy reinventing itself and there's plenty to see and do in town. But for those who like their activities to be organized, the Pfister offers an assortment of special breaks that reflect its quality ethos. These include cookery schools hosted by leading chefs, family packages for Discovery World on Lake Michigan with its fascinating interactive exhibits featuring innovation, technology and conservation of the Great Lakes, or an invitation to the city's all-singing-and-dancing WinterFest. For those who enjoy luxury hotel living, the Pfister won't fail to tick all the right boxes.

Old Talbott Tavern

Across the road from historic Nelson County Courthouse in Bardstown, Kentucky, stands another tasty slice of American history – the Old Talbott Tavern. This long-established inn is on the National Register of Historic Places and has operated continuously since its construction in 1779, during which period it has seen many famous guests, including legendary frontiersman Daniel Boone, an exiled King of France, future presidents including Andrew Jackson and Abraham Lincoln, plus one star turn in the outlaw Jesse James, who left bullet holes in the walls after firing at imaginary butterflies when drunk. In those early years the tavern had just two guest bedrooms – one for men, one for women – but nowadays the place is altogether more enlightened and operates as a five-room bed-and-breakfast establishment.

Each of the five rooms is beautifully furnished with elegant period antiques but includes modern necessities such as a private bath, cable TV, refrigerator, coffee maker, telephone, data port and wifi. In addition to the breakfast that comes with the room, the tavern offers lunch and dinner in the excellent restaurant with its classic American menus. There are two bars in which to unwind after a hard day's travelling or sightseeing, one named after Kentucky's greatest contribution to the honour roll of world-famous alcoholic drinks, Bourbon whiskey.

Rumour has it that the Old Talbott Tavern is haunted, and a respected travel writer once described the place as having 'slightly spooky charm'. Ghosts from American history may indeed swirl about this grand old inn, but they are surely benign and haven't yet stopped anyone having a good night's sleep. But if it's any consolation, the old Nelson County Jail right next door is said to be even more prone to nocturnal manifestations.

WHERE:
Court Square, Bardstown, Kentucky
COST:
Reasonable
BEST TIME OF YEAR:
Spring to fall (April to November); winters see plenty of rain, sleet and snow
DON'T MISS:
Live evening entertainment in the Bourbon Bar on Thursdays, Fridays and Saturdays; a bowl of popular local speciality Kentucky Burgoo
THINGS TO DO:
Step out of the tavern door to stroll around the Bardstown Historic District centred on Court Square; visit Museum Row, based around one of America's largest Civil War museums, also including a Civil War and American wildlife museum
YOU SHOULD KNOW:
As a result of the aforementioned evening entertainment, it can be difficult to get to sleep before 01.00 at the weekend. Many guests stay at the tavern when following the well-established Bourbon Trail, which takes in six traditional distilleries nestled among the most beautiful countryside in the Bluegrass State. The state's official Kentucky Bourbon Festival takes place in Bardstown.

Beckham Creek Cave Lodge

WHERE:
Near Parthenon, Arkansas
COST:
Expensive (but worth every penny for the frisson factor alone)
BEST TIME OF YEAR:
Any time (although pessimists will note that a typical Arkansas year will see thunderstorms, tornadoes, hail, snow and ice storms)
DON'T MISS:
The Spanish Piano, an amazing rock 'waterfall' in the main room; the spectacular view from the Rec Room at night, over to the floodlit bluff across the cove; local fine dining
THINGS TO DO:
Explore the nearby Ozark National Forest; rock climbing and spelunking; wildlife-watching and birdwatching; hiking and nature trails; horseback riding and mountain biking; fishing
YOU SHOULD KNOW:
Advance booking is essential (sometimes quite far in advance) as the Haven is popular with family parties that take over the whole place. There's no in-house catering unless ordered in advance; the most exclusive accommodation is the tucked-away Honeymoon Suite (non-newbies also welcome); there's a heli-pad for those making the grandest of entrances.

Fancy a stay in a Cold War bomb shelter? That may not sound compelling, but add the word 'former' and this becomes one of the most unusual and appealing places to stay in the whole USA. Beckham Creek Cave Lodge was meticulously created from the aforementioned bomb shelter, to take full advantage of a totally secluded location in Buffalo National River country, amid the wild beauty of the Ozark landscape.

Four years in the building, this unique cave dwelling would have Wilma Flintstone swooning with pleasure. It sits in a 115-ha (284-ac) private estate and the Lodge grandly claims 'This is truly a modern accommodation literally fit for royalty'. But surely that accommodation must be a tad gloomy for royal taste, right? Wrong! The walls and ceilings may be of spectacular living rock, but the Lodge has been meticulously planned to ensure that the interior is flooded with light from vast windows, bringing the outdoors in. But it must surely at least be a little dank for a crowned head? Nope! Dehumidifiers, air con and central heating make the internal atmosphere a relaxing comfort zone. This is definitely a place to chill out without the slightest hint of a nip in the air.

There are five en-suite bedrooms, plus an impressively large Main Room with its dining area, giant TV screen and advanced sound system. Upstairs is the elevated Rec Room, which is well stocked with assorted games to help while away the evenings. As for the days, some visitors are happy simply to stay around getting a rejuvenating fix of perfect tranquillity. But get-up-and-go types will find that the Ozarks offer plenty of stimulating activities.

Treehouse Cottages

WHERE:
Eureka Springs, Arkansas
COST:
Reasonable (with discounts for an extended stay)
BEST TIME OF YEAR:
Any time, but the autumn leaves are spectacular
DON'T MISS:
A long soak in the main heart-shaped jacuzzi, surrounded by glass, enjoying (among other things) an amazing forest view; the Koi carp pond and cascading waterfall; wandering along a private hiking trail that winds delightfully down the mountain to a natural cave and spring

Hidden in its own little forest haven, Original Treehouse Cottages at Eureka Springs has been established for two decades and offers a very special opportunity to rise above the cares of a high-pressure world. At a choice of two locations, one on a wooded hillside at the edge of town and the other close by in a pine forest, these are a luxurious manifestation of the strange but compelling human desire to build secure nests above ground. The cottages in question (too luxurious to be called treehouses per se) are all built on solid pole foundations – rather than actually burdening live trees – and stand amid woodland, each around 7 m (23 ft) above *terra firma*. They may be rustic by location, but not by nature.

The beautifully sited timber-clad cottages have evocative names like Lofty Lookout, Towering Pines, Whispering Woods, Hideaway and Hidden Oak. Reached by open steps or walkways from the hillside, they offer picture windows with the greenest of views and a supreme level of comfort that would shame many an upmarket hotel. These treehouse cottages are fitted out with classy interiors that include the likes of antique furniture, hardwood floors, Jacuzzis, separate bathrooms, queen-size wooden beds, fully equipped kitchen/dining areas and love seats. All sleep two adults.

For those seeking a permanent reminder of a wonderful aerial break, the Treehouse Gift Shop offers a selection of tasteful branded items, as well as the work of local artists – including the hostess, a potter who can be seen working in her studio within the grounds. Typical purchases include scented candles, bath and body lotions, designer jewellery, wind chimes and original pictures. It's that sort of place.

THINGS TO DO:
Exploring historic Eureka Springs; any of the nearby outdoor activities for which the Ozarks are famous, from canoeing to fishing, hiking to biking – and many more

YOU SHOULD KNOW:
No children are allowed in the treehouses, but there is a firmly grounded family cottage on site (sleeps two adults and two kids). There is strictly no smoking (indoors) and no pets (anywhere); the treehouses have log fireplaces to create a cosy winter atmosphere.

The Hotel Monteleone

WHERE:
Royal Street, New Orleans, Louisiana
COST:
Reasonable (rooms) to astronomical (top suites)
BEST TIME OF YEAR:
Any time (winters are short and mild, summers long and humid)
DON'T MISS:
A good ol' mint julep (or Bourbon rocks) in the hotel's extraordinary Carousel piano Bar & Lounge, sitting at a rotating 25-seater bar that describes a complete revolution every 15 minutes

Visitors to New Orleans are magnetically drawn to the colourful French Quarter. Once there, it isn't hard to spot somewhere to stay, because the Hotel Monteleone is the only high-rise building in the *Vieux Carré*. There's probably a room available, too, because the hotel has around 600 of them. It's often said that the French Quarter begins in the hotel's grand lobby, and it's easy to see why.

It wasn't always so impressive. Cobbler Antonio Monteleone arrived in New Orleans from Sicily around 1880, and by 1886 had saved enough to buy a small hotel. A second followed soon after and that was the start of today's something big (still owned and run, incidentally, by the eponymous founding family). Successive waves of development continually enlarged the original premises, culminating in a complete rebuild in 1954. The latest enhancement is topped by a

sensational Sky Terrace with heated pool, cocktail lounges and one of the best views in New Orleans.

The Monteleone has always been favoured by the literary set, with great writers like Ernest Hemingway, Tennessee Williams and William Faulkner staying when in town, and such was its reputation that author Truman Capote of *In Cold Blood* fame actually claimed (inaccurately) that he was born there. They're all gone now, but the place retains a strong sense of tradition. The Monteleone may only be one block away from pulsating Bourbon Street, but inside all is calm. Guests are enveloped in a comfortable cloak woven from a genteel mix of Southern charm and good old-fashioned personal service. There are plenty of excellent hotels to choose from in New Orleans, but it's certainly hard to trump the Monteleone when it comes to character and style.

THINGS TO DO:
Explore the French Quarter. Eat out – the hotel offers fine food, but New Orleans has an international reputation for exceptional cuisine and many of its signature restaurants are close by the hotel.
YOU SHOULD KNOW:
A free audio self-tour that describes the colourful history of this splendid hotel is available, and well worth taking. High-speed wifi is available throughout the hotel.

Sinya on Lone Man Creek

Americans have always done the Great Outdoors rather well, and nothing proves the point more convincingly than Sinya, a unique hideaway overlooking secluded-but-not-remote Lone Man Creek in famed Texas Hill Country. Actually, 'lone man' isn't quite it, because this exclusive backcountry retreat actually accommodates two, and couples find it to be the perfect romantic haven in which to spend some quality time.

Actually, it's the perfect *tent* in which to reaffirm relationships, but don't let that fool you. This is glamping (for which read luxury safari living) at its very best, and calling the accommodation a 'tent' is akin to describing the Ritz Hotel as a comfortable B&B. In fact, the place is best described as a luxury eco-lodge where communing with nature and pampered living go hand in hand. This impressive canvas eerie is equipped with everything needed for a relaxing break, from the vintage claw-footed Victorian bath to a fully fitted kitchenette, not to mention the couple-friendly king-sized platform bed with its goose-down pillows and quilt, or that comfortable love seat looking out over the tree tops. Outside, it's a pleasure simply to sit on the open verandah, cares washed away by the soothing sound of a rushing waterfall in the creek below.

From the moment you walk down the rock-lined path (beautifully lit at night), you'll be aware that you've found somewhere truly special. But don't expect to book in on a whim when those romantic batteries need recharging – there's a waiting list, and when you finally make it to Sinya you'll understand why. As magical getaways go, this place is a fabulous hilltop chart-topper.

WHERE:
Lone Man Creek, near Wimberley, Texas
COST:
Reasonable edging towards expensive (but you can get seven days for the price of six)
BEST TIME OF YEAR:
Any time (glorious in summer, cosy in winter, both in between)
DON'T MISS:
Seeing the moon rise over the tree tops, and rising early to hear an amazing dawn chorus and watch the sun come up over Hill Country
THINGS TO DO:
Wild swimming when the creek is full; looking for Native American artefacts along the creek banks; Wimberley market (first Saturday of the month, April to December)
YOU SHOULD KNOW:
Remote it may be, isolated it isn't – Sinya has wifi for those whose empires might crumble if they're off the net; recycled 'grey' water is used to irrigate the environs, so all soaps, detergents, shampoos, conditioners, body lotions and milk bath are eco-friendly (and are supplied as part of the deal).

Paws Up Resort

WHERE:
Greenough, near Missoula, Montana
COST:
Astronomical (but the place really does offer a uniquely satisfying luxury ranch experience and the price covers everything)
BEST TIME OF YEAR:
Any time, depending on preferred accommodation
DON'T MISS:
Traditional ranch activities like trail riding, cattle drives, chuck wagon meals; a hot-air balloon flight; horse-drawn sleigh rides in winter
THINGS TO DO:
The summer activities are almost too numerous to list, but include legendary Montana fly fishing, horseback riding, clay-pigeon shooting, archery, ATV tours, guided expeditions, river and lake adventures, zorbing (also special activities for kids). Winter activities include skiing, snowmobiling, dog sledding and horseback riding.
YOU SHOULD KNOW:
The resort's slogan is 'The Last Best Place'. Luxury homes are available all year round, glamping tents from late May to early October. For those who really want to get away from it all, the three-day wilderness experience based on the Encampment at Bull Creek is the answer, requiring a 19-km (12-mi) horseback ride before reaching the (still luxurious) creek-side camp.

If you don't like creaky puns, turn the page right now. A great place to pause for a special stay is . . . Paws Up. Unlike classic dude and guest ranches, this is not a place where roughing it in wide, open spaces beneath a big sky is part of the deal. Paws Up is indeed a modest – at 13,000 ha (32,000 ac) – Montana ranch in God's Own Big Country. It is indeed a working ranch with cowboys, horses and cattle roaming the pristine range. But Paws Up is also a ranch resort like no other. For this is where the appealing western ranch experience of frontier life and ultimate luxury 21st-century collide in a most auspicious fashion.

Firstly, decide on preferred accommodation in advance. Forget bunkhouse living, instead choose between attractive ranch houses and tented camps. The former are rich in comfort, offering a choice of locations and sizes suitable for four to eight people. The latter delivers glamping – glamorous camping – at its most spectacular, again with a choice of fabulous locations and tents for two to four people (and each camp does, of course, have a dedicated butler and its own chef). There are 28 homes to choose from, with two, three or four bedrooms, all within walking or short driving distance of the central Paws Up Village. If you can't decide which option suits you best, it's possible to book a combined luxury home/tent combo.

Secondly, turn up and move in to the chosen accommodation, instantly disconnecting from the cares and pressures of a modern world (although TV and wifi ensure that the divorce isn't too traumatic). Then reconnect with this wonderful place and consider which of the many ranch-based activities most appeals . . . and start to enjoy a vacation you'll never forget.

Wort Hotel

Opened back in 1941 to cater for a growing interest in the West's spectacular natural attributes (and Wyoming's unspoilt wonders in particular), the Wort Hotel in Jackson is built in traditional style and takes pride in combining historic charm with western hospitality (and luxury facilities) to create the town's finest lodging. The hotel has around 60 well-appointed guest rooms, including themed suites, which are appropriately furnished with lodge-pole pine beds and western fabrics and also offer such Wild West essentials as media centres with flat-screen TVs, refrigerators, humidifiers and Starbucks coffee on tap.

If sleeping arrangements are no problem, neither is in-hotel dalliance. The Wort Hotel has one of the West's most famous watering holes: the Silver Dollar Bar. With precisely 2,032 uncirculated 1921 Morgan silver dollars embedded in its surface, the name is not hard to fathom. It also happens to be the town's social centre, enjoyed by locals, cowboys and millionaires alike, with visitors guaranteed a warm welcome. There's live music three nights a week and the atmosphere is never dull for a moment. The Silver Dollar Grill (with a mere 300 embedded silver dollars, vintage stained glass, black walnut tables, western artwork and an original roulette wheel to set the scene) offers fine dining that encompasses both classic cuisine and dishes prepared with wild game and other regional fare.

This is a wonderfully laid-back place to stay, but a good part of the attraction lies in exploring the surrounding landscape. The valley of Jackson Hole itself is a scenic marvel, but that's as nothing compared to the nearby wonders to be seen in Grand Teton and Yellowstone National Parks.

WHERE:
North Glenwood Street, Jackson, Wyoming
COST:
Reasonable to expensive, depending on season and accommodation chosen
BEST TIME OF YEAR:
Any (May to September for National Parks, the cold months of October to April for winter activities)
DON'T MISS:
The famous elk-antler arches around Jackson's Town Square; Bluegrass Tuesdays in the hotel's Silver Dollar Bar, the most popular free weekly entertainment in town; the town's National Museum of Wildlife Art; Jackson Rodeos (Wednesdays and Saturdays in season)
THINGS TO DO:
Hiking; mountain biking along marked trails; fly fishing; hot-air balloon rides; marvelling at regular-as-clockwork geyser Old Faithful in Yellowstone; taking to the slippery slopes of Jackson Hole in winter, notably the steep Snow King area (if you know no fear, whizz down at night under lights) or Jackson Hole Mountain Resort; a winter horse-drawn sleigh ride in the nearby National Elk Refuge
YOU SHOULD KNOW:
Every visitor gets to sleep with the hotel's complimentary signature Silver Dollar Sam teddy bear.

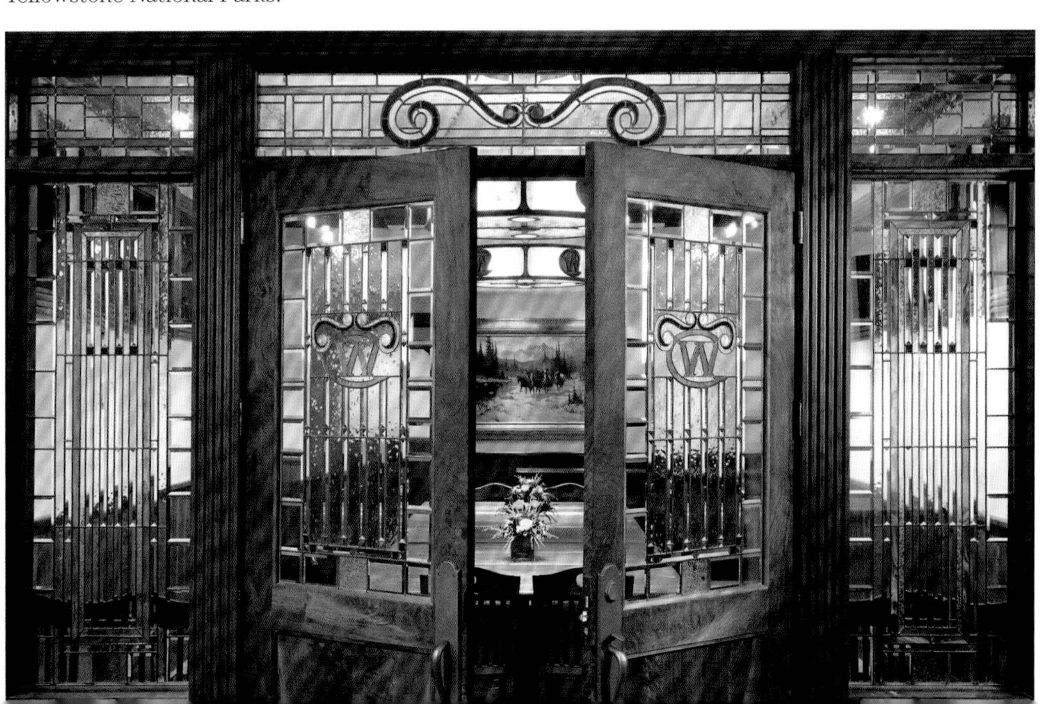

The Stanley Hotel

WHERE:
Estes Park, Colorado
COST:
Reasonable
BEST TIME OF YEAR:
Any time, depending on what outdoor pursuits you are interested in
DON'T MISS:
The hotel's fascinating Ghosts & History Tour; the spectacular scenic drive along Trail Ridge Road that crosses the Continental Divide
THINGS TO DO:
Hiking; climbing; cycling; horseback riding; golf; fishing; hunting; whitewater rafting; birdwatching; snowshoeing; sledging; cross-country skiing; ice skating; shopping; galleries; wine tastings at one of the local wineries
YOU SHOULD KNOW:
The hotel is listed on the US Register of National Historic Places and gets very booked up in the summer months, so reservations must be made well in advance. Although the Stanley was the inspiration for *The Shining*, the hotel was not the actual backdrop in the film – although the Stanley is said to be haunted.

Anyone who has seen the film *The Shining* must have wondered how such a gruesome horror story could ever be dreamed up. Well, the answer lies in the Stanley Hotel. Author Stephen King was holidaying there at a time when there happened to be hardly any guests and was inspired to write his best-selling novel as a result of staying in the almost-empty building.

The stately neo-Georgian mansion was built in 1909 by Freelan Oscar Stanley, a powerful business magnate renowned for manufacturing the Stanley Steamer automobile. He suffered from tuberculosis and took his doctor's advice to come and stay in a cabin in Estes Park for the mountain air. His health immediately improved and he was so smitten by the beauty of the surroundings, he decided to turn the area into a resort. The Stanley soon became one of Colorado's best-known grand hotels. It is beautifully situated on a mountain shelf, towering nearly 3,000 m (10,000 ft) over the Estes Valley, from where the panoramic views are simply stunning. The 138-room hotel stands in 22 ha (55 ac) of grounds where an elk herd roams and you may even catch sight of the odd coyote from the hotel verandah.

Rocky Mountain National Park is on the doorstep and Estes Park is reputed to be one of the best holiday destinations in the United States. Go for a mountain hike, picnic beside a lake among the scent of pine trees and dine beside the waterfall fountain in the hotel courtyard. The Stanley combines old-world charm with all the latest modern comforts and conveniences. It's perfect for romantic getaways or for parties of friends and family reunions.

Hotel Colorado

The Hotel Colorado reeks of 19th-century opulence. Built in 1893, in the last days of America's Gilded Age, it is a magnificent Italianate *palazzo*. Built out of pale-pink sandstone with cream-coloured Roman brickwork, it was designed to emulate the Renaissance Villa Medici in Rome, with a courtyard and beautifully planted garden.

Inside, the hotel was modelled on the grand hotels of Europe in terms of both decor and service. The intention was to inject a bit of European *belle époque* sophistication into Colorado's Wild West and to provide wealthy socialites with a suitably glamorous place to stay when they came to take the waters at Glenwood's famous hot mineral springs. After Teddy Roosevelt stayed here in 1905 the hotel's reputation was made, and it became known as the 'Little White House of the West'. Later, it attracted a rather different class of guest – during the 1920s it became the classy hangout of choice for Chicago mobsters.

As soon as you walk in you can feel the hotel's character and history oozing from every corner. It has antique armchairs and open fires in the lobby, high ceilings and old-fashioned ceiling fans in the plushly furnished rooms and broad corridors lined with fascinating old photographs of historic figures from the hotel's glory days. The Colorado is superbly located just a couple of minutes from Glenwood Hot Springs Pool and it is only a short walk to all the downtown shops and attractions. The staff here are courteous and attentive – nothing seems to be too much trouble for them. This is a great place to spend a romantic weekend in a grand historic setting.

WHERE:
Glenwood Springs, Colorado
COST:
Reasonable
BEST TIME OF YEAR:
Go any time, but perhaps December to February is the most dramatic season when the hotel is Christmassy and the surrounding mountains are covered in snow.
DON'T MISS:
Glenwood Hot Springs Pool
THINGS TO DO:
Skiing; hiking; cycling; rafting; shopping; visiting museums and galleries
YOU SHOULD KNOW:
The hotel is listed on the US National Register of Historic Places and the origins of the teddy bear are said to be here – when President Theodore ('Teddy') Roosevelt stayed here on a bear-hunting trip in 1905 the hotel staff gave him a gift of a stuffed bear to make up for the fact that he hadn't shot one. Glenwood Hot Springs pool was revered by the Native American Ute tribe as a healing place.

Devil's Thumb Ranch

WHERE:
Tabernash, Colorado
COST:
Expensive, but for a budget option you can stay in the Bunkhouse down the road and still make use of all the ranch's facilities
BEST TIME OF YEAR:
March to April for those who want to commune with nature in solitude; May to August for summer sporting activities and wild flowers in bloom; September to November for perfect horse-riding weather; November to February for winter sports
DON'T MISS:
A hot-stone massage in the spa; a boat trip down the Colorado River to Hot Sulphur Springs

A luxury wood cabin at Devil's Thumb Ranch is the perfect place for outdoor adventurers, sports enthusiasts, or anyone who just wants to escape from the daily urban grind. It's a mere 90 minutes' drive from the city but feels as though it's in the middle of nowhere. The ranch stretches over 2,000 ha (5,000 ac) of idyllic meadows and woodland, overlooked by the dramatic rocky peak that gives the ranch its curious name. According to Native American folklore, this is where the devil is buried – only his thumb was left above ground to remind the world of his existence!

The ranch cabins are beautifully situated, with plenty of privacy. They nestle among the trees on a forested ridge, overlooking the pasture and ponds below. They are very comfortably furnished with rustic antiques and down bedding and have built-in fireplaces for a log fire. At night, in the stillness, with

only the whisper of the trees and twinkling stars overhead, you can get a real sense of being part of nature.

There is a multitude of outdoor activities on offer and the ranch has a fabulous spa, swimming pool and stables. There's also a games room and movie theatre for teenagers who just want to mooch around. Devil's Thumb is run along strictly eco-friendly lines. The ranch uses geothermal heating, practises water and energy conservation, recycles, and only uses environmentally friendly cleaning materials. The ranch restaurant sources organic meat and locally grown fresh produce. This is a great place for anyone who has a conscience about leaving a heavy footprint but doesn't much enjoy roughing it. Give the Devil's Thumbs-up to the best of both worlds!

THINGS TO DO:
High-altitude hiking; shooting; horse riding; fly fishing; mountain biking; nordic skiing; snowshoeing; sledging; outdoor ice skating; yoga; kids camp
YOU SHOULD KNOW:
The ranch restaurant has won awards for its magnificent wine cellar; there is no TV in the cabins and sporting activities are not cheap, so expect these to set you back quite a lot extra. Rocky Mountain National Park is just a 45-minute drive away.

Kokopelli's Cave

Stay 21 m (70 ft) underground in a wilderness cave dwelling and cast yourself back to the Stone Age in true Flintstone style – with 21st-century mod cons. Kokopelli's Cave is not the easiest place to access. You have to drive down a bumpy dirt track and then, lugging your bags, wend your way down a steep path and negotiate a ladder to get there – but the schlep is worth every inch of the effort, because staying in this extraordinary B&B is a truly wondrous experience.

The man-made cave was blasted out of a 65-million-year-old sandstone cliff in 1980 and was, for a while, used as a full-time home before being turned into a B&B in 1997. Inside, you might expect it to be cold and dank, and perhaps a bit claustrophobic, but it's not in the least. The first thing that strikes you is the carpeted floor and then the spaciousness – 150 sq m (1,620 sq ft) of interconnected cave rooms. The luxury doesn't stop there – attractive rustic furnishings, hot and cold running water, a waterfall shower, stone Jacuzzi, terrace barbecue, and well-equipped kitchen stocked with all the food you could possibly want for making snacks and breakfast. And there's even a TV.

There is an amazing sense of solitude and calm here, even though you're only a few miles out of town. Sitting on your cliff terrace at sundown, gazing at the phenomenal mountain views, you are suddenly aware that you've got company as chipmunks, squirrels and ringtail cats come scurrying right up to the cave entrance begging for titbits. Kokopelli's Cave really is a completely unique place to stay – a once-in-a-lifetime experience.

WHERE:
Farmington, New Mexico
COST:
Expensive, but reduced rate for more than two people
BEST TIME OF YEAR:
September and October; avoid March and April when it can be very windy; closed from December to February
DON'T MISS:
Four Corners National Monument in Mesa Verde National Park, where the four states of Colorado, Arizona, Utah and New Mexico meet
THINGS TO DO:
Clambering around on the cliffs; feeding the wildlife; taking photographs; watching the sunset
YOU SHOULD KNOW:
Kokopelli's Cave sleeps four and can accommodate more if you bring your own bedrolls; children must be aged 12+ and kept under adult supervision. Pack sensibly and only take what you need – you're going to have to lug your bags back uphill.

St James Hotel

If you're after an authentic taste of the Wild West then it doesn't get any more genuine than St James Hotel. Buffalo Bill met Annie Oakley here and Billy the Kid, Pat Garrett, Wyatt Earp and Jesse James are just a few among the many famous people who stayed here.

Built in 1872 to cater for travellers along the Santa Fe Trail, the hotel was originally called Lambert's Inn after its owner Henry Lambert, President Abraham Lincoln's personal chef. After his employer was assassinated, Lambert set off in search of his fortune and his inn became one of the best-known hostelries in the west.

Lambert's Inn was frequented by cowboys, outlaws and bounty hunters and, unsurprisingly given the nature of its clientele, soon gained a reputation for being the scene of numerous brawls, gunfights and murders. At least 26 men were shot and killed here. In later years, during the course of repairs, more than 400 bullet holes were discovered in the roof.

The hotel has a marvellously antique atmosphere, complete with brocade wallpaper, chandeliers, velvet drapes, a steep creaking staircase and period furniture. Room 18 is always kept locked. It is said to house the malevolent ghost of Thomas James Wright, who was mysteriously shot in the back on his way into his room after he won ownership of the hotel in a poker game with Lambert. Wright is not the only ghost in the hotel. The St James is renowned among psychics and paranormal investigators for being full of ghosts and strange phenomena. Ghost hunters, historians and Wild West enthusiasts alike will all find St James a thrilling place to stay.

WHERE:
Cimarron, New Mexico
COST:
Reasonable
BEST TIME OF YEAR:
Late September to early October for beautiful weather and few tourists
DON'T MISS:
The old hotel register with its famous guests' names; the 22 bullet scars in the hotel's dining-room ceiling; a walking tour around the historic little town of Cimarron; the Old Mill Museum in the Aztec Grist Mill
THINGS TO DO:
Ghost hunting; historical research; Cimarron Canyon State Park for hiking and fishing
YOU SHOULD KNOW:
The hotel is listed in the National Register of Historic Places; book a room in the historic part of the hotel rather than the modern annexe.

Dog Bark Park Inn

Do you have to be barking mad to volunteer for a night in the doghouse? Not if you happen to be passing through Cottonwood you don't. For here on the rolling prairie of North Central Idaho you will find America's most striking canine bed-and-breakfast establishment – not in the sense that it's intended for pampered pooches, but because this is where you get to stay inside the world's biggest beagle. His name is Sweet Willy and he's accompanied by wee Toby, a mere stripling at just 3.5 m (12 ft) tall. Bow wow!

This particular beagle is unlike any other. Sweet Willy (officially The Dog Bark Park Inn) has entrance stairs, a lofty verandah and windows. The main room is a cosy bedroom with queen-size double bed, complete with a headboard featuring numerous cut-out dogs, while there are two fold-out futon beds in the elevated loft (actually the mighty hound's muzzle) that are ideal for youngsters. The equipment's pretty impressive, too, at least by normal beagle standards. There's a bathroom, breakfast table, refrigerator, microwave oven, air conditioning, hairdryer and a selection of games and puzzles to make up for the (welcome) absence of a TV.

The Dog Bark Park Inn harks back to the early days of automobile travel, when all sorts of weird and wonderful constructs arose to catch the passing eye, with gas stations, diners and houses shaped like anything from milk bottles to a coffee pot, a chicken to a shoe. They're long gone, but Sweet Willy (with suitable mod cons for the 21st century) is with us still, and long may this imaginative B&B remain as a whimsical extension to the prairie landscape.

WHERE:
Highway 95, Cottonwood, Idaho
COST:
Budget
BEST TIME OF YEAR:
Any time (although winters can be hard and summers hot, albeit with refreshingly cool evenings)
DON'T MISS:
The inn's unique self-serve continental breakfast featuring the renowned secret recipe, The Prairie's Best Fruited Granola; one of seven rodeos held annually within one hour's drive
THINGS TO DO:
Order you favourite breed of dog from the Chainsaw Art Gallery and Giftshop, lovingly sculpted by renowned chainsaw artists Dennis and Frances, your hosts and the creators of Dog Bark Park.
YOU SHOULD KNOW:
Going to the dog is popular, so it's best to book in advance; mobile phone reception in North Idaho is patchy to non-existent.

Storm Creek Glamping

WHERE:
Accessed from Darby, Montana, although taking place mainly in Idaho
COST:
Reasonable (with all accommodation, meals, snacks and beverages included)
BEST TIME OF YEAR:
The summer season (July to early September), although winter snowmobiling can be booked
DON'T MISS:
A soothing open-air encounter with the camp's qualified massage therapist; the area's history and lookout tour
THINGS TO DO:
Take classes from experts in useful wilderness survival skills such as mountain orienteering, Dutch oven cooking and backcountry horse riding. Wildlife and landscape photography is another activity beloved of glampers.
YOU SHOULD KNOW:
Chamber pots are discreetly placed in each tent for middle-of-the-night emergencies. Storm Creek Outfitters and local winemaker Keith Smith from Trapper Peak Winery also offer a Cork and Fork wine and fine-dining experience at the camp in Selway-Bitterroot Wilderness. The package includes one night's luxury tented accommodation and features five gourmet courses, each paired with a complementary local wine.

Frank Church River of No Return and Selway-Bitterroot Wilderness combine to create the largest wilderness area in the continental US, spanning the borders of Montana and Idaho and stretching to a mind-boggling 1.7 million ha (4.2 million ac). This country reveals little sign of human habitation, save traces of the Nez Perce Indians who once travelled through the area on their way to buffalo-hunting grounds and long-abandoned mines. There couldn't be a better place for adventurers yearning to escape the stressed modern world for a while, and such seekers after the tranquillity and solitude offered by wild places will find that Storm Creek Outfitters make it all possible.

It all starts in the old western town of Darby, midway between Yellowstone and Glacier National Parks. The adventure begins with a hike or horseback ride down the Magruder Corridor, part of the Nez Perce Trail named for a merchant murdered in 1863 as he returned home laden with gold dust (his killers were later hanged in Idaho's first legal execution). It's an expedition into stunning landscape with few people and lots of fascinating flora and fauna. The remote camp consists of cabin tents suitable for four, cosily furnished and in close proximity to the spacious (and private) shower tent with hot water and fluffy towels. Simple but clean vault toilets and a kitchen tent complete the encampment.

Days are spent enjoying the pristine surroundings, with a choice of activities ranging from fly fishing to trail riding. Lavish picnics are prepared for these outings, and in the evening it's back to the warmth of the kitchen for a splendid meal and good conversation. Reconnecting with nature doesn't have to involve privation, and is no less satisfying for choosing the glamorous camping option.

Houseboat on Lake Powell

WHERE:
Lake Powell, Utah/Arizona border
COST:
Prices range from $600 per day for a simple patio boat with awning right up to $2,200 per day for the top luxury houseboats with state rooms and all the trimmings.
BEST TIME OF YEAR:
Any time, but April to June and October are best for pleasant weather, while the summer months are usually scorching hot
DON'T MISS:
The Rainbow Bridge National Monument in the Utah section of Lake Powell, said to be the world's highest natural bridge

Scenically, it's like John Ford's classic Western movie *Stagecoach* – on water. The famous film was shot in Utah's Monument Valley on the Colorado Plateau, and Lake Powell is not far away, although part of it meanders into Arizona. It's actually a vast reservoir (the USA's second largest), created by damming Glen Canyon. Those colourful Navajo Sandstone bluffs rising from the water give the irregular lake stunning visual impact, as though shining water has simply replaced the arid flatlands. In fact, Glen Canyon and its side canyons are deep, and the reservoir took 17 years to fill after the dam was completed.

The project may have been an ecological disaster, but there was a huge bonus for holidaymakers with the creation of Glen Canyon National Recreation Area, a popular summer destination centred on the new lake. And the very best way to enjoy this extraordinary landscape is to vacation on a houseboat. These come in various shapes and sizes, sleeping up to 20 people, and all are mobile, cruising the blue waters to reveal new vistas at every turn. The sun always shines, the water's always warm and Lake Powell is surrounded by some of the most spectacular scenery in the West.

Even the economy houseboats are pretty special, carrying a dozen people when cruising, sleeping up to 10 (at a squeeze) and very suitable for families. Many of these boats operate from Wahweap, Antelope Point and Bullfrog Marinas, which have all the requisite facilities. Once stocked up, it's just a matter of going for one, three, five or seven days and leaving civilization behind. It would take forever to explore around 3,200 km (2,000 mi) of shoreline, but just going afloat here is a magical experience.

THINGS TO DO:
Mooring up at night, getting around the campfire beneath a starry sky and feeling at one with nature; looking for (and often finding) evidence of Native American occupation; wake boarding; water skiing; wild swimming; scuba diving, snorkelling; great fishing; landscape photography

YOU SHOULD KNOW:
No boating experience is necessary; most houseboats require substantial deposits in advance; some smaller boats are powered by solar panels.

Cedar Creek Treehouse

WHERE:
Ashford, Washington, near Mount Rainier National Park

COST:
Moderate

BEST TIME OF YEAR:
July to September

DON'T MISS:
A guided tour through the tree tops along the Rainbow Bridge and up the Stairway to Heaven

THINGS TO DO:
Hiking; mountain biking; swimming in the creek; trout fishing; nature watching; stargazing

YOU SHOULD KNOW:
Cedar Creek has been selected as one of the top five treehouse hotels in the world. It accommodates a maximum of four but you can pitch a tent by the creek for extra guests. There is no bath or shower, but you can wash in the creek.

You'll need a good head for heights, but if you're after a fantasy backwoods adventure with some creature comforts thrown in, this is for you – an amazing and cleverly designed solar-powered two-storey treehouse in the heart of an evergreen forest.

Built in the boughs of a 200-year-old giant cedar tree, the treehouse is 15 m (50 ft) above the ground with a stunning outlook to the surrounding mountains and forests. You climb five flights of steps to reach your lodging for the night and, once inside, you won't forget for a moment that you're in a tree – a huge trunk rises majestically through the centre of the living room and disappears through the roof. The sleeping loft has skylights for stargazing and all the mod cons needed can be found in the natty little kitchen and compact bathroom. Immediately below the treehouse a fire pit and picnic table await, right next to a swiftly flowing creek with a tempting swimming hole.

Cedar Creek Treehouse has been a real labour of love on the part of its owner. He started building in 1981 and has been making additions ever since. The 13-m (43-ft) long Rainbow Bridge runs 25 m (82 ft) above the forest floor, and a 25-m (82-ft) spiral staircase – the Stairway to Heaven – winds its way around a Douglas fir tree up to Treehouse Observatory, an octagonal observation room which is brilliant for birdwatching, or just for being there enjoying incredible views. A new 20-m (66-ft) bridge, the Sun Bridge, has recently been constructed and plans for another treehouse are well under way. Anyone who has ever dreamed of being Tarzan will love this place.

The Luxor

If there were a contest to establish the glitziest place on earth, there could be only one winner – if only because nowhere else would bother to enter once they saw the neon-lit hat of Las Vegas blazing in the ring. This desert city almost defies description, but one truism that certainly applies is 'only in America'. Self-billed as 'The Entertainment Capital of the World' (and desperately hoping that everyone will forget the alternative handle of 'Sin City'), this Nevada hot spot is internationally renowned as a centre for gambling and shopping.

And anyone looking to appreciate the shameless verve with which the city's resort casinos seek to attract the mighty gambling dollar need look no further than The Luxor. Who needs to visit Egypt when they can go to Las Vegas – and pay for the trip at the gambling tables (or not!)? The hotel (the world's third-biggest) is fronted by a 43-m (141-ft) high obelisk and the vast Great Sphinx of Giza, (which may or may not be the real thing). Better yet, you won't just get to look at dusty old stone pyramids, but actually stay in a stunning glass one. And it's not just any old pyramid. It has 4,400 rooms (ranging from regular hotel rooms to suites fit for a pharaoh), along with fabulous headline entertainment, swimming pools, whirlpools, wedding chapel, spas, beauty salons, shops, fine dining . . . and 24/7 casino action. Sadly for dedicated followers of million-dollar jackpots, The Luxor has only 2,000 slot machines.

Quite apart from that, the vast internal atrium (the world's largest) says it all. The place is simply awe-inspiring. Like the city that spawned it, The Luxor, too, almost defies description, so perhaps the phrase that best informs would-be visitors should be 'seeing is believing'.

WHERE:
Las Vegas Boulevard, Las Vegas, Nevada
COST:
Nothing going on stratospheric, depending how you fare in the gaming salons (but regular room rates are generally in the budget/reasonable range in tried-and-tested anticipation that most visitors will turn out to be losers)
BEST TIME OF YEAR:
Any time (May to September are scorchers, but air-con takes the strain)
DON'T MISS:
The slightly weird sensation of riding up and down in one of the hotel's 'inclinators' (elevators that rise and fall along the inner surface of the pyramid at a 39° angle) – it's the cheapest game in town.
THINGS TO DO:
Gambling; eating; drinking; shopping; taking in a show (or four); gambling; eating . . . maybe sleeping a little (you get the picture)
YOU SHOULD KNOW:
Room rates are always higher (as in 'double') at weekends. Just in case you can't find the place, the world's most powerful spotlight fires a 43-billion-candlepower beam into the heavens from the tip of The Luxor's pyramid.

Palms Casino Resort

Should The Luxor be too flash for you (as if!) the hip alternative is the Palms Casino Resort. For a start, it's tucked away semi-discreetly (by Las Vegas standards) in Paradise. Actually, most of the famed Las Vegas Strip is in the unincorporated township of Paradise (not many people know that), but the Palms isn't on the Strip. With a mere 700 rooms, its hotel tower is on the skimpy side (by Las Vegas standards) and with a lowly 2,500 seats the Pearl Concert Theatre is not a large showroom (by Las Vegas standards). But wait! Small (by Las Vegas standards) can equate with exclusive, and the Palms is hugely popular with the younger set and celebs, including the inevitable parade of Hollywood stars. They'd be the ones who book the Hugh Heffner Sky Villa (that's a rather special suite, folks) at around $40,000 a night.

The resort's newish Fantasy Tower hosts more goodies, including a neat little (by Las Vegas standards) suite containing a full-sized basketball court with electronic scoreboard and locker room. The third and latest element of the triple whammy is Palms Place at a modest (by Las Vegas standards) 58 storeys of suites, penthouses and condominiums. With a lavish entertainment programme, hot night life, a dozen eateries, recording studio, swimming pools, clubs, bars, spas, a tanning centre, beauty salons, fitness room and 14-screen multiplex cinema with IMAX it's not hard for guests at the Palms to keep busy.

All that has to be fitted in between doing what comes naturally hereabouts – gambling. The Palms casino features a respectable (by Las Vegas standards) 70+ gaming tables that never sleep, offering card games from blackjack to poker, craps, roulette and *pai gow* (Chinese dominoes) – not to mention all those slots with their heart-stopping jackpot possibilities. Go for it!

WHERE:
Flamingo Road, Paradise, Nevada
COST:
Reasonable (for a modest Superior King Suite) after which in ascending order the Sky (Villa) is literally the limit
BEST TIME OF YEAR:
Any time
DON'T MISS:
A meal in the Michelin-starred restaurant
THINGS TO DO:
Being there
YOU SHOULD KNOW:
Stargazers should consider booking in when The Palms is hosting the annual Cine Vegas film festival. It's advisable to book early if planning a visit, as regular rooms at The Palms are often sold out.

Holbrooke Hotel

The Holbrooke is not just a hotel, it's an incredible monument to the era of the California Gold Rush and the oldest hotel in California's Gold Country. This picturesque mid 19th-century inn is in the historic town of Grass Valley, once the wealthiest of all California's mining towns.

Built in 1862, the Holbrooke rose from the ashes of the Golden Gate Saloon, a popular local miners' bar which burned to the ground, along with much of the rest of Grass Valley town in a devastating fire of 1855. The saloon was replaced by the present hotel building, and the bar at the Holbrooke is still called the Golden Gate. It lays claim to being the oldest continuously functioning saloon west of the Mississippi.

As soon as you enter the hotel lobby you step back into the past. It's all marble and mahogany with antiques and curios in every corner, an old-fashioned cage lift, creaking floorboards and the sort of character and charm that only comes with great age. There are 28 good-sized rooms furnished with period antiques and quaint Victorian claw-foot bath tubs. Each room is named after one of the many famous Americans who have stayed here over the years.

The staff at the Holbrooke are outstandingly hospitable, making the solo traveller feel completely at ease, and the hotel restaurant serves great food at reasonable prices – the generous cooked breakfasts are especially recommended. The hotel still entertains the Grass Valley locals. Most nights you can chill out to live music with a drink and a snack in the hotel bar or, if you're feeling energetic, take to the dance floor at the Iron Door, the Holbrooke's downstairs late-night dive.

WHERE:
Grass Valley, Nevada County, California
COST:
Reasonable
BEST TIME OF YEAR:
Any time
DON'T MISS:
The historic Empire Mine State Historic Park; a visit to the North Star Mining Museum; wine tasting at one of the many wineries in the area
THINGS TO DO:
Hunt for knick-knacks in the local antique and curio shops; explore the vibrant local music and arts scene; fishing, whitewater rafting, hiking and horse riding in the Sierra Nevada foothills
YOU SHOULD KNOW:
All rooms are equipped with cable TV and free wifi. The Holbrooke is a California State Landmark and among the many famous guests have been three US presidents and the literary figures Mark Twain and Jack London.

RMS Queen Mary

WHERE:
Queensway Bay, Long Beach, California
COST:
Reasonable
BEST TIME OF YEAR:
Any time
DON'T MISS:
Admiring the parquet ballroom floor, paintings and golden-onyx fireplaces in the palatial Queen's Salon; Sunday Champagne Brunch in the Grand Salon; the RMS *Queen Mary* World War II Tour; historical prize-winning photographs in the Sun Deck Gallery
THINGS TO DO:
Take one of the 12 daily ship's tours; rent a ship's bicycle to explore Long Beach; have a massage in the spa and fitness centre; visit the ship's shopping arcade; dine in one of the award-winning restaurants.
YOU SHOULD KNOW:
RMS *Queen Mary* is listed on the US National Register of Historic Places. The ship is said to be haunted and there are endless tales of ghosts and paranormal phenomena. A free shuttle bus takes you into the tourist playground of Long Beach.

Permanently docked in Long Beach, RMS *Queen Mary* is an iconic landmark that provides unique hotel accommodation. When she made her maiden voyage in 1936 she was the grandest and fastest ocean-going liner ever built. For the next 30 years, until she was finally taken out of service in 1967, she carried the privileged and powerful to and fro across the Atlantic. The Duke and Duchess of Windsor, Fred Astaire and Winston Churchill are among the many historic luminaries who travelled on her. In World War II she was given a coat of grey paint and was transformed into a troopship, becoming known as the *Grey Ghost* on account of her speed and stealth. Carrying up to 15,000 men at a time, she transported more than 750,000 US soldiers across the Atlantic.

The *Queen Mary* was given a major facelift in 2010 and has been restored to her former glory. There are lovely Art Deco touches throughout the ship, with brass fittings and leaded glass panels. The 314 cabins (called 'staterooms' in the hotel literature – but remember you're on a ship, so don't expect an enormous amount of space!) provide varying degrees of luxury. They are done up in 1930s' decor and have the ship's original wood panelling. It's worth paying a bit more to get an outward-facing cabin for the sake of the (opening) portholes and view of Long Beach.

Strolling on the deck in the evening or sitting in the Art Deco piano bar sipping your cocktail, you can all too easily imagine yourself a wealthy 1930s socialite on a trans-Atlantic crossing. Staying on board the *Queen Mary* is a truly memorable experience.

Human Nest at Treebones Resort

Release your inner hippy spirit from the trappings of consumer culture at Treebones: a campsite on the Big Sur coast of California. You can enjoy a special eco-experience, sheltering for a couple of nights in the unique Human Nest beside the Pacific Ocean.

This extraordinary structure was created by artist Jayson Fann out of driftwood and the gnarled and knotted branches of eucalyptus trees. You ascend into it by climbing a rickety wooden ladder, hauling sleeping bags and pillows up with you. The inside is lined with a surprisingly comfortable futon mattress and is spacious enough for two people at full stretch. Perched 3 m (10 ft) above the ground with a spectacular view of the ocean, you will drift off to sleep to the sound of the waves and the distant calls of elephant seals from the beach below. And in the morning you wake up to a chorus of birdsong as the rays of sunshine filter through your cocoon of woven branches.

It is a glorious spot – a wild rocky slope tumbling down to a coast of secluded coves, surrounded by the Ventana Wilderness and the giant redwood trees, streams and canyons of Los Padres National Forest. The name comes from the silvery, sun-bleached dead wood that is scattered in the wilderness. As well as the Human Nest, Treebones has 16 yurts and seven camping pitches, all with running water. The ethos here is all about eco-friendliness and sustainability – an extension of the 1960s' counter-culture when artists and writers were drawn to Big Sur by the haunting beauty of the landscape and mesmerizing Pacific Ocean sunsets. It's a great place for getting away from it all and chilling out.

WHERE:
Big Sur, California
COST:
Budget
BEST TIME OF YEAR:
April to August
DON'T MISS:
The ocean-view pool and hot tub; the open-air sushi bar
THINGS TO DO:
Hiking; yoga; surfing; ocean kayaking
YOU SHOULD KNOW:
No cell phone reception; over 18s only; minimum two-night stay

Post Ranch Inn

The prosaic name gives no hint of the amazing experience you'll have staying here – a combination of extravagant luxury and as beautiful a natural setting as you're likely to find anywhere in the world. The Post Ranch is a perfect haven of romance and tranquillity for anyone who has had their fill of shopping malls, night clubs and madding crowds.

The Post Ranch is perched in solitary splendour nearly 400 m (1,300 ft) above the Pacific Ocean, atop the highest cliff on the dramatic Big Sur coast. Guests are accommodated in luxuriously appointed individual houses scattered over the inn's 40-ha (100-ac) cliff-top estate. The houses have been expertly constructed out of timber, slate and glass in a variety of rustic styles designed both to melt into the landscape and to ensure complete privacy from fellow guests. Every room has a king-size bed and wood-burning fireplace, a Jacuzzi and private terrace with a mountain or ocean view. This being California, the sumptuous spa offers hippy-dippy shaman sessions for soul retrieval, divination and crystal therapy as well as more conventional treatments. There is a heated pool for swimming and sunbathing and two brilliantly sited vanishing-edge cliff-top hot pools for basking in.

You are completely immersed in nature here – Pacific rollers crash into the shore below, the scent of pine trees wafts on the breeze, the cliffs are carpeted with wild flowers, the Santa Lucia Mountains form a backdrop and the ocean stretches to infinity before you. You can fill your lungs with ocean air, walk along the cliffs without meeting a soul, marvel at the spectacular sunsets and forget time as the sea and sky drift endlessly before you.

WHERE:
Big Sur, California
COST:
Astronomical
BEST TIME OF YEAR:
April to August
DON'T MISS:
A hike among the giant redwood trees of Julia Pfeiffer Burns State Park; a visit to Point Sur Lighthouse; the sea lions in the waters off Garrapata State Beach; a romantic meal in the inn's Sierra Mar restaurant
THINGS TO DO:
Morning yoga; meditation; Tai Chi; massage instruction; guided hikes; birdwatching; hang-gliding; stargazing at the on-site observatory; cookery classes
YOU SHOULD KNOW:
Nobody under the age of 18; no TV in the rooms; the hotel restaurant uses home-grown produce and has won awards for its seasonal fusion food; voted Best Leisure Hotel in the US 2011

Point Montara Fog Signal Station

WHERE:
Just south of Montara, California
COST:
Budget
BEST TIME OF YEAR:
November to April to catch the whale migration
DON'T MISS:
The infamous Mavericks, giant waves in which several big-wave surfers have met their deaths; Fitzgerald Marine Reserve, an inter-tidal shale reef rich in marine life; the coastal town of Half Moon Bay; Gray Whale Cove, a great beach for whale spotting
THINGS TO DO:
Surfing; kayaking; windsurfing; cycling; horseback riding along the shore; whale-watching; birdwatching; meditation
YOU SHOULD KNOW:
The dirt track that leads to the hostel is hard to find – stay alert to spot the sign. The hostel has a 'green' policy of composting, recycling, water and energy conservation, and use of eco-friendly cleaning products. Free wifi, linen and towels are supplied but there are no private bathrooms and no alcohol is allowed on the premises.

Just 40 km (25 mi) south of San Francisco, this offbeat little hostel is at the end of a dirt track, perched on a 2-ha (5-ac) rocky outcrop on the rugged Californian coast. The remoteness of the spot, the ocean views and the history behind the signal station all lend it a touch of romance not normally associated with budget accommodation.

The Point Montara signal station was established in 1875, after many lethal accidents on the rocks, to guide ships safely to San Francisco harbour. In 1970 the fog signal was replaced with an automated offshore signal, but the lighthouse still sends out its beacon. The 9-m (30-ft) lighthouse tower was built in 1881 and once stood in Cape Cod. It was transported nearly 5,000 km (3,000 mi) across America and went into service at Point Montara in 1928.

You don't actually stay in the lighthouse itself but right next to it in the coastguard's century-old clapboard cottage quarters. The accommodation is fairly basic, but clean and perfectly comfortable, with 30 dormitory beds and private rooms for families and couples. Outside, there is a sweet cottage garden of native plants, lovingly tended by the hostel staff, and a footpath leads down to a beach in the cove below.

The atmosphere here is really friendly. There is a cheerful common room with a cosy wood-burning stove to huddle round – a good place to meet fellow hostellers. There are two fully equipped self-catering kitchens, an outdoor picnic area and grill and a communal dining room with a view of the ocean.

Go to sleep to the roar of the waves and wake up inhaling the salty tang of the ocean air. What more could anyone want?

Fairmont Hotel

WHERE:
Mason Street, San Francisco, California
COST:
Expensive
BEST TIME OF YEAR:
Any time
DON'T MISS:
Riding in the glass elevator to see the sensational view from the Crown Room at the top of the 23-storey Tower; Happy Hour cocktails overlooking the lagoon in the Tonga Room; lunch in the hotel's Laurel Court restaurant
THINGS TO DO:
Keep fit and have a massage in Club One, the hotel spa; browse in the exclusive hotel shops; take advantage of the Fairmont's central location to sightsee and explore the city.
YOU SHOULD KNOW:
It's worth ensuring that you are given a room with a view over the bay. The Fairmont is listed on the US National Register of Historic Places and the United Nations Charter of 1945 was signed in the Garden Room. The Fairmont is the only spot in San Francisco where every cable car line meets.

Today 'Fairmont' is a global hotel brand, but it all stems from an ambition on the part of heiress sisters Teresa and Virginia Fair to build a monument to their dead father, the rags-to-riches mining magnate and US senator James Graham ('Slippery Jim') Fair.

Money being no object, the sisters decided to build a Fairmont mansion on Nob Hill (one of the original 'seven hills' of San Francisco) as a public venue in which they could hold court. Cash flow problems forced them to sell out just before construction work was completed – fortunately for them, because almost as soon as it had been built the Fairmont was gutted by fire in the great San Francisco earthquake of 1906. Undaunted, the new owners rebuilt it and the Fairmont Hotel opened its doors to the public in 1907.

The hotel's great location and grand appearance soon made it the must-be-seen-at venue for San Francisco's socialites, celebrities and sophisticates. More than a century later, the Fairmont has survived two world wars, countless economic melt-downs and several costly refurbishments. It stands today as an icon to a past golden age of elegance, still measuring up to its reputation for unashamed glamour and incomparable service.

The grandeur of the lobby has more than a hint of decadence about it – a vast expanse of marble floor, gilded Corinthian columns, and a sweeping curved staircase. You can't help but feel a *frisson* of awe as you glide through the door. Your room may come as a mild disappointment compared to the opulence of the public spaces – somewhat smaller and blander than anticipated – but really nothing can detract from the thrill of staying in this legendary hotel.

Hotel Del Coronado

The 'Del', as it is affectionately known, is a sprawling extravaganza of a building – an enormous seven-storey turreted Victorian wood folly, set in 11 ha (27 ac) of grounds fronting directly onto the magnificent Coronado beach. The hotel has an illustrious history, first opening in 1888 as the largest resort hotel in the world and also the first hotel to use electric light. The Del's presence soon made Coronado famous as a tourist resort and in the 1920s it became renowned as a playground for Hollywood stars. Today the reputation of the Del as a luxury historic hotel is as intact as ever and it has won countless awards.

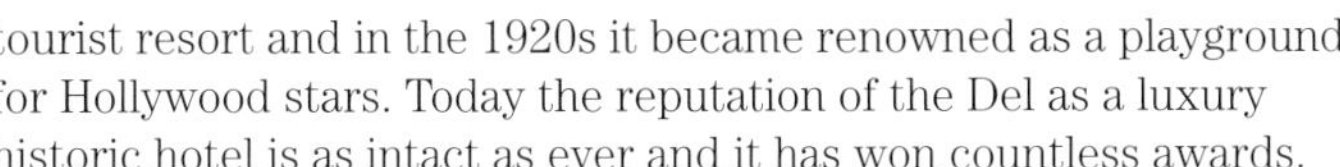

A family holiday with moody teenagers in tow is no fun for anyone. But there's no chance of that happening here as teens are exceptionally well catered for. Not only is there a surf camp, movie nights, beach bonfires and a teen lounge to hang out in but they also have the use of their own teen spa. Meanwhile parents can relax in peace on a lounger beside the pool, soak in an outdoor hot tub or rent a beach cabin for extra privacy.

The Del's luxury spa, opened in 2007, is exceptionally spacious and has 21 treatment rooms. It also boasts its own private terrace with an infinity pool overlooking the ocean, and you can get great hydrotherapy treatments and massages.

The Del is not a cheap option but you do get your money's worth. Quite apart from the hotel itself, Coronado beach is rated as one of the best in the USA, and you've also got all the attractions of San Diego on your doorstep.

WHERE:
Coronado Island, San Diego Bay, California

COST:
Expensive, and a room with a full ocean view is astronomical

BEST TIME OF YEAR:
Any time, but September and October to avoid summer crowds; the sky is often overcast in June and December

DON'T MISS:
The world famous San Diego zoo; exploring Coronado peninsula on a tandem; Birch Aquarium marine museum

THINGS TO DO:
Golf; surfing; kayaking; jet-skiing; sailing; beach sports; kids camp (four to 12 years); fine dining; shopping

YOU SHOULD KNOW:
Coronado is connected to San Diego by the Silver Strand, an 11-km (7-mi) long isthmus. The Del is listed as a US National Historic Landmark and among the many famous guests there have been 11 US presidents, the Duke of Windsor and Emperor Haile Selassie; the Del was also a backdrop in the 1959 film *Some Like it Hot* starring Marilyn Monroe.

Ahwahnee Hotel

At the Ahwahnee you will find American wilderness adventure, sophisticated multi-ethnic luxury, and historical charm all rolled into a singular memorable experience.

This extraordinary lodge was built on the site of a former Native American village. It is beautifully situated in a mountain meadow at the base of a towering granite cliff, surrounded by the majestic peaks, spectacular forests, and waterfalls of Yosemite National Park. It was built in 1926 and designed by Gilbert Stanley Underwood, a famous American architect renowned for his knowledge of folk art and rustic styles and his experimental use of materials that complemented the landscape. The hotel is built mainly out of granite and wood, echoing the natural environment, although the external timbers are in fact moulded concrete cleverly coloured and textured to look like redwood.

The interior decor is an apparently haphazard mishmash of Art Deco, Arts and Crafts Movement and Native American, with a hint of Middle Eastern influence thrown in for good measure. It shouldn't work – but it does, beautifully. In the main lounge your eye is immediately drawn to the giant stone fireplaces, stencilled wooden beams, wrought iron chandeliers, stained glass, and Native American art work and tribal artefacts.

There are 99 rooms in the main lodge, or you can stay in a woodland cottage in the hotel grounds. The rooms are gaily furnished and have lovely outlooks but you must bear in mind that you are here for the spectacular landscape and fascinating architecture rather than modern amenities. All Yosemite's best-known attractions are within walking distance. You step out of the hotel straight into a natural world full of wildlife – if you're lucky you may even spot an American black bear (before it spots you).

WHERE:
Yosemite National Park, California
COST:
Expensive
BEST TIME OF YEAR:
May and June are wonderful months just after the last of the snow has melted, when the waterfalls are in full flow and the Yosemite Valley is coming into bloom.
DON'T MISS:
Sitting in the hotel solarium – it's a wonderfully tranquil room with fountain, a jungle of plants and a superb view of Glacier Point; Yosemite Falls – the sixth highest waterfall in the world; wandering through the groves of giant sequoia trees; hiking up the Half Dome granite rock formation
THINGS TO DO:
Hiking; cycling; horse riding; climbing; hang-gliding; cross-country skiing; ice skating
YOU SHOULD KNOW:
It is incredibly difficult to get a room – bookings must be made at least a year in advance for the summer season and three to six months ahead at other times. The Ahwahnee is a National Historical Landmark.

Ojai Valley Inn

The Chumash Native Americans believed the Ojai Valley was a mystical healing place, and you certainly feel you're entering a charmed land when you come to stay at the exclusive Ojai Valley Inn. As soon as you set foot here, you feel as though you've been magically transported to the Mediterranean.

Originally built in 1923 in 90 ha (222 ac) of beautiful country grounds, this award-winning luxury resort has the ambience of an Andalucian village – wooden pergolas decked in flowers, outdoor fireplaces, Moorish bell towers and fountains. Winding terracotta tiled *paseos* lead to clusters of picturesque little *haciendas* with white-washed walls, tiled roofs and courtyards. The rooms are exceptionally spacious and opulent with four-poster king-size beds and the richly coloured fabrics of Spanish Colonial decor.

The facilities here are simply sensational. The award-winning Moroccan-influenced spa is practically a village in itself, with its own courtyard café, boutique and pool. It offers an exceptionally wide range of treatments. As well as the large outdoor family swimming pool there is a more intimate adults-only pool right next to a beautiful herb garden planted with lavender, rosemary and apple trees. The historic championship golf course has been used by countless celebrities and golf pros, and there are several tennis courts and any number of indoor and outdoor activities to keep the kids amused.

In the morning you wake up to views of the surrounding hills and the sound of birdsong, and at sundown the mountain tops are bathed in an extraordinary rosy pink glow – an almost supernatural phenomenon that occurs in only a few places around the world. This place really is magical. No wonder the Native Americans revered it.

WHERE:
Ojai Valley, California
COST:
Expensive but special offers deliver more reasonable prices
BEST TIME OF YEAR:
April to August
DON'T MISS:
The amazing 'Pink Moment' phenomenon at sunset; the resort's Artist's Cottage where you can have a drawing lesson, make your own artwork and learn to mix perfumes; dining on the verandah of the hotel's Maravilla Restaurant; cycling along a remote country path to the coast
THINGS TO DO:
Playing golf on an 18-hole championship course; tennis; horse riding; hiking; climbing; fishing; kayaking; yoga; Pilates; spa treatments; basketball; volleyball; kids camp
YOU SHOULD KNOW:
The Ojai is one of the top-ten US spa resorts. Plasma TV, high-speed internet access and exclusively designed hotel bedding is in every room. The California coast is only 23 km (14 mi) away and the nearby town of Ojai is known as an artists' and writers' retreat.

Jumby Bay Resort

WHERE:
Offshore northeast Antigua
COST:
Astronomical. However, even during high season family deals are available – and there are many more throughout the year.
BEST TIME OF YEAR:
December to April
DON'T MISS:
The hibiscus and wild orchids in extensive gardens and woods in the island's centre; the sunset cocktail cruise; the flaming torch-lit White Night beach dinner on Sundays (where everyone wears white to feast on lobster and steak); the Rumba Scrub (it's like being kneaded with exfoliating *mojitos*) and massage at the spa

Jumby Bay characterizes itself as a 'fly-and-flop' destination, meaning that the resort's level of luxury is sufficiently fabulous to subvert the most energetic visitors into somnolent appreciation of its stress-free, tropical beauty.

With the possible exception of the 'enhanced welcome experience' of spiced-up fruit juice and 'signature-scented' towel ('to refresh'), everything about Jumby Bay Resort fosters the illusion among its visitors that they are arriving on their own, private Caribbean island. It doesn't matter whether their destination is one of the magnificent villas of wildly different sizes (but uniform luxury) spread around the 7 km (4.5 mi) of coastline, or one of the newly transformed, all-dancing rooms or suites of the official hotel complex scattered along Jumby Bay itself. It's an all-inclusive playground in which every wish brings fuss-free gratification.

The entire island – just a seven-minute boat ride from the airport to this car-free paradise – has been refurbished at staggering

expense. The hotel area has been the major beneficiary and now offers beach-front suites with vaulted ceilings and four-poster beds, eight-sided 'Rondavel' cottages, and suites with private pools and gardens. At their heart is a 19th-century plantation house in Spanish Colonial style where guests from all over the island congregate in the bars and restaurants overlooking the beach. Called The Verandah, it functions like a clubhouse and – on an island where room keys don't exist, everyone rides a bike and meticulous plans are simply discarded as an affront to Caribbean empathy – it reinforces the sense of stylish, laid-back community that is Jumby Bay's biggest gift to its guests.

Parents can relax, too, as there are dedicated activities for children aged three to 12 and a nanny service for infants.

THINGS TO DO:
Tennis; croquet; putting green; all unmotorized water sports; Jungle Gym, Rose Buds, Camp Jumby and the Children's Centre (for kids); spa treatments; nightly movies
YOU SHOULD KNOW:
From June to November guests can participate in the resort's Hawksbill Turtle Project on Pasture Bay. The fruit punches at the bar use fruit grown on the island – and the various teas offered are grown in the herb gardens.

The Inn at English Harbour

Its location is incomparable. The Inn at English Harbour lies in a wooded estate contained within the Dockyard National Park, Antigua's most historic site. It has three parts. The reception and main restaurant are on the crest of the cliff, screened by forest which falls sharply towards the beach, thinning into a beautifully maintained, grassy park and gardens. Airy suites are located in three two-storey buildings with broad verandahs or balconies, darkened mahogany floors and four-poster beds that look impossibly (but very comfortably) colonial and afford views across lawns to the large infinity pool. Beyond lie just four white-washed beach *cabanas*, fringing the sand itself. Recently renovated, the whole establishment is synonymous with seclusion, privacy and intelligently sybaritic comfort – but it has a secret.

At any time, guests can take a free water taxi from their beach, across Freeman's Bay to Nelson's Dockyard itself. In five minutes they travel from beach nirvana to yachty paradise. English Harbour and the 18th-century cobbled village (restored) of Nelson's Dockyard is the headquarters of professional yachtsmen in the Caribbean. In season, its little bars, restaurants and boutiques make English Harbour the most chic and lively place in Antigua. The instant accessibility – especially as noise from one never impinges on the quiet of the other – puts a real premium on the lifestyle offered by the hotel.

The Inn at English Harbour is probably not wonderful for the super-athletic or restless teenagers. Every kind of activity is available, but not on site. The only facilities are the Astroturf tennis courts at the top of the hill – but most guests only go there to enjoy the fabulous panoramic sunsets, over a drink or dinner.

WHERE:
Southwest coast of Antigua
COST:
It's astronomical, but almost reasonable in the low season. Taxes (adding up to 15 per cent extra) are not usually included in prices quoted for meals, drinks or anything else.
BEST TIME OF YEAR:
December to April
DON'T MISS:
The steel pan music and dancing on Sundays at the top of Shirley Heights, on the cliff round Freeman's Bay; the Dockyard Museum; hummingbirds attracted to the flowers on your verandah
THINGS TO DO:
Hammock-dreaming; sunbathing; water skiing; sailing (lasers or sunfish); deep-sea fishing; kayaking; windsurfing
YOU SHOULD KNOW:
Over 10s only; there's an any-time shuttle between beach level and the reception/Terrace Restaurant; mosquito nets aren't enough – bring coils or other repellents.

Andros – Tiamo Resort

Set on white sands between virgin forest and a vast marine wilderness of shallow flats and streaming currents, Tiamo is a statement eco-destination as well as a tropical beach paradise. From its conception and building on the South Bight of Andros, the largest of the Bahamian Out Islands, it has sought ingenious ways to minimize its environmental impact on the region's authentic, wild beauty – and still deliver luxury to its visitors. The resort calls this 'barefoot sophistication'.

Tiamo's lack of eco-compromise is very attractive. It's a tiny community of just 11 comfortable bungalows spread along the beach from a communal Main Lodge (and freshwater pool) with its library, bar and seriously good restaurant. Guests appreciate both the effort put into the resort's ecological practices on a daily basis and, for the most part, the resort's earnest attempt to evangelize them. If the management can sometimes seem a bit pedagogic, it's only because they have much to be proud of, and most of the guests come for that very reason.

Practising their own principles even extends to limiting the number of fishermen allowed on the water at any one time, but it cuts both ways – those who do come know they are almost guaranteed world-class sport on Tiamo's doorstep. Divers on the fabulous coral drop-offs along Andros's reef know there will be no crowding, and honeymoon couples (they get a lot) can waft down empty white beaches in the surf. Tiamo may not provide pampering spas, but it has discovered how to combine with nature to create a luxury lifestyle in a Robinson Crusoe setting.

WHERE:
East coast of South Andros, Bahamas Out Islands

COST:
Expensive

BEST TIME OF YEAR:
November to April

DON'T MISS:
Exploring Andros's extraordinary ecosystem with the trained staff biologists; the short but eye-opening 'environmental tour' of the resort site itself

THINGS TO DO:
Snorkelling; scuba diving; sea kayaking; sailing; nature tours; fishing

YOU SHOULD KNOW:
Tiamo endorses catch-and-release fishing only. The place is accessible only by boat or seaplane. Children must be aged 14 or over.

Mullins Mill

WHERE:
Barbados, West Indies
COST:
Astronomical – or so it seems, but the house has a staff of 12 and can sleep 12 people
BEST TIME OF YEAR:
December to April
DON'T MISS:
Floodlit tennis; Jacuzzi parties; cocktails in the gazebo at sunset; the collection of Bajan antiques in what was once the entrance to the Sugar Mill; the fantastic Shell Room up the stairs next to the huge verandah
THINGS TO DO:
Playing pirates in the enormous tropical gardens – the gully by the stream makes a great hideout; going shopping in Speightstown by boat or car
YOU SHOULD KNOW:
Two of the six air-conditioned en-suite bedrooms are in garden cottages close to the main house – and usually recommended for teenagers and/or children with nannies. The staff are happy to do any shopping and cooking that you may like – but it's fun to go to the Speightstown fish market and roadside stands for yourself.

Staying at Mullins Mill is a bit like renting a castle in Europe. Few historic estates survive in Barbados, so the late 17th-century sugar mill feels as glamorous as a turreted and crenellated manor. It even has a circular tower with a spiked roof – although the open staircase descending from its central floor is more reminiscent of a Disney film than manorial grandeur. But it's fun, and in every way Mullins Mill is a completely charming conversion from long-ago working practicality to sybaritic pleasure-dome, and hang the cost.

It sits in beautifully maintained wooded gardens, on a ridge overlooking the west coast of Barbados, at exactly the point – halfway between Holetown and Speightstown – where you can begin to imagine what 'old' Barbados might have been like. It has a gazebo by the infinity pool on the edge of a cliff. The Caribbean panorama is fantastic, but to jump in the warm sea it's a five-minute drive downhill to the estate's private house on Gibbs Beach, one of the island's very best. Apart from pandering to every beach-side need, this most satisfactory outpost harbours a speedboat for waterskiing and other amusements – a sort of marine stable for a quick getaway.

You can easily feel giddy in a place like this, and the staff will encourage you to be so for all the right reasons. Mullins Mill is one of the loveliest places in Barbados to stay, and it's within easy reach of the island's best excursions like St Nicholas Abbey, Animal Flower Cave, and Bathsheba on the Atlantic Coast. With family or friends, it becomes a joyous home, however temporary.

Hotel Parque Central

WHERE:
Neptuno & Prado, Havana
COST:
Budget plus (and a little extra goes a long way towards a suite)
BEST TIME OF YEAR:
Any time except the hurricane season (June to October)
DON'T MISS:
The daiquiris at Ernest Hemingway's favourite bar, Floridita; shopping among the boutiques, bars, music stalls and mayhem of Calle Obispo; a taxi ride in a vintage Oldsmobile or Chevy
THINGS TO DO:
Exploring the World Heritage Centre of Old Havana's throbbing, music-filled streets; strolling the Malecon alongside the Caribbean to Havana's 17th-century historic fortifications and palaces; taking a friend to the Museum of Rum
YOU SHOULD KNOW:
The hotel now has a modern new section called the Iberostar Parque Central Torre, which is completely adequate but totally lacks the character of the original half; make sure you ask for a room in the Parque Central itself, ideally with a view over the park.

The hotel embodies the adult excitement of legendary 'old' Havana. In the 1950s it was at the heart of the boisterous partying and glamorous night life which fuelled Havana's reputation for the exotic. It's still a potent symbol of those glory days, but now it is more of a sanctuary from Havana's vivid street life than a let-your-hair-down destination. Guests can still soak up the hotel's thrilling ambience, while actually enjoying elegant respite from the hurly-burly.

Elegance Cuban-style is the Parque Central's only game. Its location makes a perfect statement, dominating the park square across which Old Havana's crowded alleys begin. Rebuilt in the early 1990s behind its original Spanish colonial arcades, the modernized rooms and services still retain the luxurious antique feel of their heyday in the 1950s (and the air conditioning is better). Rooms overlooking the square are at a premium for the fantastic views over the old city and across most of the important monuments, museums and the Capitol building – but the best views of all are from the guests-only rooftop pool with its tropical garden and terrace bar. Like the cigar lounge bar on the mezzanine, and the restaurant in the hotel's leafy inner courtyard, the aura of sophistication and exclusivity you get just from being there is probably the most authentic taste of 1950s' Havana you'll find anywhere (apart from the famous time-warp American cars).

If you take it with a pinch of salt it's enormous fun. The hotel is one of the best places to see those long-in-the-tooth American cars which congregate around the park. It's also good for taxis – but for guests at the Parque Central almost everything else worth seeing is walkable.

Jungle Bay Resort

Dominica, the biggest of the Windward Islands, is one of the least developed in the Caribbean. Jungle Bay, on its southeast coast, is a hardcore eco-resort built to offer a kind of rustic luxury to anyone with a taste for genuine adventure and a willingness to push themselves to get it. The rewards are phenomenal.

It's not necessary to be action man or woman, except in spirit, but it is essential to be reasonably fit. The visitors who get most out of Jungle Bay are those unafraid of toughing it through vertiginous mountains and the tangled undergrowth of steaming valleys, or with the training and experience to dive the precipitous drop-offs and explore underwater caves, springs and fumaroles that make offshore Dominica so exciting. Jungle Bay offers luxury respite to the brave and the means to make their kinds of dreams come true. At the same time, the resort is a hugely romantic idyll.

Spread around its 22 ha (55 ac) are 35 tropical hardwood cabins built on stilts beneath a jungle canopy of cedar and other trees. Each is completely private, connected by footpaths and stone stairways to the octagonal, open-air Jungle Pavilion restaurant, overlooking a volcanic-stone swimming pool and the surf beyond. All the buildings are in complete harmony with their setting – but bathed in moonlight, Jungle Bay can inspire that sense of euphoric perfection whose intensity is almost painful.

With the forested mountains of Morne Trois Pitons National Park on its doorstep, Jungle Bay can offer guided hikes to many of Dominica's finest natural wonders – but just as marvellous are the flowers, birds, and wildlife that are the staple of every expedition. They come with the cabins, too.

WHERE:
Southeast coast of Dominica
COST:
Expensive
BEST TIME OF YEAR:
December to April (the official rainy season is from July to October, but the island could not remain so verdant without regular, heavy-but-brief downpours – locals call them 'liquid sunshine')
DON'T MISS:
Sari Sari and other dramatic waterfalls within hiking distance; whale-watching (the underwater geography mimics the island's soaring mountains); the parrots; wishing by moonlight; infectious toe-tapping rhythms of *jing ping*, the local music
THINGS TO DO:
Scuba and snorkel diving; birdwatching; exploring the indigenous Carib culture; finding orchids in the forest; relaxing in the award-winning spa
YOU SHOULD KNOW:
Among many plaudits, Jungle Bay has been named as one of the 'Top Ten Island Retreats in the World'. Less well known is its conception – in the wake of the collapse of the Dominican banana trade – to promote environmental, ecological, and above all economic sustainability, for the benefit and long-term training of local people. Its success has influence far beyond its pristine setting.

Peninsula House

High on its hill overlooking the Atlantic Ocean from the northeast coast of the Dominican Republic, Peninsula House is the kind of getaway destination even celebrities dream of. Although recently built, it looks like an 18th-century Caribbean plantation house with columns supporting wrap-around verandahs on two floors. It has only six suites, furnished with first-class antiques, pictures and *objets d'art* whose sole function is to please – yet its aristocratic demeanour incorporates innovative technology aimed at ensuring the greatest comfort of its guests and the satisfaction of their every reasonable whim. It works on the principle that service is only impeccable if it is also unobtrusive. Now Peninsula House is officially the best hotel in the Dominican Republic, and regularly named by cognoscenti as one of the very best in the whole world.

As if defining luxury and the beauty of its Caribbean landscape wasn't enough, Peninsula House is perfectly sited for guests to limbo both sides of the stake. Its quiet, 6 ha (15 ac) of verdant lawns, coconut-palm-strewn hillside and beach adjoin the increasingly chic resort of Las Terranas, still small, but where of an evening the old fishermen's shacks along the waterfront now compete as bars, art boutiques and live-music jump-joints. During the daytime horseback riding, deep-sea fishing and every kind of water sport are readily available, but few of its guests want to leave Peninsula House – or its equally brilliant enclave on Coson Beach – once they have experienced its seductive charms.

Peninsula House is more about luxury as a holistic aesthetic than the mere pampering of the senses, but guests get both anyway. It doesn't have to be analyzed – just enjoyed.

WHERE:
Samana Peninsula, Dominican Republic
COST:
Expensive (but everyone agrees it's worth it)
BEST TIME OF YEAR:
December to April
DON'T MISS:
The museum quality of the art and furnishings; gourmet food
THINGS TO DO:
Explore the mangrove swamps at Los Haitises National Park; enjoy the bougainvillea-filled estate gardens; go whale-watching.
YOU SHOULD KNOW:
Guests must be aged over 18. All six suites are fabulous – but Number 6 has the best panoramic view from the verandah (and features a stunning pair of ivory-inlaid armoires).

Jade Mountain

The sheer glamour takes your breath away. By day it looks like an intergalactic spaceship perched on top of a wooded hillside facing one of the Caribbean's most spectacular panoramas. By night the cat's cradle of walkways connecting the building's different levels and individual suites is transformed into a web of twinkling, diamond lights. It is a glorious exoskeleton supporting a stupendous idea – but nothing prepares you for entering any one of Jade Mountain's 24 suites.

Behind each door, the rest of the world simply disappears. Stretching before you is a vast suite of polished hardwood floor divided by screens and exotic furniture into sleeping, lounging and sunbathing areas. There are only three walls. The fourth is open to the sky, reflected in an infinity pool extending from inside the room into the natural contours of the mountainside, and framing a unique view of St Lucia's Twin Pitons across the Caribbean 300 m (1,000 ft) below. Every suite is a different shape with a slightly different panorama of the Pitons. Between sunrise and blazing tropical sunset, every guest is regaled with their own, necessarily exclusive, album of visual memories – and at night they can create their own atmosphere by adjusting the fibre-optic lighting. With no telephone, TV, wifi or sound system, these suites are deservedly called 'sanctuaries'.

Guests emerge reluctantly, lured by the restaurant at the hotel's top floor. It has its own infinity pool set with a coloured glass mosaic; at night it provides a glamorous foil to the sarongs and beachwear of the day by invoking a requirement for as much bling and glitz as guests can carry off to live music.

WHERE:
Soufriere, St Lucia
COST:
Expensive to astronomical (and add 18% tax to all quoted prices)
BEST TIME OF YEAR:
December to April
DON'T MISS:
The waterfalls and koi-stocked pools descending through Jade Mountain's structure; the panoramic view from your chromatherapy whirlpool tub (for two); the walk-in volcano
THINGS TO DO:
Moon-gazing; snorkelling and scuba diving on pristine reefs; birdwatching and rainforest tours; water taxi to Anse Mamin
YOU SHOULD KNOW:
Guests have complete access to the beaches, water sports, restaurants and other facilities at Anse Chastanet, the resort which occupies the hill below Jade Mountain, under the same ownership. A shuttle runs between the two resorts on request; guests are asked not to use mobile phones in public areas; children must be at least 15; there's 24-hour room service.

Ladera Resort

WHERE:
Soufriere, St Lucia
COST:
Expensive+
BEST TIME OF YEAR:
December to April
DON'T MISS:
Dasheene, the Ladera's own and a St Lucia destination restaurant; the spectacular natural landscapes on the 250-year-old Fond Doux Estate tour; the market down the hill in Soufriere
THINGS TO DO:
Use the hotel shuttle to Anse Chastanet and other beaches/beach bars; sailing trips to Martinique or Marigot Bay; fishing; golf; water sports
YOU SHOULD KNOW:
If the sound of tree frogs at night bothers you, leave the waterfall in your plunge pool turned on to drown the noise.

Escapism was seldom so surprisingly possible. The Ladera is 300 m (1,000 ft) above the blue Caribbean, almost invisible beneath the rainforest climbing the steep hill behind Soufriere on St Lucia's southwest coast. The resort's nine villas and 23 suites are concealed by the lush vegetation of the former cocoa estate on which they stand, and which inspired their design in tropical hardwoods and fieldstone. Each is private from all the others and all of them are open on one side to the weather, with a magnificent view along the coast to the Pitons, St Lucia's outstanding landmark.

From such a height the views are sensational, whatever the weather or time of day. But every suite is also unique, its size and shape governed by the geography of the mountain. All of them have an infinity plunge pool on the mountain's edge (one of them with a swing), and even Gauguin would be thrilled by the abundant overhanging flowers and creeper-clad trees. In fact he'd also appreciate the combination of 19th-century-style French furnishings with the wickerwork of local artisans and folk art that characterizes the decor.

Hi-tech electronics jar with the Ladera's eco-conscious hideaway ethic, so no TVs or music centres interrupt the authentic sounds of the rainforest (although internet connections are available free in the reception area). And for guests not too sated to venture out, the hotel compounds the luxury of its suites with a full spa service, a first-class restaurant, a bar that feels (delightfully) like it's in a treehouse, and a willingness to arrange any activity that may be desired. Unsurprisingly, Ladera is unable to accept guests under 15.

The Caves, Negril

There are all kinds of exclusivity. Money or chic don't always guarantee a place in the sun. The Caves is a colony of just a dozen cottages scattered along the honeycombed cliffs right on the western tip of Jamaica. Separated from each other by a horticulturist's paradise of dense foliage, but positioned so that the sea is always visible, the cottages are concealed among limestone paths that wind through exotic gardens filled with arbours, grottos, pools and little waterfalls. Close to the water's edge, platforms hewn out of coral rock encourage both sunbathing and jumping into the deep, while steps make it easy to get out again.

There is no beach at The Caves. Instead, there's a communal saltwater pool on top of the cliffs, next to the thatched, open-air breakfast area and close to the evening restaurant and bar. Like the cottages, their style is a stunning tribute to the vivid colours and vibrancy of Jamaican folk art. Their rustic simplicity is entirely sympathetic to authentic Jamaican culture. So is the food, renowned for its inventive use of local ingredients and inspiration. It's another reason why the pool and restaurant often functions like a club. Guests tend to take a lounger to a quiet spot during the day, then congregate for the 'green flash' with a little fine music over a drink. And if not together, dinner can be served in your cottage or anywhere on the estate, including a candlelit cave next to the waves (which gets a gold star for romance).

The Caves offer tranquillity leavened by essence of Jamaica to the kind of guests who simply don't care about flashy extras. It's that hip, that funky and that cool.

WHERE:
The cliffs west of Negril, Jamaica
COST:
Expensive
BEST TIME OF YEAR:
December to April
DON'T MISS:
The lighthouse at Jamaica's western tip (it marks the concealed entrance to The Caves); the Blackwell Rum Bar – stone tables and stools in a cave grotto above the sea, like Flintstones meet Bond; the chef's truly original take on Barbecue Jerk Chicken; an Aveda spa treatment in one of the cliffside gazebos overlooking the Caribbean; 'floating' in the deep water off the cliffs (floats supplied)
THINGS TO DO:
Diving, parasailing, jet-skiing, banana boats and booze cruises off Negril's famous Seven Mile Beach, a 15-minute drive away; kayaking; snorkelling through caves (with a guide); cycling; reading; lazing in a hammock
YOU SHOULD KNOW:
Children must be at least 16. In addition to the one- and two-bedroom cottages, there's a new four-bedroom villa set in half an acre of amazing gardens, with a private pool. The estate is small enough to take over for a wedding party.

Hotel Mocking Bird Hill

WHERE:
Port Antonio, Portland Parish, Jamaica
COST:
Reasonable to expensive
BEST TIME OF YEAR:
December to April. Since the hotel is as much an ongoing community project as luxury eco-boutique, May to August and October to November are almost as good (it is closed throughout September).
DON'T MISS:
The spectacular panoramas on a gentle hike along the Rio Grande Valley; waterfalls under the rainforest canopy of the Blue Mountains; visiting the local women's paper-making co-operative, supported by the hotel; getting curious about Jamaican culture over afternoon tea, daily, with the owners
THINGS TO DO:
Beach business at Frenchman's Cove; downhill bike riding in the Blue Mountains; reading in a hammock; river rafting on the Rio Grande; learning to cook with jerk seasoning (invented by the local Maroon community); birdwatching in the forests
YOU SHOULD KNOW:
There's a minimum booking of two nights (five nights during the Christmas period). Mille Fleurs, the hotel restaurant, serves locally sourced 'slow food' and is one of Jamaica's best; the hotel has twice won the Caribbean Green Hotel of the Year award.

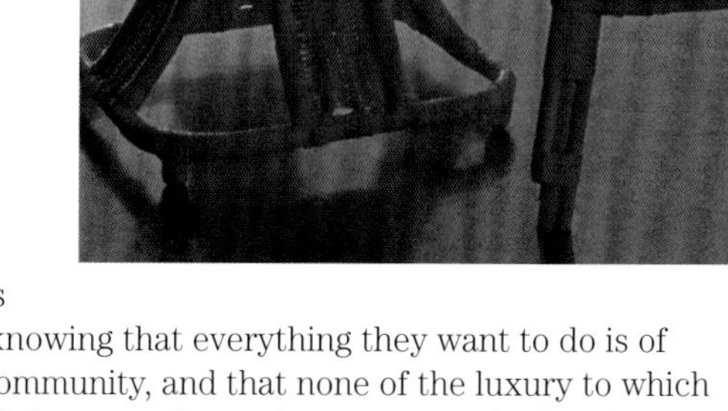

Not many hotels have the confidence to offer guests a few days of 'guiltless indulgence'. Hotel Mocking Bird Hill's unequivocal statement of environmental policy makes it vulnerable to criticism over any slip-ups or shortfalls, but the management haven't made any during 15 years of developing their principles of eco-sustainable tourism. They are justly proud of their holistic view – guests get a real kick from knowing that everything they want to do is of benefit to the local community, and that none of the luxury to which they are subjected (!) damages the environment on which it draws.

Mocking Bird Hill is wildly romantic. The hotel flourishes in an extensive area of thickly flowered gardens in the rainforest above Port Antonio on Jamaica's northeast coast. Its ten airy rooms inspire calm with a cool, predominantly blue-and-white decor. Flowers, inside and out, provide carnival-bright splashes of tropical colour – sometimes in the form of bougainvillea petals strewn with louche abandon on the bed. Louvred plantation doors and shutters catch the breeze across big terraces and balconies, a swerving racetrack for the forest birds darting low over the pool. This kind of rustic elegance makes every room a honeymoon suite, because all of them embody a philosophy based on generosity – to nature, to guests and to the local community. It's no hippy delusion. The hotel envelops guests in its ethical bubble and the invariable result is happiness. What could be more romantic?

The beach is a short drive and a whole world away. A shuttle is provided. Most guests can't wait to return to the mother ship, to plan the adventures it inspires in seeking out an alternative Jamaica.

The Seven Stars

If you do love to be beside the seaside and happen to like palm trees, the whitest sand, bluest sea and warmest sun (plus rum cocktails), then the Seven Stars in the delightful Turks and Caicos Islands could be your dream Caribbean ticket. True, the resort is a tad monumental. But that means its three large white buildings with blue roofs (matching the limpid waters of adjacent Grace Bay) can (and do) offer just about every luxury known to holidaying humankind.

The Seven Stars is on Providenciales, a small island beloved by visitors for a benign climate, rugged hills, spectacular beaches, Princess Alexandra National Park marine sanctuary and the world's third-longest coral reef. This is water sports heaven for the actively inclined, with plenty of pleasing alternatives for those who simply want to relax. The resort has a choice of accommodation from junior suites right up to four-bedroom mega-jobs for larger families or parties of friends, all equipped with pretty much everything from a kitchen with granite worktops through a luxurious bathroom via air con and ceiling fan to flat-screen TV, DVD/CD player and iPod dock.

But tear yourself away. The island's most impressive saltwater pool awaits (heated, so there isn't even the smallest hint of a shiver when you plunge in), surrounded by ample supplies of loungers, sunbrellas, towels, drinks and snacks for those who prefer not to head for the beach. The resort offers free sailing, paddle boarding, kayaking and windsurfing, plus snorkelling and scuba diving expeditions (or beginners' courses for the uninitiated). Then there's the tough choice between eateries: the Sand Dollar for *al fresco* beach/poolside meals, Seven Restaurant for fine dining or The Deck for local fare and cocktails overlooking the sea. The only drawback is that you can't stay forever (unless, like many others, you retire here).

WHERE:
Grace Bay, Providenciales, Turks and Caicos Islands
COST:
Expensive (but there are great deals to be had, especially outside high season)
BEST TIME OF YEAR:
December to April
DON'T MISS:
Yoga, aqua aerobics and other physical toning work at the resort's Fitness Centre; facials and full-body treatments from expert therapists at the spa (or the tempting couple's massage!)
THINGS TO DO:
Have a flutter in the nearby casino; test your golfing skills against the local 18-holer; kayak through the mangroves; scuba or snorkel the reef; parasailing; water skiing; kite boarding; wake boarding; horseback riding; game fishing; ATV excursions into the interior; boat trips to explore, picnic and sunbathe on uninhabited cays
YOU SHOULD KNOW:
Those who base their holiday plans on awards will be delighted to know that the Seven Stars has been voted both 'Most Romantic Resort' and 'World's Top Beach Destination'. This is a family-friendly place with babysitting, a children's play area, kids' camp and junior diving courses. The island of Providenciales didn't have a single wheeled vehicle as recently as the early 1960s, before its rapid development into today's major tourist destination.

Hotel Le Toiny

WHERE:
Le Toiny Bay, southeast coast of St Barth's
COST:
Astronomical
BEST TIME OF YEAR:
December to April
DON'T MISS:
Water sports at Grand Cul de Sac; Sunday brunch of conch ravioli and homemade *foie gras*; gossip over the barista's cocktail of the day, in the moon-shaped infinity (main) pool; surfing at Washing Machine Beach (close to Le Toiny)

The studied nonchalance of the truly sleek and slick is the signature of St Barth's. Hotel Le Toiny is its temple. It prizes the offer of total privacy above all other promises, attracting many of the world's most fabulous people to practise being alone in its adjoining suites. There are just 14, arranged in individual cottages with gardens and a small pool, plus a single three-bedroom villa.

Their style is old Caribbean, with pointed tin roofs painted pale green, clapboard walls and sliding glass fronts with louvre shutters. It's a very pleasing effect which disguises the hi-tech appointments incorporated in the wooden furniture and hidden by the drapes on the four posters. The roof extends to form a shaded terrace by the pool, and from teak sun loungers guests have a phenomenal vista to St Kitts, Nevis and St Eustatius on the horizon. Every detail shows how carefully the designers combined style with great comfort and practicality. They ought to be French, and they are.

Even with room service happy to bring three meals and anything else a day, guests can be tempted to venture out. Le Toiny's main house holds the hotel's restaurant. Called Le Gaiac, it's considered the best on St Barth's and it's as *serieux* as a French restaurant should be after flying in fresh ingredients from France itself. Few resist its splendid blandishments, and although it is admired for its gentle chic, diners' pleasure can be so great that spontaneous parties erupt on its poolside terrace. That doesn't do much for guests' privacy or nonchalant cool, but it certainly does make Le Toiny the most wonderful place to stay.

THINGS TO DO:
Walking the Cote Sauvage, the rocky cliffs of the island's undeveloped east coast on which Le Toiny is built; duty-free shopping in Gustavia; swanning around the beach bars of St Jean; Sanctuary spa treatments by your own pool; starting a backgammon tournament; reading for pleasure; practising liquid languor

YOU SHOULD KNOW:
St Barth's is within the Eurozone; it's better to rent a car full time than depend on hard-to-get taxis; children are welcome but the sophisticated ambiance isn't very suitable for them.

Villas at Stonehaven

In the Caribbean, the highest levels of chic belong to the most secluded communities. The Villas at Stonehaven take the notion a step further, by dispensing with the sense of community as well. Each of the 14 villas is identical, so there are no comparisons or advantages to be sought or avoided; and each is so completely comfortable and well-ordered that, once ensconced, lots of guests never leave the villa at all during their stay.

The villas are really unusual. They have mansard roofs with dormer balconies, arched windows with louvred shutters, and the 'bottle' balustrades of classic architecture. They resemble miniature French *châteaux* spread along a steep ridge overlooking the sandy cove of Stonehaven Bay. In fact they are invisible from each other, separated by their own large and fabulously maintained private gardens. They are solid, adult houses, the antithesis of clapboard 'rustic elegance'. Inside, under the high, beamed ceilings, rooms are furnished with proper sofas and good antique reproductions. The biggest concession to the tropics is the huge verandah, where most of the living takes place. With drawing and sitting rooms, too, and all the usual service rooms, the villas are ideal for families or groups of friends. Given staff available to shop and cook, an infinity pool in the garden and every conceivable entertainment device built into the French/Creole decor, the temptation to stay put is strong.

One definite lure is the Villas' clubhouse restaurant, famed for its high-end Caribbean cooking. Another is the cocktail bar, on a terrace next to a stunning sliver of moon-shaped infinity pool, with panoramic views across the bay. Otherwise, back 'home' is best.

WHERE:
Stonehaven Bay, northwest coast, Tobago

COST:
Reasonable to expensive

BEST TIME OF YEAR:
December to April

DON'T MISS:
Seeing giant leatherback turtles come ashore in Stonehaven Bay to lay their eggs (March to May), or the babies hatching (June to August); asking your villa chef to make traditional Tobagonian recipes like Crab & Dumpling, Shark & Bake or Callalou

THINGS TO DO:
Swimming; water sports; tennis; golf; deep-sea fishing; guided rainforest and birdwatching hikes; reading in the garden

YOU SHOULD KNOW:
Management advises that the estate is not suitable for children under seven because of low balconies, unfenced pools and steep terrain (most people just bring a nanny). Nearly everything (the beach, shops, activity centres, etc) is a short drive away, so renting a car makes sense.

Spice Island Beach Resort

WHERE:
Grand Anse, Grenada
COST:
Expensive to astronomical, even taking account of any offers or seasonal and child discounts you can combine; inclusive and half-board rates are available
BEST TIME OF YEAR:
December to April
DON'T MISS:
Beach theatre played out among the bars and playgrounds lining Grand Anse beyond the hotel; St George's, one of the Caribbean's prettiest harbour towns; the rainforest birds and orchids in the Grand Etang Lake Reserve
THINGS TO DO:
Look beautiful; choose idle elegance in the sure knowledge that every water sport and entertainment is available on your doorstep, and will be tomorrow, too.
YOU SHOULD KNOW:
There is no smoking allowed anywhere in the resort. Children are fully catered for by the Nutmeg Pod, but their presence is subject to strict and complicated rules. An 'elegantly casual' (no shorts or t-shirts) dress code is enforced for dinner in the restaurant.

By its name, location and style, Spice Island Beach Resort has a long-standing claim to offer the best of Grenada. Historical chance made Grenada 'the spice island' of nutmeg, cloves, ginger, cinnamon and cocoa, instead of another giant sugar plantation. The hotel has appropriated the nickname as its own, and occupies a generous proportion of the best beach on what is one of the Caribbean's loveliest and most verdant islands. With its natural advantages burnished by serious investment, it now epitomizes the full-on, luxury, tropical beach extravaganza beloved of honeymooners and chocolate-bar advertisements.

The resort consists of 64 suites ranked according to degree of luxury, ranging back from the sugar-spun white sand of Grand Anse, a 3-km (2-mi) curve of breathtaking, uninterrupted bliss. They stretch either side of the centrally positioned 'Club', with its open-fronted restaurants, free-form pool and bars. Shaded by palm trees, and with flowering shrubs to create semi-private alcoves, it's a really pretty and sociable communal area. The real privacy begins with the fantastic beach suites along the surf line. Behind them are ranged ten mega-suites with private gardens and large swimming pools, and seven more with plunge pools. Further back through the trees and beautiful gardens slightly less grand suites occupy two floors in a series of balcony blocks – but everybody gets a full set of air conditioning, double whirlpool bath, fans, Frette linen, Molton Brown accessories, and the latest wifi, TV and entertainment gadgetry fitted into the Caribbean-bright colours of the decor. The standard of luxury never falters.

Spice Island Beach is owned and run by a Grenadian family – so its atmosphere is charged with the warmth, humour and generosity for which Grenada has always been justly famous.

Coqui Coqui Spa

A serenely unspoilt stretch of white-sand beach edging the turquoise waters of the Caribbean is the setting for this intimate little hotel and spa. Coqui Coqui lies on the east coast of the Yucatán peninsula, midway between the coastal villages of Tulum and Boca Paila. Understated luxury is the watchword here, where the minimalist chic of the seven bedrooms blends Asian and European influences, clean contemporary lines with traditional handmade furniture. Coqui Coqui is the creation of former supermodel Nicolas Malleville and his personal touch is to be seen everywhere in his 'residences', as he likes to call them (there are three more of them on the Yucatán), not least the candles which fill each room with delicate scents from his own perfumery. Coqui Coqui also gives its name to the range of perfumes and creams which Nicolas produces in the inland town of Valladolid.

The tiny spa is an elegant, no-frills affair which offers an enticing menu of massages, skin scrubs, botanical baths and other body treatments, all of which make use of the firm's own products – essential oils, lotions and herbal preparations, many derived from local plants like mint, agave and coconut. This level of pampering doesn't come cheap, of course, but even so that doesn't stop the rooms here being booked up months in advance.

Should you feel the need for some local history and if you can bestir yourself from the torpor of Coqui Coqui, then there are two spectacular ancient Maya sites – at Tulum and Muyil – and both are within an easy drive.

WHERE:
Tulum, Quintana Roo State
COST:
Expensive
BEST TIME OF YEAR:
October to April
DON'T MISS:
The Ocean Bath Ritual, a comprehensive spa treatment promising three hours of bodily bliss
THINGS TO DO:
Sunbathing; swimming; diving; spa treatments
YOU SHOULD KNOW:
If you do visit the Mayan ruins and want to beat the crowds, its best to arrive at breakfast time.

La Purificadora

Travellers hurrying along the highway from Mexico City and making a beeline for the colonial splendours of Oaxaca to the south are all too likely to give Puebla a miss. But this would be a pity, because Puebla is another city with a rich and fascinating colonial legacy which, like Oaxaca, has been given World Heritage status by UNESCO.

A significant new reason for breaking your journey and stopping over in the 'City of the Angels', to give Puebla de los Angeles its full name, has been the opening in recent years of this smart boutique hotel, just a few blocks east of the city centre. Designed by celebrated Mexican architect Ricardo Legorreta, La Purificadora takes its name from the fact that it is housed in a late 19th-century water-purifying plant and ice factory. The imaginative conversion boasts the best of contemporary design mixed with an impressive respect for the building's history. Much of the original stonework has been left exposed, which together with many old wood features has created an effect best described as 'industrial chic'.

The lobby is a huge, airy affair, with purple sofas scattered around a bare floor of customized tiles. Everywhere you are drawn to the link between indoors and outdoors. For example, the restaurant opens out onto a broad patio area. Best of all is a rooftop terrace, complete with a 30-m (100-ft) lap pool with glass sides – a perfect place to enjoy the sunsets over the Puebla roofscape. The 26 bedrooms are as comfortably appointed as you would expect, many having balconies with lovely views out over the gardens and the glorious colonial architecture of the 16th-century church of San Francisco.

WHERE:
Paseo San Francisco, Puebla City
COST:
Reasonable
BEST TIME OF YEAR:
February to October
DON'T MISS:
The clever use of found materials such as fragments of bottle and glass in the hotel's public spaces
THINGS TO DO:
Sightseeing; fine dining; sauna; spa treatments
YOU SHOULD KNOW:
The terrace is a popular gathering place for evening cocktails among the city's *beau monde.*

Quinta Real Hotel

Whatever your views about the sport of bullfighting you cannot fail to be captivated by the atmosphere of this most unusual hotel, which has been fashioned out of the old San Pedro bullring in the central Mexican city of Zacatecas. Rest assured that you will be completely safe from marauding bulls if you decide to stay here. There has been no *corrida* (bullfight) at the 19th-century San Pedro (said to be the second oldest in the whole of Latin America) since 1975.

Fitted out with classic colonial furniture, the 49 bedroom suites have been constructed on top of the former public stands surrounding the bullring, while the *ruedo*, the arena itself, has been beautifully converted into a colonial-style patio, complete with patterned cobblestones and floral displays. The extensive restaurant follows the line of the stands and is on three levels, affording fine views of the *ruedo* and out over the city.

Founded in 1546, Zacatecas is one of Mexico's oldest colonial cities and, at an elevation of 2,500 m (8,200 ft), one of its highest. The city has an unusual topography: the centre is squeezed into a narrow ravine, with suburbs scattered over the surrounding hillsides. Zacatecas is famous for the distinctive pink stone of its houses, many of which still retain their elegant wrought-iron balconies. It is a lovely place to explore on foot and the centre is a pleasant 20-minute walk from the hotel. Closer to hand is a fine old aqueduct, El Cubo, and the Estrada park, on the far side of which the handsome former governor's mansion now houses a museum of modern Mexican art.

WHERE:
Zacatecas
COST:
Reasonable
BEST TIME OF YEAR:
The climate is pleasant all year round, although the altitude means that winter nights can be chilly.
DON'T MISS:
The hotel bar in the brick vaults where the fighting bulls were once kept penned before their release into the ring
THINGS TO DO:
Visiting an old silver mine; exploring the streets and alleys of the old town; a cable-car ride to the top of Cerro de la Bufa
YOU SHOULD KNOW:
Zacatecas grew wealthy on the back of the silver mined in the area. Appropriately enough, the hotel has its own silver shop.

Las Ventanas al Paraiso

WHERE:
Cabo San Lucas
COST:
Expensive
BEST TIME OF YEAR:
Any time of year is good, although December to March is the dry season and the peak time for visitors.
DON'T MISS:
You can arrange your own private cinema screening on the beach.
THINGS TO DO:
Swimming; sailing; scuba diving; sport fishing; golf; tennis; riding
YOU SHOULD KNOW:
The winter months (December to March) are the time to come for dolphin- and whale-watching.

Baja California is the enormous peninsula which projects more than 1,250 km (780 mi) south from the US border into the Pacific Ocean. You will find this exclusive seaside resort right down at its southernmost tip, on the coast between the small towns of San José del Cabo and Cabo San Lucas. With a white-sand beach and sapphire sea on one side and an imposing backdrop of mountains and desert on the other, this complex of private suites and residences offers the last word in discreet luxury and pampered indulgence.

Las Ventanas al Paraiso translates as 'windows on paradise', and the management cannot be faulted on its efforts to live up to the heavenly moniker. The high standards of service and comfort expected by contemporary travellers in the luxury market are amply catered for here – by personal butlers, for example, and many suites have their own private infinity pools. But what gives the resort its special flavour is the way this is combined with decor and design features – smoothly curving adobe walls, sturdy timber furniture – that evoke a bygone era of hospitality in the grand *haciendas* of old Mexico.

Not surprisingly Las Ventanas is popular with honeymooners and those looking for a romantic hideaway. Should you ever tire from gazing into your beloved's eyes the resort offers plenty of more active pursuits, including excursions into the desert. For real excitement, though, you should try fishing. This is one of the world's great sport fishing destinations and just the place to see a big 'trophy' fish, such as the legendary marlin, being landed. Or catch it!

Playa Viva

Playa Viva is a place that will appeal to anyone in search of rest and relaxation – but not at the expense of their surroundings. Recently created by a US couple, this small beach resort has been established on determinedly ecological principles with a commitment to what they call the 'triple bottom line' – good for business, good for the ecology and good for the community.

Situated on the Pacific coast some 200 km (125 mi) north of Acapulco, Playa Viva is far enough away from major resorts to boast some of the cleanest beaches and waters in the region. The complex makes use of local, renewable materials and solar power. All the accommodation offers uninterrupted views of the ocean, from basic suites to the more elaborate *casitas* – free-standing structures with one or more bedrooms.

Sustainable living and development are very much the name of the game at Playa Viva. According to the dedicated hosts, a stay here is designed to 'remind you of the interconnection between all living things'. As you would expect, there are plenty of opportunities for exploring the natural environment. Because the resort is located between two river estuaries, the presence of both saltwater and freshwater ecosystems makes for an unusually rich diversity of flora and fauna. You can explore Playa Viva's own 65 ha (160 ac) of private nature reserve, or else head off on a mountain bike into the hills of the Sierra Madre behind. And you may be lucky enough to help the staff at the turtle sanctuary to collect newly laid eggs from the beach for protection from predators until they are ready to hatch.

WHERE:
Juluchuca, Guerrero State
COST:
Reasonable
BEST TIME OF YEAR:
December to April
DON'T MISS:
The small archaeological site and evidence of ancient terraced farming behind the resort
THINGS TO DO:
Swimming; diving; kayaking; hiking; yoga; birdwatching; community development
YOU SHOULD KNOW:
As part of its commitment to the local community Playa Viva has ambitious plans to restore much of the land laid waste by 'slash and burn' agriculture to its original state as coastal forest and wetland.

Verana

WHERE:
Yelapa, Puerto Vallarta
COST:
Expensive
BEST TIME OF YEAR:
November to May
DON'T MISS:
If you take the boat trip to the protected Marietas Islands you may be lucky enough to spot the blue-footed booby. This is one of only two places (the other is the Galapagos Islands) where this rare and lovely bird is still found.
THINGS TO DO:
Hiking; riding; swimming; diving; whale-watching; yoga; massage
YOU SHOULD KNOW:
Verana does not accept children under 16 – for the unusual reason that young ones' vulnerability to scorpion bites, together with the remote location, mean that they are unable to guarantee sufficiently prompt medical attention.

Arriving at this remote and exclusive retreat high up in the lush green hills of western Mexico feels like taking a step or two out of time. An intrepid 19th-century traveller would not find anything unfamiliar about the 30-minute boat ride from the small beach at Boca de Tomatlan along the coast to Yelapa, where mules wait to bear your luggage up to the hotel (and you, too, if you can't face the short climb up the hill). As you will have gathered, Verana is about as isolated and secluded as it gets. By the time you finally arrive you will have left the sounds of cars and busy roads far behind.

This is a seriously classy establishment, featuring just eight rooms described as private guest houses. Each room has its own unique character, reflected in the names: *casa piedra* (stone house); pool house; jungle suite; tea house; *casa amor*. Verana's location overlooks the lovely Bahía de Bandares (Bay of Flags) where you can watch dolphins disporting themselves.

All the rooms have spectacular views of the ocean but at the same time you are enveloped by the dense Mexican jungle. On top of all the facilities you would expect from a top-end resort – spa, massage, fitness centre, infinity pool – there are guided jungle treks on offer; the 90-minute hike to the cascades at Cathedral Fall is particularly recommended as it has a fine wild-swimming area. The closest beach is a 10-minute walk away and boat trips are available to more remote beaches and to offshore islands where there is an abundance of birdlife.

Ka'ana

Hidden away deep in the Belizean rainforest, this charming boutique resort allows you to immerse yourself in the myriad sensations of the jungle while enjoying international standards of comfort. Ka'ana's low-impact villas and suites are scattered discreetly around a luxuriant tropical garden. Many have been designed in the style of a *hacienda* so you can sit on your private verandah and let the forest's sounds and scents waft over you.

Service is attentive to a fault – even the paintings on your bedroom walls (works by local artists) are changed after four nights. You can take your meals inside or *al fresco* and the restaurant prides itself on the home-grown produce it uses from its extensive organic kitchen garden. Although sustainability and respect for the environment are important themes at Ka'ana you need have no fear of being brainwashed here. The approach is a much more subtle one, based on the principle of 'you know it makes sense'.

This part of Western Belize, close to the border with Guatemala, offers a wealth of interesting sights and activities and Ka'ana lays on a wide range of excursions and adventures. Get a novel view of the forest canopy as you whizz down an aerial runway, or lie back in a giant rubber ring and let the current of a forest stream bear you along through great chambers in the rock where the only light comes from your own headlamp. For the more dedicated thrill-seeker there are guided tours into dramatic limestone cave complexes and the chance to join a jaguar tracking expedition, although sighting of this elusive big cat is never guaranteed.

WHERE:
San Ignacio
COST:
Expensive
BEST TIME OF YEAR:
November to May
DON'T MISS:
The ancient Maya cities at Xunantunich and Caracol – at the latter a Ka'ana tour grants you exclusive access to the site and an unforgettable night beside the ruins
THINGS TO DO:
Trekking; horse riding; cave tubing; visiting archaeological sites; exploring cave systems
YOU SHOULD KNOW:
Although it is not peak time, Ka'ana recommends a stay during the rainy season (August to October) – prices are lower and the short mid-afternoon showers bring the forest to life as well as providing welcome refreshment.

Canopy Tower Ecolodge

An old communications tower built by the USA at the height of the Cold War to form part of the Panama Canal's defence system has found a novel use in these more settled times, as a perfect observation centre for nature lovers. The tower has been ingeniously converted into what is effectively a giant bird hide, albeit one that you can stay in, and in considerable comfort.

The bedrooms occupy the upper two floors of the circular tower; there are just seven double rooms, all equipped with huge observation windows, enabling you to lie in bed and watch the natural world unfold outside. For an even closer experience you climb up to the top of the tower where a broad outdoor observation deck encircles the old radar dome. The unparalleled view of the rainforest canopy means you will not wait long before spotting some spectacular neighbours.

Canopy Tower sits on a hill in the middle of Soberanía National Park. This is one of the richest parts of the planet for birdlife, with some 400 species recorded in the park alone. The astonishing biodiversity has a lot to do with a location close to the continental divide; the Canopy Tower sits on the Atlantic Slope which has fascinatingly different habitats from the Pacific. In the short time it has been open Canopy Tower has become a veritable mecca for serious twitchers, its facilities finely honed to maximize your sightings. But don't worry if you're not a keen birdwatcher; there is still much else to enjoy about life in the jungle, including the noisy antics of howler monkeys and cute little tamarins feeding on the fruit ... favourite cecropia tree.

WHERE:
Soberanía National Park, near Panama City
COST:
Expensive
BEST TIME OF YEAR:
October to May
DON'T MISS:
The dawn chorus when the birdlife is at its most active – grab a cup of coffee and a fresh roll from the dining room, climb up to the observation deck and feast your eyes.
THINGS TO DO:
Birdwatching; hiking; trips to the Canal and Panama City; boat rides on Lake Gatún
YOU SHOULD KNOW:
...nderful place to watch ...ring migrations. ... funnel

Gamboa Rainforest Resort

On a small hill overlooking the town and the Chagres River the Gamboa Resort lies roughly at the midway point of the Panama isthmus and its famous Canal. The Chagres meets the Canal a short distance away and one of the more surreal sights of a stay here is that of the tops of huge ships gliding noiselessly through a carpet of green. Gamboa is a smart and substantial resort built on the site of what was once an American golf course.

Most of the rooms have views of the river and come with private balconies where you can laze in a hammock while watching the river traffic and keeping an eye out for toucans, *cotingas* and other exotic birds of these parts. Facilities include a large split-level swimming pool and a state-of-the art spa complete with hydro massage hot tub, thermal baths, sauna and gym.

Gamboa is amazingly quiet and relaxing, given that you are just 30 minutes from Panama City itself. Shopping expeditions are easily arranged, as are visits to the sights of this colourful and cosmopolitan capital. The resort offers an extensive menu of tours and excursions, including guided tours of the Canal itself, river trips, boat rides to Monkey Island and freshwater fishing on Lake Gatún. For the more energetic there are hiking trails and night safaris which give you the chance to see some of the rainforest's more reclusive inhabitants. A ride on the aerial tramway brings you eye to eye with the wildlife in the tree tops; with the help of a local guide you should be fortunate enough to spot monkeys and sloths as well as the tropical birdlife.

WHERE:
Gamboa, near Panama City
COST:
Expensive
BEST TIME OF YEAR:
December to April
DON'T MISS:
The stunning new Biomuseo outside Panama City, designed by the architect Frank Gehry
THINGS TO DO:
Swimming; hiking; kayaking; wildlife-watching; boat trips; fishing
YOU SHOULD KNOW:
If your budget stretches that far and you are looking for accommodation with a little more character, Gamboa also offers 'historic apartments'.

Royal Decameron Beach Resort

WHERE:
Farallón, Coclé Province
COST:
Reasonable
BEST TIME OF YEAR:
December to April
DON'T MISS:
One of the best optional day trips is a partial transit of the Panama Canal on a ferry.
THINGS TO DO:
Swimming; diving; golf; tennis; horse riding; deep-sea fishing
YOU SHOULD KNOW:
The Royal Decameron is particularly welcoming to families with children. As well as three special pools, younger guests have their own nightly live entertainment.

If your idea of a good holiday involves not looking at the contents of your wallet or purse from beginning to end, then checking in at the Royal Decameron will be just the ticket. The tariff covers all meals and drinks consumed on the premises so, apart from the odd souvenir, tipping and any presents for the folks at home you really should be able to forget those bits of plastic and paper which run your life for the rest of the year.

Mind you, if you subscribe to a 'small is beautiful' philosophy then this vast resort on the Pacific coast west of Panama City is probably not for you. With over 1,000 rooms the Royal Decameron is a hub of activity in high season, and with 10 restaurants offering everything from prime steaks to Japanese sushi, spicy Thai cuisine to freshly caught seafood, a dozen bars and no fewer than eight pools, you'll have the chance to eat, drink and swim in a different location every day of the week.

The benefits of scale make for a huge range of activities on site, including the complex's own casino and 18-hole golf course. There are tennis courts, a discotheque, a well-equipped spa and many water sports on offer on the extensive stretch of white-sand beach, including snorkelling, windsurfing and beach volleyball. And if you want a change of air, the resort's own tour operator offers a bewildering array of excursions and day trips (extra charge), including river-rafting on the Rio Grande and riding quad bikes in the hills and valleys behind the resort.

La Loma Jungle Lodge

Some 70 islands make up the Bocas del Toro archipelago which lies off the Caribbean northwest coast of Panama. One of the largest, Isla Bastimentos, is home to La Loma, a tropical farm which offers lodgings to a handful of guests. There are just three *ranchos* – individual cabins built in traditional style and using local materials. The hillside site overlooks a secluded bay and there are fine views from the *ranchos'* private verandahs. This is a place for lovers of nature, not of mod cons; there is no TV, no air conditioning and no internet. The loan of rubber boots and a pair of binoculars on arrival encourages you to explore and immerse yourself in the teeming natural world surrounding you.

La Loma is a working farm and its owners are always happy to involve guests in the daily round. The main crops are bananas, coconuts and cacao, whose beans are used for cocoa and chocolate. Much of the food you will eat at La Loma comes from the farm's organic gardens. There are no roads or vehicles on the island so the principal means of getting about is by boat; traditional wooden *cayucos* (dugout canoes) are available to help you explore the creeks and mangrove swamps of the coastline, much of which is protected as a marine park.

The owners of La Loma are deeply committed not only to their stewardship of the environment but also to being responsible neighbours. In addition to providing valuable employment to the island's traditional inhabitants, the Ngobe Indians, La Loma donates a percentage of its profits to development projects in support of the local community.

WHERE:
Isla Bastimentos, Bocas del Toro
COST:
Reasonable
BEST TIME OF YEAR:
January to March
DON'T MISS:
The chance to roast your own cacao beans and produce pure cocoa for the chocolate cake that accompanies your afternoon tea
THINGS TO DO:
Walking; birdwatching; butterfly spotting; helping out on the farm; surfing; indigenous cookery classes
YOU SHOULD KNOW:
You need to be reasonably fit to stay at La Loma as your accommodation can only be reached via a short but fairly steep climb.

Morgan's Rock Hacienda

WHERE:
San Juan del Sur
COST:
Expensive
BEST TIME OF YEAR:
November to April
DON'T MISS:
The chance to see giant sea turtles laying their eggs on the beach and, if you're very lucky, baby turtles hatching and scurrying down to the sea
THINGS TO DO:
Wildlife-watching; hiking; nocturnal nature walks; kayaking; surfing; fishing; mountain biking
YOU SHOULD KNOW:
November to April may be the dry season but many nature lovers prefer to come during the other months when prices are lower and the rains (less intense in these dry tropical forests) create a truly green and vibrant paradise.

The Pacific coast of Nicaragua has so far managed to escape the worst of the commercial mass development that has blighted many other areas of the Central American littoral. The pressures are growing, however, so now is the time to head for this lovely spot in the south of the country, close to the Costa Rica border. With its own expanse of pristine sand beach Morgan's Rock is a discreetly upmarket eco-lodge in a remote location north of San Juan del Sur. It takes its name from the fact that this was the original location for the proposed waterway linking the Atlantic and Pacific oceans. US Senator John Tyler Morgan was its most enthusiastic advocate, until the superior influence and business clout of the Panama lobby won the day.

The lodge's 15 bungalows are constructed from a variety of local woods and have openings on all four sides to allow natural ventilation from the tropical breezes. All have ocean views; a highlight of a stay here is watching the sunset from your private deck. Some bungalows even have trees growing through their roofs! Morgan's Rock takes its eco-credentials very seriously, although it is perhaps a little difficult to square this with the recent opening of a small private runway to facilitate guests' access.

Nevertheless, the lodge manages an impressive reforestation project as well as its own private nature reserve where sloths, deer, spider and capuchin monkeys are all to be seen. Solar power is the principal energy source and treated waste water is recycled for irrigation purposes. Even the complex's lighting system has been carefully designed so as not to disturb sea turtles nesting on the beach.

Tree House Lodge

Whatever part treehouses may have played in your early life, this one is guaranteed to exceed your wildest childhood dreams. Hidden away on the Caribbean coast in the far south of Costa Rica, the Tree House Lodge is a small complex of self-contained holiday homes. The description does not begin to do them justice, for each of the four houses has its own distinct character and they are as different one from the other as you could imagine.

Thus the Beach House, just 80 m (260 ft) from the shoreline, has rattan walls and a thatched roof, while the Garden House is constructed from bamboo and resembles an oversized Wendy house, complete with angular roof and vermilion walls. The funkiest design is to be found in the split-level Beach Suite. With its three double bedrooms it is the largest accommodation on site. As for the eponymous Tree House, this is a splendid affair, built on stilts around a 100-year-old giant tree (your toilet nestles in the folds of its trunk). If your inner child is not already aroused, it surely will be by the suspension bridge that provides the means of entry.

What all the houses do have in common is a construction based on firmly ecological principles. Timber is the main material used, much of it from fallen *níspero* trees that have been retrieved from the jungle. Sustainable woods have also been used in making the furniture. The houses each have a full kitchen and eco-friendly Jacuzzi. And there's no need to worry about mosquitoes either; all the windows have screens to keep the little critters out, so they are not as troublesome as you might have feared.

WHERE:
Puerto Viejo, Limón province
COST:
Reasonable
BEST TIME OF YEAR:
September to December
DON'T MISS:
Even if you are not staying in the Beach Suite you should try and get a peek inside its amazing bathroom – it's a riot of colours and wacky features.
THINGS TO DO:
Jungle hikes; swimming; snorkelling; cycling; watching howler monkeys and sloths; visiting the green iguana conservation project
YOU SHOULD KNOW:
The lodge has no bar or restaurant but there are grocery stores and eating places within easy walking distance, and also a bakery that sells daily fresh bread.

Rafiki Safari Lodge

WHERE:
Near Quepos
COST:
Reasonable
BEST TIME OF YEAR:
December to April
DON'T MISS:
If shooting rapids does it for you the nearby Savegre River provides some of the best whitewater rafting in Central America.
THINGS TO DO:
Birdwatching; hiking; horse riding; swimming (pool and giant waterslide); massage
YOU SHOULD KNOW:
You may prefer to visit in the months of May to November when the wet season makes for better wildlife viewing and more exciting conditions for rafting on the river.

Rafiki means 'friend' in Swahili and that is how you will be greeted when you arrive at this jungle eco-lodge, even if it is your first visit. The warmth of the welcome is matched by the tropical heat but the specially designed safari tents which constitute the accommodation here (and which sleep up to four) provide the perfect conditions for getting close to nature while not allowing its less desirable representatives to get close to you.

This is camping with the mod cons. Canvas walls keep the insects and the elements out but let the evening breezes waft through, while your bathroom has everything you would expect from a modern facility. The tents sit on raised hardwood decks and their private terraces, as well as the observation deck by the central bar, are great places for sitting quietly and watching life in the jungle as the mists lift off the surrounding highlands.

A little bit of the *veldt* is what Rafiki's owners, the Boshoff family from South Africa, have sought to introduce to this part of Central America. Their inspiration and primary motivation have been a desire to help the country's largest land mammal, the tapir. The twin pressures of hunting and habitat destruction have driven this magnificent animal close to the point of extinction. But the Boshoffs have ambitious plans to create a wildlife refuge at Rafiki, which is adjacent to a known tapir corridor, and eventually to re-introduce tapirs to the wild using a model of sustainable tourism (essentially tourism revenue from the lodge generates the funds for capital development) which has worked well on conservation projects in South Africa.

Alvear Palace Hotel

Tree-lined Avenida Alvear is the most exclusive shopping street in the smart inner-city suburb of Recoleta. It is also the location of the *grande dame* of Buenos Aires' hotels, the Alvear Palace. This famous and historic establishment occupies a whole city block and is located on a site where the British Embassy once stood. Rising to 11 storeys, with a further five below ground, the hotel opened in 1923, towards the end of what is generally regarded as the city's golden age.

Buenos Aires is often described by visitors from the northern hemisphere as the most European of Latin America's cities and the Alvear Palace reflects the influences of the old continent in spades. Unashamedly lavish in its decor and fittings, the hotel evokes the old-fashioned elegance and discreet opulence of the *belle époque*. The Parisian-style touches are everywhere, from the rich burgundies of the drapes and fabrics to the antique French furniture and the architecture of the surrounding streets.

Staying at one of the world's grand hotels does not come cheap but you do get solid luxury for your money. The furnishings of the 200 rooms are in Empire and Louis XVI style and are complemented by sumptuous displays of fresh flowers and fruit, while original works by modern Argentine artists adorn the walls. If you are after a little more space, then the Presidential and Royal suites are among the largest you'll find anywhere. The hotel boasts an enormous spa and fitness centre and has two top-class restaurants. Sunday brunch or afternoon tea in the glass-roofed L'Orangerie – the latter being an institution among well-heeled *porteños* (as the locals are known) – is a particular delight.

WHERE:
Buenos Aires
COST:
Expensive
BEST TIME OF YEAR:
Spring (September to November) and autumn (March to May)
DON'T MISS:
The spa's ludic pool and sensations path, where the soles of your feet are massaged by gentle currents of water passing over a bed of heated pebbles
THINGS TO DO:
Sightseeing; people watching; Museo Nacional de Bellas Artes (the city's fine art gallery); Plaza Francia handicrafts market
YOU SHOULD KNOW:
The hotel is a short walk from the splendid Recoleta Cemetery, the final resting place of the great and the good of Argentinian society, including, most famous of all, Evita herself.

Estancia Peuma Hue

In the heart of Argentina's Lake District, this luxurious *estancia* has a stunning location on the southern shore of Lago Gutiérrez, a short distance south from Bariloche, the principal town of the region. *Peuma Hue* means 'place of dreams' in the language of the Mapuche, the original indigenous inhabitants of the area, and the dreams and ethos of the founder-owner, a former psychotherapist, certainly underpin every facet of a stay here. Guests come here to discover or renew a deep connection with nature and to draw spiritual nourishment from the energy and tranquillity of Peuma Hue.

The accommodation comprises a number of large alpine-style cabins scattered over 200 ha (500 ac) of green pasture and woods by the lakeside. Large observation windows afford outstanding views of the turquoise waters and the imposing slopes of D'Agostini Mountain. Meals are taken in the central lodge, much of the produce coming from Peuma Hue's organic gardens. The *asados* (Argentinian barbecues) are a particular culinary highlight.

There is no off-season at Peuma Hue because it is right beside the peak of Cerro Catedral, one of Argentina's premier skiing and winter sports centres. During the warmer months you can experience the great outdoors in all the ways you would expect at such an establishment, while inner serenity is helped along by yoga and Tai Chi classes. There is even a separate building designated as a non-denominational temple which is used for special gatherings as well as for meditation and personal contemplation. And if all this starts to get too removed from reality, a tango workshop is sure to toss you back into the hurly-burly of your Latin surroundings.

WHERE:
Lago Gutiérrez, near Bariloche
COST:
Expensive
BEST TIME OF YEAR:
October to May for nature lovers; June to September for winter sports
DON'T MISS:
If you are looking to reward yourself after a vigorous day's trekking, the famous chocolate shops of Bariloche should do the trick.
THINGS TO DO:
Hiking; birdwatching; mountain biking; horse riding; river-rafting; climbing; fly fishing; kayaking
YOU SHOULD KNOW:
Horseflies can be troublesome in high summer (December and January), so you should bring insect repellent.

Llao Llao Hotel

This strikingly named resort hotel sits on its own peninsula jutting out into mighty Lago Nahuel Huapi, the largest of the lakes in Argentina's northern Lake District. It is a spectacular setting, as befits one of the country's most illustrious hotels. The lakeside rooms present you with a breathtaking panorama of the lake, framed by forested slopes and the ridges and peaks of the Patagonian Andes. It is no wonder that the early immigrants who were attracted to settle in these parts hailed from Switzerland and Germany, although nowadays the ruggedness and sense of isolation offered by this landscape are increasingly hard to find in the European Alps.

The legendary hotel first opened its doors in 1938 but the following year the whole place burned to the ground. It was promptly rebuilt and resumed its business catering to the needs of an exclusive clientele. Arriving at the Llao Llao can make you feel a bit like a visiting head of state, such is its grandeur and the level of attention from the staff. But you need not worry about causing a diplomatic incident, since this is in fact a thoroughly relaxed and relaxing place which nowadays caters almost exclusively for holidaymakers, albeit ones with deep pockets and refined tastes.

The 200 rooms range from basic economy to palatial suites and Llao Llao offers no fewer than five restaurants and both indoor and outdoor heated infinity pools. A challenging 18-hole golf course, private beach and well-equipped spa complete the on-site facilities and, unusually for an establishment of this class, there are excellent arrangements for children, including a daily kids' club.

WHERE:
Lago Nahuel Huapi, near Bariloche
COST:
Expensive
BEST TIME OF YEAR:
All year round. The spring (September to November) and autumn (March to May) colours are fantastic and there is excellent skiing during the winter months (June to August).
DON'T MISS:
Abseiling down nearby cliffs (assuming you have a head for heights)
THINGS TO DO:
Hiking; swimming; golf; kayaking; wildlife-watching; winter sports
YOU SHOULD KNOW:
The hotel has a mountain refuge at the base of the Cerro Catedral ski resort, which is for the exclusive use of its guests.

Rio Hermoso Hotel

WHERE:
Lago Meliquina, near San Martín de los Andes
COST:
Reasonable
BEST TIME OF YEAR:
All year round
DON'T MISS:
The northern parts of the park are home to forests of *araucaria* trees, one of the world's most ancient and peculiar-looking species (better known to one and all as the monkey puzzle tree).
THINGS TO DO:
Fly fishing; hiking; birdwatching; horse riding; biking; hunting; rock climbing; skiing; snowboarding; massage
YOU SHOULD KNOW:
There is one family room which sleeps up to four. There is no room charge for children under 11; children 11+ are charged extra.

Combining the rustic snugness of a mountain cabin with the primary colours and sleek lines of urban chic, then coming up with an utterly convincing synthesis, is no mean feat. But that is what they have pulled off at this gorgeous little hotel in northern Patagonia.

The aim is to get you as close to nature as possible, but not with any notable sacrifice to comfort and elegance. The hotel lies in a secluded rural setting a short way south of San Martín de los Andes, close to the north shore of Lago Meliquina. Six gorgeous rooms all offer views over the 'beautiful river' from which the hotel takes its name and three have their own private terraces to enhance the experience. The thoughtful use of local building materials, principally timber and stone, is evident throughout the public spaces – look out for the odd fossil imprint in the walls.

This is a year-round destination, with the displays of flowers and colours in spring and autumn respectively vying with the months of high summer in their visitor appeal. In winter Rio Hermoso is ideally situated for Cerro Chapelco, one of Argentina's top winter-sports resorts. Coming back to roaring log fires in the hotel's great stone fireplaces after a day on the slopes or out trekking is one of the special joys of a stay here. Rio Hermoso lies within the Lanín National Park, the third largest in the country and one of its loveliest. The park's rivers, including Rio Hermoso itself, are famed for their trout fishing and there are unlimited opportunities to explore its natural marvels, whether on foot, by bike, by boat or on horseback.

Las Hayas Resort Hotel

Journeying to the planet's wilder extremities these days no longer means having to forgo the comforts you are used to at home. On a hillside overlooking the Beagle Channel and the small port of Ushuaia – generally regarded as the southernmost city in the world – stands this stately hotel and resort complex. The building is in the style of a French *château* and no efforts have been spared to create an atmosphere of refinement and discreet luxury.

The 90 or so rooms, half of them suites, have a south-facing bay view or a view of the glowering granite steeples of Cerro Martial (Mount Martial) to the north. The furnishings are expensive but restrained and the facilities are every bit as good as you would expect from a five-star establishment. Of the hotel's two restaurants Le Martial is without question the best in town, serving up an eclectic range of international cuisine, with an unsurprising emphasis on seafood, against a backdrop of sweeping views of the bay.

Although you might get tired of the endless reminders from the *fin del mundo* products on sale everywhere, this really does feel like the end of the world. The Antarctic landmass is actually closer to this area than the country's capital, Buenos Aires, some 3,000 km (1,900 mi) to the north. Ushuaia itself retains the feel of a frontier town, with its jumbled streetscapes of wooden cabins, Scandinavian prefabs and more modern concrete structures. Behind Las Hayas the trek up to the Martial Glacier is a definite recommendation. Don't leave it too long, though, as experts are predicting that the glacier will disappear altogether within the next 50 years.

WHERE:
Ushuaia, Tierra del Fuego
COST:
Expensive
BEST TIME OF YEAR:
November to April, although the winter months (June to September) give you excellent skiing at Cerro Castor, the world's most southerly ski resort
DON'T MISS:
The fabulous autumn colours of the *lenga* beech trees, a species native to the southern Andes; and sampling freshly caught and cooked *centolla,* king crab
THINGS TO DO:
Squash; swimming (hotel pool); boat trip on the Beagle Channel; watching sea lions and seabirds; trekking in the Tierra del Fuego National Park; spa treatments; winter sports
YOU SHOULD KNOW:
If your budget doesn't extend this far, Las Hayas's sister establishment, the Los Acebos Hotel, occupies a similarly fine position next door but is a more modest, family-oriented affair.

Campo Cielo Grande

WHERE:
Lago Rosario, south of Esquel
COST:
Expensive
BEST TIME OF YEAR:
November to April
DON'T MISS:
A day trip to Los Alerces National Park, one of Patagonia's most pristine and home to the beautiful, towering *alerce* (cypress) trees
THINGS TO DO:
Fly fishing; wilderness trekking; horse riding; whitewater rafting
YOU SHOULD KNOW:
Even in high summer the temperature can drop dramatically at night. There is a minimum four-night stay here.

There are times when the sheer size of Argentina can seem to be overwhelming, nowhere more so than in the vast empty spaces of Patagonia. If you are looking for a knowledgeable helping hand to guide you around the wilderness, you can do no better than sign up for the bespoke service offered by Trey and Shelby Scharp at their small *estancia* in one of the more remote areas of northern Patagonia.

Situated on the shore of Lago Rosario, Campo Cielo Grande is surrounded by scenery that will take your breath away with its majestic snow-capped mountain chains, dense green forests and dramatic river valleys. And the accommodation is set up to make the very best of the sublime setting. It offers two safari-style tents, pitched on solid wooden platforms. Each tent sleeps up to four and has a fully equipped bathroom and wood-burning stove, which is lit ready for your return from the day's activities. All meals are included and on one night of your stay the feast will feature a lamb *asado* (barbecue).

The Scharps are Americans with a long-standing love affair with Patagonia, which culminated in them opening Campo Cielo Grande in 2006. Because it is a small establishment you are pretty much guaranteed the personal attention of your hosts at all times. Trey is a skilled fly fisherman and will show guests the best spots to catch the region's famous trout. He also guides whitewater-rafting expeditions on the Rio Corcovado. Shelby is an experienced horsewoman and leads day-long treks into the surrounding country for anyone wanting to see the world *gaucho*-style from the back of a local *criollo* horse.

Eolo Lodge

Unless you have a serious amount of time to explore Argentina and are travelling overland between its major sights, it is not always easy to appreciate the sheer extent of the barren expanses you pass through. This is nowhere truer than the interior of Patagonia. You can capture something of its raw essence by staying at this luxury country lodge, part of the Relais & Chateaux chain.

With no other traces of civilization anywhere in sight its situation on the featureless Patagonian *steppe* south of El Calafate presents a decidedly incongruous spectacle. The lodge is a timber-framed building set around a large central courtyard. Built in the style of a ranch, it has been designed to maximize the magnificent views – north to Lago Argentina (appropriately enough, the country's largest lake), east to La Anita valley and south to the distant craggy outlines of the Torres del Paine mountain range in Chile.

There has been no scrimping on space here and the wide-open expanses outside are matched by the lodge's broad and commodious interiors, with large picture windows to make the most of the views. The suites – just 17 in all – are large and the public spaces equally so. These include a library, lounge, dining room, sauna and a small indoor pool. Rates are inclusive of all meals – they have to be as it's a long way to the nearest restaurant! There are plenty of ways of enjoying the stunning scenery surrounding you, but you may get as much pleasure from taking a book from the library and hunkering down in an armchair before a roaring fire.

WHERE:
30 km (19 mi) south of El Calafate
COST:
Expensive
BEST TIME OF YEAR:
The lodge is only open from mid September to mid April.
DON'T MISS:
A trip to the Perito Moreno Glacier, one of the planet's great natural sights, is an absolute must.
THINGS TO DO:
Hiking; horse riding; mountain biking; 4x4 expeditions; fly fishing; glacier walking; swimming; sauna; stargazing; wildlife-watching
YOU SHOULD KNOW:
At the beginning and end of the season Eolo offers a 'three-nights-for-the-price-of-two' deal.

Estancia Dos Lunas

WHERE:
Orgamira valley, Córdoba province
COST:
Expensive
BEST TIME OF YEAR:
Any time (although you will have to book well in advance if you want to stay during the high season, December to March)
DON'T MISS:
If your horsemanship is up to it, you can indulge your Lone Ranger fantasy and ride your mount to the top of one of the sandstone ridges, there to pose impressively against the skyline.
THINGS TO DO:
Horse riding; trekking; birdwatching; swimming; board games; massage
YOU SHOULD KNOW:
One of the guided rides takes you up to a hill where there is a good chance of spotting condors.

You don't have to be a horse-lover to stay at this country ranch, deep in the rolling hills of central Argentina, but it helps mightily if you are. The clue to the *estancia*'s main activity is in the strap line: 'horse riding lodge'. Don't worry, though, if you're not that confident in the saddle since this place is seriously well equipped for all ability levels and they will have no difficulty finding you a suitable mount from among their superbly schooled horses.

Although this is no longer a working farm and you will only see active *gauchos* if you are very lucky, the great appeal of riding here is the landscape. For a start, the *estancia* itself presides over 2,300 ha (5,700 ac) of land, encompassing fields, meadows, woods and streams. The most striking feature of the estate, though, is the weird but imposing sandstone rocks that rise up ruddily from the surrounding green forest.

'Boutique farmhouse' would be an apt description of the design and decor of this elegant *estancia*. The original farmhouse is over 100 years old but has been lovingly restored; antique features have been preserved and the public spaces have old settler furniture and magnificent ponchos hanging on the walls. There is only a handful of rooms, some of them suites with two bedrooms and old-fashioned bathtubs with claw feet. For all the designer chic, Dos Lunas manages to be a homely place, too. An outdoor circular swimming pool and an indoor playroom, well stocked with films and board games, are both popular with families.

Cavas Wine Lodge

Although Argentina has been producing wines ever since Jesuit missionaries introduced grapes in the 16th century for their communion wine, it is only in the past two decades that the country has become a serious player on the international scene. Now the world's sixth biggest producer, Argentina creates wines of real distinction – most notably the dark, full-bodied reds from the Malbec grape. The Mendoza area west of Buenos Aires and close to the Chilean border is the centre of the country's wine industry and, not surprisingly, touring the many *bodegas* or wineries and tasting the products of the noble grape are what most visitors to the region come to do.

For a fully immersive experience you could do no better than stay at this luxury wine lodge a short drive south from Mendoza city. Each of the 14 *cabañas* – sleek adobe huts with smooth stone walls – has its own plunge pool, rooftop terrace and outdoor shower

as well as all the internal appointments you would expect from this class of accommodation. Even better, the free-standing buildings are scattered among the lodge's own 14 ha (35 ac) of vines, so you couldn't ask to be closer to the raw material.

A walk through the rows of vines as the sun sets over the spectacular backdrop of the snow-capped Andes is an unforgettable experience, particularly as your taste buds contemplate the evening's cuisine and fine wines. Cavas has an extensive cellar featuring some 250 of the region's best vintages and the lodge's helpful *sommelier* will be only too happy to arrange a tasting and offer advice on your selection for dinner.

WHERE:
Luján de Cuyo, near Mendoza
COST:
Expensive (but note that rates are almost half during the winter months, June to August)
BEST TIME OF YEAR:
January to March (during the grape harvest)
DON'T MISS:
The unusual treatments available in the lodge's own spa – try the vino-therapy bath, the grape-feed exfoliation or the crushed-malbec body scrub
THINGS TO DO:
Wine tasting; swimming; massage; hiking; river-rafting; horse riding
YOU SHOULD KNOW:
Cavas does not allow children under 12. A sensible option if you intend to visit a number of wineries is to hire a car and driver for the day.

Estancia La Margarita

WHERE:
Tapalqué, Buenos Aires province
COST:
Reasonable
BEST TIME OF YEAR:
All year round
DON'T MISS:
Milking a cow – La Margarita is a working farm and you can have a go at the traditional skill of milking by hand
THINGS TO DO:
Horse riding; walking; birdwatching; small game hunting (hares and partridges); swimming (outdoor pool in summer); *bochas* (like French *boules*); cycling; massage
YOU SHOULD KNOW:
To help preserve the tranquillity of the place there are no TVs in the rooms. There is a set in one of the outbuildings, though, for that football game you simply can't miss!

For many people Argentina is the land of the tango, the dark and intense music that has spawned one of the world's great dances. But tango is an urban phenomenon which originated in the crowded docksides of Buenos Aires. An altogether different Argentina is represented by the pampas, the grasslands that form the vast, flat heartland of this enormous country, and for many others a stay on an *estancia*, or ranch, deep in the pampas will provide the quintessential Argentinian experience.

A good choice would be La Margarita, a traditional *estancia* in the heart of Buenos Aires province which was founded in 1870 and remained in the same family until as recently as 2006. La Margarita now belongs to a British ex-professional musician who has opened it to paying guests who come here to enjoy the unrivalled peace and serenity.

Guests may either opt to stay in rooms in the original farmhouse, which has been sensitively restored and updated, in which case this is on a full-board basis (including afternoon tea, which is something of an institution in *estancia* life); or they can take the self-catering option and stay in one of the fully equipped rooms in the adjacent Casa Rosada. This is the land where the *gaucho* is the acknowledged master and both options include a daily ride in the room price to give you the chance to see how your own skills in the saddle measure up. You needn't worry if you've never sat on a horse before because the well-trained *criollo* horses are suitable for all ability levels and you are likely to find the traditional *gaucho* saddles rather more comfortable than the western version.

Don Enrique Lodge

The thought of being lost in a dense and remote jungle filled with strange, sinister sounds may be the stuff of nightmares, but that is precisely the experience this eco-lodge offers, albeit in an altogether safer and more benign context. Don Enrique is a stylish little hideaway deep in the jungle of Misiones province, the crooked finger of Argentina's far northeast. The region is also known as Mesopotamia as it lies between the two mighty rivers of the Paraná and the Uruguay, which form the borders with Paraguay and Brazil respectively. The lodge itself is situated in the east of the province on the banks of the Paraíso River, its handful of buildings imaginatively constructed from native woods and almost entirely surrounded by lush rainforest.

This is a beautifully peaceful place where you will have no trouble giving yourself up to the sounds and smells of the jungle. The guest cabins each have their own sitting room complete with fireplace – even though this is a subtropical climate, temperatures can drop sharply at night. The hammocks slung on your private verandah are perfect for watching the gentle course of the river and the sudden, intense downpours so characteristic of this environment. In the public spaces of the main building the emphasis is on cosiness and rusticity, with wood-burning stoves and sofas galore.

Misiones Province has some of the largest surviving tracts of Atlantic rainforest and is home to one of the planet's most diverse and precious ecosystems. Toucans, parrots, hummingbirds and eagles are all to be seen here and skilled native guides are on hand to help you spot the more reclusive mammals of the jungle, such as anteaters, deer and tapir.

WHERE:
El Soberbio, Misiones Province
COST:
Reasonable
BEST TIME OF YEAR:
Spring (October to December) and autumn (April to June)
DON'T MISS:
The boat trip to the nearby Moconá Falls on the Rio Uruguay – these spectacular waterfalls run parallel to the river for an astonishing 3 km (2 mi)
THINGS TO DO:
Jungle trekking; guided nature walks; birdwatching; wild swimming; mountain biking; kayaking; visiting a native Guarani village
YOU SHOULD KNOW:
If you are planning to make your own way to Don Enrique, you will need a 4x4 vehicle to do so.

La Candelaria

WHERE:
Lobos, Buenos Aires province
COST:
Reasonable
BEST TIME OF YEAR:
September to April
DON'T MISS:
Seeing the local talent – every Saturday the *gauchos* entertain visitors with a terrific display of their skills
THINGS TO DO:
Walking; tennis; horse riding; sulky (carriage) rides; swimming; cycling; pool and billiards; wine tasting; parachuting
YOU SHOULD KNOW:
The park at La Candelaria was designed by the famous French landscape architect Charles Thays, who was also responsible for the Botanic Gardens in Buenos Aires.

A couple of hours' drive southwest of Buenos Aires, La Candelaria offers an *estancia* experience in the grandest surroundings imaginable. At the end of the 19th century, inspired by his memories of Europe, the estate owner built a large country mansion in the style of a French *château* and surrounded it with manicured lawns and elegant parkland that would not look out of place in the English home counties. Nowadays it is given over entirely to tourism, and guests can stay in the baronial splendour of the main building. No expense was spared in the fittings and fixtures, which include chandeliers of Venetian glass, tapestries, stained-glass windows, wall panels of silk, Carrara-marble fireplaces and a mighty oak staircase. The architectural styles referenced are an eclectic bunch; there is a Gothic library, for example, while the dining room has been fashioned in the Renaissance manner.

If all this sounds a bit overpowering you could opt instead for the simpler, cleaner lines of a family suite housed in the former servants' quarters. These contain a living room as well as a bedroom and several have a fireplace. For a particularly unusual experience – and extra privacy – you could book the old Dutch mill house in the park which has been converted into a cosy guest apartment.

There are certainly plenty of activities to keep you amused at La Candelaria, including an outdoor swimming pool and two clay tennis courts. But the highlight of a stay here is without question the chance to watch a game of polo and even to have a go yourself, provided you have basic horsemanship skills.

Machu Picchu Sanctuary Lodge

It costs an arm and a leg but – afterwards – nobody has ever complained about not getting value for money. Even if it were a shack instead of a very good hotel, the cost would be worth it. The Sanctuary Lodge is the only hotel of any kind at the gates (literally) of the sacred Inca city of Machu Picchu. The nearest alternatives are miles away by bus in the valley at Aguas Calientes or even Cuzco, or in a designated camp for hikers on the Inca Trail.

Only the Sanctuary enables you to be first in to the ruins, and last out. Its location guarantees having the place almost to yourself for the 90 minutes of dawning and sunrise, before the buses arrive with the first of thousands of daily visitors – and again after the last bus leaves, for two hours of mind-boggling sunset. There is no other legal way to gain this access, since the rules on hiking up, even with the compulsory guide, were recently tightened.

In fairness, the Sanctuary is good. It is owned by Orient-Express, who call it a 'lodge' because space and other restrictions (not least making every effort to be genuinely environmentally pro-active) prevent them from offering as sumptuous a service as usual. But in this location, none of that matters. Guests can saunter in and out of the sacred city at will, returning for meals, a nap, or research in the Sanctuary's library. They can see what few others will – Machu Picchu by moonlight, and the Sun God renewing his daily promise by splitting his newborn rays between the mountains.

WHERE:
The mountaintop end of Carretera Hiram Bingham, Machu Picchu
COST:
It's astronomical – but if you can possibly afford it, do it. You will never regret it for the rest of your life.
BEST TIME OF YEAR:
May to October is the dry season, and warmer. November to March has heavy but predictable rain – just as good, with the right clothing.
DON'T MISS:
The Peruvian dishes at the Lodge restaurant; allowing time for peaceful contemplation; a hot tub, outside, with a direct view of the ruins (awesome!)
THINGS TO DO:
Enjoy the spa treatments at the hotel to ease the strain on long-disused muscles; explore the cloud forest; walk some of the shorter Inca trails.
YOU SHOULD KNOW:
Don't go for New Year's Eve – there's a mandatory dinner which adds more than US$250.00 per person to your bill. Ask for a room at the back, the other side from the uphill bus terminus, to avoid the noise of grinding gears. If you want to go off on your own for a mountain walk, tell someone – it's very easy to get lost.

Yavari on Lake Titicaca

WHERE:
At the end of a very long pier outside the Sonesta Posadas Del Inca Hotel, 5 km (3 mi) outside Puno – entry is either through the hotel or, more charmingly, by water-taxi from Puno direct to the pier

COST:
Budget

BEST TIME OF YEAR:
February to May – offering a choice between afternoon rainstorms and increasing mountain cold

DON'T MISS:
The fully restored 1914 Bolinder engine (you may have to give prior notice to gain access); the guided tour of the ship, including its history, restoration and future evolution

THINGS TO DO:
Order dinner and wine from a nearby hotel (such as the Sonesta) and have an onboard party.

YOU SHOULD KNOW:
For its first 40 years, *Yavari* was fuelled by dried llama dung. The ship is open to sightseers between 08.00 and 17.00 – if you want to stay, register during that time. Although it is fully restored, *Yavari* cannot make a commercial voyage without being (expensively) certified for passenger use, and undergoing further modifications.

Lake Titicaca is the world's highest navigable lake. It straddles the border 3,810 m (12,500 ft) up in the Andes between Peru and Bolivia. The *Yavari* is a former gunboat, built in Britain in 1862 then disassembled into 2,766 pieces. Over the course of six years the sections were carried by mules over the mountains to Puno, on the lakeshore; and on Christmas Day 1870, *Yavari* was finally launched. Now it's the oldest propeller-driven working ship in the world, as old as the ocean clipper *Cutty Sark* and (since 1990) just about as comprehensively restored. Its history belongs to Titicaca. It played a vital part in developing the Andean mining industries and as a bridge for trade and travel routes across the mountains from the Atlantic to the Pacific. It has long been one of the sights of the lake. Now it is also a floating B&B – the only place you can spend a night afloat on Lake Titicaca.

It's a supremely elegant ship with gleaming Victorian brass work and varnished wood. As a State Registered Museum it costs nothing to visit but, if you're not staying on board, you don't see the trim, spotless little cabins that turn sightseeing into pure adventure. They are much cleaner and more comfortable than in *Yavari*'s prime, but they still resonate of old ways and hierarchies. You sleep knowing that the ship is ready to sail, and you long for it to take motion. Only a government permission is wanting and that will certainly come. Soon the *Yavari* will again become a passenger ship around Titicaca – and its bed and breakfast will be one of the wonders of the lake.

Casa Cool Beans

Santa Teresa is Rio de Janeiro's boho artists' neighbourhood. Far from the touristic Rio of Copacabana or even Botofogo, it sits high on a hill where trams still rattle, looking down on the Sugar Loaf and Guanabara Bay. Its small bars, cafés and bistros discharge life and music into its cobbled streets, but the pace is laid-back. *New York Magazine* has described the quarter as 'the drop-dead-sexiest' in Rio, a rendezvous of the community of creative spirits in constant, cosmopolitan flux.

And Casa Cool Beans fits right in. It occupies one of the old mansions with big and glorious gardens for which Santa Teresa is famous. It has just nine suites (with private baths, air conditioning and even minibars), all decorated by local artists and artisans. The gardens offer several verdant 'rooms' to hang out in and there's a huge terrace where guests, owners and friends naturally gravitate round the communal table and excellent plunge pool. Like some Latin-American Algonquin, the table is the arena for creative cut and thrust, ruminative exchanges, travellers' tales and amiable bonhomie. It's what happens.

Casa Cool Beans gets most travellers closer to the 'real' Brazil than most have any right to expect. The American owners have been around town for 25 years and their intimacy with what's on and what's going on is available on request. Their *pousada*'s success is due not just to the first-class food and standards, but to the fact that it exemplifies what's great about Santa Teresa. Casa Cool Beans is both a peaceful and friendly refuge – and at the heart of the action.

WHERE:
Santa Teresa, Rio de Janeiro
COST:
Budget
BEST TIME OF YEAR:
Any time
DON'T MISS:
The excellent artworks; informal samba in one of the many music bars
THINGS TO DO:
Go dancing down the hill in the Lapa district. Ride a moto-taxi over the cobbles (!) down to Gloria, from where the metro runs to the beaches at Copacabana, Ipanema and Leblon.
YOU SHOULD KNOW:
Casa Cool Beans is unfortunately not suitable for people who experience mobility problems.

Hotel Fasano

WHERE:
Avenida Vieira Souto, Ipanema Beach
COST:
Very expensive to astronomical
BEST TIME OF YEAR:
September to October for the lush green of spring, and dry weather; November to February for big summer heat on the beach (and heavy rain, usually from 16.00 to 17.00); June to August for the best surfing
DON'T MISS:
The yellow fruits of *caipirinha* in the Londra bar; the hotel's private *cabana* on Ipanema itself, where guests are regaled with beach chairs, sunscreens, magazines and bottled water
THINGS TO DO:
Find treasures (among the tat) of the Feira Hippie artisanal market in Ipanema's Praca General Osorio (Sundays 09.00 to 17.00); watch beach life – all the beaches in Rio's Zona Sul are divided into lifeguard *postos* (sectors), each with its distinctive character and community (*Posto* 10 is Ipanema's cool one, where you might share a game of *futivollei*, unique to Rio, with staggeringly beautiful young people).
YOU SHOULD KNOW:
Staff seek to be as stylish as their hotel, so service, while charming, is often very slow; some bathroom doors carry an image of a dancer wearing top-hat and tails in a pose which suggests that designer Starck couldn't tell his tango from his bossa nova.

The Fasano opened in 2007 as the hottest place in Rio. Celebrities, fashionistas and the wealthiest of hip international socialites descended like gannets to feed on its clever PR branding. It was the first venture outside Sao Paolo for Brazil's legendary restaurateur and hotelier Rogerio Fasano, and he commissioned Philippe Starck to design every detail of his new hotel down to the last soap dish. It was, and still is, a temple to luxury minimalism.

The Fasano's success has flourished in defiance of shifting tastes for two reasons. It commands a fabulous position on Ipanema Beach (forever associated with Astrid Gilberto and Stan Getz's 1960s' song) between Copacabana and Leblon and its rooftop terrace, with infinity pool and bar, has sensational panoramas both along the coast and behind, to Christ the Redeemer looking down from Corcovado. The building itself is a standout among the million-dollar concrete anonymities around it and its stylish glass and steel inspires guests to dress to match. *Cariocas* (as the locals call themselves) and high fliers who want to frequent the rooftop, the disorienting extremism of the public spaces, the excellent al Mare seafood restaurant and the dotty chic of the ultra-exclusive Baretto Londra nightclub (keynote decor of Union Jacks in Italian colours) need at least four designer outpourings a day in order to blend in.

The 91 rooms share a Starck uniform of dark hardwoods leavened by angular slabs of yellow on the coverlets and tautly arranged whites on everything else. But apart from the top ten suites, most are small and dark, their marble bathrooms have no baths, and the clever intricacies of their basic functions often don't work. Nevertheless, the show goes on because the show is what people pay for. In Ipanema, style like this is much more important than substance.

Copacabana Palace Hotel

As stylish as the Negresco in Nice which inspired it, the Copacabana Palace is one of the very best hotels in the world. It is a classic grand hotel of proven pedigree. Like the very restricted number of its peers worldwide, its Golden Book is a chronicle of global royalty, statesmanship, talent and celebrity. Since 1923 its stucco grandeur has been the principal landmark on the magnificent crescent of Copacabana Beach. Although the neighbourhood as a whole is dingier, the Copa's standards are higher than ever thanks to a $40-million overhaul in the early 1990s, and its sybaritic comforts have been completely restored and underpinned by the best available technology.

The Copacabana Palace is a heart's-desire destination and, although it is equally compelling as a rendezvous for the highest echelons of politics and business, it remains at heart a beach hotel. It's still synonymous with fun. There's a tennis court on the roof, and Rio's finest swimming pool exudes a languorous invitation to the 'swellegant' crowd at the *al fresco* Pergula restaurant alongside. A second, predominantly Italian, gastronomic treat – the Cipriani – serves as the main dining room, but is also revered as one of South America's best restaurants of any kind. Like the high-ceilinged, deep-cushioned opulence of the Copacabana's other lounges and bars, these meticulous services cosset guests from Rio's more sordid experiences. On the beach, across the famous black-and-white mosaic sidewalk of Avenida Atlantica, staff not only pamper you with drinks, culinary baubles, towels, chairs and umbrellas – they guard you and your valuables while you brave the rolling surf.

Inevitably, some fabulous rooms are better than others. Satisfy your inner plutocrat and go for a balcony and ocean view.

WHERE:
Avenida Atlantica, Copacabana Beach
COST:
Astronomical – and at least 15 per cent extra should be added to the quoted rate for 'hotel taxes'; state taxes may add more
BEST TIME OF YEAR:
Any time. At the Copa, if there's something you can't have, they'll find an alternative that will make you just as happy – and that includes the weather.
DON'T MISS:
The dazzling gala balls on New Year's Eve and during Carnival; the *trompe l'oeil* murals by Dominique Jardy in the public spaces and even the lifts; aperitifs at sundown in the *uber*-cool Bar do Copa next to the pool; the *feijoada* at the Pergula – Brazil's national dish without any short cuts.
THINGS TO DO:
Surfing, jet-skiing, cruising and snorkelling around Rio's offshore islands; golf, volleyball or any other sport the concierge can arrange; clubbing in Lapa for informal samba sessions; promenade with the *Cariocas* along the edge of the surf to Ipanema, Leblon and back (but don't wear watches or jewellery)
YOU SHOULD KNOW:
The rooms in the hotel annexe are just as wonderful, but only the penthouse suites face the ocean. If you ask politely, the manager may show you the 'Golden Book' recording the signatures of many of the world's most famous people.

Ariau Amazon Towers

WHERE:
Right bank of the Rio Negro at Ariau Creek, 55 km (34 mi) upstream from Manaus
COST:
Expensive to astronomical
BEST TIME OF YEAR:
April to October is the rainy season, when many islands are submerged and the forest appears to be floating. November to March is dry, when the waters recede, opening white sandy beaches on every shore. It depends what you prize most – birds, botany, or something else.
DON'T MISS:
Swimming with wild, pink river dolphins; the 'Meeting of the Waters', where for 8 km (5 mi) the Rio Negro's black waters run alongside the sand-coloured Solimoes River, without mixing.

It's the biggest tree-top hotel in the world. Suspended above the Amazon rainforest on the bank of the Rio Negro, eight circular wooden towers form the principal links in a complex that includes 268 tree-top rooms, suites and whole tree-top houses set at various heights between 10 to 20 m (33 to 66 ft). There are conference rooms, restaurants, bars, cyber cafés, two heliports and even two (small) tree-top swimming pools, all connected by over 8 km (5 mi) of walkways raised high into or above the forest canopy. The treehouses – built into living mahogany trees – all have balconies, play and living rooms, spacious bathrooms and cable TV.

Imagine Swiss Family Robinson gone electric, but still open to capuchins, inquisitive sloths, parrots, macaws and many other birds who share the canopy. The Ariau Amazon Towers is ecotourism at its most luxurious – although no visitor should expect luxury in this context to equal Four Seasons-style cosmopolitanism. The real achievement is to transform rustic necessity into something so comfortable, while barely impinging on the delicate ecosystem over which it is built.

The complex was inspired directly by Jacques Cousteau and it fulfils his vision by engaging visitors in the adventure of practical Gaia theory. Every day expeditions head deep into the rainforest, over the sleek black waters of the Rio Negro to untouched islands in the Anavilhanas archipelago, or through the creeks downstream to the Amazon itself. Guides expert in botany, zoology, ornithology and field-craft stimulate curious imaginations – and gently remind visitors expecting something rougher and tougher 'up the Amazon' that without the comforts of the eco-lodge, they probably wouldn't be able to be in the rainforest at all.

THINGS TO DO:
Sign up for guided excursions, including piranha fishing, caiman spotting by night and backwater boating through the lianas, bromeliads and vines of virgin rainforest filled with monkeys, butterflies and birds.

YOU SHOULD KNOW:
Despite the heat and humidity, the water's high acidity means there aren't many mosquitoes; but take a repellent anyway. In response to complaints that an eco-lodge running helicopter transfers and several spluttering motorboats can't be truly eco-friendly, it's pointed out that without them the Amazon Towers could not host the VIPs and conferences which influence environmental policy all over the world.

Pousada des Arts

You don't have to be the slightest bit romantic for the Pousada des Arts to capture your heart. Just the sight of it makes a skylark of your soul. Its elegant facade is a burnished golden-yellow picked out with Dali-pink and cherry window frames, overhung with trailing tropical flowers. Inside, the riot of colour has no inhibitions.

This 18th-century colonial mansion has been immaculately restored to create eight rooms on two floors, looking down on an internal courtyard filled with flowers and a splashing fountain. Local artists used the same range of colours for completely different designs in each room – but a four-poster bed, soft white muslins, a balcony or tiled terrace with striped hammock, a wicker chair and beautifully painted wooden furniture are common to all. Down the steep stairs a comfortable library provides utter peace and on the other side of the courtyard the whole ground floor opens out to an enormous terrace with a panoramic vista of Salvador and the bay. The Pousada's charm is infectious, and the terrace is where guests gather to share stories and goodwill. It's also the year-round venue for art exhibitions, lectures and jazz or bossa nova concerts, all of which draw guests seamlessly into the fabric of local life and culture at no extra charge.

The Pousada is in the pretty district of Santo Antonio, in the upper town close to Salvador's World Heritage historic centre – Pelourinho – where narrow lanes of bright, pastel-coloured houses are crammed with craft shops, bars and food stalls. Pelourinho is where the action is and is what visitors bring to mind when they think of Salvador. The Pousada offers a deeper insight into Salvador's creative verve, and with even more charm.

WHERE:
Santo Antonio, Salvador de Bahia

COST:
Budget to budget+ (but no amount of money could cover what you actually get out of the place)

BEST TIME OF YEAR:
November to April

DON'T MISS:
The baroque churches of Pelourinho (Salvador's pride); the original art works spread around the Pousada; a sunset sail in the Bahia de Todos os Santos on the owner's catamaran; breakfast – sensational food, joyous surroundings and astonishing view

THINGS TO DO:
Drop 70 m (230 ft) in the elevator linking upper and lower towns and visit the traditional market, Mercado Modelo; join one of the frequent street parties in Pelourinho; seek refuge in the hammock on your terrace.

YOU SHOULD KNOW:
Salvador is known as 'Brazil's capital of happiness'. Ask for rooms 5 or 6 (with mezzanine) if your children are with you. The 18th-century stairs are too steep and thus unsuitable for people with reduced mobility.

Hotel das Cataratas

WHERE:
Foz do Iguacu, Parana
COST:
Expensive
BEST TIME OF YEAR:
Any time, depending on your priority. From May to July the falls are at maximum flow and so is the rain. January to February is high season for crowds, humidity, heat and prices, but there's no rain. September to October are the months for all-round comfort.
DON'T MISS:
Devil's Throat, the U-shaped drop at the cataracts' heart; riding the bucking jet, a speedboat thrill *à la* James Bond to the base of the falls; the Full Moon Walking Tour, to see a lunar rainbow over the cataracts (exclusive to hotel guests)
THINGS TO DO:
The Macuco Safari (rainforest by jeep then upriver by boat to the Three Musketeers); '3 Borders' helicopter trip over the gorge; rafting on the Rio Iguacu; fine dining; rainforest walks in the park (and exclusive falls viewing platforms); crossing the Tancredo Bridge into Argentina to see the panorama in reverse; abseiling; biking; rock and tree climbing; swimming; birdwatching; yielding to 'rainforest treatments' in the spa
YOU SHOULD KNOW:
Take a raincoat and waterproof camera – the mist is more than just damp. Rooms with a falls view cost more, but that's why you came. *Iguazu* with a 'z' is the Argentine (Spanish) spelling.

In full spate, the mighty Iguacu Falls crash 82 m (269 ft) over 275 separate drops spread along some 3 km (2 mi) of vertiginous lip that forms the international border between Brazil and Argentina. They are surrounded by tropical rainforest, itself protected in both countries by a National Park which prohibits any development. The Hotel das Cataratas on the Brazilian side is the sole exception. Its unique location means it is the only hotel that can guarantee unfettered access both to the falls and the wealth of rare flora and fauna that thrives in the remote forest.

It's expensive, but the hotel takes no advantage of its guests. Both parties understand the privilege they share. Excellent as only a first-rate establishment can be, the hotel takes possessive pride

in the natural wonders all around. Trained naturalists act as guides on early morning and evening walks (when the park and falls are deserted, before and after the tourist buses) to spot rarities like the giant anteater or giant otter among the raccoon-like coatis, peccaries and black howler monkeys that frequent the area; and to show how the drifting spray has created uniquely lush flora that attracts hundreds of rare species of butterflies and a kaleidoscope of tropical birds to the wild flower wilderness. They bring out the sheer adventure of the falls, where swallows plummet through cataracts to nests hidden from predators and flocks of red, blue and gold parrots soar across the mist of spray.

But if you'd rather luxuriate by the pool, this is the kind of hotel where every half hour staff emerge with fruit, cocktails or water, and a cold flannel to soothe away the heat.

Casas Brancas Boutique Hotel and Spa

Casas Brancas doesn't have any existential problems. It is the coolest hotel (and spa) in one of the country's coolest boutique resorts. Buzios is a two-hour drive from Rio. It is always described as 'the St Tropez of Brazil', and not just because it is set on the scything curve of a placid little bay, with boats drawn up to the quay and bobbing offshore, or because the pretty, pastel-painted houses lining the cobbled lanes still house a multitude of little shops, music bars, folk crafts and very good restaurants or indeed because Buzios's original Portuguese-colonial character hasn't yet suffered developer's rhinoplasty. It's because Brigitte Bardot herself discovered the little town. And BB adored Casas Brancas back in the 1960s as an ideal refuge of a kind then already impossible in most of Europe. It still is, and so is Buzios.

The hotel is enviably positioned above the shore on a tiny peninsular, just like Bambi's antler. It has only 32 spacious, stone-floored rooms, fashioned from the *hacienda*-like conversion of two colonial mansions. Too comfortable to be called minimalist, they have the elegance of crafted, rustic simplicity. Everything facing the sea has a balcony or hammock-slung terrace. Below them lies the spa and a series of wooden decks holding bars, restaurants, the pool and convivial hideaways. Casas Brancas Hotel radiates long-established confidence in its own style and tranquillity. Yes, its success is in the detail, but it's not in the fresh posies, fruit baskets or flower petals strewn before you, but in the charm of their presentation. The staff are genuinely interested in their guests, and their spontaneous thoughtfulness is that of good companions. You want to stay forever.

WHERE:
Alto do Humaita, Armacao, Buzios
COST:
Reasonable to expensive
BEST TIME OF YEAR:
Low season (March to June and October to December); the crowds come in the heat and humidity of high-priced December to February
DON'T MISS:
Hiring a beach buggy to explore Buzios's 26 beaches and coves; releasing your inner lounge lizard with backgammon after the fabulous weekend brunch in the Deck restaurant; the pool loungers for two; getting pampered in the world-class spa; shuddering at the statue of BB on the Buzios town boardwalk – she deserves better
THINGS TO DO:
Catamaran or schooner trips to the islands in the bay; diving; cycling; horse riding; tennis; golf; surfing (on the peninsula's southern side at Geriba and Ferradura); relax with the view and a jug of *caipirinha* to the sophisticated chic of ambient music and very flash, scented candles
YOU SHOULD KNOW:
Staff don't want to pester guests – so do ask if there's anything you want; if you'd rather not re-enact scenes from the Hellfire Club, don't come in high season when the *juventud dorada (jeunesse doree)* pack the town.

Pousada Maravilha

Anticipation and imagination make arriving quite a shock. For once, the pleasurably familiar notion of a tropical paradise is tinged with childlike apprehension about what is and is not possible on an island ruled by environmental and military restrictions. Fernando de Noronha, 347 km (216 mi) off Pernambuco, is a World Heritage site in a marine National Park. Its delicate ecosystem attracts naturalists and biologists whose studies would seem to conflict with the demands of high-end tourism, and especially those of honeymooners promised solicitous comforts and solitude in a sun-kissed Eden. Yet Pousada Maravilha manages to keep that promise.

For once the infinity pool merges seamlessly with the Atlantic Ocean behind. On an island of legendary vistas and three of Brazil's top-ten beaches, Maravilha offers the best of all. From the landward side, the dull-green roofs of the main reception lodge and five bungalows are heart-sinkingly like a municipal boy's camp – but they all share the incredible view from private decks furnished with hammocks, huge day beds and small hot tubs. Inside, the rooms are enormous, with a neutral decor to set off the tropical colours all around. Large bathrooms and even the separate shower and toilet have windows on that view, and big flat-screen TVs, music systems and other toys are ready for those who want them.

Maravilha is on the other side of the island from the resident community and what action there is, apart from dune buggy duels (not exactly eco-sensitive, but apparently inevitable between those testosterone-charged honeymooners), is on or under the water. Almost every day spinner dolphins – very often by the hundred – corkscrew in formation out of the clear, turquoise water by way of greeting. And so another day in paradise begins.

WHERE:
Sueste Bay, Fernando do Noronha, South Atlantic
COST:
Expensive to astronomical
BEST TIME OF YEAR:
October to February (dry, high season); March to September (rainy in short, intense bursts, low season)
DON'T MISS:
The volcanic rock formations, especially 321 m (1,053 ft) Morro de Pico, a basalt menhir rearing above Conceicao, one of the world's loveliest beaches; live *forro* music, as swampy as Cajun and hypnotic, peculiar to northeast Brazil; being lazy, and appropriately romantic
THINGS TO DO:
Eat fresh barracuda on the Praia do Meio; take an adventure walk to Baia do Sancho which involves climbing two ladders up sheer cliff faces; snorkel or dive in water clear to 50 m (164 ft), among sea turtles, dolphins, tuna, billfish and lemon, nurse or reef sharks (all visible daily in their protected environment – and safe to swimmers); take a glass-walled sauna from which you can dive direct into the infinity pool (like Naomi Campbell, allegedly); surf; beachcomb.
YOU SHOULD KNOW:
Nature goes into overdrive when it rains – be prepared for armies of frogs, yellow-eyed *mabuya* lizards, and really annoying *borrachudo* mosquitoes; marine park rules include a ban on swimming in sunscreen in certain eco-sensitive places; the luxury comforts of the Pousada can't keep up with mainland equivalents, so you'll have to forgive the odd rough edge to the facilities.

Hotel Palacio de Sal

WHERE:
25 km (16 mi) from Uyuni
COST:
Reasonable
BEST TIME OF YEAR:
April to October, when the *altiplano* is dry and sunny; from December to March the ground can be waterlogged
DON'T MISS:
Flocks of pink flamingoes at Laguna Colorada; giant cacti at Isla de los Pescadores; antique locomotives at the Train Cemetery, Uyuni
THINGS TO DO:
Guided trips across the salt flats; billiards; photography; playing golf on the unique saltpan course (May to November only)
YOU SHOULD KNOW:
Guests are asked not to lick the walls as they might dissolve if enough people had a taste! The hotel's website gives the impression of a luxury hotel but remember this is Bolivia, a developing country, and in the middle of a high-altitude desert to boot, so you're lucky to have even hot water and electricity. The Palacio de Sal is listed among the top ten of the world's most unusual hotels by all the travel industry's major magazines.

The Palacio de Sal (Palace of Salt) certainly lives up to its name. Apart from the corrugated tin roof, this bizarre hotel is built entirely of salt bricks, cemented with a salt-and-water-based glue. Most of the furniture is salt too – armchairs carved from salt, a salt-block dining table, salt-block stools, even salt-block beds (surprisingly, rather comfortable). The floors are carpeted in a thick layer of salt granules, so you make a satisfying scrunching sound wherever you walk. The 16 rooms have their own bathrooms (thankfully, the fittings aren't made of salt). There's a recreation room and a cheery bar and lounge with blazing log fires in the evenings. The restaurant menu serves a tasty selection of food – the speciality dish is (surprise!) salted chicken.

The landscape around the Palacio de Sal is just as bizarre as the hotel – an endless flat white plain, the largest saltpan in the world. The Salar de Uyuni covers a vast 10,500 sq km (4,050 sq mi) in the Bolivian Andes *altiplano*, a high-altitude plateau 3,600 m (12,000 ft) above sea level. Until tourists started spreading the word about the incredible beauty of this strange land, the only people here were salt miners, who still extract some 25,000 tonnes of salt every year.

The view from the bedroom windows is simply mind blowing – the glistening white salt desert meets snow-covered mountain peaks at a distant horizon, beneath a huge sky. You feel as though you've landed on another planet. It's difficult to think of another place in the world more weird and wonderful.

The Magic Mountain at Huilo Huilo

WHERE:
Huilo Huilo Biological Reserve, Panguipulli, Northern Patagonia, Chile
COST:
Reasonable
BEST TIME OF YEAR:
October to March
DON'T MISS:
A game of mini-golf on a course 12 m (40 ft) up in the trees; flying along the 42-m (138-ft) zip wire through the forest canopy; soaking in an outdoor hot tub made from a hollowed-out tree trunk; dipping into volcanic hot springs; Huilo Huilo waterfall
THINGS TO DO:
Year-round cross-country skiing and snowboarding; trekking; horse riding; mountain biking; fly fishing; kayaking; birdwatching; wildlife-watching; learning about conservation
YOU SHOULD KNOW:
Huilo Huilo is a privately sponsored ecological project set up to 'protect, conserve and restore the temperate rainforest', and to provide a refuge for endangered wildlife.

Huilo Huilo Biological Reserve covers 600 sq km (232 sq mi) of enchanting natural scenery in the pristine forest wilderness of southern Chile, a sparsely populated region of snow-capped volcanoes, waterfalls, lakes, rivers, woods and streams where the human footprint is hardly visible. Wandering in the woods here is rather akin to stepping straight into fairyland.

The Magic Mountain is just one of several places where you can stay in Huilo Huilo, each with its own peculiar charm. It is a fantastical conical edifice built entirely out of local wood and stone, shrouded in a cloak of moss and plants, with a fountain cascading out of its peak and a swaying wooden walkway leading to the front door. Inside, you are surrounded by wood: walls lined with roughly hewn planks, branches apparently growing through the floor of the lounge, kitsch wooden sculptures of mythical forest creatures in every nook and cranny.

A central spiral stairway leads to hotel rooms with picturesque chapel windows and quaint rustic furniture constructed from bits of tree and chunks of wood – the bedside tables are upended logs. The higher you climb inside the cone, the smaller the rooms. Kids will love being right at the top in a cosy loft, where they can pretend to be a tree sprite, or at least a gnome. There is a Magic Corner children's playroom, a reading room, and a spa with heated swimming pool, sauna and whirlpool, while all the outdoor activities anyone could wish for are in the forest right on your doorstep.

Back-to-nature types who have a whimsical streak will be in heaven in this tangled fairytale forest where Mother Nature has waved her magic wand.

Indigo Hotel

This backpackers' and trekkers' boutique hotel opened in 2006. It is in a large warehouse building that stands on the waterfront in the tourist town of Puerto Natales, gateway to the spectacular Torres del Paine National Park at the southern tip of Chile.

The Indigo has been designed in a minimalist, Scandinavian style and you are immediately struck by how clean, light and airy it feels. The 29 rooms are small but functional, with streamlined wooden furniture and super-comfortable beds – a real treat for weary travellers. All the rooms have huge windows, which make them seem far larger than they really are, and you may easily find yourself lying flat out on your bed for a lot longer than you intended, mesmerized by the sight of the clouds scudding across constantly changing Patagonian skies.

There is a superb spa on the roof, with open-air hot tubs. Here you can sit up to your neck in water, easing away the aches and pains of the day's trekking, sipping a glass of Chilean wine and watching a sunset to die for. The open-plan lounge not only has comfy sofas but also, an unusual touch, hammocks to curl up in with a book (and nod off for a snooze). The bar has a relaxed, convivial atmosphere and the hotel restaurant serves good hearty food and provides packed lunches for those out for the day.

The hotel staff organize tours, outdoor activities and sightseeing, and are only too happy to help with travel plans. The Indigo combines a really friendly, laid-back atmosphere with efficiency, sparkling cleanliness and great service. One of the best backpackers' hotels you're likely to come across anywhere.

WHERE:
Puerto Natales, Patagonia, Chile
COST:
Expensive, but well worth it
BEST TIME OF YEAR:
The weather is changeable and windy throughout the year but the months from September to May are more benign than June to August.
DON'T MISS:
The Glaciers Cruise; Cueva del Milodón (Mylodon's Cave); Indigo Hotel tour round a Patagonian ranch
THINGS TO DO:
Sea kayaking in the Ultima Esperanza Sound; trekking; horse riding; sightseeing
YOU SHOULD KNOW:
The hotel's design is so open plan that showers and loos (albeit with a screen) are in the rooms rather than attached in the conventional en-suite arrangement, so friends who are not on sufficiently intimate terms might feel a bit inhibited about sharing.

EcoCamp Patagonia

EcoCamp allows you the luxury of comfortable accommodation in completely natural surroundings. Not just any old natural surroundings, mind, but one of the most awe-inspiring landscapes and some of the best trekking country in the world – the Torres del Paine National Park.

The ethos of EcoCamp is to harmonize with nature and protect the environment from a heavy tourist footprint. You stay in a tent modelled on the shelters of the indigenous nomads who once inhabited Patagonia – their dome-shaped huts, made of bent branches covered in animal skin, maximized internal space, conserved heat and deflected the gale-force winds that sweep through the wilderness. The updated EcoCamp version is a geodesic dome of galvanized iron tubing and insulated canvas. The

25 domes are 2 m (6.5 ft) high and nearly 4 m (13 ft) in diameter, giving plenty of headroom and ample space for two single beds. There's a wood-burning stove and fleece sheets so, whatever the weather, you always feel snug and warm inside. You go to sleep at night counting the stars that twinkle through the dome's transparent roof and in the morning wake to the dawn sunlight and a chorus of birdsong.

There are three large community domes that serve as restaurant, bar and library. There's also a communal terrace where you can sit and chill out after a hard but rewarding day's trekking. All the domes rest on raised wooden platforms connected by walkways, minimizing EcoCamp's impact on the wilderness. The camp guides are incredibly knowledgeable and their enthusiasm is infectious. It's worth signing up for as many of the guided treks and wildlife excursions as you can, in the happy knowledge that EcoCamp is environmentally friendly tourism at its absolute best.

WHERE:
Torres del Paine National Park, Patagonia, Chile
COST:
Reasonable
BEST TIME OF YEAR:
September to May (the EcoCamp is dismantled and does not operate in June, July and August)
DON'T MISS:
The sight of a glacier calving; watching the myriad stars in the unpolluted night skies from the camp terrace as you drink delicious Chilean wine
THINGS TO DO:
Trekking; horse riding; birdwatching; wildlife- and nature-watching; photography
YOU SHOULD KNOW:
Electricity supply is limited so there is no power for the internet, hairdryers, electric razors, etc. EcoCamp offsets its carbon emissions, recycles waste and has composting toilets to ensure that it is environmentally neutral. The place takes a maximum of 56 people at a time so you never feel there are too many tourists around. The relentless Patagonian wind can come as a shock to people who aren't prepared for it.

WHERE:
On the Pastaza River, near Puyo, Ecuador
COST:
Expensive
BEST TIME OF YEAR:
There's a steady temperature of around 25°C (77°F) throughout the year but going from June to January avoids the worst of the rainy season.
DON'T MISS:
Witnessing the amazing spectacle of the bird conference at a *collpa* (a clay bank where birds and mammals supplement their diet by feeding on mineral deposits); visiting an Achuar village (and even spending a night in the community); going on a guided night hike
THINGS TO DO:
Learn the art of using a blowpipe gun (useful in marital disputes); fishing; swimming with freshwater dolphins; canoeing; birdwatching; observing wildlife; jungle hiking
YOU SHOULD KNOW:
The Amazon is home to more than 50 per cent of the world's flora and fauna. There are only 6,000 Achuar left, living in 64 jungle villages. You will need to take anti-malarial medication. No children under the age of seven are allowed. There is an emergency-only internet and phone connection. Electricity is solar generated, water is filtered and purified and all rubbish is either recycled or taken back out of the rainforest for disposal.

Kapawi Eco-lodge

The Achuar are one of the last indigenous peoples in the Amazon Basin. They live in 8,000 sq km (3,100 sq mi) of rainforest along the border of Ecuador and Peru, pristine territory as yet untouched by the destructive logging, mining, and oil industries. Established here in 1993, Kapawi Eco-lodge is an ecologically responsible and culturally aware tourist resort that brings badly needed funds to the Achuar to help them preserve their ancient way of life.

Kapawi is as remote as it gets – a ten-day walk from the nearest road. The only other way to reach it is by air. The one-hour flight in a light aircraft is an experience in itself, soaring above a brilliant green carpet of rainforest that seems to stretch forever. The plane drops you off on a dirt airstrip in the back of beyond where you get into a dugout canoe and are taken up river to the eco-lodge.

You are housed in one of 18 picturesque thatch-and-wood circular huts built on stilts, each with its own bathroom and solar-heated water supply. They are amazingly clean and comfortable considering you are in the middle of the rainforest. There are protective mosquito nets and the roof, floor and windows are screened to keep out creepy crawlies.

Almost all the staff are native Achuar. They're genuinely warm, welcoming people who seem only too happy to introduce you to their culture. There is an incredible variety of fauna and flora in the rainforest around the eco-lodge – more than 570 species of bird alone; and you'll see gaudily coloured butterflies, giant river otters, monkeys and freshwater dolphins. Kapawi is a truly awesome eco-adventure and a fascinating cultural experience.

Galapagos Safari Camp

Glamour camping – or 'glamping' – is the hip alternative to roughing it for anyone who doesn't see why outdoor adventures should preclude a few indoor comforts. If you're into discovering new and amazing out-of-the-way places, and appreciate a bit of glamour thrown in, you'll thoroughly enjoy a stay at Galapagos Safari Camp.

Santa Cruz is one of the larger islands in the Galapagos, with few people and beautiful natural scenery. The Safari Camp is wonderfully situated, secluded but not remote, right next to national parkland and less than 30 minutes from the ocean. Nine 27 sq m (290 sq ft) vast and unbelievably opulent tents, complete with wooden decking floors and private porches, are pitched on a ridge overlooking rolling wooded hills that tumble down to the Pacific. They are stunning inside – less a tent, more a luxury hotel suite – with elegant custom-made furniture and an en-suite bathroom with granite basin, hot-water power shower and flushing lavatory system. You can wallow in the camp's infinity pool, screened by trees and with a staggering ocean view, and drink and dine in a charming central lodge perched on top of the hill.

The accommodation, food and service are all superb. You will want for nothing. The hospitable couple who own and run the camp will arrange drivers and naturalist guides for you, and help you organize your itinerary and inter-island travel. The Galapagos Safari Camp is a dream come true for nature lovers, birdwatchers, scuba divers, or just anyone who wants an adventure in one of the most remarkable places on the planet, and you'd be hard put to find a campsite anywhere that's more glamorous than this one.

WHERE:
Santa Cruz, Galapagos Islands, Ecuador
COST:
Astronomical, but you get what you pay for
BEST TIME OF YEAR:
The temperature is pleasantly warm throughout the year but it is best to avoid June to November when thick mists descend and it often drizzles.
DON'T MISS:
The tortoise-breeding centre at Charles Darwin Research Station; Caleta Tortua Negra (Black Turtle Cove) lagoon to see the tropical fish, rays and sharks; the famous lava tunnels; land iguanas and flamingoes at Cerro Dragón (Dragon Hill)
THINGS TO DO:
Nature walks; birdwatching; boat trips to neighbouring islands; cycling; sea kayaking; scuba diving; snorkelling
YOU SHOULD KNOW:
The Galapagos Islands are 972 km (604 mi) off the coast of Ecuador. One of the world's most important marine reserves is in the Galapagos. Eminent Victorian naturalist Charles Darwin sailed here in the *Beagle* in 1835 and discovered endemic species and evidence for natural selection which led to his Theory of Evolution.

AFRICA

WHERE:
Derb Taht El-Khochba, Zaouia El-Abbassia, Marrakesh
COST:
Reasonable (cheaper in low season from July to September)
BEST TIME OF YEAR:
Any time, but mid March to late May is particularly pleasant, when the fruit trees have come into bloom before the shimmering heat of the summer.
DON'T MISS:
Watch snake charmers in the main square. Visit the Saadian Tombs, Badi Palace and Menara Gardens. Take a day trip to the Atlas Mountains.
THINGS TO DO:
Have a mint tea on the terrace and drown in the view. Sharpen your bargaining skills in one of the bustling *souks* (markets). Take a trip to the New Town of Gueliz for fabulous leather goods. Enjoy some authentic Moroccan cuisine at Dar Moha in the *medina*.

Riad Sbihi

There are all sorts of *riads* for those seeking accommodation in Marrakesh's teeming *medina*, ranging from updated boutique hotels offering every modern comfort to complement their Moroccan architecture to spectacular old houses whose interiors hardly seem to have changed for centuries. There is no doubt which category Riad Sbihi falls into. Blessed with the family name of its owners, every visitor who enters through the humble studded entrance door will be instantly entranced by the sight that meets their eyes. This grand edifice is the most authentic of *riads*, lovingly restored over two generations and featuring all the classical elements of these fine dwellings.

The central courtyard is simply stunning, with its intricate *zellij* tiling, sculpted plaster and four lush gardens around the impressive central fountain. The surrounding arcades give access to comfortable ground-floor facilities and the upper level, behind intricate iron balustrades, is where the bed chambers may be found. The terraces

offer wonderful views of local landmarks such as the 12th-century sanctuary of local saint Sidi Bel Abbès es Sebti, together with a sweeping panorama across the medina to the High Atlas Mountains. Two dining salons offer local cuisine or pretty much anything guests request, and the latter are positively encouraged to visit the kitchen to watch their meal being prepared.

There are two suites at Riad Sbihi, along with a *douiria* (double suite) and five rooms, all decorated and furnished in traditional style – although, happily, dedicated adherence to the old way doesn't extend to the exclusion of modern comforts such as air conditioning, satellite TV and a welcoming bathroom. There is a small but perfectly formed heated plunge pool and pampering *hammam* (Turkish bath) that freshens and fortifies after a day on the town. Simply enchanting!

YOU SHOULD KNOW:
A *riad* is a family town house of a particular architectural design, built around an enclosed courtyard garden with all the rooms facing inwards. If you decide to stay in one, it's worth researching thoroughly beforehand – many Moroccan hotels have added the word *riad* to their names to give a touch of romance but aren't the real thing. However, Riad Sbihi is most definitely as authentic as they come. Children are welcome (a small supplement is payable for older kids, and there are also modest local taxes that will add to the bill).

Riad Noir d'Ivoire

Marrakesh, the 'red city', is one of the most romantic cities in the world. Founded in the 11th century, this 'Land of God' at the foot of the snow-capped High Atlas Mountains was the capital of the medieval Berber empire. Its imperial past is evident even today in the faded pink ramparts of the ancient city walls and the historical buildings in the *medina* (old town).

By far the best way to get a feel for the atmosphere and culture of this thousand-year-old city is by staying in a *riad* (a traditional town house) in the *medina*. From the street the houses are all but invisible: you shuffle along featureless winding alleyways, hemmed in by high blank walls, passing the occasional closed doorway. But behind those anonymous doors is another world. Open any one of them and you are in a miniature Garden of Eden – a courtyard with fountains, ponds and fruit trees, overlooked by colonnaded terraces dripping with plants – an oasis of calm in the midst of the stifling heat and frenetic atmosphere of the *medina*.

The Riad Noir d'Ivoire is just such a haven, offering stunning traditional interiors combined with thoroughly modern temptations like a boutique, club room, library, spa and gym. The two courtyards with their pillars and arches feature greenery and tranquil pools beneath the bluest of skies. The fine-dining restaurant has an intimate atmosphere all its own and there's a fabulous roof terrace sun-seekers will find irresistible. There are five suites, some with private roof terraces and Jacuzzis, two junior suites and two double rooms. All rooms have air conditioning, minibars, flat-screen TVs wall safes, and music centres. You'll find that Riad Noir d'Ivoire really is the happiest of marriages between 21st-century comforts and the beguiling spirit of Old Morocco.

WHERE:
Derb Jdid, Bab Doukkala, Marrakesh
COST:
Reasonable to expensive, depending on choice of accommodation at the *riad* (rates don't vary by season)
BEST TIME OF YEAR:
It's lovely at any time but late March to mid June is perfect.
DON'T MISS:
After a hard day bargain-hunting in the *souk*, unwind with a relaxing soak in one of the *riad*'s limpid pools. Take a short stroll through the *medina* to Dar Marjana, there to enjoy a traditional Moroccan meal with all the trimmings (live music, belly dancers, a traditional tea man and all the spicy food you can eat).
THINGS TO DO:
Take one of the special excursions you can book through the *riad*. Choose between a visit to the Atlas Mountains to explore Berber villages and marvel at the rugged landscape, a stroll around the charming seaside town of Essaouira followed by a fresh seafood lunch at the harbour, or a two-day expedition into the vastness of the desert, to include camel riding thorough dunes at dusk followed by local food and entertainment beneath the stars. Better yet, try all three!
YOU SHOULD KNOW:
The central courtyard has a refreshing mist system that takes the sizzle out of warmer days. The *riad*'s house donkey is called Couscous. Families are welcome and an extra bed can be added for a reasonable charge.

La Sultana

Slightly off the usual tourist trail, near the Atlantic fishing town of Oualidia, La Sultana stands in solitary splendour – an imposing building reminiscent of a Moorish fortress. It is in a wonderfully tranquil pastoral setting overlooking a beautiful lagoon, with views of the ocean beyond and nothing but fields all around. The hotel's lovely terraced gardens are a little private paradise in which to stroll among palms, cacti and trailing bougainvillea.

La Sultana's 11 fabulously furnished rooms are incredibly luxurious with magical views across the lagoon and each private, walled patio has a saltwater Jacuzzi. The hotel also has a heated indoor pool in the magnificent vaulted spa and there is a sensational *trompe l'oeil* infinity pool – you really can scarcely tell where the pool ends and the lagoon begins.

La Sultana is special, even for a luxury boutique hotel, and offers a level of service quite beyond the norm. The staff are never in the least intrusive yet they look after your every need before you've even realized what it was you wanted and without any of the aloof starchiness that is so often passed off as 'good service' in luxury hotels. The hotel restaurant serves marvellous food and wine – you will taste some of the best seafood of the Atlantic coast.

This part of the coast never gets overcrowded except at the very height of the summer season, when the nearby town of Oualidia fills with Moroccan holidaymakers. La Sultana is an idyllic place for anyone who wants a quiet, relaxing seaside holiday in a peaceful, secluded retreat made for pampering and romance.

WHERE:
Oualidia
COST:
Expensive
BEST TIME OF YEAR:
April to June or September and October; avoid July and August when Oualidia gets very crowded
DON'T MISS:
Fresh Atlantic oysters; an open-air dinner on the jetty; a boat ride and picnic on the other side of the lagoon; a cookery lesson with the head chef
THINGS TO DO:
Boat rides; hiking; windsurfing; swimming; quad biking; birdwatching
YOU SHOULD KNOW:
Oualidia lagoon is in an area of coastal wetlands and reefs, rich in birdlife. The hotel is a good 20-minute walk from the town or any other restaurants.

Kasbah Tamadot

WHERE:
Asni, an hour's drive from Marrakesh
COST:
Astronomical
BEST TIME OF YEAR:
Any time of year is wonderful here but the Atlas Mountains are perhaps at their very best from the beginning of April until mid June and from mid September to early November.
DON'T MISS:
A local Berber village on market day; a mule ride through the mountains with a Berber guide
THINGS TO DO:
Hiking; guided treks; horse trekking; mountain biking; tennis; table tennis; sightseeing excursions by car
YOU SHOULD KNOW:
The Berbers are the indigenous pre-Arab inhabitants of the Atlas with their own culture and customs. Richard Branson's mother has been helping the local economy with women's education projects and employment. Kasbah Tamadot won an award for being the Best Small Hotel in Africa 2011.

Kasbah Tamadot is Richard Branson's Moroccan retreat, bought for his mother in 1998 when she fell in love with both the place and the people. To get here you drive up winding roads, climbing higher and higher through the Atlas foothills, passing through the ancient villages of the Berber heartlands as you head towards the glorious snow-capped peaks of the High Atlas.

Finally, at an altitude of 1,320 m (4,330 ft) you arrive at Branson's sensational pink sandstone castle, perched dramatically on a terraced outcrop overlooking the valley below. You can stay in the *kasbah* itself – a picturesque maze of passageways, twisting staircases and hidden courtyards – or more adventurous souls will have a great time in one of the hotel's luxury Berber tents with its own plunge pool and a deck looking out across the mountains.

The hotel restaurant provides superb international cuisine and you can dine in the fresh air, on a lovely garden terrace, enjoying the awesome mountain views. As well as an indoor heated pool there is what must be the most spectacular infinity pool of all time – a vast heated sheet of water which reflects the clouds and the sky and gives the terrifying illusion that you'll swim straight off the edge of the mountain. There is also a relaxing spa where, among a multitude of treatments, you can have a traditional *hammam*.

Kasbah Tamadot has families in mind as well as couples. There are lots of activities and amusements in and around the hotel for children and adults of all ages. Even the most recalcitrant teenager will have difficulty being grumpy when surrounded by such heady luxury in this atmospheric mountain setting.

Riad Dar Nour

WHERE:
Kasbah, Tangier
COST:
Reasonable
BEST TIME OF YEAR:
Late March to mid June and September to the end of October; Tangier gets very overcrowded at the height of the summer season in July and August
DON'T MISS:
The Dar el Makhzen (17th-century Sultan's Palace) in the Kasbah; mint tea in the famous Cafe Hafa; the lighthouse at Cap Spartel, where the Atlantic and Mediterranean meet
THINGS TO DO:
Watching the fishermen at the port; exploring the seafront; strolling to the Mirador of Perdicaris; visiting Mendoubia Gardens; shopping for leather goods and carpets; sightseeing
YOU SHOULD KNOW:
The hotel will provide dinner on request; it also owns a tea room and restaurant – Le Salon Bleu, just three minutes' walk away – and the food there is also excellent.

Tangier is the gateway to North Africa. Neither Europe nor Morocco, it is a cosmopolitan port notorious for its tourist touts and rip-off hotels. But sooner or later travellers are likely to find themselves passing through, and coming across Riad Dar Nour is like finding a blessing in this city of sin.

Although it's magnificently situated, perched up on the ancient city walls, this little hotel is almost impossible to find. The first time you come here you'll need a guide to lead you through the maze of back alleys that is the old quarter of Tangier. The simple white-washed

facade and stripped-wood window frames hint at the picturesque charm within. There are only eight rooms, all immaculately clean, air-conditioned and gaily decorated with Moroccan antiques and carpets, each with a bathroom en suite. It also exudes an arty, faintly bohemian atmosphere with its shelves of books and DVDs all over the place, personal knick-knacks, artworks and wall hangings.

The staff are extremely hospitable and even if you're a lone traveller you'll feel perfectly at ease sitting in one of the cosy salons, watching a DVD, hooking up to wifi, reading, or just chilling out. The pretty plant-filled roof terrace has a wonderful view over the *medina* and the Bay of Tangier. You can all too easily while away the evening here with a bottle of wine or a cocktail or two, watching the huge orange sun sink into the Atlantic.

The Dar Nour breakfasts are legendary. In fact, it's worth staying here for the food alone – fresh-baked pastries, homemade yogurt and crème caramel, pancakes and fresh fruit juices. Memories are made of such stuff . . .

La Maison des Oiseaux

La Maison des Oiseaux (The House of Birds) is aptly named. This little B&B, just outside the fishing village of Moulay Bousselham, is on the edge of a 4.5 sq km (1.7 sq mi) coastal lagoon, cut off from the ocean by an extraordinary cordon of sand dunes, some of which are more than 70 m (230 ft) high. The lagoon is a major stopping point along the East Atlantic bird-migration route – birdwatchers will truly be in heaven here.

As you walk up to the front door through the beautifully tended garden, La Maison des Oiseaux has a welcoming air with its cheerful spick-and-span white-washed walls and sky-blue painted shutters. The rooms are simple but sparkling clean, with tiled floors and Moroccan carved-wood furniture. The beds are extremely comfortable and there are delightful artistic touches all over the house – unsurprisingly, since the French owner is an artist.

As well as rooms in the main house, there's a separate bungalow tucked away in a corner of the garden which is perfect for families or groups. In the evenings you can sit under a vine-covered pergola on the terrace with a bottle of wine and listen to the *cicadas* and frogs as you watch the stars appear. The home-cooked food is superb and children are welcomed and have free run of the garden,.

Nature lovers, environmentalists and walkers will all be in their element here – as will anyone looking for somewhere quiet and restful that's off the beaten track, where tourists are few and far between. La Maison des Oiseaux is a haven of tranquillity.

WHERE:
Moulay Bousselham
COST:
Budget
BEST TIME OF YEAR:
December to January for thousands of wildfowl, waders and flamingoes; March to June or September to early November for the most clement weather
DON'T MISS:
Watching the fishermen land the morning's catch; a meal of fresh seafood
THINGS TO DO:
Birdwatching; walking; boating; cycling; exploring the shore
YOU SHOULD KNOW:
Moulay Bousselham is about 40 km (25 mi) south of Larache. The village has little tourist infrastructure but there are several restaurants. The Moulay Bousselham lagoon is a biosphere reserve protected area. The tidal currents are very strong so swimming is not safe on this part of the coast.

Riad Chbanate

WHERE:
Essaouira
COST:
Reasonable
BEST TIME OF YEAR:
Any time. The climate is temperate throughout the year but the wind, always strong here, is particularly fierce from mid June to September.
DON'T MISS:
A massage in the hotel's *hammam*; the hotel's homemade pancakes at breakfast; eating fresh seafood from a fisherman's stall at the port; a camel ride along the beach; walking along the city ramparts
THINGS TO DO:
Windsurfing; snorkelling; fishing; canoeing; hiking; cycling; horse riding on the beach; arts and crafts shopping in the *souk*
YOU SHOULD KNOW:
Essaouira's *medina* is a UNESCO World Heritage Site. The annual Gnaoua World Music Festival is held in Essaouira every June.

Essaouira, otherwise known as the 'windy city', is a picturesque Atlantic coastal town of white-washed houses and old fortress ruins. In the 1960s hippies, artists and musicians were attracted here by the charm of the town, the ocean air, and the immaculate 10-km (6-mi) windswept beach. Today Essaouira is a well-known tourist destination and hotels have sprouted up accordingly.

You won't find anywhere to beat Riad Chbanate, a picturesque 18th-century building in the historic old quarter, just minutes from the main square. The hotel is spotlessly clean and has its own restaurant which serves wonderful Moroccan food. The spacious rooms all have old, beamed ceilings and are beautifully furnished with traditional Moroccan rugs and antique knick-knacks but with desirable modern touches like air conditioning and satellite TV. The en-suite bathrooms are unexpectedly luxurious and have beautiful stone baths.

But it's the common areas and the service that really make this hotel so special. You'll feel completely at home here, whether you're sitting by the fountain in the downstairs courtyard, relaxing in the comfortable lounge, lying on a lounger in the shade of the patio or having a cocktail on the roof terrace watching the sun go down.

After a busy day of outdoor activity, being battered by Atlantic winds or battling your way through the heat and crowds of the *souks*, it's a relief to come back to the welcoming hotel staff and calm atmosphere – and then find rose petals strewn round your bath tub and a bottle of ice-cold water by your bed. The Riad Chbanate is an outstanding hotel in one of Morocco's loveliest cities.

Kasbah Tombouctou

WHERE:
Merzouga
COST:
Reasonable
BEST TIME OF YEAR:
September to February
DON'T MISS:
Dayet Srji salt lake; trying to clamber up Erg Chebbi
THINGS TO DO:
Camel excursions; 4x4 excursions; birdwatching; stargazing

There's only one reason for coming to Merzouga, a dead-end oasis village in the Sahara Desert – and that's the wondrous Erg Chebbi, a 150-m (490-ft) high dune that stretches for 50 km (31 mi) and is 5 km (3 mi) wide. There's literally nothing else here apart from the local Berber tribesmen and a few date palm trees.

Inevitably a desert adventure involves rather a lot of roughing it, and it really helps to stay somewhere that offers more than a hard bed and a dribble of water. Kasbah Tombouctou looks like a palatial desert fortress, standing in surreal splendour surrounded by sand, 3 km (1.9 mi) outside town next to a cluster of date palms at the foot of Erg Chebbi. The rooms are large, very clean and attractively furnished with gaily painted lime-plaster walls . . . and air-conditioned – a godsend in this part of the world.

There's a decent spa and *hammam* – where a massage will ease away the inevitable aches and pains of your camel treks – and a lovely outdoor swimming pool, which is pure bliss after a swelteringly hot, sandy ride back from the desert. The hotel restaurant serves hearty *tagines* and *couscous*, which go to the right spot after a day exploring the dunes.

But best of all is the desert itself. In the changing light and shadow of sunrise and sunset, the dunes glow in a rainbow of reds, peaches and pinks. And at night the sky is a myriad of twinkling stars. Staying here is like being in a hotel on Mars, only with all the earthly comforts you could possibly want.

YOU SHOULD KNOW:
The hotel can arrange guides, camels and 4x4 transport for you, as well as night stays in a Berber desert camp under the stars. The local people here are entirely dependent on the tourist industry for their living, which encourages cut-throat competition and endless trickery – so keep your wits about you.

Dar Raha

Dar Raha is not your average tourist hotel. It is secreted away in a village at the foot of the Jebel Zagora mountain in the far south of Morocco, an authentic old *pisé* (mud-brick) family house that has been painstakingly restored by the French owners. It's up an anonymous little side street and you'll wonder at first if a hotel can really be there, or whether you've been misdirected.

Inside, the house is far larger than it looks. There are nine guest bedrooms opening onto shared terraces, with three communal bathrooms. The salon has an eclectic assortment of books, magazines and board games, and there is a 'culture room' with a display of local artists' paintings and cultural information. All the rooms are simply but comfortably furnished, each with its own individual touches. The hotel serves wonderful, imaginatively prepared fresh food – a welcome change from the usual tourist fare.

Dar Raha has an intellectual atmosphere of almost meditative calm about it – a pleasing respite after a day spent haggling with camel drivers and market traders. From the third-floor roof terrace there are wonderful views of the town, palm groves, the mountain and the castle ruins.

The owners really care about sustainable tourism and do their utmost to conserve water and electricity, minimize the use of plastics, and recycle as much as possible. They are deeply knowledgeable about the history and culture of the area and will organize reliable guides for you.

This is the perfect base for lone travellers or couples who want to explore the desert and is very different from the usual backpacker hotels. Staying at Dar Raha is as close as it gets to experiencing the real Morocco.

WHERE:
Amezrou, Zagora
COST:
Budget
BEST TIME OF YEAR:
April and October; December and January can be uncomfortably humid and from June to August the daytime heat can be unbearable
DON'T MISS:
Hiking to the top of Jebel Zagora mountain; the rock art of the Draa Valley
THINGS TO DO:
Camel rides into the desert; having your hands decorated with henna; cookery lessons; walking through the palm groves and learning how dates are harvested; discovering the history and culture of the Draa Valley; visiting the workshops of local artisans
YOU SHOULD KNOW:
Zagora is an oasis town in the Draa Valley in the far south of Morocco, 367 km (228 mi) southeast of Marrakesh. Zagora is one of the hottest and also one of the coldest places in Morocco – the desert nights can be freezing.

Dar Melody

WHERE:
Quartier Seffah, Fez
COST:
Budget
BEST TIME OF YEAR:
From April to June or September to November, to avoid the intense heat of summer and the grey skies of winter
DON'T MISS:
Shopping in the *souks*; the Karaouine Mosque; sitting on the terrace at sundown
THINGS TO DO:
Seeing the sights; exploring the *medina*; looking round the leather workshops
YOU SHOULD KNOW:
The *medina* is a car-free zone so you have to get around on foot. Dar Melody is in the tanneries (leather) district, a half-hour walk from the tourist restaurants and a few minutes from the nearest taxi drop-off.

Fez is a daunting city for the tourist. The *medina* is a chaotic labyrinth of medieval alleyways in which you can all too easily get overwhelmed with culture shock and hopelessly lost. Venturing out from a secure base makes all the difference and staying at this welcoming family home immediately puts you at ease. The delightful French couple who run Dar Melody will meet you at the airport or station, show you the best places to eat, organize guides for you and give you tips for getting around the *medina* – all with a kindness that goes way beyond the call of duty.

The beautiful old building is in the heart of the *medina* and has been meticulously restored, with the original latticed woodwork and exquisite painted ceiling carefully preserved. The three enormous air-conditioned B&B rooms have their own bathrooms and are beautifully decorated in traditional Moroccan style, but with an added French *je ne sais quoi*. There is a delightful rooftop terrace with a great view over the *medina*, as well as a charming courtyard.

The Dar Melody is on the other side of the *medina* from most of the tourist action, so you feel an integral part of the city rather than an awkward outsider. Instead of being hassled by a throng of tourist hustlers, you just melt into the daily life of the *medina*. And when you arrive back exhausted after a hard day's sightseeing, you are greeted with chilled fruit and sweetmeats on the house, plus a receptive ear ready to listen to the story of your day's adventure. Dar Melody is a welcome haven in this fascinating but frenetic city.

Riad Le Calife

WHERE:
El Makhfia, Fez
COST:
Reasonable
BEST TIME OF YEAR:
April to June or September to November
DON'T MISS:
Cooking lessons in the hotel kitchen; a traditional massage and henna session
THINGS TO DO:
The hotel can organize golf, tennis and horse riding, and lays on guides and excursions to the historic sites around Fez.
YOU SHOULD KNOW:
Le Calife has come third in *Trip Advisor's Travellers' Choice* list of the Top Twenty-Five Hotels in the World.

Steeped in 1,300 years of imperial history, Fez is a deeply traditional city. The culture shock of the *medina* is tempered by staying at this palatial Moroccan Art Deco 1930s family home which has recently been converted into a boutique guesthouse. The Riad Le Calife bridges the cultural divide, offering some insight into the *medina* but with a western degree of comfort.

First impressions count, and you enter the courtyard to be dumbstruck by the amazingly intricate 19th-century mosaic tile work on the floor, walls and columns, the enormous carved and painted wooden doors, plus the profusion of trees and plants. It just goes on getting better and better, too. The atmosphere here is warm and welcoming and the fabulous decor and ambience throughout the hotel has been considered down to the smallest detail.

There are seven guest rooms, all with bathrooms en suite, some with living rooms attached, all overlooking the courtyard in

traditional *riad* style. There is an indoor lounge with richly coloured rugs and antiques, a library with Moroccan artwork on the walls and a relaxation room where you are bound to succumb to one or other of the treatments on offer. You can also relax on one of the two roof terraces with a pot of mint tea or a drink and look down on the activity in the *medina* below.

The food at Le Calife is superb – the very best of traditional Moroccan cuisine. It's not worth even bothering to search for a local restaurant in the *medina* that measures up – you won't find one. This is a place that gives you the best possible experience of Fez at a remarkably good price.

Riad Dar Zitoune

WHERE:
Taroudant
COST:
Reasonable
BEST TIME OF YEAR:
Any time, but June to September can be very hot; the best walking weather is from October to May
DON'T MISS:
An evening of Moroccan music in the cellar bar; The Berber *souk* in Taroudant
THINGS TO DO:
Mountain trekking; exploring the *medina* and city walls; horse-drawn carriage rides; visiting local crafts workshops
YOU SHOULD KNOW:
The hotel has its own *hammam*, sauna and massage room. There is wifi in the main reception area.

In a beautiful setting, nestling at the foot of the High Atlas Mountains just outside the southern Moroccan town of Taroudant, the Dar Zitoune or 'House of Olives' is not a *riad* in the traditional sense. It is an attractive, modern building with a walled garden – and it is the garden that is the real attraction. You stay in your own bungalow, hidden among palm and fruit trees, citrus and olive groves with trailing bougainvillea, jasmine and datura. The 14 air-conditioned bungalows are delightfully furnished in local Berber style and each has its own bathroom and private patio.

The Swiss owners of Dar Zitoune came to the picturesque walled town of Taroudant in 2003 and fell for its charms. They live on the premises and both they and their staff are hospitable and helpful without ever being intrusive, organizing transport and guides for you and ensuring that you've got everything you want. Indeed, it can be quite hard to tear yourself away from lazing around in the hotel gardens to face the scrum in the *souks* or steel yourself for the rigours of a mountain trek.

A lovely 25-m (82-ft) swimming pool in the shape of an arched Moorish doorway is bordered by a broad terrace where you can relax and drink mint tea or feast on a delicious selection of European and Moroccan dishes, with lots of fresh fruit and vegetables and excellent wines. You may also have meals served on your bungalow patio. If it's romance you're seeking, you'll certainly find it here.

Adrere Amellal

At night, with only starlight to see it by, it looks like a ghost town. If it ever rained, it would simply wash away. It radiates the intensity of the peace, comfort and emotional tranquillity it has given and re-absorbed from its guests. It should be a church, but it's a luxury eco-resort at the foot of the mystic White Mountain on the edge of the Siwa Oasis, between the glitter of Lake Siwa and the relentless dunes of the Great Sand Sea.

Adrere Amellal has literally grown from the earth on which it stands. Its 40 rooms are built of *kershef*, a traditional Siwan material of salt rock worked with mud and straw. Doors and windows are olive wood and roofs are thatched with palm. The furniture, too, is a credit to local artisans' skill with salt rock. Eco-integrity is guaranteed by the complete absence of electricity and therefore light pollution, TV, and phones. Instead, by night hundreds of beeswax candles create pools of diffuse gold throughout the complex. Daylight reveals the aesthetic genius in more surprising ways. Adrere Amellal faces the shimmering waters of Lake Siwa, but by some optical illusion the lake makes the whole complex seem to disappear in a reverse mirage. And, as the sun turns, it creates a shifting abstract of shadowlands formed by the random curves, straight lines, whorls and cylinders of the builders' original inspiration.

It's all about harmony of place, function and people. The groves of olive and date palm shade a self-sufficient organic garden, from whence comes sensational food, cooked and served in a different area of the complex each night. The luxury you don't see is the universal harmonic – but you're invited, and you can resonate.

WHERE:
Siwa Oasis
COST:
Expensive going on expensive+
BEST TIME OF YEAR:
Any time (coal braziers deal with cold nights)
DON'T MISS:
The hard, geometric shapes of dune shadows crossing the Great Sand Sea; the historic fort of Old Shali; the contemporary take on (organic) Pharaonic cooking; the Temple of the Oracle Ammun (Alexander the Great consulted it); Cleopatra's bath
THINGS TO DO:
Horse riding through the palms and olive groves; a 4x4 drive in the Great Sand Sea – in the afternoon sun, the dunes are luminous; chilling in the Roman spring-fed swimming pool (no chemicals); yielding to the resort's flexible environment (no reception area, no way of finding out where dinner will be) by finding the party
YOU SHOULD KNOW:
The only limitation on activities at the resort is 'the desert's mood'. The hotel has revived the local community by involving it in every way, and by making itself dependent on their participation in sustainable local businesses. This does not, however, include a new airport to service eco-competitors with forked tongues – so help reject modernization by staying longer at the real thing.

Winter Palace Hotel

Bellboys in red fezzes with fancy embroidery on their waistcoats set the tone. They deftly relieve you of your baggage and stand aside for you to sweep up the grand staircase, as through a portal, into a bygone era. Luxor's Winter Palace Hotel is the real thing. King Farouk of Egypt built it to entertain the late 19th century's travelling elite, including the very fashionable Egyptologists then making almost daily discoveries at sites like Luxor. Now, among the wrought-iron Art Deco curlicues, rich oriental carpets, and the two-storey-high Ottoman blown-glass chandelier in reception – all of them quite genuine and very valuable – travellers are culturally seduced into participating in a similar experience to that enjoyed by their Victorian forbears.

The management love it when guests want to poke around the lofty public salons, and even some of the rooms, to examine their treasures. Rich brocades on sofas, striped velvet armchairs, satin swags and plush are to be found everywhere. Of course the 86 rooms and six suites are thoroughly up to date with the quality of linens, slippers, plus expected bathroom and technological amenities. Those all seem a bit irrelevant in the face of total immersion in the profoundly stylish comforts of an earlier time. Nobody has to like the Victorian splendour – just enjoy its munificence.

It's certainly a Grand Hotel, able to twist in the air and catch any problem, but it's not formal. Guests who enter into the spirit of its historic and actual grandeur will have the best time. There's no need to play a part. Just allow the hotel to cosset you.

WHERE:
Corniche El Nil Street, Luxor
COST:
Expensive
BEST TIME OF YEAR:
Any time
DON'T MISS:
The Theban necropolis and the Valley of the Kings, across the Nile from the Winter Palace; the Luxor Temple, a few metres' walk down the riverbank; the *son et lumière* at Karnak Temple; the Hatshepsut Temple
THINGS TO DO:
Stroll round downtown Luxor – Art Deco, ancient Egyptian and a mix of local architecture worth gawping at; Howard Carter's house; 'high tea' in the Palace's Victorian Lounge; ask to see some of the hotel's valuable first editions, over an after-dinner drink in the exquisite Royal Bar
YOU SHOULD KNOW:
The Winter Palace is a great place for family holidays – there are lots of monitored activities for children while adults go to temples or dine by candlelight in the Belle Epoque restaurant '1886'. If you're unwilling to haggle, use the Palace's back entrance to avoid the babble of importuning taxis at the front.

Ras Sinai Desert Village

The spirit of the commune is alive and well on the Gulf of Aqaba. Two Bedouin families found a place they loved, stopped, stayed, and as other travellers of like mind joined them, gradually formalized their encampment into a means of survival and contentment. Ras Sinai Desert Village is a business collective designed to make money, but not (by intention) a profit. It is a rare example of alternative philosophy being carried through to a sustainable enterprise. Rarer still is that the end result is untainted by cynicism and is successful because it caters to those least likely to be able to enjoy a Red Sea holiday by any other means.

The Desert Village is endearingly ramshackle. *Hooshas* (bamboo huts on a base of cemented stones) of various sizes are scattered along the water's edge and dug into the stony hill above. They share the wonderful view across the sea to the Saudi Arabian mountains and all have private 'balconies' (an open bit), bamboo shutters hanging at odd angles and inside comfortable carpets, mattresses and bright-coloured cushions. Bathrooms and showers are communal, western-style, and scrupulously clean. Hot water can be arranged. Delicious food comes from the renovated restaurant. It's the heart of the camp, economically and socially. Musical instruments abound. In fact music is everywhere, improvised fusions of wildly different cultures. Music inspired the settlement – and now the very best building (with clay walls and a ceiling!) is the village 'studio', where the acoustic is brilliant and people play daily for the pleasure of it.

Ras Sinai sits four square between the elements, driven by that model of harmony as its guiding muse.

WHERE:
Red Sea shore, Nuweiba, southeast Sinai
COST:
Budget-budget
BEST TIME OF YEAR:
Any time (December to March if you're fleeing north European winter)
DON'T MISS:
The Camel Safari (eight people minimum) to feel the 'desert vibes' and see mountains flooded with colour from pale gold to deep rust-red; St Catherine's Monastery, either by day, or at night with a two-hour climb to see sunrise from 'Moses Mountain' (both including air-conditioned bus).
THINGS TO DO:
Yoga by the water's edge; meditational walks while beachcombing; snorkelling on one of the world's great reefs (just off shore); riding *Hasake*, a flat-bottomed boat; Tai Chi or free dance in the circular Temple building available for all creative impulses; studying the stars from a hammock; hiking the desert
YOU SHOULD KNOW:
By taxi or by bus, ask the driver for 'Ras Shitan', and specifically 'Ayash Camp'. Bring your musical instrument(s) if at all possible. There's a minimum daily food 'spend' of roughly three times the per person cost of a hut – or about US$15 (in high season) to US$5. The village is ideal for groups of family or friends, and any number of children.

Kyambura Gorge Lodge

WHERE:
Eastern border of Queen Elizabeth National Park
COST:
Expensive – as in 'very'
BEST TIME OF YEAR:
December to March, June to September (the two dry seasons)
DON'T MISS:
Game drives on the plains for lion, buffalo and elephant; tracking chimpanzees in Kyambura or Kalinzu Forest (their constant screaming and whooping can be exhausting); guided birdwatching in QENP for spoonbill stork, blue-headed bee eater and some 570 other species; search Ishasha for tree-climbing lions
THINGS TO DO:
Take a boat ride on the Kazinga Channel to spot hippos and crocs; walk the restored wetlands among flamingoes and exotic water birds; go swimming in the pool overlooking the gorge; count red-tail, black-and-white colobus, and other monkeys
YOU SHOULD KNOW:
Kyambura Gorge is one of Africa's great secrets. It is the geographical centre of the greater Virunga landscape, at the heart of the Albertine Rift that straddles Uganda, Rwanda and the DR Congo – hence the amazing biodiversity.

This lodge is at the forefront of eco-friendly development in Uganda. Recently built as a model for community projects employing sustainable local materials and local management, it's a triumph of interior sophistication and comfort, and exterior camouflage. The conversion from coffee plantation to eco-lodge has created a community of eight *bandas* (pyramid-thatched pavilions) and a bigger building housing reception, dining area and bar. The *bandas* have individual decor, but are all exceptionally spacious. Beamed ceilings and wooden floors hit exactly the right 'frontier' note of safari adventure – but the bathrooms are hallmarks of contemporary, urban luxury. Outside, they blend into the hillside. Their balconies have one of Africa's finest panoramas – across the forested gorge to the savannah country, rolling away to the ever-mysterious blue screen of the Rwenzori mountains.

Its position gives the Kyambura Gorge Lodge exclusive access, as the gateway to Queen Elizabeth National Park (QENP) which protects that view. Kyambura Gorge itself is machete-thick tropical rainforest, and the savannah is lush on either side. Lion, hippo, leopard and elephant vie with a hundred lesser species in this freakishly biodiverse region, but the speciality of the Lodge is tracking chimpanzees. Nowhere else in the western arm of the Rift Valley is there a better chance of getting close to humankind's closest relative, and it's a lifetime thrill if you succeed.

Between staring intently into the canopy and gazing through long grass at lions, guests can also simply appreciate the forest from their balcony hammock. Everyone who comes here is directly contributing to saving the chimpanzees, by creating viable local jobs that preserve the forest for tourism. A bit of luxury is a great way to do it.

Fatuma's Tower

Just like Africa itself, Fatuma's Tower is full of unexpected surprises. Once the home of a Swahili noblewoman and her attendant slaves, this extraordinary place is on the Indian Ocean island of Lamu. The island's Lamu Old Town is a historic Swahili settlement with simple but charming buildings of coral stone and mangrove wood, embellished with carved doors.

The car-free island is stunningly beautiful, drawing innumerable tourists. But their conventional experience is not for guests at Fatuma's Tower, for this is a place that takes the cliché out of the word 'retreat' and delivers the real thing. Fatuma's Tower is a place with vision, and that vision is of a totally stress-free environment where people can commune with their inner selves, as gently suggested by the house motto: Peace, Space, Tranquillity. Departure from the care-filled modern world begins with a leisurely boat trip (a wooden boat, of course), while journey's end is set against sand dunes amidst lush green foliage where birds sing and a soothing fountain tinkles into a plunge pool.

The attentive owners call this a house for guests (a subtle distinction from 'guest house'). The tower has five large bedrooms and a yoga hall, for yoga is an essential part of a visit for those who wish to participate. Additionally, the Sand Castle has a ground-floor family apartment and the Garden Cottage has two en-suite doubles. All rooms are simply furnished with local antique furniture and fabrics appropriate to the tower's Swahili history. Meals are a light but delicious combination of Italian and Swahili cuisine, majoring on local seafood, while kitchen staff discuss menus before shopping for fresh-that-day produce and cooking to your requirements. If total relaxation isn't enough, there's plenty to see and do, but many guests are content simply to recharge those flat batteries in the uniquely restful ambiance of Fatuma's Tower.

WHERE:
Near Shela, Lamu Island
COST:
Budget, inching up into reasonable for the best accommodation
BEST TIME OF YEAR:
Any time
DON'T MISS:
Daily yoga sessions; eating under the stars in the lantern-lit courtyard or amidst garden greenery
THINGS TO DO:
A trip to the village of Matondoni, surrounded by mangroves, where traditional sailing dhows are built and repaired; a sunset cruise on one of those dhows; a visit to the nearby tourist haven of Shela with its striking Friday Mosque and white-sand beach; the usual Indian Ocean holiday activities (fishing, snorkelling, scuba diving, windsurfing)
YOU SHOULD KNOW:
All the rooms have solar-powered hot water, fans and mosquito netting (even so, pack insect repellent). It's possible to book the whole place for a group visit (and many groups interested in yoga do just that). Lamu's proximity to Somalia is a continuing worry.

Treetops Hotel

WHERE:
Near Nyeri, Aberdare National Park
COST:
Reasonable (and that includes the Queen Elizabeth Suite!)
BEST TIME OF YEAR:
Any – the wildlife never sleeps, or so it seems
DON'T MISS:
Best not to nod off and miss the (you guessed it) wild animals (especially elephant, buffalo, rhino and warthog) – but actually there's no excuse, because an optional buzzer service alerts guests when something stirs at the waterhole; the distant view of Mount Kenya
THINGS TO DO:
Watching (you guessed it) the wild animals; socializing with fellow guests in the communal dining room
YOU SHOULD KNOW:
Treetops was burned in 1954 during the Mau Mau uprising, but rebuilt in 1957 close to the original site. Overnight guests at Treetops are required to observe a 'low decibel' regime to avoid spooking the wildlife, which includes a ban on shoes with hard soles. Lord Baden-Powell of Boy Scouts fame frequently visited Treetops and lived in the grounds of the Outspan Hotel. Children under the age of five are not allowed.

If you want to feel like a Queen (or her Prince Charming) Treetops has track record – for it was here that Princess Elizabeth and the Duke of Edinburgh were spending the night in 1952 when George VI died, elevating her to the British throne. Treetops had been around since the early 1930s, when it was created by swashbuckling adventurer Major Eric Sherbrook Walker as a game-watching outstation that added a dimension to his Outspan Hotel, which overlooks the nearby gorge of the Chanai River.

Originally Treetops was a simple two-roomed platform built into a large fig tree in the heart of dense lichen-hung forest, specifically designed for night-time observation of the varied wildlife attracted to the adjacent waterholes and salt lick. But publicity generated by the Royal connection ensured that demand rocketed, so Treetops Hotel 'growed and growed' over the years to become today's compact 50-room lodge. The place has four decks, and rather than maintain the original policy of 'no game, no charge', Treetops has an artificial moon that ensures animals can be seen even on moonless nights. In addition to a roof-top viewing platform, guests can observe through windows in the communal space and from ground-level photographic hides.

Recently refurbished without losing its original *zeitgeist*, Treetops Hotel now offers facilities somewhat closer to 21st-century expectations. Although it has the basics, this will never be a luxury safari lodge – but that's the point. This is a place to get up close and personal with some of Africa's most impressive wildlife species, without risk to life and limb. It's also been more than good enough for the many rich, famous and fashionable guests who have enjoyed a Treetops adventure (including Queen Elizabeth II, who made a return visit in the 1980s).

Campi ya Kanzi

Going on safari in Kenya is a popular and well-subscribed activity for adventurous holidaymakers, to the point where it can almost seem that too many tourists are chasing the same spectacular indigenous wildlife. So for those who like avoiding the herd, Campi ya Kanzi (full marks to anyone who guessed the owner is Italian) in southeastern Kenya is a refreshing alternative. This bush camp is located at the foot of the Chyulu Hills, between two game reserves (Tsavo West and Amboseli). It is an unspoilt part of the country with magnificent views across the plain to Mount Kilimanjaro, and notably bereft of competing safari traffic. Just the job for those who don't like to share their piece of Africa with the wider world!

This is ecotourism at its best, a joint venture with the Maasai people that sees $100 of each visitor's daily charge going to conservation work that helps preserve the very wilderness, people and wildlife that make a stay so rewarding. And this isn't gesture ecotourism, because Campi ya Kanzi operates a strict ten-point code that ensures an absolutely minimal environmental impact. But that doesn't mean that guests have to suffer the slings and arrows of outrageous primitive camping merely to satisfy their (and the camp's) principles. No indeed!

Up to 16 guests are accommodated in six tented cottages with thatched roofs, luxuriously equipped, or the slightly grander Hemingway and Simba suites. Each has a dedicated Maasai attendant. With so few guests and 114,000 ha (282,000 ac) of wilderness on the 'tentstep' the safari experience itself is magical, with a choice of habitats (savannah, cloud forest, river and lake) where lions, elephants, giraffes and zebras roam free. For people who really care about the environment and like savouring unspoilt nature at first hand, Kenya simply can't offer a better experience.

WHERE:
Chyulu Hills
COST:
Astronomical (but everything is included)
BEST TIME OF YEAR:
Any time (but the coolest month is July, while January and February are the hottest)
DON'T MISS:
Taking full advantage of the various safari options – tailored to your requirements, outings can include dining in the bush, game drives in an open Land Rover and going afoot with a guide and local tracker to bush-hike or find animals
THINGS TO DO:
Relaxing; wildlife-watching (including birds); photography; visiting a Maasai village to learn about the culture; stargazing (no light pollution here!)
YOU SHOULD KNOW:
If you can rustle up a party of ten, it's possible to book the associated Kanzi bush lodge. Allow for the cost of flying in using the camp's light aircraft. Unlike the rule in Kenya's national parks, visitors to Campi ya Kanzi can go afoot rather than having to observe wildlife from a vehicle.

Diamonds Dream of Africa

WHERE:
Casuarina Road, Malindi
COST:
Budget and slightly beyond, depending on choice of room (garden or sea view)
BEST TIME OF YEAR:
The coastal climate is a warm and humid climate all year round.
DON'T MISS:
A lobster dinner served at a candlelit table on the beach; the mid morning cold sorbet served to guests on the beach or beside the pool; barbecue lunch at the pool bar; cocktails served before dinner; a session in the Thalassotherapy spa

Malindi is located where the Galana River discharges into the Indian Ocean, and this former Swahili trading port has become one of Kenya's most popular tourist destinations. Those seeking to explore this enchanted coast from a base in Malindi could do a lot worse than head for the beach-side Diamonds Dream of Africa, a small and affordable resort hotel that promises much, and delivers. The place offers large, comfortable guest rooms furnished with Italian-designed furniture in teak and, although this is billed as one of the 'Luxury Small Hotels of the World', these are not quite at the cutting edge of modern tropical best practice (for example, the en-suite bathrooms lack air conditioning, which can mean that they almost double as an impromptu sauna).

No matter, for the hotel is beautifully situated on the beach, is distinctively designed in a quirky Indo-Arab style and sits in

immaculate gardens complete with palm trees. Best of all, the level of service is uncompromising and friendly staff go the extra distance to ensure that every guest enjoys a memorable holiday. The package is all-inclusive and the wining and dining is exceptional, especially the caught-that-day seafood, while the open-air restaurant has a wonderful outlook over the sea.

The hotel offers the use of a spa, beauty centre and gym. So, combined with the tempting comfort of loungers by the pool, in the grounds or on the beach, it isn't necessary to stray far to enjoy a memorable holiday. But then again Malindi is also an ideal starting point for expeditions to some of Kenya's wonderful natural attractions. The choice is entirely yours!

Thinking of having a Diamonds Dream of Africa? You won't regret it, because this place is a real gem!

THINGS TO DO:
Beach stuff; snorkelling and scuba diving (ideally at Malindi Marine Park, although this doesn't come cheap); a trip in a glass-bottomed boat for non-divers; checking out nearby Malindi market; a visit to the famous Gedi ruins; a safari out to one of the great national parks (Maasai Mara, Tsavo, Amboseli or Nakaru)

YOU SHOULD KNOW:
The coral pillar that stands prominently above the sea in Malindi was erected by Portuguese explorer Vasco da Gama in 1498, when he called in search of a guide who could direct him towards India. There are numerous 'beach boys' in Malindi who tend to pester tourists relentlessly.

Giraffe Manor

WHERE:
Karen, Nairobi
COST:
Fairly but not excessively expensive, and the experience is worth it
BEST TIME OF YEAR:
The giraffes are always there!
DON'T MISS:
One of the house specialities – Mount Kenya smoked trout pâté; superb views of the Ngong Hills
THINGS TO DO:
Eat a lantern-lit dinner on the terrace, beneath burning equatorial stars; visit the Karen Blixen Museum, where the Danish author of *Out of Africa* lived for many years; hike the short nature trail at the Giraffe Centre, which runs a conservation programme; a trip to the Maasai Market for crafts, curios and ethnic artefacts
YOU SHOULD KNOW:
The Nairobi National Park is adjacent to Giraffe Manor and staff can arrange dawn drives and/or day trips.

Hustle, bustle – for all that each one is different, modern cities are all the same in that respect. Kenya's capital, Nairobi, is no exception. East Africa's most populous city has three million inhabitants and a serious traffic problem, so it's definitely not the place to go looking for a fantastic wildlife break, right? Wrong, actually, for Giraffe Manor – in the suburbs just 20 km (12 mi) from the city centre – may have a Nairobi postal address, but it's in another world.

This is definitely a place to write home about – a private green enclave within 57 ha (141 ac) of indigenous forest, where visitors enjoy the soothing charms of a classic boutique hotel . . . and giraffes with everything. Built in the 1930s to serve Kenya's European elite and pioneering tourists, Giraffe Lodge has a famous resident herd of Rothschild Giraffes (along with assorted animals such as bush buck, warthog and dik dik, plus nearly 200 species of bird).

The place looks like an old-fashioned English country house, and the comfortable interior and superb level of service maintain the impression of stepping back into a bygone era of elegance and style. The rooms are large and furnished with antiques. A wonderful country-house sitting room is the perfect place to relax, while those using the shady verandah and terrace invariably find inquisitive giraffes wandering up in anticipation of a treat. Open fires dispel any evening chill, and fine dining is the order of the night. Just don't be surprised to look up and find a giraffe spying through your bedroom window, or a horned head dipping down eagerly in the hope of sharing your breakfast. Not only the best place to stay in Nairobi, but magical with it!

Chumbe Island

Chumbe Island punches well above its weight. It is a tiny coral island 19 km (12 mi) off mainland Zanzibar which lacks even one decent beach, yet has carried off major awards for ecotourism. Its appeal rests on exclusivity. The whole island is part of a major marine national park put in place when the Tanzanian military closed its base. By then it had already started the long cleansing process which stringent park rules completed. Now Chumbe is encircled by a shallow reef containing 90 per cent of more than 200 coral species found in East Africa, with 350 species of fish, turtles and lobster flourishing in its waters. This is the famous Chumbe Island Coral Park.

Chumbe Island Lodge is run for the Park's benefit. Only 14 visitors are allowed on the island at any one time, housed in the seven beautifully sympathetic eco-*bandas* lined up beside the lodge. Their grass-thatch roofs bend and curl gracefully to the sky, a harmonious vision that masks really thoughtful eco-solutions to the provision of luxury. The lodge itself is a work of art, its soaring *makuti* thatch reminiscent of the Sydney Opera House. Its green credentials are a draw in themselves, but there is a huge range of activities to absorb visitors. Few are conventional. Guided walks through the island's lush forest regularly tease out giant coconut crabs, the world's biggest (and one of the rarest), which scramble to the top of palms for their prey.

The multi-coloured corals, dense coral-rag forests, breeze-filled palms and even the wonderful food all belong in a beach paradise that Chumbe could be. But by devoting itself to genuine eco-economics, it has made itself unique. Visitors – even honeymooners – agree.

WHERE:
Off the coast of southwest Zanzibar
COST:
Reasonable to mildly expensive
BEST TIME OF YEAR:
Mid June to mid April
DON'T MISS:
The coral gardens and coral-rag forest; stress-free(!) snorkelling with the *Floating Information Module*, an inflatable ring with illustrated colour plates for underwater identifications; opening the front wall of your *banda* to the starlight – and getting a view over the ocean at sunrise
THINGS TO DO:
Walks around the rock pools and tideline interchange; climbing the 131 steps to the top of the old lighthouse; joining the staff in whatever projects they could use some help with – it's the Chumbe ethic; taking the boat out and meditating above the reef
YOU SHOULD KNOW:
Chumbe Island is a malarial area. Scuba diving is banned on the reefs. On a coral island like Chumbe there's no groundwater – but all the buildings are ingeniously designed to trap, filter and store their own rain. Day trips to Chumbe are possible – but only if there are fewer than 14 people staying the night.

Ngorongoro Crater Lodge

WHERE:
Ngorongoro Crater, Ngorongoro Conservation Area
COST:
Astronomical
BEST TIME OF YEAR:
Any time, but there are fewer people and the crater is at its greenest in the rainy season, April to June
DON'T MISS:
Excursions to Lakes Ndutu and Eyasi; the flamingoes at Empakaai Crater
THINGS TO DO:
Walking safaris; game drives; birdwatching; watching Maasai herdsmen at work; visiting a Maasai cultural village; tucking into a delicious bush breakfast

Ngorongoro Crater Lodge has been described as 'Maasai meets Versailles', and that just about sums it up. This must surely be the most spectacular Safari lodge in all of Africa.

The natural setting alone is enough to enchant. The lodge is perched at an awesome altitude of 2,375 m (7,800 ft) on the rim of the Ngorongoro Crater. You look down to a 260 sq km (100 sq mi) crater floor 600 m (2,000 ft) below, where 30,000 wild animals – including all of the Big Five – roam free. The almost mystical beauty of this view, a primeval African landscape seen through swirling mists of low cloud, is heart stopping – and unforgettable.

A Maasai warrior greets you when you arrive and escorts you past the zebras that placidly graze in the lodge's grounds. There are 30 guest huts, built out of traditional mud and thatch and arranged to look

like a fairytale version of a Maasai *manyatta* (village). But there any resemblance to Africa ends. The hut's interior of wood-panelled walls, open log fire, king-size bed, soft furnishings of brocades and velvets, silk curtains and crystal chandelier is like walking onto a period film set. The African bush is the last place in the world one would expect to stumble across such baroque artifice. And the bizarre, over-the-top theme extends to the main lodge where you are served your evening meal amid leather armchairs, brocade sofas, rococo gilt mirrors and yet more crystal chandeliers.

A personal butler attends to your every whim. He even prepares your evening bath for you, scattering rose petals into the running water. The Ngorongoro Crater Lodge aims to make you feel like royalty and guess what? It succeeds.

YOU SHOULD KNOW:
The Ngorongoro Crater is the largest intact caldera in the world. The 'Big Five' is a game-hunting expression for the five wild animals that are most dangerous and difficult to kill – lion, leopard, African elephant, Cape buffalo and rhinoceros.

Shamba Kilole Lodge

WHERE:
Mafia Island
COST:
Budget
BEST TIME OF YEAR:
For diving, October to March; for sea-turtle hatching, June and July
DON'T MISS:
The traditional boat-building yards on Chole and Jibondo islets; the lighthouse at Ras Mkumbi, for great views and magnificent baobab trees; a picnic at Kanga beach

Anyone who is concerned about the environment yet wants to escape from the crowd will be in their element at Shamba Kilole. It is an unpretentious guesthouse on Mafia Island, the main island of a little coral archipelago south of Zanzibar. Even though Mafia is in some of the best diving waters of the Indian Ocean, it is barely on the tourist map and is still almost completely unspoilt – so the charming Italian couple who own Shamba Kilole are doing their bit to keep it that way.

There are several places to stay on Mafia but Shamba Kilole is the only certified eco-lodge. It is small and friendly, with a really personal atmosphere. There are six bungalows built with local stone and brick in a lovingly tended 5-ha (12-ac) palm-tree garden. They offer a blissful view of the white sands and aquamarine ocean of Kilole Bay. The air is filled with a chorus of exotic birds and there are mangrove forests and shoreline rock pools to explore.

The bungalows are simply furnished in an attractive ethnic style, with small private terraces. Each has its own bathroom with (drinkable) water from a bore well. All the basic comforts are here – a 16-m (52-ft) swimming pool (with an environmentally friendly chlorination system), a bar with free internet access and exceptionally good home-cooked dinners in the evening – but no superfluous frills. The hospitable staff at the lodge will organize diving lessons, boat trips and cultural trails for you.

There is hardly any tourist infrastructure on Mafia Island so don't expect a vibrant nightlife. Come here for serenity, warm hospitality and the glorious Indian Ocean.

THINGS TO DO:
Snorkelling; diving; swimming with whale sharks; boat trips in a *dhow*; watching turtles hatch; cycling; birdwatching; visiting archaeological sites; cultural excursions
YOU SHOULD KNOW:
Mafia Island has some of the richest coral reefs in the world – there are more than 400 species of fish and terrific dive sites. Shamba Kilole is on a mangrove forest shoreline but there is a beach nearby.

Serengeti Bushtops Camp

At Bushtops Camp you'll experience elemental natural wonder but with all the cosseting service a luxury hotel can offer. The camp is in remote wilderness in the northernmost part of the Serengeti Plains where mile after mile of golden grassland is interrupted only by the occasional thicket of acacia trees and the weird granite *kopjes* (isolated rock outcrops) that sprout dramatically from the ground in this part of the Serengeti.

The 12 luxury tents are not just lavish – they're also absolutely vast. You get 120 sq m (1,300 sq ft) of accommodation, including a huge verandah with an open-air shower and outdoor hot tub, and a telescope for observing the animals. The tents are pitched on a west-facing ridge, well apart for complete privacy, facing towards the evening sun for sensational sunset views over the Serengeti grasslands. A communal lounge bar and dining tent serves excellent food with an outstandingly fine selection of wines. In the evenings you can choose to dine inside by flickering lantern light, outdoors around a camp fire under a canopy of stars or, if you prefer solitude, in the privacy of your own tent.

Bushtops is the perfect place to witness one of nature's most awe-inspiring marvels – the Great Migration, when more than two million wild animals cross the River Mara. At nightfall the grasslands pulsate with life. You can listen to an orchestra of animals establishing their territory – the roar of a lion, the sharp growl of a leopard, the raucous yips and whoops of hyenas and an elephant trumpeting in the distance. Here, notions of time lose all meaning and you find yourself enveloped in the infinite mystery of nature.

WHERE:
Near Kogatende Ranger Post, Serengeti National Park
COST:
Astronomical
BEST TIME OF YEAR:
June to November for huge herds of migrating animals; February and March to witness topi antelopes giving birth
DON'T MISS:
The Great Migration; trying to spot the Big Five (lion, leopard, African elephant, Cape buffalo and rhinoceros); crocodiles in the River Mara
THINGS TO DO:
Game drives; guided game walks; birdwatching
YOU SHOULD KNOW:
There is plenty of wildlife all year and you can enjoy round-the-clock butler service, complimentary massages in your tent, satellite wifi and cellphone (erratic signal), meals and two game drives a day – all included in the price.

Vamizi Island Lodge

WHERE:
Quirimbas Islands
COST:
Astronomical (but feel good about it!)
BEST TIME OF YEAR:
December to January, March to April, July to September
DON'T MISS:
Neptune's Arm – one of the world's top-ten dive sites
THINGS TO DO:
Scuba diving; snorkelling; kayaking; windsurfing; *dhow* trips; beachcombing; nature walks; whale-watching; turtle-watching; fishing; cultural visits; picnics
YOU SHOULD KNOW:
Vamizi is one of the best diving sites in the world. The island lies at a point where the ocean floor drops suddenly and there is a convergence of cool and warm equatorial currents. The 1-km (just over half a mile) deep underwater cliff off the coast is a habitat for a vast amount of marine life, including big game fish like tuna and marlin.

Over the past century, the tourist industry has spread its imprint all over the planet, despoiling pristine landscapes and exhausting natural resources. But on Vamizi only the tourist trade can actually save the island from human desecration. Setting up a resort here was fraught with problems, but determination to preserve this idyllic little slice of heaven has resulted in the concept of 'barefoot luxury', whereby tourism contributes vitally needed funds towards local conservation projects.

Vamizi is a Robinson Crusoe romance – a tiny crescent-shaped tropical island, just 12 km (7.5 mi) long and 1 km (just over half a mile) wide which supports 112 species of bird and endangered Samango monkeys and (offshore) 180 kinds of coral and 400 species of fish. There are just 12 thatched wooden villas on the beach. Shaded by trees, the villas are super-large (170 sq m/1,830 sq ft) with living areas open to the elements, furnished in 'castaway chic' style with enormous beds and marble bathrooms.

Dine by lantern light in the communal lodge or gather round a beach grill to eat freshly caught fish; have reiki and shiatsu treatments; do dawn yoga exercises on the sand and meditate on the vast Indian Ocean stretching before you in an ever-changing kaleidoscope of turquoise, cobalt, emerald and viridian. You will experience some of the best diving in the world, see dolphins, watch a humpback whale breach and turtles nesting on the beach. The calm water and gently sloping beach is perfect for children to frolic in. You and they can swap the trappings of 21st-century urban life for beach living at its best – pure 'barefoot luxury'.

Moremi Crossing Camp

If you thrive on back-to-nature adventures, Moremi Crossing in the Okavango Delta is a marvellous place to stay. You journey by light aircraft and then by river to a 16-tent camp on a remote island in the Moremi Game Reserve, a 5,000-sq-km (1,930-sq-mi) wetland wilderness full of birds and animals.

The amenities are quite simple here. You sleep in a spacious twin-bedded, vintage safari tent pitched on a raised wooden deck, and have your own shower and toilet facilities. It's very comfortable but don't expect any frills. Moremi Crossing is committed to ecotourism. Hot water and power are supplied by solar energy and there is a hi-tech waste-disposal system, ensuring that the camp's imprint on the environment is kept to the bare minimum.

The communal bar and dining area is a picturesque, multi-level, balustraded wooden deck covered with a thatched roof that blends in with the surrounding woods of fig, palm and giant ebony trees. It has a spectacular view across the Boro River to Chief's Island, the largest land mass in the delta. Once the Batawana tribal chief's personal hunting ground, Chief's Island is a natural habitat for countless animals that are attracted by the copious water supply, sweet-tasting grasses and thorn trees.

The camp guides are knowledgeable and enthusiastic, and you are likely to see just about every kind of wild animal you can think of – elephants, hippos, giraffes, antelopes, rhinos, lions, and cheetahs – and more than 450 species of bird. And, as a high point in your wilderness adventure, you can go on a *mokoro* (dug-out punt) expedition to bivouac under the stars – a magical experience of primeval Africa in all its pristine glory.

WHERE:
Okavango Delta
COST:
It's expensive, but everything (meals, drinks, guides, boat trips, etc) is included in the price.
BEST TIME OF YEAR:
Early July to the end of October, when the rainy season is over but the waters are still high
DON'T MISS:
A sunset boat cruise; a night of wilderness camping
THINGS TO DO:
Guided game walks; boat and *mokoro* cruises; gazing at beautiful views
YOU SHOULD KNOW:
Okavango Delta is the largest inland delta in the world. Water pours down from the Angolan mountains and drains into the Kalahari Desert, creating a seasonal oasis in an otherwise arid country. The rising waters between June and August attract hordes of birds and animals. Expect to see a greater concentration of wildlife here than anywhere else in Africa – there are an estimated 200,000 animals.

Hotel Heinitzburg

WHERE:
Windhoek
COST:
Reasonable
BEST TIME OF YEAR:
May to late October
DON'T MISS:
Historical paintings in the Knight's Room; exploring Katutura township on a bike tour; a day trip to Arnhem Caves
THINGS TO DO:
Sightseeing; hiking; horse riding; mountain biking; golf; swimming
YOU SHOULD KNOW:
Children are welcome here. There is no wifi in rooms and the connection is rather temperamental in the lobby.

Beautifully situated on top of a hill, the Heinitzburg is one of three castles in the city of Windhoek, all local landmarks designed by German architect William Sander. It was built in 1914 and bought by Count von Schwerin as an extravagant gesture of love for his fiancée Margarethe von Heinitz. When the castle was turned into a boutique hotel in 1966, an attractive annexe was added to provide extra rooms.

The Heinitzburg has an old-fashioned charm. Its 16 unusually large, airy rooms all have big windows looking out over the city below and are elegantly appointed with hand-carved furniture and opulent fabrics in muted tones. The hotel surroundings are luxurious and the service is impeccable. It's all faintly reminiscent of the *belle époque*: an air of romantic luxury pervades the entire building.

The hotel grounds are beautifully planted and well maintained, and the open-air swimming pool, although small, is especially inviting. The Garden Terrace is a perfect place to sit and watch the glorious African sunset, with evening cocktail to hand. And Leo's, the hotel restaurant, has a well-deserved reputation as one of the best places to eat in Namibia. The food and wine is of a consistently high standard and the ambience is delightful, offering another lovely view over the city.

The Heinitzburg is perfect as a gentle introduction to Namibia at the start of a trip, or as a last couple of days' treat right at the end, to recover from the rigours of the Namib Desert and enjoy a bit of luxury in the form of a friendly welcome of canapés and champagne, a slap-up meal and a comfortable bed.

Manolo Boutique Hotel

This intimate little hotel brings urban chic and cutting-edge design to a Cape Town suburb. Ensconced in the quiet residential area of Tamboerskloof, which spreads around the lower slopes of Table Mountain, Manolo is a brilliant location for exploring this most vibrant of South Africa's cities. You are just a short taxi ride from the sights and attractions of the city centre, while you are on the right side of town for making the most of the country's most iconic mountain. The views from the cableway that whisks you up to the summit plateau are stupendous but, if you are in reasonably good shape, it would be a shame to miss out on tackling one of the hiking routes to the top.

Each of the rooms at Manolo has its own character and there are quirky little design touches everywhere. The prevailing white of walls and furniture is punctuated by dazzling splashes of colour, including some funky modern art, and the urban cool is further mitigated by the warming presence of fireplaces. There is a small lap pool and a retractable sun roof in the public lounge area. But the chief glory of a stay here is the fabulous views – of Table Mountain and over the city and harbour. The rooms are designed to take full advantage of the elevated setting and there can be few more seductive experiences than lying on a lounger on your own private patio, a glass of the hotel's own chilled bubbly in your hand, and feeling the ocean breeze waft over you as the sun's dying rays play on the spectacular mountain face.

WHERE:
Leeukloof Drive, Cape Town
COST:
Reasonable
BEST TIME OF YEAR:
Any time (Cape Town is not a weather-sensitive destination)
DON'T MISS:
That rewarding climb for a view to die for – of the various hiking routes up Table Mountain the one up Platteklip Gorge is probably the best
THINGS TO DO:
Sightseeing; watching the sunset; swimming; hiking
YOU SHOULD KNOW:
At certain times of year Manolo offers a fourth night free when you book a three-night stay.

Mount Nelson Hotel

WHERE:
Orange Street, Cape Town
COST:
Expensive
BEST TIME OF YEAR:
All year round
DON'T MISS:
Afternoon tea at the Mount Nelson is a Cape Town institution – it's a splendidly indulgent affair with sandwiches, cakes and fancies of every description.

The Mount Nelson is a Cape Town landmark and one of the most famous legacies of the colonial era. Although this grand establishment opened its doors when South Africa was still a British colony, the year – 1899 – was a troubled one in the country's history, marking the start of the bitterly fought war between the British and the Dutch settler community – the Boers. Nevertheless, the hotel flourished and rapidly built a reputation among the international travelling elite. In the modern era the 'Pink Lady', as Mount Nelson is affectionately known, has adapted effortlessly to the no less discerning demands of mass tourism and the jet-age globetrotter.

This is a place to stay if you enjoy being reminded of earlier, more glamorous times and don't mind the odd over-the-top decorative flourish. An atmosphere of old-fashioned refinement and luxury greets you from the moment you approach the main building along the grand palm-lined avenue, yet it comes together with the highest contemporary standards of service and amenities.

The rooms and suites are symphonies of chintz and floral fabrics and the old-world charm of the place is continued in its two restaurants, including the award-winning Planet Restaurant. Mount Nelson's most precious asset is the 3.5 ha (9 ac) of landscaped gardens surrounding it, forming an oasis of green calm at the heart of this bustling city. The gardens feature two heated swimming pools and a delightful row of historic homes which have been converted into suites in the style of English country cottages, complete with rose garden – the perfect setting for a romantic break.

THINGS TO DO:
Sightseeing; shopping; swimming; tennis; squash; spa treatments; fitness centre
YOU SHOULD KNOW:
The Pink Lady does not stand on its dignity these days and is genuinely welcoming to families with young children – there is a dedicated activity centre for the under 12s, and even a lounge set aside for teenagers.

Molori Safari Lodge

The Madikwe Game Reserve in the far north of the country is one of South Africa's better-kept secrets. Situated some 400 km (250 mi) northwest of Johannesburg, Madikwe's nearest major settlement is Gaborone, the capital of neighbouring Botswana. As its location suggests, the reserve – the fourth largest in the country – is less visited than places like the Kruger so it is a good place to come for a more peaceful safari experience. And because day visitors are not allowed here, tourism is effectively restricted to those who come to stay at one of Madikwe's luxury safari lodges.

One of the very best lodges is Molori, which is strategically sited by a water hole and has sweeping views of a broad valley and distant mountains. Molori promises 'an authentic connection to your surroundings', while unashamedly offering the last word in comfort and refinement. You may be in the middle of the bush, but there's absolutely no reason for you to slum it. The five attractive suites are all different and make imaginative use of local materials and colourful African prints. Each airy suite has floor-to-ceiling glass doors which fold back onto an expansive wooden deck and your own private infinity pool. A telescope is thoughtfully provided to help with your wildlife-watching and the espresso coffee machine is a welcome extra touch.

Being here is, of course, all about the wildlife and your Molori experience is tailored to giving you the best possible opportunities to spot a range of wildlife – including the Big Five, all of which are found here. Indeed, Madikwe has South Africa's second-largest elephant population.

WHERE:
Madikwe Game Reserve, North West Province
COST:
Expensive
BEST TIME OF YEAR:
June to September
DON'T MISS:
The lodge has its own planetarium in which one of the largest privately owned telescopes in southern Africa enables you to explore the breathtaking night skies.
THINGS TO DO:
Wildlife-watching; safari drives; bush tracking; swimming; spa treatments; massage; fishing; stargazing
YOU SHOULD KNOW:
Molori arranges daily shuttle flights from Johannesburg airport to its own airstrip. Rates include all meals and two 4x4 game drives per day.

Grootbos Private Nature Reserve

This well-established eco-resort has won numerous awards in the 20 years it has been open, for pioneering work on flora conservation and land management – all achieved without compromise to the visitor experience. Grootbos's 27 free-standing luxury suites are grouped around two lodges, each with a different character. The Garden Lodge has a distinctly African feel with its use of stone, thatch and dark woods, while the brickwork and paler woods used throughout the Forest Lodge create an altogether lighter, more airy impression. Each suite comes with sun deck, infinity pool, fireplace and even under-floor heating. The latest addition to the Grootbos complex is a separate villa with six suites. Sleeping up to 12, this is available for exclusive hire only and comes with a personal chef, butler and guide.

The star attraction here is the location, a few kilometres inland from the Atlantic coast of the Western Cape. The buildings have been designed to make the most of the setting. A mountain slope above Gansbaai offers incredible views over Walker Bay and to the distant Cape of Good Hope. And as the prospect is a west-facing one, you are guaranteed some truly memorable sunsets over the ocean.

This area is noted for its distinctive flora, especially the *fynbos* plant, and Grootbos's 1,000 ha (2,470 ac) are covered with numerous species of the shrub, creating a riot of colour when they are in flower. Walker Bay is also one of the best places in the world for watching whales. Because the bay has deep water, these magnificent creatures can be seen easily from the shore, as well as from the customary boat trips.

WHERE:
Gansbaai, Western Cape
COST:
Expensive
BEST TIME OF YEAR:
July to December
DON'T MISS:
For the ultimate adrenalin experience try being submerged in a steel cage (no diving experience necessary) in order to get irrationally close to a great white shark.
THINGS TO DO:
Guided nature walks; horse riding; 4x4 jeep safaris; whale-watching; swimming; enjoying sunsets
YOU SHOULD KNOW:
If your ecological principles (and wallet) permit, Grootbos's private airstrip allows you to access the reserve by light plane or helicopter.

La Residence

Set in the heart of South Africa's wine country, this exclusive retreat will have a particular appeal to anyone with a serious appreciation of fine cuisine and great wines. La Residence lies on the edge of Franschhoek, a charming little town of white-washed Victorian houses set in a verdant valley of rolling vineyards ringed by mountains. The name pays homage to the place's French origins (*Franschhoek* translates as 'French corner' in Afrikaans) when Huguenot refugees – Protestants fleeing persecution in their native France – settled here at the end of the 17th century. The French influence remains very much in evidence – in the place names, the architecture and the remarkable number of high-class restaurants.

As its own name suggests, La Residence enters into the Gallic spirit of things with gusto and its elaborate interiors are redolent of an *ancien regime* establishment where no expense has been spared on the fixtures and fittings. Each of the 11 suites has a contrasting character; some sport exotic and oriental touches, while others show a more contemporary flair. All have private balconies looking out over rose gardens and fountains that would not look out of place in the grounds of a French château.

The most significant legacy of those early French settlers has of course been wine-making. With over 20 wine estates in the Franschhoek valley alone, this is an excellent base from which to sample the wines of the Cape and to learn more about their production. Franschhoek is often described as the country's gourmet capital, so you will have no difficulty finding world-class cooking to accompany the local vintages.

WHERE:
Franschhoek, Western Cape
COST:
Astronomical
BEST TIME OF YEAR:
September to June
DON'T MISS:
Alfresco lunches among the vineyards and ancient oaks
THINGS TO DO:
Wine tasting; fine dining; swimming; golf; trout fishing; horse riding; carriage rides; quad biking; hot-air ballooning
YOU SHOULD KNOW:
La Residence has its own vineyard and has recently produced its first vintages, of Shiraz and Cabernet Sauvignon.

Phinda Game Reserve

WHERE:
Northern KwaZulu-Natal
COST:
Astronomical
BEST TIME OF YEAR:
This is an all-season destination.
DON'T MISS:
The sunset cruises on the lovely Mzinene River
THINGS TO DO:
Wildlife-watching; 4x4 game drives; guided bushwalking; birdwatching; horse riding; swimming
YOU SHOULD KNOW:
You are only a short drive away from some beautifully unspoilt beaches and a dip in the Indian Ocean.

Phinda is a private reserve in the tranquil north of KwaZulu-Natal. Located close to the World Heritage site of iSimangaliso Wetland Park, Phinda is special because within its relatively small area – some 230 sq km (89 sq mi) – it encompasses no fewer than seven distinct habitats: mixed bushveld savanna, open woodland, palmveld (grassland dotted with palm trees), wetlands, evergreen forest, tree-covered hillsides and, most precious of all, dry sand forest – a rare survival of the ancient dune forests which once carpeted this coastline. This unique natural cocktail makes for a wonderful diversity of wildlife viewing opportunities.

The accommodation options at Phinda are correspondingly

varied. You can choose from four lodges sited in dramatically different environments. The Mountain Lodge has split-level suites, while the suites at the smaller Rock Lodge are adobe structures designed in the style of a *hacienda*. Both offer sweeping views over the southern part of the reserve. In the north the Vlei Lodge has six thatched suites which border the wetlands and their stunning birdlife (over 400 bird species have been recorded at Phinda). The most unusual dwellings are at the Forest Lodge, whose suites lie deep in the sand forest. Raised up on stilts and with floor-to-ceiling glass walls, they have won numerous awards for their eco-sensitive design.

Wherever you choose to stay you are guaranteed exceptional wildlife experiences. All the Big Five are found at Phinda, including the rare black rhino, and the keen-sighted park rangers will help you see as much as possible on bush walks or the twice-daily game drives. It is particularly known for the chance to observe cheetahs in the wild.

Makkedaat Caves

You can't go much further back to basics than sleeping in a cave and that's just what is on offer at this site in the Eastern Cape, around 120 km (75 mi) west of Port Elizabeth. There are five accommodation options from which to choose. These range from Makkedaat itself and Van Terrebert – natural caves which have been enclosed with timber and rock and can sleep up to eight and ten respectively – to the Aalwyn and Dawid se Baks, which are rock overhangs that have been left open to the elements.

For romantics and nature lovers there is also the Dassiebak, a cosy cliffside hideaway meant for two. Each cave is kitted out for basic self-catering and has running water, hot shower, flushing toilet and a small kitchen with sink and gas stove. Van Terrebert and Dawid caves are equipped with solar-powered electricity, but you'll get a more primal experience at one of the others where paraffin lamps and candles are your only source of illumination at night.

All the caves are east-facing so, while you may not get much of a lie-in, you will have grandstand views of the sunrise to compensate. They also have a large outdoor area perfect for a traditional African *braai* (barbecue) and for spinning yarns of an evening around a crackling fire. The Makkedaat caves are located within the Baviaanskloof Wilderness Area that comprises 270 sq km (105 sq mi) of rugged mountainous terrain, river valleys and red sandstone hills. The area was populated by Khoisan hunter-gatherers tens of thousands of years ago – early ancestors who may well have used these same rock shelters themselves.

WHERE:
50 km (31 mi) east of Willowmore, Eastern Cape
COST:
Budget
BEST TIME OF YEAR:
All year round (the caves are cool in summer and warm in winter)
DON'T MISS:
The numerous examples of prehistoric rock art in the area
THINGS TO DO:
Hiking; birdwatching; mountain biking; 4x4 trips; stargazing
YOU SHOULD KNOW:
You can reach the caves in a conventional vehicle but you will need a 4x4 to head any further east into the Wilderness Area. You need to bring your own bedding and it's best, for obvious reasons, to avoid arriving in the dark!

River Lodge, Lion Sands Reserve

WHERE:
Sabi Sand Game Reserve, Mpumalanga province
COST:
Expensive
BEST TIME OF YEAR:
August to November, February to May (this avoids the South African school holidays when the Kruger becomes extremely busy)
DON'T MISS:
The unforgettable experience of a fully catered breakfast or dinner in the bush
THINGS TO DO:
Game drives; bush walks; swimming; fishing; spa treatments; stargazing and guided night walks
YOU SHOULD KNOW:
This is a malaria risk area so you should take appropriate medical precautions before your visit.

The Kruger National Park is synonymous with big game and big wildlife experiences. South Africa's largest and most famous national park extends for 350 km (217 mi) on a north-south axis along the border with Mozambique in the country's far northeast. Acting as important buffers along the park's western boundary, a string of private game reserves includes the Sabi Sand Reserve, which has been a pioneering force in the development of sustainable wilderness tourism.

With a lush landscape kept fresh throughout the year by the two rivers – the Sabie and the Sand – that traverse the reserve, this place takes some beating as a safari location. The guaranteed water sources attract an astonishing range of animals and birdlife, including of course the Big Five (lion, leopard, elephant, rhino and buffalo), but also other stars like cheetah, sable antelope, zebra and wildebeest. No fence separates Sabi Sand along its 50-km (31-mi) shared boundary with the Kruger itself, so the wildlife is able to range freely.

Lion Sands is a small, family-run reserve within Sabi Sand and River Lodge is a beautifully appointed safari lodge at its heart. The lodge sits on the banks of the gently flowing Sabie River, looking east over the Kruger. The 18 thatched units have air conditioning in the bedrooms and both indoor and outdoor showers. With two swimming pools, wooden viewing decks, fireplaces and a luxury spa, this is the perfect place to unwind after a busy day in the bush and swap those tales of big-game encounters. In fact, the peace and serenity are only likely to be disturbed by the inquisitive local monkey population.

Singita Kruger

The South African company Singita has for some years been a leading name in the market for safari experiences that combine top-end luxury with sustainable and environmentally responsible tourism practices. Their portfolio of safari lodges throughout southern Africa includes two within the Kruger National Park. Singita has a 13,500-ha (33,360-ac) concession in the central part of the park, close to the border with Mozambique. The area is dominated by the Lebombo mountain range and the diverse habitats include rocky outcrops and stands of imposing euphorbia trees.

There is an astonishing richness and variety of wildlife here. In order to maximize viewing opportunities, Singita's two lodges are strategically sited beside rivers and waterholes where the animals come to drink. Lebombo Lodge, with 15 suites the larger of the two, is artfully concealed in a thickly wooded hillside and commands sweeping views of the park, while more intimate Sweni has just six suites raised on stilts beside the tranquil river of the same name.

Singita's immaculate suites exude discreet luxury with all the trappings you would expect at these sky-high prices, including air conditioning and both inside and outside showers. Your own viewing deck gives you the option of sleeping under the stars if you so choose. The public areas include a swimming pool, health spa, gym and traditional *boma* area for alfresco dining. Singita's overall philosophy is based on the promise of 'touching the earth lightly'. During your stay, in addition to the safari drives and bush walks, you will be given the chance to learn more about the many conservation and community projects with which the company is involved.

WHERE:
Kruger National Park
COST:
Astronomical
BEST TIME OF YEAR:
All year round (the chillier mornings and evenings of the winter months – June to September – are compensated by the enhanced visibility of wildlife due to the sparser vegetation)
DON'T MISS:
This part of the Kruger is particularly noted for its lions and you may be lucky enough to see the famous Mountain Pride.
THINGS TO DO:
Game drives; guided bushwalking; mountain biking; swimming; archery; stargazing; wine tasting
YOU SHOULD KNOW:
No children under 10 are allowed at Lebombo Lodge. You should take anti-malarial precautions before staying at either of these lodges.

Tsala Treetop Lodge

As its name might indicate, Tsala really does place you up in the forest canopy. And this is not any old forest but one of the most ancient on the whole continent. The dense woodlands that tumble down the slopes of the Tsitsikamma Mountains to the Indian Ocean constitute one of the few tracts of indigenous coastal forest to have survived in South Africa, although aggressive logging in the past has sadly left only 650 sq km (251 sq mi) of the original woodlands today. All the same, there's plenty to lose yourself in and Tsala is the ideal base from which to explore an environment which is home to some true giants of the forest, including the kalander, ironwood and stinkwood trees.

The lodge's buildings are perched high on stilts in the heart of the forest. Connected by wooden boardwalks, their stone, wood and glass construction helps them blend naturally with their surroundings. The interior decoration is described as 'Afro-baroque' – earthy tones, multi-coloured print fabrics and solid hand-made furniture. The suites each have a separate sitting room with wood-burning stove, private infinity pool and timber deck. The views out over the forest roof to the distant hills will make it hard for you to move, although the spectacular meals cooked up in the Zinzi restaurant will probably win out in the end. If you are part of a larger group and would like more self-sufficiency, the two-bedroom villas recently opened at Tsala are a good option and are equipped with small kitchens.

The Tsitsikamma forest is famous for its birdlife. Over 250 species have been recorded here, including the African crowned eagle, one of the country's most awesome birds of prey.

WHERE:
Near Plettenberg Bay, towards the eastern end of the Garden Route
COST:
Expensive
BEST TIME OF YEAR:
Any time (this coastline enjoys a temperate climate throughout the year, although you might want to avoid the crowds that descend on the Garden Route during the high season, December to February)
DON'T MISS:
A sunset cruise on the lovely Knysna lagoon
THINGS TO DO:
Hiking; birdwatching; forest picnics; canopy tour (aerial runway); horse riding; swimming; massage
YOU SHOULD KNOW:
Unusually for an establishment of this class, Tsala does not make a single supplement levy.

Heritage Le Telfair Golf and Spa Resort

The Indian Ocean island of Mauritius is an idyllic holiday destination – guaranteed climate, enchanting natural scenery, a wealth of flora and fauna, plus pristine beaches. Heritage Le Telfair is a veritable paradise in this island haven, situated in what was once an 18th-century sugar plantation, the 25-sq-km (10-sq-mi) estate of Domaine de Bel Ombre on the secluded southwest coast.

A plantation-style house stands next to the ocean in lush tropical gardens, sheltered by wooded hills which dramatically descend to the coast in an awesome 500-m (1,640-ft) drop. Your room is in one of 20 villas around the grounds. The French windows open out onto a private verandah, while dark wooden floors, ceiling fan, period-style furniture and spacious bathroom almost make you feel you're in the colonial age – until, that is, you're reminded of the 21st century by amenities such as air conditioning, TV, CD/DVD player, internet access and even a hairdryer.

The resort is particularly clean and well maintained with magnificent service, delicious food, a children's club, and an in-room child-minding service. The 18-hole hillside golf course overlooks a sparkling blue lagoon, and the immaculate private beach is pure-white sand. The wondrous spa has the tranquil atmosphere of a sanctuary with splashing fountains and burbling brooks flowing through its garden. It has sensational *ayurvedic* treatments as well as more conventional ones, two gazebos to unwind in and a secret hideaway with private pool.

Whatever your age and whether you want a family holiday, romantic honeymoon, cultural and historical adventure or just want to laze on the beach, Heritage Le Telfair will measure up to even the most exacting expectations of five-star luxury.

WHERE:
Domaine de Bel Ombre, Mauritius
COST:
Expensive
BEST TIME OF YEAR:
All year round, although it's at its hottest with highest humidity from January to April
DON'T MISS:
Le Morne Cultural Landscape UNESCO World Heritage site; Chamarel Falls beauty spot; dinner at the 19th-century Chateau de Bel Ombre; Ganga Talao crater lake; exploring Frédérica Nature Reserve on a quad bike
THINGS TO DO:
Golf; tennis; table tennis; hiking; cycling and mountain biking; horse riding; swimming; scuba diving; snorkelling; parasailing; waterskiing; boating; fishing; birdwatching; yoga; historical and cultural sightseeing
YOU SHOULD KNOW:
Heritage Le Telfair is named after Charles Telfair, an early 19th-century Irish botanist and plant collector who established a botanical garden in Mauritius and worked to improve the conditions of the slaves on the sugar plantations.

Conrad Maldives Rangali Island

WHERE:
Rangali Island, Alif Dhaal (South Ari) Atoll
COST:
Astronomical
BEST TIME OF YEAR:
The dry season is from December to April but it's warm throughout the year. May to November is the best time for diving.
DON'T MISS:
A dolphin- and whale shark-watching cruise; the mini-submarine or glass-bottomed boat trip around the reef; dining 4 m (13 ft) underwater in the glass-walled Ithaa Restaurant while you watch the fish go by
THINGS TO DO:
Scuba diving; snorkelling; sailing; canoeing; windsurfing; fishing; boat trips; tennis; table tennis; beach volleyball; yoga classes; gambling in the casino
YOU SHOULD KNOW:
The Conrad Maldives is very family-friendly – there is a kids' club and child-minding service, children's menus and diving lessons for children aged over five. For safety reasons you cannot stay in the water villas with children aged under 12.

People stay in Conrad Hotels to bask in the unashamed hedonism that this luxury brand offers, and the Conrad Maldives is no exception. Rangali is a tropical island paradise offering a coral reef, palm-fringed sandy beach and crystal-clear blue lagoon. The natural surroundings alone are tempting enough, but add the lavish amenities of Conrad and you'll find yourself wallowing in your own personal version of heaven.

The Rangali resort runs across two coral islands which are linked by a 500-m (1,640-ft) causeway. You stay in an exceptionally roomy, luxurious private villa that is either on the beach, perched over the water's edge, or standing on stilts out in the lagoon. You can socialize as much or as little as you want – the villas all have a marvellous sense of seclusion and resort staff are charmingly attentive yet always unobtrusive.

The spa is not just a spa – it's an entire village within the resort, offering an astounding array of treatments, pools, chill-out sanctuaries and exercise regimes. For evening entertainment there's a casino and an outdoor cinema and you will eat wonderful food and savour a fantastic selection of wines in your choice of seven restaurants and four bars. It's definitely no hardship working your way through an international cuisine that ranges from Italian to Japanese, with everything in between.

The Maldives is renowned for its outstanding diving and, whether you're a beginner or an expert, this is the perfect place to chalk up some incredible underwater experiences (not least, eating in the underwater restaurant!) You will see manta rays, whale sharks, and turtles among the multitude of tropical fish. The Conrad Maldives is a holiday resort *par excellence*.

Soneva Gili Six Senses Floating Hotel

The Soneva Gili is the only resort in the Maldives which has all its villas afloat on the water. To get to this exclusive floating hotel you take a 20-minute speedboat taxi from the Maldives capital, Malé, to arrive at a picturesque village of 45 rustic villas strung out across the lagoon, accessed by a pontoon bridge.

Each spacious thatched villa floats in semi-seclusion, with its own water garden and sun deck, separate living and dining areas and a semi-roofless bathroom with steps down to the lagoon. For total escapism, go for one of the seven Crusoe villas. You can only get to these by rowing boat. Far out in the lagoon, surrounded by ocean and sky, with only the gentle sound of the lapping waves and the birds calling, you can unwind in complete privacy and peace.

The resort offers a huge range of activities on both land and water. It has a 30-m (100-ft) swimming pool for anyone who prefers pool to lagoon swimming, a great gym and the fabulous Six Senses Spa with glass-floored treatment rooms over the water, so you can gaze down at the mesmerizing view of the lagoon's coral garden while you have a massage.

The island restaurant serves wonderful fusion food in a lovely ambience, with beautiful views across the Indian Ocean. Or you can enjoy a private moonlit dinner on your floating deck and then climb up to your roof terrace to watch a night sky shimmering with countless stars before you turn in. The Floating Hotel is blissfully romantic, a place to relax and immerse yourself in the sensuous and spiritual beauty of your surroundings.

WHERE:
Lankanfushi, North Malé Atoll, Malé

COST:
Expensive or astronomical, depending on time of year

BEST TIME OF YEAR:
The dry season is from December to April, but it's warm throughout the year. May to November is the best time for diving.

DON'T MISS:
A sunset champagne cruise; a cultural excursion to nearby islands

THINGS TO DO:
Scuba diving; snorkelling; windsurfing; canoeing; sailing; deep-sea fishing; tennis; volleyball; *boules*; badminton

YOU SHOULD KNOW:
Soneva Gili has featured in *Condé Nast Traveller UK's* Gold List and has been the *World Travel Awards* winner as Indian Ocean's Leading Luxury Resort.

Anantara Dhigu Resort and Spa

WHERE:
Dhigufinolhu Island, South Malé Atoll
COST:
Astronomical
BEST TIME OF YEAR:
The dry season is from December to April, but it's warm throughout the year. May to November is the best time for diving.
DON'T MISS:
Sailing around the lagoon on a catamaran
THINGS TO DO:
Scuba diving; snorkelling; surfing; windsurfing; waterskiing; parasailing; kayaking; sailing; sea fishing; tennis; volleyball; badminton; island hopping
YOU SHOULD KNOW:
There's a kids' club for children aged three to 11 and babysitters are provided for infants. All villas are equipped with flat-screen TV, CD/DVD player, MP3 player and minibar.

The first Anantara spa resort opened in 2001 in Thailand. Since then Anantara has gained an enviable international reputation for its 'experience-based' resorts and Dhigu more than lives up to its reputation. Just a 35-minute water-taxi ride from Malé, Dhigu has 110 private villas, either on the beach or over the water, with private sun decks, outdoor splash tubs and a vast living space ranging from 110 to 400 sq m (1,184 to 4,305 sq ft), decorated in soothing tones that mirror the colours of the ocean, the sand and the sky outside.

The spa is perched over the lagoon and has a range of superb treatments aimed at getting your body and mind balanced and working together in harmony. The *ayurvedic* treatments really work – you emerge from the spa feeling completely calm and relaxed, yet bursting with renewed vigour. As well as the treatment programme, the spa holds yoga classes and guided morning meditation sessions on the beach.

Nine food outlets present guests with a selection of creative menus unequalled anywhere else in the Maldives, and you can arrange to have cooking classes with the resort's chefs to find out the secrets behind their delicious food. You can swim in the clear waters of the lagoon or in the beach-side infinity pool and have a workout in the gym, while internet addicts can retreat to the library to do some secret electronic surfing.

There is a phenomenal number of activities on offer and the resort is extremely well equipped. This is a brilliant place for chilling out, for honeymoon couples and for water-sports enthusiasts of all ages and abilities.

Veligandu Island Resort

WHERE:
Veligandu, North Ari Atoll
COST:
Expensive
BEST TIME OF YEAR:
The dry season is from December to April, but it's warm throughout the year. May to November is the best time for diving.
DON'T MISS:
Snorkelling; a *dhoni* (traditional Maldives fishing boat) trip; a sunset boat trip to see dolphins
THINGS TO DO:
Scuba diving; snorkelling; windsurfing; catamaran sailing; kayaking; surf biking; fishing; deep-sea trips; volleyball; football; badminton; lots in the indoor games room
YOU SHOULD KNOW:
Internet access is very expensive, as is the villa's minibar and the resort shop. Veligandu is geared for adults wanting a relaxing time in an idyllic setting. There is little in the way of children's entertainment here.

The Maldives is renowned for having some of the best spa resorts in the world but, even by Maldivian standards, Veligandu is outstanding in terms of value and atmosphere. It is on one of the more distant Maldives' tourist resorts, a small island standing alone at the tip of North Ari atoll. The waters here are unusually clear and you can see shoals of fish swimming around your villa. The resort staff are truly exceptional – always willing, with a ready smile and a charm that cannot fail to rub off on even the most out-of-sorts guest.

The island is outstandingly clean and well maintained with 76 villas of 86 sq m (925 sq ft) standing either on the beach or in the water, each with king-size bed, ceiling fan, separate sitting area, partially open-air bathroom, private patio with Jacuzzi and a wooden sun deck. A freshwater infinity pool overlooks the lagoon and there is a children's pool as well. The bar has a peaceful ambience with breathtaking views of the ocean – and you can watch any sports fixtures you might be missing, or even have a game of scrabble. Both the *à-la-carte* restaurant and less-formal buffet serve stupendous food.

There are 20 dive sites around the lagoon representing varying degrees of difficulty and the water is teeming with marine life so, whether you're a beginner or an experienced diver, you'll find all the sites you need to get your kicks.

Veligandu is a quiet, laid-back resort with the most tremendous service and a wonderfully tranquil atmosphere in an idyllic setting – a truly wondrous place for a completely relaxing, romantic break.

Maia Luxury Resort and Spa

The Seychelles Islands are tropical havens with breathtaking scenery in a perfect climate. And Maia is the Seychelles at its legendary best – an absolutely breathtaking 5-ha (12-ac) tropical garden on a rocky peninsula that has deservedly won an award. More than 300 species of exotic plants grow here and you are immersed in a paradise of orchids, hibiscus and sweet-scented spice trees where the only sounds are the calls of the birds, babbling streams tumbling down the moss-covered granite slopes and thundering ocean waves crashing into the shore.

There are 30 Balinese-style villas hidden around the peninsula, each in its own private, gated garden. Your villa's secluded terrace has an enormous infinity plunge pool, an outsize day bed and a heavenly view across the hillside to the ocean beyond. Inside, it is splendidly furnished in dark wood and plush silks, with a luxurious mosaic-tiled bathroom. You are waited on hand and foot with discreet and charming service. Each villa is allocated a personal butler, on call 24 hours a day, who attends to your every whim, whether it be the arrangement of a candlelit dinner on the beach, setting up a barbecue, or preparing a rose-petal bath.

The spa here is superb. It has three luxurious private pavilions, each with its own garden, a fitness centre where you can work out a personal exercise regime and a hillside meditation deck where you can greet the dawn sun. The restaurant serves fusion food of an incredibly high standard and the fresh seafood is to die for. Maia is the ultimate in sanctuaries for recharging your physical and spiritual batteries.

WHERE:
Anse Louis, Mahé
COST:
Astronomical
BEST TIME OF YEAR:
All year round – March to May and September to November for best diving conditions; May to September for hiking
DON'T MISS:
Birdwatching on Bird Island; a picnic on La Digue Island; a scenic helicopter tour of the Seychelles
THINGS TO DO:
Scuba diving; snorkelling; canoeing; kayaking; fishing; meditation; *hatha* yoga; *qi gong*; self-shiatsu; hiking; horse riding; exploring the island
YOU SHOULD KNOW:
Only non-motorized boats are allowed around Maia to preserve the tranquillity – there is an easily accessible off-site water-sports centre for motorized sports. Maia is not primarily a family resort, but children of all ages are well catered for and there is a child-minding service. There is free wifi throughout the resort and each villa is equipped with a Bose sound system, iPod dock and flat-screen TV. Maia has featured on the *Condé Nast Traveller* Gold List.

Frégate Island

WHERE:
Frégate Island
COST:
Astronomical+
BEST TIME OF YEAR:
All year round (March to May and September to November for the best diving; May to September for walking)
DON'T MISS:
The island museum to learn about the fascinating maritime history of Frégate; the view from the top of Mont Signal; meeting a giant tortoise
THINGS TO DO:
Swimming; snorkelling; scuba diving; kayaking; yachting; tennis; volleyball; badminton; cycling; yoga; gym; walks
YOU SHOULD KNOW:
Frégate is a private island owned by German billionaire Otto Abel. It features in all the top-ten lists of the world's best resorts.

The most distant island of the Inner Seychelles, Frégate was a 17th-century pirate base and tales of buried treasure abound. But the island itself is a tiny treasure. It is only 2.2 sq km (less than 1 sq mi) but has the world's best beach and is a habitat for 50 species of bird and its own endemic turtle. No wonder this privately owned island is a favourite haunt of celebrities seeking a bit of rest and relaxation away from the public glare.

There are just 16 beach-front villas in this exclusive resort, all sumptuously furnished and with every amenity you could wish for. All the villas are completely secluded, with amazing views of the ocean, and two of them are specifically designed for families so that children can play safely outdoors. There are two restaurants and two bars on the island. The restaurants use island-grown produce as much as possible. Some of the produce is grown hydroponically, so the creative menus are based around deliciously fresh, seasonal food. Fresh fruit and vegetables are daily fare here and of course the locally caught seafood is incomparable. What's more, you can have your meal brought to you in any chosen spot on the island.

The entire ethos of Frégate is one of conservation, harmony with nature and the re-energizing of body and soul. The ambience is one of complete seclusion and tranquillity, far from the madding crowd. There is only ever a maximum of 40 guests at any one time and you come here to experience breathtaking scenery, seven pristine beaches, wonderful food and the clean ocean air. Frégate is quite simply a paradise playground for the super-rich. Take out a second mortgage and enjoy!

EUROPE & THE MIDDLE EAST

Savoy Hotel

WHERE:
Savoy Place, Strand, London
COST:
Expensive (and upwards, for suites)
BEST TIME OF YEAR:
Spring, summer, autumn or winter
DON'T MISS:
Afternoon tea in the Thames foyer, beneath a wonderful stained-glass dome that was covered in World War II and not revealed again until refurbishment in 2007, or try the new Savoy Tea *patisserie*; a work-out in the glass-walled fitness gallery with pool and spa above the Savoy theatre; cocktails in the Art Deco Beaufort Bar with its black-and-gold decor, or a dalliance in the famous (and famously unchanged) American Bar; grazing at the equally renowned Savoy Grill
THINGS TO DO:
Explore London
YOU SHOULD KNOW:
The hotel's name originates from the first great edifice that was built on the Thames-side site – the grand 13th century Savoy Palace erected for Count Peter of Savoy, uncle of Henry III's Queen Eleanor. The Savoy might be the last word in traditional opulence, but that tradition does not include the thousands of fixtures and fittings auctioned off before the recent works.

It's the sort of place where the great and the good have loved staying since the doors opened in 1889. It's the sort of place where César Ritz once hovered by Reception and Auguste Escoffier created amazing cuisine below stairs. It's the sort of place where royalty felt at home, and stars of stage and screen from Charlie Chaplin to Marilyn Monroe liked to be and be seen. It's the sort of place where Noel Coward tinkled the ivories and sang risqué songs, or Frank Sinatra did it his way. It's the sort of place where Winston Churchill held cabinet meetings and aristocratic women appeared wearing full regalia.

It is, of course, London's iconic Savoy hotel, recently returned to its full glory after a comprehensive restoration, the bill for which had lots of zeros on the end. Generally accepted as London's most famous and possibly now finest hotel, the Savoy was the brainchild of Victorian entrepreneur Richard D'Oyly Carte, who had made a fortune staging Gilbert and Sullivan operettas at his Savoy Theatre. Enthused by similar ventures in America, he created a magnificent hotel that embodied lots of innovations such as first British hotel lit by electricity, with electric lifts, en-suite bathrooms and hot running water throughout.

Today's Savoy more than lives up to those ambitious beginnings, with 268 luxurious rooms that maintain the hotel's illustrious tradition and the interior accent definitely on refined opulence rather than modern glitz. One tough decision is between Edwardian room decor (river side) or Art Deco (Strand side). Once settled in, there's a further choice – remaining within doors and basking in the hotel's almost unlimited delights, or venturing forth into the exciting metropolis. That's another tough one! But either way, staying at the Savoy is the ultimate London hotel experience – one which says 'you've arrived' (at least for one night).

SAVOY
to the role. A HUGE HIT!

St Pancras Renaissance London Hotel

Once upon a time, there was one of the world's finest railway hotels – no, make that *the* finest – standing proud on London's Euston Road. In the 1870s the British Empire was at its zenith and the nation's rail network was booming. The Midland Railway Company wanted an eye-catching prestige hotel adjacent to its new terminus of St Pancras to enhance its corporate reputation. Ambitious directors opted for the most expensive design by leading architect George Gilbert Scott and the resulting 300-room Midland Grand Hotel must have exceeded their expectations. With its advanced construction techniques, hydraulic lifts, revolving doors, a fireplace in every room, a grand staircase and lavishly decorated public rooms, this was an awesome structure. But two omissions, then revolutionary, would prove fatal within 60 years. With no central heating or en-suite bathrooms, the army of staff needed to hump coal, empty chamber pots and fill washbowls made operations uneconomical and the hotel closed in 1935.

A gloomy period followed, when the building was used for railway offices and there was an ever-present threat of demolition. Finally, permission was granted for redevelopment in 2004 and the result has been suitably impressive. With the top floors turned into loft-style apartments, the new five-star St Pancras Renaissance London Hotel certainly lives up to its name. Public areas have been restored to their former grandeur and a new wing has been built. Travellers in rail's golden age would recognize the fairytale red-brick facade and dazzling Grand Staircase, while today's guests can marvel at the opulent interior but also enjoy every modern convenience.

There couldn't be a more iconic choice of London hotel for those who revel in tradition (without sacrificing their home comforts, naturally). The original building contains ultra-grand suites awash with authentic Victorian character, including the magnificent Royal Suite in the original ballroom, while the new wing (Barlow House) contains the regular guest rooms with their contemporary character.

WHERE:
Euston Road, London
COST:
Can be reasonable (deals available online), but generally expensive depending on season and accommodation chosen
BEST TIME OF YEAR:
Any time
DON'T MISS:
A splash in the Victorian tiled pool; personalized butler service for those able to afford a suite; a meal in the signature Gilbert Scott bar and restaurant; a meal or drinks on the lower level of the Booking Office Bar, overlooking the Eurostar platforms; a soothing session in the sumptuous subterranean spa
THINGS TO DO:
Er, this is London, folks
YOU SHOULD KNOW:
The formal Grand Opening of the St Pancras Renaissance was on May 5 2011, exactly 138 years after the original hotel opening in 1873. Sir John Betjeman once called this Victorian Gothic treasure 'too beautiful and too romantic to survive' – and would have been ecstatic when the building's subsequent resilience proved him wrong. Parking at the hotel is expensive.

Brown's Hotel

WHERE:
Albermarle Street, London
COST:
Expensive (and you would expect nothing less)
BEST TIME OF YEAR:
London is a year-round destination (but it's best to avoid July and August when tourist crowds engulf all, and the January sales when consumer wars break out in Oxford and Regent Streets).
DON'T MISS:
The world-famous afternoon tea at Brown's, accompanied by piano playing and with a choice of 17 different blends; Donovan's Bar, a homage to celebrated photographer Terry Donovan and decorated with his work (the naughty pictures are in a corner); Britart in the hotel's Albermarle restaurant, along with superb food

The Savoy might be top dog when it comes to the capital's historic hotels and the St Pancras Renaissance London Hotel may have the last word when it comes to Victorian opulence married to modern comfort, but the city's oldest-established hotel can hold a candle to both. Brown's in prestigious Mayfair was opened in 1837 and expanded with the purchase of adjoining premises in 1889. It has retained its signature Victorian character, albeit tempered with a contemporary feel introduced when a major refurbishment was completed in 2005.

The list of notable guests over nearly two centuries reads like a who's who of royalty, the upper classes and international movers and shakers, also attracting the literary set represented by luminaries like Robert Louis Stephenson, J M Barrie, Rudyard Kipling, Bram Stoker, Arthur Conan Doyle, Oscar Wilde and Agatha Christie (who based her classic murder mystery *At Bertram's Hotel* on the place). Brown's was acquired by the rise-fall-and-rise Forte hotel dynasty in 2003, and the revamped interior decor was created under the direction of family member Olga Polizzi. The result is a pleasing mix of traditional and modern, adding up to refined sophistication that amply justifies a five-star rating. Each room and suite is individually decorated (no Holiday-Inn thinking here!), featuring antiques and contemporary artworks that (combined with impeccable service) emphasize the main message – this is the modern face of British luxury hotelmanship at its best.

Another advantage is the hotel's proximity to top shopping areas like Bond Street and Regent Street, and also two wonderful open spaces, Green Park and Hyde Park. It is also handy for theatres, galleries and some of the capital's most iconic sights, so this makes a great base for enjoying London (although only oligarchs would now be able to contemplate the sort of nine-year stay enjoyed by King George II of Greece after he was deposed in 1924).

THINGS TO DO:
Plunging into the London maelstrom, or alternatively sinking back into the pampered clutches of the hotel's state-of-the-art spa
YOU SHOULD KNOW:
Britain's first-ever telephone call was made from Brown's Hotel by inventor Alexander Graham Bell in 1876.

Church Street Hotel

Anyone for the passionate atmosphere of Latin America, say Cuba or Mexico? Sounds good? Good enough to make your way to bustling Camberwell in South London, where the eclectic Church Street Hotel smoulders (metaphorically speaking, of course)? Not everyone wants (or can afford) to stay in one of Central London's upmarket hotels, and those who want something completely different should be tempted by this quirky establishment that describes itself as 'a Spanish Americana boutique hotel' that is 'an oasis of Latin sensuality'. And so indeed it might be, for those who don't mind a fiesta atmosphere (sometimes until late at night) and can live without an en-suite bathroom – some guest rooms have them, some (the budget ones) don't, and room sizes vary from petite (budget) to spacious (doubles).

The decor is all about the brightest of colours, arched doorways, wooden furniture and lots of hand-painted tiles. Service is friendly and attentive, but when it comes to alcoholic refreshment there's an honour system, with the self-service bar well stocked with whiskies, rum, tequila, spirits, wines and (nice touch) Spanish/American beers. Guests are expected to write down what they consume, but those IOUs can soon mount up if a party gets under way. The morning-after breakfast is special, including freshly made coffee, cereals, organic bread, delicious pastries, free-range eggs, jams and the hotel's legendary hot sauce. The adjacent Angels & Gypsies restaurant provides decent Spanish fare, with many ingredients brought in fresh from nearby Borough Market.

This idiosyncratic B&B-style establishment may not please the purists, but it brings a splash of carefree character to this gritty part of town, and will certainly provide an affordable night's accommodation that is – which nobody can deny – refreshingly different from anything any other hotel in this great city of eight million inhabitants can offer. *Viva* Camberwell!

WHERE:
Camberwell Church Street, London
COST:
Budget to reasonable, depending on season and choice of accommodation
BEST TIME OF YEAR:
January to December
DON'T MISS:
A complimentary tea or coffee in the wood-panelled Havana-style lounge, with its comprehensive DVD library; a decent supper at the Dark Horse pub opposite the hotel; using up the classy free Korres bathroom products
THINGS TO DO:
A stroll around Camberwell Green getting a flavour of the 'real' London (all human life is there!); catch the bus to the West End's fleshpots; stay in and imagine you're chilling at a genuine Mexican *casita*
YOU SHOULD KNOW:
The reception desk looks as though it's an ornate altar 'liberated' from a Mexican church, and the thought is reinforced by the considerable quantity of religious iconography (along, it must be said, with plenty of secular art) to be found throughout the hotel.

The Lugger Hotel

WHERE:
Portloe, near Tregony, Cornwall
COST:
Reasonable
BEST TIME OF YEAR:
Take your pick – Portloe is crowded in summer, bracing during the winter and delightful during spring and autumn.
DON'T MISS:
A session with the hotel spa's rejuvenating therapists; a leisurely *al fresco* lunch on the terrace overlooking the harbour; an evening drink in front of the blazing log fire
THINGS TO DO:
Fishing; hiking the Cornish Coastal Footpath; exploring local history
YOU SHOULD KNOW:
The Lugger was recently named as 'Best Seaside Hotel' by *The Sunday Times*. No Cornish inn would be Cornish without a good smuggling pedigree and the Lugger is no exception – a former landlord was convicted of smuggling French brandy and executed.

Anyone chasing a romantic notion of traditional Cornwall should race past the tackier manifestations of the tourist-dependent economy and make their way to the stunningly beautiful Roseland Peninsula between Falmouth and St Austell, and there discover the small but characterful village of Portloe. Here be ye olde Kernow of popular legend – a cluster of stone buildings nestling snugly above a secluded cove that punctuates a rugged coastline of soaring cliffs, jutting headlands and pounding surf. There's a perfect small harbour with weathered breakwater that protects a couple of working fishing boats, and a Cornish flag flutters proudly in the sea breeze to complete the picture.

A central component of this enchanting scene is the 17th-century waterside Lugger Hotel, now occupying three buildings around the harbour. People travel from far and wide for the fine-dining experience to be enjoyed in the restaurant (seafood landed that morning in the harbour a speciality), but the Lugger is also a wonderfully soothing place to stay. Recently made over, it now has 22 guest rooms that have simple, clean modern decor and feature luxurious en-suite bathrooms with deep baths and power showers. The views from bedroom windows can only be described as spectacular.

The whole atmosphere of the place is friendly and completely relaxed, so you may well choose to stay close to the hotel and savour the picturesque charms of Portloe and environs. But those seeking to visit some of the county's major attractions will find that the hotel makes an ideal base for sorties to such should-visit destinations as the Eden Project, Lost Gardens of Heligan (now happily re-found) or Falmouth's National Maritime Museum. And a rewarding day out will be all the better for knowing that the Lugger's warm 'welcome home' awaits.

Botelet Farm

Carefully nurtured for 150 years and more by successive generations of the same family, Botelet Farm is a wonderful contradiction in tourist terms, for it pulls off the difficult trick of not only welcoming visitors to unspoilt countryside but also preserving the very things that attract them in the first place. This classic Cornish farmstead sits above Fowey and Liskeard, with sweeping views across an ancient landscape to the sea, and it offers an imaginative choice of accommodation possibilities for those who would like to enjoy the unique 'Botelet experience'.

The stone farmhouse offers two bed-and-breakfast rooms with shared bath, and the lived-in interior is an eclectic mix of traditional and modern, seasoned with a display of curios to surprise and enchant. A healthy organic breakfast is served at a scrubbed table in the large kitchen, where guests returning from a brisk walk are welcome to warm up beside the wood-burning range cooker. Those seeking to embrace nature more closely can choose between two Mongolian-style yurts in remote locations, both sleeping two adults. Each has a wood-burning stove and offers barbecue self-catering (cooking equipment provided). One has electricity, one does not, depending just how authentic you want the experience to be. There's also a wild flower meadow where a couple of tents can be pitched, or a camper van parked.

Families have the choice of two self-catering cottages. There's 17th-century Manor Cottage, rich with historic features (sleeps five) or the white-washed 19th-century Cowslip Cottage with valley views (also sleeps five, with two pets allowed). It's another world at the end of Botelet's winding lane. The wind turbines strike a thoroughly modern chord amidst the patchwork of ancient fields and woods, but merely serve to emphasize the farm's avowedly green credentials.

WHERE:
Herodsfoot, near Liskeard, Cornwall
COST:
Budget for B&B, yurts and camping; budget to reasonable for multi-occupation cottages – rates vary considerably by season
BEST TIME OF YEAR:
Cottages available all year (but note that high summer tends to get booked up well in advance), otherwise Easter to late autumn
DON'T MISS:
A relaxing massage in your yurt; the views to Dartmoor and Dodman point from the nearby neolithic hill fort of Bury Down
THINGS TO DO:
Mooching around the farm simply enjoying being there; horse riding at nearby Polmartin Stables; visiting Lanhydrock House and gardens; driving to Looe and going out on a mackerel boat to catch supper (landlubbers can peek at the fascinating fish market, before landing the evening meal at Pengelly's famous fish shop)
YOU SHOULD KNOW:
As a modern touch, digital radios are supplied for the yurts and wifi is available close to base station (the farmhouse). Toilet and washing facilities for yurt glampers and meadow campers are also available near the farmhouse, along with a fridge and recycling bins. The water supply is pumped from a natural mineral borehole beneath the orchard.

Bodrifty

WHERE:
Newmill, near Penzance, Cornwall
COST:
Budget
BEST TIME OF YEAR:
Any (winter storm watching a speciality!)
DON'T MISS:
The authentic Iron Age settlement, one of Britain's best-preserved examples containing the visible remains of at least nine houses; the sensational 360-degree panorama from Mulfra Hill, crowned by a 4,000-year-old burial chamber

An Iron Age house in a Mousehole sounds, well, more like the set for a Walt Disney cartoon than the setting for a memorable experience. But guess what? It is in fact the latter. Bodrifty Farm is in the wild west of Cornwall, sited on the rugged moorland of the Land's End Peninsula, overlooking Mount's Bay and the pretty fishing village of Mousehole. Bodrifty is on the site of a late Bronze Age and Iron Age village once home to up to 100 people, and owner Fred Mustill was inspired to create a replica roundhouse in order to understand more about the lives of those enigmatic former inhabitants. He learnt the first lesson about their harsh existence when it took two years to complete the project, moving huge stones and using local materials.

But the result is impressive, bringing history alive. The roundhouse, with its granite walls and conical thatched roof, appears to grow from the Cornish landscape in this Area of Outstanding Natural Beauty. Those who choose to stay in this unique B&B will enjoy simple comforts that were not available to Iron Agers, in the form of subtle lighting and a rustic four-posted bed made up with the finest linen, plus an old but serviceable rug. The place has an extraordinarily peaceful atmosphere, with starry skies, no light pollution, no passing traffic (and not a caravan to be seen). Where could be better for that romantic break unlike anything else you've ever experienced?

Bodrifty's rural delights may also be sampled in a more conventional manner by taking the charming self-catering Swallow Barn, a converted 16th-century farm building that has sensitively morphed into a pleasing space that is ideal for a get-away-from-it-all couple. But whatever the roof, the experience will be magical.

THINGS TO DO:
A trip to arty St Ives and Tate St Ives (including the Barbara Hepworth Museum and Sculpture Garden); tramping the wild, gorse-covered Penwith moors; walking the ancient Tinners' Way ridgeway; a stroll to and meal at the award-winning Gurnard's Head gastropub; head for the beach
YOU SHOULD KNOW:
A stay at the roundhouse is for a minimum of two nights or a maximum of seven. Once your booking is confirmed, you will receive *The Guide*, Bodrifty's insider tip-sheet to the attractions of West Cornwall.

Deerpark Cabins

Set around an old mill pond in a superb wooded-valley setting just a few miles from the spectacular south coast of Cornwall, Deerpark Cabins provides a tempting location for those who simply want a relaxing country break in unspoilt countryside – although this little haven makes an equally good base for those intent on venturing forth to sample Cornwall's wider attractions.

The self-catering waterside cabins are ideal for families. The Golden Oak Treehouse should be the preferred choice for those who like something a little different, because the luxurious accommodation includes a beguiling treehouse extension. But don't expect to be roughing it in the back of beyond. The wooded setting may give the impression of rustic isolation, but you'll enjoy a raft of luxury trimmings. Suitable for a large family or group of friends, these cabins sleep up to eight in four bedrooms (no fighting over the treehouse, which is accessed by a bridge from the main cabin's terrace and makes a cosy hideaway for a couple).

The firmly grounded regular Golden Oak cabins, with a choice of bedrooms from one to four to suit every family or party, are also pretty special and offer log-burning stoves and a terrace. Golden Oaks have sumptuous furnishings, private outdoor hot tubs and fully fitted kitchens. Flat-screen TVs and DVD players are standard, along with a games console to keep little (and larger) hands out of trouble. Silver Birch cabins come with two or three bedrooms for smaller families, but are equally well equipped. The park has strong 'green' credentials and makes every effort to minimize the human impact on this special location, so enjoy with a clearish eco-conscience!

WHERE:
Near Liskeard, Cornwall
COST:
Reasonable
BEST TIME OF YEAR:
April to September
DON'T MISS:
Book one or more of the extra goodies – like the romantic evening in with champagne, rose petals and aromatherapy, or the chef who whips up a fine-dining meal in your cabin. Spoil yourself!
THINGS TO DO:
Hire bikes (or a tandem) to ride the park's forest trails – or explore on foot; visit the famously popular fishing villages of Looe and Polperro (but sharpen your elbows in high summer); find a beach (they're not in short supply hereabouts); take a ride on the nearby Liskeard Virgin Hot-Air Balloon Flight; or experience a zipline thrill at Adrenaline Quarry.
YOU SHOULD KNOW:
The old gunpowder mill was sited here because it was a suitably remote location far away from potential collateral damage. A grocery pack to get you started can be pre-ordered. Dogs are allowed in some Golden Oak and Silver Birch cabins. The park has a total of 45 cabins and there's an on-site launderette to deal with any muddy clothes.

Burgh Island Hotel

WHERE:
Burgh Island, off Bigbury-on-Sea, Devon

COST:
Top end of expensive, with the Garden Suite and Beach House toppling into astronomical

BEST TIME OF YEAR:
March to October, but a winter visit can be rewarding for lovers of (pampered) solitude and wild weather

DON'T MISS:
Riding to/from the island at high tide on the extraordinary custom-built sea tractor; a dip in the hotel's natural salt-water Mermaid Pool

THINGS TO DO:
Explore the island using the network of footpaths and find the ancient chapel later used as a huer's hut, where a watching fisherman would set off a hue and cry when shoals appeared in the bay; have a leisurely drink at the island's historic Pilchard Inn, as ancient as the hotel is modern, or sample the inn's legendary Friday curry night; batter the green baize in the original 1930s Billiards Room; enjoy the many services provided by the thoroughly modern spa and fitness centre.

YOU SHOULD KNOW:
In keeping with the 1930s' flavour there are no TVs in the rooms, although compulsive viewers will find a set (plus a selection of DVDs) in the library room (but cheats can watch streamed TV on their laptops in bed via the free wifi service).

It looks just like a film set constructed for a classic Agatha Christie murder mystery, but why build a set when you can use the real thing? The Art Deco Burgh Island Hotel was *the* place to be seen in the 1930s and the author was a frequent visitor, along with other glitterati like Noel Coward. Never one to waste experience, the crime writer liked the place so much that she used it as a setting for not one but two books: *And Then There Were None* and *Evil Under The Sun* featuring Hercule Poirot. Naturally, when it came to filming the latter for TV no set was needed – the hotel and island were the real thing.

Burgh Island is just off the seaside village of Bigbury-on-Sea in South Devon's picturesque South Hams district, and the angular white hotel building stands in a commanding position on the site of an old monastery, looking for all the world like an ocean liner from the great age of sea travel. The hotel was erected in 1929 and extended in 1932, but declined steadily from its early peak after World War II. However, a full refurbishment in 2006 restored its former glory, and re-created the glamorous aura that was once the hotel's trademark. Each room is named after a celebrity. Each one is different, but beautifully appointed.

The fine-dining experience is exceptional and features much local produce. In keeping with the re-created 1930s' experience, many guests dress for dinner and there's live music in the ballroom on Wednesdays and Saturdays. And yes, it is possible to book in for a murder mystery house party, no doubt watched approvingly from on high by the *grande dame* of crime, Agatha Christie herself.

Gidleigh Park Hotel

Over many years, publishing tycoon Andrew Brownsword and his wife Christina found that Gidleigh Park Hotel on Dartmoor was the ideal place to forget the stresses and strains of high-powered business life. Indeed, they liked the hotel so much that they bought it. Since then, the Brownswords have added a number of guest rooms but ensured that the hotel retains the relaxed atmosphere that attracted them in the first place, and with their dedicated team they have created a country-house hotel that's second to none.

The attractive half-timbered house was built for a shipping magnate in Arts & Crafts style and sits in a commanding position overlooking extensive gardens and woodland. The Michelin-starred restaurant, famed throughout the West Country and beyond, specializes in French cuisine and regularly features near or at the top of fine-dining award lists. But impeccable food is but a part of the Gidleigh Park package (although the late Poet Laureate Ted Hughes was so impressed that he wrote a poem about it), because the hotel itself is equally impressive. The rooms are all different and all are special. There are three spa rooms with bathrooms designed to pamper (including one with a rooftop hot tub from which to appreciate the starlit heavens). Spacious wood-panelled Master Rooms pay homage to the hotel's Arts & Crafts pedigree, Deluxe Rooms have balconies overlooking the Teign Valley, while Classic rooms at the top of the house (the old servants' quarters, though you'd never know it) are elegantly styled and also have wonderful views. Families can choose the secluded thatched garden Pavilion or the Loft Suite.

This is as good as staying at a county-house hotel ever gets, and anyone who can afford the best (even if only for a couple of memorable nights) will soon appreciate that they have experienced just that.

WHERE:
Gidleigh, near Chagford, Devon
COST:
If you have to ask you probably can't afford one of the spa rooms, but most rooms are merely reasonable to expensive (for two people sharing).
BEST TIME OF YEAR:
Any time (Dartmoor can be bleak in winter, but staying indoors is no hardship)
DON'T MISS:
The fact that dinner should be accompanied by a fine wine from the renowned cellar; a Temple Spa package that offers treats like relaxing oils and scented candles, or one of the sensuous beauty treatments available in the privacy of your own room
THINGS TO DO:
A walk in wooded grounds (find the romantic bridge over the rushing River Teign); a guided walk on Dartmoor (or explore for yourself); a game of tennis on the hotel court (or some cut-throat croquet); fly fishing; wildlife spotting (badgers and deer a speciality)
YOU SHOULD KNOW:
Families are welcome and there are plenty of open-air activities locally to stimulate adventurous kids, plus attractions like the Dartmoor Miniature Pony Centre or South Devon Steam Railway. There's a small charge for dog owners who want to introduce their hounds to the delights of Dartmoor (unless they happen to be called Baskerville), and the pampered pooches get to sleep in a heated kennel (or one of three nominated guest rooms if they won't be parted from their parents).

Bovey Castle

WHERE:
North Bovey, near Moretonhampstead, Devon
COST:
Expensive (but there are special offers and lodges are reasonable per person if shared by a family or party)
BEST TIME OF YEAR:
May to October for outdoor activities
DON'T MISS:
Afternoon tea on the South Terrace; a romantic *al fresco* meal in the secluded summerhouse; a self-indulgent treatment in the flagship SUNDĀRI spa

Dartmoor has an appeal all its own and everyone likes a romantic castle. Put the two together and come up with a memorable place to stay, especially for all-action types who like outdoor activities and adventure. Actually, Bovey Castle isn't as old as its weathered Jacobean appearance might suggest, having been built in the early 20th century for Viscount Weymouth. And it soon became the Great Western Railway's Manor House Hotel, eventually being made over and renamed Bovey Castle by ambitious entrepreneur Peter de Savary. But it certainly looks the part, in a wooded location overlooking a lake and the River Bovey, with dramatic views across Dartmoor National Park, and was ideal for the new owner's vision of offering an experience that made guests feel they were on their own private estate, complete with a wide choice of leisure activities.

And that's the deal on offer today. Bovey Castle itself is a suitably luxurious hotel offering excellent service, the warmest of welcomes, a choice of rooms and essentials like fine dining and a spa. For anyone who wants to (almost) do their own thing, there is a choice of impressive lodges in the grounds, offering private sanctuary for those who value independence. They each have three double bedrooms and sleep up to eight (ideal for families), while having access to the main hotel's services.

But the real joy is the range of stimulating activities on offer, ranging from archery to yachting. And children are not overlooked. The Bovey Rangers keep children from seven to 14 years old comprehensively entertained indoors and out during school holidays and at weekends (think supervised delights such as campfire building, canoeing, dance classes and moorland adventures). There is also a playroom for younger children.

THINGS TO DO:
There's lots on offer, as in archery, air-rifle shooting, art classes, clay-pigeon shooting, cider making, cocktail shaking, falconry, fly fishing, game shooting (in season), guided walks, gliding, horse riding, hot-air ballooning, off-roading, quad biking, rock climbing, tennis – being bored is not an option.

YOU SHOULD KNOW:
The hotel grounds include an 18-hole golf course constructed in the 1920s. There is a helipad for guests in a hurry. Lodges are offered on a 'room only' basis to suit self-caterers, so services such as meals delivered from the hotel are extra.

Burnham High Lighthouse

WHERE:
Berrow Road, Burnham-on-Sea, Somerset
COST:
Reasonable to expensive, depending on occupancy level and time of year
BEST TIME OF YEAR:
April to October
DON'T MISS:
The slightly scary experience of peering down through the copper-domed lantern room's glass floor; watching sunsets over the sea from the top of the tower; an undemanding stroll along Burnham's pier, Britain's shortest, to sample the amusements; a glass (or two) of local Somerset cider
THINGS TO DO:
Kite surfing (or simply fly a kite); windsurfing; beach combing; swimming; sand yachting; a foray into the distinctive Somerset Levels; an outing to Cheddar Gorge's show caves; a steam-train journey from Minehead on the West Somerset Railway; hiking in the Mendip Hills; visiting Exmoor
YOU SHOULD KNOW:
It's best to be fit – there are 120 steps plus a ship's ladder before you reach the dizziest heights. Well-behaved pets are welcome (but not in the bedrooms). Sandy boots, shoes, feet and pets should be hosed down before entering the tower. There is free wifi throughout the tower.

It's pretty obvious, when it comes to it – a soaring white tower with bright-red stripe rising 33 m (108 ft) above the glorious 10-km (6-mi) sandy beach at Burnham-on-Sea, close to the mouth of the River Parrett where it meets treacherous Bridgewater Bay with its marshes and mudflats. This is Burnham High Lighthouse, big brother of the still-operative Burnham Low Lighthouse that stands close to the water's edge, raised on stilts and decorated to match the 'big un'.

The High Lighthouse was built in 1830, automated in 1920 (one of the first in Britain to be so modified), sold by Trinity House to a member of the Rothschild family in the 1990s, now converted into a holiday let. End of history lesson, start of a memorable seaside break. Today's holidaymakers (families or friends, as the lighthouse sleeps six) have the run of the soaring eight-storey tower, which has three en-suite bedrooms (shower, toilet and washbasin), bathroom, ground-floor reception room, living room, galley kitchen on the seventh and dining area with splendid views across the bay in the historic restored lantern room at the top.

With its small private patio and barbecue area just a short walk from the golden sands, the lighthouse is the ideal rental for families that want a classic seaside holiday (stag and hen parties not welcome!). The Victorian resort of Burnham-on-Sea is rather more old-fashioned and genteel than nearby Weston-super-Mare but has plenty to keep youngsters (donkey rides on the beach) and parents (a round on the adjacent Burnham & Berrow Links golf course) entertained. The High Lighthouse also makes an excellent base for day trips to Somerset's many attractions.

Clavell Tower

It was about to vanish for ever over a crumbling cliff when the Landmark Trust – saviour of interesting 'at-risk' buildings for posterity and holidaymakers – stepped in to rescue the elegant Clavell Tower from a watery grave. This extraordinary rotunda has 12 columns and pierced parapets in local stone, and has stood as a folly on a stretch of wild Dorset coast since 1830, serving only as a landmark for passing shipping. Following the Trust's intervention, it was taken down and painstakingly reassembled close to its original site, but far enough from the precipitous edge to ensure its future safety.

Clavell Tower is now a romantic holiday let that will appeal mightily to a couple (it only sleeps two) who appreciate the combination of impressive historic building and fabulous location overlooking the sea – while their dog (if they have one) will love the freedom. But the experience requires a little effort. Car parking is at the foot of the cliff and access is via a steep footpath, so it's as well to travel light (albeit with enough food and drink for your stay). The rooms are small, round and beautifully appointed, ensuring that Clavell Tower has everything you need for a comfortable stay (bathroom, kitchen, double bedroom and top-floor sitting room).

This is part of the famous Jurassic Coast World Heritage Site. The Tower stands atop Hen Cliff immediately to the east of the great sweep of Kimmeridge Bay, with its famous Flats, an extensive rocky platform cut by the sea over many millennia. This is one place where you will never tire of messing about by the water – especially as your unique nest awaits at the end of each day.

WHERE:
Kimmeridge, near Wareham, Dorset
COST:
Budget to reasonable (for two sharing, depending on time of year)
BEST TIME OF YEAR:
Whenever you can get a booking (although winters can be bleak, there's a cosy gas fire)
DON'T MISS:
Sweeping views of coast and sea from the balcony (it's a circular walk that starts and ends at the bedroom door); inspecting BP's 'nodding donkey' oil well on a cliff west of Kimmeridge village
THINGS TO DO:
Exploring the South West Coastal path (both ways, it goes right past the door); surfing when the waves are right; beachcombing; sallying forth to nearby beauty spots such as Corfe Castle and Lulworth Cove
YOU SHOULD KNOW:
Make your plans to stay in this idyllic spot early, as Clavell Tower is always heavily booked far in advance. Open days are held for those who just want a sneaky peek. A young Thomas Hardy used the Tower as the frontispiece for his Wessex Poems (and courted a local coastguard's daughter). Crime writer P D James was also captivated by the place, using it as inspiration for her novel *The Black Tower*.

Coalport Station

WHERE:
Coalport, near Telford, Shropshire
COST:
Budget to reasonable (per person, for at least two people sharing, varying by season)
BEST TIME OF YEAR:
Any, but the garden's at its best in spring and summer and the trees are spectacular in autumn
DON'T MISS:
A refreshing drink and/or good pub meal beside the river at the adjacent Woodbridge Inn; spirited Irish music at the nearby Boat Inn (unsurprisingly also beside the river) on Thursdays; loafing around in the station's tranquil wooded gardens, right beside the River Severn
THINGS TO DO:
Ride the real thing on the Severn Valley Steam Railway, 15 km (9 mi) down river, or the smaller nearby Telford Steam Railway just 8 km (5 mi) away. Walk along the Severn Way track path into the heart of Ironbridge to admire Thomas Telford's famous 1781 bridge across the Severn (and visit one or more of the six fascinating museums). Enjoy riverside strolls and exploring the unspoilt countryside on bike or afoot.
YOU SHOULD KNOW:
The nearest active station for those who want to make it a completely authentic railway break is Telford Central Station (arrange to be collected, or take a cab to Coalport). There's wifi on site. Local supermarkets will deliver to the station. There's no smoking on site and no cheating (like airline loos, the carriages have sensitive smoke-detection systems).

The train now standing at the platform of Coalport Station in the picturesque Severn Valley's Ironbridge Gorge is going . . . absolutely nowhere. It may be because there's no locomotive, or the fact that the tracks begin and end in the station, but actually the real reason is that the Shrewsbury to Bridgnorth line upon which it stands was axed in 1968. No matter, railway enthusiasts and lovers of romantic non-journeys will delight in the opportunity to stay in one of two Mark 1 railway carriages, refettled to be far more comfortable than the originals ever were.

Coalport Station is a mellow old building right beside the river that serves as a poignant reminder of England's lost rural railway heritage, as do those Mark 1 carriages built in the 1950s and early 1960s before the culling began. This pair are very special, with interiors finished to a very high standard that offers every luxury, and they have been awarded four-star-plus status – the highest available for non-hotel accommodation. The carriages are centrally heated and the larger rooms have air conditioning. There are flat-screen TVs, music centres, fridges, ceramic hobs, microwaves, dish washers and washing machines (German appliances, obviously, as British rolling stock tends to be manufactured by German companies nowadays).

The 'basic' Carriage 1 sleeps six and has an en-suite master bedroom with whirlpool bath, family bathroom, two twin-bedded rooms, kitchen and spacious lounge. The 'posh' Carriage 2 sleeps just four, offering two en-suite rooms with Jacuzzi baths and power showers, well-fitted kitchen and a super-relaxing sitting room (First Class, of course). This is luxury living, unusual style, and you'll be as reluctant to leave as the carriages themselves.

Walcot Hall Estate

Even though it was the 18th-century cradle of the Industrial Revolution that would change the world, Shropshire remains one of England's great rural counties. It has rolling hills, picturesque market towns . . . and hidden surprises, not least on the Walcot Hall Estate. This handsome Georgian mansion was remodelled from an earlier house by Clive of India in the 1760s and is set in the remote countryside of the Welsh borders. And for holidaymakers looking for quirky accommodation those hidden surprises await, tucked away in various quiet corners of the grounds with stunning views. These surprises come in various forms. Each is privately located in woodland and must be reached on foot (bring stout footwear and no more luggage than you can carry). They have no electricity, but cooking facilities are supplied and there's a gen-u-ine privy.

The *tipi* (tepee) for two provides a simple but romantic bolthole for really good friends (campfires a speciality). Close by (but well hidden) is a slightly more sophisticated option – the brightly painted gypsy caravan that sleeps two plus one. Surrounded by a sea of bluebells in spring, the yurt has a cosily furnished interior and also sleeps two (plus junior). The wheeled shepherd's hut has four single bunks and a sitting area, plus wood-burning stove (but no sheep). Also sheepless in Walcot is the old dipping shed, a superior option. It still requires a brisk hike up a steep path but this timber building has an open-plan layout that includes a kitchen, reception hall, dining room, living room, bathroom and double bedroom (with a second double on a mezzanine floor reached by ladder). The ultimate in rural decadence, it has electricity (own generator), Rayburn range cooker and wood-burner. For the non-fleet-of-foot Walcot Hall also has two wonderful showman's wagons that are accessible by car. For that genuine get-away-from-it-all experience, you need look no further.

WHERE:
Lydbury North, near Ludlow, Shropshire

COST:
Budget (but varying by choice of 'surprise')

BEST TIME OF YEAR:
May to September

DON'T MISS:
The estate's wonderful arboretum – especially the Great Douglas Fir, a magnificent sight at 4 m (13 ft) wide and over 30 m (98 ft) tall; exploring the tranquil parkland; fishing (the estate has a lake and two angling ponds); horse riding within the grounds

THINGS TO DO:
Visit the quaint nearby town of Bishops Castle, known for hearty home-cooked food at pubs such as the Three Tuns, Six Bells and Castle Hotel, also famous for their own-brewed beers. Dine finely in historic Ludlow, gastronomic super-town (and visit the atmospheric castle). Sally forth to the fascinating Ironbridge Gorge, where the aforementioned Industrial Revolution began. Hike a section of nearby Offa's Dyke.

YOU SHOULD KNOW:
Book early if you want weekend or high summer dates. For those who prefer more conventional accommodation, it's possible to rent family apartments in outbuildings and the hall itself. In addition, Walcot has a campsite with 12 spaces for touring caravans and additional pitches for tents, behind the Powys Arms pub at the entrance to the estate. The lake was dug by French prisoners during the Napoleonic Wars.

WHERE:
Near Tetbury, Gloucestershire
COST:
Can be reasonable (two sharing or families) to expensive, depending on season and choice of accommodation
BEST TIME OF YEAR:
Any time, but midsummer in the Cotswolds is tourist high noon
DON'T MISS:
The opportunity for some seriously sensual beauty treatments and relaxing therapies at Calcot's new spa; strolling around the manor grounds as though you owned them
THINGS TO DO:
Explore the delightful centre of Tetbury and visit the Police Bygones Museum (unless you have a guilty conscience). Go and call on Prince Charles at Highgrove (he'll be out, but for a not-altogether-small charity donation you can explore the gardens and grounds). Check out nearby Westonbirt Arboretum. Drool over Owlpen Manor, one of the most romantic early manor houses in England.
YOU SHOULD KNOW:
Calcot Manor started life in the early 1300s as a tithe barn for Kingswood Abbey. Book early if you want to stay at Calcot Manor for Tetbury's famous annual Woolsack Day (the last Bank Holiday in May), to enjoy the lively street fair and races where beefy competitors rush with (obviously!) heavy sacks of wool up a steep hill.

Calcot Manor

The Cotswold Hills are the hunting ground (often quite literally) of those steeped in money old or new, who pay millions for prestigious country houses with a bit of precious land. These are not only trophy homes (often *second* homes), but frequently mellow stone manors with centuries of history behind them that are incredibly pleasing to the eye, seeming to grow from the rolling countryside.

Few can be privileged to own such a property, but locals and visitors alike can enjoy the authentic 'Cotswold experience' at Calcot Manor, near the ancient market town of Tetbury. Dating back to the 14th century and surrounded by that must-have park and meadowland, Calcot is a delightful country-house hotel that really does pull out all the stops to make guests feel at home. The welcome is warm and it's not hard to close your eyes for a moment and imagine that you're returning from a hard week's fund-management to your luxurious Cotswold retreat.

The hotel has 35 individually designed and furnished rooms, including suites and family accommodation, much of it around the courtyard. The main house has a dozen rooms that are perfect for couples. All the guest rooms have essentials such as satellite TVs and state-of-the-art music systems, plus trimmings like fluffy robes, fresh fruit, books, magazines and a generous supply of aromatherapy goodies. The elegant Conservatory Restaurant serves fine food with a Mediterranean flavour, using the best local ingredients. Some may prefer the Gumstool Inn for superior pub grub and *al fresco* summer dining. Expect to meet and mingle with savvy locals in both, although they may not actually include the likes of Prince Charles, Jeremy Clarkson, Damien Hirst, Hugh Grant, Kate Winslet, Stella McCartney or similar Cotswold luminaries. Even so, Calcot Manor will make *you* feel pretty special.

Pavilion Cottage, Osborne House

Osborne House is the (vast and more than somewhat ornate) country love nest created by Prince Albert for his darling wife Victoria on the Isle of Wight, with wonderful views across the Solent to the mainland. But sadly Pavilion Cottage was not a place where the lovers went to pass a few romantic rural hours together away from the cares of state. Indeed, the place was not built until the early 1900s after the old Queen had passed away, and the only people who entertained there were cricketers. For truth be told Pavilion Cottage was not so much a cottage, more a . . . cricket pavilion, outside which naval officer cadets and their opponents exchanged broadsides over 22 yards (sorry, some things just don't sound right in metric-speak) of close-mown grass.

Still, this single-storey half-timbered building (now surrounded by a hedged garden, the cricket pitch having long vanished, along with the naval cadets) certainly is a charming little cottage now, and one that makes a wonderful holiday bolthole for four. It has two bedrooms, a sitting room, kitchen and bathroom. The main rooms are all light and airy, opening out onto a verandah that runs along the front of the building. The cottage has every mod con, including appliances galore, and has a peaceful setting within the grounds of Osborne House, overlooking a sweep of unspoilt countryside.

And that's not the best of it. Guests at Pavilion Cottage have the run of Osborne House's extensive grounds after the *hoi polloi* have been turfed out for the night, and that includes Queen Victoria's private beach. It's all too easy to imagine that this is your personal estate, which may explain why Pavilion Cottage gets so many repeat bookings. As for kids, they just love having the run of the place.

WHERE:
Osborne House, East Cowes, Isle of Wight
COST:
Reasonable (for four sharing)
BEST TIME OF YEAR:
Any time is good, summer is best (although the grounds do get crowded during opening hours).
DON'T MISS:
A tour of Osborne House (restricted opening in the winter months); enjoying the eclectic exhibits inside the Swiss Cottage and children's museum created by the royal couple to educate and amuse their children; Queen Victoria's extraordinary, caravan-like bathing machine
THINGS TO DO:
A carriage ride within the grounds; splashing around on the beach; forays out to enjoy some of the island's tourist attractions; a walk along the scenic coastal path
YOU SHOULD KNOW:
A naval college was based at Osborne House (given to the nation after Queen Victoria's death here in 1901) until the 1920s. Pavilion Cottage is operated by English Heritage and is mightily in demand, with the most popular dates booked up well in advance. In addition to the two double bedrooms, Pavilion Cottage has a tot-cot.

Le Manoir aux Quat' Saisons

WHERE:
Church Road, Great Milton, Oxfordshire
COST:
Astronomical (but you won't regret a single penny)
BEST TIME OF YEAR:
Whenever you feel like a country break with food to die for (not literally, of course)
DON'T MISS:
A stroll round the kitchen garden to see where many of the restaurant's ingredients are lovingly nurtured; exploring the grounds with wonderful features like the English Water Garden; afternoon refreshment in the Japanese Tea Garden
THINGS TO DO:
Eating the seven-course lunch, then the splendid nine-course tasting menu in the evening – should there be time for anything else, the helpful hotel staff can arrange activities like fishing, horse riding or entertainment for kids.
YOU SHOULD KNOW:
If you're in an unseemly hurry to address that mouth-watering restaurant menu, arrive via Le Manoir's helipad. Should you dream of whipping up fine food *à le Manoir*, consider enrolling for one of the in-house cookery courses.

You may guess that Le Manoir aux Quat' Saisons (generally referred to simply as 'Le Manoir') has a French connection, and you wouldn't be wrong. It comes in the form of self-taught chef Raymond Blanc, which means that a foray into rural Oxfordshire can not only offer the relaxed delights of a classic country-house hotel in an idyllic setting, but also an experience that should make every gourmet start to salivate in anticipation of delights to come – two-Michelin-star fine dining in the manor's renowned restaurant (a coveted status sustained and honed over three decades). The 15th-century manor has recently been restyled with the lightest of touches for a clean modern feel, without devaluing the charming historic building.

The place has a wonderfully intimate atmosphere, and there are over 30 individually designed guest rooms and suites to choose from. All are beautifully furnished and decorated. The choice for guests who appreciate a touch of humorous nomenclature might be Blanc de Blanc, a suite with private garden that comes in (surprise!) gradations of white. Those of romantic bent who perhaps fancy some super-private quality time between meals might opt for the detached Dovecote, on two levels with a queen-sized bed. But even the regular rooms are of deluxe quality, well up to the overall standards of this meticulous establishment.

Let's give the last word to Raymond Blanc, who made it all happen: 'Le Manoir aux Quat' Saisons is the fulfilment of a personal vision, a dream that one day I would create a hotel and restaurant in harmony where my guests would find perfection in food, comfort, service and welcome.' And so they do.

The Dovecote

What's for lunch? Nowadays a traveller might stop off at the Little Chef to be found at the end of Oxfordshire's Kingston Bagpuize bypass, but in olden times the nearby 18th-century Dovecote would have been the handy source of instant protein. So ignore the Little Chef and turn off into Beech Lane (ironically bordered by pine trees) to find the aforementioned Dovecote, a delightful listed building that now serves as a cosy love nest for romantic couples.

This quatrefoil structure is capped with a central lantern, and within may be found over a thousand brick-built nesting boxes, together with the rotating wooden ladder used to collect the tasty squabs from distraught pigeon parents. This is encouragingly called a 'potence'. But if that all sounds a little primitive to anyone seeking a relaxing break, don't be disheartened. The historic character of this fascinating building may have been preserved, but suitably 21st-century bells and whistles have been added to ensure a memorably comfortable stay. Think under-floor heating, a handy kitchen, spacious lounge with dining area, TV and sound system, glass-fronted bedroom above with king-size bed and a view of those original features, sauna to stew you and shower to cool you down again (each accommodating two, if you must know).

Then it's a matter of preparing supper, closing the curtains, lighting the candles . . . and getting on with it. But if you awake refreshed and are determined to stray, the Dovecote makes a great base from which to explore Oxford's dreaming spires and the many and varied attractions of the Cotswolds.

WHERE:
Buckland, near Faringdon, Oxfordshire
COST:
Budget (per person, two sharing)
BEST TIME OF YEAR:
April to October (but the romantically inclined should be very happy with an intimate winter break)
DON'T MISS:
An *al fresco* meal (find the garden chairs and picnic table stashed under the stairs)
THINGS TO DO:
Find the River Thames (hint – head north for a couple of miles); stroll to the village of Buckland for a swift half (or two) at the Lamb Inn; check out Blenheim Palace
YOU SHOULD KNOW:
A travel cot can be arranged if a small person is already part of the team. A 'welcome' food pack will be supplied, tailored to your requirements.

Spring Cottage

WHERE:
Near Taplow, Buckinghamshire
COST:
Cliveden House's Platinum Club sandwich was confirmed as the world's most expensive in 2007, with a price tag of £100, so you might expect that the cost of a stay at Spring Cottage would be astronomical (and you'd be right).
BEST TIME OF YEAR:
April to September for the best of the weather
DON'T MISS:
The opportunity to explore Cliveden's magnificent riverside grounds with formal gardens, temples, pavilions, follies, water garden, wonderful sculptures, statuary and superb landscape views
THINGS TO DO:
Look around the stunningly furnished main house; attempt to beat Cliveden's original yew maze (the butler will send a search party if you don't return by nightfall); a Thames champagne cruise in one of Cliveden's vintage day launches; a soothing session in the Pavilion Spa (or swim in one of the heated pools)
YOU SHOULD KNOW:
Guests at Spring Cottage will not only be following in the footsteps of John Profumo, but also the smaller spectral imprints of Queen Victoria, a frequent visitor who drove over from Windsor Castle to share her sorrows with confidante the Duchess of Sutherland after Prince Albert died.

And now for something rather naughty (once upon a time). The imposing Astor stately home at Cliveden (now owned by the National Trust but run as a grand hotel) was the scene of an infamous 1960s scandal. For it was here that Secretary of State for War, John Profumo, lit a fire that badly scorched the British government. The Profumo Affair exploded when he lied to Parliament about his affair with Christine Keeler, who was simultaneously involved with senior Russian Naval Attaché (thought by many to be a polite way of saying 'Soviet Spy') Yevgeny Ivanov. The minister's deadly dalliance took place in part at Cliveden's Spring Cottage, which may now be rented by those with a scurrilous sense of history, or merely seeking the relaxing break of a lifetime.

Actually, 'Cottage' is something of an understatement. Spring Cottage was built in the early 1800s as a summer retreat for the Countess of Orkney, and it was later extended by the Duchess of Sutherland. With its tall chimneys, mock-Tudor half-timbering and stunning woodland setting right beside the water, this must surely be one of the most romantic buildings along the entire length of the River Thames.

Then as now the place was a haven of tranquillity, and today's guests (up to six at a time) enjoy the traditional services of a butler, coupled with the thoroughly modern convenience of a car waiting to whisk them up to the main house at any time, offering the perfect combination of peaceful hideaway, complete privacy and swift access to all the services provided by a modern luxury hotel. Staying at Spring Cottage is a once-in-a-lifetime experience (naughtiness optional).

Pelirocco Hotel

Brighton has had a somewhat racy reputation ever since the Prince of Wales (later King George IV) entertained here in his fabulous seaside retreat, the Royal Pavilion. And nowadays this South Coast city is renowned for vibrant street life (and night life second to none). The place represents a special mix of heritage, culture and cosmopolitan fun, and the 'alternative' aspect of this buzzing resort is nowhere better encapsulated than in the extraordinary Pelirocco Hotel, close to the seafront in the city's 'hottest' area. The Pelirocco is loudly billed as 'The original Rock 'n' Roll boutique hotel' and is generally regarded as the sauciest stopover in town.

The hotel's sedate Regency exterior hides the fact that this is quite possibly the quirkiest hotel in the world. Inspired by pop subculture, driven musicians and some of Brighton's zaniest characters, the Pelirocco Hotel is constantly presenting events such as fashion launches, assorted exhibitions and art projects, gigs, book readings and (if there's nothing else going on) wildish parties.

Expect a room that's . . . unusual. Typical choices from the 19 themed rooms might include Do Knit Disturb, the bizarre knitted room created by Brighton artist Kate Cardigan (pun intended), the knockout Ali's Room for dedicated followers of 'float like a butterfly, sting like a bee' Muhammad Ali, the Pin Up Parlour dedicated to the UK's answer to Marilyn Monroe (aka the buxom Diana Dors), Dollywood (Dolly's Deep South Cabin), Cloud Cuckoo Land (where everything is perfect), the Sputnik pod room or rather decadent Play Room with its huge round bed (mirror above), giant plunge bath and pole-dancing area. But don't assume that anything will remain static, as change and excitement are the Pelirocco Hotel's middle names. Sign yours in the register and prepare for a rollercoaster stay.

WHERE:
Regency Square, Brighton
COST:
Budget going on reasonable
BEST TIME OF YEAR:
Brighton swings all year round, as does the hotel.
DON'T MISS:
The hotel's very own radio show (wacky Pelirocco Platters, broadcast twice weekly on Brighton's Radioreverb); a (somewhat expensive) photo shoot by the hotel's celebrity photographer after a makeover, so you take away a professional portfolio as a reminder of your stay
THINGS TO DO:
Soak up the hotel's undoubted vibe – and join the in-house funky fun; bring your own vinyl and spin the hotel's decks; visit the Royal Pavilion, because it's there and just as jazzy (in its own time) as the Pelirocco (today); check out the pier; scorch your plastic around Brighton's famous Lanes shopping area.
YOU SHOULD KNOW:
Stay for two weekend nights at the Pelirocco and get a third free. In case you're wondering if the place is actually *clean*, it is – spotless, in fact.

Safari Britain

WHERE:
Firle, East Sussex
COST:
Budget (per person)
BEST TIME OF YEAR:
Open from May to September
DON'T MISS:
Sitting on the privy scanning the great sweep of countryside with the binoculars thoughtfully provided; the ingenious hot shower hidden inside an ancient beech tree, powered by a wood-burning stove; hiring the country cook who will whip up a special meal for you if kitchen duties weigh heavy
THINGS TO DO:
Genuine country living; a hike along the nearby South Downs Way; guided nature/wildlife-watching/adventure walks (extra charge); a 25-minute stroll to The Ram in Firle village
YOU SHOULD KNOW:
Non-compostable rubbish must be taken away in the heavy-duty bags provided. No dogs allowed. The focus is on group bookings but individuals, couples and families can be accommodated when there is no group in residence.

The adventure starts with a drive into the Sussex countryside, culminating in a short ride along an unmade former coach road and ending with an assignation at an old shepherd's cottage and barn. Park in the clearing and await transport to the campsite, located on a chalk escarpment owned by the Firle Estate. Hardy campers can walk, carrying all they need, but it takes 15 uphill minutes before the encampment on a grassy plateau is reached. This is getting away from it all in spades, surrounded by beech woods and stunning South Downs scenery.

Don't expect to see wild animals (apart from the occasional deer or fox), because the 'Safari' bit refers to the rewarding pleasures of simple living, entirely without unnecessary frills. There will, however, be frequent visits from sheep and ponies who regard the area as home. A maximum of 20 visitors at any one time maintains the uncluttered 'at-one-with-nature' atmosphere encapsulated in the site's slogan, 'High on Pleasure, Low on Carbon'. They are accommodated in eight 'Boy Scout Camp' canvas bell tents containing foam mattresses, cotton bottom sheets, pillows and pillow cases.

Cooking gas, wood, charcoal, drinking water, cool boxes, candles, matches, fire lighters, cleaning kit, loo paper, soap and condiments are provided, so all you need to bring is food and drink, a sleeping bag and a torch to facilitate reading in bed or nocturnal forays to the composting toilet. Meals are self-cooked using bottled gas in the large kitchen yurt (all necessary equipment provided), with the big central fireplace or barbecues as alternatives. The communal living area is another super-comfortable yurt with hide rugs, a wood-burning stove, books and games for rainy days. Those who fancy *really* getting away from it all will be in Safari Heaven!

Folkestone Martello Tower

WHERE:
East Cliff, Folkestone, Kent
COST:
Budget (per person, with a full house)
BEST TIME OF YEAR:
April to September
DON'T MISS:
The original door to the gun deck at the top, complete with hatch through which to pass cannon balls (if you have any); relaxing in front of a log fire in the evening; buying seafood fresh from the boat at Folkestone Harbour; enjoying the secluded garden with its barbecue area, children's play house and large trampoline

Look out, there's a Napoleon about! Duly rattled, the British government built 100-odd small round forts to defend England's south and east coasts. These self-contained Martello Towers housed 25 soldiers, had thick walls to resist cannon fire from invading men o' war and could reply in kind with a single heavy gun on the roof that could traverse through 360 degrees. But the Little Corporal's invasion never came, and not one Martello fired a shot in anger.

They were so solidly built (each used 250,000 bricks) that some – like equally under-employed concrete World War II pillboxes a century and more later – were simply too much trouble to demolish. So many remain, and some have taken on a new life as quirky homes with a sea view. One such is Martello No 2 (of four still standing in Folkestone). This is the only Martello along the south coast available as a short-term holiday let, to delight those who like to stay somewhere rather more than a little different that is inescapably redolent of history, complete with atmospheric original features like vaulted brick ceilings.

The entrance is via a stairway to the original first-floor entry point, leading to an open-plan area with a kitchen, dining area and sitting room with a balcony. The old ammunition store below has two double bedrooms and the family bathroom. A stone staircase in the wall leads up to the tower's crowning glory, the former gun deck with its sweeping views of Folkestone Harbour and shoreline, the White Cliffs of Dover, the French coast (on a clear day), Dungeness and the North Downs. There is also an en-suite double bedroom, ensuring that there's ample room for the average family. And if the French should invade, simply bar the door!

THINGS TO DO:
The seaside – there are beaches galore within easy walking distance (the Warren and Sunny Sands being the nearest) and Folkestone has the usual attractions; ride the Romney, Hythe and Dymchurch Railway; visit one (or both) of the nearby zoo parks – Howletts and Port Lympne

YOU SHOULD KNOW:
The seaward walls of Martellos are 4 m (13 ft) thick, so putting in new windows with sea views during residential conversion is no easy task. The other Martello you can stay in is the largest and most northerly ever built – the Landmark Trust's four-gun quatrefoil tower at Aldeburgh in Suffolk. The Martello at Dymchurch (No 24 of 74 built along the south coast) has been restored and is now a museum showing how the original garrison lived and worked.

Leeds Castle

WHERE:
Near Maidstone, Kent
COST:
Expensive
BEST TIME OF YEAR:
House parties are held all year round.
DON'T MISS:
Guests at house parties have exclusive use of the castle, so make the most of it by exploring the interior.
THINGS TO DO:
The tourist thing starts up again next morning, and it's well worth checking out attractions like the maze, grotto and (somewhat bizarrely) dog-collar museum. There's a pay-and-play golf course (sadly the butler won't carry your clubs), regular hot-air balloon flights and ziplining at Go Ape! for youngsters. One unusual option is the Segway tour (those amazing devices touted as *the* 21st-century mode of personal transport).
YOU SHOULD KNOW:
If you fear that your manners might not be quite up to a stay in the castle itself (or you're on a budget), you can still enjoy the Leeds Castle experience by taking one of the Stable Courtyard bed-and-breakfast rooms. They're spacious, nicely furnished and guests have access to the castle and grounds (it's great to stroll around the latter after day-visitors have departed). There are also three self-catering holiday cottages within the scenic Leeds Castle Estate.

If ever a Hollywood director needs a romantic medieval castle to star in his latest historical epic, the cry 'send for Leeds Castle' will surely be heard. Once described by a noble visitor as 'the loveliest castle in the world' (perhaps after a little too much champagne), Leeds Castle certainly is as pretty as a postcard, sitting on its fortified river island with mellow stone battlements and turrets reflected in the surrounding water.

Built in 1119 as a Norman stronghold and with royal associations over several centuries thereafter, the place owes its survival to the owner during the English Civil War who shrewdly sided with the winning Parliamentarians. It has been made over a couple of times since – notably when the interior was revamped by the last private owner, Lady Baillie, who bought the castle in the 1920s and made it an essential port of call on the social circuit. She died in 1976 after instructing that Leeds Castle should not merely become a heritage museum, but be used and enjoyed. And that's where you come in (if

you've ever dreamed of living like an aristocrat, however briefly).

Leeds Castle hosts regular country-house parties that allow everyone to experience the sort of elegant living once reserved for the upper classes. The evening begins with aperitifs in the library, warmed by an open fire. The butler is on hand to serve drinks, naturally, as guests mix 'n' mingle. Then it's on for a splendid meal in the grand banqueting hall, followed by recovery time in the withdrawing room (happily with both ladies and gents in attendance, rather than going their separate ways as once was *de rigeur*). After everyone is suitably partied out, a luxuriously furnished bedroom awaits, and the visit ends with breakfast the following morning.

House in the Clouds

There's only one place to head for if you crave a holiday 'for people who want to experience life as it was when England was Merrie England'. That may sound naive to modern ears (was England ever really that merry?), but it was the passionate dream of barrister, railway designer and landowner Glencairn Stuart Ogilvie, who believed in all things English and healthy open-air pursuits (although ironically he was Scottish). So he made his dream come true, building the fantasy holiday village of Thorpeness – just along the Suffolk coast from the ancient town of Aldeburgh – in the 1920s.

Ogilvie created a country club, golf course, holiday homes in Tudor and Jacobean revival styles, a windmill, out-of-time almshouses and a boating lake called the Meare. The place is little changed today and it's impossible to miss the village's most extraordinary sight. The House in the Clouds is a fairytale red cottage perched atop a square black tower. The cottage did in fact hide the tank that contained the Thorpeness water supply (pumped by the mill), while the supporting tower was a house occupied by one of Ogilvie's friends. When mains water came, the cottage was converted into a large games room and upper viewing gallery, and the House in the Clouds is now available as a holiday let.

It's expensive, but can accommodate at least two average families or a large party of friends. Beautifully appointed, it has a well-fitted kitchen, five double bedrooms plus additional double sofa bed, three bathrooms, drawing room and that sensational 'room at the top' with incomparable sea and countryside views. There are 67 stairs with resting places on each landing, and a spiral staircase to the upper gallery. One thing is absolutely guaranteed – you'll never stay in another place remotely like the quirky House in the Clouds.

WHERE:
Thorpeness, Suffolk
COST:
Astronomical, particularly in summer, but reasonable per person if you can round up a full complement
BEST TIME OF YEAR:
March to October (but make it July and August if you like a buzz, as two-thirds of the villagers only arrive for the summer holidays and the lively Thorpeness Regatta on the Meare and Aldeburgh Carnival are held then)
DON'T MISS:
In-house games tournaments (table tennis, snooker, lawn tennis, *boules*); messing about in boats on the Meare (kids will love it, as there are tiny islands based on locations from *Peter Pan,* such as Wendy's home and the pirate lair); a barbecue evening in the garden; Maggi Hambling's controversial sculpture *The Scallop* (dedicated to former local resident Benjamin Britten) on the blue-flag shingle beach at Aldeburgh
THINGS TO DO:
Explore North Warren RSPB reserve (and the Aldringham Walks area of heathland to the north). Visit nearby Snape Maltings for a concert or its specialist shops. Check out Aldeburgh's medieval Moot Hall and its local museum.
YOU SHOULD KNOW:
In high summer the minimum stay at the House in the Clouds is one week, but at other times it's possible to book by the night. The house soars above a large private garden. It's advisable to secure your reservation in good time as this appealing holiday home has a very high occupancy rate.

Cley Windmill

WHERE:
Cley Next the Sea, Norfolk
COST:
Budget to reasonable, depending on the room (two sharing)
BEST TIME OF YEAR:
Any time (busy in summer; often bleak in winter but with lonely grandeur and lots of migratory wildfowl; spring or autumn for room to swing a camera)
DON'T MISS:
Cley Marshes bird reserve (look out for avocets and listen out for bitterns); relaxing in the walled garden adjacent to the River Glaven; sensational sunsets; dining by candlelight at the mill (book with the room for a guaranteed reservation and a discount)
THINGS TO DO:
Visit the House of Windsor's Sandringham Estate; venture onto the wide expanse of Holkham Beach and dunes; take the Coasthopper bus to explore the coast (runs between Kings Lynn and Cromer, and yes, you hop on and hop off as you please); enjoy a seal-watching boat trip to nearby Blakeney Point
YOU SHOULD KNOW:
The windmill was owned by the family of singer James Blunt for many years. Be sure to book early – this enchanting guesthouse has one of the highest occupancy rates in Britain, with good reason.

North Norfolk Heritage Coast is often referred to as 'Chelsea on Sea' for the number of wealthy second-home owners who have chosen the area as an ideal refuge from the stresses and strains of city life, and their 'Chelsea Tractors' (top-of-the-range 4x4s) are much in evidence during the summer months. But they can't and don't invade and conquer the lonely salt marshes, mudflats and wide beaches where the tide rushes in at alarming speed, all of which give this haunting coastline its special character.

If you want to explore for yourself, and have a hankering for unusual accommodation, an ideal choice is Cley Windmill, a prominent landmark built around 1820, nestling beside an old quay on the edge of the marshes. This really is a bed-and-breakfast (or self-catering) experience second to none. The busy coast road runs through this pretty village at the mouth of the River Glaven, but the mill is in a peaceful spot beneath those big Norfolk skies, with breathtaking views across waving reed beds to Blakeney Point and the sea.

There is a choice of nine en-suite rooms with a view, in the mill and its picturesque complex of flint-walled outbuildings, some of which can accommodate up to four people (if they're family or very friendly), while those preferring to self-cater can opt for the Dovecote. Breakfast is included, and taken in the mill's beamed dining room. The circular ground floor of the mill makes a most inviting sitting room full of antique furniture where guests can meet, mingle and relax around an open fire. Once discovered, visitors tend to return time after time, and it's easy to understand why.

The Rotunda

Part of the original Bull Ring development that modernized (some said) or devastated (claimed others) the centre of England's second city in the 1960s, the aptly named 25-storey Rotunda (yes, it is indeed round) has finally come into its own. After numerous calls to demolish a symbol of post-war Britain's least favourite architectural period, this instantly recognizable cylinder was awarded listed-building status in 2000 and is now no longer an office building, but a sought-after residential complex.

And the top floors are given over to some of Britain's most unusual self-catering accommodation – 26 serviced apartments in this cool glass tube that reaches for the sky. They come in studio, one-bed and two-bed configurations. They're all different and all special, representing urban chic at its slickest. The wedge-shaped apartments radiate out from a central lobby and all have window walls of glass

WHERE:
Bull Ring, Birmingham
COST:
Budget, reasonable or expensive, depending on season and apartment chosen (rates are per apartment rather than per person)
BEST TIME OF YEAR:
'Any toime' sounds good in a Brummie accent.
DON'T MISS:
The special discount available by booking direct with the Rotunda by phone or on line
THINGS TO DO:
Some serious retail therapy (the Rotunda is right in the centre of the city); see the famous jewellery quarter (and its pen museum); visit Birmingham Museum and Art Gallery for one of the world's best collections of romantic pre-Raphaelite paintings; take in the Custard Factory for the Ikon Gallery (contemporary art) plus specialist shops and a Saturday flea market
YOU SHOULD KNOW:
If you take an apartment for Friday and Saturday, you get Sunday night thrown in for free. The infamous Birmingham pub bombings in 1974 that killed 21 devastated the Mulberry Bush on the ground floors of the Rotunda – and cost the wrongly convicted Birmingham Six 16 years apiece in prison.

with a step-out balcony beyond (enjoy sensational city views by day and night). There are echoes of the Swinging Sixties that marked the Rotunda's genesis, but also modern musts like Poggenpohl kitchens, Italian espresso makers, white bathrooms, funky furniture, Apple computers, iPod docks and free wifi. And rest assured that the beds are the most comfortable money can buy.

The apartments are family-friendly – kids just love the bright decor and are wowed by the views. They are also welcomed with a small gift and dressing-up box (under tens) or pens and crayons for slightly older ones, plus games for all ages (including dads). It's possible to eat in together, too, rather than dining out, although guests get a Gastro card offering discounts at recommended restaurants. The apartments are named after famous British cars made down the road at Longbridge, but don't be fooled – they are run by Staying Cool, and self-catering doesn't come much cooler.

The Old Lock-Up

Wirksworth was once (amazing though it may seem today when gazing upon the area's wonderful scenery) a busy lead-mining centre – and 19th-century miners were not noted for sobriety come pay day. So no doubt the Old Lock-Up saw more than its fair share of drunken troublemakers, duly thrown into a cell to sober up. That cell is now, ironically, the bar that serves visitors to this welcoming (another *volte face*!) bed-and-breakfast establishment in the Derbyshire Peak District National Park. The Old Lock-Up on the outskirts of town was once a magistrate's house, then a police station, and one cell has been left just as it was so that visitors can imagine where transgression would have led them in the 1800s.

But there the hardship ends. For the Old Lock-Up is no longer a dour house of detention, but has the friendliest of atmospheres and four splendid guest rooms. The Magistrate's Room was where justice was dispensed before local police forces were established in the 1850s. Prisoners could have a private chat with their lawyer in the Solicitor's Room, while the other two bedrooms are in the coach house where once the horses needed for hot pursuit of felons were stabled.

For those who prefer not to be luxuriously banged up for the night, there's an alternative – Derbyshire's smallest B&B. But even this one is not without issues, for it is a tiny Gothic chapel sitting in a peaceful graveyard. This romantic hideaway was built in 1812 and has been carefully renovated to maintain its original character, while also including the bare necessities (beautiful antique bed, bathroom and shower, TV and radio, fridge and tea-making facilities).

WHERE:
Wirksworth, near Matlock, Derbyshire
COST:
Budget
BEST TIME OF YEAR:
April to October
DON'T MISS:
Breakfast (not the buffet option, the plate-busting 'full English'); the fascinating display of historical artefacts associated with the Old Lock-Up
THINGS TO DO:
Walking (the surrounding countryside is magnificent); hiking the High Peak Trail; the 'Drive a Train' experience at Ecclesbourne Valley Railway (a five-minute walk away) – or just take a ride; visit Chatsworth House; journey beneath the earth at Poole's Cavern
YOU SHOULD KNOW:
Writer D H Lawrence and his German wife Frieda had to report to the Old Lock-Up once a week in World War I, as she was a registered alien. You might get to sleep in the room where murderer George Victor Townley admitted stabbing his former fiancée to death in 1861 (he controversially escaped the gallows on the grounds of insanity but later committed suicide in Pentonville Prison – and no, no ghost has ever been spotted in the Old Lock-Up!).

WHERE:
Helmsley, North Yorkshire
COST:
Reasonable going on expensive (but deals to be done); a session in the spa costs extra
BEST TIME OF YEAR:
Any season but winter for outdoor activities; winter for a snug stay-indoors break with some refined Christmas shopping thrown in
DON'T MISS:
A dip in the heated outdoor pool, or simply taking a glass of wine or afternoon tea on the delightful surrounding terrace; the restaurant's tempting tasting menu; imposing Helmsley Castle
THINGS TO DO:
Shopping in town (a surprising choice of goodies on offer); gentle riverside walks; wild and suitably wuthering moorland walks; a visit to Duncombe Park (mansion and gardens); a trip to historic York; nearby Flamingo Land for kids (theme park with zoo and farm, open from April to November); also for the young (or young at heart) – the Go Ape! high-wire adventure in Dalby Forest.
YOU SHOULD KNOW:
A two-night stay is compulsory at weekends. Leave the stuffed poodle (toy) outside the door in lieu of a 'Do Not Disturb' sign if you want to lie in.

Feversham Arms

If awards tell you anything, they communicate the fact that the Feversham Arms in North Yorkshire will deliver a memorable stay. The hotel won an AA Hotel of the Year Award when Gleneagles got the Scottish crown and the Connaught scored for London, also securing the accolade of 'Britain's Favourite Hotel'. So far so very good. So what's the special deal?

Location: the peaceful backwater of Helmsley, once a thriving weaving centre but now a historic market town that retains its compact medieval layout, renowned as a perfect place for a relaxing country break on the edge of the North York Moors. The building: a sturdy old stone-built Victorian inn turned boutique hotel beside the church, with a homely log-fire feel plus modern comforts. Accommodation: 33 beautifully furnished rooms with fireplaces including 22 suites, some of which resemble small country cottages. Eating: breakfast (included) served in your room, restaurant with top chef offering a rich English menu well served with the finest local produce. Drinking: two bars, the lively one at the front where the locals gather and the snug at the back for a peaceful pint. Pampering: decadent bathrooms, in-room spa treatments available, the Verbena Spa (reached by a glass bridge from the main building) for full-on self-indulgence including champagne, juice bar and spa food. Entertainment: flat-screen TV with DVD player in every room, extensive DVD film library. Families: well catered for with a babysitting service, free cots for toddlers, in-room folding beds for older children available for a small supplement, children's menu in the restaurant – and dogs welcome. Atmosphere: warm, friendly and a refreshingly genuine 'nothing-is-too-much-trouble' approach to customer satisfaction.

So what's not to like, what more is there to know? Enjoy!

La Rosa Gypsy Campsite

The clue is in the 'Camp Karma' which visitors are expected to observe, covering the need for gentle sustainable behaviour while in residence. This is most definitely not your average campsite, although its setting in the North Yorkshire Moors National Park near Whitby is everything a happy camper could possibly dream of. La Rosa Gypsy Campsite is simply . . . extraordinary. It's a place with a vision, and that vision is something that would have been recognized and applauded by 1960s hippies high on alternative culture (among other things).

This is a delightfully different place, with on-site accommodation on the extensive 8-ha (20-ac) site consisting of scattered static caravans of various vintages, along with wild cards like a converted truck and *tipi* (tepee). But you'll never feel crowded, because no more than 18 people can stay at any one time. All the accommodation is funkily decorated and, while beds are comfortable, the facilities are basic to say the least. Don't expect newly fashionable 'glamping' (glamorous camping), but an almost primitive experience that fulfils La Rosa's avowed sustainability mission. The only bath sits in the middle of an orchard (bring a swimming costume), showers are in a converted byre and the composting loo is in an old shepherd's hut. Caravans have no electricity but the price includes bedding, cooking gas, candles and firewood. Bring torches, wellies, warm clothing and food, but no more than you can carry easily as it's a bit of a hike to caravans in the top field.

The last word goes to the laid-back management: 'We like to hope that being green does not mean you can't be comfy, have a laugh or eat chocolate cake. We welcome and aim to provide for all ages and types of people (except racists, bigots or puritans!).' You get the picture!

WHERE:
Near Goathland, North Yorkshire
COST:
Budget (with a discount for those arriving by public transport, on foot or by bike)
BEST TIME OF YEAR:
April to October
DON'T MISS:
Gentle contemplation of the meaning of life; gentle woodland walks around the site
THINGS TO DO:
Visit the Birch Hall Inn in nearby Beckhole, a winner of the coveted (by traditionalists) 'Most Untouched Pub Award'. Enjoy a steam-train ride on the North Yorkshire Moors steam railway – it runs from Pickering to Whitby with local-to-La-Rosa stations being Grosmont and Goathland, the latter doubling both as Aidensfield in the long-running TV drama *Heartbeat* and Hogsmeade in the first Harry Potter film. Take out a traditional rowing boat on the River Esk at Ruswarp.
YOU SHOULD KNOW:
Non-campers who'd like a slice of quirky La Rosa character with sea views and a real roof should head for the La Rosa Hotel on Whitby's West Cliff. This flat-fronted Victorian building was once the regular haunt of *Alice in Wonderland* author Lewis Carroll and has been kitted out with an astonishing mixture of antiques and car-boot kitsch that definitely add up to a unique 'wonderland'.

Chillingham Castle

WHERE:
Near Wooler, Northumberland
COST:
Budget to reasonable (depending on choice of accommodation and number sharing the chosen apartment, as multiple occupation does not raise the cost by much)
BEST TIME OF YEAR:
Any time (but Northumbrian winter weather can encourage the idea of staying in beside the fire)
DON'T MISS:
The castle tour (April to October only, not Saturdays, but self-catering guests are allowed to visit many parts of the castle after hours); Chillingham's unique herd of wild cattle (the only ones left in Britain); the gardens and woodland walks

Although a single family line has owned and occupied Chillingham Castle since 1246, it's now possible to share their home and soak up the historic atmosphere. The castle developed over the centuries with the addition of essentials like 14th-century battlements, Elizabethan long galleries, grounds by Capability Brown in the mid 1700s and a stunning Italianate garden in the 19th century. After falling into disrepair it was rescued by Sir Humphry Wakefield in the 1980s, whose wife Katharine is descended from the family that established Chillingham.

Now, the castle is surrounded by stunning gardens and a 150-ha (370-ac) park and there are eight self-catering apartments dotted around the castle and outbuildings. These allow visitors to get a flavour of Sir Humphry's impeccable if eccentric restoration and are suitable for individuals, couples, groups of friends and well-behaved families ('off to the spooky dungeon' for troublemakers!).

The intimate Guard Room sleeps two, with its own entry from the courtyard. Grey is in the heart of the main building, sleeps four and includes a spectacular long gallery with timbered ceiling and carved chimney piece. Lookout for five is high in the castle and has wonderful views. The Tower overlooks the arched courtyard and can accommodate four. The popular Victorian artist Sir Edwin Landseer was a regular visitor and the apartment that bears his name can sleep six. Courtyard on two floors also sleeps six. The characterful Old Dairy (sleeps six) has views across the valley, while the Coaching Rooms harbour the largest apartment. Each is beautifully furnished with antiques and has its own very individual character redolent of history, so the only questions to answer are 'what's not to like about castle life?' and 'which one?'.

THINGS TO DO:
Fishing on the River Till; exploring Northumberland's famously beautiful wild countryside (and the rugged coast close by); ghost hunting (as a result of dark deeds done here over all those centuries, Chillingham Castle is said to be one of the most haunted buildings in England)
YOU SHOULD KNOW:
Some apartments are unsuitable for children under the age of ten. That fierce old 'Hammer of the Scots', Edward I, based himself at Chillingham Castle before sallying forth to give William Wallace a good drubbing in 1298.

Sykeside Camping Park

The Lake District is a jewel in England's natural crown and the centrally located Dovedale Valley is surrounded by magnificent upland landscape – Dove Crag, Fairfield and Hart Crag – and Brotherswater (formerly Broad Water) is nearby. Situated at the northern foot of the Kirkstone Pass, Sykeside Camping Park is as scenic as it gets, and wherever your tent is pitched a great view is guaranteed. Sykeside has been carefully planned to retain a variety of dispersed sites, thus ensuring that the natural feel of the place is not compromised by regimented rows of cheek-by-jowl tents.

For caravanners there are five hard-standing sites with electrical hook-ups, located in a secluded corner of the park, while there are 19 sites likewise empowered for those increasingly popular RVs (once merely called 'camper vans'). Any tentless families or groups who want a piece of this special place can book into the bunkhouse, which has nine rooms with between two and six beds apiece, plus basic cooking facilities. And those who like a life of (relative) luxury can opt for a well-equipped self-catering cottage that sleeps four.

The park's atmosphere is super-relaxed and visitors want for nothing. The modern toilet and shower facilities have shaving sockets and power points. There are laundry, drying and washing-up rooms, plus a well-stocked shop that has camping supplies and equipment, fresh produce and general provisions, guides and maps. Good food and drink are served in the Barn End Bar (summer only), which inevitably acts as the camp's social centre where campers can meet, mingle and discuss the day's discoveries. There couldn't be a better place for those who like open-air holidays to experience the magic of the Lake District.

WHERE:
Brotherswater, Patterdale, Cumbria
COST:
Budget, budget, budget = super-affordable (including the cottage, shared between four)
BEST TIME OF YEAR:
April to June, September (the Lake District's narrow roads are ill suited to the sheer volume of summer holiday traffic, and the site is open all year for hardy adventurers)
DON'T MISS:
A pie and a pint at the adjacent Brotherswater Inn; the choice of walks (to suit any level of ability including smallish children) that start from the campsite; casting a line into Brotherswater
THINGS TO DO:
The Lake District, as in sightseeing, hiking and cycling (if you're fit), boat trips, sailing and canoeing, birdwatching, a ride on the Lakeside and Haverthwaite heritage railway and more
YOU SHOULD KNOW:
The park is conveniently situated as a base for forays to attractive places such as Ambleside, Windermere, Grasmere, Coniston, Keswick, Penrith and Kendal. The valley-bottom location means there's poor TV reception and there's no mobile phone signal, either (so teenagers may be unimpressed).

Hell Bay Hotel

WHERE:
Bryher
COST:
Expensive
BEST TIME OF YEAR:
April to October
DON'T MISS:
A boat trip round the islands; the view from the top of Samson Hill; a drink at Fraggle Rock Bar – England's westernmost pub; the renowned Tresco Abbey Garden
THINGS TO DO:
Rambling; cycling; swimming; diving; snorkelling; boating; kayaking; tennis; golf; croquet
YOU SHOULD KNOW:
It's not easy to reach Bryher. You can get there by boat from Land's End or by flying to Tresco or St Mary's in a helicopter or light aircraft (the Skybus) and then taking the ferry.

Bryher is the smallest and wildest of the inhabited Scilly Isles. Just 2 km (1.25 mi) long and 1 km (0.5 mi) wide with only 80 inhabitants, it is one of the very few places in Britain that still feels really remote. The sea is exceptionally clear here and there are beautiful deserted beaches, virtually no cars and few tourists.

Hell Bay is the only hotel on the island, a coastal estate in a heavenly spot, hidden away in its own secluded grounds overlooking the sea. The 25 large, comfortable and spotlessly clean rooms and family suites are in assorted outbuildings surrounded by lovely gardens. Many of them have sea views, and you may even spot a seal on the beach from your window. Within a few moments' walk of the hotel grounds you'll find yourself on a deserted beach watching the Atlantic breakers rolling in and the seabirds whirling overhead.

There is a whole-heartedly child-friendly attitude here. Kids will have a wonderful time collecting their own breakfast eggs from the hotel's chicken coops, frolicking in the heated swimming pool, playing outdoor chess and hanging out in the children's games room. The hotel also serves a role as the island's informal art gallery, with sculptures and paintings by many well-known locally connected contemporary artists on view in the public areas. Hell Bay is a really stylish hotel, a great place for a restful family holiday or a romantic interlude, chic yet unpretentious with an excellent restaurant that serves food of a quality way beyond what one might reasonably expect on a small, remote British island.

Longueville Manor

Longueville Manor well deserves its reputation as the best hotel in Jersey. It's set in 6.5 ha (16 ac) of beautifully landscaped gardens at the end of a pretty wooded valley, with formal plantings, fountains, a lake, ancient trees and a Victorian kitchen garden. The 16th-century manor house fell into a state of complete neglect during World War II but the forebears of the present owners saved the estate from ruin and Longueville has now been in the family and continuously maintained as a hotel for the past three generations. It is exceptional in offering unstinting luxury, fantastic food and impeccable service at the same time as being thoroughly family orientated, even going so far as to welcome pet dogs.

There are 30 spacious rooms all individually decorated in a harmonious blend of styles that somehow manages to combine an aura of ultra-chic, hi-tech sophistication with personal homely touches. The bathrooms are especially plush with bespoke toiletries and even a scented candle on the shelf. One of the hotel suites is a 17th-century stone cottage in the grounds with its own kitchen and private garden – perfect for a family break, or anyone who wants complete privacy.

Longueville prides itself on its food. You can enjoy grilled lobster *al fresco* on the swimming pool terrace, tuck into an old-fashioned afternoon tea in one of the cosy lounges and feast on a sensational dinner in the oak-panelled dining room. There is none of the snooty pretension that one so often finds in luxury hotels – just outstandingly courteous, unobtrusive service in a thoroughly relaxed atmosphere. The Longueville is everything one could possibly want of a five-star hotel, and more – a place for wallowing in unashamed self-indulgence.

WHERE:
St Saviour
COST:
Expensive, but various special offers help to keep the price down
BEST TIME OF YEAR:
April to October
DON'T MISS:
The 'Nun's Walk' trail through Longueville Manor's woods; the seven-course Discovery Menu dinner in the hotel restaurant
THINGS TO DO:
Hiking; mountain biking; horse riding; fishing; sailing; diving; kayaking; tennis; golf; croquet
YOU SHOULD KNOW:
Longueville Manor has won numerous awards. It is the only AA Five Red Star hotel on Jersey and is a member of Relais & Châteaux.

La Corbière Radio Tower

WHERE:
La Corbière
COST:
Reasonable
BEST TIME OF YEAR:
April to October
DON'T MISS:
Crossing the causeway to La Corbière lighthouse; the granite monument *St Malo* by sculptor Derek Tristram on the headland; Jersey War Tunnels Museum
THINGS TO DO:
Walking; cycling; birdwatching; beaches; golf; exploring the island
YOU SHOULD KNOW:
At the end of the war, rather than being demolished, La Corbière Tower had years of useful existence as a marine radio tower and was only converted into self-catering holiday accommodation in 2004. The tower is not suitable for toddlers, small children or anyone with mobility problems – the staircases are very steep. Bookings must be made well in advance.

The island of Jersey is renowned for its beautiful beaches, unspoilt scenery and leafy country lanes – plus its fascinating history, in which La Corbière Radio Tower at one time played a peculiarly threatening role.

Standing in a commanding position on a rugged headland overlooking the Gulf of St Malo, the tower has a vaguely menacing, indestructible look about it which, given its history, is not really surprising. It was originally built as an observation tower during the World War II German occupation of Jersey as part of Hitler's chain of Atlantic defences and was only transformed into a radio tower after the war. The brutalist architecture of solid concrete with narrow window slits makes the tower's original purpose of directing artillery fire at passing Allied shipping only too clear.

You need to be athletic to stay here. The tower is six storeys high with just one room on each floor. It sleeps six in three double rooms and has three shower rooms and a fully equipped kitchen. The lookout centre at the top was once the main purpose of the tower's existence and, now converted into a living area, is still the most compelling reason for staying here.

Perched up in the sky, you are blessed with a fantastic all-round view of the island and for miles out to sea, with the famous landmark of La Corbière lighthouse perched on an outcrop in the foreground. It is all too easy to lose track of time, mesmerized by the waves as you contemplate the dramatic history of the wild Jersey coastline. Anyone who relishes the out of the ordinary will delight in the novelty of staying in La Corbière Tower.

WHERE:
Alderney, Channel Islands
COST:
Budget or reasonable, depending on number of people and time of year
BEST TIME OF YEAR:
April to October
DON'T MISS:
Views from Fort Clonque's old gun emplacements; the tidal race in the Swinge Strait; Les Etacs gannet colonies; remnants of the German World War II fortifications
THINGS TO DO:
Cliff walking; swimming; rock pooling; cycling; birdwatching; fishing; sailing; tennis; boat trips
YOU SHOULD KNOW:
The Landmark Trust is a charity that rescues and preserves all sorts of old buildings. Many of its properties are available for holiday rentals and the proceeds go back into the charitable trust to help with restoration costs. You must book months in advance to be sure of getting the property you want for the dates you want. However, if you're not too choosy about where you stay, there are always late availability options posted on the Landmark Trust website.

Fort Clonque

Fort Clonque is one of the most important historical buildings on the tiny island of Alderney. It is a rambling 19th-century pile of a fortress sitting on a rock stack at the steep southwestern tip of the island, overlooking the Swinge strait and accessible only by causeway. This amazing Victorian building almost looks as though it has sprung organically out of the rocks. It stands picturesquely on various different levels and encloses swathes of open grass and samphire pasture, lichen sprouting on its granite walls that coil unevenly round the rock stacks, following the lie of the land.

The fortress was originally built by the British in the 1840s but was abandoned a few years later and left to decay. In 1940 Hitler took over the Channel Islands and refortified it, converting part of the Victorian army quarters into a massive gun emplacement. Now, thanks to the work of the Landmark Trust, it is possible to rent Fort Clonque as a holiday let. The Trust has furbished it to accommodate as many as 13 people in five twin-bedded rooms and a triple room. There are two bathrooms and a shower, an open fireplace and an immense vaulted kitchen which is a joy to cook in, equipped with all the implements anyone could possibly need.

At high tide the fortress is often cut off from the main island, as it is in rough weather when giant waves dash against the thick 6-m (19-ft) walls and the causeway is flooded. The ever-present danger of being isolated is all part of the thrill of staying here. It is an absolutely superb place for a family holiday or group adventure.

A Cottage at Portmeirion

Portmeirion is a wondrous 20th-century folly, a fantasy seaside village designed and built by Welsh architect Sir Clough Williams-Ellis between 1925 and 1975. Williams-Ellis had a vision of erecting a unified built environment which would enhance the natural landscape of the rugged Cardigan Bay peninsula he owned. Eventually, the development of the Portmeirion estate turned into an idiosyncratic labour of love that took almost an entire lifetime to complete.

Portmeirion is an extraordinary architectural achievement – a 'classical confection' of unlikely shapes and styles cascading down the hillside to the shore, in which Georgian colonnades and Greek temple architecture blend sympathetically with Italianate domes, quaint clapboard fishermen's houses and picturesque pantiled cottages with colour-washed walls, all set in 28 ha (70 ac) of subtropical woodland and wild gardens known simply as *Y Gwyllt* (The Wild Place). Some 5,000 plant species grow here, including Californian redwoods and holm oaks, and there are tree-lined avenues of exotic evergreens. Wonderful views, lakes, a classical temple here, a Chinese pagoda there punctuate the 32 km (20 mi) of criss-crossing pathways that eventually lead to the windswept beach.

Seventeen of the Portmeirion cottages are available for self-catering holidays, many of them with beautiful views of Cardigan Bay. They sleep between three and eight people and are let by the week. Once here, there's no need to leave the estate – the two hotels offer all their facilities to Portmeirion village guests and there are restaurants, coffee shops, a bookshop, art gallery, and even a spa for seaweed treatments, aromatherapy and massages. Portmeirion is a one-off. Staying here, you are transported into a perfectionist's fantasy land and, whatever time of year, it always feels secluded, peaceful and utterly surreal.

WHERE:
Minffordd, Gwynedd
COST:
Reasonable
BEST TIME OF YEAR:
It's beautiful at any time, but go in May or early June to catch the rhododendrons in flower, and September to October for the glorious autumn colours.
DON'T MISS:
A ride on the narrow-gauge Ffestiniog Railway; views from the headland as you walk to the lighthouse; having tea in the gardens of Plas Brondanw, the Williams-Ellis ancestral home
THINGS TO DO:
Woodland and village walks; swimming; tennis; exploring the coast; beachcombing; sightseeing
YOU SHOULD KNOW:
The Portmeirion estate is a Grade II listed conservation area run as a charitable trust. It is frequently used as a set for films and music videos, and most notably was the location for the cult classic 1960s TV series *The Prisoner*.

Cae Du Campsite

WHERE:
Rhoslefain, Tywyn, Gwynedd
COST:
Budget
BEST TIME OF YEAR:
April to early October; closed from end of October until Easter
DON'T MISS:
Climbing Cadair Idris; the historic church at Llanegryn; the walk around Dolgoch Falls; a steam-train trip on the narrow-gauge Talyllyn Railway; a visit to the old-fashioned seaside town of Barmouth
THINGS TO DO:
Coastal walks; hill walking; beachcombing; bouldering; mountain biking; sightseeing
YOU SHOULD KNOW:
Cae Du, on the coast at Rhoslefain, is not to be confused with a much larger and more commercialized campsite of the same name 50 miles to the north. It can be very windy so choose your pitch wisely and take a windbreak and your own firewood if you can – it is quite pricey locally and you can spend hours hunting for driftwood on the beach. Also take plenty of food as there are no shops nearby. Dogs are welcome as long as they're kept on a lead and well away from the sheep.

It appears almost impossible nowadays to find anywhere along the British coastline that is not subject to some pettifogging restriction or other, so it's a rare thrill to discover somewhere to spend the night by the sea and sit round a campfire without being ordered to move on.

The Cae Du campsite is an idyllic spot right beside the beach, a bit off the beaten track at the end of a bumpy, pot-holed dirt road. You can pitch your tent anywhere on the cliff or down by the shoreline, the most important priority being to find somewhere that is both flat and conveniently near one of the empty fire pits that are dotted around the place. The peaceful, unregimented atmosphere makes Cae Du very different from most campsites. The friendly owners are busy running their farm. They do come round with firewood, and sell fresh eggs and the most delicious home-made minted lamb burgers you've ever tasted, but those are the only signs of authority you'll see. The washing facilities are basic but scrupulously clean and there's a cosy barn where you can hang out in the evenings if you feel like socializing.

Sitting on the boulders beside the sea with the wind blowing in your hair, watching the waves as the sun goes down, clambering along the beach and exploring the rock pools, seeing herons, oyster catchers and cormorants or catching sight of dolphins frolicking in the bay it's easy to get the feeling that all is right with the world. If you're after amenities, entertainment and internet connections this is definitely not the place for you, but if space, simplicity and sanity are what you're seeking then Cae Du is pretty much heaven.

West Usk Lighthouse

Lighthouses are always strangely attractive, coastal sentinels that guide men at sea through hazardous waters. But even for a lighthouse, West Usk has an unusually romantic atmosphere. Built in 1821 at the confluence of the Severn and Usk estuaries, this picturesque Grade II-listed two-storey tower stands at the end of a winding bumpy track in a picture-postcard setting overlooking the Bristol Channel on one side and miles of pastureland on the other. The lighthouse was decommissioned in 1922. Its present owners rescued it from dereliction in 1989 and have dedicated themselves to restoring this fine landmark, while running it as a delightfully eccentric B&B.

Inside you'll find a treasure trove of nautical artefacts, a wishing well and, most bizarrely of all, an original Dr Who Dalek waiting to greet you at the bottom of the spiral staircase. Each wedge-shaped room is furnished in a completely individualistic style. Alternatively, you may choose to stay in the Mongolian yurt pitched in the grounds.

From the top of the lighthouse there are breathtaking panoramic views of the estuary, the sea and the Welsh hills. You may sit on the roof, soaking in an outdoor hot tub or enjoying a barbecue as you watch the boats passing. If the weather is inclement and you need shelter, the cosy lantern room at the very top of the winding staircase also offers a glorious 360-degree view.

As the flood tide comes racing up the Severn Estuary, waves start lapping around the foot of the walls and the lighthouse really comes into its own as the charming, quirky little holiday hideaway it is.

WHERE:
St Brides Wentlooge, Newport, Gwent
COST:
Reasonable
BEST TIME OF YEAR:
April to October
DON'T MISS:
A soak in the rooftop hot tub; a chauffeur-driven ride in the lighthouse owner's Rolls Royce Silver Spirit; the ancient parish church of St Bride's; a hot-rock-cooked steak at the local Lighthouse Inn
THINGS TO DO:
Coastal walks; cycling; golf; fishing; birdwatching
YOU SHOULD KNOW:
At various times of year you can see the Severn Bore – a tidal wave that rolls up the estuary into the River Severn. It's worth checking the tide timetable so that your stay here coincides with this amazing natural phenomenon.

The Grove

WHERE:
Narberth, Pembrokeshire
COST:
Expensive, but worth it – and plenty of special offers
BEST TIME OF YEAR:
May to October
DON'T MISS:
Dinner in the Grove restaurant; an in-room aromatherapy massage; a country walk in Canaston Wood; the coastal walk around St David's Head
THINGS TO DO:
Walking; hiking; mountain biking; horse riding; fishing; sailing; exploring the picturesque villages and bays of the Pembrokeshire coast
YOU SHOULD KNOW:
The Grove has won numerous accolades and awards for its food, wine list and accommodation, including *AA* Notable Wine List, *AA* Highly Commended Award, *The Good Food Guide*, *The Sunday Telegraph* Britain's 20 Cosiest Hotels and many other tourist industry awards.

The owners of the Grove have done an incredible job of transforming a decrepit 18th-century house and 10.5 ha (26 acres) of unkempt grounds into a magnificent estate which they run as a luxury boutique hotel. The house has been extensively renovated and the Georgian walled garden restored to its former glory. Four guest cottages lie within the grounds, where ancient oak and beech trees, a rhododendron border, rose garden, orchard, summer house and a stream that meanders through a wild flower meadow complete the scene.

The interior of the main house has been imaginatively decorated in an inspired mixture of Georgian and Arts and Crafts style. The result is relaxed and comfortable while also being sophisticated and artistic. The 12 rooms all have inviting decor, lovely views and super-luxurious bathrooms. You may choose to stay in the main house, an attached 17th-century coach house or the original 15th-century long house. Or if you want a family break with some independence and privacy, the estate cottages are ideal for either B&B or self catering – you're even allowed to pick vegetables for your own use from the hotel's kitchen garden.

The Grove's reputation rests as much on its superb food as its luxury accommodation. The award-winning restaurant uses locally sourced meat, line-caught fish and vegetables that have been freshly dug from it's own garden. Sitting in the old-fashioned comfort of the wood-panelled dining room or in the airy Orangery looking out onto the beautiful gardens, you'll be served one delicious seasonal dish after another. The Grove is an outstanding boutique hotel that offers great service and really bothers to make its guests feel at home.

Inshriach Yurt

Camping in Scotland might not yet have featured on your life's 'must-do' list but this novel facility in the Highlands could just change your mind. True, the weather in the Cairngorms can be famously challenging but it presents no problem to the thick canvas tents designed to withstand the harsh conditions of the central Asian steppes. The yurt at Inshriach is based on the traditional dwellings used by the nomadic horsemen and shepherds of Mongolia. A circular tent 5 m (16 ft) in diameter, the yurt is a surprisingly lavish affair; inside it features a grand Victorian double bed, an armchair and antique mahogany writing table. A thoroughly modern and efficient wood-burning stove makes it all very cosy and keeps the chill at bay, although you are still advised to pack your thermals and woollens if you are making a winter visit. The stove has a hot plate and oven for basic cooking and there's also an outdoor hearth which doubles as a barbecue.

The yurt presents a rather incongruous sight on a hillside above the River Spey. It is on the Inshriach estate – 81 ha (200 ac) of natural woodland and pasture – which offers spectacular views of the Monadhliath Mountains to the west. This is definitely a place to come to escape the madding crowd although, as always, getting away from it all does come at a price – not in terms of finance so much as amenities. The shower and toilet facilities are located in an outbuilding by the main house, which is a ten-minute walk away over fields, so a degree of adaptability will come in handy for a stay here – as well as a box of matches for the fire and a torch!

WHERE:
Near Aviemore, Highlands
COST:
Budget
BEST TIME OF YEAR:
April to October (unless you are a serious winter-sports enthusiast)
DON'T MISS:
If you are a keen angler you'll be delighted that Inshriach offers excellent fishing on a 5-km (3-mi) stretch of the famous salmon-bearing River Spey, which is included in the price of a stay.
THINGS TO DO:
Hiking; wildlife-watching; canoeing; swimming (summer); climbing; stargazing
YOU SHOULD KNOW:
The yurt only sleeps two so cannot accommodate a family. There is a two-night minimum stay.

Invereshie and Inshriach National Nature Reserve

Carbisdale Castle

WHERE:
Dornoch Firth, Sutherland
COST:
Budget
BEST TIME OF YEAR:
April to October
DON'T MISS:
The nearby Falls of Shin are one of the best places in the whole of Scotland for watching the spectacular leaping of the Atlantic salmon as the fish make their annual migration upstream to breed.
THINGS TO DO:
Mountain hiking and climbing; woodland walks; mountain biking; birdwatching; visiting Dornoch Cathedral
YOU SHOULD KNOW:
As well as the traditional dormitories, Carbisdale has a number of four-bedded family rooms which can be pre-booked.

These days it is no longer necessary to wangle an invitation as a house guest in order to sample the life of a Scottish laird in his ancestral lair. Many a baronial pile that once presided imperiously over a vast estate has now found a new function in these more democratic times as a hotel or country club. Even so, the prices usually charged ensure a degree of exclusivity every bit as daunting as a raised drawbridge. So it comes as a pleasant and very welcome surprise to discover that you can actually stay in an authentic Scottish castle without breaking the bank, still less needing an introduction.

Carbisdale Castle towers over the River Kyle in Sutherland. Now run as a youth hostel by the Scottish YHA this brooding neo-Gothic pile was built for the dowager Duchess of Sutherland in the early years of the 20th century. In fact, it was deliberately designed in three distinct styles to create an illusion of longevity – an example of aristocratic one-upmanship if ever there was one. What makes this place so special – and surely one of the most sumptuous youth hostels anywhere – is the fact that so much of the original decor and interior opulence have been preserved. Thus at Carbisdale you find standard hostel facilities such as dormitories, self-catering kitchens and games rooms alongside a gallery of exquisite Italian marble sculptures, magnificent drawing rooms and sweeping staircases hung with grand paintings. And like any self-respecting building with a distinguished history, it comes complete with a putative resident ghost or two. Scary but nice!

The Pineapple

In 18th-century Britain there was something of a craze in aristocratic circles for growing pineapples in hothouses. As if the real thing were not enough, they also became a popular motif in architectural decoration. Usually this would take the form of a finial on a gable end or gateway but John Murray, Fourth Earl of Dunmore, decided to celebrate the exotic fruit on an altogether more extravagant scale when in 1777 he had an 11-m (36-ft) high example meticulously carved in stone and added to the roof of a recently completed summer house on his estate by the Firth of Forth.

On any account it is a wonderfully bizarre sight, and one that you can feast your eyes on to your heart's content because the whole complex has been painstakingly restored by the Landmark Trust and is available to rent as holiday accommodation. The living and sleeping quarters are actually in the old bothies, stone cottages which abut the Pineapple itself on either side and which once served as houses for estate gardeners. There are two bedrooms, a kitchen and a generous living room with large open fireplace. The Pineapple presides over the former walled garden laid out by Lord Dunmore on a south-facing slope. Now owned by the National Trust for Scotland, it has been replanted as a crab-apple orchard and provided with a pond. A small private garden on the north side of the building is for the exclusive use of residents and there are numerous walking routes to enjoy in the surrounding woodland.

No one knows for sure why Lord Dunmore erected the Pineapple, but one theory has it that it commemorates his time as Governor of Virginia in America.

WHERE:
Dunmore, near Stirling
COST:
Reasonable
BEST TIME OF YEAR:
April to October
DON'T MISS:
The four decorative urns on the roof are in fact cleverly disguised chimney pots.
THINGS TO DO:
Walking; spotting pond life; cycling; visiting Stirling Castle and the amazing Falkirk Wheel
YOU SHOULD KNOW:
There is a minimum three-night stay. You should note that you have to go outside to get from the living and eating areas to the bedrooms.

Gleneagles

WHERE:
Auchterarder, Perthshire
COST:
Expensive
BEST TIME OF YEAR:
All year round (there are some good deals on rooms in the off-peak winter months with, for example, children 14 and under going free)

Without doubt Scotland's most famous hotel, Gleneagles sits comfortably amongst the world's elite establishments. The grand old building may not be architecturally striking but it has a commanding presence in an appropriately central location near Perth, at the very heart of the country. Built by the Caledonian Rail Company, Gleneagles still has its own station on the main London to Inverness line. When it opened its doors in 1924 the hotel was described as the 'eighth wonder of the world', and although World War II inevitably took some of the shine off its high-society allure the 1950s saw its revival to become a firm fixture in the British establishment's calendar, most importantly for the start of the grouse-shooting season on the Glorious Twelfth (of August).

Nowadays Gleneagles offers every comfort and facility you would expect from a five-star luxury establishment. The hotel has over 230 rooms, including 26 suites, two award-winning restaurants, numerous bars and cafés, two swimming pools, grass tennis courts, an exclusive spa and several upmarket shops selling the finest Scottish products. A huge range of countryside activities are offered on the 345-ha (853-ac) estate. For many people Gleneagles is inevitably synonymous with golf. With no fewer than three championship courses in its grounds this may be the place to try and finally penetrate the heart of that mystery: the appeal of spending hours striking – or searching for – a little white ball around the countryside. The backdrop for your round certainly doesn't come any more stunning, with the Ochil Hills to the east and distant views of the Trossachs and Grampians.

DON'T MISS:
The hotel's cellars, which contain many original features from the 1920s, such as the railway bay where wines were once delivered from all over Europe. They are also home to some 350 varieties of single-malt whisky.

THINGS TO DO:
Golf; tennis; swimming; spa treatments; walking; fishing; horse riding; falconry; shooting; archery; 4x4 driving; mountain biking; wine and spirit tasting; visiting whisky distilleries

YOU SHOULD KNOW:
You can learn how to handle a trained gundog at what Gleneagles claims is the first school of its kind in the world.

Trigony House Hotel

Travellers making a beeline for the Scottish Highlands are likely to miss out on a landscape that remains one of the country's undiscovered scenic treasures. The Lowlands south of Glasgow may not be as spectacular as their more rugged Highland cousins but they do offer the significant advantage, especially in the summer months, of being noticeably less busy. So if you're looking for somewhere to get away from it all, whether it be a quiet romantic hideaway or a full-on communion with untamed nature, the southwest of Scotland is strongly recommended. And this elegant country-house hotel in lovely Nithsdale, north of Dumfries, makes a superb base. Trigony House began life in the 18th century as a shooting lodge for Closeburn Castle (the castle keep still stands nearby but is not open to the public), and its ivy-clad walls of pink sandstone present an enticing picture in the afternoon sun.

Trigony House is a family-run hotel and the affection the owners have for the building is everywhere in evidence. The interiors have been lovingly restored, in appropriate homage to some exquisite craftsmanship from the 1930s when the Art Deco staircase and the striking panelling in Japanese oak were installed. Many of the rooms have views over the extensive and beautifully kept gardens, while others look out on mature woodland which hides the remains of an old Roman fort. Service comes with lots of personal touches, as you would expect, not least in the kitchen where truly outstanding dishes are cooked up, reflecting the best of the region's fare and using locally sourced ingredients such as prime Galloway beef.

WHERE:
Thornhill, Dumfriesshire

COST:
Reasonable

BEST TIME OF YEAR:
April to October

DON'T MISS:
One of the joys of a stay here is eating breakfast while watching red squirrels forage in the garden.

THINGS TO DO:
Walking; cycling; wildlife-watching; horse riding; fishing; falconry; archery; exploring the countryside in a hired vintage car (self-drive); 4x4 off-road safari; visiting Robert Burns sites

YOU SHOULD KNOW:
Unusually for a country-house hotel in this league Trigony House is a pet-friendly establishment and dogs are assured of a warm welcome.

Gearrannan Blackhouse

WHERE:
Carloway, Isle of Lewis
COST:
Budget
BEST TIME OF YEAR:
April to September (although you should note that the blackhouses are available all year round and that prices in the low season (October to March) are two-thirds of the normal rates).
DON'T MISS:
One of the blackhouses is now a museum, fitted out as it would have looked in the 1950s. In the summer months it houses regular demonstrations of the famous Harris Tweed being woven.
THINGS TO DO:
Hiking; biking – the 29-km (18-mi) Pentland Road to Stornoway is a particular favourite with cyclists; fishing; surfing; watching sunsets; visiting archaeological sites
YOU SHOULD KNOW:
From June to August the minimum stay is five nights. It is not possible to start a stay on Sunday, which is still a meaningful day of rest in these parts.

The islanders of the Outer Hebrides certainly knew how to build against the weather. Their traditional dwellings, known as blackhouses – although cottage would be a more accurate descriptor – were constructed with double drystone walls and thick thatched roofs. The materials and their profiles, low to the ground, provided protection from the buffetings of the Atlantic winds. At Gearrannan on the western coast of Lewis you will find a remarkable survival of a traditional blackhouse village which has been sensitively restored and converted into holiday accommodation (the last permanent residents left as recently as the mid 1970s).

The village comprises nine cottages, four of which have been fitted out as self-catering units: three suitable for a couple or a small family and one larger one that can sleep up to 16. While the outside appearance of the blackhouses with their stone walls and thatched roofs has been largely preserved, the interiors reflect contemporary standards of comfort and convenience. Gone are the bare earth floor and the central hearth, the glow of whose peat fire once provided the only illumination, to be replaced by under-floor heating and a welcoming stove in the cosy sitting room. It is just as well that the cottages now have electricity because little natural light gets in; the original blackhouses had virtually no windows, which were expensive and afforded poor insulation. Fortunately, one or two have now been inserted and there can be few greater pleasures than sitting at a window watching and listening to the great Atlantic rollers crashing onto the nearby beach. And for much of your time here these are the only abiding sounds you will hear.

HotelForTwo

The delightful fishing village of Tobermory

Mull is, after Skye, the largest of the islands that form the Inner Hebrides. It is also one of the most accessible for anyone after a Scottish isle experience, being just a 45-minute ferry crossing from Oban on the west coast mainland. Even so, the delightful little fishing village of Tobermory at the island's northern tip has a remote, otherworldly atmosphere that will summarily banish thoughts of a more hectic lifestyle. In the middle of a terrace high above the harbour stands this idiosyncratic little guest house. Its quirky furnishings and design touches give HotelForTwo very much the feel of a private home, which in fact it still is. The name comes from the fact that there are just two rooms, both en suite, which can be booked as two singles or by two couples. You then have the run of the whole house, with two sitting rooms and a well-appointed kitchen. There is also a pretty front garden on the other side of the quiet road, with hammocks and deckchairs available to enhance your enjoyment of the fine views over the bay.

You really do have the best of both worlds here since the owner makes herself as available or elusive as you wish. She is on hand with ideas and suggestions about things to do and see and, most importantly, to cook meals, including three-course gourmet dinners (although these have to be pre-booked). Breakfast is included in the rates but if you prefer not to have the presence of a stranger – however solicitous their attentions – at this sensitive time of day, then the ingredients will be left out for you to prepare your own.

WHERE:
Tobermory, Mull
COST:
Reasonable
BEST TIME OF YEAR:
March to September
DON'T MISS:
A chance to see a show by Mull Theatre, the island's very own professional touring company which has its production base and home venue just outside Tobermory. At one time it held the record for the smallest theatre company in the world.
THINGS TO DO:
Walking; cycling; fishing; birdwatching; whale-watching and seal tours; pony trekking (including the chance to ride on a deserted beach)
YOU SHOULD KNOW:
If you are into bagging Munros – climbing Scottish mountains with a height of over 914.4 m (3,000 ft) – Mull has its own, Ben More, which just makes the cut at 966 m (3,169 ft).

Jura Lodge

WHERE:
Craighouse, Jura
COST:
Expensive
BEST TIME OF YEAR:
April to September
DON'T MISS:
The chance to sign up as an honorary Diurach (the Gaelic word for the people of Jura). Membership entitles you to a free dram of Jura whisky at the island's hotel every month for the rest of your life!
THINGS TO DO:
Fell walking; cycling; whisky tasting; fishing; shooting; writing (who knows, the ambience may release those creative juices)
YOU SHOULD KNOW:
There is a three-night minimum stay at the Lodge. The family-run Jura Hotel offers a cheaper though more conventional alternative.

You might recognize the name of Jura as the island where George Orwell sought solitude to complete his dystopian masterpiece *1984*. The island today is hardly less remote than when the writer lived at Barnhill in the late 1940s. In fact the 200 or so permanent residents are vastly outnumbered by the island's deer population of over 5,000. The only settlement to speak of is Craighouse on the east shore; here you will find the principal source of employment and the business which ensures that, like many a Scottish island, the name of Jura continues to resonate around the world.

That business is of course whisky, the amber nectar which has long been one of the glories of the country's heritage. As well as producing award-winning single malts, the Jura Distillery in Craighouse owns the Lodge, a handsome mansion which is filled with antique furniture and grand antler displays that attest bygone attitudes to the great Scottish outdoors. Preserving a link with Orwell, the distillery now offers the Lodge as a retreat to contemporary writers at certain times of the year. At other times it is available for anyone to rent so, if you can afford it, gather together your whisky-loving, book-devouring, fell-walking friends and make a house party of it.

It seems that whisky has been produced on Jura since at least the 16th century, albeit only for domestic consumption in the early years. The first commercial distillery on the island was established in 1810 and the present business, which is nearly 50 years old, stands on the original site. The taller stills used are said to produce softer, less peaty malts than the typical Island whiskies.

The Old Church of Urquhart

Churches continue to be oases of calm and tranquillity for many amidst the hectic pace of modern life. It should come as no surprise therefore that sleeping in a former church can be a particularly peaceful experience. In the village of Urquhart, 8 km (5 mi) east of Elgin, one such has been imaginatively converted into a comfortable B&B that makes a splendidly quirkish base for an exploration of Speyside and the Moray Coast. The Old Church was built in 1843 under the influence of James Gillespie Graham, the most fashionable architect of his day and the man responsible for introducing the Gothic Revival to Scotland. Many of the church's original features have been retained in its new secular role; the two bedrooms on the ground floor have the original dark wooden wainscoting, while the first-floor room looks out on the garden through the graceful stone tracery of a Gothic window.

Two large lounges make the most of the church's tall central space. Meals are taken on a balcony which once served as the church gallery. The surrounding area is rich in ecclesiastical associations, including the ruined Elgin Cathedral, once one of the mightiest churches in the land, and the still active monastic community at Pluscarden Abbey in its beautiful valley setting.

The area is also famed for its salmon and sea-trout fishing and for its whisky distilleries. The peace and calm of the Old Church will undoubtedly encourage such gentle pursuits but if you are looking for a little more action there are fine mountain-biking trails nearby as well as boat trips in the Moray Firth where you can spot dolphins, seals and puffins.

WHERE:
Urquhart, near Elgin, Moray
COST:
Budget
BEST TIME OF YEAR:
March to October
DON'T MISS:
With a little notice your hosts will cook up a three-course dinner, using the freshest local ingredients, that is terrific value.
THINGS TO DO:
Walking; mountain biking; horse riding; fishing; whisky tasting; marine wildlife-watching
YOU SHOULD KNOW:
If you are in a larger group and would like more independence the Old Church also offers a self-catering apartment, created in the chancel at the former east end.

Aikwood Tower

WHERE:
Near Selkirk, Scottish Borders
COST:
Reasonable if full occupancy of ten (expensive if there are six or fewer of you)
BEST TIME OF YEAR:
All year round
DON'T MISS:
Settling into an armchair in the cosy Laird's Study with a book from its library of political biographies, personally chosen by Lord Steel
THINGS TO DO:
Croquet; table tennis; walking; mountain biking; horse riding; fishing; shooting; kayaking; golf; birdwatching
YOU SHOULD KNOW:
Aikwood can be booked for exclusive use only and sleeps up to ten. Stays are usually for one week or a weekend (three nights) although sometimes two-night midweek stays are possible.

Aikwood is the former home of well-known British politician David Steel who was this area's MP for over 30 years, as well as being the leader of the Liberal Party for a dozen years in the 1970s and 1980s. The area in question is the Scottish Border country around Selkirk and Peebles, a timeless landscape of rolling hills, mixed woodlands and meandering valleys that has captured the imagination of travellers for centuries, including no less a personage than Sir Walter Scott.

Scott in fact claimed descent from the family who built Aikwood in the 1540s in the form of a fortified tower house – a popular architectural style at the time but also something of an enforced choice given the prevailing unrest and lawlessness of the Borders region. The building had fallen into disrepair and neglect when in the late 1980s Baron Steel of Aikwood (as he now is) acquired it from the Duke of Buccleuch, owner of the neighbouring Bowhill Estate. Lord Steel immediately set about a complete restoration, turning the tower house into a comfortable family home while retaining many of its historic features, including a carved stone in one wall that commemorates a 1602 family marriage.

In recent years Lord Steel has made over Aikwood to a son who has now given it a new lease of life as the Borders' first 'boutique stronghold'. A recent addition to the roster of Scotland's unusual holiday stays, Aikwood Tower promises 'understated luxury', whether you are warming your toes in front of a roaring fire in what was once the great hall or relaxing in an antique claw-foot bath in one of five en-suite bedrooms.

The Fitzwilliam Hotel

Neither charm nor elegance was greatly valued during Northern Ireland's years of sectarian division. Their reappearance as characteristics of The Fitzwilliam Hotel is a reassuring statement of Belfast's determination to match the cosmopolitan chic on tap in other major cities. The Fitzwilliam is 'neck-or-nothing' brave – a steel and glass boutique hotel of unremitting modernist style. Its 130 rooms could scarcely be more comfortable, or better provided with Egyptian linens, whole levees of soft pillows and the finest electronic connections for every purpose. Yet the decor betrays uncertainty. The predominant lime green, grey and black furnishings sit on carpets patterned with violent geometrics, all the more strident by contrast with the dark lustre of American walnut connecting walkways. The combination is a wake-up call for a go-getting business traveller; not quite so relaxing for a tourist at leisure.

Both kinds of guest benefit from the real warmth of the Fitzwilliam's service, but the hotel's trail-blazing ambition to join the best of the best does have some rough edges caused by inexperience (read 'trying too hard', bless them). With a good restaurant and an excellent New York-style bar, it's a mystery that the hotel's savvy didn't include the 'private dining room', which consists of a very public, glass-walled cube suspended over the lobby. In fact, the Fitzwilliam's willing and friendly atmosphere is its greatest asset and the main reason that – all its designer charms being as ergonomically efficient and lovely as any other hotel's – *Condé Nast Traveller* recently included it on its 'Hot List'.

The Fitzwilliam Hotel is right in the heart of Belfast, next to the Grand Opera House. It is the perfect base from which to see how today's Belfast is changing.

WHERE:
Great Victoria Street, Belfast
COST:
Reasonable (rooms) to moderately expensive (junior suites) – but the hotel is much more sophisticated than its prices suggest
BEST TIME OF YEAR:
Any time
DON'T MISS:
Giant's Causeway Visitor Centre, in Belfast, and as good as it gets if you can't get to the real thing; the Botanic Gardens; early Irish artefacts and Armada relics at the Ulster Museum; Titanic Dock & Pump House; the historic Crown Liquor Saloon, just down the road from the hotel
THINGS TO DO:
Belfast Bike Ride tour along the Lagan river valley to the Neolithic Giant's Ring monument; the Bronze Age cairns on Divis and the Black Mountain (the backdrop to every picture of Belfast, and only recently opened); the children's museum interactives at the Odyssey
YOU SHOULD KNOW:
The Fitzwilliam is non-smoking throughout; limited parking is available if pre-booked; the Fitzwilliam Dublin is a sister hotel – known as 'the Purple Extravaganza'.

Ballygally Castle

WHERE:
Coast Road, Ballygally, Larne, Co. Antrim
COST:
Very reasonable to mildly expensive
BEST TIME OF YEAR:
Any time
DON'T MISS:
The walled gardens of Glenarm Castle; the 27 m (89 ft) Chaine Memorial Tower, an 1887 replica of an ancient Irish Round Tower at the western edge of Larne Lough; the Andrew Jackson Cottage and US Rangers Centre at Carrickfergus; the Giant's Causeway – very close to Bushmill's Irish Whisky distillery
THINGS TO DO:
Walk up Slemish Mountain, St Patrick's first known Irish home, where he made his first Christian conversion – the vistas are astonishing, and so is the 180-m (590-ft) steep and rocky climb; play golf at Cainrndhu GC or Royal Portrush; go ghost-hunting; explore the Nine Glens of Antrim.
YOU SHOULD KNOW:
In the 1950s, Ballygally Castle was bought and greatly restored by the British carpet tycoon Cyril Lord.

Ballygally Castle is a stolid, baronial keep with walls 1.5 m (5 ft) thick and conical turrets at the corners of its steeply angled roof. Built in 1625, it looks older, but its grim countenance is softened by the extensions and renovations which form the bulk of its incarnation as a 44-room hotel. Now it has the advantages of both old and new: the contemporary decor of the bedrooms is sympathetic to the historic authenticity of the quirky public spaces. Even the Garden Suite in the newest wing shares the slightly spooky atmosphere that pervades the ancient fortress. Ballygally is famous for it. The castle is said to be one of the most haunted buildings in Britain, and many guests come just to test their imaginations against its reputation in general, and the turret 'ghost rooms' in particular.

Few run screaming from their beds. The castle is far too comfortable. Even its layout delivers a benefit denied to most hotels. Woven into the keep's stone fabric by circular staircases, sudden passageways and studded doors hidden behind heavy velvet curtains, the dining rooms, bar, lounges and other amenities all make people feel like guests in a private house. Inhibitions weaken, and conversations start which often end over an excellent dinner, or a drink (and even backgammon) in the bar afterwards. The hotel is known for both its fine dining and for its 'fun' bar. Nobody has to join in, but most people do. It's a rare hotel where guests dance for spontaneous pleasure.

A short distance north of Larne, the castle stands at the head of Ballygally Bay, with a panoramic view over the soft white sands and the Irish Sea to Scotland. Stop and wonder.

Ard Nahoo Health Farm

It's a health farm in the broadest sense. Ard Nahoo offers all manner of treatments to promote well-being of body and mind, but it also promotes a self-consciously alternative social philosophy of holistic health. If it sounds a little preachy, it is – but Ard Nahoo is happy to put its own principles into action and be judged on the results.

The farm is run on the most environmentally friendly lines known to science. Guests are encouraged to make themselves aware of the local ecology by exploring the farm's own nature trail and wildlife pond. They're even given information sheets noting the historical, medicinal and culinary properties of native trees. On a personal level, eco-living at Ard Nahoo means anything from courses and workshops to yoga, holistic massage, detox sauna or hot tub. Beyond those are the riches of being at leisure among the frankly fabulous countryside of the north Leitrim hills with a great pub, Sligo Town and the sea not far away. At Ard Nahoo this combination of eco-awareness and plain fun is called 'ethical living'.

There are three eco-cabins at Ard Nahoo. Hawthorn is a snug, all-wooden studio fitted with a kitchen and a mezzanine platform for the double bed. Holly and Willow each have three comfortable double-bed rooms, a living area and full kitchen and bathroom. Any of them can be isolated for the benefit of guests seeking a private retreat and the larger two are ideal for families or groups of friends, as well as singles.

Intriguingly, most of Ard Nahoo's clientele is female. Speculation suggests this is because women are more open to wholehearted experimentation with good new ideas.

WHERE:
Mullagh, Dromahair, Co. Leitrim
COST:
Budget (although two guests wishing for exclusive occupation of a three-bedroom cabin will obviously pay much more)
BEST TIME OF YEAR:
Any time
DON'T MISS:
The *Uisce* Hour of pampering, in the luxury of perfect calm; the waterbus from Parkes Castle across Loch Gill to Sligo via the Lake Isle of Innisfree; music on Fridays at Stanfords pub in Dromahair; the subterranean rivers, waterfalls, chambers and passageways at Marble Arch Caves
THINGS TO DO:
Explore the Celtic Nature Trail; surf at Strandhill or one of Sligo's other famous surfing beaches; visit the prehistoric complex at the Cavan Burren; gallop a horse along a private beach; walk the Loch Nahoo Loop – around the Loch with the whooper swans.
YOU SHOULD KNOW:
One of the Treats of the World is to see a film at the Mobile Cinema, which stops every Wednesday in Manorhamilton. It specializes in great world cinema and Irish film, shown in a converted truck.

Glenlo Abbey Hotel

Glenlo Abbey Hotel is a prestige country-house affair designed to appeal as much to the corporate market as to upscale tourists. It is unusually lucky on both counts. Its heart is a lovely classical building created in 1740. The stone-built Abbey grew around it in the 1790s, but was never consecrated. Their combined legacy is the unusual number of elegant sitting rooms, salons and chambers that, with the library and formal dining suites, strike just the right note of luxurious leisure. The 46 rooms and suites echo their size and style without quite matching either, although they all benefit from heavily marbled and accessorized bathrooms, and stunning views either across Lough Corrib into Connemara or over the Abbey to the edge of the golf course.

The hotel's location is near perfect. Its 56-ha (138-ac) estate on the edge of Lough Corrib is just 4 km (2.5 mi) from the lively delights of Galway City. The estate is entirely given over to a highly rated double nine-hole parkland golf course with doubled greens turning it into a challenging 6,538 yd (par 71!), while the Lough offers excellent fishing and clay-pigeon shooting from its shore. These are precisely the activities that fill the conference halls and rows of executive meeting rooms packed around the 18th-century buildings, and which cater to the deluxe mini-coach parties with only a few hours to spare at every destination. The two groups are the lifeblood of western Ireland's economy, and providing them with consistent luxury is nailbitingly difficult. Glenlo Abbey Hotel may not be to everyone's taste, but it earns its five stars.

WHERE:
N59 (Galway to Clifden highway), Bushypark, Galway
COST:
Expensive
BEST TIME OF YEAR:
April to October
DON'T MISS:
Exceptional dining at The Pullman Restaurant – vintage railway carriages of dark, varnished wood and deep plush set outside the main building alongside the golf course's first tee; the Oyster Festival (or any other of Galway's amazing festivals); the Galway Races; salmon and trout fishing, in season
THINGS TO DO:
Horse riding; walking the crescent of Whitesands at low tide; boating on the lake; more golf – some of Ireland's best courses are local; getting a drink in a *Gaeltacht* pub; exploring a peat bog along the Clifden road
YOU SHOULD KNOW:
Glenlo Abbey is Galway's first 5-star '*Failte* Ireland' rated hotel.

Loop Head Lighthouse Keeper's Cottage

The Atlantic end of the Shannon Estuary is one of Ireland's least-known natural wonders. Loop Head is the tip of Co. Clare's 'forgotten peninsula', which forms the estuary's north shore, and (with Kerry Head on the south side) marks the transition from ocean to river. It is a wild place of towering black cliffs and sea stacks contorted by Atlantic gales, of screaming birds, pounding surf and miles of undulating, spongy grass flecked with cowering wild flowers. In mist, rain, ice or sunshine its solitude is filled with the transcendent beauty of a vast light show in constant motion all about. Loop Head is one of the best illustrations anywhere of live, untrammelled nature.

It's also a dangerous place for shipping, and the whitewashed Loop Head lighthouse has stood at the tip since 1670. Automation has left the centrally heated keeper's cottage, with two doubles and a single bedroom, available to rent. Its simple comforts and basic amenities do not include TV, telephone or microwave – but for the kind of visitors who yearn to envelop themselves in the spirit of the place, it is a sanctuary of luxury as appropriate as the Ritz to London. The nearest shop is 5 km (3 mi) away in Kilbaha. Good. Stoke up the fire and put the kettle on. You have what you need.

From Loop Head clifftop the view south across the Shannon includes Derry Head and Dingle; and to the north the curve of the peninsula allows you to see along the Clare coast to the Cliffs of Moher. That view encompasses a hundred things to see or do – but the best of them is to stay where you are.

WHERE:
Kilbaha, Co. Clare
COST:
Budget-budget
BEST TIME OF YEAR:
April to October
DON'T MISS:
Clambering round the caves and coves cut into the cliffs; dolphin-watching – a group of over 100 bottlenose dolphins use the outer estuary as their playground; listening to Irish, widely spoken at Carrigaholt, a historic fishing port with a stone-walled, flagstoned pub (the Long Dock on West Street) where you can hear traditional Irish music around 22.00 and eat a banquet
THINGS TO DO:
'Moonwalk' on the cliffs' springy turf; fishing from the Loop rocks (or a boat, rentable in Carrigaholt); picnicking; hiking the Bridges of Ross; swimming in one of the deserted, sandy coves; paying respects at the Church of the Little Ark of Kilbaha; cycling
YOU SHOULD KNOW:
In July and August, minimum rental is seven days. Even if the weather turns bad, the lightkeeper's cottage is so cosy, and the sitting room so very comfortable, that you are unlikely to want to leave.

Shelbourne Hotel

Since the Shelbourne opened in 1824, it has been the informal headquarters of the highest echelons of Irish society and its political and business communities. Its legendary status has conferred on it a grandeur its elegant frontage doesn't quite match, but its location opposite the lake in St Stephen's Green – the biggest garden square in the world and the epicentre of Dublin – more than compensates. Inside are Dublin's two most famous bars, immortalized in prose and poetry, and two of its best restaurants. They have witnessed almost everything that has mattered in nearly two centuries of Irish history, and they still do. Frequently crowded, and always buzzing, the bars remain supremely elegant; and the Lord Mayor's Lounge provides deeply cushioned glamour for more intense discussion or reflection.

The bedrooms at every level reflect their Georgian origins. Not even the best suites are especially big, but their high ceilings give full expression to heavy drapes and the kind of sink-into-it luxury that is completely timeless. Newer rooms added at the back during the Shelbourne's recent overhaul are Georgian by osmosis. The grandest of the originals face the park at the hotel's front. Although slightly noisier, they're worth the extra cost to feel like Oscar Wilde or Oliver St John Gogarty looking down on the throng.

If the Shelbourne excites the imagination, it's mainly because the hotel isn't pretentious about its history. Visitors do that for them, even the regular Dublin barflies who never enter the place without feeling a sense of occasion. The renovations restored the original marble staircase to the hall, and pristine glamour to everything else. The Shelbourne's enduring charm is to wear such glamour lightly.

WHERE:
St Stephen's Green, Dublin
COST:
Expensive
BEST TIME OF YEAR:
Any time
DON'T MISS:
Afternoon tea in the Edwardian splendour of the Lord Mayor's Lounge – the only true teatime event in the city; the Horseshoe Bar, heartbeat of Dublin's social scene; the Saddle Room restaurant, one of Dublin's very best (but reserve a Gold Booth banquette for a quieter time)
THINGS TO DO:
Walk in St Stephen's Green; enjoy the best of central Dublin on your doorstep, like Grafton Street, Trinity College, O'Connell Street and Georgian Dublin in the streets around Merrion Square.
YOU SHOULD KNOW:
The Shelbourne Hotel is so devoted to its service ethic that it retains a 'Genealogy Butler' for guests wishing to trace their Irish ancestry.

Kinnitty Castle Hotel

Kinnitty Castle tells the story of Ireland. Its 13th-century origins, the political changes in its ownership, its restorations, redesign as a Georgian Gothic masterpiece, rebuilding after burning during the Troubles, and eventual rescue by refurbishment as a luxury hotel are all embedded in its fabric. The story is not unusual, but the sensitivity of the hotel conversion certainly is. Kinnitty is one of only a handful of major Irish stately homes which as hotels have retained their character as a private house. None of its 37, antique-filled rooms are the same; and although all are grand, some are grander than others. The best suites are enormous, panelled extravaganzas of velvets, brocades, marquetry and curtained four-posters. Smaller rooms are only less marvellous because of the stairs needed to reach them. Public rooms are magnificent, especially the Louis XV-style drawing room and the genuine antiquarian library/bar. Even the Georgian restaurant (60 covers) feels more like a Regency club than a modern hotel.

The castle is surrounded by vast lawns and 263 ha (650 ac) of rolling parkland. Beyond that, it has sporting access to a further 8,100 ha (20,000 acres) of thick woods and open ground that used to form part of the castle's estate, and is teeming with wildlife and game. It's a paradise for field sports. Kinnitty's own equestrian centre offers riding lessons, hunting, cross-country and mountain trekking. Clay-pigeon shooting and tennis are also available – and serious fishing can be arranged. So can entry to the most exclusive golf clubs in the region. Yet there's no charge at all for walking the trails in the magnificent Slieve Bloom Mountains behind the castle.

WHERE:
Kinnitty, Birr, Co. Offaly
COST:
Reasonable
BEST TIME OF YEAR:
Any time (but note that most field sports are seasonal)
DON'T MISS:
Candle-lit dinner in Sli Dala, the castle's 'destination' restaurant; a Friday or Saturday evening at Monks' Kitchen (the castle's informal eaterie) when traditional Irish music whips up a storm; Leap Castle; the Tullamore Dew Heritage Centre
THINGS TO DO:
Walk the Silver River Eco-nature Trail at Cadamstown; explore the Birr Castle demesne; wonder at the earliest evidence of human habitation (6,500 BC) in Ireland at the Lough Boora excavations near Kinnitty.
YOU SHOULD KNOW:
The enchanting Slieve Bloom hills are famous as the birthplace and nursery of Finn M'Cool, He of The Legends. The hills are also the spawning ground of the Salmon of Knowledge, which brought him the wisdom of the world, so it did.

Gyreum Ecolodge Hostel

WHERE:
Corlisheen, Riverstown, Co. Sligo
COST:
Budget and better
BEST TIME OF YEAR:
April to October (or any other time, for the multitude of hardy folk undeterred by the fierce weather patterns of Ireland's northwest)
DON'T MISS:
Investigating the amazing range of courses/workshops/fun entertainments organized by Gyreum – above all the nine-day Pilgrim's Progress walking tour across six counties, stopping off at a range of multi-faith centres and heritage sites. It includes a boat along Lough Erne to Inish Rath, the Hare Krishna temple at Derrylin (Co. Fermanagh), through the Cuilcagh Mountains to Jampa Ling Tibetan Buddhist Centre at Bawnboy (Co. Cavan), and culminates in a glorious, collective, full moonlit hot tub.
THINGS TO DO:
Walk in the Bricklieve Mountains; surf at Strandhill; explore the greatest concentration of megalithic structures in Europe, including the Carrowkeel 'passage tombs' across Lough Arrow; gawp at the 360-degree views of lakes and hills across four counties; play pool; share the sauna.
YOU SHOULD KNOW:
There is absolutely nothing cranky or Spartan about Gyreum. It overflows with warmth, humour, intelligence and imagination. It is also the first eco-lodge in Ireland to have been awarded the prestigious EU Eco-Label for tourist accommodation.

It often seems as though Co Sligo thrums to the same earth song as San Francisco's Marin County. The Gyreum, near Castlebaldwin, is one reason why. It's a huge circular structure set into Sligo's celebrated 'cairned' mountains, aligned four ways, to both winter and summer solstices at their dawns and dusks. It's an eco-temple conceived according to spiritual geography (ley lines and other indicators) as a generator of goodwill, placed at the service of whoever wants to make use of it.

The Gyreum is the ultimate in flexible, democratic design. It has two 'dorm rooms' for five and six guests, and two double bedrooms, all of which may be single sex or mixed as required. A further seven indoor capsule tents (billed as 'two-bed mixed dorms') with air mattresses, pillows and duvets can be set up in the cavernous (and floor-heated) central hall, alongside the giant movie screen and the glass-domed library. Bathrooms and the fully equipped kitchen are communal – although catering is available to large groups. These attributes are all fundamental to a good hostel: the Gyreum regards them merely as a launch pad.

The huge space beneath the 30-m (100-ft) diameter green cone is infinitely versatile. It's been used as rehearsal space for dance, theatre and music companies; retreat space; mass yoga; wedding ceremonies and celebrations; and a favourite stopover for hill walkers, naturalists, hikers and cyclists. Some call it an 'Installation Incubator' for its influence on the organizations, groups of friends and societies which have found inspiration there. It's easy to be dismissive of someone delighting in a prism casting rainbows in sunshine. At the Gyreum, it could easily be the next Steve Jobs, drifting on the sympathetic vibe.

Boutique Camping – the Yurt

WHERE:
Mount David, Castletown Geoghegan, Co. Westmeath
COST:
Budget
BEST TIME OF YEAR:
Any time
DON'T MISS:
Storytelling at the fire pit; bat-spotting expeditions; fishing on the private lake; hanging out in the unspoilt village of Castletown Geoghegan, with genuine Irish music and dancing in its three, determinedly traditional bars; having a riotous barbecue by the lake

Glamorous camping, or 'glamping', is as ancient as history itself. Refined by a series of Great Khans, the original Mongolian yurt turned out to be the blueprint for its highest expression. At Castletown Geoghegan in Co. Westmeath Boutique Camping has nine genuine imported Mongolian yurts, set round a lake in rural parkland among some 200,000 trees. Like a Tardis, each of them is much bigger inside than appears from without. Furnished with a large double bed swathed in muslin curtains, a single bed which makes a fine sofa, chairs, table and a wood-burning stove, the yurts are lit by candles and lanterns. Their straight sides, with the cone of the roof rising high in the yurt's centre, create a feeling of spaciousness which the lighting dramatizes. These are yurts to make you feel like a prince or princess (possibly even the Queen of Sheba).

There is plenty of anecdotal evidence to show how difficult it can be to get visitors to leave their yurt – but the local amenities are compelling. The site is the glorious parkland of the Mount Druid estate, studded with Celtic folklore, Ogham alphabet symbols and *Sile na Gig* (Celtic fertility symbols). Besides the various forms of 'glamping' accommodation, there's a meditation hut, a wood-burning sauna, an informal bar at the boathouse on the lake, and a wonderful renovated barn which acts as a clubhouse. With a kitchen, deep sofas, a gym and showers, it is the venue for all manner of impromptu fun and games creatively inspired by families, romantic couples, and the regular hen parties who adore the place. Genghis would approve.

THINGS TO DO:
Go racing at Kilbeggan, or at Mullingar's Greyhound Stadium; hire a boat at Lilliput Adventure Centre; mountain biking; walking the local rural trails; paintball and laser tag; drop in to Locks Distillery museum

YOU SHOULD KNOW:
For hen parties and other 'girlie get-togethers', Boutique Camping offers a full range of spray tans, facials, massages and other treatments on site; the yurts are – deservedly – extremely popular for local festivals and many other local events, so be sure to book as early as you can.

Hotel Fox

WHERE:
Jarmers Plads, Copenhagen
COST:
Budget sidling into reasonable, depending on time of year and room size
BEST TIME OF YEAR:
April to October unless thermal underwear features in your travelling wardrobe
DON'T MISS:
Live DJ music in the hotel bar; sampling Japanese delights in the hotel's Restaurant Sushikappo (that's sushi treats lest anyone should wonder); the not-to-be-missed breakfast buffet

Finding a fox in the middle of Copenhagen might seem unusual, but not nearly as surprising as discovering the Hotel Fox, which really can claim to be one of the most unusual overnighters in the world. Indeed, to take full advantage of everything this amazing hostelry has to offer it would be necessary to stay 61 times. That may sound like an arbitrary figure, but isn't. For the hotel has 61 rooms and each is an individual work of art, so to fully appreciate this extraordinary gallery would take two months. Of course nobody is suggesting that's a realistic possibility, but the thought does serve to illustrate how unusual this place is.

Embodying the work of over 20 different artists, the en-suite rooms are all completely different from one another (apart from the standard flat-screen TV that no self-respecting hotel believes guests

can do without), with the vibrant hand-painted decor of each room ranging from street art to bold Japanese Manga characters, geometric designs to fairytales, imaginary creatures to friendly monsters. There is an in-hotel restaurant and bar, plus a lounge with café and bar services. There's also a roof terrace with a view. The staff are friendly and helpful, and will direct guests to facilities the Hotel Fox does not have. For example, there is no spa and fitness centre, but guests can use those at the sister Hotel Kong Arthur close by.

So is the Hotel Fox really the world's most exciting and creative lifestyle hotel in the world, as the management claims? Well, let's put it this way – seeing will be believing that you really haven't seen anything that's anything like it anywhere else, and that you really won't *ever* see anything that's remotely like it anywhere else.

THINGS TO DO:
Stroll through Orstedsparken, one of the city's best parks (right opposite the hotel); explore the Tivoli Gardens; visit the nearby Danish Design Centre.
YOU SHOULD KNOW:
Bicycles and MP3 players can be hired at reception. The hotel will try but cannot promise to allocate specific rooms, and it's not possible to change rooms mid stay. Wifi or wired internet is available throughout the hotel. It's advisable to book in advance as this is a popular central hotel with affordable room rates. Families are welcome and children up to the age of 12 can stay in their parents' room for free. The famous Little Mermaid statue is *not* within easy walking distance.

Lalandia Billund

Family fun is guaranteed at the Lalandia Billund resort in Central Denmark. This is not a place to stay in passing (two nights is the minimum), and the set-up with its well-equipped holiday cottages is not really structured for singles or couples. This is generally a destination for Danish families, as most countries have similar resorts of their own, but it's always interesting to see how others do it – and a huge bonus is the proximity of Legoland Park, which is just a few minutes' walk away.

Mind you, there's plenty of entertainment on offer at Lalandia and the place puts up a good fight when it comes to anchoring guests to the extensive site. That's an appropriate image, because an essential element of the package is the tropical Aquadrome water park, Scandinavia's largest. This offers a lazy river, slides for all ages, tubing, indoor swimming pools, wave pools, Jacuzzis, saunas, solariums, palm trees and a beach. There's also a seasonal outdoor pool, health club, fitness room and spa. Monky Tonky Land caters for toddlers and younger kids, and the petting zoo never fails to entice children, who are spoilt for choice when it comes to organized activities.

Over 800 guest rooms ensure that everyone is part of a happy band of brothers and sisters, all accommodated in well-equipped cottages with terraces and garden views. Self-catering is a breeze, with fitted kitchens having everything from fridge-freezers to dishwashers, although a selection of restaurants awaits those families declaring their holiday as a cooking-free zone. Bathrooms have spa tubs and wired internet access is available. This really is a great place to let it all hang out – if you can keep up with the kids, who'll adore the place.

WHERE:
Ellehammersalle 3, Billund
COST:
Reasonable, with various deals to be done (cost varies by season, length of stay and choice of holiday cottage, while there are extras on top of the basic price for services like internet and electricity that can soon add up)
BEST TIME OF YEAR:
Open all year, with plenty of indoor activities to occupy everyone on any cold or rainy days
DON'T MISS:
Legoland just down the road (guests at Lalandia can buy a good-value pass that gives the family unlimited access for the duration of their stay)
THINGS TO DO:
Quite apart from the Aquadrome's seductive delights there are endless activities to be found on site including archery, badminton, bowling, indoor mini golf and indoor tennis. Family karaoke and the children's disco are among the noisier options.
YOU SHOULD KNOW:
Lalandia is patrolled by a gang of child-friendly costumed characters. All accommodation is non-smoking. The same company also runs the Lalandia Rødby resort in the south of the country, following a similar template.

The Utter Inn

WHERE:
Västerås, Lake Mälaren
COST:
Reasonable
BEST TIME OF YEAR:
May to October
DON'T MISS:
Lovely views across the lake; a pre-ordered luxury meal delivered by boat
THINGS TO DO:
Swimming; sunbathing; canoeing; watching marine life
YOU SHOULD KNOW:
The Utter Inn is always heavily booked so you must reserve well in advance; it only sleeps two; bring your own supplies of alcohol; it's not for claustrophobics.

Adventurous souls are offered a unique sensory experience at the Utter Inn (that's the Otter Inn to English speakers), designed by Swedish alternative artist Mikael Genberg. Guests spend the night marooned in the middle of a lake, 3 m (10 ft) under the water, with just one other person and a lot of fish. To reach this extraordinary place, you are taken by boat 1 km (0.5 mi) out across the water from Västerås harbour on the shore of Lake Mälaren. The boat departs with a promise that you will be collected next morning.

Your first sight of the Utter Inn is completely surreal – a quaint red-and-white clapboard shack of the sort you might see in any Swedish meadow, bobbing up and down in the middle of a lake. But this shack is equipped with under-floor heating, camping stove, table and chairs. There is even a canoe so you can paddle to a nearby uninhabited island and stretch your legs before settling down on your 'terrace' deck to watch the sun go down.

So far, so very normal – as floating huts go, that is! But then open the hatch in the floor, descend the ladder and you'll find yourself in an underwater chamber with windows in all four walls. You are suddenly strangely aware of a bizarre role reversal, as though you are in an aquarium being observed by the fish. The room is sparsely furnished but perfectly comfortable and the passing marine life more than makes up for the lack of a television. You are not entirely cut off from civilization. Plenty of boats sail by and passing windsurfers will stop for a chat. But remember you can't get back to the lakeside until you are rescued, so it's as well to choose a like-minded companion for this amazing adventure.

Treehotel

Deep in the boreal forest of Sweden's Lapland, something hovers. Is it a UFO? Possibly. For that's the name of one of the aerial accommodation pods at Treehotel, 65 km (40 mi) south of the Arctic Circle. These are cutting-edge treehouses designed to thrill, while paying due deference to the need to leave the smallest possible human footprint on this vast and ecologically important northern forest. That means no nails or bolts are used to secure these extraordinary cabins to their living foundations. But rest assured – as if by magic, they still hang up there very solidly at a height of around 4 m (13 ft), which seems much higher once you're up than it does from *terra firma*.

It's possible to visit Treehotel as part of an organized trip that takes in this pristine wilderness destination, or pre-book an individual holiday. This is not a check-into-in-passing sort of place, as you generally fly in to Luleå, from where you are escorted to Treehotel, enjoying the spectacular scenery of the Lule River valley on the 100-km (62-mi) journey. After checking in to Brittas Pensionat at the village of Harads, it's off to meet your eyrie.

Each treehouse will amaze you. The UFO hovers in the treetops, portholes glowing, and surprises with a roomy split-level interior that sleeps two parents and two children. The Cabin is a rectangular capsule with floor-to-ceiling windows and birch panelling. You have to look hard to spot Mirror Cube, which reflects and thus vanishes into surrounding pines. Blue Cone (confusingly red) looks like a mischievous pixie's hat. Room with a View actually has three (of the forest, sky and river) and boasts a terrace, while the extraordinary Birds Nest resembles nothing more closely than . . . a scruffy eyrie. Whichever one you book will surely prove to be an adventurous traveller's delight.

WHERE:
Near Harads, Lapland
COST:
Fairly expensive, but very acceptable for something sensationally different
BEST TIME OF YEAR:
It's open all year round (24-hour days in summer, classic white wonderland in winter). January to April are favoured months for winter activities.
DON'T MISS:
Sweating it out in the tree sauna; the midnight sun or Northern Lights, depending on the time of year; a guided tour of Treehotel
THINGS TO DO:
Popular winter/spring choices include sleigh rides, dog sledding, snowshoeing, ice fishing, visiting a Sami village, igloo building and skijoring (horse-pulled skiing). Summer/autumn choices are hiking, mountain biking, kayaking, horseback riding, fishing and carriage rides (among others).
YOU SHOULD KNOW:
Breakfast is included, and taken at Brittas Pensionat. Children are welcome at Treehotel. The hotel won the Grand Tourism Prize in Sweden's Travel & Tourism Awards. Organized activities are charged as extras.

Ice Hotel Jukkasjärvi

WHERE:
Marknadsvägen 63, Jukkasjärvi, near Kiruna
COST:
Reasonable
BEST TIME OF YEAR:
The ice hotel is open from early December to mid April.
DON'T MISS:
Seeing further areas of the hotel being constructed during December and January; the Northern Lights tour
THINGS TO DO:
Self-driving snowmobile excursions (drivers must be at least 16); dog sledding, making ice sculptures; horseback riding (with every chance of meeting a moose); reindeer sledding (just like Santa!)
YOU SHOULD KNOW:
Over 100 weddings take place in the Ice Church each year. It's possible to stay in chalets during the summer, even though the ice hotel has gone down the river. Local Sami people have their own language and culture, and it's possible to arrange Sami cultural experiences that provide fascinating insight into the lives of these native Lapps.

The food may melt in your mouth, but fortunately Ice Hotel Jukkasjärvi itself won't turn to slush around you (although when the brief northern summer looms it will be abandoned to a watery fate). This super-cool Lapland destination is the first-ever (and largest) ice hotel in the world, and has had more than two decades of successful operation in a village by the Torne River, 200 km (124 mi) north of the Arctic Circle.

And this is not just any old ice hotel, but a work of art that is created for a few months of ephemeral life. The design is different each year, as directed by the imaginative vision of a team of architects, artists and experienced snow builders who come from many countries. By the time the build is finished, after around six weeks, there will suites, ice rooms, snow rooms, communal areas and a church. It's an impressive process involving snow cannons and huge blocks of ice cut and hauled from the river. The winter sun never gets above the horizon, but the snow is crisp and the icy landscape magical.

The temperature in the hotel never rises above –5°C (23°F), and sleeping on a bed of ice (admittedly insulated by a thick mattress, reindeer skins, an arctic sleeping bag and thermal underwear) is a surreal but compelling experience. There's an adjacent warm building with bathrooms, showers and a sauna, and savvy guests don't overdose on late-night coffee in a pre-emptive attempt to warm up. Nocturnal calls of nature require a trip through freezing corridors to the warm facilities, a journey best avoided if at all possible. Many guests choose to spend but a single night in the ice hotel and additional nights in the associated (warm!) nordic chalets.

Kolarbyn Eco-Lodge

Pack warm clothing, weatherproof gear, stout boots or walking shoes, sleeping bag, pillow and a towel, plus useful extras like a camera, binoculars, torch, water bottle and snacks. Then head for Kolarbyn Eco-Lodge, deep in the dense forests of Bergslagen, a region known for its many lakes, conifer woodlands and abundant wildlife. And it will be a wild life for visitors, too, for the place has 12 simple (but cosy!) primitive shelters in the backwoods, with no electricity. There is running water, but it's in the crystal-clear stream that runs through the camp. Sweet drinking water comes from a traditional well.

Each shelter has two plank beds for adults, plus a child's bed if requested. Lighting is by candles and the glow of a wood-burning stone fireplace. A generous supply of sheepskins help ward off any night chills (and soften those beds!), while essentials like firewood (for splitting), candles and matches are provided. There are composting toilets but no showers, although hardy pioneers can plunge into the stream or nearby Lake Skärsjön in lieu of more formal facilities.

Fire pits and primitive cooking equipment are to hand, and washing up is done in that handy stream. Except in winter an organic self-service breakfast is available daily, but visitors help themselves to basic cooking equipment from the storehouse, light their own fires and barbecue their own food (purchased in the local small town). The true appeal of this place is not the forest setting, however impressive, but the chance to be self-sufficient and at one with nature. No rules, no cosseting, no pressure – just living simply in a simply beautiful place.

WHERE:
Near Skinnskatteberg
COST:
Budget
BEST TIME OF YEAR:
Summer (but truly hardy adventurers will revel in the stunning winter season from November to April)
DON'T MISS:
Enjoying an evening of simple companionship (and discussing this extraordinary experience) with like-minded guests in the communal meeting hut; getting a few people together and firing up the floating sauna on Lake Skärsjön (takes 10)
THINGS TO DO:
Taking a guided trip into the wilderness to see beaver and moose; borrowing the canoe or old wooden rowing boat to explore the lake
YOU SHOULD KNOW:
Arrive by car and park on the gravel road close to the camp. It may be a wild place, but there is mobile phone reception in case of emergency. Summer's the time to hear a sound rarely heard in the industrialized world, but one that still strikes a chill into the human heart – the eerie howling of wolves.

Jumbo Stay

This is absolutely *the* place to stay for those with a fear of flying or, come to that, those who *love* flying. It works just as well either way, for Jumbo Stay is (you guessed already!) a converted Jumbo jetliner that has become a hotel. An imaginative idea indeed, and one that has been realized with considerable panache. The decommissioned Boeing 747-212B stands on a custom-built plinth with enclosed entrance tower, and is a striking sight on the edge of the busy Stockholm-Arlanda Airport. Built in 1976, this former behemoth of the airways was stripped internally and then completely refurbished in 2007.

The towering twin-deck crash-pad (only kidding!) with spiral staircase has 76 beds in 27 small rooms, most equipped with two bunk beds. But there's a variety of options, including four-bed male and female dorms, family rooms, suites, singles and doubles with private baths. The *crème de la crème* is the luxurious Cockpit Suite with private shower and toilet, a must for aviation junkies or adventurous co-pilots (sleeps two, naturally). All have flat-screen TVs and free wifi access, and there is efficient air conditioning throughout the plane. The cheaper rooms share five modern bathroom-and-toilet facilities on the main deck, which is rather more than voyagers enjoy on the real thing.

Jumbo Stay is open 24/7 for the convenience of those using the adjacent airport, and the JumboBar offers drinks, meals and snacks. Those on the tightest of budgets are welcome to use the on-board microwave ovens to take care of their catering needs. As luxury hotels go, the place may lack a certain something. But by conventional airline standards an overnight 'flight' is sheer heaven.

WHERE:
Stockholm-Arlanda Airport, 37 km (23 mi) north of Stockholm
COST:
Budget (although suites are more expensive)
BEST TIME OF YEAR:
Any
DON'T MISS:
Airport views (including the spectacular air-traffic control tower by night); chilling in the first-class lounge with its original (but rearranged) seats
THINGS TO DO:
Plane spotting; having a meal on the outdoor terrace or splash in the swimming pool (weather permitting); chewing the fat with fellow grounded travellers in the comfortable bar
YOU SHOULD KNOW:
Jumbo Stay is wheelchair-friendly. Breakfast is not included in the room price, except for those occupying suites, but may be purchased as an extra. The hotel is an easy 15-minute walk to/from the airport terminal for travellers arriving/departing in planes that actually fly, or alternatively there is a swift free shuttle service.

Gotska Sandön

The Baltic region of Gotland is a popular summer-holiday destination for Swedes and is a jumping-off point for the truly remote outpost of Gotska Sandön. This small Baltic isle is around 40 km (25 mi) north of Fårö Island, and it's just 9 km (5.5 mi) long and 6 km (4 mi) wide. That's no bad thing for intrepid adventurers looking for a slice of the simplest life, because the ferry tends to land where the wind takes it, leaving passengers to make their way to the camp on foot (occasionally requiring a hike almost along the island's full length).

With luck, a tractor and trailer will await to transport baggage, but it's not for new arrivals, who get a wonderful introduction to Gotska Sandön on a walk through dense pine forest to journey's end – a charming campsite with red-painted chalets sporting white windows and verandahs. They surround an open area filled with tempting aromas from the kitchen where earlier arrivals are busy cooking (this is a self-catering adventure). Happily for those who like to mix their wilderness experience with basic home comforts, there are excellent washrooms and toilets. Pre-booking is required, but visitors can stay in a cabin, their own tent or crude shelters.

A maximum of 165 people are allowed to stay on the island at any one time – a good number to provide comradeship at the camp, while allowing those who wish to seek solitude plenty of private space. There are numerous coastal and inland tracks to explore, including one to the island's dizzying high point, a sand dune that soars all of 40 m (131 ft) above sea level. Forest and meadowland sparkling with wild flowers, dunes and beaches combine to create a nature-lovers' paradise and a tranquil pace of life that's hard to leave behind when a return to everyday life beckons.

WHERE:
Gotska Sandön Island, Baltic Sea
COST:
Budget
BEST TIME OF YEAR:
Late spring to early autumn (mid May until mid September)
DON'T MISS:
The Nature Centre run by the Swedish Environmental Protection Agency; the island's three lighthouses; Madame Souderland's historic homestead (she was one of the first to live on the now-uninhabited island with her family in the 18th century); sunsets over the Baltic
THINGS TO DO:
Absolutely nothing beyond enjoying (and perhaps photographing) the unspoilt natural charms of this beautiful Baltic island; for those so inclined the nightly service in the island's wooden chapel
YOU SHOULD KNOW:
Take enough provisions to last for your stay (there's no shop). If sea conditions are unfavourable be prepared for an involuntary extension of your visit. The only four-legged wildlife on the island is the humble toad, although seals may be spotted off shore. Get there from Fårö or the Swedish mainland.

Salt & Sill Hotel

WHERE:
Klädesholmen, Tjörn Municipality
COST:
Reasonable to expensive (varies somewhat by season and room chosen)
BEST TIME OF YEAR:
High summer to be part of the madding crowd, any other season for some refreshing breathing space
DON'T MISS:
If you're not up for the world's best herring platter, how about trying the world's fastest sauna? The *Silla* is a catamaran sauna with twin diesel engines that can reach a speed of 15 knots. Hot stuff!
THINGS TO DO:
The tourist thing – eating, drinking, relaxing, checking out the town and visiting the Sillebua museum, doing the beaches, watching spectacular sunsets over the water
YOU SHOULD KNOW:
The Salt & Sill Inn is not exactly traditional – it was constructed on the site of a former canning factory and opened in 1999. The hotel offers various tempting packages that include one or more of the restaurant's finest meals. More than half Sweden's production of pickled herring comes from the local Klädesholmen Seafood plant.

Ready to sample the world's best herring platter? That's the bold claim made for the house speciality by the Salt & Sill Inn, gloriously located in the small island fishing port of Klädesholmen on the west coast of Tjorn, which as everyone who knows everything knows is Sweden's 'herring island'. But if a world-beating herring platter isn't your thing there are plenty of other options, as the chef focuses on the best of local produce to create an exciting fine-dining experience to titillate even the most jaded of taste buds.

The island is 45 minutes from Gothenburg by car, which is quite an expedition for the sake of a meal, however good. So the going's been made easy by the inspired creation of the adjacent Salt & Sill Hotel, Sweden's first floating hotel. This boxy construct won't win design awards, but offers comfortable accommodation in a spectacular location with great sea views over Bohuslän's outer archipelago. There are 22 rooms and one suite in six two-storey buildings on floating pontoons. The interiors are simple Scandinavian chic in style, and each has access to an outdoor seating area overlooking the water. This is a peaceful location away from the island's tourist hustle and bustle – an ideal spot to relax and unwind.

There is on-board catering for those who choose not to eat at the adjacent Salt & Sill Inn, but that should really be an essential part of the occasion. Eating fine food overlooking the sea, either inside or out on the pier, is an experience not to be missed. And Klädesholmen itself is an appealing old fishing port that just cries out to be explored.

Tipi in Dalsland

Spend a minimum of four wonderful days and three nights almost in the Great Outdoors, the 'almost' referring to a welcoming Swedish *tipi* (tepee – locally *kåto* or *goahti*) that blends naturally into lakeside trees, promising warm and snug overnight accommodation. The waterside encampment is in Dalsland, Sweden's Lake District, and welcomes individuals, couples and families who want to get away from it all and enjoy some stirring outdoor adventure, or simply relax and find a wonderful sense of freedom from the stresses and strains of everyday life.

The deal is simple, as is the lifestyle. Bring food, a sleeping bag and a pot for boiling anything you don't want to barbecue, plates and cutlery (also a camp stove if you're a non-barbecuer) and settle into a *tipi* (conical pole tent) that will have birch-twig mattresses covered in reindeer skins. There will be a fire pit with firewood and a splitting axe, matches and kindling to take care of the catering. Each *tipi* has an assigned rowing boat with lifejackets, plus a fishing permit for anglers intent on catching supper (bring your own tackle). There are dry outside toilets, and those who want a hot sluice or cooked meal can simply take a ten-minute walk to find shower and restaurant facilities.

This is an ultimate wild-camping experience, and some will be more than happy to unwind and enjoy the sense of space and freedom, simply relaxing in a wood-heated bathing barrel to the sound of water lapping the shore. But others will want to take advantage of the many organized activities that can be pre-booked, from forest ziplining through a high-rope course to kayak wildlife safaris. The choice is yours!

WHERE:
Near Brohögen, Dalsland Province
COST:
Budget
BEST TIME OF YEAR:
May to September only
DON'T MISS:
Enjoying a convivial evening meal in the collective dining tent; a game of *Tre-kamp* (the triple challenge of archery, axe throwing and air rifle target shooting)
THINGS TO DO:
Visit the moose centre to get up close and personal with Sweden's iconic animal, along with the likes of fallow deer and goats.
YOU SHOULD KNOW:
The four-day trips begin on Mondays (extra days by arrangement). The ability to swim is desirable, going on essential. Some of the adventure activities are unsuitable for children under the age of 12.

WHERE:
Flaggmansvägen 8, Stockholm
COST:
Budget, budget, budget (by expensive Stockholm standards!)
BEST TIME OF YEAR:
Open 24/365
DON'T MISS:
A meal in the ship's restaurant; a drink on *af Chapman*'s deck at night when the city lights sparkle on the water
THINGS TO DO:
Sightseeing – the hostel is handy for all the city centre goodies, which can be explored on foot; boat trips around the Stockholm Archipelago from the nearby quay; sharing the wonderful world of Astrid Lindgren at Junibacken
YOU SHOULD KNOW:
Bedding is provided and sleeping bags are not allowed. Young people under the age of 16 get a discount. Breakfast is not included but is available. Internet is available, but not free. An HI (Hostelling International) card is available at reception for those who don't have one, and gives a worthwhile discount.

Chapman Hostel

It famously floats, but there's a good alternative for landlubbers. The af Chapman & Skeppsholmen Hostel on the island Skeppsholmen in the city centre offers Stockholm's most interesting (and affordable) accommodation – a unique hostelling experience. The refurbished tall ship *af Chapman* is one of the city's iconic sights, especially when floodlit at night, and is moored overlooking the historic Gamla San (Old Town) and Stockholm's Royal Palace. Reception is in the adjacent mellow brick building that offers the non-rocking option with its own (larger) selection of rooms. This place also has an interesting history, once serving as the location for the palace firewood store.

Don't expect luxury, but the hostel provides an interesting practical overnight stay and is great for families (who should actually find the boat irresistible, even though it's slightly more expensive). All cabins and rooms have bunk beds and range from a small two-person space right up to the large attic dormitory sleeping 16 or more. Many of the ship's cabins have been restored to their original style for a genuine shipboard experience and, with 280 beds over both locations, it's easy to find a berth. There are en-suite double rooms available as a cheap alternative to regular hotels.

Breakfast is not included but the hostel's legendary eco-breakfast is not expensive but is substantial, providing fuel for a good morning's exploration of the city with its museums, restaurants and fine architecture. For those seeking an entertaining outing, a ferry gives easy access to Djurgården Island where the Skansen open-air museum, Vasa ship museum, Nordic museum, aquarium and Gröna Lund amusement park may be found.

Stenebynäs Estate

In western Sweden, close to Norway, Dalsland is renowned for spectacular lakeland scenery, and there couldn't be a better way to appreciate the tranquil natural delights of this unspoilt area than a visit to the Stenebynäs Estate. This wooded preserve extends to 100 ha (247 ac) and occupies a stunning location with 2 km (1 mi) of private shoreline on a peninsula that juts out into Lake Iväg.

There is a choice of four country cottages in which to stay, each in a beautiful setting overlooking the lake. Red-painted Svalan should be first pick for large families or two families who wish to share. It has a balcony and terrace facing the water, seven bedrooms and two bathrooms. The large living room has an open fire and the well-equipped kitchen has a verandah. The family-sized Duvan is a traditional-style Swedish house with a huge balcony enjoying sensational views. Korpen has two comfortable double bedrooms and a large open-plan living area with kitchen. Lommen is set on a private wooden knoll overlooking the lake and is perfect for a romantic break. Downstairs is a living room, kitchen and shower room, and upstairs a double bedroom nestles beneath the eaves. Lommen is also suitable for two couples, or parents with older kids, because it comes with an adjacent cabin that has twin beds.

Chilling out, letting kids run wild, exploring the estate and messing about on the water are the things to do here. Each cottage comes with a wooden rowing boat, canoes and kayaks, so anglers will have a whale of a time (happily not literally). Pike and perch abound in the pure water and are tasty with it. There are innumerable small beaches and interesting landing spots to be found around the large lake and wild swimming is popular in summer.

WHERE:
Dals Långed, Bengtsfors, Dalsland
COST:
Reasonable (varies by cottage and season)
BEST TIME OF YEAR:
The cottages are available all year round, with each season offering its own special magic.
DON'T MISS:
A leisurely picnic at one of the many remote but scenic landing places that can only be reached by boat; spotting the estate's herd of long-horn cattle
THINGS TO DO:
Horse riding; berry picking and hunting wild mushrooms in the woods (providing only that you know which ones are safe to eat); a session in the lakeside sauna
YOU SHOULD KNOW:
Aspiring tennis players will be delighted to find a hard court hidden deep in the woods.

Hotell Liseberg Barken Viking

WHERE:
Gullbergskajen Quay, Gothenburg
COST:
Reasonable (prices vary by room size and season)
BEST TIME OF YEAR:
Gothenburg never sleeps (but the hotel is closed for Christmas).
DON'T MISS:
Watching the river traffic go by while having a light meal or drinks at the ship's outside tables (with a handy tented shelter waiting should sun or rain dictate discretion)
THINGS TO DO:
The floating hotel is close to the Nordstan shopping mall, Scandinavia's biggest.
YOU SHOULD KNOW:
Children under six stay free of charge (using existing beds), but there's a small charge for a baby's cot. One of the more unusual features for an old sailing ship is the thoroughly modern elevator. The ship is a smoking-free zone (even on deck).

A luxury three-star hotel that sailed the Seven Seas is surely . . . a cruise liner? Actually, no. The Hotell Liseberg Barken Viking is still afloat, but securely (and permanently) moored in the sheltered waters of the Göta Älv River, close to the centre of Gothenburg. This handsome four-masted barque was one of the last tall ships, built in the early 20th century, and now combines the romance of a bygone maritime era with all the comforts expected by today's hotel guests. The multi-lingual staff are all very friendly and do everything possible to ensure the comfort of guests. Needless to say, kids absolutely adore the opportunity to experience shipboard life.

The hotel is open 24/7 and has 29 smallish but adequate guest rooms with cable TV and free wifi internet access. The charming marine-themed rooms (should that be cabins?) with their cosy beds are wood-panelled and feature nautical paintings by artist Franz Glatzl. The excellent on-board Kapten Clausens Salong restaurant is named after a former ship's captain (Swedish cuisine and seafood a speciality), where an excellent buffet breakfast is served within the room price. Dinner is extra, but those who wish to dine out will find a good selection of firmly grounded eateries within easy walking distance. The ship has comfortably furnished lounging areas, including reception and the library.

There are great waterfront views from the old white-painted windjammer, which is handily located for the main railway station and the city centre's tourist sights, including the nearby Maritime Adventure Centre with another 19 interesting ships to explore. In summer there is often lively on-deck music to entertain guests.

Tree-top Cabin

This is the dream fulfilment of every child who wedged a cardboard box in the branches of a tree and pretended it was a sky fortress, aerial Xanadu or space station. The difference is that every comfort is ready and waiting for intrepid explorers willing to challenge the wilderness of eastern Norway's Brumunddal forest. X marks the tree. Find it and up you go. Woven into the branches is a wooden house of consummate perfection, its amenities all the more appreciated for being so unexpected. In fact there are two such houses, respectively 12 km and 25 km (7.5 mi and 15.5 mi) from the nearest village and shop in Brumunddal. The Pine House is more rustic, a single room incorporating kitchen, sofa beds and bunks round a fireplace, 8 m (26 ft) up a 250-year-old pine. A cabin on the ground below holds firewood and an outdoor toilet. There's no shower, but the lake outside offers an authentic wilderness take on hygiene.

The Larch House is bigger and includes a separate double bedroom and room for four more people. It has a fully equipped kitchen, shower, toilet and a fireplace cunningly created to serve both the main room and the open porch/balcony, from which the benches have a fabulous view through the tree tops to the nearby lake. Up here, you become part of the forest and its wildlife. Birds and squirrels come begging for scraps and in summer it's a rare day when an elk doesn't come snuffling past below. In the depths of winter, when the fire reflects on snowy branches and all is stillness under the bright stars, it is pure Norse magic.

WHERE:
Brumunddal, between Hamar and Lillehammer

COST:
Budget (but if two people book one of the cabins, they are guaranteed to have the place to themselves, which of course raises the cost per person a little)

BEST TIME OF YEAR:
Any time (winter is popular – the lowest costs are in spring and autumn)

DON'T MISS:
Shopping – you need to bring all your food, drinks and drinking water with you, as well as your bed linen; dog sledding with polar dogs; the black grouse grazing in the top of the birch tree in front of the balcony in autumn, winter and spring

THINGS TO DO:
Cross-country skiing; hiking; fishing in the lake

YOU SHOULD KNOW:
Visitors are responsible for leaving the cabin 'as you would like to find it yourself' – but cleaning can be arranged for a modest fee. Both cabins have a container full of bird seed and visitors are asked to fill the bird tray on arrival and departure. To reach the Pine House, visitors must pass a NOKr 50 ($9 US) toll bar into the national forest (the Larch House has different access).

WHERE:
Kabelvag, Svolvaer, Vagan, Lofoten (the huts are also included in the address of *Svinoya Rorbu Hotel* ('Base Camp Lofoten') for corporate bookings involving all 33 *rorbuer*)
COST:
Reasonable
BEST TIME OF YEAR:
Any time
DON'T MISS:
The Lofoten Museum and (summer) archaeological excavations in Storvagen; scuba diving the 200 m (650 ft) underwater cliffs and surging currents of the Raftsundet strait; the wolf fish in the carpets of soft corals flourishing in the pure Atlantic waters; the boat trip to the Refsvikhula Cave and The Maelstrom (one of the world's strongest tide races); from October, the mesmerizing Northern Lights; in summer, golf at Hov, in the midnight sun
THINGS TO DO:
Eat stockfish at Borsen Spiteri in Svolvaer, the oldest (1828) quayside building and first shop; take a coastal safari by boat to Trollfjorden; cycle to the lovely mountain pass of Einangen on the Valberg-Leknes road; visit the tiny fishing villages on the islands of Flakstadoy and Moskenesoy; catch the winter cod (from March); ski
YOU SHOULD KNOW:
The Northern Lights appear as pillars, streaks, wisps and whole curtains of shimmering pink and green. The Inuit believe the lights represent the souls of their as yet unborn children, and the torches of long-departed ancestors.

A *Rorbu* (Fisherman's Hut)

Lofoten is an archipelago off the northwest coast of Norway. Although inside the Arctic Circle, it is touched by the last warming breath of the Atlantic Gulf Stream. For a thousand years, Norway's fishermen have gathered for the season at Kabelvag to chase million-strong shoals of fat cod, turning the village into Lofoten's *de facto* capital. That role has moved to Svolvaer in the next-door bay – but the whole area reflects the fishing culture that governs the islands' history. Among the most obvious indicators are the *rorbuer*, the dark-red huts built in the 19th century for visiting fishermen. Now restored, 30 of them line the shore of Svinoya, a tiny island linked by a bridge to Svolvaer – but it is the three newly built huts outside Kabelvag itself which provide visitors with the most accurate experience of the fishing tradition, plus the modern amenities to do so in the greatest comfort. Real trawlermen should be so lucky.

Each hut has three double bedrooms, two bathrooms, two sitting rooms (one with cable TV) and a first-class kitchen. They share a wide, quayside boardwalk which is ideal for soaking up the amazing vistas of the sea, of Vagakallen, Lofoten's highest (942 m/3,090 ft) mountain and of the historic, medieval centre of Storvagen. What's more, these *rorbuer* enjoy almost rural tranquillity (nobody can silence the seabirds!), although many of Lofoten's best attractions are within easy walking distance. Winter or summer makes no real difference. The essential *rorbu*'s wooden construction guarantees comfort at any temperature, especially if guests remember (as they must) to pre-order their firewood – just like fishermen in days of yore.

Turf-Roofed Highland Cabin

They are the signature accommodation of Norway's signature inland valley and traditional resort centre. The highland cabins dotting the forested hillsides above the lake at Gala, in the Gudbrandsdal valley north of Lillehammer, are showpieces of the very best of Norway's tourist industry. Dressed in the ultra-traditional external decor of red, green and blue, the cabins come in semi-detached two-bedroom, and four-bedroom sizes. Their interiors are models of neat, Scandinavian ergonomics, better furnished than many an urban apartment with a painterly mix of ochre, pale-blue and cranberry walls, woodwork and painted furniture, and muted tartan fabrics. You would never leave, were it not that outside is Norway's most staggeringly beautiful inland valley, flanked by both the Jotunheim and Rondane National Parks, whose receding snowy peaks proffer an irresistible invitation to run, jump, twirl, and hum the *Sound of Music* (there's no need for embarrassment – everyone else is doing the same).

In fact, it's only when you leave the cabins and look back that their most unusual feature becomes apparent. Most of them have a turf roof. Centuries of evolution in Gudbrandsdal have created a local version of a rural vernacular common across the globe. Around Gala, the turf roof is an art form. Thoroughly practical (warm in winter, cool in summer) and very cunningly waterproofed (draughtsmen drool over the design specifics), the best of them produce two flowerings a year. The first turns the cabin roof into a spring meadow; the second into a rampant wild-flower explosion. Both are delightfully mad and full of joy. Somehow, that feels like an expression of the highly appropriate match between Norwegian hospitality and one of its loveliest regions.

WHERE:
Gala, Gudbrandsdalen
COST:
Reasonable – but car hire usually needs to be added
BEST TIME OF YEAR:
Any time
DON'T MISS:
Walking the glacier on Smorstabbreen; a canoe safari across four mountain lakes with stops to swim; making a summer trip by chairlift to the top of Valsfjell – and mountain biking down the alpine skiing runs; a night-time elk safari
THINGS TO DO:
Explore the Venabygd and Kvam mountains, natural playgrounds of waterfalls, plateaux, ravines and forested peaks; ski some of Norway's best cross-country and alpine runs (and most of the cabins are ski-in and ski-out); enjoy the cabin's sauna, and consider the view; horse riding; whitewater rafting on the Sjoa river
YOU SHOULD KNOW:
Gala is on the Peer Gynt Trail linking Dalseter in Espedalen to Scheikampen in Gudbrandsdalen by ski tracks; every summer more than 10,000 people see the annual production of Ibsen's *Peer Gynt*, accompanied by Edvard Grieg's music, performed with Gala Lake as a backdrop; it isn't actually turf which insulates the cabins' roofs – it's the multiple layers of birch bark laid in a clever way underneath the turf.

Hellisoy Lighthouse Keeper's House

WHERE:
Off the west coast of Fedje island, Nordbordland
COST:
Budget to reasonable
BEST TIME OF YEAR:
April to October
DON'T MISS:
Fishing from the private jetty; whale-watching; enjoying the subtle interplay of moonrise and sunrise over the water from the top of the lighthouse; spreading a picnic on the grass clifftop
THINGS TO DO:
Rent a boat or canoe to explore the deep fjords and skerries near the island; go shopping in Fedje village; get some answers from the official 'tourist information' office on the right of the ferry quay – disguised as the Pernille café/restaurant (and full of delicious local cooking).
YOU SHOULD KNOW:
On February 9 1945, the British submarine HMS *Venturer* fired four torpedoes at the submerged German submarine U-864. The fourth torpedo shattered and sank U-864. This is the only known incident in the whole of naval warfare in which one submarine sank another while both were submerged. The wreck of U-864 lies in 73 m (240 ft) of water just off Hellisoy lighthouse.

The red-and-white banded Hellisoy lighthouse has warned shipping of coastal hazards between Bergen and Sognefjord since 1855. It is one of Norway's first two cast-iron round towers, 32 m (105 ft) high, with a storybook lantern and gallery at its summit. It isn't easy to reach. Visitors from the Norwegian mainland must cross the Nordbordland region's maze of waterways to the community of Austrheim; take a local ferry from Saevroy out into the North Sea, to Fedje – a place so remote it is known as 'the island in the middle of the ocean'; and then hire a boat or passage to cross the last 50 m (55 yd) of turbulent water to the tiny skerry of Hellisoy itself. The location is a byword for solitude, so it's unfortunate that many visitors come for just an hour (on 'Lighthouse Safari'), to climb the tower and gaze hopefully out to sea. But then they go, leaving up to 15 people – groups of friends, or two or three families – to enjoy the lighthouse keeper's house perched on the cliffs close to the tower. With five bedrooms, two sitting rooms, a big kitchen and a wood-fired sauna, it's extremely comfortable. Guests can bring their own, or hire, bed linen; but they must also bring their own food or go fishing for it.

The lure of Hellisoy is the elemental force of nature all around. The vagaries of microclimates around Norway's mega-fjords create startling shifts between millpond calm, sunlit storm and gale-force challenge. Exhilarating purity of light makes pinpoint sharp every colour and shape. Washed in Atlantic-clear air, every moment on Hellisoy reminds you what it is to be completely alive.

Lainio Snow Hotel and Village

The massive sense of fun that pervades the Lainio Snow Village is backed up by at least as much tact. Its proprietors know just how excited visitors are to be so high above the Arctic Circle, eating, drinking and sleeping in an all-ice world, and how little they are truly prepared for the experience. So, discreetly placed 'warm rooms' attached to each of the major ice facilities ensure that nobody need suffer from the extreme temperatures common in northern Lapland. The solicitude is exemplary, and a large part of why the Lainio Snow Village is a roaring success.

In fact, many people come to the Snow Village as an excursion from Yllas, a few kilometres away and Finland's most popular (and funky) ski resort. Most leave regretfully, wishing they had booked longer. Once inside the inter-connecting Snow Hotel, Ice Restaurant, Ice Bar and gallery of artfully lit ice and snow sculptures, visitors find imagination kicking in, causing something like rising hysteria at the bizarre absurdity of the place *and their presence in it*. Few places are entirely new, and worldly travellers are disoriented when they discover one. This is Lainio's triumph. The 16 igloo-shaped bedrooms and ten elaborate 'ice suites' actually offer very comfortable mattresses on a wooden frame, with polar sleeping bags to make sure. Yet when guests compare notes in the 24-hour Ice Bar, their ice glasses filled with iced everything, they swap tales of iced adventure to raise the hair on your neck. Human nature, pushed by northern latitudes to extremes, makes Lainio one of the best-humoured and fun gossip exchanges anywhere in the world. That alone makes it worth rebuilding every year.

WHERE:
Yllas (pronounced 'Oo-las'), close to the Swedish border in northern Lapland

COST:
Expensive, but unique

BEST TIME OF YEAR:
December/January to April

DON'T MISS:
Your first sight of the entrance to the Snow Village, like an epic film set; the Northern Lights (frequent and dramatic this far north); the longest ski run in Finland; running with huskies; full spa treatments; smoked reindeer and reindeer stew

THINGS TO DO:
At the Snow Village try everything you can find in its iced equivalent; otherwise, use the marvellous facilities based in Yllas to enjoy some of Europe's least known and unusual winter sports.

YOU SHOULD KNOW:
Lainio is obviously a marvellous location for a wedding – but with real style, the proprietors adhere to the belief that since a marriage should be built on solid ground, so should the wedding chapel. Therefore, instead of an astonishing Ice Chapel, there is a tiny wooden church, which says it all.

Kakslauttanen Igloo Village

WHERE:
Northeast Finland (northern Lapland) close to Urho Kekkonen National Park
COST:
Reasonable to moderately expensive
BEST TIME OF YEAR:
December/January to April
DON'T MISS:
The Reindeer Safari (a slow-mo sledge with a view up a reindeer's butt); the 'Biggest Smoke Sauna in the World', with up to 100 other people; the Ice Bar, with Lappish specialities like Raaku, Kultakurkku, and Russian 'Champanskoje'
THINGS TO DO:
Enduro Motocross and Forest Scooter Safaris (enjoy that Arctic tranquillity on a skidoo); snowshoe trekking; Santa's Resort (if your love of kitsch is stronger than your embarrassment for the Elves' pitiful regime)
YOU SHOULD KNOW:
Whatever the outside temperature, inside a snow igloo it's a constant -3°C (27°F) to -6°C (21°F); the beauty of the Arctic winter and the subtleties of Sami culture are simply not compatible with corporate attitudes – but snow igloos are.

The Kakslauttanen Hotel and Igloo Village is a lovely idea in danger of losing its innocence. It is close to being an Arctic theme park. The complex has three principal constituents – a hotel of 31 very fine log cabins, each with its own sauna, kitchenette and open fire; the 'igloo village' rebuilt each year; and a year-round 'Santa's Resort' which exploits locally cherished Sami culture in support of an excruciating series of Christmas clichés. Corporate thinking and development are rife – but the Igloo Village, by virtue of its annual renewal, still has the power to reduce the most cynical traveller to dumbstruck awe in the face of the Arctic's natural magic.

The Igloo Village is built a short distance from the hotel's main reception and restaurant building. The completion of the Ice Bar, Ice Chapel, World's Largest Snow Restaurant (open only for 'groups') and ten snow igloos is celebrated by an international ice-carving competition, the results of which are truly amazing and last until spring. Lights embedded in the walls create a warm glow inside the igloos, and their thickness ensures perfect quiet and deep sleep. Just as well – because close by are 20 glass igloos laid out in regimented lines, their hemispherical pods brightly lit to show the luxury twin beds and toilets within. The idea is that you go to sleep watching the stars or, with luck, the Northern Lights. It's a great idea, but don't rely on the neighbours either to keep quiet or to turn the lights out. You won't get a second chance, because the hotel relies on guests spending just one night on their 'igloo experience', and the rest in the hotel. Think lucky, and enjoy the snow.

Padaste Manor

It takes centuries and a lot of luck to create a fairytale like Padaste Manor. Its 14th-century origins are discernible behind its charming 19th-century facade and elegant interiors, but its survival as a picturebook country house, along with its historic outbuildings and the entirety of its 7-ha (17-ac) landscaped parkland and a further 22-ha (54-ac) estate of meadows and forests is due to its remote location. The Manor sits on the shore of Padaste Bay, on the south side of Muhu, a small island off the Estonian mainland. Isolated by the paranoid politics of the 20th century, it was rescued from decline at the moment when its unique location was recognized as part of one of Europe's most important natural wonders – and immediately protected as an untouched paradise of biodiversity.

The hotel is as rare and wonderful as its flora and fauna. None of the 14 rooms in the Manor itself are identical. Some have fireplaces or balconies, and one (Room 15) has a tiny mezzanine 'Poetry Loft' approached by ladder, where you can sit in a club chair beneath a convenient skylight surrounded by volumes of verse. Wooden floors are heated and the furnishings are sumptuous and sympathetic to the Manor's history. They conceal every hi-tech facility or toy anyone could wish for – but best of all are the views through the park to the varied shoreline. The Carriage House and the Farmhouse buildings flanking the Manor are if anything more luxurious, although they lack the obvious splendour of the manorial chambers. It remains only to add that the restaurant is one of the best in Estonia, and start making travel plans.

WHERE:
Padaste Bay, Muhu Island
COST:
Moderately expensive
BEST TIME OF YEAR:
March to October (Padaste Manor is closed from November to February, except for pre-arranged group bookings like weddings or conferences)
DON'T MISS:
The Spa, which abjures all global brands in favour of authentic Muhu recipes and traditions for its lotions (and insists that guests using the Roman steam bath jump naked into a freezing cold tub); the 23 species of rare orchid in their natural habitat; migratory cranes, ducks and swans among millions around Padaste Bay; the breeding pairs of sea eagles; owls, woodpeckers, June nightingales, deer, wild boar and moose in the estate forests
THINGS TO DO:
Walking the shoreline of pine, juniper, ferns, wild flowers and reed grasses; summer lunch at the SeaHouse brasserie on the terrace, and formal dinner in the main hall; riding; fishing; visiting Uugu cliffs and caves or the 12th-century Muhu Fortress; Koguva fishing village
YOU SHOULD KNOW:
The hotel is happy to collect guests (free of charge) from Kuivastu, where the ferry arrives from the mainland. Alternatively, it's possible to arrange helicopter transfer direct from Tallinn or elsewhere.

Hotel Telegraaf

WHERE:
Vene 9, Tallinn
COST:
Expensive
BEST TIME OF YEAR:
Any time
DON'T MISS:
Toompea Castle, Estonia's seat of power, dominating the Old Town since the Teutonic Knights built the first fortress in 1227, and now the Estonian Parliament; the pharmacy in the corner of 11th-century *Raekoja Plats* (Town Hall Square) in continuous use since 1422; the House of the Brotherhood of the Blackheads (don't ask!); afternoon tea and/or a champagne cocktail on the hotel's relatively tranquil Summer Terrace
THINGS TO DO:
Amble round the medieval city walls. Get curious about what's inside some of the Old Town courtyards. Steel yourself to visit the KGB Museum and small but evocative Museum of Occupations. Exult in the pink baroque palace built by Tsar Peter I, now both the Kumu Art Museum and the Estonian President's residence.
YOU SHOULD KNOW:
Get a Tallinn discount card – even for a couple of days it's worth it. Seek out the Claustrum, the surviving third of an ancient Dominican Monastery – in the middle of its cellar is the 'Energy Pillar', said to be the source of physical and spiritual health.

Built in 1878 as the city's telegraphy centre, the Hotel Telegraaf is a landmark modern conversion in the medieval heart of Tallinn. The 13th-century Old Town is a warren of cobbled alleys, gabled houses, courtyards half-glimpsed through coaching arches, lead-tiled onion domes and needle spires. The hotel is an elegant *fin de siècle* addition to the graceful patina of centuries. Behind the facade 86 rooms are divided by size into eight categories, from the Presidential Suite on down. All of them are extremely comfortable, their decor an exactly judged blend of cosmopolitan luxury and neutral modernity. Every amenity is built in, and the provision of a full spa service, a 30-m (100-ft) 'Roman' pool, sauna and Jacuzzi, chic lobby bar and award-winning Restaurant Tchaikovsky (a 'symphony of Russian cuisine' and 'flavours of Estonia') makes the Hotel Telegraaf equally alluring to leisure and business visitors.

It's impossible to exaggerate the charm of the hotel's location. All but a handful of rooms have a privileged view of the Old Town, and one of Tallinn's most picturesque and intriguing old lanes is right opposite. *Katerina Kaik* (St Catherine's Passage) is an ancient pedestrian alley along the back of what was once St Catherine's Church. It houses St Catherine's Guild, an affiliation of craft workshops where artists and artisans use traditional techniques to create glassware, fabrics, hats, quilts and ceramics. Interspersed with the kind of small bars and cafés it's a pleasure to loll about in, the place embodies the spirit of Tallinn – and Estonia – reborn. So indeed does the Hotel Telegraaf. In the centre of everything, it's the perfect oasis.

The Dylan

The Dylan is the arbiter of hotel chic in Amsterdam. In fact globally, it's one of just a handful of boutique hotels that can claim a Royal Straight Flush of perfect location, integral history, stunning design fusing modernity with classic elegance, a completely 'secret' garden, discreetly impeccable service, a world-class concierge desk and a Michelin-starred restaurant. It's even partly amphibious. You can arrive by water (on your own or the hotel's boat) at the private landing stage on the smartest section of the smartest of Amsterdam's central canal rings, Kaisersgracht; and you can dine on the delicious award-winning food while roaming the canals on a 19th-century renovated wooden 'salon' boat, the *Muze*, operated by the land-based Vinkeles restaurant.

The hotel began in the early 17th century as a theatre attended by European royalty. Vivaldi himself conducted the orchestra there in 1737. Now, you enter beneath the historic canal-side facade into the marble of reception for a welcome so low-key but smoothly efficient that it strips away stress in moments. Your room will be a combination of comfortable warmth and minimalist statement so brilliantly extreme it's a pleasure to be in, although few are exactly the same and the long corridors open onto some wild variations. The rooms occupy several houses on the canal, and completely enclose a delightful garden courtyard which acts as a bar and brasserie. But it's the sophistication of the Bar Barbou and the Long Gallery Lounge inside that attracts celebrities and Amsterdam's ultra-hip, and the hotel is always home to visiting musicians and actors. Curiously, for all the celebrity glamour, it's actually the staff and their genial efficiency that make the Dylan such fun to stay in.

WHERE:
Kaisersgracht, Amsterdam
COST:
Expensive
BEST TIME OF YEAR:
Amsterdam is a delight at any time.
DON'T MISS:
The 'High Wine' evenings during summer, when canapés and a multitude of wines are served in the courtyard; the 18th-century bread ovens once used by the orphanage on the hotel site, now part of Vinkeles' sunken restaurant
THINGS TO DO:
Take advantage of having much of the best of Amsterdam on your doorstep. The hotel can arrange a bicycle but all the museums, the infamous Red Light district and the most interesting shops are within walking distance.
YOU SHOULD KNOW:
The hotel is named after Welsh poet Dylan Thomas (the suite named in his honour has a fully stocked drinks cabinet instead of a minibar); the hotel employs a painter full time just to make sure the white paintwork stays bright white.

A Canal Houseboat

WHERE:
The central canal area, the Amstel River or the former docklands, Amsterdam
COST:
Super-budget to expensive, but comfort and privacy can be guaranteed at a reasonable price
BEST TIME OF YEAR:
Any time is a good time to go afloat.
DON'T MISS:
A moment
THINGS TO DO:
Look out for the 'Love Boat', the Houseboat Museum on Prinsengracht, the two 'Cat Boat' official refuges filled with feline strays, the 'Houseboat Under the Windmill', the enormous converted ferry 'Amstel Botel' and the stunning appeal and variety of the 2,500 houseboats on the city's central canals.

Visitors who choose to stay on a canal houseboat instead of at an ordinary hotel have the opportunity to get under the skin (though happily not the surface) of Amsterdam in a way that would be otherwise difficult. The canals are integral to Amsterdam's history and culture, and none more so than the *grachtengordel*, the central canal ring area listed as a World Heritage site. The wonderful houses lining the banks are among the city's most coveted and expensive, but moored next to them are houseboats of every size, description and state of decay. Most are privately owned and many are for rent. Whether you pay a king's ransom to frolic in luxury worthy of a seraglio, or share a scrupulously clean four-bed dorm in a friendly commune costing less than a terrestrial hostel, your perspective on Amsterdam will change for ever. The gentle rocking of your bedroom

in the wash of passing boats is the authentic feeling of belonging.

Many houseboats are literally small houses secured to a wooden or steel hull. Others are converted from working tugs, clippers and barges (and for a little extra, can be persuaded to take you on a private tour of Amsterdam's beautiful waterways). It's important to check exactly what spaces and facilities are available. Most sleep four to six people, but if the shower (or, rarely, the bath) is shared, it's often more comfortable for friends to take over the entire boat. Houseboats are generally quite cramped for living space – but they have the wonderful extra of a topside deck and perhaps flowered garden from which to view life along the canal margins, and observe other water-dwellers. You'll find your interest is reciprocated, because Amsterdammers will recognize you as one of their own. That doesn't happen in hotels.

YOU SHOULD KNOW:
There are several agencies who will put you in direct contact with houseboat owners – do make sure you get details of exact location and facilities before booking. If museums are important, ask for somewhere close to Leidseplein, if you want tranquillity a canal near the fabulous Botanic Gardens – but whichever canal you start from, everything worth seeing will still be in walking/cycling distance.

Capsule Hotel

It is forbidden to think of the capsule hotel as merely a novelty of practical recycling. It's true that each of the bright-orange survival pods dates back to a 1972 design used in the North Sea oil industry, and that they were rescued from retirement and offered for rental as part of a 2004 art project. That knowledge isn't enough. You have to share the perception of a floating capsule as elevated Concept Art to really enjoy staying in one. There are several ways to demonstrate this. The pods are designed to keep you alive in atrocious maritime conditions. They are devoid of every comfort and none were added when they were first exhibited as art objects (with the exception of an 'emergency' lavatory and a new lock on the door).

When they became successful as eccentric places to stay, their 'concept' was extended to three versions. Now, the basic capsule is furnished only with a simple hammock. For 50 per cent more money you get a lavatory as well, and the deluxe version (for twice the basic price) comes with a sheepskin rug, cushions, sparkling wine, a DVD player with the complete collection of James Bond films and a small, brilliantly incongruous disco glitter-ball. The subtlety of relating such a disproportionate sliding financial scale to largely pointless 'extras' raises the concept to genuinely high art. If you share that opinion, it also raises some merry laughter and you'll have a wonderful time playing on your pod. Those in the Netherlands in search of more rigorous artworks should avoid the capsules. When occupied, they roll in almost perpetual motion, and you have only your artistic integrity to hold onto.

WHERE:
Docked at one or more of several sites close to Scheveningen and The Hague, but the owner (sorry, artist) has announced that new capsule sites (on and off the water) are planned in Amsterdam and western France.

COST:
Reasonable (there's a premium on Art)

BEST TIME OF YEAR:
Any time

DON'T MISS:
Calling at F.A.S.T. (Free Architecture Surf Terrain), the super-artistic surfer's village near The Hague's beachside suburb of Scheveningen where the capsule pods were re-imagined as Art, and may still be moored

THINGS TO DO:
Role-play suggested by your choice of capsule mode (sleeping bag and emergency rations/astronaut splashdown; 007 kit/the escape pod scene at the end of *From Russia With Love*)

YOU SHOULD KNOW:
Officially, the 4.5-m (15-ft) diameter capsules are TEMPS (Totally Enclosed Motor Propelled Survival craft) – they may not be glamorous, but they are undeniably cool (and SAFE).

The Harbour Crane

WHERE:
The harbour, Harlingen, Friesland
COST:
Expensive
BEST TIME OF YEAR:
Any time
DON'T MISS:
Privileged views over the Waddenzee shallows in one direction and over the historic centre of Harlingen in the other (use the binoculars so thoughtfully placed in the control cabin); enjoying the night time stars and seascapes
THINGS TO DO:
Play crane driver; discover the parameters of the computerized entertainment centre; sunbathe; walk round the lovely centre of Harlingen, enjoying the crane from every angle as you return; cackle with glee
YOU SHOULD KNOW:
Receiving guests is not allowed; pets and smoking are also banned.

The genius of the Harlingen Harbour Crane hotel belongs not to the irresistibly quirky idea, but to its completely brilliant execution. By creating five-star accommodation out of a 71-ton, 46-m (151-ft) high disused 1960s lumber crane, still *in situ* on the outer mole of Harlingen harbour, the owners have transcended conventional definitions of 'designer' and 'romantic' hotels. The main living space (which housed the crane's lifting mechanism) makes art from its extremist modern decor. It embraces overt technology with all kinds of computer-controlled devices for the resident couple's comfort and fun – and laces it with consummate style in the form of Charles Eames' furniture and a huge double

bed that invites collapse. Only the plasma TV seems *de trop*. Why would anyone watch it when one end of the room is a floor-to-ceiling glass pod with a wraparound panorama of limitless sea and sky? Better than that, the entire crane revolves through 360 degrees at the touch of a button. A ladder leads from the bedroom up to a small glass cabin, and the seat of power. You can sit here day or night – in your pyjamas even – twirling the joystick and spinning the crane to your heart's delight. If that palls, the shower is built for two, the lights and music are on dimmers, and you can raid the minibar before watching the sunset from the spacious roof deck. In the morning breakfast arrives fresh on an ingenious lift, one of two that highlight the crane's novel technology.

Guests leave grinning and laughing with delight. Harlingen's luxury giant toy really does have a claim to be one of Europe's most original and romantic getaways.

Camp Spirit

Camp Spirit is aptly named. Its influence is both powerful and immediate and it reaches hidden places most visitors have forgotten they've got. This eco-camp occupies the west side of a 4-ha (10-ac) man-made island called De Kluut in the middle of Veluwemeer, one of the lakes formed when Flevoland province was reclaimed from the open sea. Only 40 km (25 mi) from Amsterdam, De Kluut feels as remote as a South Sea island, and just as peaceful. Deserted except from May to September, it's a self-regenerating miniature paradise of high trees, reed palms, dense thickets and grassy clearings.

Even in summer, only 50 people are allowed on the island at any one time. They choose to stay in *tipis* (Native American or Swedish), yurts (Mongolian or Kyrgyz) or Sahara tents, placed for privacy within a general communion. The only 'building' is a small but exemplary bamboo shower block with proper toilets and basins. A much larger *tipi* acts as a clubhouse, especially in bad weather. People drift and gather, sharing games, books, art materials and chat, or just idling in neighbouring hammocks. It's heaven for children, and their parents, because everyone looks out for everyone without being precious or interfering. In good weather that's important, because so many activities take place on the water – but Veluwemeer has an average depth of only 1.5 m (5 ft) and safety has never been an issue.

As if there wasn't enough to do on the island, the lake shores of Flevoland and Gelderland are crammed with entertainment sites and summer events. Both banks are easily accessible – but most families prefer to create their own fun where the world can't reach them.

WHERE:
De Kluut, Veluwemeer
COST:
Budget (per person, per night – even in the highest season) and astonishing value for the degree of camping comfort
BEST TIME OF YEAR:
Camp Spirit is only open between May and September.
DON'T MISS:
Day trips off-island with the kids to Flevoland leisure centre (free entry to the vast swimming pool for Camp Spirit guests), Bataviawerf national historic ships centre at Lelystad; the Lowlands Music Festival at Biddinghuizen (in August).
THINGS TO DO:
Hiking and cycling on the polder land to small fishing villages like Harderwijk or Elburg, enjoying panoramic vistas reminiscent of Breughel; water bicycling, canoeing, rowing, windsurfing and playing shallow-water games where kids are safe.
YOU SHOULD KNOW:
Fresh bread can be delivered daily to your tent and there's a camp shop selling basics. None of the Camp Spirit workshops (yoga, meditation, mosaic, creative arts, sound-healing, etc) are gung-ho – their warm informality is one of the Camp's greatest gifts.

H2Otel

WHERE:
Wijnhaven, Rotterdam
COST:
Reasonable
BEST TIME OF YEAR:
Any time (but midwinters can be bleak)
DON'T MISS:
Taking a tour of one of the world's biggest ports on a Spido boat – so ultra-modern nothing like them exists anywhere else, so astonishing the boat alone is worth a special trip to Rotterdam; Spido tours last from 70 minutes to six hours and will take you to world-beating engineering works like the Maeslant Storm Surge Barrier, or try the 'Seven Rivers and Delta Works' tour that includes beautiful Dordrecht, the 18th-century Kinderdijk windmills and the impressive engineering of the south Holland river delta
THINGS TO DO:
Admire Rotterdam's wonderful new architecture, like the Cube Houses or Blijdorp Zoo; take the 'rocket launch' to the top of the Netherlands' tallest tower – the Euromast; treat the kids to Railz Miniworld model railway extravaganza and Plaswijckpark theme park.
YOU SHOULD KNOW:
The hotel doesn't serve dinner but runs a local restaurant, one of several nearby. Upper-deck rooms are entered from outside, so you have to face the weather to get to breakfast. Ask for a room with a balcony. Beware thin adjoining walls and noisy neighbours.

The canals and rivers of the Netherlands are dotted with big and small boats offering rooms to rent. Rotterdam's H2Otel is unusual because it unwittingly reflects the city's character and the psychology that differentiates Rotterdam from any other Dutch city. Some 60 years ago, the whole of Rotterdam's historic centre was razed during World War II. Ever since, it has embraced vehement modernism to replace ancient beauties that are no longer standing. H2Otel exemplifies that thinking, as applied to a floating hotel. It's a two-decker. Like a camper van with its roof pushed up on one side, the upper storey forms a quarter-circle cross-section, high enough to fit in a comfortable bathroom by the doorway, but arching down over the bed to a rectangular window that gives guests a great view of the port and canal traffic. On both 'decks', the 49 rooms are opportunities for striking modern design on the walls and in the choice of furniture. No two rooms are the same but, bizarrely, some juxtapose reproduction 19th-century classical furniture with violently abstract walls and utterly bland bedding. They may be works in progress.

In every conventional sense, H2Otel matches or even betters its land-based equivalents. It's a remarkably quiet refuge in a very central position, and makes the most of being a boat. The reception area and lounge double as art exhibition spaces and there's a waterside terrace for sundowners. Better still is the small fleet of 'picnic boats' which guests can rent (cheaply) for breakfast, lunch or tea on the water. Use them to scud around the port and admire the extraordinary ultra-modern skyline for which Rotterdam has justly become famous.

Hotel de Vrouwe van Stavoren

Whoever wouldn't want to sleep in a gigantic wine barrel? Converting them into hotel bedrooms is an idea of almost universal appeal – practical, ecologically sound and witty. It is also cosily eccentric, an attribute appropriate to its location in Stavoren, now almost landlocked by the IJsselmeer, but once Holland's oldest city (1118) and its most important port when the lake was the open-water Zuider Zee. Stavoren, like much of the northern province of Friesland, is a tranquil, time-warp sort of a place. Flat farms merge with the wandering creeks and waterfowl-filled ponds under vast skies, and people would rather watch hares boxing than raise their voices. So sleeping in a wine barrel isn't at all extraordinary to them.

The Hotel de Vrouwe van Stavoren has grown round its wine barrels and has rooms like any other hotel. But the wooden barrels are its core. Four of them stand in line, each the former container of over 14,500 litres of wine. They have front doors, with portholes either side like tiny Swiss chalets. Inside a bed hugs each curved wall, leaving a space to exit at the back into a built-on (and unprepossessing) bathroom and sitting space. Despite their years of secondary service, the barrels are still redolent of their original content. Wine lovers relish it. Others may prefer sitting on the barrels' communal terrace being admired by hotel guests who haven't slept in a barrel (hierarchies are complicated in Friesland).

The real points are that Friesland is one of Europe's most beautiful land and seascapes, that Stavoren is as charming as it is historic and that if you're going there the Vrouwe van Stavoren's wine barrels are just the ideal place to base yourself. It's the madness of magic, and you can dine out on the story for years (don't forget to take a bottle).

WHERE:
Havenweg, Stavoren
COST:
Reasonable (but winter discounts can reduce that to super-budget and better than many hostels)
BEST TIME OF YEAR:
Any time (including cold winters when the polders are frozen for skating)
DON'T MISS:
The 'hanging gardens' of the courtyard bar and restaurant, alive with colour throughout spring and summer; watching the inward and outbound shipping from the hotel's front terrace (including occasional clippers); taking a small boat, tug or barge trip from the port round some of the Frisian lakes connected to the IJsselmeer; the glorious sunset over Stavoren harbour
THINGS TO DO:
Fishing; cycling; swimming; windsurfing; sailing; hiking; birdwatching; sand yachting; botanizing around the marshes
YOU SHOULD KNOW:
The Wadden Sea National Park lies within easy reach, on the other side of the IJsselmeer dyke.

Die Swaene

WHERE:
Bruges
COST:
Expensive
BEST TIME OF YEAR:
November to March (it may be chilly at times but you will avoid the tourist hordes)
DON'T MISS:
Every weekday the hotel offers guests a free guided tour of the historic centre.
THINGS TO DO:
Sightseeing; canal trips; fine dining; swimming; spa treatments
YOU SHOULD KNOW:
Dogs are allowed at Die Swaene (there is a small surcharge).

The name of this swish boutique hotel in the centre of historic Bruges translates as The Swan, and swans are just about the only things missing from its picture-postcard setting beside a peaceful canal lined with former merchants' houses and warehouses. A mere stone's throw from the Burg, one of the city's two principal squares, you couldn't be any closer to the heart of this wonderfully preserved medieval jewel. Whether it be ambling along the cobbled streets and embankments or taking in the sights from a leisurely cruise around the canals, Bruges invites visitors to slow down and bask in the glories of an earlier age when the city was one of the wealthiest in Europe with a population in the 15th century twice that of London.

Die Swaene provides the perfect complement to the mellow mood. The unassuming brick exterior of this ancient building may not look much but inside you are greeted with a riot of opulence, the interiors reflecting the genteel elegance and discreet glamour of its 18th-century heyday. Many of the original *trompe l'oeil* ceiling paintings and decorative door surrounds have been preserved, while the bedrooms have been carefully individualized with little design flourishes among the antique furnishings.

It's worth paying a little extra for a room with a view over the canal and the historic skyline. An annexe houses an indoor pool and sauna as well as a stylish but informal restaurant where *al fresco* dining is possible on the attractive canal-side terrace. The main building also offers a private dining room in what was once the sumptuous guildhall.

La Balade des Gnomes

WHERE:
Durbuy, Ardennes
COST:
Reasonable
BEST TIME OF YEAR:
Any time
DON'T MISS:
The Trojan Horse, a giant free-standing wooden horse which houses a family suite on its two levels
THINGS TO DO:
Dreaming; walking; cycling; canoeing
YOU SHOULD KNOW:
The little community of Durbuy, 8 km (5 mi) away, is an outstandingly pretty place that's proud of its claim to be the world's smallest town.

Nothing in the surrounding Ardennes landscape prepares you for this extraordinary little hotel attached to an unexceptional farmhouse. La Balade des Gnomes is the vision of one man, a local architect who has simply given free rein to his imagination and created what he describes as a 'world in harmony with nature and the spirit of childhood'. This is definitely a place to stay if you are looking to reconnect with your inner child.

Each of the ten rooms is themed around a particular area of fairytale or folklore; thus one room is 'a cabin in the forest' and celebrates the legends associated with those dark Germanic woods, while another, 'stars of the desert', transports you to the world of the Arabian Nights, complete with an inquisitive camel. Elsewhere, you can immerse yourself in African tribal culture or the myths of the trolls. And *Sur un quartier de Lune* ('on a moon's quarter') is

a room which celebrates the lunar landings of 50 years ago, albeit with a hefty dose of fantasy; the bed is encased in a lunar vehicle and you sleep beneath a canopy of stars.

Everything is done with tremendous verve and utter conviction. If you are someone who enjoys spending imaginative time in other realms, be it Middle Earth, Narnia or Hogwarts, then La Balade des Gnomes ('The Gnomes' Ramble') will be a source of endless delight as you explore nooks and crannies where you will be hard pushed to find a straight line or right angle. The mod cons are not forgotten amidst the welter of fantasy, although the shower cubicle or the TV cabinet may not be quite what you expected. Surprise, surprise!

Michelberger Hotel

WHERE:
Warschauer Strasse, Berlin
COST:
Budget
BEST TIME OF YEAR:
All year round
DON'T MISS:
The little details that set the Michelberger apart from the blandness of the average city hotel, such as the door key cards, the labelling on its bath products and own-brand bottled water – all designed by the hotel's in-house graphic design studio
THINGS TO DO:
Socializing; being where it's at in Berlin's lively Friedrichshain district; clubbing; sightseeing (the only substantial remaining section of the Wall is just a stone's throw away); checking out the nearby O2 World Arena; visiting the famous East Side Gallery
YOU SHOULD KNOW:
In keeping with the relaxed mood, you are invited to ask the receptionist nicely if a late night means you could be struggling to make the check-out time. At weekends there is a minimum two-night stay.

Take a disused factory building near the River Spree in the old East Berlin district of Friedrichshain, a jaded young entrepreneur tired of routine challenges, a bunch of like-minded creative spirits signed up to his dream and some sympathetic money men – and the result is the Michelberger Hotel, an utterly distinctive new addition to the Berlin hotel scene. It is hard to imagine this wonderfully wacky place appearing anywhere other than Europe's most hip and happening city. Indeed, Tom Michelberger, whose brainchild it is, says 'we wanted to create a place to stay that is as creative, honest, laid back and inexpensive as Berlin is'.

From the moment you enter beneath the regularly changing illuminated message over the front door, the prevailing atmosphere at the Michelberger is one of cheerful but controlled disorder. Staying here feels more like being in a friendly family home, which is exactly how the relaxed staff encourage you to treat it, whether it be lazing in the large comfy sofas in the lobby where stacks of old books and magazines not only line the walls but also form the tables and lampshades, or else in one of the simple but funky bedrooms with their hand-made wallpapers, mirrors suspended on ropes and bathtubs sited cheekily beside the windows.

The co-operative that now runs the hotel scoured Berlin's flea markets for the quirky features that crop up everywhere, from a wall of cuckoo clocks to the wooden restaurant chairs from a painter's studio. If at times it feels everyone's trying a little too hard to be *über*-cool it would take a hardened cynic indeed to hold out for long against so much enthusiasm and playfulness.

Hotel de Rome

WHERE:
Bebelplatz, Berlin
COST:
Expensive
BEST TIME OF YEAR:
All year round (if you are an opera-lover you will be particularly interested in staying in March and April when the Staatsoper's annual *Festtage* take place)
DON'T MISS:
The spectacular views of the city from the roof-top terrace, a beguiling place to sip a cocktail during the summer months

Situated just off Berlin's legendary Unter den Linden boulevard, the Hotel de Rome is one of the few luxury hotels in Berlin housed in a historic building – in this case the former headquarters of the Dresdner Bank which the ambitious money men commissioned at the end of the 19th century to a design in the neo-Renaissance style of an Italian *palazzo*. Ending up in the Soviet zone at the end of World War II, the bank was promptly requisitioned and closed down by the anti-capitalist occupying forces. The building served as administration offices for the East German government for a number of years before being abandoned and falling into disuse. A multi-million-euro refurbishment by an international hotel chain in the early years of the new millennium has seen it restored to something like its glory days when it would harbour the riches of Berlin's wealthy elite.

Nowadays the Hotel de Rome (it takes its name from a renowned hotel that stood on the site before the bank) looks after its guests with as much care and attention as the bank once did its gold deposits. The restoration, which was overseen by an Italian design team, is an ingenious blend of original features and strikingly contemporary touches. The Opera Court, today the setting for coffee and afternoon tea, is located in the former lobby of the bank, a grand affair with a splendid glazed ceiling, while the bedrooms have the benefit of the original high ceilings and have retained much of the old wood panelling and stucco decoration. And the hotel spa and pool now sit snugly in the bank's former strong rooms. It's an altogether enriching experience for the well-heeled traveller!

THINGS TO DO:
Sightseeing; people watching; visiting the museums on the Museumsinsel; going to the opera (the Staatsoper, run by Daniel Barenboim, is next door)

YOU SHOULD KNOW:
The hotel stands on one side of Bebelplatz, site of the Nazis' infamous book-burning in 1933, now commemorated by Micha Ullmann's remarkable subterranean monument.

Propeller Island City Lodge

WHERE:
Albrecht Achilles Strasse, Berlin
COST:
Reasonable
BEST TIME OF YEAR:
Any time (but midwinter in the city can sometimes be a little bleak)
DON'T MISS:
Propeller Island's biggest room – the Two Lions – can accommodate a family and is popular with children who get to sleep in its two cages raised on stilts.
THINGS TO DO:
Sightseeing (Schloss Charlottenburg and the Zoo are close by); shopping (the hotel is a short walk from the Kurfürstendamm, Berlin's legendary shopping boulevard); indulging your imagination; night life
YOU SHOULD KNOW:
If you have enjoyed your experience on Propeller Island and want to take something of its atmosphere away with you, the art gallery downstairs has original artworks by Herr Stroschen for sale.

When you get a hotel described as a *Gesamtkunstwerk* you know you must be in Germany. The composer Richard Wagner's doctrine of the 'total work of art' – bringing together the arts to create an all-embracing, multi-sensory experience – is given a contemporary urban twist at this absolute one-off in Berlin's Charlottenburg district. 'Hotel' actually seems a more than inadequate label for the experience of staying at Propeller Island – a more accurate description would be 'living in a work of art'.

The realization of artist and musician Lars Stroschen, City Lodge offers 30 rooms, each a unique creation and completely different one from the other. Prospective guests are invited to scope the rooms on the website to select their sleeping experience. This might be in a room with walls covered in multiple mirrors (if you like the way you look), or else one where the bed is hung on ropes from giant beams. The Gallery Room has a circular bed that rotates, while Grandma's Room hides a shower and toilet within a huge antique wardrobe and the bathroom in the Nightlight Room is the inside of a giant plastic bag.

For an even weirder experience you could opt for the Upside Down Room where, as you would expect by now, the bedroom 'furniture' is attached to the ceiling while the real beds and chairs are found in recesses in the floor. A range of coloured lighting in the Therapy Room allows you to choose the interior effect to match your mood. Most bizarre of all, and really only for budding Nosferatus, is the Tomb Room where you can literally enjoy the sleep of the dead – in a coffin, naturally!

Arte Luise Kunsthotel

A giant pair of sculpted horse's nostrils greets you as you enter the lobby, giving a vivid foretaste of what awaits elsewhere in the Arte Luise Kunsthotel. So-called 'art hotels' may have proliferated in urban settings over recent years but most use the odd dramatic splash of colour or cleverly placed *objets d'art* in the foyer to justify the label. The Luise, however, is the real deal – a hotel that is not just about art but which has been fashioned in its entirety by artists. When this former *Stadtpalais* (city mansion) built in early 19th-century neoclassical style was acquired and renovated in the late 1990s, more than 30 local and international artists were commissioned to create their own unique rooms in the hotel. The result is a wonderland of styles, colours, imagination and whimsy.

In this 'gallery where you can spend the night' you may choose to stay in one of the high-ceilinged rooms on the old *piano nobile*, such as the *Königssuite* (Royal Suite) where Thomas Baumgärtel has covered every surface in gold and flecked it with his trademark screen-printed bananas, symbols of fertility and love; or else the Cabaret Room, all red velvets and seductive lights, which harks back to the heady days of 1920s Berlin. A painting covering two walls of the *Mauerspringer* (wall-jumper) Room refers to a famous graffiti on the old Wall itself. Before 1989 this building actually formed part of that notorious barrier. In the early days of partition East Berliners would attempt escape by jumping out of windows onto the S-Bahn trains passing directly beneath. Fitted out like an old S-Bahn lounge, the Next Station Room pays tribute to these brave souls.

WHERE:
Luisenstrasse, Berlin
COST:
Reasonable (artist rooms without en-suite facilities are also available at budget rates)
BEST TIME OF YEAR:
Berlin is an all-year-round destination.
DON'T MISS:
The epigrams and brain teasers which cover the walls of the Philosopher's Stairway (it's actually the hotel's main staircase so you can't miss them, but solving them is another matter)
THINGS TO DO:
Looking at art; city sightseeing (you are a short walk from the Brandenburg Gate and the Reichstag); jogging in the Tiergarten; cycling; wine tasting in Habel (the hotel restaurant)
YOU SHOULD KNOW:
Because the hotel regards itself as a *living* art work with a policy of giving commissions to new artists (and thus regularly changing the decor of its rooms), there is no guarantee that the rooms described here will still be there when you visit. You have been warned!

Steigenberger Frankfurter Hof

WHERE:
Kaiserplatz, Frankfurt
COST:
Expensive
BEST TIME OF YEAR:
Any time (be warned, though, that rooms may be difficult to come by in October during the Frankfurt Book Fair)
DON'T MISS:
A workout in the gym and fitness centre; if you are here in the winter months look out for the traditional log cabin which takes up temporary residence in a courtyard offering alpine hospitality and *gemütlichkeit* (welcoming cosiness)
THINGS TO DO:
Sightseeing; people watching; fine dining; sampling *Ebbelwei* (apple wine) in a traditional city tavern
YOU SHOULD KNOW:
The Frankfurter Hof was the first building in the city to be equipped with electric lighting.

The Frankfurter Hof is the grand old lady among Frankfurt's five-star hotels and one of the flagship establishments in the portfolio of the Steigenberger hotel chain. Since opening its doors in 1876, a few years after the original German unification, the Frankfurter Hof has been the meeting place of choice for the movers and shakers not only of the city but of the entire country's business and political worlds.

Several careful renovations and refurbishments later, it remains a place where you feel big deals are still done and many an important rendezvous takes place. The 320 rooms and suites are a discreet blend of international chic and old-world elegance, while for eating there is a choice of four restaurants, including a gourmet restaurant serving Michelin-starred French cuisine and a Japanese *sushi* establishment. Oscar's bar and café has a more informal bistro atmosphere where you can enjoy spotting celebrity signatures scrawled on the walls.

The façades are the only parts of the historic building to have survived intensive Allied bombing raids in 1944, but with characteristic efficiency the Frankfurter Hof had been rebuilt and was open for business again within a few years of World War II's end. Fortunately, many of the old hotel's valuable antiques and furnishings had been prudently removed for safe keeping and could be displayed once again; the hotel is particularly proud of its Gobelins tapestries. As befits a premier establishment, its location on the Kaiserplatz could not be more prominent or central – a few minutes' walk from the heart of the financial district as well as the city's main shopping and cultural areas.

East Hotel

Hamburg's ultra-chic East Hotel is a must-stay for night owls who have a penchant for cutting-edge design. This converted iron foundry has become *the* meeting place for the city's hip crowd, so a robust fashion sense and a strong dose of cool will certainly help you cut it as a guest here.

The East is the vision of Chicago-based architect Jordan Mozer who has created a dazzling display of stylistic exuberance. According to Mozer, East's design is 'design which stirs all the senses' so there are delights here for the fingers and nostrils as well as for eyes, ears and palate. Curves and flowing lines predominate in the furnishings and decor, with everything having a fluid organic feel, as if it were still evolving. The humble bedroom wash basin, for example, is transformed into a free-form sculpture in stainless steel resembling a large amoeba; you half expect it to have moved when you wake next morning. Everywhere you are encouraged to touch and feel, because the East may be a work of art but is certainly no museum.

The bedrooms undoubtedly ooze designer chic but the 'wow' factor is absolutely guaranteed when you enter the hotel restaurant. This *tour de force* features enormous sinewy pillars which rise up through three floors to a coffered ceiling. The stunning space is enhanced by dramatic lighting and windows and doors of multi-coloured glass. Extending off the vast main atrium are more intimate bar areas which nestle in the brick vaults of the old industrial building. And the fourth-floor nightclub confirms the hotel's slogan that 'when the night comes in Hamburg, the sun rises in the East' (that's a pun, folks, veering dangerously close to a German joke).

WHERE:
Simon-von-Utrecht-Strasse, Hamburg
COST:
Reasonable
BEST TIME OF YEAR:
All year round
DON'T MISS:
The bedrooms have ingenious internal curtains which divide off the sleeping area but also offer the potential for fun with shadow play.
THINGS TO DO:
Night life; clubbing; sightseeing; harbour tours; Beatles nostalgia
YOU SHOULD KNOW:
Contrary to its name, the hotel is actually to the west of the city centre, close to the infamous Reeperbahn red-light district (which has cleaned up its act somewhat since the seedy 1960s when four young lads from Liverpool started to make a name for themselves).

Hotel im Wasserturm

What was once the largest water tower in the whole of Europe has (rather surprisingly but very successfully) found a new lease of life as one of Cologne's luxury hotels. Some 20 years ago the redundant and decaying tower was stripped out and comprehensively re-modelled to provide an ambience that combines the best of contemporary design with the idiosyncrasies of a heritage-listed building.

Chief among these is the shape of the building which is – you've guessed – round. By way of homage, circles and cylinders crop up as distinctive design elements throughout the hotel's sleek interiors. The use of pale woods produces a nicely contrasting effect with the original brickwork and, while the circular form may not be an interior designer's ideal, it does mean that the split-level suites on the higher floors offer unimpeded views over the city skyline (impressive by night).

There is an informal restaurant on the ground floor which serves imaginative fusion dishes, but for a really special experience it's worth pushing the boat out for a meal in La Vision, the hotel's gourmet restaurant on the 11th floor. The Wasserturm is justly proud of the two Michelin stars awarded to this temple of *haute cuisine.* In warm weather you can eat or drink outside on the rooftop terrace, which has fine views of the Kölner Dom (Cologne Cathedral) and the Altstadt. Among the prominent guests who have stayed in the Wasserturm a certain Brad Pitt left the rather fairytale-aware comment that 'Rapunzel would have been proud to let down her hair here'.

WHERE:
Kaygasse, Cologne
COST:
Expensive
BEST TIME OF YEAR:
Any time, although November and December are particularly recommended as you can visit Cologne's famous Christmas market
DON'T MISS:
The Schokoladen Museum (Chocolate Museum), a short walk away on an island in the Rhine
THINGS TO DO:
Sightseeing; shopping; discovering Cologne's Roman origins; cycling; boat trips on the Rhine
YOU SHOULD KNOW:
If you have a head for heights, sound lungs and strong legs the climb up the south tower of Kölner Dom to the base of the steeple (509 steps) is one of the most exhilarating experiences any ancient building can offer.

Brenners Park Hotel and Spa

To borrow a phrase from a famous song about another city, Baden-Baden is 'so good they named it twice'. The double-barrelled duplicate moniker serves to underline the Swabian city's position as Germany's premier spa resort, the source of its prosperity being duly honoured in its name (*baden* means 'bathe'). The country has any number of spas built around natural springs but nowhere else possesses the glamour, cachet and allure of Baden-Baden, or has been attracting royalty and European high society for over 150 years.

And *the* address of choice in this fabled haunt of crowned heads, film stars and the super-rich has always been Brenners Park Hotel. With its prime location on the legendary promenade of Lichtentaler Allee, Brenners is a temple to the refinement and elegance of the *belle époque* – that glamorous era so brutally cut short by World War I. Priding itself on offering more than the standard five-star hotel experience, Brenners claims to be a 'home to those seeking a unique trio of luxury hospitality, fitness and health in harmony with nature'.

As the label would suggest, the hotel's extensive spa facilities provide a huge range of health and beauty treatments for just about every ache and pain imaginable. And if you arrive in good shape and want to stay that way a team of in-house medical professionals is on hand with preventative health advice and programmes. Tempted as you will be not to stir from this plethora of pampering services, it would be a pity were you to miss a visit to the resort's historic thermal baths; here you can sample for yourself the health-giving properties of the natural mineral waters which put this place on the map way back in Roman times.

WHERE:
Schillerstrasse, Baden-Baden
COST:
Expensive
BEST TIME OF YEAR:
All year round (those invigorating waters stay the same!)
DON'T MISS:
The chance to immerse yourself in nature in the Black Forest (rather than water in town), whose northern limits are a short distance south of the spa
THINGS TO DO:
Spa treatments; sauna; massage; walking; jogging; taking the waters; having a flutter at the casino; golf; mountain biking; rock climbing; hiring a classic car
YOU SHOULD KNOW:
Modest or shy visitors should bear in mind that the Germans have a more relaxed attitude to nudity when using spa facilities.

Hotel König von Ungarn

WHERE:
Schulerstrasse, Vienna
COST:
Reasonable
BEST TIME OF YEAR:
Vienna never sleeps (except at night).
DON'T MISS:
Tafelspitz, the classic Viennese dish of boiled beef tenderloin – if it's not on the restaurant menu, try Plachutta just down the road
THINGS TO DO:
Watching the amazing white stallions of the Spanish Riding School; listening to the Vienna Boys' Choir at Sunday Mass; dancing to Strauss waltzes; shopping; opera- and concert-going; visiting museums
YOU SHOULD KNOW:
The hotel's name translates as 'King of Hungary' and reflects the fact that during the Austro-Hungarian Empire in the second half of the 19th century this was an establishment that was popular with Hungarian aristocrats and financiers.

If you are visiting Vienna it is probably because you are checking out the unrivalled history and culture of the Austrian capital. Where better to stay, then, than in the city's oldest hotel? The König von Ungarn has been looking after guests since 1746 – Austrians are great autograph hunters, so look out for the framed signatures of famous visitors from the past on the walls. The hotel is housed in a 16th-century building in the shadow of St Stephen's Cathedral – the very heart of the historic centre, which makes it a superb base for exploring this most pedestrian-friendly of cities.

With fewer than 50 rooms this is an intimate establishment centred around its crowning glory – an inner courtyard which has been roofed over with a dramatic pyramid skylight to create a delightfully informal lobby and lounge area, complete with a tree growing in the middle. Galleried corridors surrounding the courtyard on the upper floors give access to the bedrooms, which are furnished for the most part in a pleasant classical style making use of traditional rustic furniture. If you fancy something more modern, the conversion of an adjacent building in 2009 has resulted in 11 new rooms, including a stunning penthouse suite which shows off the best of contemporary design.

The restaurant is just as venerable (and renowned) as the hotel and has long been one of the top places to sample the varied delights of traditional Viennese cuisine. Its red vaults were almost certainly frequented by Mozart, who lived next door in the late 1780s during one of the happiest periods in the composer's short life. The building is now known as the Figarohaus because it was (allegedly) here that Mozart composed *The Marriage of Figaro.*

Hotel Sacher

In 1988 the owners of Vienna's famous Hotel Sacher took over the Österreichischer Hof, the most prestigious of Salzburg's many hostelries. Now duly renamed to bring the Sacher brand to the west of Austria, this grand mansion-style building on the north bank of the River Salzach occupies a superb position looking across to the spires and domes of the Altstadt, with the Hohensalzburg fortress towering behind. The lavishly appointed rooms come with antique furniture, precious carpets, walls hung with original works of art and imposing marble bathrooms. The historic stairwell with its glazed skylight, wrought-iron balustrades and potted plants is a perfect expression of the style and confidence of the Habsburg Empire in its 19th-century heyday.

Since opening its doors in 1866 the hotel has welcomed prominent figures from the worlds of politics, business and the arts, many of whose signed photographs are displayed on the walls of the entrance hall (that Austrian autograph-hunting gene at work again). Max Reinhardt, Richard Strauss and Hugo von Hofmannsthal met regularly at the hotel when they were planning the first Salzburg Festival and since 1920 the Festival has been held every summer. Today it attracts audiences from across the globe to hear the world's leading performing artists, many of whom stay at the Hotel Sacher. The hotel has three restaurants but its most sought-after gastronomic location has to be the café where you can taste the hotel's eponymous dish, *Sachertorte* – the divine chocolate cake that has carried the Sacher name around the world. The café terrace overlooking the river is a particularly pleasant spot to while away a balmy summer's evening as you ponder whether to succumb to another slice of *Torte* and a consequently expanding waistline.

WHERE:
Schwarzstrasse, Salzburg
COST:
Expensive
BEST TIME OF YEAR:
Visit during July and August for the Salzburg Festival (although there are plenty of other cultural events throughout the year); the cityscape also looks particularly lovely in the winter months when the peaks of the surrounding mountains are covered in snow.
DON'T MISS:
Although Salzburg is a compact city that makes exploring on foot a pleasure, you might care to borrow one of the bicycles which the hotel makes available for free.
THINGS TO DO:
Exploring the Altstadt; visiting Mozart's birthplace and family residence; concert-going; tucking in to coffee and cake; cycling; jogging along the banks of the Salzach
YOU SHOULD KNOW:
The hotel publishes recipes for a number of classic Viennese dishes on its website, although you will look in vain for a recipe for its own *Sachertorte*, which remains a more closely guarded secret than the Coca-Cola formula!

Parkhotel

WHERE:
Rodlpark, Ottensheim, Linz
COST:
Budget (there are no set rates and you are asked to pay what you wish when you leave)
BEST TIME OF YEAR:
May to October (only available in these months)
DON'T MISS:
The Latin flavours and sounds at the nearby grill and snack bar which is run by a former samba teacher from Uruguay
THINGS TO DO:
Swimming in the Danube; walking or cycling along the Danube riverbank path; enjoying *Linzer Torte* (a delicious cake made with redcurrant jam, not raspberry as is often thought)
YOU SHOULD KNOW:
There is a *maximum* stay of three nights and online booking only. When your reservation is confirmed you are given an access code for your pipe.

Unless you have been seriously on your uppers it is unlikely you will have contemplated spending the night in a sewerage pipe, but this is just what artist Andreas Strauss invites you to do at his novel accommodation in Upper Austria. Three sections of giant concrete drainage pipe sit alongside one another, presenting an incongruous spectacle on a gently sloping hillside beside the Danube. One end of each section has been blocked up, while the other provides the entrance to your sleeping quarters.

The plain, functional and not-exactly-welcoming exterior belies what turns out to be a surprisingly snug and comfortable interior. True, there is no room for any furniture other than a double bed, but there is lighting, plenty of storage for your travel items and those important power sockets for recharging your appliances. Ventilation grills ensure there is a good circulation of air and anyone suffering from claustrophobia should be soothed by the inclusion of a porthole window in the roof.

The pipes currently reside in the little town of Ottensheim, west of Linz, but Herr Strauss originally set up what he calls his 'hospitality device' in the city of Linz itself on the principle that all most people require for a city overnighter is a bed, since the existing urban infrastructure should meet every other need. This is equally true of its present site where toilets, showers and eating facilities are all within easy walking distance. Staying at the Parkhotel may resemble camping more than it does a genuine hotel experience, but it does have the decided advantage that in the event of a stormy night you can sleep safe in the knowledge that this shelter will certainly not be moving anywhere. And, fear not, neither will it fill with rushing water.

Schneedorf Igloo

WHERE:
Ötztal, Tyrol
COST:
Reasonable
BEST TIME OF YEAR:
December to March
DON'T MISS:
The chance to get a head start, hitting the slopes nice and early before the hordes from the valley start to appear

Sleeping in sub-zero temperatures won't appeal to everyone but, provided you are well prepared, a night in an igloo can be a very special experience – one you may not necessarily want to repeat but certainly won't forget. Schneedorf means 'snow village' and in the mountains 2,000 m (6,560 ft) above the Tyrolean village of Ötz a cluster of igloos have been carved out of the snow. Each igloo is equipped with two double beds and can therefore sleep up to four. These are for adventurous travellers who require no pampering – you have to make your own way to the site at the base of the Acherkogel ridge, either on skis or by taking the cable car up from the valley.

Following a welcome drink of *Glühwein* or tea you are inducted into the particular protocols of your icy quarters. A traditional fondue dinner sends you nicely warmed to bed, and hi-tech sleeping bags make sure you stay that way through the night (the bag-liners are changed daily). After a buffet breakfast in the mountain restaurant you can continue your skiing itinerary or else start regaling your friends with those exaggerated tales of extreme endurance.

Schneedorf is in the Ötztal, one of three valleys which run north from the Ötztaler Alps. This is a great area for winter sports. Schneedorf is part of the Hochötz ski area and further up the valley lie the resorts of Sölden and Obergurgl. A stay at the igloo village can be combined with other activities, including a workshop where you are instructed in the art of building your own igloo. If you are confident enough in your handiwork you can even elect to sleep in your own construction!

THINGS TO DO:
Chilling out (pun intended); swapping stories; stargazing; skiing, snowboarding; igloo building
YOU SHOULD KNOW:
You are advised to come equipped with thermal underwear and some good-quality winter-sports clothing.

Naturhotel Waldklause

One look at the clean lines and bright hues of this chic spa hotel should be enough to send those toxins packing, or at least to serve serious notice on them. The Waldklause oozes health and well-being from every carefully crafted nook and designer cranny. The architecture makes use of natural materials – stone and pale woods – so that the hotel blends in with the magnificent surroundings of the Tyrolean Alps. Huge floor-to-ceiling windows everywhere make the most of the mountain views, as does a rooftop terrace. Harmony with nature combines with stylish interiors more redolent of an urban boutique hotel – funky furniture, striking colours and unusual lighting are the order of the day in the lounge and dining areas. The invigorating but relaxing mood continues in the bedrooms and suites, each with its own balcony and supply of icily pure spring water on tap.

As you would expect, the spa facilities here are second to none and there is a bewildering menu of treatments and programmes to choose from. As well as the customary sauna and steam bath you can unwind in a whirlpool while soaking up the mountain views, or if you are after something with a more local flavour you might try the fragrant Tyrolean herbs sweat chamber.

The Waldklause is in the village of Längenfeld, halfway up the Ötztal, one of Tyrol's top winter-sports destinations. Running south to the Italian border, the valley is dominated by Austria's second-highest peak, the Wildspitze (3,774 m, 12,382 ft). Guests have free admission to the Aqua Dome, a state-of-the-art thermal baths and spa complex a few minutes' walk away.

WHERE:
Längenfeld, Tyrol
COST:
Reasonable
BEST TIME OF YEAR:
All year round
DON'T MISS:
The nearby Stuibenfall, Tyrol's highest waterfall with a drop of 159 m (522 ft)
THINGS TO DO:
Hiking; climbing; mountain biking; whitewater rafting; nordic walking; skiing; snowboarding; horse-drawn sledge rides
YOU SHOULD KNOW:
The hotel is close to the two renowned winter sports resorts of Sölden and Obergurgl.

Null Stern Hotel

WHERE:
Sevelen, St Gallen Canton
COST:
Budget minus
BEST TIME OF YEAR:
April to September (but note that it rains a lot in June and August if you're thinking of spending any time above ground)
DON'T MISS:
The nightly draw to see who gets to have a hot shower in the morning
THINGS TO DO:
Not a lot, apart from socializing with like-minded fellow-travellers – it's the experience that counts
YOU SHOULD KNOW:
Those opting for luxury accommodation get to have a go on the Glucksrad, the Null Stern's very own wheel of fortune (it's an old bike wheel decorated with clothes pegs, spun by guests to see who gets which bed, some having better mattresses or thicker duvets than others. Should nuclear war break out, you would be evicted into the radiation cloud – the Swiss Army retains the right to reclaim the place if missiles start raining down, and the Null Stern Hotel must be maintained as a viable nuclear bunker.

Here's a hotel boast you don't hear every day – 'NO STARS'. And visitors to the unique bed-and-no-breakfast Null Stern (correct, that's 'no stars' in German) Hotel soon discover that an idle boast it is not. Switzerland decided as the Cold War hotted up that there was a very real risk of being nuked if the Americans and Russians got tetchy. So this safety-first nation built nuclear bomb shelters, which unfortunately (as things turned out) proved to be a rather bad investment, leaving lots of unwanted and rather deep concrete holes in the ground. But wait, all was not lost!

Artist brothers Frank and Patrik Riklin came up with a solution, by converting the bomb shelter in the small eastern town of Sevelen into overnight accommodation. Actually, 'converting' might be putting it a bit strongly. Opening the massive front door requires two strong men and there is, of course, no natural light. The last guests get to see of the outside world (until they re-emerge next morning, blinking troll-like in the light of day) is via a row of CCTV monitors in reception. Then there's the tough choice between standard and luxury class (respectively army-style bunk beds and assorted previously used 'antique' beds).

Then it's off to bed carrying the complimentary slippers needed for padding across icy concrete floors if nature calls in the night, suitably equipped with a hot water bottle *in lieu* of central heating, plus complimentary ear plugs that offer hope that the incessant noise of the ventilation system can be blotted out for long enough to get to sleep, before the mandatory 07.00 wake-up call. Just hope you're not subjected to one of the hotel's free surprises – the word *alpenhorn* springs to mind. It all adds up to a more-than-quirky experience that is also huge fun.

Jailhotel Löwengraben

Swiss hotels are renowned for being discreet, supremely luxurious and traditional, right? Actually, not always. Step from the spartan simplicity of a former nuclear bunker to the, er, spartan simplicity of the Jailhotel Löwengraben. In fact, the management claims that this is one prison you won't try and escape from, with some justice, for it's a rather pleasant (and affordable) place to stay. The hotel occupies a plain building in the heart of Lucerne's historic old town that dates from 1862, where the last prisoners were incarcerated towards the end of the 20th century.

And of course those Swiss master criminals (really?) would have been delighted if they'd experienced the place as it is today (not least because it's open all hours and nobody tries to stop you from checking out as and when). The budget choice of accommodation is branded as 'unplugged', and this is as close as it gets to the original in-cell experience, although there is an exclusive shower right next door. Up the 'fine' a little and you get the choice of a double cell, cell with two single beds or triples and quads fitted with bunk beds. For those who feel, well, a cut above the rest of the prison population, a choice of four suites awaits. These have been created in the former visitors' room, the recreation room, the library – and (for those with an I'm-in-charge mentality) the warden's old office. All rooms come with wash basin, toilet and shower.

There is a restaurant, the front-of-house bar attracts lively young locals and this is a fun place to stay for those who don't require (or can't afford) those aforementioned discreet luxury hotels, and actually appreciate something completely different.

WHERE:
Löwengraben, Lucerne, Lucerne Canton

COST:
Budget

BEST TIME OF YEAR:
Any time is good. Rates are cheapest in the winter low season and somewhat more expensive (though still very affordable) in high season (June to August).

DON'T MISS:
The Alcatraz Club (get it?) – with free entry for hotel inmates (but will you ever manage to escape?)

THINGS TO DO:
This is a handy place to stay for those wishing to explore Lucerne's attractive old town on a tight budget. Visit the river bridges (especially Chapel Bridge, originally constructed in 1333 and Mill Bridge, the oldest covered bridge in Europe); the twin-towered Church of St Leodegar; the famous carved lion monument in a small park just off the Lowenplatz; and the Swiss Transport Museum (trains, boats, cars and planes).

YOU SHOULD KNOW:
The hotel is open 24/7; breakfast is a cold buffet served between 07.00 and 10.00; free wifi is available in public areas only; the windows are still barred but do open, although you'll need to stand on tiptoe to get there; German is the local language.

Lausanne Palace

WHERE:
Grand Chêne, Lausanne, Vaud Canton
COST:
It's expensive to astronomical (if you aspire to the Coco Chanel suite).
BEST TIME OF YEAR:
It matters not – the luxurious service never misses a beat.
DON'T MISS:
Smokers of the world unite and meet in the otherwise non-smoking hotel's Habana Bar for the heady combination of aromatic tobacco, old leather and the tipple of choice; non-smokers of the world unite and enjoy a leisurely coffee beneath a brightly coloured brolly on the outdoor terrace; there's live evening music in the trendy LP bar with its great lake view.
THINGS TO DO:
Take a cruise on Lake Geneva; explore Old Lausanne with its many historic buildings and wealth of interesting museums.
YOU SHOULD KNOW:
Lausanne has been the headquarters of the International Olympic Committee since 1915 and its Presidents are always quartered at the Lausanne Palace; use of the main spa facilities is extra; the local language is French.

Any hotel that calls itself a Palace has much to live up to, and the Lausanne Palace certainly gives it a suitably regal shot. This grand building was erected as *la belle époque* imploded with the advent of World War I – but as conflict engulfed Europe the neutral Swiss were already looking to a future where tourism would be king. The hotel they constructed has lived up to all their expectations, quickly becoming an institution in the lakeside city of Lausanne and thriving to this day.

The experience of staying there has been likened to voyaging on a luxury cruise liner, albeit one that's rather solidly moored. A major refurb in the 1990s brought the place right up to the best contemporary standards, with the addition of the sort of mega-spa now demanded by the discerning clientele top-end hotels seek to attract. The five-star Lausanne Palace offers nearly 150 guest rooms, including 30 suites, with the choice of traditional or cutting-edge modern decor. They come in various sizes and prices, with the 'luxury bedrooms' having views over Lake Geneva to the Alps, while those occupied by mere mortals overlook Lausanne Cathedral and the charming old town.

Fine cuisine perfectly complements the luxurious accommodation, with no fewer than six restaurants to choose from, ranging from the Michelin-starred *Table d'Edgard* with terraces overlooking Lake Geneva through the Palace's Sushi Zen Restaurant, to the intimate *Cellier* table in the hotel's well-stocked wine cellar. Fitness fanatics can opt for the Yogi Booster with its healthy local produce. Were it an acronym, the spa would surely stand for 'super-pampered activities'. There's everything from a heated indoor swimming pool, fitness room, Jacuzzi, sauna, solarium and relaxation rooms to a hair salon and variety of massage treatments to sooth those cares away.

Alpine Geodesic Dome Pod

Whitepod is a winter-sports resort with a big difference. It aims to minimize the impact of tourism on the Alpine environment by housing guests in geodesic dome pods. Just 15 of these hi-tech igloos are pitched around the Chalet des Cerniers, a traditional 19th-century Swiss chalet that serves as the restaurant, lounge and spa. The spherical pods are made of insulated cotton and each is mounted on its own wooden deck with a dramatic panoramic view across the towering snow-covered peaks of the Swiss Alps. On the inside the pods are pure eco-chic, with simple wooden furniture, a cosy wood-burning stove, sheepskin throws on the beds and cow skins scattered across the floor.

Camping at a height of 1,700 m (5,580 ft) in the heart of the Swiss Alps, you are immersed in a hauntingly beautiful winter world. You can explore the silent forest on snowshoes, get around by dog sledge or just quietly contemplate the mountain scenery. You are surrounded by 7 km (4.5 mi) of ski slopes which are ideal for beginners and intermediate skiers.

Over the years the tourist industry has so scarred the alpine landscape with reckless development that it is uplifting to participate in this unique project – a genuine experiment in harmonizing with the environment, making the most of resources by recycling waste, eating locally sourced food and minimizing the use of electricity.

In the evening, after a day of hearty outdoor activity, you'll be welcomed back to your pod by the light of an oil lamp and the cheery glow of a wood-burner that has been lit in your absence. And as you snuggle down under your sheepskin cover, you'll discover a hidden luxury – a hot water bottle has been strategically placed to warm your toes. What bliss!

WHERE:
Whitepod Resort, Les Cerniers, Swiss Alps
COST:
Expensive
BEST TIME OF YEAR:
December to March
DON'T MISS:
Having a sauna and massage; locally sourced food and wines
THINGS TO DO:
Skiing on piste and cross-country; snowboarding; paragliding; dog sledding; snowshoeing; mountain biking; hiking
YOU SHOULD KNOW:
There is sleeping space for up to four people in each pod; Whitepod Resort has won a prize for sustainable tourism; the concept of the geodesic dome was developed by American engineer Richard Buckminster Fuller in the 1950s.

Grand Hotel du Lac

WHERE:
Vevey, Vaud Canton
COST:
Reasonable to expensive, depending on season and choice of accommodation
BEST TIME OF YEAR:
Any time (each season is different)
DON'T MISS:
Sunday brunch – the piano plays, kids are welcome and it's an exceptional meal
THINGS TO DO:
The Alimentarium Museum, opened in 1985 by the Nestlé foundation and featuring an exhibition of cooking, eating, food, digestion (really!) and Nestlé's history; Vevey's lively morning market (Tuesdays and Saturdays); in season, folk markets (*Marchés Folkloriques*) that take place every Saturday from mid July to the end of August in one of Europe's biggest market squares, featuring brass bands, folk music and traditional craftsmen at work
YOU SHOULD KNOW:
It's usually necessary to book well in advance (and early booking attracts a discount); French is the local language; the author Anita Brookner liked the hotel and its ambience of peaceful luxury so much that she both wrote it into the story and titled her 1984 novel *Hotel du Lac* – and promptly won the Booker Prize.

The pretty town of Vevey lies on the north shore of Lake Geneva, not far from Lausanne, and everyone with a sweet tooth should make the pilgrimage – for international food giant Nestlé was founded here in 1867, swiftly followed by the invention of milk chocolate in 1875. And where better to stay upon arrival than the elegant and refined Grand Hotel du Lac?

This traditional lakeside hotel combines Victorian charm with modern comfort, a genteel atmosphere with impeccable service, serving as a reminder of bygone days when wealthy travellers and holidaymakers sought out Europe's finest hotels as they toured the Continent, or stayed for months if the charms of a particularly appealing place proved irresistible. The hotel has 50 rooms, including suites, many with balconies and a view of Lake Geneva and the distant Alps. They are decorated in restful pastel shades and equipped with everything a modern grand tourist could want, from air conditioning to satellite TV with 400+ channels.

The public rooms are everything you would expect, too, encouraging guests to linger languorously and watch the world go by. Naturally, the cuisine doesn't let the side down, with a choice between the fine-dining Les Saisons restaurant or a more casual encounter with La Veranda, overlooking the lake and mountains. For those who like to do a bit more than relax and unwind slowly, the hotel's outdoor pool is open from May to September, a fitness centre offers instruments of physical torture ranging from weights to treadmill – and the spa embraces self-indulgent types with a range of massages, reflexology and assorted body treatments (the mineral mud wrap is definitely a winner). And if you don't have a Bentley that lets you purr up in style, a stay at the hotel will encourage you to feel as though you have.

Hôtel Crillon

The Crillon is Old Money. Built in the mid 18th century as a private house (with a frontage nearly 100 m/330 ft long!), it belonged to the Comtes de Crillon until its 1909 transformation into a hotel. It dominates the Place de la Concorde at one end of the Champs Élysées and provides resuscitation to fashionistas exhausted by shopping in the Rue du Faubourg Saint-Honoré next door. Its red-and-gold bar has given 'office' space to world-famous journalists like Sam White and Martha Gellhorn, and to countless dignitaries from every country under the sun. It has 103 rooms, 39 suites, and five luxury apartments, and the only ones with the same decor are the four 'historical' suites – entirely fitted out in their original *Grand Siècle* style. It is magnificent and utterly charming, that rare kind of place which makes you feel elated when you set foot in it.

The Crillon specializes in what the French call *'l'art de vivre'*. Every aspect of service, including caring nursery staff for the children, the wine steward being helpful instead of officious, or the concierge putting fun into the logic of a city tour, is impeccable. The hotel hopes to make guests feel good about themselves and great about Paris. Comfort, quality and luxury are guaranteed staples in the rooms, bars and restaurants, but guests will find something extra on the first floor. Here there is a series of three interconnecting reception rooms (the Batailles Room, the Aigles Room and the Marie-Antoinette Room) all classified as National Monuments. Usually used for weddings, balls, cocktail parties and fabulous fashion shows, they are the epitome of the Crillon's core Parisian character and – on a grand scale – what the hotel does so memorably every day for its guests.

WHERE:
Place de la Concorde, Paris
COST:
Very expensive to astronomical
BEST TIME OF YEAR:
Any time (although springtime cocktails amid the hanging flowers of the Winter Garden Patio are rather special)
DON'T MISS:
The masterpieces of Renoir, Picasso, Cezanne, Monet and so many others at l'Orangerie, on the corner of the Tuileries round the corner; the almost sinful shopping opportunities along the Rue Royale and the Rue du Faubourg St-Honoré, the twin symbols of *haute couture* and Parisian chic; gourmet French cuisine in the Michelin-starred Les Ambassadeurs, or something light in the fashionistas' favourite, L'Obe
THINGS TO DO:
Take tea in the Winter Garden, the Crillon's most romantic setting; avoid cultural overload – before you go there, decide on just three things to look at in the Louvre; then cross the river and stroll back via the Left Bank.
YOU SHOULD KNOW:
The very best – and most expensive – rooms at the Crillon are the fifth-floor Bernstein Suite. It comes with an enormous panelled sitting room, including a grand piano on which Leonard Bernstein often played for his guests, and two huge terraces with exceptional views across Paris.

Ritz Hotel

WHERE:
Place Vendôme, Paris
COST:
Astronomical
BEST TIME OF YEAR:
Any time
DON'T MISS:
The opening of a new chapter in the history of luxury – the renovation is being overseen by Thierry W Despont, the interior designer of several of the world's most illustrious hotels and of the J Paul Getty Museum
THINGS TO DO:
Enjoy the *ateliers* of some of the household names of fashion, in and around the elegant octagon of the Place Vendôme (between the Garnier Opera House and the Louvre); spend, spend, spend in preparation for the Ritz re-opening; practise a sophisticated glide in evening dress; extend your knowledge of proper cocktails.
YOU SHOULD KNOW:
Ernest Hemingway is quoted as saying 'When I dream of an afterlife in heaven, the action always takes place at the Ritz Paris'.

Its name has entered the language. Irving Berlin gleefully defined dressing for glamour with full make-up and jewels as 'putting on the Ritz' and many a lesser establishment or event has reaped the benefit when some aspect of their operation was called 'ritzy'. Guests arrive here with expectations heightened by over a century of celebrity endorsements. With a roll-call including Proust, Chaplin, Dietrich, Sartre, de Beauvoir, Hemingway, the Duke of Windsor, Coco Chanel, Audrey Hepburn, Maria Callas and Elton John, the hotel has a unique grip on the cultural imagination of the whole world. It has the romantic elegance of a *fin de siècle* theatre, and the pale apricot, pink and gold of its decor, repeated in varied keys throughout, flatters beauty and exudes sensuous languor. Each of its exotic salons, restaurants, bars and suites is a set with its own character, inspiring guests to great 'performances' (and very often, a change of clothes to match). The combination is a formula for fun and, although it has often been imitated, it has never been bettered.

After such a long run of success, evolution is inevitable. The Ritz has chosen to meet its future head-on instead of risking its pre-eminence to fate. Despite quite extensive 'refurbishments' up to 2010, the hotel closed in mid-2012 citing the need for 'an unprecedented renovation' of 27 months, leading to 'spectacular improvement'. Until its unveiling, no details are available – but devotees of Ritz Style can be certain that the future will honour the breathtaking glamour inherent in its ambience; that we mortals will once again share the fabulous perquisites of the rich and famous; that true love will flourish in its *sympathique* bars and restaurants; and that its prices will rise to the stratospheric.

Hôtel Georges V

The Georges V has three Presidential Suites, often with three actual presidents staying in them. Since its opening in a blaze of glory in 1928, it has been first among equals of the select group of 'palace' hotels in Paris, and the first choice of heads of state and major dignitaries after the Élysée Palace itself. It is a byword for the sumptuous and the splendid. Its original Art Deco details have been restored, its bas-reliefs re-gilded, and every tessera of the mosaics on its marble floors reset, to show off the Flemish tapestries, rich brocades, crystal chandeliers and antiques that – along with staggering floral displays – fill its public salons. Its rooms and suites are decorated in the same key. At every level they are larger than those of any other hotel, and their predominantly Louis XV furniture (with subtle modern touches) conceals the very highest levels of 21st-century amenities. Many also have balconies or terraces that look over the roofs of Paris to the Eiffel Tower, the Arc de Triomphe and the pink skies of romantic sunsets. The hotel's location on one of the city's most prestigious avenues secures another aspect of its reputation – turn left off the Champs Élysées between Fouquet and Louis Vuitton, and the other end of the avenue passes the Crazy Horse Saloon, crosses the Pont d'Alma and leads you to Les Invalides and the Quartier Latin. The Georges V is central to Paris at its smartest and most sophisticated.

These days, the hotel's spa, wellness salons and special children's agenda (menus, entertainment rooms, crèche and nannies) are as immaculately served up as everything in its two-Michelin-starred restaurant (Le Cinq) and historic bars – amazingly, without sacrificing anything to its grandeur and magnificent pomp.

WHERE:
31 Avenue Georges V, Paris
COST:
Astronomical
BEST TIME OF YEAR:
Any time is unlimited luxury time.
DON'T MISS:
The *trompe l'oeil* murals of the gardens at Versailles round the pool; the ivory, gold and white Honeymoon Suite with vistas across Paris, for the romantic weekend of a lifetime; getting pampered with an Australian Sodashi body-scrub in the luxury spa; the tasting menu at Le Cinq
THINGS TO DO:
Trawl some of the most luxurious shops in Paris (Dior, Vuitton, Hermès); linger over tea or cocktails in the elegant La Galerie, the hotel's 'heart and soul' and best for people-watching; drink morning *chocolat* at Fouquet at the end of the street; cross the bridge to the Quai D'Orsay museums.
YOU SHOULD KNOW:
The Georges V may perhaps be a little less formal than 50 years ago, but it still maintains pertinent dress codes. Most of the time the hotel asks guests to be 'elegant' and never should they be less than 'smart casual' (which could easily be more expensive).

Shangri-La Hotel

WHERE:
10 Avenue Iena, Paris
COST:
Astronomical
BEST TIME OF YEAR:
Any time
DON'T MISS:
Franco-Asian fusion dining beneath the breathtaking glass cupola of the light-filled Bauhinia restaurant; TV screens embedded in bathroom mirrors; Le Bar, a tented fantasy watering hole meant to invoke Napoleon's Egyptian campaign
THINGS TO DO:
Enjoy classic French cuisine at L'Abeille or gourmet Cantonese in the Shang Palace; stroll to the Trocadero, Eiffel Tower, the museums or just the street market along Avenue d'Iena; take a drink to the secluded garden; loaf around the pool and spa, created from the erstwhile Bonaparte stables.

The Shangri-La is both a genuine palace and one of the elite few 'palace hotels' in Paris. Prince Roland Bonaparte – Napoleon's great-nephew and a cousin to Napoleon III – built it in 1896 across the Seine from the Eiffel Tower (for his wife Marie-Felix, happily the heiress to the Société des Bains de Mer hotels and casinos in Monte Carlo). It's a colossal mansion, immaculately restored and sympathetically modified where necessary. It's also a triumph of classic '*luxe, calme et volupté*' , its unaffected grandeur flying in the face of modernist extremes and preserving the original series of ground-floor rooms (the panelled sitting room, billiard and smoking rooms) as pleasingly rare, even cosy, lounges. The Grand Staircase, first-floor reception salons, ballroom and private apartments are all National Monuments, restored to gilded splendour for the joy of the Shangri-La's guests. The radical changes to the upper three floors – added by private owners after the Prince left – are in complete harmony with the rest, although remodelled to give more than half the hotel's 54 rooms and 27 suites private balconies. The decor is blue, white and ecru, worked into exotic fabrics, silk-threaded wallpapers and deep-pile carpets and these beautiful furnishings set off the carefully placed antiques – especially oriental porcelain and lacquer work which pay subtle compliment to the hotel's begetters, the Shangri-La group based in Hong Kong.

The restraint shown by the Shangri-La group in the conversion shows an extraordinary understanding of what it means to be a 'palace hotel'. You can take the marble, gold filigree, *toile de jouy* fabrics and no fewer than 18 reception rooms covering every amenity for granted. Nothing but fundamental empathy with elegance and style can account for the charming ambience which, fully formed, greets amazed guests.

YOU SHOULD KNOW:
Despite its obvious grandeur, the Shangri-La still feels as intimate as your very own *Hôtel Particulier*. Take advantage of the charming service ethic and ask to see the Shangri-La suite (aka *La Suite Panoramique*) on the very top floor. The suite, its vistas and price are out of this world.

Hôtel de l'Abbaye St Germain

It exudes the tranquillity banked during centuries as a Catholic convent. Built in the late 17th century, the Hôtel de l'Abbaye has all the beauty of its era, plus the quiet demeanour of its original function. As you pass beneath its ironwork grill into the formal elegance of the courtyard, the building closes round you in a warm welcome that leaves bustling Paris far behind. You enter the sanctuary of a green-latticed drawing room, seeing through it to a sun dappled garden court where a fountain splashes below hanging flowers and trailing vines and ivy. In winter it achieves the same effect with a blazing fireplace in one of the deep-pile salons opening off reception and the reading room. In any season the hotel is one of the most romantic hideaways in Paris, known locally as a *hôtel de charme*. In fact, locals as much as guests enjoy the combination of slightly poker-faced reticence in the reception areas and the thoroughly un-monastic, voluptuous luxury of the 44 rooms and suites upstairs. Decorated in warm florals across walls, bedspreads and curtains, the rooms aren't big, but they could scarcely be more comfortable or better equipped with flat-screen TVs, marble bathrooms, enclosed glass showers and all the other amenities that make modern hotel life half-bearable. And that's especially true if there are two of you.

Tucked away between Saint-Sulpice and the Jardin du Luxembourg, the hotel is sited perfectly for more lively parts of St Germain des Prés. The Café Flore and Les Deux Magots may be tourist magnets but they, or at least the multiplicity of cafés, bars and creative arts centres all around them, are still the epicentre of Left Bank culture. The Hôtel de l'Abbaye is the appropriate refuge.

WHERE:
10 Rue Cassette, Paris
COST:
Expensive
BEST TIME OF YEAR:
Any time (. . . is Valentine's time)
DON'T MISS:
Incongruous but witty touches like the Warhol screenprint in some of the rooms; the room with the private terrace that has a view of *les toits de Paris* (as Piaf put it) to die for
THINGS TO DO:
Explore antiquarian bookshops, the Boulevard St Michel and the bars round the Sorbonne; find a new 'favourite' bistro for yourself; take a romantic walk, kicking autumn leaves all the way to Notre Dame and back.
YOU SHOULD KNOW:
Keep knowledge of the Hôtel de l'Abbaye as your special secret. No-one else must know.

La Croix du Vieux Pont

WHERE:
Berny Rivière, Vic Sur Aisne, near Soissons
COST:
Budget
BEST TIME OF YEAR:
Treehouses, like the tents, are open from the third week of April to the second week of September (the chalets open earlier and close later).
DON'T MISS:
The pool complex (a heated indoor pool with water slides, a lazy river, a pool with a retractable roof, an open-air 'lagoon'); the lakes (one with a shallow beach, one for pedalos and canoes, one for fishing); the chocolate factory at Lachelle; the medieval chateau at Pierrefonds; the family theme park of La Mer de Sable
THINGS TO DO:
Trampolining in the children's playground; archery; pool; video arcade; mini-golf; Soccer Station for football-loving kids; separate teen and children's discos
YOU SHOULD KNOW:
Treehouses can sleep six (minimum age is two); the restaurant has a large children's menu, high chairs, and early eating times; some treehouses and tents are near open water; only conventional trunks may be worn in the pools (no surfer shorts, etc).

The setting is idyllic. Willows bend to the gently flowing river in the heart of the Aisne Valley and tall poplars march across the green *paysage* of Picardy. In this tranquil parkland, the campsite of La Croix du Vieux Pont belongs like butter to a cow. Families can choose to stay in mobile home 'chalets' with little gardens, squared-up in hedged rows around one of several small lakes, or in various kinds of super-sophisticated tents, including multi-roomed safari tents. A lucky few can stay apart and even above the crowd, in one of the all-singing, all-dancing treehouses. Sturdily built around two or more trees, the houses have two separate bedrooms, divided by a large, furnished deck on which the whole family can invent new games of Robin Hood or jungle adventures. The thatched rooms – each with a small (dry) toilet attached but no kitchen or running water – are made and furnished entirely in wood, with a double bed in one, and four singles in the other. In the twilight of a summer's evening, parents may feel a fairytale coming on.

Everyone staying in a treehouse also gets a Frontier Tent, pitched on the ground close by. It's there as insurance against little children who might suddenly feel frightened up in the tree canopy, and also as a fully kitted-out kitchen. If cooking doesn't appeal, there's an on-site restaurant in a converted barn, a *crêperie* by the lake and a takeaway next to the shop. There's also a bar. With so much to do around the four pools, three lakes and parkland, all four will prove welcome, and you can always retreat back up to the treehouse deck for a family foodfest.

Staying on a *Péniche*

WHERE:
Most rivers and canals throughout France, including moorings in the heart of great cities and beautiful hamlets
COST:
Budget to astronomical (a week for two people on one particularly fabulous barge with an onboard swimming pool costs a fraction under $12,000)
BEST TIME OF YEAR:
Any time for the B&B variety, particularly those moored in or near popular venues like Avignon, Paris or Carcassonne; March to November for boats travelling the Canal du Midi

France has the most agreeable waterway system in the world. The combination of languorous rivers and long-distance canals means the whole country is accessible by boat. A *péniche* is the name given to a working barge converted to take passengers. It can be of any age or size, provided it can fit the width of the canals and the height of the bridges. It can even be static, a floating B&B, but most of them are perfectly capable of travelling very long distances at a pace measured in passing beauty instead of kilometres per hour. France is at its loveliest from the water, the singularities of its ancient church spires marking medieval hamlets curled up within protective fields and woods with history written in châteaux along the river banks and in every bridge.

Les péniches can be a bit tatty, shared with cheerful owners who want to enjoy your company as you both go where the wind blows. They can also be (and increasingly, are) beautifully decorated creations of quite stupendous luxury, on which just two or four people recline like *nabobs*, hovering (metaphorically) between larks' wings and *foie gras* for lunch, and attended by a proper chef, bi-lingual guide, maid and sundry *matelots* to steer and haul ropes. Neither mode is better or worse. Like hotels, these boats have infinite variety, but they also have one thing in common. Nearly all of them are privately owned. Whatever level you choose – either of price or amenity or location – that distinction is what makes staying, and hopefully travelling, on a *péniche* the single most glorious way to visit any part of France. It's astonishing how much culture you can absorb trailing a languid toe in the water.

DON'T MISS:
Exploring the huge range of boats available; most aren't at all pricey and many offer specialist trips

THINGS TO DO:
Relax into the pace of *péniche* travel – on the Canal du Midi alone there are 45,000 specially planted plane trees and cypresses to admire along the banks; almost anywhere in France you might stay or travel through, there will be a local wine to discover (let your enthusiasms guide your choice).

YOU SHOULD KNOW:
It is almost as much fun choosing where you want to go, and on what kind of *péniche*, as it is being there. But not quite.

Le Fort du Cap Levi

WHERE:
Cap Levi, Fermanville, Cotentin
COST:
Budget (and a sensational breakfast is included)
BEST TIME OF YEAR:
Any time (wrap up well in winter)
DON'T MISS:
A quick study of the original fortifications – the fort had a 24-gun battery firing from 30 m (100 ft) above the sea, so would have been lethal; big seas, vast skies; that big breakfast

The stone fort at Cap Levi is the last survivor of 11 coastal batteries built by Napoleon to defend the great harbour at Cherbourg. It stands on the very lip of the Cotentin Peninsular at the eastern end of Cherbourg Bay. It was restored as a rare example of Napoleonic military thinking, notably the 35-m (115-ft) semi-circular gun platform with a broad field of fire that enabled it to protect coastal shipping from the depredations of the British navy. The renovation included turning the guard house and magazine buildings into delightful guest accommodation. It has five bedrooms and a dining room with a sublime view of the crashing sea below. The rooms are attractively done up in a nautical theme, and comfortably snug even when the wind starts whistling (it will, it will). They benefit from the protection of the fort's stout outer wall, but even though the owners

pierced holes in it, to improve the view and make it less austere, only one bedroom has a view of the sea.

It matters little. Everyone meets around the table in the conservatory with the day- and night-time view, swapping tales of the day's adventures. A windswept track once used by customs men adjoins the fort and leads across the cliffs and headland to the Fermanville lighthouse, then onwards to Port Pignot – one of the smallest harbours in France. The other direction quickly leads to Levi Port, a hamlet with a rugged mole protecting its stone quay. The fort is ideally placed for hikers on one of the Departmental *Randonnées* (cross-country routes). Hikers, particularly, will appreciate the double whammy of a warm welcome and a place so redolent of its authentic history.

THINGS TO DO:
Walk loose and breathe deep – having got here, drink it in.
YOU SHOULD KNOW:
You don't have to hike to the fort – you can drive, and it's still worth it because you'll want to come back and stay.

Le Spa Bleu

There are no motorways and no major highways in the Ardèche; the vineyards of the Rhône's west bank give way to rich farming country. Low hills crowned with broken woodland merge into the foothills and cherry orchards of the high Cévennes, blue on the horizon. Just thinking about it can make people misty-eyed. Without knowing why, they feel somehow better. It was observing this truism that inspired its proprietor to turn a beautiful 18th-century Provencal *mas*, or large farmhouse, into Le Mas Bleu. The hills and dry hollows and rivers of the Ardèche itself were to be a metaphor for human health. Wellness (*bien-être*) was to be achieved by helping guests to rediscover their inner strengths through treatments and their relationship to the natural world outside. The Spa Bleu is the result.

In fact it is impossible to separate the Mas from the Spa, because to use one you have to stay in the other. There is no overt pressure to do anything. Many people bring partners, friends and families, who can be accommodated in a variety of really gorgeous *gîtes* sleeping one to a dozen people. For anyone not disposed to luxuriate in the Spa's enormous range of treatments, there are endless ways to have a good time. Sooner or later the Spa always wins, seducing new clients with massages (Californian, Indian, Chinese, Swedish, Korean, and 'four-handed' – oh the bliss!) reflexology, yoga, facials and a good few more. Add in the hot Jacuzzi and the *hammam*, and with guests sauntering round glowing with obvious, clear-eyed renewal, it is no wonder queues keep forming. The Mas Bleu alone is a star destination for laid-back time off. The Spa makes the horizontal experience nigh on perfect.

WHERE:
Balbiac, Rosières, southern Ardèche
COST:
Budget to reasonable (on a per person per night basis – but it depends on which *gîte* you choose and on the season)
BEST TIME OF YEAR:
Any time (all the *gîtes* have both central heating and wood fires), although the Mas is especially enticing during the lavender season and during the grape harvest
DON'T MISS:
Exploring the four local rivers – l'Ardèche, la Beaume, la Drobie and la Chassezac; the markets in one or all of six medieval villages including Joyeuse, Balazuc and Vinezac; the lavender-perfumed *hammam* followed by the heated whirlpool; whole-body massages
THINGS TO DO:
Boules; billiards; walking in the Cévennes; cycling; strolling in the 100-year-old vineyards surrounding the Mas and other local farmhouses and hamlets;
YOU SHOULD KNOW:
Smoking is allowed and guests are encouraged to help themselves to a bottle of wine from the cellar at any time. Its 'Liberty Hall' philosophy makes the Mas Bleu one of the most agreeable places to stay in the south of France.

Haut Toupian Camping

WHERE:
Goudargues, Ardèche
COST:
Reasonable
BEST TIME OF YEAR:
March to October
DON'T MISS:
The weekly food market in Goudargues, especially for its cheeses, sausages and wines
THINGS TO DO:
Walking; cycling; canoeing; horse riding; rock climbing; wine tasting; visiting caves
YOU SHOULD KNOW:
Only full-week bookings are accepted.

The Ardèche, south of Lyon, allows you to experience rural France at its loveliest. This distinctive region of woods and plateaus studded with lavender fields and vineyards also features dramatic swift-flowing rivers that cut through the limestone landscape and carve out spectacular gorges. The Cèze is one such river and like the Ardèche, its bigger neighbour to the north, boasts a series of spectacular towering canyons as it pursues its meandering course southeast to the Rhône.

Goudargues is the small village in the Cèze valley where you will find Haut Toupian, an old stone farmhouse on whose land stands a very superior camping facility. Two rectangular safari tents have been erected, with canvas walls on a timber frame and the whole mounted on a wooden deck. The interiors are spacious and very well appointed. In addition to a double bed and a self-contained bathroom at the rear, each tent boasts a fridge and a coffee machine. Two sofa chairs open into single beds, making this ideal for a family stay, and *oui*, this is definitely 'glamping' rather than camping.

The tents have no cooking facilities but your hosts will provide you with a tasty continental breakfast and will, if you wish, prepare delicious evening meals using local organic produce and featuring typical dishes of the region. They can also supply picnic hampers for your day trips, although you may find yourself reluctant to move far afield. While the children frolic in the (unheated) pool, you can hang loose on the deck outside your tent with a glass of local wine and soak up the glorious panorama of hills and forests.

Phare de Kerbel

WHERE:
Lorient, Brittany
COST:
Reasonable
BEST TIME OF YEAR:
March to October
DON'T MISS:
The trip to the coastal island of Ile de Groix, a 45-minute ferry ride to a different world
THINGS TO DO:
Swimming; sauna; beachcombing; collecting shellfish; walking; visiting the citadel at Port-Louis
YOU SHOULD KNOW:
Only full-week bookings are accepted during high season (April to September).

When it comes to 360-degree views it doesn't come any better than the top of a lighthouse. This redundant lighthouse on Brittany's south coast has been cleverly converted into holiday accommodation which, together with the lighthouse keeper's cottage, sleeps up to six people. The area where the light was once housed, at a height of 25 m (82 ft), has been cannily transformed into a comfortable living space with a kitchen recess and a shower and toilet. A sofa bed means that two people can sleep up here and feast on sunsets and sunrises, as well as those sweeping views in every direction – over Lorient harbour, out to the Ile de Groix and south down the coast to Quiberon Bay. As you can only rent the complex as a whole (the cottage comes with the lighthouse) to avoid arguments you may need to take turns in your group so that everyone can spend a night or two up on high – assuming of course that no one minds the climb!

The cottage has a further two double bedrooms, plus kitchen and bathroom. Alongside there is a heated swimming pool for your exclusive use and a nifty little sauna cabin, which is perfect for taking mind and body off those stiff Atlantic breezes. Kerbel Lighthouse stands just back from a sandy beach and a popular local pastime at low tide is to gather shellfish (aka 'lunch') on the foreshore. The huge natural harbour formed by the Blavet estuary is a magnet for yachtsmen, so there is usually plenty of activity to keep you interested out on the dancing waves.

Castel Camping le Brévedent

WHERE:
Pont-l'Evêque, Calvados
COST:
Budget
BEST TIME OF YEAR:
May to September
DON'T MISS:
The talk given by the owner every Sunday evening in the château's drawing room in which she describes the history of the building and her family
THINGS TO DO:
Swimming; hiking; cycling; guided nature walks; tennis; lake fishing; mini-golf; canoeing; billiards; cider and Calvados tastings
YOU SHOULD KNOW:
The camp encourages music-making on site. On Friday evenings there is an 'open stage' acoustic concert in front of the château.

Le Brévedent is an elegant 17th-century hunting lodge whose grounds are turned into a family-run campsite in summer. There are good-sized pitches for over 100 tents scattered around a picturesque lake in front of the house (which is more like a small château than a mere house). It is a delightful spot and the owners pride themselves on maintaining a relaxed and informal atmosphere. There is also a serious respect for nature and the environment, which is reflected in many of the talks and activities on offer.

Young children will feel especially at home here, with a large heated swimming pool, playgrounds and plenty of games and organized activities to keep them amused. The site has a restaurant and takeaway in addition to a well-stocked shop where you can buy freshly baked bread and other local produce. Best of all is the bar set up in the old house itself which provides an atmospheric and convivial setting in which to while away a summer's evening.

Situated north of Lisieux, le Brévedent is in the heart of the Pays d'Auge, a classic Normandy landscape of green valleys, rolling hills and patchwork fields. Everywhere the pastures, orchards and half-timbered farmhouses remind you that this is one of France's most important agricultural areas, famous above all for its cheeses and ciders. There are plenty of opportunities to sample world-famous brands such as Camembert and Livarot and to wash them down with farmhouse *cidres* (ciders) that taste completely different from anything you can buy in the supermarket. As summer draws to an end you may get the chance to be involved in harvesting the fruit in le Brévedent's orchard and making your own apple juice.

Cerza Safari Lodge

WHERE:
Lisieux, Calvados
COST:
Reasonable
BEST TIME OF YEAR:
March to October
DON'T MISS:
The private guided safari tour available only to lodge guests and for groups of up to six, which takes you behind the scenes and enables you to get up close and personal with some of the animals, including the rhino

If you don't fancy the idea of sweltering tropical heat and doing battle with unnerving creepy-crawlies on a real African safari then the people who run Cerza Zoological Park in Basse-Normandie have come up with a more than passable alternative. Over 800 wild animals roam more or less freely in a 60-ha (148-ac) area of Normandy woods and parkland near Lisieux. Some 125 species are on display, representing wildlife from around the globe, including the big stars of Africa itself – lion, giraffe, zebra and antelope – plus bison, brown bear, wolf and kangaroo. There are designated trails around the park but if you are looking for a more immersive wildlife experience, why not stay in one of the safari lodges?

There are 26 eco-lodges on the edge of the park, each with its own terrace offering views across the lake to the animals in the 'wild valley'. The air-conditioned lodges are heated by solar power and waste water is purified and recycled to ponds and waterholes throughout the park. Each lodge can sleep up to six and is fitted out for self-catering, although a buffet breakfast is always available in the entrance pavilion. The bamboo furniture in the lodges, the use of warm colours and the odd exotic ornament all contribute to the illusion of being on safari, as does waking in the morning to find wallabies and muntjac deer grazing just outside.

Cerza is particularly proud of its captive breeding programme for white tigers and the conservation work it undertakes for the Indian rhinoceros, supported by income generated from visitors. Seeing this mighty but endangered beast roaming the grasslands is a truly memorable spectacle.

THINGS TO DO:
Wildlife-watching; walking; cycling; horse riding (outside the park); a trip to the seaside at fashionable Deauville or Trouville; visiting the Normandy beaches (site of World War II's D-Day landings)

YOU SHOULD KNOW:
Other, less expensive accommodation options available at Cerza include a wooden wigwam (the 'Zoobservatory') and a 'Normandy' yurt.

Château de la Barre

If you have ever wondered what it must have been like to be a house guest at one of those grand country houses of old, staying at this château may well be as close as you will ever get. Dating from the 14th century and enlarged over the succeeding three, Château de la Barre has remained in the hands of the same family for a trifling 600 years. As a paying guest you will be staying at the invitation of the present Comte and Comtesse de Vanssay, who have only recently opened their venerable home to ordinary visitors. This is still very much the family home and the Comte and Comtesse will be on site to ensure that your stay is as select and refined as the setting promises (you too!).

Nestled deep in the countryside to the east of Le Mans the Château has a discreet yet confident air characteristic of the established aristocracy. The five guest rooms are all in the main house which is filled with beautiful antiques, Persian carpets, family portraits and crystal chandeliers. The undoubted highlight of a stay, and one which you should on no account miss, is the weekly formal dinner at which the Comte and Comtesse are your genial hosts; after champagne cocktails in the Salon Rose you eat in the Dining Room off the family silver and the finest porcelain, before completing the evening with coffee and liqueurs in the Grand Salon. It probably takes a certain amount of poise and *savoir-faire* to carry this off but you can rest assured that your hosts will remain impeccably polite and tolerant of any minor lapses in etiquette.

WHERE:
Saint-Calais, Sarthe
COST:
Expensive
BEST TIME OF YEAR:
March to November
DON'T MISS:
The 18th-century armchair in which you relax while sipping your *digestif* probably still has its original embroidered upholstery. Tradition, don't you love it?
THINGS TO DO:
Walking around the estate; learning about French history; exploring the Loire Valley with its wonderful ancient churches and manor houses
YOU SHOULD KNOW:
The wines which accompany your formal dinner will have been personally chosen by the Comte from the château cellars.

Bois Landry Treehouses

If you are happy to forgo a few creature comforts for the benefits of recapturing that long-forgotten sense of childhood excitement, while also reconnecting with nature, then this magical place is worth serious grown-up consideration. Deep in an ancient forest on the edge of the Parc Naturel Régional du Perche, a cluster of huts and cabins have been built high in the trees. The host trees are carefully selected for their health and strength and each cabin has been specially designed around the contours and features of its tree.

The cabins are constructed using renewable woods and according to strict environmental guidelines. There is no running water or electricity and the toilets are composting ones. The overriding principle here is of respect for the trees themselves. Thus there is no invasive damage to the trunks from the construction; no screws are used and the tree is protected from any metal surfaces by wooden wedges. The cabins are braced and supported by tensile cables hung from higher branches.

Usually when you are choosing somewhere to stay you are guided by considerations such as location, price and the views. At Bois Landry, however, your chief criterion is likely to be the access to your room. The 14 tree houses are between 4 m (13 ft) and 13 m (43 ft) off the ground so a head for heights, though not actually essential, certainly helps. Access might be by rope ladder, spiral staircase winding round the trunk, swing bridge, gangway, zipline, or a combination of any of these. In the case of the higher cabins and the ziplines, safety harnesses and helmets are provided and there are minimum age restrictions.

WHERE:
Champrond-en-Gâtine, Perche, west of Chartres
COST:
Reasonable
BEST TIME OF YEAR:
April to October
DON'T MISS:
Take full advantage of the numerous walking trails in the privately owned forest.
THINGS TO DO:
Hiking; cycling; birdwatching; horse riding; golf; fishing; a trip into town to marvel at the stained glass in mighty Chartres Cathedral
YOU SHOULD KNOW:
Depending on your cabin, there is a walk between 700 and 1,000 m (765 to 1,100 yd) to the showers, washing facilities and parking area.

Les Hautes Roches

WHERE:
Tours, Loire Valley
COST:
Expensive
BEST TIME OF YEAR:
March to October
DON'T MISS:
A visit to Tours' wonderful Musée du Compagnonnage, which celebrates France's rich heritage of traditional crafts and the historic guilds that nurtured them
THINGS TO DO:
Walking; cycling; river cruises; visiting one of the Loire's renowned châteaux; canoeing; wine tasting
YOU SHOULD KNOW:
Tours was a major pilgrimage centre in the Middle Ages, with pilgrims coming from all over the country to worship at the tomb of St Martin, a fourth-century bishop of the city.

In medieval times the monks of Marmoutier Abbey built caves in the riverside cliffs at Rochecorbon on the outskirts of Tours. These were once simple monastic cells carved out of tufa, but have now been transformed into luxury hotel rooms, contemporary in design but each with a distinctive colour scheme and atmosphere to complement the natural rock of the walls. The hotel has an attractive 18th-century frontage and stands on a terrace overlooking the majestic River Loire. The bedrooms are all south-facing, giving uninterrupted views over the river to the surprisingly undeveloped south bank. The hotel does have its own heating and air-conditioning systems but, as cave dwellers since time immemorial have discovered, the natural rock ensures that interiors maintain a relatively even temperature at all times of the year.

Still, sleeping in caves has certainly come on a long way since our hunter-gatherer ancestors first tried it out. Les Hautes Roches bills itself as one of France's first 'troglodyte hotels' but you are unlikely to detect any sense of slumming it in a bat-filled cave when you stay here. The best of the region's cuisine is featured on the menus of the award-winning restaurant, tempting you after working up an appetite in the outdoor pool or by striding along the riverbank into the city. In fine weather the large riverside terrace is a perfect spot for outdoor dining, under the shade of lime trees. The Touraine is a renowned wine region (Vouvray is but a few kilometres upriver) and naturally the caves at Rochecorbon provide superb cellarage for the wines that accompany your meals.

Les Hautes Roches bills itself as one of France's first 'troglodyte hotels'.

Le Ty Nadan Campsite

Family holidays are always a tricky business, especially when you're on a tight budget and have kids of differing ages and interests. Le Ty Nadan is a perfect solution: an award-winning holiday park beside a river in the depths of the beautiful Brittany countryside, next to 40 ha (100 ac) of woodland. And it's only a 20-minute drive to the sea, so you can easily nip off to explore the rugged coves and sandy beaches of Brittany's scenic west coast.

You can just pile the kids into a camper van or, if you don't want to be burdened with equipment, rent one of the site's pre-pitched safari tents or a woodland cabin. There are 325 pitches available, varying in cost according to size and amenities. All have electricity and some have private running water and drainage – the sort of pitch you choose is a matter of weighing amenities against cost.

The exceptionally well-maintained site is renowned for its range of activities and helpful, competent instructors. As well as lots of river and woodland pursuits, there's an outstanding water park with huge indoor and outdoor heated swimming pools, complete with thrilling water slides and paddling pool. Swimming and diving lessons are also on offer. Small children can use the kids' club for supervised play and there's a babysitting service so that teenagers and adults can take advantage of the assorted night-time entertainment.

Le Ty Nadan is a great place for a family activity holiday that won't break the bank. You can pretty well guarantee that everyone, whatever their age, will find plenty to enjoy about a holiday here. You'll all come home having had new experiences and feeling a lot fitter, healthier and happier.

WHERE:
Locunolé, Arzano, Brittany
COST:
Budget. Water park and evening entertainments are inclusive but a supplement is charged for most of the sports activities.
BEST TIME OF YEAR:
April to October
DON'T MISS:
Having a go on one of Brittany's longest zip wires; seeing the beauty spot of Les Roches du Diable
THINGS TO DO:
Cycling and mountain biking; horse riding; pony trekking; quad biking; hiking; rock climbing; swimming; diving; canoeing; kayaking; water cycling; angling; archery; golf; paintballing; tennis; football; *boules*; badminton; volleyball; table tennis; beaches; sightseeing
YOU SHOULD KNOW:
Le Ty Nadan is not conveniently close to a town. However, the site has excellent amenities and facilities – there's a laundrette, wifi internet access and a fairly decent restaurant, takeaway and bar. The campsite shop is reasonably priced for day-to-day provisions.

Le Couvent d'Hérépian

This former convent on a cobbled lane in the sleepy little village of Hérépian is somewhere very special indeed. Even if you didn't know that nuns had once lived here, it wouldn't be hard to guess – the beautiful 17th-century building is suffused with an aura of calm and the hotel staff radiate welcoming warmth. The place has beautiful period features including winding stone staircase, vaulted ceilings, flagstone floors and wrought-iron lights. The 13 suites are all decorated in muted tones and natural fabrics with plenty of space and light, and they are extremely well equipped – kitchenette and fridge, free wifi, flatscreen TV, DVD/CD player and even a pre-loaded iPod and dock.

There is a delightful cellar bar where you can just pour yourself a drink any time of day or night and are trusted to put it on your tab. The charming garden has an outdoor pool and a view of the mountains and there's a wonderful subterranean heated relaxation pool in the basement spa. The salon has an open fire in winter but is snug and welcoming at any time, with comfy armchairs and a good choice of books, DVDs and CDs.

The atmosphere is so pleasant and laid back it scarcely seems worth making the effort to leave the convent's confines, even when beckoned by the scenic joys of Haut Languedoc Regional Park just outside the door. A day passes so easily here. After a late breakfast on the garden terrace, hanging out by the pool, reading, napping and a spa treatment, it's suddenly time for the hotel's superb evening meal. Le Couvent is a blissfully romantic bolthole – a complete respite from the stresses of real life.

WHERE:
Hérépian, Languedoc-Roussillon
COST:
Reasonable
BEST TIME OF YEAR:
Any time. If you want total peace and quiet choose December to February when the weather is mostly dry and sunny, although often cold. May is a beautiful month, with the flowers in full bloom before the start of the tourist onslaught.
DON'T MISS:
A meal at local restaurant l'Ocre Rouge; antique shopping in the town of Pezenas; visiting the caves of Courniou
THINGS TO DO:
Rambling, cycling, horse riding, climbing, rafting and all the other outdoor pursuits of the Haut Languedoc; golf; visiting vineyards
YOU SHOULD KNOW:
The Daily Telegraph ranked Le Couvent d'Hérépian tenth of the 50 best hotels in the world.

Tipi at Le Tuilerie

Run by an admirably enterprising Scots couple with six children, Le Tuilerie started off as an eco-experiment in self-sufficiency when the family came here in 2004. From small beginnings they have developed it into a 95-ha (235-ac) working Limousin livestock farm, but still firmly uphold the principles of low-impact living which brought them here in the first place.

They genuinely enjoy having their temporary summer guests and the amenities here have been extraordinarily well thought out so that you enjoy all the pleasures of camping without any of the miserable discomfort that can so often dampen the spirits. The *tipis* (teepees) are pitched in a tree-fringed pasture beside the farmhouse, with masses of space around each one; they can sleep a family of six (or you can stay in a yurt for eight) and are comfortably kitted out with futon beds, sheepskins, rugs and a central wood-burning stove. Table, chairs and all the utensils for campfire cooking are provided, but there's also a really civilized communal kitchen in the farmhouse for 'proper meals' as well as a common room, laundry room, wifi connection and use of the farmhouse garden, while each *tipi* or yurt is allocated its own indoor private shower facilities.

The farm children are only too happy to show visiting kids around and involve them in vegetable picking, pig feeding and egg collecting, and the farm is next to 100 ha (250 ac) of woodland that is a haven for wildlife. It's a joy to watch children running free, experiencing country life and having backwoods adventures. Staying in a *tipi* at Le Tuilerie is indeed an inspirational lesson in natural living.

WHERE:
Le Tuilerie, La Souterraine, Limoges, Limousin
COST:
Budget
BEST TIME OF YEAR:
Open from May to September. June is a good month to see the calves and lambs and in September you can watch haymaking.
DON'T MISS:
The farm's freshly baked cakes; a cultural trip to Limoges; swimming in Lake La Souterraine
THINGS TO DO:
Walking; cycling; birdwatching; nature spotting; horse riding; canoeing, kayaking and sailing on nearby lakes; exploring the local villages
YOU SHOULD KNOW:
Breakfast, linen, towels, and as much wood as you need are all included in the rental price. The farm shop sells its own meat, fresh eggs and home-grown fruit and vegetables. Travel cots, high chairs, push chairs, baby baths, toys, etc are freely available for use by campers, so you can travel relatively lightly. The campsite field is completely enclosed for safe outdoor play.

Le Nid dans l'Arbre

WHERE:
Vieux Moulin, Oise, Picardy
COST:
Reasonable
BEST TIME OF YEAR:
Open from April to October
DON'T MISS:
A visit to Pierrefonds Chateau; a walk in the Forest of Compiègne
THINGS TO DO:
Swinging through the trees; gazing at the view of the forest; walking; cycling
YOU SHOULD KNOW:
Cabins accommodate from two to eight people. Bathroom facilities are limited – showers and toilets are in a barn at ground level. Children must be aged ten or over.

Ever wanted to escape from the helter-skelter of urban life and recapture the spirit of a long-lost childhood? Well, here's your chance. There's nothing quite like sleeping in a treehouse perched in the ancient oaks of the Compiègne Forest just 80 km (50 mi) from Paris. The rustic little wooden huts at Le Nid dans l'Arbre (The Nest in the Tree) are all different, depending on the natural architecture of the tree supporting them and how many people they're designed to accommodate. You access them by zip wire and ladder, so you need to be reasonably agile and unafraid of heights.

Each of the ten huts is individually themed – a honeymoon suite, a fisherman's cottage, and even a Zen tea garden – with suitably *kitsch* whimsical touches. Your treehouse has an open terrace so you can sit under the forest canopy as the sun goes down and watch the darkening shadows to the sound of whispering leaves and the mysterious rustles and scuttlings of the forest night life.

The treehouse is lit only by candlelight, has a water cylinder, and is equipped with a dry toilet. There are no cooking facilities but you can have a picnic basket delivered up to you. Whether you regard the lack of basic amenities as romantic or not is entirely a matter of personality, but you can be sure that this escapist little treehouse estate will bring out the inner child one way or another. The adventure is designed to appeal to the hidden Peter Pan in everyone's soul – however grown-up you may think you are, those first few moments on waking in the morning when you glimpse the rays of sunlight filtering through the trees are just magical.

Hotel Boscolo Exedra

Originally called the Hotel du Rhin, the Exedra was built in 1913. It was at the height of the *belle époque* – when the romantic epithet 'Côte d'Azur' was first coined for the coast of Provence and when Nice, along with Cannes and Menton, had become the fashionable place for the international glitterati to congregate. The hotel was purposely built in the city centre, on the prestigious tree-lined Boulevard Victor Hugo, instead of the increasingly crowded sea front, to avoid the *hoi polloi* who hung around on the Promenade hoping to spot celebrities.

The hotel facade and sumptuous foyer are magnificent examples of the *belle époque* style. In striking contrast, the hotel's 113 suites have been completely refurbished as 'contemporary chic' – parquet floors, soothing tones of white, cream and ivory and fully integrated bathrooms. Everything is the latest in design excellence and works brilliantly as a restful retreat from the buzz of the city streets. The hotel's supposedly 'futuristic' bar has a wonderfully retro 1960s appeal, and the Sardinian head chef at the hotel restaurant La Pescheria creates delectable Italian-influenced food, served from an open kitchen. The hotel spa has a marvellously funky swimming pool – a tree sculpture in the middle jets out cascades of water – and the Exedra even has its own reserved area at the prestigious Ruhl Plage beach terrace, a ten-minute stroll away.

The service, ambience and food in the Exedra are all exactly what one expects from a five-star hotel. Sometimes it's just pure pleasure to wallow in the lap of luxury without counting the cost, and where better to do that than on the Côte d'Azur?

WHERE:
Boulevard Victor Hugo, Nice, Provence

COST:
It's expensive, bordering on astronomical in high season, but reasonable if you plump for low-season special offers.

BEST TIME OF YEAR:
Provence is lovely at any time of year but May and June are usually good months for sunshine without the hordes of tourists that flock here in the hotter months of July and August.

DON'T MISS:
A stroll along the Promenade des Anglais; the flower market on Cours Soleya; exploring the pedestrian streets of the old quarter

THINGS TO DO:
Swimming; cycling; shopping; fine dining; sightseeing

YOU SHOULD KNOW:
The Exedra is owned by Boscolo, an Italian company which specializes in the renovation and refurbishment of old grand hotels and historical buildings, refitting them for the 21st century. Boscolo only completed the overhaul of the Exedra in 2009 and the hotel is variously known as Hotel Exedra, Nice; Hotel Boscolo, Nice or even Boscolo Hotel Exedra, Nice. Nice!

L'Abbaye de la Bussière

WHERE:
La Bussière-sur-Ouche, Dijon, Burgundy
COST:
Expensive or astronomical depending on suite, but probably worth it
BEST TIME OF YEAR:
May to June and September to October
DON'T MISS:
Wine tasting in the Côte d'Or vineyards; sightseeing in Dijon on market day; a visit to Fontenay Abbey
THINGS TO DO:
Cycling; horse riding; walking; fishing; kayaking; golf; cultural and historical sightseeing; touring the wine district
YOU SHOULD KNOW:
L'Abbaye de la Bussière is a member of Relais & Chateaux, and the hotel restaurant has a Michelin star. The Dijon-Prenois racetrack is on the doorstep for motor-racing enthusiasts.

Anyone with a strong sense of history and an appreciation of fine architecture will love this luxury hotel – an ancient Cistercian abbey in Burgundy wine country. The Cistercian Order of monks built the abbey in the 12th century and ran a monastery here for the next 650 years, until the French Revolution. Over the following 200 years, the building fell into a state of ever-increasing dilapidation as it passed through one pair of hands after another. It is now under English ownership and has been extensively and sensitively renovated to preserve its historical features and aura of spiritual tranquillity.

The abbey is set in 6 ha (15 ac) of beautifully tended grounds with a botanical garden, a stream and lake. The Gothic architecture is simply breathtaking – fireplaces with beautifully carved mantelpieces, ornate stone mouldings and ancient great timbers. Throughout the building and grounds you can feel the loving attention that has been paid to every single detail. The 18 rooms and suites all have sublime views over the abbey gardens and are elegantly furnished with a wonderful sense of antique style.

The three restful lounges are equally beautifully furnished with antique armchairs, books and curios. The hotel restaurant is in what was once the abbey cloister, overlooking the garden. It feels like a cathedral – a vast room with a gallery and vaulted ceiling. The food is simply out of this world – completely true to its Burgundy culinary heritage but with novel, inventive touches (and of course every meal is accompanied by a superb choice of local wine). L'Abbaye de la Bussière is an absolute gem – peaceful, luxurious and with food and service as outstanding as the surroundings.

Les Tilleuls

WHERE:
Saussa, Gèdre, Hautes-Pyrénées
COST:
Budget
BEST TIME OF YEAR:
From mid May to mid September – it's closed for the rest of the year
DON'T MISS:
The stunning view of Cirque de Gavarnie from the Saugué Plateau; hiking round the Cirque de Troumouse, Lourdes and Mauvezin Castles

Les Tilleuls is a small, out-of-the-way campsite more than 1,000 m (3,280 ft) up in the mountains of the World Heritage Pyrenees National Park. There are just 25 pitches, with plenty of space between them, spread across four grassy mountain ledges, shaded by trees and overlooking a valley.

The campsite facilities are simple but clean and everything you need is here – an electrical hook-up, five basins and toilets, four showers, three washing-up sinks, a washing machine and barbecue area. Amazingly, there's wifi up here, in the middle of nowhere – although it's scarcely conceivable that anyone would want to spend their time messing around with technology here, surrounded by some of the most beautiful scenery in the world.

The views from the campsite are straight out of a picture book.

Look down and see flocks of sheep grazing along the valley, quaint stone cottages, cows the colour of cream-toffee in green meadows, rhododendron woods and pine forest. Then look upwards at the snow-covered peaks up in the clouds, gnarled crags and the great natural amphitheatre of the Cirque de Gavarnie, hewn out of the mountainside by glacial force with a waterfall cascading down its wall. There are few places in the world with landscapes comparable to the dramatic beauty of the High Pyrenees. Just sitting outside your tent will make your spirits soar.

The great joy of Les Tilleuls, aside from the heavenly environment and invigorating mountain air, is the blissful quiet up here in the mountains. It's a perfect place for communing with nature, being active and simply letting your cares float away. It's a rare treat to stay somewhere quite so tranquil.

THINGS TO DO:
Hiking; climbing; canyoning; horse riding; birdwatching; wildlife-watching; fishing; rafting

YOU SHOULD KNOW:
Les Tilleuls accepts tents, caravans or camper vans on the site. The family who owns the land also has two old-fashioned wooden caravans permanently on site for holiday lets, as well as three summer *gîtes*.

A Yurt at Ferme Terre d'Aromes

WHERE:
Séranon, Grasse, Alpes-Maritimes
COST:
Reasonable
BEST TIME OF YEAR:
It's open all year but is best between May and July when the plants and herbs are in flower.
DON'T MISS:
Chapel of Notre-Dame du Roc in the picturesque village of Castellane; Gorges du Verdon
THINGS TO DO:
Hiking; mountain biking; canyoning; rafting; kayaking; paragliding; swimming; courses in plants and essential oils; cookery classes; Tai Chi
YOU SHOULD KNOW:
The farm also has rooms with en-suite bathrooms available to let for those who prefer four-walled comfort.

The rather whimsical farm name Ferme Terre d'Aromes (Scents of the Earth) is not nearly as pretentious as it sounds when the penny finally drops that it's only a 40-minute drive to Grasse, the perfume capital of the world, and that the 'crops' grown here are aromatic plants – pine, hawthorn, yarrow, lavender, St John's wort, juniper, wild roses, and more – all produced for their essential oils, which this unconventional farm distils itself.

The farmhouse is a converted old barn in a small mountain village at an altitude of 1,250 m (4,100 ft) only 20 minutes from the Verdon Gorge (renowned as the most scenic canyon in Europe). The setting of the campsite is absolutely glorious; the yurts are scattered among pine trees on a 5-ha (12-ac) south-facing mountain shelf with a panoramic view to die for – of the Mediterranean Sea to the east and mountains to the west.

The farm is dedicated to alternative living. Solar panels produce all the electricity, water is drawn from a spring and there are composting toilets. There are 12 yurts in two different sizes. The smaller size (27 sq m/290 sq ft) is really spacious for a couple and can easily house a family of four or five; the larger ones (35 sq m/377 sq ft) sleep up to eight people. Inside, they're funkily done up with brightly painted and patterned ethnic furniture – a reference to the yurt's oriental origins. At night, fold back the ventilation flap in the yurt's roof and let the pine scented breeze waft in as you gaze up at the stars. And once you've spent the night cocooned in a yurt, you'll never want to sleep in an ordinary tent again.

Camping La Brouquere

WHERE:
Gondrin, The Gers
COST:
Budget
BEST TIME OF YEAR:
May to October
DON'T MISS:
Visiting an Armagnac *domaine* and trying a glass of Floc de Gascogne; the chapel and park of Sanctuaire de Notre Dame de Tonnetcau; market day in Gondrin
THINGS TO DO:
Rambling; cycling; horse riding; canoeing on the River Baise; golf; visiting historical sights

La Brouquere is in a heavenly spot right in the heart of Armagnac country. Well away from the main road, right at the end of a little country lane which you think is never going to end, you find yourself at a picturesque farmhouse where you are welcomed in by the English-speaking Dutch owners. They are spectacularly good hosts – immediately putting you at your ease and offering you a glass of wine as they show you round and explain that the farm was in fact once a winery. The 2-ha (5-ac) campsite is surrounded by vineyards and has wonderfully scenic views of the gently rolling hills and huge skies typical of rural Gascony.

One of the many joys of La Brouquere is that it is so small and tranquil – there are only six pitches, shaded by ancient oak trees to provide relief from the sometimes fierce sunshine, and with masses of space between them. The site is beautifully maintained, immaculately clean, and has extraordinarily good amenities: a fair-sized swimming pool to splash around in, darts board, *pétanque* balls, bikes for hire, a children's playground and a communal internet terminal plus wifi on the pitches. The farmhouse sells its own vegetable produce and homemade snacks, organizes a daily delivery of freshly baked bread for campers and offers a *table d'hôte* evening meal a couple of times a week so that you can get to know your hosts and other campers if you so desire.

The relaxed pace of life in the sleepy ancient villages and peaceful countryside is like stepping back in time to another world. La Brouquere is a very special place indeed. You will want to come back.

YOU SHOULD KNOW:
La Brouquere accepts tents, caravans and camper vans. For only a small extra charge you can have your own private bathroom if you don't want to share the communal facilities. Dogs are welcome and there's an area set aside for them to run around off the lead. According to *The Sunday Times,* La Brouquere is among the best 15 campsites in France.

Chateau de Nieuil

A natty new concept in ecotourism, the *carré d'étoiles* (star square) is a prefabricated transportable box made of wood from sustainable forests, which provides living and sleeping quarters for two and can be plonked down wherever you like. The *carré* has giant porthole windows and a star-viewing window in the roof. It comes with a telescope and star chart, the idea being that the *carré*'s occupants will connect closely to the world outside at the same time as they enjoy indoor comfort.

Inside the *carré* a sleeping gallery just large enough for two is accessed by ladder, while down below has been ingeniously kitted out with shower, separate WC, fully equipped kitchenette and wall-mounted TV, miraculously still leaving enough space to fit in a sofa and a couple of tables – with legroom to spare.

The Hotel Château de Nieuil, a fairytale castle with a moat, formal gardens and a lake, has recently installed a *carré d'étoile* in a grassy wild meadow next to 40 ha (100 ac) of beautiful park and woodland. Guests are offered full access to all the château's amenities – bar, restaurant, art and antiques gallery and swimming pool.

This must be the most ironic B&B ever – a wooden box in the grounds of a palatial 16th-century château. But if you're a committed eco-warrior who wants to stay ahead of the game, and have ever wondered what it would be like to live in a Tardis, then a couple of nights (or at least one!) in the *carré d'étoiles* at Chateau de Nieuil is an absolute must!

WHERE:
Nieuil, Charente-Limousin
COST:
Reasonable
BEST TIME OF YEAR:
It's open from April to October but the Charente countryside is at its most beautiful in May and June.
DON'T MISS:
Having a glass of cognac in Cognac; a visit to Château La Rochefoucauld ; the medieval town of Confolens
THINGS TO DO:
Hiking; cycling; fishing; tennis; river boat trips; sightseeing
YOU SHOULD KNOW:
Carrés d'étoiles were designed by Louis and Nathalie Blanco of the Bocages Company, who are pioneering new sustainable ways of living for the 21st century.

A *Roulotte* in Normandy

Who hasn't at one time or another yearned for the freedom of the open road, a wandering gypsy life? Well, even if you can't take to the road, you can at least enjoy a temporary escape from the worries and restrictions of everyday life by staying in a *vardo* or traditional gypsy wagon, known in France as a *roulotte*.

These quirky wooden huts on wheels are of various sizes and two basic shapes – box or barrel – usually with decoratively painted exterior woodwork and plush interiors. They date from the 19th century; before that gypsies travelled by foot or pony. In France the gypsies were known as *les bohèmes* because they were thought to have come from Bohemia; they roamed through the countryside as peddlers, fortune tellers and

WHERE:
Various locations in Normandy
COST:
Budget
BEST TIME OF YEAR:
Late May to early September
DON'T MISS:
The Normandy beaches; Rouen Cathedral; having a glass of Calvados (apple brandy) with ripe Camembert
THINGS TO DO:
Hiking; cycling; horse riding; swimming; historical and cultural sight seeing; discovering the incomparable regional gastronomy

poachers, living off the bounty of the hedgerows. Their *roulottes* were easy to hide from the scrutiny of local landowners and villagers, secreted amongst the outlying orchards, woods and meadows of the vast French country estates.

These days you can stay in a restored *roulotte* in the most delightful surroundings. Choose from the grounds of historic Chateau Bellenau, with a view of the formal landscaped gardens; nestling among the silver birch trees at Chateau de Monfreville; or tucked away in an orchard under the branches of the apple trees at Les Roulottes de la Risle. La Roulotte des Crins d'Or is next to the Brotonne Forest with its ancient woods of oak and beech trees, or you may prefer La Roulotte de Matis, surrounded by open pastureland grazed by ponies, horses and cows and with sweeping views across the Normandy countryside. Wherever you choose, you'll be casting off society's straitjacket and enjoying the carefree life of a bohemian – if only for a little while.

YOU SHOULD KNOW:
Staying in a *roulotte* has recently become a very popular holiday activity among the French. Until recently they were hard to find but nowadays, if you research carefully, you should be able to find one for rent in most regions of France.

Ferme du Bois Joli

In the depths of absolutely glorious countryside in the French Alps, high up in the mountains at 1,100 m (3,610 ft), Ferme du Bois Joli (Pretty Wood Farm) is a traditional 250-year-old Savoy farmhouse in a small hamlet at the foot of Mont Blanc. It has a large back garden, with an orchard and field, looking out onto wooded mountainside and there's a view of Mount Joly from the front of the house.

The picturesque three-storey farmhouse sleeps up to 15 people in four double bedrooms, two twin-bedded rooms and a triple. The original exposed roof beams, struts and timbers give the interior a warm traditional atmosphere and the attractive ground-floor living area is huge, with a wood-burning stove, lovely picture window and large farmhouse table. Upstairs there's a cosy alcove with an open fire and a pool table, and a separate TV room at the top of the house. It's a really cleverly organized, uncluttered arrangement of space, enabling a lot of people to live together without getting on top of each other.

The farmhouse is situated between two charming ski resorts, the delightful 19th-century spa town of St Gervais-les-Bains and the historic village of Contamines-Montjoie, so it's a perfect place for a skiing holiday. But it's just as wonderful outside the skiing season, when you can enjoy hiking, climbing and mountain biking. The farmhouse is right next to a 55 sq km (21 sq mi) nature reserve – forest, mountain pastures, rock fields, glaciers and breathtaking views on your doorstep.

Whatever time of year, Ferme du Bois Joli has a wonderfully authentic farmhouse atmosphere. Here you can get a glimpse of the real Savoy.

WHERE:
St Gervais-les-Bains, Haute Savoie, Rhône-Alpes
COST:
Budget
BEST TIME OF YEAR:
Any time (it just depends on what outdoor activities you're interested in)
DON'T MISS:
Taking the Mont Blanc tramway to the Nid D'Aigle at the top; the church of Notre-Dame-de-la-Gorge
THINGS TO DO:
Skiing; snowshoeing; skating; mountaineering; rock climbing; *via ferrata* (for bolt and cable climbing); hiking; glacier trekking; canyoning; whitewater rafting; caving; fishing; horse and pony riding; mountain biking; walking
YOU SHOULD KNOW:
Savoy is a fascinating region. For most of its history the region was a separate state, annexed first to Italy and then to France only some 200 years ago. The region still retains its own very distinctive culture, customs and food, and the Savoyard people have a spirited sense of independence.

Le Val de Cantobre

WHERE:
Cantobre, Nant, Aveyron, Midi-Pyrénées
COST:
Budget
BEST TIME OF YEAR:
May to September
DON'T MISS:
The Gorges du Tarn; pedalling along the Vélorail du Larzac; the village of Roquefort-sur-Soulzon where the 'King of Cheeses' comes from; Millau viaduct, the highest bridge in the world designed by British architect Sir Norman Foster
THINGS TO DO:
Hiking; climbing; paragliding; abseiling; canyoning; pot holing; horse riding; cycling and mountain biking; rafting; canoeing; fishing; birdwatching; tennis; golf; badminton; *boules*; football; table tennis; volleyball; basketball; snooker
YOU SHOULD KNOW:
Le Val de Cantobre has been rated as No 4 in the world's top 50 campsites by *The Independent* newspaper.

This lovely family campsite will appeal to nature lovers and people who enjoy activity holidays. It is situated in the most rugged part of the Massif Central in a stunning position on the border between Grands Causses Regional Park and Cévennes National Park. The site is surrounded by breathtakingly beautiful natural scenery on all sides – high plateaus and wild hills, deep cavernous gorges and towering cliffs. There is a huge variety of wildlife in the area – deer, wild boar, beavers and vultures who wheel in the skies above.

The campsite is set on terraces on the wooded valley slope of the River Dourbie, looking towards the picturesque hill village of Cantobre, perched precariously on a sheer rock face. The site itself is extremely clean and well maintained and unusually attractive. The land was once a farm and the site's restaurant, bar and pizzeria are housed in the medieval farm buildings while all around the site there are trees and greenery.

There are 215 spacious pitches, some with wonderful sweeping views across the valley to Cantobre, and on the lower ones there is direct access to the River Dourbie – one of the best angling rivers in France. The site contains a great water park with four pools and a wild river, two playgrounds and a games room, plus an excellent shop and a varied evening entertainment programme.

But the joy of this site is its amazing location, relaxed atmosphere and the huge selection of activities offered, either on the site or in the immediate area, not to mention the nearby medieval fortified towns worth visiting. Anyone of any age, from the very young to the elderly, will have a whale of a time here.

Domaine du Haut des Bluches

WHERE:
La Bresse, Hautes-Vosges
COST:
Budget
BEST TIME OF YEAR:
All year round, except from November to mid December when the site is closed
DON'T MISS:
The *Schlitte* Mountain – year-round sledging; visiting the gardens of Wesserling; climbing up the hill to the Brabant Chapel; a tour of the Thillot copper mines
THINGS TO DO:
Hiking; nordic walking; mountain biking; cycling; horse riding; fishing; climbing; paragliding; swimming; skiing; cross-country skiing; snowshoeing; sledging; snowboarding; ice skating
YOU SHOULD KNOW:
The site is suitable for the disabled. It has small chalets to rent with a B&B option and a large chalet with 13 bedrooms – perfect for large winter-sports groups.

This excellent campsite is in a beautiful location, beside a river among the rolling forested hills and mountain lakes of the Vosges. It's exceptionally clean and spacious with 140 pitches spread out informally among the trees on 4 ha (10 ac) of terraced land 700 m (2,300 ft) up in the hills.

The site has a decent shop, bar, restaurant and takeaway, play area and games room, but nothing else in the way of entertainment, which goes a long way towards explaining the calm, unhurried atmosphere here. It's perfect for people who just want to go off and do their own thing. And there is certainly plenty to do, all year round. The Vosges countryside is marvellous for hiking, mountain biking and other outdoor pursuits, while the campsite is only 5 km (3 mi) from La Bresse-Hohneck, the largest winter sports resort in the Vosges.

As well as the glorious Vosges countryside, all the amenities of the historical town of La Bresse are just down the road – museums and galleries, artisans' workshops, a superb swimming pool, adventure park, great restaurants and a cinema. The Vosges heritage is a rich one and the surrounding area is not only outstandingly scenically beautiful but also stuffed with historical and cultural sights. And then there's the crowning glory: the Route des Cretes, a spectacularly beautiful scenic mountain road running along the ridge that marks the boundary between Lorraine and Alsace, with jaw-dropping views round every bend.

The Domaine du Hauts des Bluches is a rarity – a campsite that is just as wonderful in the winter snow as in the green of summer.

A view from the Route des Cretes

WHERE:
Luz Saint Sauveur, Hautes-Pyrénées
COST:
Budget
BEST TIME OF YEAR:
The site is open all year but May to September are the best months unless you're a winter-sports enthusiast – Gèdre is a well-known ski resort.
DON'T MISS:
Seeing the eagles and raptors at Donjon des Aigles; the ancient mill at Gèdre; having a donkey ride at the Cirque de Gavarnie; Gloriettes dam and hydroelectric plant, the second biggest in Europe

An Indian *Tipi* in the Mountains

The owners of a traditional mountain farm in the High Pyrenees have four *tipis* (teepees) on their land. At an altitude of 1,300 m (4,260 ft), surrounded by stunning mountain scenery, this is a wonderful place for a family camping and activity holiday – a completely different experience from the hurly burly of a normal campsite.

The *tipis* are in an idyllic spot – a grassy terrace in front of a picturesque barn. Sheep and dwarf goats wander among the trees, and the mountain views are simply incredible. Each *tipi* sleeps a family of four, or even six if some are tinies. *Tipis* are far less

restricting, more comfortable and better ventilated than conventional tents and these are delightfully decorated with Native American ornaments. Each has its own camp fire, with logs provided, and you have full use of the barn, which has been converted to hold two bathrooms, a well-equipped kitchen and a dining/living/TV room. The farm is only 2.5 km (1.5 mi) from the charming Pyrenean village of Gèdre, where there is a superb swimming pool, and you can sign up for any number of mountain-sports activities.

This is a wonderful way to introduce children to the wild. The lakes, mountains and forests of the High Pyrenees are a joy to the senses, and the role-play involved in *tipi* living will delight the kids – as well as you. You can enjoy the best of both worlds here – sleeping under the stars but with all the convenience of protective walls to simplify the business of providing for the basic needs of the family – while they get on with the serious stuff of being a Native American tribe.

THINGS TO DO:
Climbing; canyoning; rafting; kayaking; hiking; mountain biking; horse riding; *via ferrata* (for bolt and cable climbing); swimming; tennis; bungee jumping; paragliding; adventure parks; winter sports

YOU SHOULD KNOW:
Les Tipis Indiens is an excellent place for two or more families to stay as a group – the dining room has four large tables and the barn seats up to 24 people.

Le Moulin de Maître Cornille

Named after a famous story by 19th-century French novelist Alphonse Daudet, this 18th-century Provencal windmill is an absolutely enchanting place. Still with its sails intact, it is set on a hill in a hectare (2.5 ac) of land surrounded by woods and hills. The air is balmy with the scent of wild aromatic herbs and shrubs such as rosemary, thyme, cistus, cypress and broom, and alive with the chatter of *cicadas*. This heavenly setting is further enhanced by a mind-blowing view of the Pont du Gard – an ancient Roman aqueduct described by Daudet as a 'rainbow in stone'.

The mill sleeps five with ease (and seven quite comfortably if two people are prepared to sleep on a sofa bed in the living area) in two double bedrooms and a single. There is only one bathroom but it's a pretty ritzy one, which more than compensates for a lack of the en-suite facilities that everyone seems to expect nowadays. Anyway, you can always wash outside – there's a lovely bathing pool in the courtyard, set in flagstones with stone steps leading down to the water. The ground floor of the mill still has its beautiful vaulted ceiling and has been converted into a kitchen, dining and living area, charmingly furnished in traditional Provencal fashion.

Surrounded by natural parks and just outside the picturesque 12th-century hill-top village of Castillon – one of the loveliest villages in the whole of France with its ancient cobbled streets, fortified walls, gate houses and gargoyles – the mill couldn't be in a more perfect situation. Le Moulin de Maître Cornille, steeped as it is in history and literature, is an extraordinarily romantic place to stay.

WHERE:
Castillon du Gard, Provence Gard (Languedoc-Roussillon)

COST:
Budget

BEST TIME OF YEAR:
Provence is beautiful at any time of year but from the end of September to the beginning of April it is very quiet and a lot of the local businesses and restaurants are closed. May and June are perhaps the most beautiful months.

DON'T MISS:
Wallowing in the mill's bathing pool with a glass of wine, gazing at the incredible view of the Pont du Gard; Provencal market and antique shops in the nearby town of Uzès; tasting the Côtes du Rhône wine at Chateau de Bosc, Domazan

THINGS TO DO:
River swimming; kayaking; cycling; horse riding; tennis; golf; hot-air ballooning; going to the sea; playing *pétanque* in the mill garden

YOU SHOULD KNOW:
Le Moulin de Maître Cornille is within easy driving distance of the historic cities of Avignon, Arles, Nîmes, and Montpelier and only 45 minutes from the sandy beaches of the Mediterranean coast.

Palazzo Ruspoli

WHERE:
Via della Fontanella di Borghese, Rome
COST:
Astronomical
BEST TIME OF YEAR:
Any time, but choose April to June and September to October if you want to be fairly certain of good weather; avoid the oppressive heat and hordes of tourists in July and August.
DON'T MISS:
Throwing a coin in the Trevi Fountain; the daily market in Campo de' Fiori; having a meal or at least a drink at Ristorante-Caffe Lo Zodiaco

Live like royalty in Rome by staying in a stupendous apartment in the 16th-century Palazzo Ruspoli. The rooms were the lodgings of the young Napoleon, nephew of Napoleon Bonaparte, while he was living in exile in the 1830s before following in his uncle's footsteps and muscling his way to the top job – Emperor Napoleon III of the Second French Empire.

The grand entrance to the palazzo leads through an arched gateway with enormous wooden doors, along a Doric-columned colonnade and on up a sweeping marble staircase. The suite has three enormous rooms with vast windows, carved wooden ceilings, silk damask wallpaper, massive gilt-framed paintings and beautiful antique ornaments everywhere. A huge wrought-iron chandelier hangs from

the bedroom ceiling, which has a wonderful canopied bed dripping with silk drapes and tapestry cushions.

All this antique splendour could be intimidating but the atmosphere is so relaxed and welcoming that you're immediately put at ease as you sink into an antique silk sofa as though you were born to it. Amid all the period splendour there's every amenity you could possibly wish for, including wifi, plasma TV and iPod dock. The service matches the surroundings – a butler to carry your bags and a maid to fetch you a drink. At night a turned-down bed strewn with roses awaits and breakfast turns up as if by magic in the morning, presented on a solid-silver tray.

The Ruspoli Palace is on the corner of Rome's smartest shopping street and very close to the main historical sights. The family still lives there and you can't help feeling privileged to be staying somewhere so special – at last you've found yourself in the lap of *la dolce vita*.

THINGS TO DO:
Window shopping (or even buying something) in the Via Condotti; visiting the Vatican and St Peter's Basilica; exploring the splendours of Ancient Rome
YOU SHOULD KNOW:
The Palazzo Ruspoli is in an area that was known in Ancient Rome as Campo Marzio or 'Field of Mars', a large plain between the hills of Rome and the River Tiber. It was gradually absorbed into the city and some of the most famous monuments in the world are here.

Villa Spalletti Trivelli

The Spalletti Trivelli family home is an elegant late 19th-century villa, set in its own gardens and facing the Quirinale – the President's official residence – in a quiet residential area of central Rome. After extensive restoration, the villa was opened as a boutique hotel in 2009.

The villa has 12 palatial guest rooms with high ceilings and large shuttered windows enjoying views either of the Quirinale gardens or the villa's own garden, all beautifully furnished and with marble bathrooms. At first the faintly museum-like atmosphere can be awe-inspiring, but you soon realize that all this opulence is intended for your enjoyment and you're meant to treat the villa like a family home. You can hang out in one of the salons with a cup of coffee or look at the books in the library without feeling remotely self-conscious, and the staff are superb – courteous and helpful but never intrusive. Revel in civilized little touches like expensive china, free aperitifs, a bar where you can just help yourself to a drink and the constantly topped-up complimentary minibar in your room – all of which makes you feel that you're a special house guest rather than just another business proposition.

Rome is a noisy city throughout the day and into the small hours, so after a day of sightseeing or shopping it's bliss to escape from the hubbub of the city into the tranquillity of the villa. Retreat to the inner sanctum of the softly lit hotel spa and revive yourself in the *hammam* or simply flop into a garden chair and listen to the birds chirruping. The Villa Spalletti Trivelli is an absolute treasure.

WHERE:
Via Piacenza, Rome
COST:
Expensive
BEST TIME OF YEAR:
Any time is good but choose April to June or September to October if you want to be fairly certain of fine weather; it's best to avoid the oppressive heat and hordes of tourists in July and August.
DON'T MISS:
Having a glass of wine on the rooftop balcony; the mosaics in the Basilica of Santa Maria; exploring the catacombs; an evening meal in one of the restaurants around Campo de' Fiori
THINGS TO DO:
Hop-on, hop-off bus tour of Rome; sightseeing; shopping in the Porta di Roma mall; discovering Rome's gastronomic delights
YOU SHOULD KNOW:
In the early 20th century the Villa Spalletti Travelli was a well-known literary salon where writers and poets gathered. The Spalletti Trivelli family book collection, still housed in the villa's library, is a designated part of Italy's national heritage, curated by the Ministry of Culture and Heritage.

Hotel Hassler

WHERE:
Piazza Trinità dei Monti, Rome
COST:
Expensive (astronomical for the best rooms)
BEST TIME OF YEAR:
Any time
DON'T MISS:
Having dinner in the hotel's Imàgo restaurant; drinking a Veruschka (pomegranate juice and sparkling wine) in the Hassler cocktail bar; the Keats-Shelley Memorial House in Piazza di Spagna; the Borghese Gardens; Capuchin Crypt in the church of Santa Maria della Concezione; the evening street performers in Piazza Navona

Perhaps the most outstanding thing about this iconic family-owned hotel, apart from its venerable age and celebrity cachet, is its prime position – overlooking the Spanish Steps. It must surely be one of the world's most romantic places to stay.

The Hassler is an atmospheric old-style European hotel of a kind that hardly exists nowadays, with service to match. Rooms vary in size but even the smaller ones have lovely high ceilings which makes them feel more spacious than they really are, and each room is individually furnished in lavish film-star fashion with opulent mirror-walled and marble bathrooms.

Eating at the Hassler is a wonderful experience. The sixth-floor Michelin-starred restaurant has the best view over Rome to be found anywhere in the city. The intimate 1930s cocktail bar transports you into a bygone age of glamour with its wood panelling, red-leather

bar stools, gilt-framed mirrors and a live pianist tinkling away in the background. And the garden bar, enclosed by ancient, ivy-covered stone walls with wrought-iron furniture and *jardinières*, is a wonderfully secluded little niche for breakfast at the start of a hard day's sightseeing.

The Hassler has an air of discreet but very real exclusivity about it. As soon as you walk into the marble foyer and have a peek into the opulently furnished salon you are aware that you are one of the privileged few, that this is far too sophisticated a place to welcome children, and that anybody who isn't actually staying here doesn't have a chance of getting beyond the front door. Standards are high and it is expected they will be maintained. But if you fall for old-fashioned, individualistic charm, this is *the* place to stay when in Rome.

THINGS TO DO:
Taking a guided walking tour; sampling Rome's nightlife; shop in the Porta Portese flea market; eat pizza in one of Rome's renowned pizzerias.

YOU SHOULD KNOW:
Ask for a room overlooking the courtyard. It's worth giving up the view of the Spanish Steps for a quiet night and you can always look at the view from the roof terrace, which is the largest in Rome. Attached to the Hassler is Il Palazzetto – four rooms run and owned by the Hassler, all of 30 seconds' walk away and with full use of all the amenities. It's just as good as the main hotel and is quite a bit cheaper.

Beautiful countryside and ancient hill-top towns and villages are yours to explore when you stay in a Tuscan farmhouse.

A Tuscan Farmhouse

WHERE:
Tuscany
COST:
Budget
BEST TIME OF YEAR:
Most of the *agriturismo* farmhouses are open all year round but from May to September is best in terms of weather.
DON'T MISS:
Going to a wine tasting; exploring medieval hill villages; climbing the Leaning Tower of Pisa (it's a must, and the journey itself will take you through breathtaking landscapes)
THINGS TO DO:
Walking; horse riding; mountain biking and cycling; swimming; sightseeing; sampling Tuscan food and wine

The Tuscan soil has been cultivated for millennia and the old farmhouses here are indescribably picturesque, nestling in the shade of cypress trees among the rolling wooded hills, vineyards and olive groves of this ancient land.

As farming becomes less profitable and the tourist industry grows, Tuscan farmers are increasingly converting their spare rooms and under-used outhouses into *agriturismo* tourist accommodation. *Agriturismo* is as environmentally friendly as tourism can ever get – it allows farmers to augment their income and townies to experience the reality of rural life. You can rent an entire farmhouse, or just a room or apartment. Most *agriturismo* farmhouses have swimming pools and other essential tourist amenities.

The farmhouse at Il Vecchio Maneggio is on a hill top in the heavenly countryside near the World Heritage village of San Gimignano. It has five rustically furnished rooms with private bathrooms and provides home-cooked food. The farm produces honey and saffron and breeds horses, which guests may ride.

South of Siena, Podere Cunina has been converted into seven self-catering apartments. It is just one of several *agriturismo* farmhouses around Buenconvento, a medieval village in the sparsely

populated Crete Senesi (Siennese Clays), a spectacularly surreal landscape where regimented lines of dark cypress trees march across the domed hills, a flowing patchwork of raw and burnt sienna, red ochre and golden fields. Or stay among the vineyards in Chianti country at Fattoria Viticcio, or at La Valentina Nuova in the Maremma Natural Park surrounded by olive trees and grazing cattle, only 3 km (2 mi) from the coast near the picturesque fishing town of Talamone. Whichever farmhouse you stay in, one thing's for sure – you'll lose your heart to Tuscany.

YOU SHOULD KNOW:
The idea of *agriturismo* started in Tuscany and was codified into Italian planning law in 1985, enabling farmers to change the use of their outbuildings and install extra amenities on their land. Nowadays there are *agriturismo* farms in most parts of Europe. It takes about three hours to drive across Tuscany – most of the roads are winding and single lane, so progress can be slow. The best way of getting around is by train and bus as public transport is pretty reliable and a reasonable price.

Agriturismo I Mandorli

Three sisters run this wonderful Umbrian farm in the hills of Trevi, under the watchful eye of their Italian mama and with their children in tow. The 50-ha (124-ac) farm has been in the same family since the 18th century, passed down from one generation to the next. In 1996 there was no male heir so the women plucked up their courage and decided to run it themselves, producing organic extra virgin olive oil as their main occupation.

The farmhouse is a traditional Umbrian *case padronale* (manor house) full of cherished family heirlooms – including a 17th-century oil press that's still in working order. In the shade of some ancient almond trees a cluster of four little outhouses, one of them a former shepherd's hut, have been converted for *agriturismo*. You can either stay in a self-catering apartment or just have a double room with en-suite bathroom. A mouth-watering homemade breakfast of freshly baked bruschetta, cake and biscuits is served in the farmhouse every morning.

This is an idyllic place for children. There's a horse, chickens, cats basking in the sun, plus a welcome swimming pool shaded by olive trees with a glorious outlook over the Umbrian hills. I Mandorli oozes a sense of the past – the ancient gnarled trees of the olive grove, the quaint farm buildings, the old farmhouse kitchen table and household treasures all speak of a long history. The farm is brilliantly located for exploring the countryside around Trevi and the lovely Umbrian hill towns of Assisi, Spoleto and Orvieto. Umbria is one of Italy's smallest and most traditional regions and I Mandorli is traditional Umbria at its best.

WHERE:
Trevi, Umbria
COST:
Budget
BEST TIME OF YEAR:
Go in October if you want to see the olive harvest and taste the freshly pressed oil.
DON'T MISS:
The springs and ancient temple at the source of the Clitunno River; the medieval hill town of Montefalco; eating regional food at La Prepositura restaurant in Trevi
THINGS TO DO:
Exploring the local hill towns; walking in the Umbrian countryside; cycling; horse riding
YOU SHOULD KNOW:
Incongruously, the farm looks down onto a railway line, about 800 m (2,625 ft) away, and you can hear the trains in the distance.

Treehouse at La Piantata

WHERE:
Arlena di Castro, Viterbo, Lazio
COST:
Very expensive
BEST TIME OF YEAR:
All year round, but June and July are especially lovely, with the lavender fields in full flower just before the harvest
DON'T MISS:
Bathing in the Terme dei Papi thermal springs; the church of San Flaviano at Montefiasconi, a picturesque village overlooking Lake Bolsena with a view all the way to the sea; the Renaissance gardens of Villa Lante; the Etruscan hill town of Tuscania; the medieval Castello Gugliemi on the coast at Montalto di Castro
THINGS TO DO:
Walking; horse riding; cycling; swimming; sailing; boating; golf; tennis; visiting the numerous sights in the area
YOU SHOULD KNOW:
La Piantata also has charming B&B cottages and another less sophisticated and smaller but equally appealing treehouse in the branches of a century-old holm oak tree. Reservations for the treehouses must be made well in advance – they are always very heavily booked.

If you really *do* care about the environment yet just can't help yourself from wanting the biggest and best of everything, how about eco-living Italian style? You can stay in the largest (and most chic) treehouse in all Europe, the stuff of childhood fantasies but with a distinctly sophisticated twist.

The treehouse at La Piantata organic farm is an interior-designed 87-sq m (936-sq ft) cabin constructed from Canadian cedar, plate glass and black steel. It's been built 7 m (23 ft) up in a 200-year-old maritime pine and has a stunning all-round view of lavender fields, olive groves, the Cimino Mountains and Tyrrenhean Sea. The cabin has every hi-tech appliance under the sun – flat screen TV, Bose home theatre system, CD and MP3 player, heating, air conditioning, LED lanterns – plus a four-poster bed with a crystal bedhead, a huge furnished terrace, refrigerated bar, and even a telescope.

At night the heady scents of lavender and pine hang in the air as you watch the sun slowly sinking into the sea. And you wake to the sound of birds twittering and breakfast being winched up by pulley onto your terrace. Then it's time to start the day with a whirlpool dip in the farmhouse's sensational swimming pool, set in volcanic stone.

La Piantata is in the wooded hill country around Lake Bolsena. Constantly fed by volcanic spring water, Bolsena is the cleanest lake in Europe. Nearby are ancient Etruscan ruins and the medieval towns and villages of the Via Francigena, the old pilgrim route to Rome. The treehouse at La Piantata is a very special romantic place, in a beautiful region of Italy as yet undiscovered by tourist hordes.

Tenuta di Spannocchia

Who hasn't wondered what it would be like to live on a country estate? Well now you can try it for yourself at Tenuta di Spannocchia. Owned by an aristocratic Italian family, the estate is 430 ha (1,060 ac) of rolling grain fields, chestnut woods, pasture, olive groves, vineyards and vegetable gardens in the Natural Reserve of Alto Merse, just 19 km (12 mi) from the city of Siena.

At the heart of any great estate there has to be a historical mansion and here it's the registered historic site of Castello di Spannocchia, a magnificent centuries-old Tuscan manor house with a 12th-century tower. The estate is run as a fully functioning, self-sufficient organic farm, but it is also a wildlife refuge and education centre. The farm produces olive oil, wine, honey and jam, fruit and vegetables, pork, beef and lamb. The animals here are all endangered breeds: Cinta Senese pigs, Calvana cows, Pomarancina sheep, Monte Amiata donkeys, and Monterufolino ponies.

There are picturesque farm cottages scattered around the estate dating as far back as the 13th century, once the homes of tenant farmers. Seven of these, each with its own charm, have been beautifully restored for holiday lets. They vary in size and design but all are completely authentic and each sits in its own lovely setting. Tenuta di Spannocchia is a magical place, whether for a romantic break in a secluded cottage on the edge of the woods or for a family holiday – the children can simply open the front door and tumble out into the fields. Staying here is like stepping back into the rural Tuscany of long ago.

WHERE:
Chiusdino, Siena
COST:
Budget
BEST TIME OF YEAR:
May to October
DON'T MISS:
A cookery demonstration; hiking to the Hermitage of Santa Lucia; the head of St Catherine of Siena in San Domenico church; seeing how crystal is made at Colle Val d'Elsa; sightseeing in Siena
THINGS TO DO:
Walking the woodland paths on the estate; watching the farm at work; hiking; cycling; swimming; food, wine and art courses; sightseeing excursions
YOU SHOULD KNOW:
In order to rent one of the estate cottages you must pay a small fee to become a member of the Spannocchia Foundation (the money goes towards supporting the Foundation's conservation and education work to encourage sustainable cultural landscapes). All sorts of educational courses are run at the Castello – from cookery and art to photography and archaeology – which guests can participate in.

Grand Hotel Tremezzo Palace

WHERE:
Tremezzo, Como, Lombardy
COST:
Expensive
BEST TIME OF YEAR:
May and June are beautiful months for flowers in bloom; the autumn colour in September is also lovely but July and August are the best months for water sports. Lake Como is pretty flat (metaphorically speaking) from mid October to April.
DON'T MISS:
A trip around the lake on the hotel's private boat; the beach at Lido di Lenno; the lakeside walk from Colonno to Griante; the 17th-century Villa Carlotta and botanical gardens; a pizza in Pizzeria Balognett
THINGS TO DO:
Lakeside walks; hiking; mountain biking; horse riding; climbing; bouldering; *via ferrata* (for bolt and cable climbing); swimming; water sports on the lake; tennis; golf; billiards; sightseeing
YOU SHOULD KNOW:
Rooms have either a lake or garden view. The view over the lake is stunning but there is a road between the front of the hotel and the lake and passing traffic might bother some people.

The Tremezzo Palace is a stunning Art Nouveau palace in a prime position on the edge of Lake Como. The hotel first opened its doors in 1910 to cater for wealthy tourists making the obligatory stop at Lake Como on their European Grand Tour. Over a century later, having survived two world wars, the hotel still stands as proudly as ever, commanding the best outlook of any hotel on the lake – a view that encompasses the Grigne Mountains, Bellagio – the 'pearl of Lake Como', and the wooded peninsula and villa at Punta Balbianello.

Although it's undergone several refurbishments, the 90-room luxury hotel still retains its *belle époque* period decor and ambience. The superb reception rooms include a lavish dining room decorated in blue and gold, a 'winter' room with vast picture windows looking out onto the lake, a billiard room with an antique billiard table and dark-red walls that has the atmosphere of a gentlemen's club, and a secluded reading room – plus a lakeside terrace bar. The hotel's beautiful 20-ha (50-ac) semi-tropical terraced gardens are a riot of colour and winding paths lead up the hillside, past statuary and *jardinières,* to a gazebo at the top. There are two outdoor swimming pools, one in the privacy of the hotel gardens and another floating out on the lake, and an amazing indoor infinity pool that, even through the plate-glass barrier, appears to segue into the water of the lake.

It's rare to find a *belle époque* grand hotel that isn't under corporate ownership with the frosty, impersonal stamp of a managed chain. But Tremezzo still has all the hallmarks of a family-owned hotel – wonderful personal service, glamour and exclusivity.

Villa d'Este

The 16th-century Renaissance palace Villa d'Este has always been *the* place to stay on Lake Como. It was built by the Cardinal of Como as a summer retreat. Smitten by the location, he ordered that the convent which already stood there be demolished to make way for his new home. The palace was acquired by Princess Caroline, unhappy wife of the Prince of Wales (later King George IV) when her marriage to the British monarch broke down in 1814 and she ran away to Como. She entertained lavishly and turned the palace into an open house for the European aristocracy and their hangers-on. In 1873 Villa d'Este, already a hotel in all but name albeit a very exclusive one, started charging its guests and opened its doors to a wider public.

Villa d'Este really is palatial. It has 152 guest rooms – 125 in the palace and 72 in the Queen's Pavilion, a mid 19th-century villa erected in the palace grounds to commemorate Caroline. Every room is individually furnished in extravagant silks, velvets and brocades, and the corridors and salons are stuffed with paintings and antiques. The lovely 10-ha (25-ac) hillside Renaissance garden has formal topiary hedging, a 600-year-old plane tree, a stupendous 16th-century mosaic *nymphaeum* and two secluded villas for guests who want complete privacy. The hotel spa has a lovely large and airy indoor pool, and the outdoor one floats on the lake (in competition with the Grand Tremezzo – the only other Lake Como hotel to have a floating pool).

The romantic history of Villa d'Este seems to seep out of its walls. Staying here is the sort of once-in-a-lifetime experience that you'll always remember with fondness.

WHERE:
Cernobbio, Como, Lombardy
COST:
Astronomical, but worth it for the experience
BEST TIME OF YEAR:
May and June are beautiful months for flowers in bloom; the autumn colour in September is also lovely but July and August are the best months for water sports. Lake Como is pretty dead from mid October to April.
DON'T MISS:
Exploring every inch of the Villa d'Este and its garden – you are staying somewhere completely unique; a steam-ferry trip around Lake Como; a tour of Villa del Balbionello; walking the scenic trail of Via dei Monte Lariani
THINGS TO DO:
Hiking; mountain biking; horse riding; climbing; bouldering; *via ferrata* (for bolt and cable climbing); swimming; using the hotel's kayaks and having a go at other water sports on the lake; golf at the hotel's own club; investigating the Villa d'Este's extraordinary history; sightseeing
YOU SHOULD KNOW:
Villa d'Este regularly appears in 'The Best Hotels in the World' lists in *Leisure & Travel*, *Condé Nast Traveler* and *Forbes Traveler* magazines.

Villa Feltrinelli

Nestling at the foot of a vertiginous mountain slope overlooking the sparkling blue waters of Lake Garda, Gargnano is a picturesque little lakeside town. Less than five minutes' walk from the main square, set back from the road behind a gated driveway, a peach-and-cream stucco villa with perky little turrets peeks out from between the trees. This is the Villa Feltrinelli – one of the most exclusive hotel hideaways you're ever likely to stumble upon.

The villa was built in 1892 as a summer retreat for the Feltrinellis, a prominent family of business magnates. After World War II the house gradually fell into disrepair. It was eventually sold in 1997 and has since been beautifully refurbished as a boutique hotel. The inside of the villa is seriously sophisticated, with dark-wood panelling, stained glass, huge chandeliers, murals, ceiling frescos, antique ornaments and period furniture arranged with uncluttered chic.

There are 21 suites: 13 in the villa and seven in outbuildings at either end of a heavenly 3-ha (7-ac) garden with a terraced lemon grove and ancient magnolia trees. The rooms and attached bathrooms are all huge and the atmosphere is like staying in someone's extremely opulent home. You arrive to find flowers in your room and a complimentary minibar, there's a free laundry service and honesty bar and you can have breakfast wherever you want – in bed, beside the lake, a chosen spot in the garden, beside the swimming pool. And, of course, the hotel restaurant has a Michelin star.

Naturally, unstinted luxury comes at a price. If you need to count the cost of exclusivity, Villa Feltrinelli definitely isn't the place for you; if you don't, it is.

WHERE:
Gargnano, Brescia, Lombardy
COST:
Astronomical
BEST TIME OF YEAR:
May to September
DON'T MISS:
A trip across the lake in a vintage launch; the *sardí* (lemon houses); Rocca Scaligera medieval castle at Sirmione; Il Vittoriale Museum at Gardone Riviera
THINGS TO DO:
Lakeside walks, hiking, climbing; cycling; horse riding; swimming and water sports; fishing; sightseeing
YOU SHOULD KNOW:
Lake Garda is the largest and cleanest of the Italian Alpine lakes. The Germans expropriated Villa Feltrinelli from the family during World War II and housed Benito Mussolini there.

Sextantio *Albergo Diffuso*

Abruzzo is a wild and sparsely populated region of Italy. Wolves and bears still roam in the forests and golden eagles nest in the mountain crags. The beautiful medieval village of Santo Stefano, more than 1,250 m (4,100 ft) up in the rugged mountains of Gran Sasso, has only 120 remaining inhabitants. This once-thriving mountain village was gradually decaying until it was revitalized by Sextantio *albergo diffuso*. A mansion in the main square and five peasants' houses scattered around the village have been converted into 27 guest rooms. The sensitive restoration has ensured that the rooms retain their original quaint character but have been made fit for the 21st century with wifi, under-floor heating and swanky Philippe Starck bathroom fittings.

On arrival you are greeted with a wine tasting and tour of the village then given a massive, ancient-looking iron key – a hint of what's to come. You open the house door and step straight into the Middle Ages – finding bare stone walls, narrow windows, exposed beams, tiled floors, heavy timber doors, simple rustic furnishings, woollen mattresses (surprisingly comfortable) and a log pile beside the working fireplace.

You can curl up beside the hearth and watch the flickering flames of your open fire, hang out in the village wine cellar sampling local wines and liqueurs, eat hearty regional food by candlelight under the vaulted ceiling of the atmospheric 16th-century hotel restaurant, and wander along cobbled streets that have scarcely changed in 700 years or more. The *albergo diffuso* is a brilliant touristic idea. The advent of tourism in Santo Stefano gives the few remaining villagers a chance of retaining something of their cultural heritage and the authenticity of this memorable experience is remarkable.

WHERE:
Santa Stefano, Abruzzo
COST:
Reasonable
BEST TIME OF YEAR:
The dramatic mountainous countryside is beautiful at any time of year but early May is particularly lovely, when the wild cherry trees are in blossom. Think winter sports from December to March, or other activities from April to October.
DON'T MISS:
Visiting Castel del Monte to see how cheese is made; Rocca di Calascio medieval mountain-top fortress; tasting *genziana* herbal liqueur and eating *chitarrini*, the local pasta
THINGS TO DO:
Hiking; climbing; mountain biking; horse riding; cross-country skiing; snowshoeing; visiting hill-top villages and medieval castles; wildlife-watching in the Gran Sasso National Park; gastronomy; educational courses
YOU SHOULD KNOW:
Santa Stefano is considered to be one of the most beautiful medieval villages in Italy. There is no in-room phone, TV or turn-down service but there is a swimming pool and tennis court. Sextantio runs an events and education service – you can take courses in wine and food, cookery, creative writing, social history or yoga.

Oltre il Giardino

WHERE:
Casa i Frari, Fondamenta Contarini San Polo, Venice
COST:
Reasonable
BEST TIME OF YEAR:
April to early June (Venice can be hot and muggy in July and August)
DON'T MISS:
A ride in a gondola; the Church of the Frari round the corner from the hotel; the nearby Legatorio Polliero traditional bookbinders and stationery shop in San Polo
THINGS TO DO:
Seeing all the sights of the city; going to art galleries and museums; exploring Venice's quaint alleyways; cycling along the Venice Lido; souvenir shopping
YOU SHOULD KNOW:
In the 1920s the house belonged to Alma Mahler, widow of the composer Gustav Mahler.

Venice is like a Renaissance stage set and wherever you turn your head there's yet another historic treasure or architectural gem to admire. But even the most enthusiastic sightseer may find themselves exhausted by the end of the day and in need of respite. Il Giardino is the perfect antidote for tourist burn-out, a godsend in a city which, for all its charm, may sometimes feel overwhelming.

The hotel is centrally located in a quiet residential street just off San Polo and overlooks a canal on one side and its own garden on the other. It has six light and spacious double rooms and another two in an annexe. The rooms are all simply but stylishly furnished and the attached bathrooms are sparkling clean. If you're travelling as a family you can simply ask for an extra bed or cot to be installed in your room. Il Giardino's secluded walled garden is a haven in a city with little greenery where, footsore from tramping round the sights, you can flop down among the rosemary and oleander shrubs in the shade of the magnolia, olive and pomegranate trees, watch the chirpy sparrows pecking at crumbs, and restore your zest.

The breakfasts here are superb and more than a match for any five-star hotel. You wake to the smell of baking bread and come downstairs to a banquet. But perhaps the best thing of all about this hotel is the staff – they're not just efficient but truly *sympatico*. When you come back after a day's sightseeing you are greeted with genuine warmth and interest.

Offering a great location, great service, and great value, whether you're travelling alone, as a couple or *en famille*, Oltre il Giardino is a real diamond.

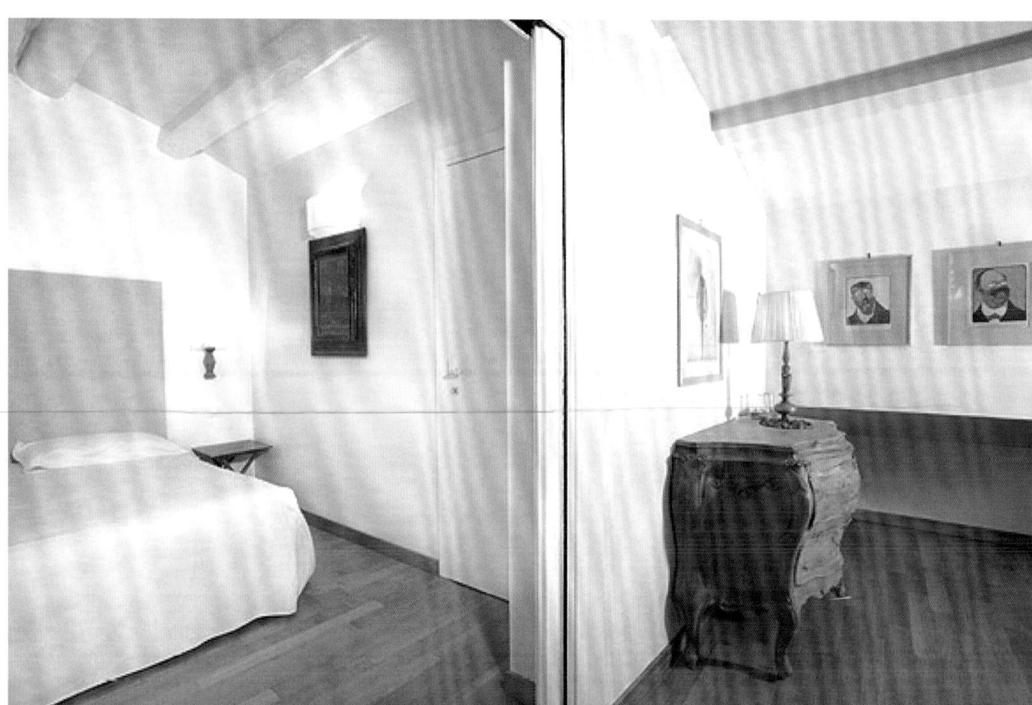

Venissa

Escape the bustle of Venice by staying in rural tranquillity on an island in the lagoon. Mazzorbo, next to the picturesque island of Murano and linked to it by a footbridge, is a lovely island of orchards and vineyards. The bucolic charm of the surroundings makes a delightful break from the city centre which, stunningly beautiful though it is, can become exhausting in the summer heat.

The owner of Venissa runs a *prosecco* winery and a restaurant. He opened a hotel in 2010 as an afterthought – six rooms in a picturesque restored outbuilding beside a 2-ha (5-ac) walled vineyard. It could be described as 'minimalist chic veering toward the spartan' as the rooms are furnished with all the essentials, but only the essentials, in impeccable designer style.

The service here is friendly and casual but the real delight of this place, apart from the blissfully peaceful rural environment and wonderful views over the lagoon, is the superb restaurant to which the hotel is attached. It is an open secret among foodies that Venissa not only serves the best food in Venice but also some of the most inventive dishes in the whole of Italy. It's worth staying here for the food alone although, unlike the rooms, a meal cannot be said to be particularly cheap,

Although the lagoon islands are a boat ride away from the city centre, you are still within relatively easy reach of all the city sights, and the islands have an independent life about them that gives you a completely different take on Venice. If you're into gastro-chic, romance, and places off the usual tourist trail, then Venissa is very hard to beat.

WHERE:
Fondamenta Santa Caterina, Mazzorbo, Venice
COST:
Budget
BEST TIME OF YEAR:
April to early June
DON'T MISS:
The island church of Santa Caterina; visiting the famous Venetian glass-making workshops on the neighbouring island of Murano; the 7th-century Basilica of Santa Maria Assunta on the island of Torcello
THINGS TO DO:
Eating wonderful food and sampling the island's *prosecco* wine; boat trips to the other islands in the lagoon; seeing the sights of Venice and visiting its museums and art galleries
YOU SHOULD KNOW:
Mazzorbo is 40 minutes by *vaporetto* from the city. It's a very pleasant journey across the lagoon and the daytime service is frequent and reliable.

Villa San Michele

WHERE:
Via Doccia, Fiesole, Florence, Tuscany
COST:
Astronomical
BEST TIME OF YEAR:
April to June and September to October
DON'T MISS:
The 17th-century fresco of The Last Supper in the hotel; street artists outside the Uffizi; an ice cream at Vivoli Gelateria; Farmacia di Santa Maria Novella, an old-fashioned apothecary shop in a 13th-century chapel; San Lorenzo market; Anticio Setificio Fiorentino silk factory
THINGS TO DO:
Mountain biking; horse riding; tennis; golf; gastronomy; browsing among the silver and jewellery shops; cultural sightseeing
YOU SHOULD KNOW:
The hotel runs its own cookery school so this is a great opportunity to have a holiday and learn new skills at the same time. Children are made welcome here and there's a great kids' club.

This luxury hotel, a former Franciscan monastery, was nabbed by Napoleon for his Italian headquarters. He certainly had an eye for a nice piece of real estate – the 15th-century villa is superbly situated among the rocks of a high hill top, surrounded by a terraced woodland garden of olive, cypress, oleander and lemon trees, with a stunning view over Florence and the Arno Valley. And the building itself is an architectural gem, with a facade attributed to Michelangelo.

Inside, the villa is full of beautiful ornaments and pictures. The 46 individually furnished guest rooms, with terracotta-tiled floors, parchment lampshades and marble bathrooms, are sublimely comfortable. The hotel restaurant serves phenomenal Tuscan food and there are three bars. You can relax in the monastery's cloister, among the ivy-entwined statues in a shaded garden loggia dripping with wisteria and climbing roses, laze by the swimming pool on a terrace shaded by olive trees where a cascade tumbles into the pool or dip into the water, drink in hand, listening to the birds singing in the trees and seeing the whole of Florence spread out before you.

The villa still has the ethereal, timeless atmosphere of a monastery and feels like a sanctuary. There's a free shuttle car service for the 15-minute journey to and from the city centre so you can nip back and forth at will, escaping to your palliative retreat in the Tuscan hills whenever you've had your fill of Florentine art and can't endure another moment of the heat and crowds. The monastic calm and sybaritic luxury at Villa San Michele cossets the body and revives the spirit.

Munta e Cara *Albergo Diffuso*

WHERE:
Apricale, Liguria
COST:
Reasonable
BEST TIME OF YEAR:
May to October
DON'T MISS:
The dolphins and lighthouse at Capo Mele; tasting the delicious local speciality *fugassun* (green vegetable cake); Bussana Vecchia artists' village
THINGS TO DO:
Exploring the village; walking; mountain biking; canyoning; rafting; swimming; fishing; yachting; sightseeing
YOU SHOULD KNOW:
Do not expect to find all the conventional hotel services and amenities at Munta e Cara. Your room is cleaned for you every day and a good breakfast is included in the price but you carry your own bags along the steep little cobbled alleyways and there is no telephone in the room, or room service.

During the 20th century many of Italy's beautiful ancient villages became virtual ghost towns, gradually crumbling into ruins as the young moved away to find work in the cities and older generations died. The concept of the *albergo diffuso* is an inventive way of injecting new life into these picturesque uninhabited villages – a hybrid of hotel and home stay where tourists can enjoy the romance of village surroundings but with hotel services.

Apricale, in the foothills of the Maritime Alps, is just such a place. Perched on top of a steep hill and with stupendous views of the mountains and Mediterranean Sea, it has hardly changed since the 14th century and is rated one of the ten prettiest towns in Italy. With only 600 inhabitants the village was in a state of terminal decline until Munta e Cara set up *albergo diffuso* tourist accommodation here and brought it back to life.

Rooms and apartments are in renovated cottages scattered around the village, all charmingly furnished in a cheerful rustic style. The local bar is Munta e Cara's hotel reception desk and the breakfast room is in one of the village houses. You are plunged straight into the daily world of a traditional Italian hill village – quaint stone houses huddled on the hillside, winding cobbled streets, the inevitable stray cats and no cars – just the chimes of the church clock and the occasional tinkling of mountain goat bells to disturb the peace. Apricale is only 12 km (7.5 mi) from the sea, so the Italian Riviera is almost on your doorstep. Munta e Cara is a novel sort of hotel and staying there is a real adventure.

Apricale, rated one of the ten prettiest towns in Italy

Castello Vuillermin

WHERE:
Via General Enrico Caviglia, Finale Ligure, Savona, Liguria
COST:
Budget
BEST TIME OF YEAR:
May to early October
DON'T MISS:
The Roman remains in the Chiesa dei Cappuccini; Giardini Hanbury Botanici, one of the most famous gardens in Italy originally planted by 19th-century English botanists; the ancient coastal town of Noli
THINGS TO DO:
Coastal walks; hiking; cycling and mountain biking; climbing; swimming and water sports; golf; tennis; exploring caves and Roman remains
YOU SHOULD KNOW:
Castello Vuillermin does not advertise itself widely, but it can be tracked down through websites listing hostels. You have to climb quite a long flight of steps to get to the castle.

You don't normally expect a youth hostel to be housed in a grand building. The great castles, stately homes and old palaces of Europe have more often than not been converted into luxury hotels way beyond the pocket of the average tourist. So the hostel at the coastal town of Finale Ligure is a real find – a neo-Gothic fairytale castle at the top of a hill, complete with impressive fortifications and turrets.

The hostel is clean, comfortable and quiet. It has 69 beds, arranged by floor – females on the first, males on the second, with family rooms in an attached manor house. The atmosphere is one of welcoming, laid-back calm. The ground-floor reception area invites you to flop down with a bottle of wine and chat with fellow travellers, or you can laze in the garden and enjoy the marvellous view from the terrace. And if you want to be king of the castle you can always make the effort of climbing the ladder to the top, where the panoramic view of sparkling blue sea, sky and green hills from the battlements is to die for.

Castello Vuillermin overlooks Finale Ligure, an atmospheric boho beach resort right next to the Rock of Caprazoppa, near Capo di Noli. The town has picturesque streets and plenty of historic buildings from pre-Roman remains to romantic 17th-century churches and is famous for its white-sand beaches. The more adventurous can go climbing and rambling in the limestone plateaus and canyons of Il Finale, the beautiful backcountry hills. Castello Vuillermin is very different from the usual hostel accommodation and is a great place to use as a base for an Italian Riviera holiday.

La Scalinatella, Capri

WHERE:
Via Tragara, Capri, Naples
COST:
Astronomical at the height of the summer season but reduced rates available at other times of year
BEST TIME OF YEAR:
May to September
DON'T MISS:
The best lunches in Capri on the hotel pool terrace; the Faraglione rocks; Casa Malaparte on Punta Massullo, a fine example of pre-World War II Italian modernist architecture; Villa Jovis, Emperor Tiberius's cliff-top palace; taking the chair lift (or even walking) to the top of Monte Solaro, the highest point of the island; enjoying a boat trip round the island

Enchanted island of the Blue Grotto, Capri has been a party place ever since the decadent Emperor Tiberius decided that his clifftop palace on the island was a more pleasant place than Rome from which to govern his Empire. Throughout the 19th and 20th centuries poets and writers, musicians and artists, celebrities and sybarites all flocked here, attracted by the island's magnetic charm. With rugged mountain slopes, carpets of wild flowers and the bluest of blue seas it is little short of heaven, so it's not surprising that Capri is still a favourite haunt of the glitterati.

The most exclusive hotel on this exclusive island is an unassuming white Moorish villa perched on a cliff overlooking the sea, modestly hiding its charms behind a flower-festooned hedge. Inside, the intimate atmosphere feels more like a private club than a hotel. The sophisticated, understated decor is immaculate and everything from bed linen to tableware is top-notch, including the hand-painted majolica floor tiles, antique gilt furnishings and expensive curios. The hotel's 30 spacious and stylish rooms all have vast patio terraces which are the equivalent of an outdoor room. There are two swimming pools on separate terraces, both with captivating sea views, and the hotel restaurant serves outstanding food.

The discreet and charming staff go to endless lengths to ensure that guests are looked after. They will help plan your day's itinerary, book restaurant tables, order taxis – all with smiles and genuine civility. La Scalinatella is within easy walking distance of the bars, boutiques and nightclubs in La Piazzetta, the island's vibrant main square – probably the most glamorous public square in the world. In the 'paradise of idleness' that is Capri, the Scalinatella is quite simply *the* place to stay.

THINGS TO DO:
Coastal and mountain-path walks; swimming; scuba diving; boating; tennis; day trips to neighbouring islands, Naples, Sorrento or the Amalfi coast; nightclubbing; celebrity spotting; shopping in designer boutiques
YOU SHOULD KNOW:
La Scalinatella was awarded Best Hotel in the World by *Condé Nast Traveler*. Non-residents are not permitted to bring a car to Capri in the summer months. You can get round the island by bus, taxi or funicular railway.

WHERE:
Positano, Salerno
COST:
Expensive (astronomical for the most prestigious rooms)
BEST TIME OF YEAR:
Mid April to late October only (Le Sirenuse is closed for the rest of the year)
DON'T MISS:
A coastal excursion in the hotel's vintage wooden boat; dinner in the Michelin-starred hotel restaurant; works of art in Santa Maria Assunta church; hiking along the Path of the Gods; taking the bus trip along the scenic coast road to Amalfi, the most beautiful road in Italy; Il Museo della Carta (Paper Museum) in Amalfi, a fascinating museum that is much more interesting than it sounds!
THINGS TO DO:
Hiking; cycling and mountain biking; swimming; snorkelling; scuba diving; windsurfing; deep-sea fishing; boating; kayaking; tennis; exploring the alleyways of Positano; watching the street artists at work; relaxing in cafés, observing the street life
YOU SHOULD KNOW:
Travel & Leisure magazine has rated Le Sirenuse sixth in the World's Best Hotels awards. In high season (mid May to early October) no children under six are allowed. There's free wifi throughout the hotel building and all rooms have plasma TV, CD/DVD player and iPod dock. The hotel provides free loan of pre-loaded iPods and has a DVD library of more than 700 films.

Le Sirenuse

The little fishing port of Positano is so picturesque it feels unreal – a jumble of quaint 17th- and 18th-century colour-washed houses with terracotta tiled roofs climbing all higgledy-piggledy up an impossibly steep cliff face. The one proper street runs along the harbour front from where flights of steps and winding passages wend their way up and down through the town.

Halfway up this vertical village, a Moorish baroque *palazzo* stands majestically overlooking the harbour and Positano Bay. Built in the 18th century as a summer residence for the aristocratic Sersale family, Le Sirenuse has been counted among the most glamorous hotels in Italy ever since it first opened its doors in 1951. Members of the Sersale family still run the place and you can feel the aristocratic presence in the atmosphere. It's like staying at an exceptionally grand private house, stuffed with family treasures, and has staff for whom nothing is too much trouble. The 59 airy rooms have white-washed walls hung with attractive paintings and prints and are individually furnished with a dashing eclecticism – contemporary and antique with a touch of the East thrown in. The opulent marble bathrooms have whirlpool tubs and are stocked with exclusive Eau d'Italie products – the Sersale family's signature brand.

There's a marvellous state-of-the-art spa, a swimming pool surrounded by lemon trees and a terrace champagne bar decked with sweet-smelling roses and frangipani, where you can sit in the evening with an aperitif as you watch the sun sink into the sea. And the superb hotel restaurant, where you can dine by the light of 400 candles, is unbelievably romantic. If you're a glamour seeker, you need look no further.

Palazzo Belmonte

This magnificently rambling 17th-century royal palace is right next to the sea in Cilento National Park on the beautiful coast south of Naples. The present Prince Belmonte still lives in one wing and guests are accommodated in a variety of elegantly furnished, very clean and comfortable suites, either in the palace itself or in the Villas Belmonte and Edoardo in the grounds.

The 2-ha (5-ac) palace grounds are enchantingly wild, a secret garden enclosed by high stone walls, filled with the sound of birdsong and the warm scent of honeysuckle and jasmine, with ancient trees and giant agapanthus flowers, old stone steps leading to secluded corners, and an ancient private chapel. There is also a splendid 24-m (80-ft) swimming pool hidden behind a curtain of bougainvillea, and it has a poolside bar. If you prefer the sea, follow a hidden pathway down to a secret gate which opens onto the hotel's private stretch of golden-sand beach.

The restaurant terrace looks out onto the sea and serves delicious traditional Mediterranean food. You can dine on freshly caught sea food *al fresco* by candlelight, watching the moonlight play on the water and the twinkling lights of the island of Capri in the distance. And if you want a change of scene, there's an excellent choice of local restaurants in the pretty little seaside village of Santa Maria di Castellabate, a short stroll away.

Palazzo Belmonte exudes a wonderfully romantic atmosphere of gently faded aristocratic grandeur. Royal history oozes out of the walls and you can't help but feel thrilled to be staying at a place where Kings of Spain and Italy have been guests, however long ago that may have been.

WHERE:
Santa Maria di Castellabate, Salerno
COST:
Expensive
BEST TIME OF YEAR:
Any time between April and October will be wonderful, but the palace gardens are at their most beautiful during May and early June.
DON'T MISS:
The Doric Temples of Paestum; eating the locally grown white figs; exploring the World Heritage medieval town of Castellabate; visiting the picturesque inland villages of Campora and Felitto in the heart of Cilento National Park
THINGS TO DO:
Lazing on the private beach; swimming; scuba diving; windsurfing; water skiing; sightseeing day trips; hiking along the beautiful coast of Cilento National Park; mountain biking; tennis (but you need to bring your own racquets)
YOU SHOULD KNOW:
The Palazzo Belmonte is 120 km (75 mi) south of Naples – a two-hour drive. The hotel arranges private cars and drivers for you to take day trips to Pompeii or Herculaneum, and you can cross the bay by hydrofoil to the Amalfi coast.

A *Trullo* in Puglia

WHERE:
Itria Valley, Puglia
COST:
Budget if you rent a privately owned *trullo*, reasonable if you stay at Trullidea
BEST TIME OF YEAR:
April to September (*trulli* are cold and damp in winter)
DON'T MISS:
The World Heritage *trulli* town of Alberobello; the amazing karst caves of Grotte di Castellana; the beautiful village of Cisternino; the rock dwellings and chapel of Santa Maria della Grazia in the lovely town of Fasano; Torre Canne Beach, a beautiful long stretch of sand
THINGS TO DO:
Rambling; cycling; going to the coast; swimming and water sports; exploring this little known part of Italy; sampling the regional food and wine
YOU SHOULD KNOW:
Puglia is one of the poorer regions of Italy and has only recently found its way onto the tourist map. It has Italy's longest coastline – 800 km (500 mi) of sand beaches – and it basks in hot sunshine for most of the year. More olive oil is produced here than in any other region of Italy (fill your boots with extra-virgin).

The *trullo* is a house design unique to the Itria Valley, a beautiful agricultural area of rolling hills in Puglia, in the heel of Italy's boot. These quaint little round dry-stone huts with conical roofs look like gnomes' houses. Originally used as temporary shelters for field workers and farm tools, they were adopted as permanent homes by impoverished landless labourers. Whole families would live in the single circular room, with wall recesses curtained off as sleeping quarters. *Trulli* villages sprang up and larger, more sophisticated versions were built with several vaulted rooms contained within two, three or more cones.

Old, abandoned *trulli* are dotted around everywhere among the small vineyards and olive groves. You see their little conical roofs peeking out from behind copses of holm oaks, sometimes singly, sometimes in clusters. In recent years many of the derelict 19th- and 20th-century *trulli* have been renovated. These quirky little houses are perfect for holiday accommodation. They are located in unspoilt countryside near the sea and are ideally suited to the hot Puglian sunshine.

You can rent *Trullo negli Alberi*, a huge seven-coned *trullo* attached to a *lamia* (traditional farm building), which sleeps eight. Surrounded by olive, oak and fruit trees, with a courtyard swimming pool and only 15 km (9 mi) from the sea, it has been lovingly restored by an English couple who lost their hearts to this part of Italy. Or you could stay in Trullidea *albergo diffuso* in the amazing World Heritage *trulli* town of Alberobello. There are plenty of other restored *trulli* of various sizes to rent, but you won't find them anywhere except Puglia – a *trullo* is a unique local offering.

Masseria Torre Coccaro

As soon as you turn into the driveway you know you've arrived somewhere really special as you take in the beautiful 17th-century rural architecture, the heavenly surroundings of orchards and olive groves, the little courtyard chapel – and then soak up the scent of citrus in the clean sea air.

The picturesque farmhouse tower and fortifications were originally built as a defence against marauding Turkish pirates who habitually pillaged the Puglian coast. Now the tower and outbuildings have been transformed into 39 stylishly furnished luxurious suites, all with their own terraces, little private gardens, or both. The hotel restaurant is in the old stables and you can dine under a pergola dripping in jasmine and bougainvillea. There is a sensational spa in the caves once used to shelter sheep. It has a blissful womb-like atmosphere of complete tranquillity and all the facilities of a top-notch hammam, with ayurvedic herb treatments.

On the Coccaro Estate, which is still a working farm, there's a beautiful botanical garden enclosed by stone walls built by Benedictine monks in 1500, and a superb nine-hole golf course set among almond, carob and olive trees. The hotel is just under 2 km (1 mi) inland but it has its own Coccaro Beach Club on a fabulous 5-km (3-mi) private stretch of sand backed by dunes and offering a seafood restaurant, oyster and sushi bar, and massage pavilion. Or you can just as happily laze beside the lovely outdoor swimming pool among palm and olive trees and eat at the poolside bar. The Masseria Torre Coccaro is a rural paradise – an idyllic retreat from the urban jungle where children and adults alike will be thoroughly pampered, eat wonderful food and be spoilt for choice of things to do.

WHERE:
Savelletri di Fasano, Brindisi, Puglia
COST:
Expensive (and the best suites are astronomical, but special offers can lower the price a bit)
BEST TIME OF YEAR:
May to October (but note that Puglia is very hot indeed in August)
DON'T MISS:
A trip on the hotel's private yacht to see the caves of Polignano a Mare and the ancient port of Monopoli; an early morning or evening horse ride along the beach; a visit to the World Heritage *trulli* town of Alberobello
THINGS TO DO:
Swimming; jet skiing; windsurfing; kite surfing; scuba diving; kayaking; fishing; sailing; beach volleyball; hiking; mountain biking; quad biking; go-karting; horse and pony riding; golf; tennis; billiards; Tai Chi; yoga; ceramics and cookery lessons
YOU SHOULD KNOW:
Mr and Mrs Smith hotel guides rate the Masseria Torre Coccaro among the top 100 most romantic hotels of the world, and Coccaro Beach Club among the top ten beach clubs in the world. The Torre Coccaro is one of only ten hotels in Italy to have been awarded three gold keys by the prestigious *Gambero Rosso Guide*. The hotel runs a cookery school. The 18th-century farm chapel is often used for weddings. Children are really well catered for with lots of activities and an excellent kids' club and babysitting service.

WHERE:
Piazza San Pietro Caveoso, Rione Pianelle, Matera, Basilicata
COST:
Reasonable
BEST TIME OF YEAR:
May to mid October
DON'T MISS:
The 13th-century Matera Cathedral of Santa Maria della Bruna; the *chiesi rupestri* (cave churches) – San Pietro Caveoso, entirely carved out of the cliff face, and Santa Maria d'Idris and San Nicola dei Greci where there are beautiful rock frescoes; Casa Grotto di Vico Solitario cave house to get an insight into the living conditions of a typical troglodyte; the fabulous view from Belvedere Luigi Guerricchio Pittore terrace
THINGS TO DO:
Exploring the labyrinthine alleys and narrow streets of the *sassi*, eating in one of the little restaurants you pass; renting a bike from the hotel; visiting the museums, palaces and historic churches of Matera; hiking in Murgia Materana Regional Park, a limestone plateau where there are caves, rock churches and neolithic sites; day trips to Policoro and Metaponto on the South Italian coast to see the ancient Greek remains
YOU SHOULD KNOW:
There are two separate cave districts in La Gravina gorge – *Sasso Caveoso* and *Sasso Barisano*. The *sassi* of Matera were used as the backdrop to Mel Gibson's controversial 2004 film *The Passion of Christ*.

Hotel Sant'Angelo

In the cliff face of La Gravina, a 200-m (660-ft) deep limestone gorge, the *sassi* (ancient natural caves of Matera) have been inhabited for at least 9,000 years. With an ever-increasing population, the *sassi* districts grew from Neolithic beginnings into sprawling cave townships. The inhabitants built porticoes and house facades at the cave entrances and the narrow streets that wind their way up the gorge are simply the porticoes of *sassi* below. Entire families and their livestock lived here without running water, sewage disposal or electricity until the 1950s, when the entire population was forcibly removed and rehoused. Since then the *sassi* have become of historical and romantic interest. Many of the caves have been renovated and you can now stay in the *sassi*.

At the Hotel Sant'Angelo you can experience the atmosphere of cave dwelling without any of the discomfort of troglodyte living. The hotel looks out onto a little piazza, a cave church and the gorge – a sensational position in the heart of the *sassi*. Its 16 air-conditioned rooms are stylishly furnished with every mod con and most of them have small outside seating areas. Some rooms are more cave-like than others – the more authentic, the more claustrophobic – or you can opt for space and fresh air. The breakfast room is a wonderfully atmospheric cave that recedes deep into the cliff and has an incredible view from its terrace.

Behind the regeneration of the *sassi* is a story of desperate hardship and human struggle. It's impossible not to be moved by the melancholy beauty of the faded *sassi* house facades. Staying in the caves of Matera is an awe-inspiring experience that will leave a lasting impression.

Grand Hotel Timeo

Taormina is one of the loveliest towns in Europe, high up in the hills of eastern Sicily overlooking the Bay of Naxos. In the town centre, directly in front of the famous Ancient Greek Theatre, stands one of Europe's most glamorous old grand hotels. Built in 1873, the Grand Timeo was the first hotel in Taormina and can count among its famous guests over the years such luminaries as Oscar Wilde, Tennessee Williams, Christian Dior, Liz Taylor and Audrey Hepburn.

The Grand Timeo is surrounded by 2.5 ha (6 ac) of stunningly beautiful parkland filled with cypress, magnolia and palm trees and has a sweeping view – from the rugged coast and the sea to the awesome presence of Mount Etna. The entire hotel has an opulent baroque air about it with vast public areas designed to impress. Everything, from the Murano light fixtures to the oil paintings and flower-decked dining room loggia, is stylishly arranged down to the last detail. The 70 palatial rooms and suites are elegantly furnished in tranquil shades of cream and taupe with parquet floors, marquetry bedsteads and swagged curtains over the bedhead.

You've got the charming little piazzas and picturesque winding streets of Taormina conveniently on your doorstep and a free Mercedes shuttle service to transport you to and from the hotel's private beach. Or you can simply lounge around beside the hotel pool in the tranquil surroundings of the hotel garden being pampered by the charming waiters. If you want to be treated like royalty, wallow in unstinted luxury, eat divine food, gaze at spectacular views and be treated to flawless service, the Grand Timeo will do it for you.

WHERE:
Via Teatro Greco, Taormina, Sicily
COST:
Astronomical
BEST TIME OF YEAR:
April to October
DON'T MISS:
Going to a play at the 3rd-century BC Greek Theatre; travelling on the narrow-gauge Circumetnea railway for a walk on the slopes of Mount Etna; a boat tour around Mazzaro Bay; the 13th-century Ursino Castle at Catania
THINGS TO DO:
Swimming, scuba diving and other water sports at Mazzaro Bay; boating; hiking; mountain biking; golf; tennis; browsing in the antique shops of Taormina; sightseeing
YOU SHOULD KNOW:
You can stay either in the main building or at the more secluded Villa Flora annexe in the grounds. Most but not all of the rooms have a terrace and sea view, but all have every amenity you would expect from a five-star hotel, including free wifi. There is a spa, gym, tennis courts and outdoor swimming pool.

Antica Dimora del Gruccione

WHERE:
Santu Lussurgiu, Oristano, Sardinia
COST:
Reasonable
BEST TIME OF YEAR:
April and May are lovely months when this beautiful island is still green and lush and it's not yet too hot. July and August are great months for swimming and water sports but the sun is very strong.
DON'T MISS:
Savouring the seven-course tasting menu at the hotel; sampling *mirto*, a Sardinian liqueur; the Bronze Age Nuraghe Losa, one of the best-preserved stone towers on the island; the World Heritage site of Barumini; the dunes at the Sinis Peninsula
THINGS TO DO:
Hiking, horse riding, mountain biking, birdwatching and guided nature tours in the Natural Reserve of Sinis-Montiferru; swimming, scuba diving and other water sports on the coast; golf; cookery and crafts courses; visiting the archaeological sites in the area
YOU SHOULD KNOW:
The *gruccione* or bee-eater is a beautiful little bird that migrates to Sardinia every summer. Antica Dimora del Gruccione runs workshops and seminars on food, crafts, personal development and yoga. The area around Santu Lussurgiu is of great archaeological significance and the village is well placed for day trips to the rest of the island.

The sleepy little town of Santu Lussurgiu is one the best-preserved medieval villages in Sardinia. It sits high up in the crater of an extinct volcano, surrounded by oak forests with breathtaking views of the distant sea.

A family of women run a small *albergo diffuso* called Antica Dimora del Gruccione (The Bee-eater's Old Home) from their romantic 17th-century Spanish-style courtyard mansion. Imposing wooden gates in a high stucco wall lead through an enchanting courtyard garden to a beautiful rambling house with barrel-vault ceilings, stone arches and exposed chestnut beams. The 12 clean and bright, funkily furnished single, double or treble rooms are scattered around the mansion and two nearby village houses. Alternatively, you can rent a charming self-contained apartment in the mansion's picturesque courtyard.

In the morning you awake to the lovely sound of birdsong and church bells. During the day you can explore the village and the countryside, have a cookery lesson, relax on one of the patios or in the mansion's wonderful living room, or drive to the coast which is only 35 km (22 mi) away. The evening meal here is cooked (and eaten) strictly according to the principles of the 'slow food' movement. It's a gastronomic delight and the menu consists solely of regional dishes using only locally sourced products. Dinner is the event of the day – a long, relaxed evening of food, wine and conversation, sitting around the table in the courtyard under the lemon trees.

It feels like a privilege to stay in beautiful surroundings in an authentic traditional village environment. You get a real insight into Sardinian culture and heritage and your eyes are opened to the possibility of an altogether less hectic (and perhaps healthier and happier) way of life.

Terre di l'Alcu

The Emerald Coast of northeast Sardinia used to be an exclusive haunt of the super rich. You'll still see plenty of oligarchs' yachts but every year it attracts more *hoi polloi*. If you want to be near the coast but escape the crowds and see something of the real Sardinia, it's far more relaxing to stay in the tranquil hinterland.

The Terre di l'Alcu is an organic farm only 20-minutes' drive inland from the seaside tourist town of Santa Teresa di Gallura and the white-sand beaches of the Emerald Coast. This *agriturismo* farm is off the tourist map, in the hills with a river running beside it and a superb view of the mountains. The farmhouse is newly built according to the traditional picturesque Sardinian *stazzo* design – a longhouse that blends in with the landscape, built from local materials of granite, wood and terracotta. It sits on 4 ha (10 ac) of land where the delightful owners grow vegetables and herbs, tend an orchard and vines and keep honey bees.

There are six bright, uncluttered rooms with large bathrooms. Each room has its own entrance and terrace overlooking the garden so you have complete privacy from other guests. The owners are wonderfully warm and welcoming, immediately making you feel at home – and they cook superb evening meals made entirely from local produce and using their own freshly picked fruit and vegetables. This is a heavenly place to stay, in the heart of the breathtaking Sardinian countryside where you can amble through the fields, walk along the river in perfect peace, gorge yourself on healthy organic food and at the same time enjoy all the tourist attractions of the Emerald Coast.

WHERE:
Luogosanto, Olbia-Tempio, Sardinia
COST:
Very reasonable
BEST TIME OF YEAR:
April to October (July and August can be baking hot)
DON'T MISS:
The medieval palace of Baldu; Castle of Balaiana; Arzachena Archaeological Park; a boat trip through beautiful La Maddalena archipelago, a protected geomarine park
THINGS TO DO:
Rambling; nature walks; birdwatching; cycling and mountain biking; horse riding; clay-pigeon shooting; swimming; diving; windsurfing; kite surfing; sailing; canoeing; day trips to see Roman remains
YOU SHOULD KNOW:
The farm does B&B or half board (dinner included) all year except at the height of the season in August when it is half board only. Children are given a 50 per cent discount and children under three go free.

Bella Pineta

WHERE:
Martis, Sassari, Sardinia
COST:
Budget
BEST TIME OF YEAR:
April to October. Sardinia is green and lush in the spring. By the end of the summer the landscape has been transformed into a romantic bleached wilderness with silver olive trees. In July and August it's too hot to do anything very strenuous.
DON'T MISS:
The little 18th-century church of San Pantaleo; the museum in Chiesa San Giovanni; the petrified forest of Carrucana; Badde Traes Gorge; a day trip to Capo Falcone and the paradise beach of La Pelosa 88 km (55 mi) away; the food market in the medieval quarter of Alghero 74 km (46 mi) away
THINGS TO DO:
Hiking; mountain biking; horse riding; swimming; boat trips; birdwatching; wildlife-watching; archaeological sightseeing; day trips to other historical sights
YOU SHOULD KNOW:
Breakfast is not included in the price. Bella Pineta is not suitable for children under ten and it is a non-smoking site.

Camping is meant to be romantic but more often than not it means ending up dirty and dishevelled. By taking an Emperor Tent at Bella Pineta you can camp in style and enjoy all the romance with none of the discomfort.

Two 6-m (20-ft) tents are pitched far apart under tall pine trees near a stream in 2.5 ha (6 ac) of wild grounds attached to a quaint 16th-century cottage. The tents have plenty of head room (2 m/6.5 ft high) and are properly furnished with colourful rugs and a comfortable double bed complete with sheets and pillows. Each tent sits on its own terrace and has a separate little kitchen and its own bathroom with a stylish hand basin, hot shower and dry compost toilet. At night you go to bed by the light of solar-powered and wind-up lanterns and, of course, the moon and the stars. Breakfast and an evening meal can be served to your terrace if you want and your bed is made up every day. The nearby historical village of Martis has several bars, little churches and two museums. You can eat in the restaurants in the nearby country towns of Nulvi or Chiaramonti or you can dine on excellent home-cooked meals at various *agriturismo* farms in the area.

Bella Pineta is a lovely pastoral spot, off the beaten track in the volcanic rolling hills and deep valleys of northern Sardinia where the only sounds are the chatter of crickets, gurgling water, birdsong and sheep bells. It feels as though you are miles from anywhere yet it's only 30 km (19 mi) to the north coast. This is conscience-free eco-camping with all the luxury of a country hotel.

Hotel Torre Ruesga

The Tower Hotel is situated in a wonderful natural setting in the El Alto Asón west of Bilbao, a dramatic area in Cantabria that features rugged mountains and deep wooded valleys. Rural Spain at its most bucolic is the setting for this boutique hotel, a fine early 17th-century former palace sitting on the bank of the River Asón. Upon arrival pedants will swiftly notice that it hasn't merely got the one tower enshrined in the name, but two. No matter, for the bonus dual-tower experience couldn't be bettered for those seeking a warm welcome and the most relaxing of country breaks.

The hotel has ten en-suite guest rooms and five cottage suites. Each one is different but all are spacious and beautifully decorated in a traditional style fully in keeping with the historic building. The rooms have the full complement of expected facilities including wifi, satellite TV and air conditioning. The delightful restaurant with its rough stone walls is small and intimate. The speciality is Cantabrian cuisine, which majors on simple dishes cooked with the finest local ingredients. The public rooms are both comfortable and suitably impressive, to maintain the atmosphere of gracious living at its best. The inviting sitting room has an open fireplace, and active guests will soon find and use the snooker room, sauna and gym. The Tower Hotel is also surrounded by exceptional gardens and has an open-air swimming pool.

If merely enjoying the hotel or exploring rural Cantabria isn't enough, the hotel offers specialist breaks with organized activities – golf weekends, a fine-dining experience, wine tastings or guided visits to Cantabria's natural wonders.

WHERE:
Barrio de la Barcena, Ruesga, Cantabria
COST:
Budget to reasonable (depending on season and choice of room)
BEST TIME OF YEAR:
April to October (but winters are mild if you choose an off-season break)
DON'T MISS:
The hotel's interior features wonderful 19th-century frescos by the Catalan painter León Criach.
THINGS TO DO:
Hiking; mountain biking; fishing; an expedition into Asón Collados Natural Park; a trip to the nearby Atlantic coast
YOU SHOULD KNOW:
Families are welcome. The hotel is on the outskirts of a village that rises early (and not always quietly). The best recommendation is the fact that so many Spanish people choose the Hotel Torre Ruesga for their own breaks. Cantabria is in 'Green Spain', the strip of land between the Cantabrian Sea and the Cantabrian Mountains so called because of its particularly lush vegetation.

Marques de Riscal Hotel

WHERE:
Calle Torrea, Elciego, Álava Province, Basque Country
COST:
Expensive
BEST TIME OF YEAR:
March to October
DON'T MISS:
The hotel's delicious tasting menus; a tour of the famous Marques de Riscal winery, right next door; finding out what the hotel's Spa Vinothérapie has to offer
THINGS TO DO:
Watch the Gehry building changing before your very eyes as the light plays on it; borrowing and using one of the hotel's complimentary bicycles; sightseeing around the scenic Rioja region; joining in the wine harvest (in September)
YOU SHOULD KNOW:
There are guest rooms in the spa building, so choose between staying in the Gehry architectural masterpiece and having quick 'n' easy access to the pampering programme (and great views of the main building). Children are welcomed with a kids' pack and there is a special menu on offer for them.

Anyone who has been to Bilbao's striking Guggenheim Museum (architect Frank O Gehry), and been impressed, will surely love to spend time at the Marques de Riscal Hotel in Basque Country. The name might suggest a former nobleman's grand historic home, sensitively converted to a luxury hotel – an impression underlined by its location in the ancient village of Elciego with its jumble of red-tiled roofs, soaring Church of San Andrés and blue mountains beyond – but no. The village previously best known as an important wine centre, now has another claim to fame; for the aforementioned Marques de Riscal Hotel has already attracted international renown, so extraordinary is Frank O Gehry's modernist design.

Bolted onto the side of the winery that bears the same name, the hotel looks as though some superior being has unwrapped a giant present and thrown down discarded purple and silver titanium ribbon to land among the vineyards in this unspoilt corner of rural Spain. Is this art as luxury living, or luxury living as art? It hardly matters, for you won't be coming here for the countryside views, pleasant though they are. Instead, simply staying at this 21st-century icon is a trip in itself, with the added benefit of two superb restaurants (think Michelin star plus complimentary breakfasts) and a fine wine cellar.

The hotel has 43 spacious rooms, furnished in keeping with the zany exterior and equipped with the likes of satellite TVs, DVDs, games consoles and free wifi. They have huge bathrooms and power showers. There's an indoor pool, health club, spa tub and massage facilities, steam room, library and coffee shop/café. It all adds up to an unexpected, surprising but delightful experience. And yes, it *is* art, but also luxury living – the best of both worlds!

Hotel Viura

Venture into the Sierra de Cantabria and make your way to the village of Villabuena de Álava in Rioja, there to admire the imposing 16th-century San Andrés Church. Then move your gaze sideways (as if you hadn't instantly done so) and be amazed. For there stands the Hotel Viura, surely one of the most unexpected sights to be found anywhere in rural Spain. This extraordinary architectural confection does, however, undoubtedly reflect the Spanish love of *avant garde* design when it comes to new buildings. The hotel consists of a whimsical scatter of stacked cubes with glazed fronts in brown or white, many with outside space atop the cube below, piled haphazardly as if abandoned by a bored juvenile giant.

These geometric statements add up to over 30 guest rooms, including four suites, each one provided with cutting-edge technology and featuring ultra-modern furniture in keeping with the Viura's general ambiance – although, by way of contrast, views from the windows are of unspoilt countryside and mountains. Plasma TVs are complemented by friendly touches such as minibars stocked with free bottled water and soft drinks plus (this being Rioja country) the hotel sommelier's selection of local wines. Free wifi is available throughout, the rooms have DVD players and there is a DVD library, but you definitely won't be wasting any time gazing at a screen.

Regional cuisine using local ingredients can be enjoyed either in the hotel's own restaurant or at one of the many eateries that make culinary magic in the hill towns and villages. Hurrying good food is simply not the done thing, and an accompanying bottle or two of the best Rioja also deserves due care and attention. As for the days, the hotel makes a perfect base for exploring La Rioja.

WHERE:
Calle Mayor, Villabuena de Álava, Álava Province, Basque Country
COST:
Reasonable (with good discount for advanced booking)
BEST TIME OF YEAR:
March to October
DON'T MISS:
A tone-up in the hotel gym; sampling that famous Basque staple *pintxos* (the local equivalent of *tapas*, served on a skewer, very much part of social life hereabouts) – and the hotel will give you a dozen different recipes to take home as a tasty reminder of your visit to Basque Country
THINGS TO DO:
A session at the local vinotherapy spa, close to the hotel (we're talking baths, wraps and massages rather than copious imbibing of wine); borrowing a mountain bike from the hotel and exploring the area; having a go at that traditional Basque game, *pelotta* (there's a court right beside the hotel); vineyard tours (or join the autumn grape harvest in return for a hearty lunch)
YOU SHOULD KNOW:
If you can't make your own entertainment, the hotel offers special packages such as romantic breaks, adventure experiences, food and wine tasting.

Corte de Lugás

WHERE:
La Pedrera, Santa Maria de Lugás, Lugo Province, Asturias
COST:
Budget (off season), affordable (high season) – breakfast included
BEST TIME OF YEAR:
The warmest of welcomes is guaranteed at any time.
DON'T MISS:
A generous helping of the most famous Asturian regional dish, *fabada asturiana*, a rich stew made with large white beans (*fabes*), shoulder of pork (*lacón*), black sausage *morcilla* and spicy sausage (chirizo) – ideally accompanied by a glass or two of the famous local cider
THINGS TO DO:
Visit the superb little 13th-century church of San Salvador de Valdediós at nearby Villaviciosa; chill out on Rodiles Beach, a long stretch of golden sand starting at the mouth of the Villaviciosa Estuary
YOU SHOULD KNOW:
To the owner's surprise and delight, Corte de Lugás featured in *The Daily Telegraph* list of the world's Top 50 hotels. The hotel offers bargain romantic and gastronomic breaks.

It doesn't get much more remote than the timeless farming hamlet of Lugás, near the town of Villaviciosa, at the head of an estuary on Spain's north coast. Anyone who takes the trouble to make their tortuous way to Lugás will be rewarded with the nicest of surprises – a typical Asturian 17th-century farmhouse chock-full of original character that has been sensitively converted into a comfortable hotel with seven double rooms and three superior double rooms. Additional flexibility for families (extra beds for children can be supplied) or groups of friends is provided by cabins and the self-catering Contina House. Despite the hotel's undoubted physical charms and tranquil rural location, the most impressive aspect of a visit is the genuinely enthusiastic welcome extended by the family who own the place.

The rooms have the usual facilities – en-suite bathrooms, TV/DVD, air conditioning, internet access – and the hotel's cosy stone-walled King Favila Restaurant serves excellent food crafted from local produce, with an extensive menu to work through. This is an essential part of the experience, and the appeal of the cuisine may be gauged by the number of locals who eat here. There's also a magnificent sitting room with a fireplace and high, beamed wooden ceiling in which to relax with a post-prandial coffee or liqueur.

The Corte de Lugás makes a great base from which to explore Spain's Atlantic Coast and the Picos de Europa mountains, or hike the fascinating local trail along the wooded banks of the Profundo River with its evocative succession of ruined water mills. Another popular walk with great views is the Peña Cabrera trail through Lugás to the recreational area of the same name. That said, many guests may prefer to simply stay put and enjoy the relaxing ambiance of this special little rural hotel.

Casa do Sal

WHERE:
Combarro, Pontevedra Province, Galicia
COST:
Budget (weekly rental for a couple)
BEST TIME OF YEAR:
All year round (winters are mild and tourists are notable by their absence at this time of year)
DON'T MISS:
Try sampling a (small) glass of *aguardiente*, a spirit produced only in Galicia, Distilled from grape skins, it can pack quite a kick (and the grapes themselves make a very drinkable local wine).

For a waterside break and a genuine reminder of a vanished Spain, try staying in the charming old fishing village of Combarro, packed along the shoreline on the north side of the Ria de Pontevedra, one of Galicia's three great estuaries. The village is notable for its narrow stepped streets, colourful fishing boats and extraordinary *hórreos* (stone-built storage buildings on stilts, topped with crosses called *cruzeiro* to ward off evil – witches having once been seen as a particular threat in these parts). This part of Galicia may be a top tourist destination, but nothing can spoil the historic character of the old village (and there's no law that says you have to follow the crowd

and use the popular sandy beach on the edge of town, tempting though it may be).

If you believe in that old pearl of wisdom 'location, location, location', then the Casa do Sal should be just the ticket (and you might even find that pearl by jumping straight out of the window into the water, or at least enjoy a good swim when the tide's in). This holiday rental for a couple (although there is room for three at a pinch) was the old salt warehouse used by fishermen to preserve their catch. Casa do Sal is a romantic stone-walled retreat right on the water in the heart of the historic village, now brightly converted into a cosy bijou studio apartment complete with elevated sleeping platform, miniature sitting room with TV and cooking facilities.

But cooking will probably be the last thing on your mind. The village is a historic monument, with lots of old streets to explore. There are numerous bars and restaurants with terraces, and there's nothing better than sitting outside to enjoy Galician cuisine as the evening shadows lengthen. Combarro is famous for good food and fish recipes are a speciality.

The narrow streets of Combarro are perfect for exploring.

THINGS TO DO:
An outing to interesting local towns such as Sanxenxo and Pontevedra; a bracing hike to the top of Mount Castove, with wonderful far-reaching views across the Pontevbedra and Arose Estuaries

YOU SHOULD KNOW:
No communication worries are likely here – the helpful owner speaks English, French, Spanish, Portuguese and Italian. That said, many locals still speak (and use) the ancient Galician language. If you like the sound of Combarro but Casa do Sol is too small for your family/party, there are plenty of pensions in the village that offer good accommodation at affordable prices.

Hostal l'Antic Espai

WHERE:
Gran Via de les Cortes Catalanes, Barcelona
COST:
Budget to reasonable, depending on season and choice of room
BEST TIME OF YEAR:
To see Barcelona? Catch it whenever you can!
DON'T MISS:
The optional reflexology and massage services; chilling out in the café-bar after some serious sightseeing
THINGS TO DO:
Everyone should gaze in wonder at Gaudì's towering but unfinished masterpiece, the Sagrada Familia basilica, and visit his surrealistic Parc Güell; visit the Picasso museum; wade into the traditional market in the Barceloneta (old port area, now a seriously entertaining 'have-fun' zone); eat and drink; go nightclubbing (if so inclined).
YOU SHOULD KNOW:
The TV Room shows international channels for those who worry that their home digital recorder may have malfunctioned. Parking can be arranged.

Is there a more lively city than Barcelona in all Spain? Some may say that's a trick question, as the locals would indignantly say that this fine city is in Catalonia and add that it's the liveliest city in the world. Either way, there's no denying its appeal. This place will steal your heart, and the Hostal l'Antic Espai is at the heart of the action – close to the central Plaza Catalunya and the world-famous Ramblas, one of Europe's liveliest streets, and some of the extraordinary architecture created by Anton Gaudì.

Actually, the word *hostal* is misleading, for this is no hostel but an unusual boutique hotel offering elegant accommodation in the old L'Antic Espai residence. The place is full of the owners' eclectic collection of pictures, furniture and *objets d'art*, creating the atmosphere of a much-loved home. There are ten rooms in a mix of en-suite singles, twins and doubles, all lavishly furnished in contrasting styles, many with antiques. Others are based on Catalonia's 20th-century modernist tradition with inlaid furniture reflecting naturalistic themes. Some have access to the elegant terrace, an ideal spot to take a leisurely *al fresco* breakfast. The rooms have everything from plasma TV through wifi to air conditioning, while the level of service is exceptional.

The hotel's prime location makes it an ideal base for sightseeing. It is in the bustling Eixample district, cradle of architectural modernism, where the astonishing Casa Battló and La Pedrera (Casa Milà) by Gaudì can be found in Paseo de Gracia. And it's but a short walk to one of Barcelona's signature buildings, the incredible Palau de la Música Catalana, a modernist theatre constructed in crystal and enamelled glass. For traditionalists, the place to head for is Barrio Gótico, a place of crowded medieval streets and beguiling squares. But that's but a small sample of what Barcelona has to offer – as you'll soon discover!

Les Cols Pavellons

WHERE:
Avinguda Mas Les Cols, Olot, Girona Province, Catalonia
COST:
Expensive
BEST TIME OF YEAR:
A great meal is great whenever consumed, a bizarre experience is bizarre whenever experienced.
DON'T MISS:
The *al fresco* breakfast (the table is a mat on a glass deck, so the ability to sit cross-legged helps); a day picnic – a bag packed with a blanket and lunch to eat while you're out and about

Start with a sensational Michelin-starred restaurant in a 13th-century former farmhouse outside the town of Olot, amid the dramatic landscape of Catalonia's Garrotxa Volcanic Zone National Park. The architect-designed interior of Les Cols is stunning, as are the accompanying pavilions where diners can spend the night – as indeed can any enquiring traveller seeking another unique stopping place to add to their 'stayed-in-that-amazing place' list (although in truth anyone who could resist the associated fine-dining opportunity would have to be a super-disciplined dieter, or a fast-food junkie).

The five pavilions are a wonderful expression of Spain's love affair with modern architecture, each consisting of a glass-and-steel box with glass floor that seems to make it float above the black rocks below, in tribute to the area's volcanic past. Don't expect any frills within – or indeed anything at all, apart from the mandatory minibar. The only furniture is a large, green futon. Is it actually possible to sleep in a goldfish bowl? Yes indeed – one touch on the control screen and the walls fade to black (what else?) to ensure privacy, while subtle lighting plays on the under-floor rocks to create a soothing ambiance. There's a self-flushing loo within a steel shape that grows from the glass, and anyone in need of a bath can repair to the patio, a space set aside for contemplating the meaning of life or simply plunging into the pebbled soaking pool fed with a steady trickle of hot water if Zen isn't your thing.

One thing's for sure. A night in one of these cutting-edge crystal cubes is unlike any other hotel stay ever – different, unsettling, exciting and ultimately hugely stimulating. And, once experienced, Les Cols Pavellons will most definitely go straight to the top of your 'stayed-in-that-amazing place' list.

THINGS TO DO:
For an abrupt return to normality visit Olot's Museu Comarcal de la Garrotxa (the regional museum) and check out the town's Claustres del Carme (Carmelite Cloisters) dating back to Renaissance times. Hike up one of the local (extinct) volcanoes (Montolivet, Montsacopa, Garrinada or Bisaroques) to work off any excess poundage acquired through shameless over-indulgence in fine food.

YOU SHOULD KNOW:
Bring a brolly – the Garrotxa has a famously humid climate and a local saying goes 'if it isn't raining in Olot, it isn't raining anywhere'.

Cabanes als Arbres

For those who appreciate the simple life when exploring the world (that means no electricity or running water, folks), Cabanes als Arbres will be a super-satisfying experience. It's in the Guilleries Forest, a beautifully green mountainous area in the north of Catalonia notable for elms, holm and cork oaks, chestnut trees and conifers. Nesting in the trees is certainly different (for humans), but doesn't have to involve privation. This collection of ten treehouses represents ecological tourism at its best and provides a wonderful opportunity to be at one with nature.

Each house is different, and reflects the tree in which it is constructed. But all are roundish or octagonal in shape, with wood-shingle roofs and the main tree trunk going up the middle of the inside space. Interiors are cosily furnished in

WHERE:
Carretera de Vallclara, Sant Hilari Sacalm, Girona Province, Catalonia
COST:
Budget (two or more sharing; some treehouses sleep four)
BEST TIME OF YEAR:
April to September
DON'T MISS:
The dawn chorus (no chance!); an evening meal delivered to your treehouse (for an extra charge, but well worth it)
THINGS TO DO:
Enjoy more adventure at nearby La Selva de l'Aventura (a zipline-style forest adventure park); visit the reservoir at Sau for water sports; sample the spa at the Hotel Font Vella in Sant Hilari Sacalm; walk the local 'Route of the Fountains'; explore on two wheels or two feet.
YOU SHOULD KNOW:
No children under the age of ten are allowed in the treehouses for safety reasons, but families with younger children are welcomed at the Vileta, which has five double rooms (but no en-suite bathrooms). Most treehouses have to be reached on foot.

an appropriately rustic style and each has a balcony upon which to relax and eat (you haul up the breakfast provided from the ground below in a basket, or bring your own picnic) while chilling among the foliage and enjoying distant views of the Pyrenees. Access is by ladder and bridge, which should be perfectly manageable for anyone who's reasonably fit.

Bedding, towels, drinking water, head and hand torches, candles and a paraffin heater are supplied, along with a walkie-talkie to summon assistance in the unlikely event of an emergency. When night falls, those candles and torches provide romantic illumination. A jug and basin await for old-fashioned ablutions and there is a composting toilet. If you'd like the use of hot showers, a visitor lounge, swimming pool and garden with bar service, this can be found in Masía la Vileta – an old stone-built Catalan farmhouse that has a reception area which is open 24 hours a day.

Hotel Adler

One of Madrid's grandest 19th-century buildings stands at the intersection of two great thoroughfares in the fashionable Salamanca district of the city. Once a palace, the place has now been refurbished and stands proudly as the five-star Hotel Adler, one of Madrid's newest. The historic exterior is mirrored by a gracious atmosphere within for, despite the inclusion of every modern convenience you could possibly need and some cutting-edge design, every care to preserve the hotel's timeless charm was taken during the extensive make-over.

The public areas are certainly impressive, and there are 45 beautifully furnished and inviting guest rooms and junior suites from which to choose. Anyone looking for an elegant and refined base from which to explore the delights of a great capital city will be delighted by the spacious accommodation. All rooms are en suite, with both bath and shower, plus all the expected in-room luxury touches from large flat-screen satellite TV with DVD player through air conditioning and an in-room safe for valuables, to free wifi. If there are any better hotel bathrooms in all Madrid they're decidedly hard to find, and the level of service from the dedicated staff is outstanding – as rather suggested by the high percentage of 'nothing-but-the-best' business people who stay at the Adler on expenses. For anyone thinking of drinking/eating in, there is a bar and excellent restaurant specializing in Mediterranean cuisine, although eating out can be a most rewarding gastronomic voyage of discovery in this cosmopolitan city.

Is this the most stylish, fashionable and sophisticated boutique hotel in Madrid? The management certainly thinks so, and after sampling the Adler's special experience you may well agree.

WHERE:
Velázquez and Goya Streets, Madrid
COST:
Reasonable to expensive (but packages are available)
BEST TIME OF YEAR:
Any time
DON'T MISS:
A pre-sightseeing workout at the hotel's fitness centre (perhaps after a leisurely breakfast in the restaurant)
THINGS TO DO:
Madrid, Madrid and Madrid. In the unlikely event that you need help in making a start, try the wonderful green spaces of Retiro Park, power shopping in Serrano Street or culture in the 'Golden Triangle of Art' (the world-famous Prada, Reina Sofía Centre and the Thyssen-Bornemisza Collection).
YOU SHOULD KNOW:
Valet parking is available at a reasonable fee. Breakfast is not included in the room price. A babysitting service is available and baby cots can be supplied on request. Some of Madrid's most famous tourist attractions are actually a brisk walk away.

Hotel Marquis de Villena

WHERE:
Avenida Amigos de los Castillos, Alarcón, Cuenca Province, Castile-La Mancha
COST:
Reasonable/expensive for basic double room/superior double room or suite
BEST TIME OF YEAR:
Any time
DON'T MISS:
The four historic churches within easy strolling distance of the castle; local delicacies including *morteruelos* (a hot meat pâté), *cordero en caldereta* (lamb stew) and *suspiros* (sweet almond sauces); views from the top of the castle, and nearby Alarconcillos Tower
THINGS TO DO:
The Júcar River feeds the huge Alarcón Reservoir, near to the hotel, for fishing and water sports; the hotel has a tour desk to arrange outings or activities to keep you busy; visit the Cassasimarro craftsmen who specialize in handmade guitars, lutes and bandurrias.
YOU SHOULD KNOW:
The castle offers lively Young Getaway promotions for under 35s (no boring oldies), and also (separate!) refined Golden Days promotions for over-55s (no noisy young revellers). The decor has a military theme in keeping with the castle's origins (it was captured by King Alfonso VIII from the Moors in the 12th century).

Parador de Alarcón is an 8th-century Moorish castle that sits impressively next to the Júcar River to the southeast of Madrid. The four-square battlemented *parador* (state-run hotel) with its fortified gateway and tower is located on a promontory above the medieval village whose name it bears (which came first, chicken or egg, castle or village?). The place is now home to the four-star Hotel Marquis de Villena, often referred to simply as Parador de Alarcón. This castle-cum-hotel has an historic feel, with wooden beams and traditional furnishings complementing stone walls – although the interior has been cleverly designed to introduce the sort of modern features expected by today's travellers and tourists, albeit without unduly compromising the original character. This was once the home of the Marquis de Villena, and guests can still see fine examples of the works of painters such as Tapies, Redondela, Sempere, Amadeo Gabino, Alvaro Delgado, Martinez Novillo and Menchu Gal.

The 14 guest rooms at the Parador de Alarcón are spacious and comfortable, decorated with warm colours and featuring luxurious fabrics. All have a private en-suite bathroom, air conditioning and a satellite TV/DVD player. There is 24-hour reception, a lift giving access to upper floors and guest parking on site. The castle has a café and bar, while the restaurant offers traditional local food, using seasonal ingredients. There is also a good selection of fine Spanish wine and, should you fancy a change of menu, there are several good restaurants in the village.

Staying at the Hotel Marquis de Villena is a pleasure *per se*, but the castle also makes a great base for sallying forth to explore the countryside and local attractions such as Embalse de Alarcón, Belmonte and Ciudad Encantada.

Parador de Zafra

WHERE:
Plaza Corazón de María, Zafra, Badajoz Province, Extremadura
COST:
Budget to reasonable, depending on room and season
BEST TIME OF YEAR:
Any time (but be aware that winters can be very cold and midsummers very hot)

Anyone who fancies being King of the Castle (or more accurately *Duke* of the Castle) for a night or two will be suitably ennobled by the state-run Parador de Zafra in Extremadura (sometimes known more formally as Parador Duque De Feria). This majestic castle, dating back to the 15th century, was indeed once the residence of the Dukes of Feria. The spectacular stone facade with its nine towers serves as a reminder of former defensive duties, and the beautifully maintained interior with its wrought-iron detailing, high ceilings and historic furnishings would still be familiar to long-ago guests such as the feared conquistador Hernan Cortes, who stayed awhile in the early 16th century before laying waste to the New World.

DON'T MISS:
Making the difficult choice from the hotel restaurant's extensive menu that features regional cuisine, before enjoying the chosen meal (hint: the lamb stew is divine)

THINGS TO DO:
Stroll straight out of the castle into Zafra's historic centre and visit the town churches, Santa Clara Convent, two impressive squares and the Palace of the Marqués de Solanda (not forgetting the great *tapas* bars). Hire a bike from the hotel and do some exploring; go horse riding; drive the scenic Ducado de Feria route; visit the Roman remains at Merido (and the Museo Romano).

YOU SHOULD KNOW:
Baby cots are supplied on request and most rooms will accommodate an extra bed for a youngster (under 12s stay free of charge).

Happily for today's guests, a few improvements have been made since then. In fact, the Hammer of the Incas would have been amazed, and probably settled in far too comfortably to even think about heading off for a little overseas conquest. The four-star Parador de Zafra has 50 rooms, consisting of a single, doubles, suites and two with disabled access. All the rooms have a private en-suite bathroom, telephone, satellite TV, safe and minibar. There is central heating and air conditioning throughout, a lift, free wifi, bar, restaurant, central courtyard with arched arcade and tranquil garden with swimming pool. This confident hotel has a noble past and notable features include a majestic lounge with open fireplace and corridors lined with portraits, which all help to tell the story of this grand castle's noble history.

It all contributes (my lords and ladies of the road) to that rather special aristocratic feeling, which can make a stay at this fine fortress seem so memorable.

WHERE:
Alájar, Huelva, Andalucia
COST:
Very Reasonable for two people (budget for more than two)
BEST TIME OF YEAR:
It's open throughout the year. Under-floor heating and a hearth make it perfectly feasible to stay in the colder months of November to March. From mid June to the end of August it can be too hot for very much activity.
DON'T MISS:
A wonderful meal at El Padrino, a local restaurant only open on Fridays; La Peña de Arias Montano – clamber up the hill to the hermitage on the rocky outcrop towering over Alájar and admire the stupendous view; Gruta de las Maravillas – dramatic limestone caves with underground lakes; the 13th-century castle at Cortegana; sampling the world-famous regional *jamón* (dry-cured ham) and sherries in the town of Jabugo

Molino Río Alájar

The rugged wooded hills, high mountains and little white villages of Andalucia are a world apart from the sprawling coastal developments and crowded beaches of southern Spain. Molino Río Alájar is a restored watermill deep in the hills of the Sierra de Aracena, surrounded by wild woods of chestnut and cork oak trees. The Dutch owners have built six charming hillside guest *casitas* (traditional cottages) from local materials of chestnut, sandstone and terracotta. Standing in complete harmony with the surrounding landscape, the *casitas* are already full of character, with rustic furnishings, tiled floors, wooden timbers, furnished patios with stunning views for outdoor eating and well-equipped, spacious kitchens.

There's a lovely 11-m (36-ft) swimming pool among the oak trees and a beautifully maintained tennis court. Kids can roam in the woods, climb trees, feed the pigs and play with the friendly dogs. You can pick your fruit and vegetables straight from the orchard and kitchen garden or, should you want to eat out, Alájar – one of the region's prettiest villages with little white houses and cobbled streets – is only a 15-minute walk away and it has several excellent *tapas* bars and restaurants.

Each *casita* is completely secluded, screened by trees and greenery. However, if you feel like mingling with the friendly owners and other guests, there's a communal living room and kitchen in the millhouse, with a stone barbecue on the terrace, which you are welcome to use. The mill is on the ancient network of cobbled drovers' paths that runs through Andalucia and you step out of your front door straight into the countryside. Molino Río Alájar is a tranquil sylvan paradise in the heart of hidden Spain – a perfect place for walkers and lovers of the countryside.

THINGS TO DO:
Hiking; cycling; horse riding; donkey trekking; birdwatching; nature walks; *pétanque*; table tennis; table football; flamenco guitar lessons; Spanish lessons; having tennis coaching; visiting local villages and sights
YOU SHOULD KNOW:
There is free wifi in public rooms and a TV, DVD/CD player and phone in each *casita*. Bikes can be hired, and a babysitting and shopping service is provided. Larger cottages sleep up to six and are ideal for a family of four. You'll need to hire a car – it's a 90-minute drive from Seville airport.

Cuevas el Abanico

Once upon a time describing someone as a 'troglodyte' might have caused offence but, in the context of Spanish holidays, underground living bears no stigma – quite the reverse, with uprated cave accommodation eagerly sought. It's actually been a time-honoured Spanish way of life, particularly in the south where those rock walls ensure a constant temperature that creates a cool environment during hot summers and a warm one during chilly winters. Nowadays, these former dwellings (often forcibly cleared by the authorities as recently as the 1960s) have become sought-after (and different) places to stay, suitably improved with the sort of home comforts essential to modern life as we prefer it.

One such establishment is Cuevas el Abanico, which has an eye-popping location in Granada itself – its garden terrace overlooks the Alhambra Palace. This is the Sacromonte district, where Roman mines became Christian catacombs, and the flamenco-loving Gitano people established a lively cave-dwelling community in the 19th century. Now, the restored Abanico Caves offer cheerful rustic decor with white-washed walls, comfortable beds, modern bathrooms and kitchenettes featuring microwave, fridge and washing machine. It's all a far cry from the basic troglodyting of times past, although the *frisson* of subterranean dwelling remains. This is definitely not a hotel, despite the modern trimmings, but definitely an authentic cave complex, complete with arched ceilings and intriguing passageways.

The surprise and delight upon arrival is enhanced by the contrast between the entrance – a classic Spanish white-washed facade complete with tiled roof and wrought ironwork at door and windows, off a narrow cobbled lane – and the labyrinth within. The irregularity of the caves contributes to their charm, but they also offer clean, modern accommodation.

WHERE:
Verea de Enmedio, Granada, Andalucia
COST:
Reasonable (for at least two sharing)
BEST TIME OF YEAR:
Any time (off-season bookings are easier to secure)
DON'T MISS:
Granada's stunning heritage sights (as if you could!)
THINGS TO DO:
Visit the adjacent Sacromonte Cave Museum; get with the local vibe at one of the flamenco bars in various nearby caves; stroll through Granada's historic Albayzin district (overlooked by the caves) and enjoy the narrow medieval streets of the former Moorish quarter.
YOU SHOULD KNOW:
Early booking is essential – these caves are hugely popular with holidaymakers and are always reserved well in advance (book direct with the venue). Private parking (at a reasonable daily cost) is available nearby. Children under three stay free of charge but there is a supplement for older children who require an extra bed (and there's a maximum of one per room).

Cortijo del Marqués

WHERE:
Camino del Marqués, Albolote, Granada Province, Andalucia
COST:
Budget
BEST TIME OF YEAR:
March to October offers the best of the weather (but sitting in front of a roaring log fire on a winter's evening is no hardship).
DON'T MISS:
A hearty meal in the restaurant; a moment of peaceful reflection in the wonderful private chapel, built in 1878
THINGS TO DO:
Simply enjoy the peace and quiet of this beautiful building and the Spanish countryside; cycle or hike locally (bike rental available at the manor); sally forth to explore Granada's striking countryside and historic monuments (starting with the awesome Alhambra, naturally)
YOU SHOULD KNOW:
Most visitors simply find the manor chapel interesting. In fact, it actually sees several weddings each year, with the happy couple and their guests accommodated in the big house. The manor does cater for guests with mobility problems.

For an authentic flavour of traditional Andalucian rural life (which happens to be available conveniently close to Granada and the A-44 motorway for ease of access), look no further than Cortijo del Marqués. This fine old restored *cortijo* (manor house) is located between the Pozeuelo and Arana mountains, set amid olive groves and surrounded by fields of sunflowers and wheat. Happily, 'traditional' does not mean 'basic' when it comes to the facilities. The stone-built Marqués does have wonderfully authentic charisma, and the guest rooms have pleasing rustic decor, with wooden or tiled floors and wooden beams. But every one of those spacious rooms has central heating, a fan, private bathroom with a bathrobe and hairdryer provided, and also a seating area. There is free wifi in public areas.

The rooms are all different and with names such as Tower, Pigeon Loft, Granary, Cistern, Church, Lookout and Carpenter's, the character of the spotless accommodation is easy to imagine – and the *actualité* doesn't disappoint. In addition there is a detached cottage that is perfect for families or two couples. Outside, the set-up is excellent, especially for families with kids. The manor house has a terrace with beautiful views of the surrounding countryside, while garden patios provide ideal spots in which to soak up the sun. Children can play safely in the walled garden and an outdoor swimming pool (protected from unauthorized junior incursion by a gate) perfectly complements those hot summer days.

The management cannily proclaim that Cortijo del Marqués is Granada's best-kept secret, but will probably be less than heartbroken to discover that their secret's out.

Posada la Plaza

Canillas de Albeida

The traditional mountain village of Canillas de Albeida may be in Malaga province, but couldn't be more different from coastal package-holiday central if it tried. This is one of the so-called white villages in the Axarquia region of Andalucia, on the slopes of the Sierra de Tejeda and Almijara Mountains Natural Park with spectacular panoramic views across the valley below to the coast. The Posada la Plaza is a delightful rural inn with 16th-century origins in the village centre. Although recently restored, the interior retains much of its traditional charm, with decor that has an appropriate hint of Moorish influence, featuring chestnut-beamed ceilings and much decorative wrought ironwork inside (beds and light fittings) and out (balconies overlooking the pedestrianized village square with its grand fountain).

Initial impressions of the white-painted *posada* can be misleading. The modernization has introduced excellent facilities that you might not expect to find in a rural Spanish village hotel. Each of the nine guest rooms (standard, superior or suite) has a bathroom with all the trimmings, air conditioning for hot summer days and heating for chilly mountain nights, satellite TV and wifi. Posada la Plaza has its own restaurant and honesty bar, an indoor residents' lounge, an outdoor seating area with great views to the Natural Park and – surprise! – a rooftop terrace with enclosed Jacuzzi, which is part of an intimate spa.

This is a wonderful base for those who like to fill their lungs with bracing mountain air and it's a pleasure to wander through fields full of rosemary and lavender or explore the pine woods (make the effort to get to the top of La Maroma, the highest peak in the Sierra Tejeda, and be rewarded with truly awe-inspiring views). And Posada la Plaza is equally good for those who want to whizz down to sample those Costa del Sol seaside pleasures.

WHERE:
Canillas de Albeida, Malaga Province, Andalucia
COST:
Budget to reasonable (seasonal tariff)
BEST TIME OF YEAR:
April to October
DON'T MISS:
Eating an *al fresco* meal at the sun-shaded tables in the village square, or simply nursing a cold drink as you watch the locals going about their leisurely business; taking a steam bath
THINGS TO DO:
This is hiking country, but also heaven for (fit) mountain bikers (yup, real mountains), while those who prefer to let something else do the hard work can opt for horse riding. The village has a municipal swimming pool and tennis court. *Bon viveurs* can descend into the valley for wine tastings or to sample the cuisine at several restaurants in Canillas de Albeida itself.
YOU SHOULD KNOW:
The right choice for families is a suite that sleeps two adults and two children. Toddlers are free of charge and older children attract but a modest supplement for the extra bed.

Kaliyoga

WHERE:
Orgiva, near Granada, Andalucia
COST:
Reasonable (per person, per night)
BEST TIME OF YEAR:
There are retreats all year round.
DON'T MISS:
The cookery workshop on Wednesday evenings (if you don't want to cook, just eat!); plundering the book exchange
THINGS TO DO:
Do what you've come to do. If you want to take time out to see the sights, this is not the place for you, although many (suitably energized) participants do stay at a pension in the local small town of Orgiva so that they can spend time exploring the dramatic landscape before or after their retreat at Kaliyoga.
YOU SHOULD KNOW:
English is the language of choice. Meals are included. Retreats begin on Sundays and end on Saturdays. Holistic therapies are optional and cost extra, so bring some folding money to pay the therapists direct if you intend to give the (highly recommended) holistic therapy team a go. Retreats are not suitable for children under the age of 12.

Away from the 'We're off to sunny Spain' coastal strip, Andalucia has some stunning unspoilt scenery. It isn't hard to find a little place in the hills and recharge the batteries in rural splendour. But for those who find merely getting away from it all is not enough, this stunning region presents a more proactive option. Kaliyoga offers week-long well-being retreats designed to refresh the body and lift the soul, with the aim of encouraging a complete mental and physical detox .

As the name suggests, the experience revolves around yoga, with the most popular option being the centre's Dynamic Yoga Retreat. But within a yoga framework there are a number of choices. Special weeks include Yoga and Mountain Hiking, Superfood Cleanse, Juice Fasting Detox and Yoga at Christmas or Easter. The sun always seems to shine in Andalucia and the welcome at Kaliyoga matches its warmth. Every effort is made to create a home-from-home atmosphere. The accommodation is comfortable, ranging from singles with a separate bathroom to large en-suite doubles, all with crisp linen and climate control. For true communers with nature, there are *tipis* (teepees).

And if it all sounds a bit like working hard for your relaxing break, it isn't. There's a definite accent on having fun even as you regenerate, and there's plenty of time for hitting the sauna or hot tub, sunbathing around the oval pool, hanging about in a hammock and laughing with like-minded guests over a leisurely *al fresco* meal as *cicadas* call and night falls in the rolling green Andalucian hills. For those who like to do a bit extra, afternoons can be taken up with the likes of horse riding and hiking. How will you feel at the end of the week? Like a million dollars!

Casa la Trancada

The tiny, low-lying island of Isla de Tabarca is the largest of a small archipelago off the coast of Alicante. It is just under 2 km (1 mi) long and there are only around 100 permanent residents, who make their living out of fishing and tourism. The island has a romantic history; it was a hideout for Berber pirates who used to raid the Costa Blanca until 18th-century King Carlos III ordered a fortress town to be built and forcibly settled some Genoese fishermen and their families here.

Until recently there was no overnight accommodation on Tabarca but now you can stay in a quaint 18th-century fisherman's house in the island village of San Pedro. The house has been converted into a charming little hotel and the facade retains its original picturesque appearance, with cheerful Mediterranean-blue shutters. The inside has been carefully converted to preserve much of the original character. There are just four snug air-conditioned rooms with bathrooms, minimally furnished but with extremely comfortable beds. The hotel is scrupulously clean and has a lovely atmosphere – the hospitable owners speak no English but are all smiles and serve a fabulous breakfast spread.

The waters around Tabarca have been designated a marine reserve. The unpolluted sea, little coves, rocky beaches and tidal pools are a paradise for marine life, so it's a wonderful place for exploring the undersea world, sunbathing and eating fish straight out of the sea. Outside the height of the tourist season there is hardly anyone here and you can enjoy the crystal-clear waters and your fisherman's cottage in perfect peace.

WHERE:
Isla de Tabarca, Alicante, Costa Blanca
COST:
Reasonable
BEST TIME OF YEAR:
April to June and September to October are good choices. In July and August the island tends to be packed with day trippers – there can be as many as 3,000 every day.
DON'T MISS:
The town walls and 18th-century ruins; the Church of San Pedro y San Pablo; the Tower of San José; the archaeological museum in the 16th-century castle fortress of Santa Pola on the mainland; flamingoes on the salt flats Salinas de Santa Pola
THINGS TO DO:
Swimming; snorkelling; scuba diving (with permit); fishing (with permit); sunbathing on the long sandy beach; eating freshly caught fish in the island's restaurants
YOU SHOULD KNOW:
It takes an hour by boat to get to Tabarca from Alicante and half an hour from Santa Pola (there are also boats from Guardamar del Segura or Torrevieja). Tabarca is a protected marine area so fishing or scuba diving without a permit is prohibited (and permits must be arranged in Alicante). No cars are allowed on the island. The island village of San Pedro y San Pablo is one of the best examples of old military architecture in Spain.

Cas Gasi

WHERE:
Camino Viejo de Sant Mateu, Santa Gertrudis, Ibiza
COST:
Expensive
BEST TIME OF YEAR:
From April to October (this is an especially welcome retreat in the high season party months of July and August, when the island is invaded by noisy clubbers)
DON'T MISS:
Wandering around the hippy village of Santa Gertrudis; Dalt Vila – the fortified old quarter of Ibiza; the hippy street market in Ibiza town; views from the cliffs at Es Cubells; the celebrity beach of Las Salinas
THINGS TO DO:
Swimming; diving; sailing; boating; hot-air ballooning; cycling and mountain biking; horse riding; walking; tennis; golf; exploring the island by car; going to the beach
YOU SHOULD KNOW:
Cas Gasi is listed by *Tatler* magazine among the 101 Best Hotels in the World. Robert de Niro and Kate Moss have been among the celebrity guests. You can hire bicycles and speed boats, and charter the hotel's yacht.

Even the most dedicated clubber is likely to suffer from burn out on the party island of Ibiza. Cas Gasi is the place to counterbalance the exhaustion from too many late nights. In the middle of the island, a world away from the coastal club scene, this exclusive family-run hotel is a beautifully restored 19th-century *finca* (farmhouse) with an enchanting garden – a profusion of colourful flowers amid wild pine, almond and fig trees. The *finca* is in an idyllic hill-top setting, attached to a 4-ha (10-ac) organic farm that has vegetable beds and orchards of citrus, apricot, cherry and pomegranate tumbling down the hillside terraces, while the surrounding hills are clothed in olive trees.

There are ten air-conditioned rooms of various sizes plus two suites, all with beamed ceilings and tiled floors, individually furnished in bohemian-chic style with fine fabrics and vases of fresh-cut flowers. You can chill out on the terrace or shaded porch, or relax in the airy living room, browsing through the library of books and DVDs, with a fresh organic juice or Cas Gasi cocktail from the bar. The restaurant serves simple but sublime Mediterranean food using seasonal organic fruit and vegetables grown on the estate, fresh eggs from the farm's chickens, hand-pressed olive oil, cheese from neighbouring farms and line-caught local fish.

The hotel has an excellent wellness centre with a gym and sauna. It offers massage and beauty treatments, yoga or Pilates sessions and workouts. There's a choice of two outdoor pools, one of them a counter-current training pool. Only 12 km (7.5 mi) from the main beaches, Cas Gasi is a blissful, exclusive sanctuary – a perfect place for romance and self-indulgence.

Petit Hotel

Majorca has an unfortunate reputation as a cheap package-tour destination crammed with ugly hotel complexes, but the rugged northwest of the island is completely unspoilt by tourism, a breathtakingly beautiful region of wild pine-clad mountains and lush valleys. Fornalutx is a picture-postcard village of quaint green-shuttered stone houses with red-tiled roofs. High up in the fertile Sóller valley, 8 km (5 mi) from the sea, the village is surrounded by orange groves and has beautiful mountain views.

Tucked away down a narrow side street, the Petit Hotel was once a convent and the building emanates a welcoming aura of restorative calm. The airy rooms have beamed ceilings and shuttered windows and are as neat as a new pin, with immaculate white curtains and bedspreads. The breakfasts are exceptionally good – a sensational spread of hams and cheeses, bread still warm from the oven, eggs laid by the village hens, and a basket of local oranges for you to squeeze your own juice. You are made to feel completely at home in the public rooms and can pour yourself a drink from the honesty bar or use the sauna.

The tranquil hotel garden is a terraced orange grove with a glorious outlook on the mountains. You can all too easily while the day away in a hammock under the orange trees, reading, having a dip in the pool, snoozing or just gazing meditatively at the view and breathing citrus-scented mountain air. Le Petit Hotel is a real gem and a recuperative haven for jaded spirits or for anyone who wants a quiet walking holiday. It's rare to stumble across such simple comfort and unpretentious charm.

WHERE:
Fornalutx, Majorca
COST:
Reasonable
BEST TIME OF YEAR:
Go between March and May for the orange and almond blossom or between September and October for mountain hikes. Many of the island's amenities are closed between November and February.

DON'T MISS:
The thrilling narrow-gauge railway journey through the mountains from Palma to Sóller – the train goes through 13 tunnels; a walk to the Mirador de ses Barques for spectacular views of the Sóller valley all the way to the sea; the scenic coast road between Port d'Andratx and Sóller; Cap Gros lighthouse; the artists' village of Deia, where writer Robert Graves lived

THINGS TO DO:
Hiking; mountain biking; walking; swimming and water sports on the beaches at Puerto de Sóller; exploring the island by car or bike; lazing under the orange trees in the hotel garden
YOU SHOULD KNOW:
Petit Hotel provides no meals except breakfast. There are several bars and restaurants in and around Fornalutx and more in Sóller, 3.5 km (2 mi) away.

WHERE:
Rua 1 de Dezembro, Lisbon
COST:
It's expensive but still good value for a luxury inner-city hotel, especially one with such style – and there are plenty of special offers which help to reduce the price.
BEST TIME OF YEAR:
Lisbon is a year-round destination but it's as well to avoid mid June to the end of August when it is uncomfortably hot for city sightseeing.
DON'T MISS:
Using the Santa Justa street elevator to get up and down hill; listening to *fado* singers; the wondrous view from the Miradouro de Sao Pedro de Alcantara; an Italian ice cream at Santini – better than any in Italy; taking the route 28 tram ride; a day trip to the World Heritage town of Sintra 30 km (19 mi) away.

Avenida Palace

The Avenida Palace stands in the centre of Lisbon, a monument to Beaux-Arts architecture. It first opened in 1892 and soon acquired a reputation as one of the best hotels in Europe for its glamour, service and location. Nothing has changed. The Avenida Palace is still going strong, always keeping up with the times. During a century of revolutions and wars, its public rooms have been frequented by political dissidents, schemers and spies – many a plot has been hatched here – and as you go through the main door into the huge marble-floored atrium, you cannot help but be bowled over not only by the elegant grandeur of the decor but also by the polite and discreet service.

The period furnishings make you feel you've stepped back a century. The 82 luxurious, high-ceilinged rooms have glamorous black, golden-cream or white marble bathrooms and are completely soundproofed – even though you're in the heart of the city, you won't be disturbed by traffic noise. Breakfast is served in the palatial ballroom. The hotel bar is just like a Victorian pub, all mahogany, red leather stools and crimson velvet drapes, with a live pianist tinkling away and there's also an old-fashioned library, tea lounge and even a special smoking room.

The service is superb, of a sort you don't expect nowadays – courteous, charming and deferential without being remotely unctuous – and the concierge will fix absolutely anything for you. The hotel is in a fantastic and convenient location, right next to Lisbon's central station and within walking distance of the main sights and shopping streets. The Avenida Palace is the *grande dame* among Europe's historic old hotels. It's not often that one comes across such classy accommodation.

THINGS TO DO:
Visiting historical sites, museums, galleries and art exhibitions; discovering the city on foot; taking a boat trip on the River Tagus; exploring parks and botanical gardens; relaxing in coffee shops and local restaurants; shopping

YOU SHOULD KNOW:
The Avenida Palace was designed by distinguished Portuguese architect José Luis Monteiro who trained at the Ecole des Beaux-Arts in Paris and who was also responsible for the design of Rossio Railway Station next door to the hotel. Both buildings are outstanding examples of the Parisian neoclassical architectural movement.

Quinta da Cumieira

Minho is a beautiful, green region of northwest Portugal encompassing old manors, farm cottages and medieval hamlets dotted around the fertile valleys and rugged granite hills which are covered in cedar and chestnut forests. There are far fewer tourists here than in the south and the province is still firmly rooted in its traditional livelihood of subsistence farming. Sheep graze on hillside pastures and the valleys are a patchwork of smallholdings with hedges of tall grapevines separating each little field or meadow.

In the depths of this beautiful countryside, the owners of a 17th-century farmhouse have pitched two huge 45 sq m (485 sq ft) luxury tents in their vineyard. With plenty of headroom and lots of space to move around, each tent can easily accommodate up to four people. They are furnished with very comfortable twin beds, top-drawer bed linen, a sleeping couch, sitting area, minibar and coffee machine. But what really makes them so very special is that the bathroom, with its proper porcelain fittings, is actually inside the tent. And to cap it all, you are supplied with fluffy towels, bathrobes, slippers and complimentary shower products. Pretty glamorous for a camping holiday!

The setting is idyllic, surrounded as it is by 3 ha (7.5 ac) of vineyards and orchards. There is also a 15-m (50-ft) terraced swimming pool among the vines and a trout-fishing river running past. A general store and a couple of cafés are nearby in the hamlet of Cumieira and the country town of Cabeceiras de Basto is only ten minutes' drive away. It's hard to imagine camping more comfortable than this; Quinta da Cumieira is rural bliss.

WHERE:
Cumieira, Cabeceiras de Basto, Minho

COST:
Budget

BEST TIME OF YEAR:
June to September

DON'T MISS:
The extraordinarily quaint ancient village of Agra; the Travassos Museo do Ouro, gold-filigree museum and workshops; tasting *aguardente*, a spirit made from fermented grapeskins; the picturesque medieval bridge and chapel at Vieira do Minho; the World Heritage town of Guimarães; the baroque churches and 18th-century houses in Braga

THINGS TO DO:
Hiking; mountain biking; trout fishing; going to the beach (a 50-minute drive); wine tasting in the *quintas* on the *vinho verde* wine route; day trips to cities and towns

YOU SHOULD KNOW:
Quinta da Cumieira is under an hour's drive from the World Heritage city of Porto and not far from the Spanish border. It takes around two-and-a-half hours to drive to the World Heritage pilgrimage site of Santiago de Compostela in Galicia.

Grande Hotel do Porto

WHERE:
Rua de Santa Catarina, Porto
COST:
Reasonable
BEST TIME OF YEAR:
May to September
DON'T MISS:
Cafe Majestic, a renowned Art Deco café where artists, intellectuals and political activists used to hang out; Bolhão Market – a vibrant covered market that sells everything under the sun; a boat trip up the River Douro; having a glass of port in Livrario Lello, an old bookshop famous for its beautiful interior; Fundacao de Serralves – modern art museum and exhibition centre; visiting Porto's port wine cellars
THINGS TO DO:
Seeing the World Heritage sights; exploring the labyrinthine streets; port-wine tasting; nightlife in the Ribeira district; shopping
YOU SHOULD KNOW:
There is wifi in all the public areas of the hotel and one of the rooms has been specially adapted for use by guests with disabilities. Edward VIII, Duke of Windsor is said to have stayed at the Grande – unfortunately the hotel register with his signature has been lost.

Rather like the city itself, the Grande is a magnificent hotchpotch of styles and eras. Opened in 1880, it is among the oldest hotels in Porto and is full of character. The sandstone mansion with its wrought-iron balustrades has a beautiful 19th-century facade and the lobby is a grand *fin de siècle* set piece – imposing russet-coloured marble columns, plush furnishings in warm gold and apricot tones, random collections of ornaments, and a stairwell lined with old photographs of famous guests.

After the impressive entrance, the rooms come as something of a shock. They're high-ceilinged but small, with modern, minimalist furnishings – scrupulously clean and perfectly comfortable, but just not at all what you were expecting. Yet go down to the huge, airy dining hall and your perception will immediately be set to rights as you are served a fabulous meal under an elaborately moulded ceiling and crystal chandeliers. Slowly, very slowly, it dawns on you that the Grande is a *kitsch* masterpiece, decorated with an idiosyncratic ebullience that has a charming quirkiness and a wonderful sense of fun about it.

The bar is a shrine to the British royal family. It has funky pink lighting and a silver brocade sofa with crown-embroidered scatter cushions. The silver-papered wall is covered with photographs of pre-war royals and a large Andy Warhol-imitation pink multi-print of the young Queen Elizabeth II hangs in pride of place. A nightcap or afternoon tea here is positively surreal.

The Grande is superbly located right in the city centre and the hard-working, enthusiastic hotel staff ensure that you enjoy every minute of your stay. This is one of a kind, a true reflection of the World Heritage city of Porto.

The beautiful city of Porto

Aquapura

Once a traditional 19th-century manor house with outbuildings and stunning views along the World Heritage Douro Valley, with its broad river and terraced hillside vineyards, Aquapura has been reinvented as a sprawling but stylish spa hotel offering an astonishing interior. It's moody, cutting-edge design was created by Portugal's most innovative architects and designers.

This waterside boutique hotel offers a choice of 50 guest rooms, including nine suites, and 21 self-catering villas. The accommodation has the usual essentials – flat-screen TVs and DVD/CD players, air conditioning and minibar with free bottled water – and there's free wifi throughout the complex. The exceptional facilities are complemented by attentive staff who make sure that guests feel at home throughout their stay.

This is a place in which to enjoy the ultimate in self-indulgent relaxation. The sensational subterranean spa includes an indoor hydrotherapy pool complemented by heated water beds, herbal sauna, laconium and a steam room. Assorted massage techniques are a speciality and there is a choice of detox programmes to try, including anti-ageing and keeping trim. The stunning outlook from the heated outdoor pool makes it ideal for lazy lounging. It is surrounded by olive trees and a clematis- and honeysuckle-clad stone wall that turns the air heavy with scent. Needless to say, the hotel's two fine-dining restaurants offer superb wine lists, with the emphasis on the very best from Douro's own vineyards.

Families are very welcome; baby cots are provided free and babysitting can be booked. But note that there are extra charges for beds put into parental rooms for older kids. There's also a children's menu in one of the restaurants. Aquapura's two- or three-bedroom villas are the best choice for families, though, as they include kitchens and private pools.

WHERE:
Quinta do Vale Abraão, Samodães, near Lamego, Norte Region

COST:
Reasonable (and there are various tempting packages on offer) to expensive, depending on room/suite and season

BEST TIME OF YEAR:
Actually, with a spa like that you don't even need to know what the weather's like outside.

DON'T MISS:
Riverside woodland walks around the grounds; a workout in the gym; eating and drinking your fill on the dining patio in the charming old stone courtyard; a seriously satisfying encounter with the spa

THINGS TO DO:
River-based water sports; a wine-tasting tour of the neighbouring *quintas*; tennis on the hotel courts; a river tour organized by the hotel; exploring historic Lamego town

YOU SHOULD KNOW:
Couples intent on gazing into each other's eyes in rapt and undisturbed mutual contemplation should avoid August, when there are lots of boisterous children about the place.

Canvas Moon

WHERE:
Near Tábua, Coimbra District, Centro Region
COST:
Budget (two sharing)
BEST TIME OF YEAR:
The tents are pitched from April to September.
DON'T MISS:
A game of badminton or *boules* in the cool of the evening (challenge the other tent and make it a tournament!)
THINGS TO DO:
Water sports on the nearby Aguieira Reservoir, including swimming, canoeing and fishing; mountain hiking and biking; climbing; wildlife-watching (try to spot the pine martens); a day trip to Figuera De Foz for beach time (and/or surfing/bodyboarding) – it's an hour by car; skiing in winter (by arrangement)
YOU SHOULD KNOW:
For families with a couple of kids the Barraco (a refurbished barn) provides equally good accommodation. Bring your own provisions, including eco-friendly toiletries, as this is a self-catering break. A basic welcome pack is provided, but after that you need to organize your own supplies.

Let's go glamping! Yes, luxurious tent dwelling is very definitely roof of the day (and night) at the Canvas Moon eco-retreat. It's a great place to spend a rewarding break, at one with nature and appreciating the comforting certainty that not one volt of generated electricity will be used, nor one drop of water wasted. The surroundings – Canvas Moon is near the Serra da Estrela Mountains and Mondego River in Central Portugal, well away from the usual tourist haunts – are simply stunning, as are the mountain views.

The retreat consists of just two bell tents with a diameter of 5 m (16 ft); each sleeps a couple. Choose between Marrakesh on the middle terrace and Parisienne on the lower terrace, furnished as each name suggests. They have an outside decked area, solar lighting, wind-up radio sets, a solar-powered hot shower and odourless composting toilet. The site is sheltered by pine forests and the terraces are vibrant with tropical plants, palms, fruit trees and vines.

Catering is what you make it. An efficient cool box and ice are supplied, along with a good old backwoods Kelly Kettle to boil up water from the mountain spring. There is a barbecue area with awning on the middle terrace and all necessary cooking equipment is supplied. But then again the local town of Tábua is just 5 km (3 mi) away and offers a good selection of bars and restaurants, including a highly recommended pizzeria, plus shops for your provisions. There are plenty of opportunities in the area for active types, but in truth Canvas Moon is so beguiling that most visitors will find that this super-relaxing camp and its immediate environs are hard (going on impossible) to leave.

Yurt Holiday Portugal

WHERE:
Near Arganil, Coimbra District, Centro Region
COST:
Budget
BEST TIME OF YEAR:
April to October
DON'T MISS:
An information pack is provided giving details of possible activities, plus nearby historical and cultural destinations that are worth visiting. Shop at the weekly market in either Arganil or Góis.

Ecotourism is a movement that has really come of age in the 21st century, helping to support rural economies and preserve the unspoilt natural beauty that attracts aware visitors in the first place. And Portugal is one of the best ecotourist destinations in Europe because, away from coastal tourist hotspots like the Algarve, the central mountains not only have natural grandeur but also a timeless rhythm of life that pays no heed at all to the frenetic pace of modern urban existence. Yurts have migrated far from the Mongolian steppes in support of this process, and the call-a-spade-a-spade Yurt Holiday Portugal, an hour inland from the old university town of Coimbra, offers two of these suitably uprated nomadic dwellings, luxuriously furnished in a superb setting.

They may be found on an organic smallholding, with its own spring and powered by solar energy. Chestnut Tree Yurt has a double bed with

room for two younger children's beds, or an accompanying bell-tent can provide accommodation for two older kids. So, families welcome! Outside the yurt is a private bathroom with hot shower, sink and composting loo. There are reading lights and enough power for a laptop. Apple Tree Yurt has an attached mini-yurt and sleeps four. It, too, has its own private facilities and a solar panel provides lighting. A substantial breakfast is included, and can be served outside your yurt in the shade of a chestnut tree. Packed lunches and hearty evening meals can be arranged, or the local towns have good restaurants.

You will surely be tempted to wander in the surrounding hills, or drive a short way to enjoy splendid mountain scenery, explore abandoned hill villages, discover lakes and reservoirs or eat at country restaurants that offer traditional cuisine using only fresh, local ingredients. This is rural Portugal *par excellence*, with not a heavy tourist footprint to be seen.

THINGS TO DO:
River-beach activities, including wild swimming and kayaking; horse riding; mountain biking (bikes provided); walking; fishing; stargazing (the night sky is indeed heavenly!)

YOU SHOULD KNOW:
English is spoken! There is a minimum stay of two nights. The terrain is rugged and not suitable for the infirm. You will need transport (car, motorcycle or bike).

WHERE:
Zambujeira do Mar, Odemira District, Alentejo Region
COST:
Budget to reasonable (peaking in the summer season)
BEST TIME OF YEAR:
April to September
DON'T MISS:
Borrowing one of the mountain bikes and whizzing along the cliffs; taking a cool drink at the bar atop the cliff above Praia do Tonel
THINGS TO DO:
This is beach-holiday time, folks, but if you want to get beyond lounging in the sun, surfing or bodyboarding, spread more than your waterwings and head for Évora (on the Unesco World Heritage list) and Beja for a flavour of historic Portugal. Inland, there are a number of wine *quintas* that offer tastings.

Herdade do Touril

For a special beach holiday in a location the Brits and Germans have yet to discover in large numbers (the Portuguese know how to keep a secret), head for the Alentejo between Lisbon and the Algarve. On this stunning coastline it's possible to find wonderful sandy beaches that don't get overcrowded, even in high summer. Once there, as pleasing a stopping-point as any is the charming fishing village of Zambujeira do Mar. With its cluster of white houses and jumble of terracotta roofs it's actually more like a small and eminently respectable holiday resort possessed of a fine sandy beach – although there are several excellent fish restaurants which testify to the fact that the locals haven't forgotten how to shoot a net. Better still is the amazing small bay on the edge

of town, Praia do Tonel. This is surrounded by low cliffs, is reached by a steep path and never seems to be crowded. The golden sand is immaculate and, when the scorching sun reaches its zenith, welcome shade can be found beneath the cliffs.

Zambujeira do Mar is about all those classic holiday Ss (sun, sea and sand to name but three). Once there, Herdade do Touril is a super place to stay. It's a small complex consisting of a farmhouse and converted outbuildings, with the added benefit of attentive staff who really do seem to think that nothing is too much trouble when it comes to ensuring that guests have a wonderfully relaxing time. This small and welcoming rural complex offers a choice of double rooms, suites or cottage accommodation. It has a pool, breakfast is included, and the location is private, even though the cliffs and sea are no more than a short walk away.

YOU SHOULD KNOW:
Be prepared to avert your eyes if nudity offends – the beaches don't have an official 'naturist' section, but Portuguese attitudes to such matters seem relaxed and it happens. The popular Sudoeste Festival, one of Portugal's biggest summer music festivals, takes place in Zambujeira do Mar in early August – it features national and international bands playing through the day and evening, with disco into the small hours.

Muxima

After years spent working on humanitarian projects in Africa, the returned owners of Muxima have created a leafy eco-retreat that has something of the bush-village feel. Not that anyone is asked to suffer privation – quite the opposite. The two rustic guest houses are simply but more than adequately furnished, there's a terrace eating area and a spring-fed, reed-filtered swimming pool ready for you to plunge into when the midday sun is really sizzling.

The scene is set as you approach along a winding sandy track through Muxima's own cork and eucalyptus forest. The original farmhouse, La Casa de Eira, is a long building with an open verandah which houses one suite and three double rooms. Each has its own section of verandah and that helps to create an intimate feel. Casa do Monte is in the forest, along a narrow path up through the eucalypti (but reachable by car). This building also has thick walls made of traditional *taipa* (packed adobe) and houses three suites, each with an independent entrance. The accent is on bright ethnic decor beneath beamed ceilings, while those plastered mud walls create a cool interior beneath lazily turning ceiling fans – even in the heat of the day.

A huge buffet breakfast is included, but otherwise it's a matter of cook your own (if you have a suite) or eat out (if you don't). The latter is no hardship – a stroll to the local village of Aljezur soon leads to a leisurely home-cooked meal and a bottle of local wine by the river at Restaurante Pont'a Pe. Alternatively, put together a sumptuous picnic at the shop by the bridge and eat by candlelight back at Muxima while the cricket-orchestra plays. Despite being so close to the packed beaches of the Algarve, this is unspoilt rural Portugal at its very best. Parents can unwind while kids run wild, so relax and enjoy!

WHERE:
Near Aljezur, Faro District, Algarve Region
COST:
Budget (per person with at least two sharing)
BEST TIME OF YEAR:
April to October (the beaches will be packed in July and August, though)
DON'T MISS:
Leading the kids around on the resident donkey; lingering over breakfast at one of the colourfully painted tables overlooking the wonderful garden
THINGS TO DO:
Archery (bows supplied); commandeer the mountain bikes that are there for the pedalling; birdwatching; explore nearby Southwest Algarvian Natural Park and the Vicentina coast; fishing; horse riding; beach fun and water sports at Monte Clerigo or Amoreira; golf; dolphin-watching trips
YOU SHOULD KNOW:
In case you were wondering, 'Muxima' means 'heart' in Kimbundu – an Angolan dialect. *Muxima* is also the name of a town in Angola's Bengo Province.

Algarve Surf & Yoga Camp

WHERE:
Near Aljezur, Faro District, Algarve Region
COST:
Budget to reasonable, depending on season and number sharing the chosen accommodation
BEST TIME OF YEAR:
The camp is open from May to October.
DON'T MISS:
Local seafood restaurants (plus the renowned coffee and cake shops); relaxing encounters with the on-site wellness practitioners and masseuses (extra cost, but well worth it)
THINGS TO DO:
Enjoying the simple life; surfing and yoga sessions
YOU SHOULD KNOW:
Guests are asked to bring their own eco-toiletries (shampoo and soap). Mountain biking, nature walks and canoeing can be arranged.

Surf's up! Portugal's growing ecotourist credentials are further enhanced by '*tipi* valley' – affectionate shorthand for the Algarve Surf & Yoga Camp in beautiful Costa Vicentina Natural Park. But wait – how can a surfing camp be located in a secluded inland valley covered with cork trees (even if they theoretically make staying afloat easier)? Actually, it's a really good trick. The camp allows eco-conscious visitors to stay in an idyllic rural spot that couldn't be more different from (or less stressed than) the crowded and energy-guzzling coastal strip. Yet at the same time it's close enough to wonderful Algarve beaches with their rolling Atlantic breakers for riders and bodyboarders to be in surf heaven in no time at all.

Yoga platforms overlook the valley, so can-do practitioners of both surfing and yoga have all they need close to hand. But instruction can be part of a typical five-day programme, with yoga classes twice daily and also surfing instruction (all equipment provided). Numbers are kept small to maintain the camp's intimate, relaxed atmosphere as reflected in the house motto 'Simple Living'.

Accommodation requires a choice between Native American *tipi* (sleeps five comfortably), the one-person Island *tipi* or the Safari tent for couples. The tented Moroccan Lounge is the place for guests to relax, mingle and discuss the day's adventures. A stream runs through the camp but water is drawn from a traditional well and heated by solar energy to power two showers built from local cane and bamboo. Odour-free toilets are self-composting. There is an organic garden that provides much of the food consumed (three good meals a day are included). It's comfortable, but this is not luxurious 21st-century 'glamping' but rather a genuine opportunity to live close to tranquil nature without electricity or distraction, while refreshing the mind and exercising the body.

Walnut Tree Farm

In the extreme south of Portugal, just around the corner from Gibraltar, is somewhere that sounds rather English – Walnut Tree Farm in the Monchique hills. The name may be English, but the location is definitely Portuguese. The farm is set in a secluded green valley in sparsely populated Aljezur municipality, close to the splendid beaches at Arrifana, Monte Clerigo and Amorreira. It's possible to rent the restored farmhouse, which has four double rooms and two bathrooms, along with extra accommodation for large families or parties of friends. This takes the form of a treehouse in a sturdy century-old walnut tree (sleeps two), plus a yurt with sky deck that can accommodate four. Each has a simple kitchen, outside shower and composting toilet.

The three different options may be rented together or separately, although there are no prizes for guessing where kids (who invariably love the farm) will want to stay. This is a great get-away-from-it-all, back-to-nature experience, with the house energized by solar power and water drawn from a pure spring, although there's nothing primitive about the experience. The low, white-painted farmhouse is very comfortable and has an excellent beamed kitchen with rustic furniture, which opens onto a terrace. This is the place to eat *al fresco*, against the stunning background of conical wooded hills.

There are plenty of activities to be found locally for those who like to keep busy on holiday, but in this tranquil spot there is serious temptation to spend time in a sun-dappled hammock while the kids scamper about, or perhaps even explore the unspoilt surroundings. Walnut Tree Farm is about as idyllic a retreat as you'll find in rural Portugal, just the job for chilling in the sun.

WHERE:
Near Aljezur, Faro District, Algarve Region
COST:
Budget (per person, with a full complement)
BEST TIME OF YEAR:
The farm is available from April to November.
DON'T MISS:
A dip in the farm's swimming lake
THINGS TO DO:
Letting the kids run wild; heading for the coast and bodyboarding, surfing or kite surfing; mountain biking or hiking; horse riding; birdwatching, stargazing (no light pollution here); simply relaxing in a beautiful natural environment
YOU SHOULD KNOW:
Unsurprisingly in view of that name, English is spoken.

Reid's Palace Hotel

WHERE:
Estrada Monumental, Funchal
COST:
It's expensive at best, and the better rooms are astronomical, but there are special offers and Reid's is generous with its upgrades.
BEST TIME OF YEAR:
Madeira is a year-round destination. From October to April it is very mild, but it can be a rainy. From May to September it is very pleasantly hot.
DON'T MISS:
Quinta do Bom Sucesso, a botanical garden; afternoon tea on Reid's tea terrace; the cable-car ride from Funchal up to the village of Monte and the return journey on the thrilling Monte Toboggan; Fortaleza do São Tago, a coastal fort housing a museum of contemporary art; São Vicente Caves – eight dramatic lava tunnels
THINGS TO DO:
Walking the *levadas*; exploring the picturesque island villages; swimming; scuba diving; wind surfing; fishing; whale and dolphin spotting; tennis; golf; billiards; dancing classes; wine tastings; relaxing in cafés, bars and nightclubs
YOU SHOULD KNOW:
Madeira is famous for its ancient *levadas*, a 2,150-km (1,336-mi) network of irrigation channels that you can walk along, going from village to village through the breathtaking mountain countryside.

Some 650 km (400 mi) off the coast of Africa, the 'floating garden' of Madeira was colonized in the 15th century by the Portuguese and is culturally entirely European. This beautiful Atlantic island is a subtropical paradise with dramatic volcanic scenery of mountains, high cliffs and rocky coves surrounded by an azure ocean.

William Reid, a 14-year-old cabin boy, landed on Madeira in 1836. A go-getting fellow, he made a fortune in the wine trade and went on to realize his dream of building a palace. He found the perfect spot on a high cliff with spectacular views of the ocean, had tons of earth transported in preparation for his paradise garden, but never saw his venture through. He died before the building work was completed and it was left to his sons to open the doors of Reid's Palace in 1891. It was soon established as one of Europe's grandest hotels and all sorts of luminaries have stayed here.

The rambling palace straddles the clifftop, surrounded by its world-famous 4-ha (10-ac) subtropical terraced garden. All 163 of the opulently furnished rooms have terraces with views of the ocean or Funchal harbour. As well as the grand formal dining room, there are three restaurants, a breakfast room and poolside café, cocktail bar, tea terrace, bridge room and smoking room. A secluded spa in the garden, a magnificent gym, a choice of seawater or freshwater heated pools on cliffside terraces, and an unheated seawater pool beside the ocean complete the scene. Every amenity anyone could possible want is contained within the palace walls. Reid's Palace is a diamond among luxury retreats, the glamorous pleasure paradise that William Reid always dreamed of.

Xara Palace

On a prominent hill top in the centre of Malta, the medieval fortified city of Mdina offers commanding views across the whole island and the sea beyond. It was therefore an obvious choice to become the capital and administrative centre of the Knights of St John when they first arrived in 1530. Soon afterwards, the order's Grand Master ordered the construction of a brand-new capital on the coast, which became Valletta. Although no longer at the centre of power, Mdina remained a site of strategic importance and a valued refuge for Maltese nobility from the searing summer heat of the plains, as is evident from the many handsome Baroque palaces and mansions scattered around the citadel.

Nowadays, with a resident population of just a few hundred, Mdina is known as the 'Silent City' and has become a popular destination for day trippers from the coastal resorts. Wandering Mdina's narrow streets and enjoying the shade from its stone walls is a soothing experience at any time, but the best way to appreciate this magical place is to stay here overnight when at either end of the day you have the place more or less to yourself.

And without question the very best place to stay is the Xara Palace, close to the cathedral and the Vilhena Palace. This 17th-century *palazzo* has been lovingly restored and converted into a luxury boutique hotel where antique furniture, expensive fabrics and original artworks are judiciously deployed to evoke its heyday as the home of an aristocratic Maltese family. Several of the bedrooms are built into the old bastion walls and offer stunning vistas over the island, while a glass roof over an inner courtyard has created a cool and fragrant atrium in which you can relax.

WHERE:
Misrah il-kunsill, Mdina
COST:
Expensive
BEST TIME OF YEAR:
All year round (but note that prices and crowds are lower in the winter months – November to March)
DON'T MISS:
If you've decided to push the boat out for a stay here you might as well dig that bit deeper and book a suite with its own private terrace where you can gaze at the stars as you soak luxuriously in the outdoor Jacuzzi.
THINGS TO DO:
Exploring the citadel; visiting archaeological sites; walking; fine dining on an outdoor terrace; golf; horse riding
YOU SHOULD KNOW:
The Baroque architecture which pervades much of the Mdina townscape is the consequence of rebuilding after a major earthquake in 1693.

Canaves Oia Hotel

WHERE:
Oia, Santorini
COST:
Expensive to astronomical (every category costs slightly less at the caves than its equivalent at the Suites)
BEST TIME OF YEAR:
March to October/November
DON'T MISS:
A boat trip to Nea Kameni in the middle of the lagoon, where a 20-minute walk leads you to the volcano's crater, and onwards to bathe in the hot springs of Palia Kameni; hiring *Iguana*, the hotel's luxury speed boat (takes six) for the day; the gourmet dining at the Canaves Oia Suites restaurant – exclusive to all the hotel's guests
THINGS TO DO:
Feed your imaginings at the Venetian castle of Gizi Manor in Fira (just one of many historic churches, monasteries and castles on the island); dance a night away at Kamari or Fira, described as 'the more vivid' parts of Santorini (Oia is more laid back, even sophisticated); enjoy the hotel spa.
YOU SHOULD KNOW:
The hotel owns a fully crewed, 68-ft Feretti yacht that sleeps eight in sybaritic luxury. You can hire the magnificent M/Y *Alexandros* and cruise the Greek islands, combining the cruise with a sojourn at the hotel – before, during, or after – for a really memorable (if expensive) holiday.

Developed from original cave dwellings down a steep cliff on the northwest edge of Santorini's caldera lagoon, the Canaves Oia Hotel is the dream destination of every self-respecting troglodyte. These are caves with attitude. Everything about them radiates discreet class, but it's important to distinguish between the 'caves' and the Canaves Oia Suites. Effectively the hotel's other half, and close by, the Suites boast some of the biggest rooms on the island. They are built to resemble the ultra-traditional island style of the caves, are just as beautifully furnished, share the same stunning views, and if anything are probably more comfortably appointed. They even have air conditioning.

The caves, burrowed deep into the rock, don't need it. Each *canave* is quirkily different. None follow any geometric rule, consisting instead of smooth, rounded surfaces that meld whole rooms, terraces and corridors into a sinuous elegance of brilliant white and dark wood flooring. Furnishings are few but exquisitely chosen and placed, making aesthetic masterpieces of at least several rooms. They may be smaller, but their atmosphere outclasses the best of the neighbouring Canaves Oia Suites.

Outside, on individual terraces or from the pool, you can immediately see why Oia has the reputation of Santorini's most beautiful village. It faces southwest across the sea to the still-smoking remnants of the volcano which blew out the island's centre. With the islet of Thirasia placed just so in the foreground, it's no wonder that Oia is credited with the most amazing sunsets anywhere in the Cyclades. The hotel is very much part of the village (although you don't notice it from any of the rooms) and that puts a wide choice of restaurants, bars, good local music and other facilities within easy reach.

Fresh Hotel

The architects of ancient Greece would love the Fresh Hotel. It is uncompromisingly modernist, a nine-storey block of geometrical purity. Its form disguises its repetitious function by the artful placing of eye-catching slabs of violently bright colour. By night, clever lighting emphasizes its use of shocking pink, orange and lilac as something playful, but a closer examination of how the revivifying strong colours are muted by calming blues and greens in the rooms reveals the building as a modern classic that fully justifies its prime position in the heart of Athens. The hotel would be chic in any capital city. In Athens, and overlooking the Western World's ultimate symbol of architectural perfection, the Acropolis, the Fresh Hotel offers a refreshingly cheeky and cheerful antidote to the gravitas of its neighbours.

Its design aesthetic never falters. The 130 rooms and three suites share variations of the same palette and sophisticated elegance. Their subtle luxury includes everything that business or leisure travellers could wish for without surrendering their minimalist feel. The public rooms achieve the same effect with more drama. Three restaurants have vividly different characters, like the Orange Bar with its *nouveau grec* menu, orange Corian bar counter, and folding walnut floor, or the cool, terrazzo-floored Magenta with a pink-and-white decor pleasantly bearable to the most ragged-headed morning-after sufferer. The *pièce de résistance* is the oversized rooftop swimming pool. The sun-loungers are a brilliant way to study the Parthenon, but it's the 'Air Lounge' bar alongside, bursting with cushioned comfort and outrageously hip, that takes the biscuit with a panoramic view of the illuminated Acropolis in all its glory. Fresh Hotel is a blaze of colourful imagination worthy of that view.

WHERE:
Sophocleous Street and Kisthenous Street, Athens
COST:
Reasonable (rates include breakfast but not tax)
BEST TIME TO GO:
Any time
DON'T MISS:
Midnight skinny dipping to celebrate the Parthenon; taking the funicular up Lycabbetus Hill for the panorama of Athens' hills all the way to the sea; checking out the all-in-one cultural quarter of Technopolis, out towards Piraeus (once the city gasworks, now an industrial museum with some of the best exhibitions, concerts and international and local gigs)
THINGS TO DO:
Two minutes from Omonia Square, and close to the Acropolis complex, explore the narrow alleys of Plaka, Psirri District and central Athens – you are spoilt for choice; sauna; *hammam*; partying with the locals
YOU SHOULD KNOW:
Fresh Hotel may be hip, carefree and resemble a giant toy assembly, but it really does welcome children. Child menus, furniture and care experts are on hand (invaluable if parents need sitters any time in the day or night) and the rooftop pool always has a lifeguard on duty.

Mykonos Grace Hotel

WHERE:
Agios Stefanos Beach, Mykonos
COST:
Expensive to astronomical
BEST TIME OF YEAR:
Late June to mid September
DON'T MISS:
The hanging lights in the State of Grace bar, made with upside-down teacups and saucers; sunset from the balcony over the port towards Delos; dining by the pool (fabulous view, sheltered from the Meltemi wind); making the effort to stay up late for some of the *outré* events that fill the long summer; enjoying the famed Mykonos windmills
THINGS TO DO:
Visit Paradise Beach, one of Europe's most famous nudist beaches (if you're in shape); discover the Aegean Maritime Museum; explore the labyrinth of alleys in the ancient town of Mykonos (among the charming antiquity there are some racy bars and clubs, and enjoyably idiosyncratic shops); hit the excellent spa; update your jet-set wardrobe

The Cyclades island of Mykonos is renowned for its freewheeling ways. Nothing could demonstrate its cosmopolitan sophistication better than the fashion-plate elegance of the Mykonos Grace Hotel. It's a hybrid of modernist minimalism and the traditional idiom of a Greek village. That means the hotel complex consists of geometric arches and rectangles spilling down the hillside above Agios Stefanos beach in a symphony of pure white, contrasted with a (usually) azure sky and the turquoise quilt of private plunge pools. It's all about aesthetics, and they are brilliant for every grade of room and suite. Their amenities begin with luxury and work up to the two enormous VIP suites with indoor/outdoor private pools, private elevators and, rather endearingly, a daily delivery of fresh flowers and two cocktails.

Of course, Mykonos is about being seen as well as seeing, and the Grace Hotel is one of the hippest places to 'want to be alone' on the island. Accordingly, the State of Grace hotel bar and restaurant not only serves champagne breakfast all day and night from its vantage next to the large infinity pool, but is also surrounded by four-poster day beds with billowing gauzy drapes on which glitterati can recline and be adored. Yet the ambience remains calm and cool, because the hotel is in fact a super-smart refuge from the real action on Mykonos, which is to dress fabulous and sample the legendary pleasures of a night on the town. Towards midnight, the reception area fills with sheer glamour, and the twin triangular chrome pillars shimmering with cascading water by the hotel's entrance start to flash the reflected sparkle of mega-bling as guests leave in search of *nostalgie de la boue*. Oh to be back!

YOU SHOULD KNOW:
Two rooms have been adapted for different preferences, including oversize bathrooms (and one has its own lift, guaranteeing total privacy); congratulate yourself if you spot Petros the Pelican, the island's mascot for 50 years – it is said to bring you luck.

Dalabelos Estate

At least as many people are drawn to Crete by its endlessly fascinating history as by its potential as a Mediterranean beach playground. The Dalabelos Estate near Rethymnon is an attempt to show how Crete's semi-mythical past is bound into a still-living tradition. Begun as an ecotourism project by the Petrodaskalakis family, the completion of a community of ten studios on a 3-ha (7.5-ac) site of olive trees, vineyards and aromatic shrubs within a working agricultural estate, broke the bounds of its original imagination. Instead of just offering ecologically responsible R & R in a beautiful rural setting, the family has opened itself to proactive visitors willing to make a small emotional (and sometimes physical) investment in the farm. The reward is direct access to authentic Cretan culture. It's an offer beyond price.

The traditional stone-built studios are fully equipped little homes, with fireplaces and many another warming touch. All of them have wonderful views across the Cretan landscape to the sea and misty blue mountains. There's no pressure to do anything except read, walk, breathe in the aromatics of the hot countryside while the crickets chirrup, and perhaps play backgammon over a drink. But at any time you're welcome to look at (it's moral support!) or join in any of the daily or seasonal farm routines. Produce includes organic olive oil, raki, wine, seasonal fruit and vegetables and many different herbs, so the work never stops. The more you join in (not necessarily with physical labour – goodwill is everything) the more you penetrate the charmed circle of legendary Cretan hospitality. Good rapidly gets even better. The Dalabelos Estate is how you make friends for life. In Crete, that's family.

WHERE:
Ageliana, Rethymnon
COST:
Budget
BEST TIME OF YEAR:
Any time – Dalabelos is in the nature of cyclical things
DON'T MISS:
Participating in the wine pressing (end of August to mid September) or distillation process for raki (mid October to end of November); the restaurant's traditional Cretan cuisine made from ingredients grown on the estate; giving your all to the evenings of wine and laughter and local music, with their kids playing tag between your feet
THINGS TO DO:
Make pottery under the guidance of local experts in the estate's own studio; walking; swimming – the sea is only 5 km (3 mi) away; maybe prepare a song or silly poem to entertain everyone else on some fun-filled night; feel stress melting away
YOU SHOULD KNOW:
It's advisable to hire a car if you plan to visit historic sites like Knossos or the Gorge. If you only plan to go as far as the nearest beach, the estate will find you a bicycle.

WHERE:
Tripiti (also spelled 'Trypiti'), Milos
COST:
Budget (based on per person, per night, and full occupancy – visitors seeking exclusivity can obviously pay more)
BEST TIME OF YEAR:
April to October (although fireplaces and heating systems ensure lots of winter interest)
DON'T MISS:
The *syrmata* (fishermen's houses) carved into the rock at Klima, the island's most picturesque fishing village; the beaches at Agia Kiriaki, Papafrangas and Provatas; the folk and archaeological museums, and wonderful Cycladic architecture of the flower-filled, narrow streets of Plaka (which effectively combines five villages in one); the early Christian (1st to 4th centuries) catacombs, the biggest in Greece
THINGS TO DO:
Hiring a fishing boat and helping the children explore secret coves, smugglers' caves and coastal villages; swimming on and under the water; Tripiti is famous for its *meze tavernas*, and many bars and restaurants are in walking distance; eat a pirate feast under the stars by the windmill – or a candlelit dinner *à deux*
YOU SHOULD KNOW:
The windmills are serviced daily, and local cooks can be arranged; if you are booking a windmill, check if the 'outhouses' have been rented separately; credit cards are not accepted (cash or bank transfer only).

The Windmills

Aphrodite has long gone to take up a permanent post as the Venus de Milo of the Louvre in Paris. Like the ancient statue, the island of Milos is a unique beauty even among the island gems of the Cyclades, and the Aegean as a whole. Although it lacks the forests, lush vegetation and rivers that variously characterize neighbouring islands, its volcanic origins have dressed Milos in a scheme of chalk white, terracotta, ochre and jet-black rock that is found nowhere else. Equally unique among the islands are its 72 big and small beaches of sparkling silver sand. With these assets, and a location off the beaten track in the southwest Cyclades, Milos has remained unprettified. What you see is real, and what you get is genuine.

Milos has eight villages, clustered round the 'capital', Plaka, on the flat land on the north side of its fabulous natural harbour. Tripiti village has stunning views over Plaka and the comings and goings of the seaway; and on its highest ridge is a row of four 16th- to 19th-century windmills. They are round towers of thick rock, but three are whitewashed. All of them have a living room with kitchen facilities on the ground floor, a mezzanine of two single beds, and a private, double bedroom under the beamed 'tent' of the roof. Two have extra rooms built outside, studios with cooking facilities which can be included or rented separately. Imaginatively, any one of them is paradise, especially for children, extended families, and groups of friends. With enclosed gardens and shaded terraces, their unpretentious comforts conjure authentic Greek culture and history – and they make the perfect base for exploring everywhere else.

Levendi's Estate

Levendi's is the word given to the alchemical mystery that transmutes ordinary hospitality into something like kinship for life. It's also the name of a 3-ha (7.5-ac) olive farm set in a broad cleft between two thickly wooded mountains on the north coast of Ithaca. It is a place of deep tranquillity, tinkling goats' bells, and thyme and myrtle in the salt-borne breeze. A stone-flagged path snakes down into the trees from the entrance to this idyllic refuge. It passes four cottages, serene little homes surrounded by beautiful flowered gardens, each with two double bedrooms, kitchen, bathroom, living room and shaded terrace. Each is private from the others, but shares the vista of the bay, and the endlessly murmuring surf.

The descending path leads to a gorgeous infinity pool, placed to unite sea and sky in reflections framed by pencils of dark cypresses, and winds through bougainvilllea to a secluded cove of gravelly sand. Beside the pool guests find organic breakfasts, an honesty bar and an outdoor kitchen where everyone congregates to eat and talk of an evening – if they haven't chosen to be private in their cottage, or to cruise any of the bars and *tavernas* in the local villages.

Without TV or internet access, Levendi's Estate is an almost instant stressbuster. Families rediscover each other, helped by a first-class nanny and childcare service. The olive groves, woods and gardens are a paradise for energetic children, and completely safe. Peace reigns. It is the luxury of simplicity, applied to recreation as it is to every other facet of the organic estate. Levendi's alchemy is in making guests feel that this is home (or wish that it were).

WHERE:
Aphales Bay, Ithaca
COST:
Expensive (but includes the cost of a hire car and boat transfers to Cephalonia or Patras)
BEST TIME OF YEAR:
May to November (closed December to April)
DON'T MISS:
One of Ithaca's summer church festivals (all-night song and dance and roast meats and wine, at Kioni, Stavros, Exogi or Piatrithia); riding the estate motorboat; exploring the Cave of Nymphs and other sites associated with Homeric myth
THINGS TO DO:
Biking (the hotel has ten mountain bikes, including children's sizes); swimming in the pool or off one of Ithaca's beaches; reading in one of the dozen hammocks hung in dappled glades throughout the estate; marvel at linens and lace in the pretty island capital, Vathi; enjoy *tavernas* on the waterfront of the unspoilt and typical Ionian villages of Kioni and Frikes
YOU SHOULD KNOW:
Slightly tongue in cheek, Levendi's calls itself eco-chic. A list of all their eco-responsible touches (from home-made toiletries to bug-proof screens instead of air conditioning, to the swinging branch used to dry laundry) is pretty boring. Live with them all and you will appreciate their true effort.

An Island Lighthouse

There are some 1,244 islands in Croatia. On the map they appear like a careless streak of paint dashed down the coast of Istria and Dalmatia. From the water they are a fearsome mixture of looming promontories, jagged headlands and sheer cliffs. Their shores are littered with the wrecks of Roman, Byzantine and Venetian ships that failed to cope with the powerful tide races of the deep water funnelled between them. Only in the 19th century did Croatia's Austro-Hungarian masters systematize the haphazard braziers and beacons set up by local communities into a practical chain of 48 permanent lighthouses to protect seafarers. And now 11 of these are available for holiday rentals. In a country of legendary natural beauty (Shakespeare's Illyria, no less) their locations are among the best of the best.

The 11 lighthouses cover an extraordinary range of terrain and character. Savudrija, built by Metternich for a Croatian lover, and the oldest and northernmost, is actually on the mainland, although you can't see that. Sveti Ivan (St John) is a tiny rock formation with two miniscule beaches suitable for children. Porer, near Pula, is a 35-m (115-ft) tower on top of a circular white cliff. It takes a single minute to walk round the islet, but its sunsets are widely admired as the best in the Adriatic. Palagruza, way out in the open sea, is an exceptionally beautiful showcase of natural Mediterranean flora, and Struga lighthouse sits on a sheer cliff on the south side of Lastovo, an island big enough to have its own local (and extremely laid-back) culture. So, 11 different kinds of drama to feed the imagination, fabulous vistas by day and night, and the sea, the sea.

WHERE:
The Dalmatian archipelago, on Croatia's Adriatic coast

COST:
Budget (but the minimum stay is one week from the end of May to mid September everywhere except Porer and Sveti Ivan, where it is two days all year – perhaps for fear that any longer in such restricted spaces might drive people crazy)

BEST TIME OF YEAR:
High season (July to August)

DON'T MISS:
The opportunity – even if you've already visited Croatia, the lighthouses are 11 of the country's best-kept secrets and most-rewarding destinations

THINGS TO DO:
Swimming; sunbathing; drawing and painting; cooking and eating; guileless introspection; practising the noble art of *pomalo* (Dalmatian island philosophy characterized as 'relax, it'll keep – have some coffee and a drink . . .')

YOU SHOULD KNOW:
All but four lighthouses come with lighthouse keepers. Lighthouse buildings sleep between two and 14 people in up to four separate apartments at any one. Apartments all have TV and Sat-TV, full kitchens and shower rooms; guests must bring all their own food (including spices) and drink. Finding the lighthouse that suits you best is easy through one of several official agencies that know all the owners.

Hostel Celica

For older Slovenians the building in which this lively youth hostel is housed carries grim reminders of darker days in the country's recent history. In the former Yugoslavia it was a military prison where more than a few dissidents were incarcerated over the years. Nowadays, you don't need a criminal conviction to sleep within its walls and, best of all, you get to decide how long your 'sentence' should be.

Within a few years of Slovenia gaining its independence in the mid 1990s the old prison cells were being subjected to ingenious makeovers at the hands of more than 80 artists. Sleeping either two or three, each of the 20 cells has been given a unique new look, with many incorporating split-level sleeping areas. Mosaics and other artworks have been introduced to soften the plain surfaces and there's a funkiness about the designs that gives them a contemporary edge.

While the cells may be cosy enough there's no escaping the fact that these were once rather more Spartan quarters. The cells are arranged in two single-sex blocks with a communal bathroom at one end (true to form, the men's is blue, the women's red). There are also a few en-suite rooms for four or five people and two dormitories sleeping seven and 12 respectively. The hostel is run by the students union at Ljubljana University and there is always lots going on in its two cafés and bar, including free weekly concerts and jam sessions, a regular club night and popular 'all you can eat' nights in the restaurant that feature different cuisines from around the world.

WHERE:
Metelkova 8, Ljubljana
COST:
Budget
BEST TIME OF YEAR:
All year round (although the summer months – June to August – are particularly good for the number of free events and for hanging out in the lovely garden)
DON'T MISS:
One cell has been converted into a Point of Peace, a non-denominational place for contemplation and prayer, with niches for the world's five major religions and a sixth niche to represent all the others.
THINGS TO DO:
See the sights of Ljubljana, one of Europe's smaller and most appealing capital cities.
YOU SHOULD KNOW:
The hostel is deservedly popular among holidaying students and the backpacker set so you will need to book well in advance, especially in high season (May to September).

WHERE:
Cesta Svobode 12, Bled
COST:
Reasonable
BEST TIME OF YEAR:
April to November (although a blanket of snow in the winter months, December to March, transforms the Bled landscape into a veritable wonderland for hardy types)
DON'T MISS:
Take one of the hotel's old wooden rowing boats out on the lake and soak up the views.
THINGS TO DO:
Taking the waters; spa treatments; swimming; hiking; golf; casino; visiting caves; wine tasting; cross-country skiing (December to March)
YOU SHOULD KNOW:
Drinking the mineral-rich water from the natural springs at Bled is said to be beneficial to the stomach and other internal organs.

Grand Hotel Toplice

Lake Bled is perhaps Slovenia's most famous beauty spot and has been attracting lovers of nature for the best part of two centuries. The iconic view of the lake – its tiny island and pilgrimage church, the ancient castle perched on a rocky crag by the shoreline, all set against the backdrop of the majestic Julian Alps – graces the covers of endless brochures advertising this small country the world over. The invigorating qualities of the region's mountain air had always been recognized but it was the discovery of thermal springs at Bled in the mid 19th century that led to its development as a major tourism centre. The original Luisenbad Hotel and Spa on the lake shore, a favourite with the fashionable elite of the Austro-Hungarian Empire, was replaced in 1931 by the present building and renamed the Grand Hotel Toplice.

Still the premier establishment at this busy resort, the Grand Hotel may have been modernized over the years to meet contemporary standards of comfort and service, but its interiors with their opulent period furnishings still carry echoes of the glory days of the 1930s when the King of Serbia would move his court to Bled for the summer, and the hotel became the haunt of politicians and film stars. Its lustre survived regime change when after World War II Marshal Tito also chose Bled as his summer residence, presiding over international conferences of the non-aligned nations.

Today the Grand Hotel welcomes guests in search of rest and relaxation in a fabulous setting, whether dining beneath the chestnut trees on the lakeside terrace or bathing in the thermal waters of the beautiful colonnaded swimming pool.

Marrol's Boutique Hotel

Five minutes' walk from one of Central Europe's best-preserved old towns can't be a bad location for any hotel. Tucked away down a quiet side street in Bratislava, this smart boutique establishment doesn't disappoint when it comes to service and facilities, either. Housed in a 19th-century town house, Marrol's offers 54 rooms, including three suites, which look out either on the Old Town or the hotel's garden courtyard. The decor has a distinct flavour of retro chic, with large armchairs in black leather and plain but stylish wooden furniture.

The hotel prides itself on creating an informal but attentive atmosphere. If you are visiting in the winter months you will be greeted by a roaring fire in the lobby, while the garden terrace is a delightfully cool and secluded spot in which to enjoy a summer drink. The small spa features a sauna and Jacuzzi and the hotel restaurant, the Messina, is one of the Slovak capital's best, serving a fusion of Mediterranean cuisine and local Carpathian specialities.

The warren of lanes and alleys which make up Bratislava's Old Town are a delight to explore on foot. The hotel owes its unusual name to the charming story of Lady Mary Ann Marrol, daughter of a wealthy Scottish merchant who stayed the night while her carriage was being repaired in the workshop (as the building then was 100 years ago); while there she saved the young nephew of the workshop's owner from being run over by galloping horses. In gratitude the owner renamed his business after her and it is Lady Mary's features that welcome you above the hotel entrance to this day.

WHERE:
Tobrucka 4, Bratislava
COST:
Reasonable
BEST TIME OF YEAR:
All year round
DON'T MISS:
While here you really should try the *brynzové halušky*, a much loved national dish of potato dumplings covered with sheep's cheese and bacon.
THINGS TO DO:
Walking around the Old Town; visiting Bratislava Castle; a river cruise on the Danube; immersing yourself in Middle European café culture
YOU SHOULD KNOW:
Because the hotel spa accommodates a maximum of six guests, a session must be pre-booked – although it is then exclusively yours for two hours (or longer).

Aria Hotel

WHERE:
Tržište 368/9, Prague
COST:
Expensive
BEST TIME OF YEAR:
It's excellent all year round (although you would be advised to avoid the serious crowds in July and August). For lovers of classical music spring (May) and autumn (September) are particularly good times, when music festivals book-end the summer.
DON'T MISS:
The panoramic views of Prague Castle and the historic city from the rooftop terrace
THINGS TO DO:
Listening to music; exploring Malá Strana and the Old Town; watching the world pass by on Charles Bridge; river trips; visiting museums and galleries
YOU SHOULD KNOW:
The hotel overlooks Prague's oldest Baroque garden, the Vrtbovská, to which its guests have private access.

Music is likely to be high on many people's list of reasons for visiting Prague. Turn any corner of the old city in the summer months and you are practically guaranteed to come across live music in a square or baroque courtyard, be it folk, classical, ethnic or a group performing Mozart in period costume. Capitalizing on all this activity, the Aria Hotel in the city's Malá Strana district has been designed with the music-lover in mind.

A row of modest grey-stone and yellow-stucco buildings has been transformed by two leading Italian architects best known for their work for Versace to create what the hotel describes as a 'luxurious musical haven'. Clean lines and bright colours reflect the best of contemporary Italian design, which is subsumed to a celebration of musical culture in its many guises. Each of the hotel's four floors is devoted to a different genre – jazz, opera, classical and contemporary – the rooms on that floor being themed accordingly. Taking things a stage further, the suites are each dedicated to an individual artist or composer; thus there is a Mozart suite and a Beethoven suite, and also suites honouring King Elvis and Billie Holiday.

Not surprisingly, the Aria does not overlook the country's national composers, Dvorák and Smetana. The hotel certainly hits all the right notes, with each room including a computer and sound system loaded with relevant data and music. Under the guidance of its own music director the hotel also features a well-stocked music library and two areas for watching recordings of your favourite concerts or operas on plasma screens and surround-sound audio.

Ještęd Tower

The Ještěd-Kozákov mountain ridge in North Bohemia has been a magnet for walkers and climbers for centuries. The relative flatness of the surrounding landscape means that the ridge offers some spectacular views, nowhere more so than from its highest point, Mount Ještěd. It comes as no surprise to discover that this 1,012-m (3,320-ft) peak was chosen in the 1960s as the location for a television transmitter and relay station. The resulting Ještěd Tower was built to a radical design by a local architect who used an unusual hyperboloid shape to extend the profile of the mountain. From the outset it was intended that the 94-m (308-ft) tower should be put to recreational use as well as fulfilling its broadcasting brief, so accordingly the lower floors were fitted out as a hotel and restaurant.

Still a working transmitter, the tower is today a much-loved landmark in the Liberec region and a popular venue for rallies, concerts and sporting events. The hotel has rooms on two levels, with 12 spacious double rooms and two suites on the first level and five more basic double rooms (not en suite) on the level above. The views out of the porthole-style windows are of course stupendous, as they are from the circular restaurant beneath; in good conditions you are able to see far into neighbouring Germany and Poland. At night Ještěd Tower is illuminated with dramatic lighting effects. A road leads to the summit but you might prefer to make the ascent by cable car, or else follow in the footsteps of the early hikers and take one of the walking trails from Liberec.

WHERE:
Mount Ještěd, near Liberec
COST:
Budget
BEST TIME OF YEAR:
April to October
DON'T MISS:
The hanging cubicle chairs in the corridors are a nice touch – and very cosy!
THINGS TO DO:
Hiking; climbing; mountain biking; stargazing; exploring the bizarre rocky landscapes of the Ceský Ráj
YOU SHOULD KNOW:
In 2000 the Ještěd Tower was awarded the title of Best Czech Building of the 20th Century.

Palazzo Zichy

WHERE:
Budapest
COST:
Reasonable
BEST TIME OF YEAR:
Budapest is an attractive destination at any time of year.
DON'T MISS:
The Dohány Street Synagogue is well worth a visit. Built in the mid 19th century, Europe's largest synagogue has seating for 3,600 people and miraculously survived World War II.
THINGS TO DO:
Sightseeing; bathing in thermal baths; shopping; lingering over coffee and cakes; visiting museums and galleries; clubbing and nightlife
YOU SHOULD KNOW:
Free tea and coffee are available in the lounge throughout the day, one of several little touches that mark this hotel out.

In the smart Józsefváros district of Budapest, this former residence of a Hungarian aristocrat has been cleverly converted into a very desirable boutique hotel which has built up a loyal following among guests who enthuse about the friendly staff and conscientious service. Cutting-edge interior design sits cheekily alongside historic spaces where the original colour schemes and stucco work have been carefully re-created. It shouldn't work, but it does; when you first enter the hotel and pass through the original palace lobby into the split, modern reception area, the effect is simply breathtaking.

The contemporary theme continues into spacious bedrooms that are welcoming havens at any time, but especially after a long day's sightseeing. The inner courtyard of the old palace has been covered with a glass roof to create a light and airy atrium which houses a bar, lounge area and breakfast room. The hotel does not have a restaurant but, with so many good dining options nearby, this is hardly a drawback.

One of the reasons why Palazzo Zichy inspires such loyalty among its guests is its wonderfully central location. You are just a few minutes' walk from the Hungarian National Museum and the Applied Arts Museum – two of the city's top collections – and Budapest's main shopping area is also easily accessible from here. It would be nice to think that Count Nándor Zichy, who was an early advocate of rights for Hungarians of all classes as well as a devout Catholic, would have approved of the new use to which his town residence had been put and the appreciative patrons it now attracts.

art'otel

The German art'otel chain has carved out a distinctive niche in the market for the discerning leisure traveller, with a design concept for its upmarket hotels that is based on the extensive display of original work by important living artists. For its first venture outside Germany the company chose the contemporary US artist Donald Sultan to be the presiding creative genius within the walls of this stylish boutique hotel in the Hungarian capital. Sultan is best known for his use of vibrant, contrasting colours in large paintings which allude to the historical genre of still life. His trademark technique involves the use of linoleum tiles mounted on a frame; the surface is coated in black tar which is burned off and paint then applied in the exposed areas. Nearly 600 of Sultan's dazzling original artworks are displayed throughout the hotel, in the guest rooms as well as in the public areas.

The sizeable hotel has been fashioned out of a number of 18th-century town houses, with the addition of a modern wing with a determinedly 21st-century feel. An inner courtyard gives the best view of the two styles; you can sit here with a drink and enjoy the contrasts, especially the way the afternoon sun warms the yellow plasterwork of the old facades, so characteristic of 18th-century Baroque architecture in Central Europe. The art'otel occupies a prime riverside site in the Víziváros district on the left bank of the Danube; many of the rooms have outstanding views of the river and the Hungarian Parliament, Budapest's most iconic building, on the opposite bank.

WHERE:
Bem Rakpart, Budapest
COST:
Reasonable
BEST TIME OF YEAR:
All year round (but you should note that there can be uncomfortably high humidity levels in the summer months of June to August)
DON'T MISS:
The hotel is well situated for exploring Buda Castle and the surrounding historic area.
THINGS TO DO:
Sightseeing; looking at art; taking thermal baths; jogging along the Danube and on Margaret Island; cycling; river cruises
YOU SHOULD KNOW:
If you are planning on some serious sightseeing the Budapest Card is well worth buying – it gives you unlimited travel on public transport together with discounts at many restaurants, museums and attractions.

WHERE:
Széchenyi Square, Budapest
COST:
Expensive
BEST TIME OF YEAR:
All year round
DON'T MISS:
No trip to Budapest is complete without a visit to one of its celebrated thermal baths, the most obvious legacy of the 200-year Turkish occupation of the city. The Széchenyi and the Gellért Baths are the two best known.
THINGS TO DO:
Sightseeing; shopping (the hotel is close to Váci utca, the main shopping street); spa; swimming (there is an indoor infinity pool on the top floor); river trips; enjoying the lively café culture of Middle Europe; wine tasting
YOU SHOULD KNOW:
The Four Seasons puts itself out for its younger guests in ways you don't always find at this level. There is no additional charge for children up to 18 who share their parents' room.

Gresham Palace

As befits a major European city with a rich history, Budapest boasts a range of styles in its public and private architecture. The Art Nouveau movement, which held sway throughout the continent at the end of the 19th century, here finds its most impressive manifestation in the Gresham Palace on Széchenyi Square. With a prime location on the Danube embankment, facing the city's famous Lánchíd or Chain Bridge, the palace's facade is once again visible in all its dramatic splendour thanks to a six-year restoration of the complex by the Four Seasons hotel group.

No expense has been spared in bringing this sleeping princess back to life following years of decay and neglect in the Communist era. The Gresham Palace was originally commissioned by a British insurance company to serve as its European headquarters, and when it opened in 1906 it took its name from the Elizabethan financier Thomas Gresham. The building was designed in the Sezession style – the Austro-Hungarian take on Art Nouveau – which tended to emphasize architectural form over ornament and extravagance. Not that there was a lack of brilliant flourishes in the interiors, and these are on view once again thanks to the work of top modern crafts people who restored the tiled walls, mosaic floors, stained-glass windows and wrought-iron work. Highlights to look out for are the tiled lobby and the Páva Udva or Peacock Passage, the central arcade with a glass cupola and splendid twin peacocks on the wrought-iron entrance gates. Since opening in 2004, the Gresham Palace has quickly established itself as a connoisseur's choice – gracefully combining vintage architecture with all the comfort and amenities expected of a modern luxury hotel.

Hotel National

Thoroughly overhauled to include all the gizmos that guests expect from luxury hotels, the National is probably closer now to the intentions of its original 1902 design than at any time since 1917. It's been a rough ride. The hotel is next to the Kremlin and to Red Square – a location that guaranteed it a leading role during Russia's colossal 20th-century upheavals. In 1918 it became the fledgling Soviet government's first official home. Ever since, idealogues have wavered between preserving its heritage and inducting it into the monolithic system of socialist hospitality known as Intourist. Happily, heritage has won. Now the National provides the wonderful frisson of access to Russia's spectacular artistic inheritance, and still fulfils its intended role of catering to high politics, business, and luxury tourism.

It's big. It's also practical. The 206 single, double and studio rooms are very comfortable according to their status, but of neutral style. They all face inwards to the courtyard. The big guns are the 46 suites with panoramas of the Kremlin and Tverskaya Street. No two are identical, but they are collectively gorgeous evocations of classic Russian opulence. Rich brocades and exotic carpets are set off by some of the finest antiques you will ever see, and in their proper context. Most were gathered from aristocratic palaces, but now you can only be grateful they were preserved. Best of all are the five 'National' Suites, typically with deep yellow/peach walls, carpets of sublime subtlety, grand mirrors, most beautifully crafted furniture and first-class pictures throughout their three rooms, which might also include a grand piano or (!) a Jacuzzi. Except for the conference rooms, the public rooms are equally exhilarating. Treat yourself.

WHERE:
Mokhovaya Ulitsa, Moscow
COST:
Expensive (dull) to astronomical (really exciting and worth it)
BEST TIME OF YEAR:
Any time (there's always skating in Gorgy Park come winter)
DON'T MISS:
The grand swags and princely views over the floodlit Kremlin spires from the semi-circular grandeur of the Suzdal Room in the Moskovsky restaurant; the stained glass windows surrounding the sweeping white marble and gilt grand staircase; a performance at the Bolshoi Theatre down the street
THINGS TO DO:
Visit the Arbat, a pedestrian street of small shops, for history (it's one of Moscow's oldest streets) and pure Russian chic. Ask the National's concierge to arrange your visit to the Kremlin and to the Tsars' treasury in the Armoury Chamber (Oruzheynaya Palata) – you may well get a privileged view not open to others.
YOU SHOULD KNOW:
A Russian maths problem – if it takes five minutes to walk from the Hotel National to the State Historical Museum at No 1 Red Square, and ten minutes to walk to the GUM department store at No 3 Red Square, how enormous is Red Square?

Grand Hotel Europe

The pale-lilac and white baroque facade unites a terrace of early 19th-century houses into a single magnificent building. Even on Nevsky Prospekt, the most elegant thoroughfare in St Petersburg, the 130-year-old Grand Hotel Europe stands out as a landmark. It's impossible to exaggerate the excitement you feel as you go in. It's been a hospital, orphanage and government offices, but since 1991 it has been fully restored to the neo-baroque and *fin-de-siècle* Art Nouveau glory of its heyday. From the most ordinary 'Classic' room to the 'Belle Chambres' everything is touched by exquisite 19th-century charm.

The suites are even more fabulous, graded according to degrees of opulence that are simply off the scale of most grand hotels. Antique furniture and hand-made fabrics are combined with impeccable taste to express both cultural significance and the highest standards of comfort and luxury. Best of all are the Terrace suites at the very top of the hotel, with views over the heart of St Petersburg, and the ten 'historic' suites named after celebrated icons of music and the arts, like Stravinsky and even Pavarotti (who loved the place).

The irreproachable taste of such magnificence and grandeur is – incredibly – surpassed by the public rooms below. The double-height, balconied L'Europe Restaurant is not only one of St Petersburg's best, but features a sensational end wall of Art Nouveau stained glass. Four other restaurants are hardly less exotic, and along with the two bars each contributes to a fairytale feeling of other-worldliness. The Grand Hotel Europe makes you feel weightless when you are in it, and sends you out to St Petersburg's cultural masterpieces on a little cloud of insouciant well-being.

WHERE:
Nevsky Prospekt, Mikhailovskaya Ulitsa, St Petersburg

COST:
Expensive to astronomical – daily rates do not normally include taxes and service charges (typically around 18 per cent) so do ask when you book

BEST TIME OF YEAR:
Any time is a good time for the ultimate Russian hotel experience.

DON'T MISS:
Live ballet on 'Tchaikovsky Nights' (Fridays) in L'Europe Restaurant (Saturdays it's jazz!); chocolates made in the hotel's own chocolate factory; cocktails outdoors on the Grand Terrace during St Petersburg's 'White Nights' summer festivities

THINGS TO DO:
Visit the Cathedral of Our Lady of Kazan opposite the hotel, next to the arcaded elegance of Gostiniy Dvor department store; walk down Nevsky Prospekt to the golden spire of the Admiralty, via Palace Square, lined by the Winter Palace and the Hermitage; go to any performance at the Mariinsky or Mikhailovsky Theatres, round the corner in Arts Square (as is the Church of the Saviour on the Spilled Blood, with its soaring, photogenic onion domes)

YOU SHOULD KNOW:
Besides Russian cuisine and Russian music, the hotel's Caviar Bar has Russia's only full-time, professional vodka sommelier.

Pera Palace

As soon as the Orient Express through-train service started to run from Paris to Istanbul in 1889, western high society flocked to this exotic new tourist destination – only to complain that there were no suitable places to stay. And so it came to pass that the Pera Palace was built.

A graceful architectural pastiche of neoclassical, Art Nouveau and oriental design, the Pera Palace opened in 1895 and immediately established its credentials as one of Europe's most glamorous hotels. It vied in splendour with the Ottoman Sultan's Palace, the only other building in Istanbul to have electric lighting.

The Pera Palace saw the decline of the Ottoman Empire, two world wars and the founding of the Republic of Turkey, opened its doors to countless luminaries and appeared in numerous works of fiction, but by the turn of the 21st century its charms were wearing distinctly thin. But now a major makeover has restored all its former glory. More glamorous than ever, the hotel reopened in 2010 with the latest technology and a state-of-the-art spa. Two rooms have been turned into museums – one of them dedicated to Agatha Christie, who wrote *Murder on the Orient Express* in Room 411, and the other to Atatürk, the founding father of modern Turkey.

As you arrive, a liveried footman opens the door and you step into an enchanting oriental romance where the service is fastidious and the extravagant Ottoman decor is unstinting. Sunlight filters down through six huge turquoise glass domes in the ceiling of the marble-walled Kubbeli Salon and the rooms are furnished with hand-woven carpets, opulent antiques and Murano chandeliers. Both as Ottoman museum and 21st-century luxury hotel, the Pera Palace is iconic.

WHERE:
Mesrutiyet Caddesi, Beyoglu, Istanbul
COST:
Expensive
BEST TIME OF YEAR:
Istanbul is a year-round destination but late April and May are especially pleasant months when the tulips are in bloom and it is not yet too hot.
DON'T MISS:
English afternoon tea in the Kubbeli Salon; a ride in the original cast-iron and wood-panelled hotel lift; the view from the top of the Galata Tower; window shopping in the famous Istiklal Avenue; taking the Tünel underground funicular railway from Beyoglu to Karaköy; the Egyptian Spice market; the Ortaköy Mosque
THINGS TO DO:
Seeing the historical sights and visiting museums; cruising up the Golden Horn and Bosphorus; frequenting the cafés and bars in the narrow streets of Beyoglu; shopping in designer boutiques and bazaars
YOU SHOULD KNOW:
The writers Ernest Hemingway and Graham Greene were both regular guests, as was Greta Garbo. Among the countless other luminaries who have stayed at the Pera Palace are Edward VIII, Queen Elizabeth II, Emperor Franz Joseph, Sarah Bernhardt, Alfred Hitchcock and Jacqueline Kennedy Onassis.

Verystanbul House

WHERE:
Fener, Istanbul
COST:
Reasonable (or you can use just one of the bedrooms for 20 per cent less)
BEST TIME OF YEAR:
Any time is good but it can be cold and damp between November and March and uncomfortably hot in July and August.
DON'T MISS:
Eating *simit* sesame-dough rings for breakfast, fresh from the local bakery; climbing the ancient city wall; a traditional Turkish meal looking out over the Golden Horn on the roof terrace at Tahiri Halic restaurant; artefacts and relics in the Patriarchal Cathedral Church of St George, the worldwide headquarters of the Greek Orthodox church; Byzantine frescoes and mosaics in the Chora Museum; a genuine Turkish bath in Çemberlitas or Cagaloglu *hammam*.
THINGS TO DO:
Exploring the picturesque Fener area; visiting museums; shopping and haggling in the bazaars; walking along the bank of the Golden Horn; taking a boat trip on the Bosphorus; eating and drinking in local cafés and restaurants
YOU SHOULD KNOW:
Fener is a World Heritage site. Since it is a traditional area, only one or two of the local shops sell alcohol. The house is at the top of a steep hill, so you need to be quite fit, and an open stone staircase means you have to keep an eye on toddlers.

Staying in a private house is always the best way of getting to know any place, but this is especially true in the bewitching city of Istanbul, that gloriously confusing medley of East and West.

An old three-storey house in the Fener district has been beautifully renovated by its French owners. A picturesque area of narrow, cobbled lanes and historical town houses, Fener was once home to Istanbul's Greek community but since the 1960s has metamorphosed into a Muslim family neighbourhood. Veiled housewives chatter on their doorsteps, children play in the street, men sit around braziers drinking tea. You may get a few curious glances when you first arrive – tourists aren't often seen in this district – but as soon as the locals realize you are guests at Verystanbul they are genuinely friendly and the local shopkeepers and street vendors are delightful. Even at night it feels remarkably safe here.

Verystanbul sits at the top of a hill and is one in a row of quaint colour-washed houses with stucco facades and medieval-looking first-floor bay windows overhanging the street. The inside is gorgeously furnished in a boho-chic style. There's a wonderful roof terrace where you can sit in the evenings looking out on the city, plus a well-equipped, spotlessly clean kitchen, spacious living room and two double bedrooms with beautiful wood ceilings.

It's very easy to get buses and taxis to other parts of the city and close enough to the main sights, but also far enough from tourist areas to get a real insight into the daily life of this magical city. Staying at Verystanbul you'll see a side of Istanbul that you won't find in any guidebook – an unusually rewarding and thoroughly memorable cultural experience.

Sirkeçi Konak

WHERE:
Hüdavendigar Caddesi, Sirkeçi, Istanbul
COST:
Reasonable
BEST TIME OF YEAR:
Istanbul is enchanting at any time of year but it can be cold and wet between November and March. From late April to early June it is usually sunny without being too hot.
DON'T MISS:
A walk in Gülhane Park; the Basilica Cistern, an eerie Roman underground water reservoir; the Archaeology Museum; local restaurants and street food in the port area of Karaköy; the hotel tour of the Fatih farmers' market

In a city as overwhelming as Istanbul, with so many tourist hotels all superficially appearing much of a muchness, it's difficult to be sure that you've found a hotel that is good value for money. Sirkeçi Konak is a real find – a very attractive modern *konak* (mansion) tucked away down a quiet side street in the heart of the old city, right next to the Topkapi Palace and the Blue Mosque. Its location alone ensures that this hotel has plenty of custom, which makes it all the more pleasing that the management puts so much loving care into looking after its guests.

The hotel prides itself on combining the desirable amenities of a 21st-century western hotel with a traditional atmosphere – as can be

found in the spa, which has a proper Turkish bath – and good old-fashioned Turkish hospitality, such as the dish of *loukoum* (Turkish Delight) that you'll find in your room. The 52 bedrooms are not large but they have an air of 19th-century opulence, heightened by their Ottoman furnishings, under-floor heating and spacious bathrooms with tubs. The Ottoman mansion theme extends to the atmospheric public rooms and there are two excellent restaurants – one serving fish and the other traditional Turkish food. Dinner on the roof terrace looking out on an enchanting panoramic view of Gülhane Park and the Bosphorous is wonderfully romantic.

It's the little extra touches that make Sirkeçi Konak so special, such as the thought behind the hotel's guided walks introducing you to parts of the city you'd be unlikely to stumble on otherwise. The staff give the impression that they derive genuine pleasure in enabling you to enjoy every minute of your stay in their mesmerizing city, and Sirkeçi Konak is one of its gems.

THINGS TO DO:
Seeing the sights; visiting museums; shopping in the Grand Bazaar; boat trips along the Bosphorus; exploring the lesser known parts of the city; gastronomy

YOU SHOULD KNOW:
Sirkeçi Konak lays on free cookery lessons and wine tastings. It is unusually accommodating to people travelling with kids – there are triple and family rooms and the staff are not just tolerant and patient, but actively kind to babies and children.

A Cave in Cappadocia

WHERE:
Goreme National Park, Nevesehir, Cappadocia
COST:
From budget to expensive, depending on the degree of luxury
BEST TIME OF YEAR:
From March to November (the high-altitude plateau is bitterly cold between December and February)
DON'T MISS:
Goreme Open Air Museum; Kaymakli and Derinkuyu ancient underground cities; the 5th-century Church of John the Baptist in the village of Çavusin; the fairy chimneys of Pasabagi valley; wine tasting in Ürgüp; potteries and handicrafts workshops in Avanos
THINGS TO DO:
Trekking; horse riding; mountain biking; hot-air ballooning; visiting archaeological sites and old monasteries and discovering early Christian cave art; enjoying the nightlife in Ürgüp
YOU SHOULD KNOW:
The name Cappadocia is from the Persian *Katpatuca* (Land of the Beautiful Horses) and was the Roman name for the region now officially known as Nevsehir – a highland plateau in central Anatolia. The extraordinary landscape has been shaped by thousands of years of the wind and rain wearing away volcanic tuff, the hardened lava and ash from primeval volcanic eruptions.

Goreme National Park in Cappadocia is unlike anywhere else on earth, a fantastical other-worldly landscape of deep ravines and cliffs, awesome caves, and bizarre 'fairy chimneys' sprouting out of the ground and up to 40 m (130 ft) high.

From the Bronze Age onwards troglodytes have inhabited the fairy chimneys and caves of Cappadocia. From the 4th century, Christian converts hid here to escape persecution. They carved monasteries and churches out of the rock face, decorating the interiors with exquisite religious frescoes. Whole networks of caves have been dug out to create underground villages and even entire towns complete with secret passageways, storehouses, stables and barns, churches and sarcophagi; and fairy chimneys have been ingeniously converted into multi-storeyed houses with staircases and windows.

People still live in this bizarre wonderland and there are numerous cave hotels where you can stay. Cappadocia Cave Suites in Goreme has 35 rooms with bedrock walls, windows and wooden ceilings. Or you can stay in a fairy chimney at the wonderful Kelebek Hotel, which has rooms to suit all pockets, or at the Fairy Chimney Inn, a 1,500-year-old Byzantine monastery with magnificent views from the courtyard terrace. In the lively town of Ürgüp you can stay at Yunak Evleri in one of 30 beautifully furnished cave rooms carved into a cliff face that dates back to the 5th century. Or sidetrack off the main tourist route to stay in the fascinating little village of Ayvali at the beautifully restored caves and fairy chimneys of Gamirasu, a 1,000-year-old Christian retreat. Witnessing the human ingenuity that has made this haunting no-man's land habitable is an awe-inspiring experience and the caves of Cappadocia are truly memorable.

Marmara Antalya Revolving Hotel

The Marmara Hotel Group has opened a revolutionary new hotel, literally! Yes, prepare to take a spin in a hotel that revolves – it's the only one in the world. The 'revolving loft' is a three-storey, 24-room circular building annexed to the main hotel. It gently rotates to give a constantly changing panoramic view. You can't actually feel yourself moving but you may feel mildly disorientated on waking in the morning to find yourself gazing at the mountains, when last night you were admiring the moonlight rippling over the sea. The limited number of rooms means that most guests are accommodated in the main hotel, but there's a lounge area in the revolving annexe where guests who haven't managed to obtain a room there may sit and enjoy a drink while watching the continuously changing view.

The hotel is in a superb setting on high cliffs in a lush, landscaped garden. There is a vast infinity pool surrounded by flowers, a sensational artificial river which you can canoe along, and a private stretch of beach reserved for hotel guests. All the rooms and public areas, revolving or otherwise, are done up in brightly coloured modernistic decor designed to be fun and put you in a light-hearted holiday frame of mind.

Antalya is an attractive coastal city built on cliff terraces tumbling down to the sea and surrounded by the spectacular scenery of beautiful tree-clad mountains. The city plays host to some two million tourists every year, attracted here by the sunshine, blue sea, miles of golden beach, a vibrant night life and superb shopping as well as cultural sites and a picturesque old town. Marmara could not have picked a better spot for its revolutionary experiment in hotel design. Enjoy the fun!

WHERE:
Eski Lara Yolu, Sirinyali, Antalya
COST:
Reasonable
BEST TIME OF YEAR:
June to September
DON'T MISS:
The Archaeological Museum, onc of Turkey's most important museum collections; the view from the landmark Hidirlic Tower; Kesik Mosque, formerly a Byzantine church; the ancient city of Termessos 30 km (19 mi) from Antalya; Düden waterfalls
THINGS TO DO:
Swimming; waterskiing; jet-skiing; windsurfing; diving; catamaran sailing; canoeing; golf; cycling; hiking in the beautiful countryside; shopping; enjoying the vibrant night life; exploring the picturesque streets of Antalya old town
YOU SHOULD KNOW:
The 'revolving loft' cost $12 million to build and was an incredibly complex feat of engineering. Unsurprisingly, Marmara won an award for the Most Innovative Concept in Luxury Hotels.

Bayram's Treehouses

WHERE:
Olympos, Kemer, Antalya
COST:
Budget
BEST TIME OF YEAR:
May to September
DON'T MISS:
The ancient ruins of Olympos; the natural wonder of the Chimaera (of mythological fame) at night time, where blue flames shoot out from the rocks; climbing to the top of Mount Olympos for spectacular views
THINGS TO DO:
Kayaking; swimming; snorkelling; boat tours; hiking; rock climbing; canyoning; mountain biking
YOU SHOULD KNOW:
Olympos is 90 minutes by bus from the huge resort of Antalya on the southern Turkish coast. It is a tiny village with no bank or cash facilities and it can get crowded in high season but, because it is in a protected national park, it hasn't suffered from the tourist developments that blight most of the Antalya coast.

You'd never know that Olympos was once an important ancient Lycian city. All you'll find today are a few houses and orange groves leading through some ancient ruins to a shallow, rocky bay in the middle of nowhere. It is a hippy paradise – a long stretch of sand and fine-shingle beach fringed by wild vines, pine, oleander, bay and fig trees, a river that runs into the sea, high mountains in the background . . . and not much else.

A stay at Bayram's treehouses offers days lazing on the beach, swimming in the warm blue sea, hiking in the beautiful back country, reading, eating and sleeping. And when darkness falls you can sit around a campfire with a *nargile* (water pipe) playing backgammon, drinking beer, making music, drumming and partying.

The accommodation is basic but a lot more comfortable than camping. The quaint little wooden huts sit on raised platforms, nestling among the orange trees. They sleep two to five people and you can either rough it with floor mattresses on kelim rugs and use the communal washing facilities, or go for a superior air-conditioned cabin with proper beds and a private bathroom. There's a decent restaurant and a bar on the site and wooden lounging platforms with mattresses and cushions, as well as hammocks strung between trees, where you can relax, chat, read or take a nap.

There are several places to stay in Olympos but the ambience of Bayram's is especially pleasant because of the exceptionally friendly staff and the broad cross-section of people – from those who are retired, to children, as well as backpackers and hippies. Anyone on a tight budget looking for an off-the-beaten-track, back-to-nature but lively beach holiday will be completely in their element here.

Hotel Azur, Çirali

If you love the idea of a foreign family holiday by the sea but can't stand the thought of the noisy, crowded beaches of the Turkish Riviera, then the out-of-the-way resort of Çirali in the Olympos National Park is a dream come true. This sleepy little village is not much more than a smattering of small farmhouses, a mosque and a few tourist restaurants at the end of a winding mountain road. Not only is it almost the last unspoilt part of the Antalya coast, but it is also on one of the best beaches – and you can stay in a garden paradise at the Hotel Azur.

Close to the beach, Hotel Azur has been owned and run by a local family for two generations. It provides hearty hospitality, superb Mediterranean food and faultless service. Guests are accommodated in charming four-person, air-conditioned bungalows and timber lodges secluded among the greenery of a huge, beautifully maintained semi-tropical garden. Butterflies flutter around the exotic flowers, geese and peacocks strut under the trees, rabbits hop in and out of the flowerbeds and cats laze in the sun. Children will love the animals and the freedom to roam, while parents or the non-encumbered can lie languidly in a hammock inhaling the scent of citrus and pine, listening to the cries of the sea birds and plucking ripe fruit from the trees.

The broad 3.5-km (2-mi) long sand and fine-shingle beach slopes gently down to the sea and the water is exceptionally calm and clear – perfect for youngsters. Çirali is in a region of outstanding natural beauty, surrounded by rugged pine-clad mountains. You can't really get much closer to heaven.

WHERE:
Çirali, Kemer, Antalya
COST:
Very reasonable
BEST TIME OF YEAR:
May to September (late July to the end of August to see the hatching of baby sea turtles)
DON'T MISS:
The walk from Çirali to the waterfalls at Ulupinar; the ruins of Olympos; the Chimaera eternal flame
THINGS TO DO:
Çirali is on the Lycian Way, the coastal footpath, and there are lots of good short-distance hikes in the area. Other possible activities include swimming, snorkelling, kayaking, taking boat tours, trekking, canyoning, rock climbing and mountain biking – or just lying on the beach.
YOU SHOULD KNOW:
Çirali is in the same bay as Olympos but there is no direct connecting road, so the easiest way to get to Olympos is by walking along the beach. Çirali is a peaceful family- and couples-orientated resort with little nightlife and few backpackers.

Güllü Konaklari Hotel

WHERE:
Sirince, Selçuk, Izmir
COST:
Reasonable
BEST TIME OF YEAR:
May to September for sunshine; October to April for visiting archaeological and historical sites
DON'T MISS:
St John the Baptist Church; the 4th-century House of the Virgin Mary; frescoes at the Sütini Cave
THINGS TO DO:
Walking in the hills; exploring the village; visiting ancient ruins and other historic sites; shopping in the village handicrafts shops; tasting the local wines
YOU SHOULD KNOW:
As there is a good bus service to Sirince you don't need your own car to come and stay here. It is only 8 km (5 mi) from Selçuk (Ephesus). Sirince is famous for its wine and has a rich history.

The west coast of Turkey has been a centre of civilization since the earliest times. Tourists are attracted here in their millions and the coastal hills are now blighted by unsightly hotel complexes and holiday apartment blocks. If you want to visit the ancient cultural and historical sites, but would prefer to stay somewhere more picturesque, you can still find a more traditional Turkey in the hills of the hinterland.

The delightful Güllü Konaklari (Rose House) is a restored mansion set in a walled hillside garden with a fountain, fruit trees, masses of roses and tubs of geraniums, lavender and fuchsias, just above the town of Sirince. This picturesque little inland town has cobbled lanes and old stone houses and although the main street is geared for tourists, you only have to turn the corner to bump into an old man with a donkey going about his business.

The hotel has a dozen air-conditioned rooms, each named after one of the rose varieties in the garden. They are furnished differently but all have rustic charm and elegant, spacious bathrooms. The hotel overlooks beautiful countryside and there are panoramic views over the town to the surrounding hills. The hotel restaurant is excellent and you can sit on the delightful terrace admiring the view as you savour the wonderfully fresh Mediterranean fare. There are divans in secluded spots around the garden where you can read or have an aperitif as you watch the sun going down behind the hills. The tranquil and romantic atmosphere at Güllü Konaklari is in welcome contrast to the hectic coastal scene and it makes a perfect base from which to visit the ancient sites.

The Aegean Gate

WHERE:
Kumbahçe, Bodrum
COST:
Reasonable
BEST TIME OF YEAR:
May to September
DON'T MISS:
The Castle of St Peter, a Crusader fortress; the well preserved ancient amphitheatre; the Tuesday market; riding a camel; the windmills of Bodrum; a trip on a *gulet* (a traditional Turkish wooden sailing boat)
THINGS TO DO:
Swimming; windsurfing; diving; snorkelling; jet-skiing; parasailing; boat trips; river rafting; horse riding; jeep safaris; eating and drinking; clubbing and live music nights; shopping for leather goods and beads; exploring the coast and seeing the historic sites

You wouldn't choose to stay in the chic port town of Bodrum, the birthplace of Herodotus, unless you were up for enjoying the legendary nightlife in this sophisticated, vibrant Turkish Riviera resort. Yet however much fun you have in the waterfront *tavernas*, lingering over a bottle of wine or clubbing until the small hours, a bit of respite can also be very welcome.

In a quiet part of town yet less than 15 minutes' walk from the centre and close to a 24-hour taxi rank, the Aegean Gate is a peaceful sanctuary from the bustle of harbour-side life. This wonderful boutique hotel is a large, renovated town house in a magical setting – on a rugged hill top next to a dramatic rock outcrop – with a beautifully landscaped garden and stunning views of the sea. There are six suites, each consisting of bedroom, living room and bathroom, sleeping a maximum of three people. Two are self-catering poolside apartments with their own terraces and kitchenettes and the other four have balconies looking out to the island of Kos. The rooms are spacious, tastefully furnished and sparkling clean.

The relaxed, informal atmosphere is just like staying with friends. You'll feel completely at ease spending the day lazing on the pool terrace, having a drink from the poolside bar and wandering around the garden. The delightful Irish owners go out of their way to make guests feel at home and will help you organize your sightseeing expeditions, tell you the best places to eat and give you the low-down on what's what in town. The Aegean Gate is really special – as soon as you leave you'll be dreaming of when you can return.

YOU SHOULD KNOW:
This is a hotel for animal lovers – the owners have several cats and the local strays turn up for feeding every day, there are two very friendly rescue dogs and tortoises living among the rocks in the garden. No children under the age of 16 are allowed and there is a minimum stay of two nights.

Mehmet Ali Aga Konagi

WHERE:
Datça, Mugla
COST:
Expensive
BEST TIME OF YEAR:
April to October – the garden is at its best between late April and mid June
DON'T MISS:
Having a traditional Ottoman bath and massage in the mansion's wood-fuelled *hammam*; the windmills of Datça; the Seljuk mosque in the nearby village of Hizirsah; swimming at the ancient site of Knidos where the Aegean Sea meets the Mediterranean
THINGS TO DO:
Trekking and nature walks; birdwatching; mountain biking; swimming; scuba diving; windsurfing; kayaking; boat trips; fishing trips; whiling away the afternoon under the vines in the waterfront restaurants of Datça; exploring the beaches and villages along the peninsula; shopping in the local craft and jewellery workshops
YOU SHOULD KNOW:
Datça is a narrow 100-km (62-mi) long peninsula in southwestern Turkey, famous for its fish, honey and almonds. It is one of the few places on the Turkish Riviera that is not developed and there are unspoilt beaches in little coves all along the coast. The water here is exceptionally clear and unpolluted. Mehmet Ali Aga Konagi is 3.5 km (2 mi) from the sea and runs a free shuttle service to its own beach club.

To get to Mehmet Ali's mansion you take a narrow winding road through wild mountains forested with pine, eucalyptus and myrtle, with breathtaking views of the sea, passing little white-washed houses surrounded by olive groves and vineyards. You finally arrive at your destination – an authentic Ottoman mansion.

One of the oldest examples of Ottoman architecture still surviving, the mansion was built in 1809 for Mehmet Ali, governor of the Datça Peninsula. The building has been painstakingly restored by the present owners and the interior is simply incredible – a superb period piece with arches, pillars, ornate frescoes, carved and painted wood, decorative ceilings, finely cobbled and tiled floors, and the original marble family *hammam*.

The atmosphere is one of utterly relaxed grandeur. You can stay in one of five historical rooms in the mansion itself, each beautifully furnished in the original opulent Ottoman style. Or, if you prefer modern amenities to period authenticity, plump for one of the attractive stone buildings around the edge of the garden – former stables and servants' quarters converted into elegant rooms opening out onto a covered terrace dripping with jasmine and bougainvillea.

The garden is a romantic paradise full of scent and colour, with lush semi-tropical plants and medicinal herbs, a citrus orchard and rose terrace, pergolas in secluded corners, a garden pond and a swimming pool shaded by almond trees. The food is positively delicious here – Turkish cuisine at its best – and the ambience is as good as the food when you eat by candlelight in the beautiful colonnaded courtyard. Mehmet Ali's is everything you would expect from an Ottoman mansion – a dream hotel in magical surroundings, a world away from the Turkish Riviera tourist mayhem.

Zeytindali Hotel

When you land on the island of Gökçeada, it feels as though the clock has been turned back 50 years. It's exactly as the Aegean islands used to be before they were 'discovered' – an idyll of sun, sea and simple rustic pleasures. The air is heady with the scent of wild thyme, the rugged mountain slopes are clothed in pine trees, sheep graze placidly in the pastures around ancient hill-top villages and quaint stone cottages are dotted among the island's vineyards and olive groves.

The Zeytindali Hotel occupies two romantic stone houses in the picturesque hill village of Zeytinliköy, one of the oldest settlements on the island. Each of the 16 rooms is named after a figure from Greek mythology and is individually furnished. The decor is simple but charming and the rooms are immaculately clean and have decent bathrooms. Lovely sea or village views are on offer and you can have a room with its own little garden. The staff are friendly and efficient and the hotel has an atmosphere of warm informality. Its restaurant serves wonderful, fresh food and it's only too easy to spend hours dawdling on the terrace, lingering over a breakfast spread of home-produced salty sheep cheeses, local olives and thyme honey, watching village life go by. Life here has changed little over the centuries and there is a sense of continuity and unhurried calm that will soothe even the most frayed of nerves.

No doubt the tourist industry will ensure that this beautiful unspoilt island eventually becomes as overcrowded as the rest of the Aegean. Now is the time to visit Gökçeada, to enjoy the beautiful natural scenery and secluded sandy beaches before it's too late.

WHERE:
Zeytinliköy, Gökçeada, Çannakale
COST:
Budget
BEST TIME OF YEAR:
April to October
DON'T MISS:
Having coffee at Madam Dibek, a famous coffee house in Zeytinliköy; Pinarbasi Beach, the longest and sandiest beach on the island; the underwater wrecks at Maviköy (Bluebay), the first National Underwater Park in Turkey; the abandoned village of Dereköy; Barba Yorgo, a Greek *taverna* in the village of Tepeköy; having a curative mud bath in Aydinçik
THINGS TO DO:
Swimming in the sparkling unpolluted sea; scuba diving; snorkelling; windsurfing; boat trips; trekking; mountain biking; birdwatching; exploring the island's nine villages; shopping in the local markets
YOU SHOULD KNOW:
Gökçeada used to be known by its Greek name of Imbros. It is the largest of Turkey's Aegean islands and the westernmost point of Turkey. For centuries the island was inhabited by Greeks, but it was ceded to Turkey in 1923. During the 1960s, when relations between Greece and Turkey grew increasingly strained, most of the islanders were coerced into leaving. There is still a small Greek community but the vast majority of Gökçeada's inhabitants are Turkish settlers.

The King David

WHERE:
King David Street, Jerusalem
COST:
Astronomical but discounts and upgrades can often be wangled
BEST TIME OF YEAR:
A year-round destination
DON'T MISS:
Walking along the ramparts of the city wall; 'The Night Spectacular' *son et lumière* show at the Tower of David Museum; the swanky shops in Mamilla Mall; Mahane Yehuda *shuk*, a labyrinthine open-air market; Jerusalem Botanical Garden, with more than 6,000 plant species; eating waffles in Babette's coffee shop on Shamai Street
THINGS TO DO:
Historical walking tours of the Old City; visiting the numerous museums and religious and archaeological sites; shopping in the markets and malls; listening to live music in Jerusalem bars; checking out the nightclub scene
YOU SHOULD KNOW:
The south wing of the King David was requisitioned by the British as their administrative headquarters in 1938. In July 1946 the extremist Zionist Irgun organization planted a bomb in the hotel basement which killed 91 people and injured 45. This terrible terrorist atrocity is writ large in the history of the hotel and, while the wing was rebuilt, if you look carefully you can see a slight difference in the stone.

You can't help feeling a tingle of excitement as you enter the foyer of the King David, wondering whose famous face you're going to spot. For more than 80 years this iconic Jerusalem hotel has been a stamping ground for the great and the good. Royalty, celebrities, prime ministers and presidents from all over the world walk daily through its doors and a sense of privilege and class pervades the atmosphere.

Opened in 1931, before the state of Israel was founded, the King David stands in a prime position just outside the Old City, overlooking the Western Wall and Mount Zion, a palace of delicate pink limestone quartz. It was built by an influential consortium of Egyptian Jewish bankers and no expense was spared on the construction. Externally, the building is a grand neoclassical mansion but set foot through the door and you are magically transported to the East – graceful arches and domes, ancient biblical motifs and oriental Art Deco features meld stylishly into the classic western symmetry.

The 233 rooms and suites combine timeless luxury with every hi-tech amenity. Four plush restaurants offer a vast range of gourmet food and the King David breakfasts are legendary – reputedly the best in Israel. The extensive gardens are a welcome sanctuary from the heat of the city, with secluded corners to relax in, and the service is renowned for its polish – whether you're having a spa treatment, arguing for a room upgrade or simply ordering a poolside drink, you are treated with unfailing charm and courtesy by a faultlessly professional team of staff.

This world-famous historic hotel represents all that's best about old-fashioned glamour and dignity – a surprisingly thrilling experience.

Evason Ma'In Hot Springs

In the spectacular desert mountains around the Dead Sea, 264 m (865 ft) below sea level, the Ma'In sulphur springs of Wadi Mujib gorge have been enjoyed for thousands of years – Herod the Great is said to have sworn by the healing properties of the mineral-rich waters here. More than 100 natural springs and waterfalls, fed by winter rain seeping through the rock of the highland plateau, bubble and splash out of the cliff face at the bottom of the gorge, the water pre-heated to a balmy temperature of 45°C (113°F) by underground thermal energy.

The prestigious Evason spa company has built a luxurious spa lodge in these romantic desert surroundings. Nestling in the oasis of Wadi Mujib, overlooked by precipitous rock outcrops, the lodge has 94 rooms and three luxury suites, all soothingly decorated with simple yet stylish furnishings and calm colour tones, designed to harmonize with the landscape. You can meditate under a pergola in one of the outdoor relaxation areas, retreat behind the doors of the peaceful reading room, swim in the open-air pool, wallow in the indoor thermal pool, work out in the gym, and watch the sun sink behind the mountains over a long and lazy meal in the clifftop restaurant. And at the traditional Roman baths, just five minutes' walk along the gorge, you can indulge yourself in therapeutic beauty treatments, have an underwater massage, and frolic under the gushing Ma'In waterfall as it cascades down into a cliffside pool.

Ma'In hot springs is a restorative sanctuary, the perfect place to escape from urban stress. You can breathe unpolluted air, eat freshly grown, healthy food, and marvel at the dramatic desert scenery.

WHERE:
Hammamat Ma'In, Wadi Mujib, Madaba
COST:
Expensive
BEST TIME OF YEAR:
March to May or September to November to avoid the high summer heat and the winter rains
DON'T MISS:
A therapeutic mud bath; an underwater massage; the impressive Al Megheirat dolmens (prehistoric burial chambers); a day trip to the ancient rock city of Petra; the famous Byzantine mosaics of Madaba
THINGS TO DO:
Bathing in the hot springs; spa treatments; outdoor workouts with a personal trainer; hiking and nature walks; mountain biking; birdwatching; day trips
YOU SHOULD KNOW:
The Ma'In hot springs are just 18.5 km (11.5 mi) from the Dead Sea and 30 km (19 mi) from the city of Madaba. Wadi Mujib is the lowest-lying nature reserve in the world and there is a wealth of flora and fauna in the mountains around the Ma'in springs.

Dana Tower

WHERE:
Main Street, Dana,
Wadi Dana Nature Reserve
COST:
Budget
BEST TIME OF YEAR:
Choose the spring months of March to May, or from September to November to avoid chilly winter nights and rain.
DON'T MISS:
The ruins of Khirbet Feinan, 6,000-year-old copper mines; hiking to the summit of Rummana Mountain to see the strange rock formations, amazing views, and griffon vultures; a day trip to the World Heritage rose-pink city of Petra 40 km (25 mi) away
THINGS TO DO:
Hiking (with or without guides); horse riding; camel trekking; mountain biking; jeep tours; overnight camping in the wild; birdwatching; studying the flora and fauna; visiting some of the 100 nearby archaeological sites; looking round the silver and pottery shops
YOU SHOULD KNOW:
Wadi Dana is extraordinarily rich in flora and fauna. There are 700 plant species, three of which are endemic, 200 bird species and 40 species of mammal – including the endangered Syrian wolf and sand cat. The Dana Tower organizes guided hikes, night walks, wilderness camping and jeep tours for guests.

The Dana Tower is a world away from the skyscraper city hotel its name conjures up. Miles off the beaten track, and far from being a high-rise, it's a delightful little tourist inn in the picturesque 15th-century village of Dana. The village comprises a jumble of higgledy-piggledy stone houses clinging precariously to a precipitous rock face in the middle of the Wadi Dana Nature Reserve.

The charmingly eccentric and hospitable owner of Dana Tower is a local man who has converted several traditional hillside cottages into a single rambling building. There are 12 spotlessly clean, individually decorated single, double and triple rooms, some with their own bathrooms, and they are all funkily furnished and have been given whimsical names like Flying Carpet, Crazy Camel, and the Harem. Or you can choose to sleep under the stars on the sprawling split-level roof terraces from where you get staggering views over the Wadi Dana canyon.

You will find all the traditional charm of the Middle East here: amazingly generous-spirited hospitality and gregarious communal meals. In the evening, guests can lounge in a Bedouin tent among embroidered cushions and brightly coloured woven rugs, sipping mint tea, smoking *shishas* (water pipes) of fruit-scented tobacco in the twilight, and watching the purple sunset shadows deepen over the crevasses and cliffs of the canyon.

The Wadi Dana is Jordan's largest nature reserve – a 320 sq km (125 sq mi) canyon of dramatic red and white sandstone rock, impressively deep with narrow side ravines, sheer escarpments and craggy mountains. The desert terrain ranges from 50 m (165 ft) below sea level up to 1,500 m (5,000 ft) high and supports an incredible diversity of wildlife. It is absolute magic here – heaven for adventurers, walkers and nature lovers.

Fujairah Rotana Resort

Fujairah is the most beautiful part of the United Arab Emirates, on the Gulf of Oman with a 90-km (56-mi) coastline of immaculate sand and mountains that tumble down to the Arabian Sea. The pace of life is much less hectic here than in the other Emirates and the culture still relatively traditional.

For a holiday of sun, sand, sea and spa, whether as a couple or a family, you couldn't choose a much more perfect spot than the Rotana Resort. The palatial neo-colonial complex nestles at the foot of the Hajar Mountains overlooking a pristine white-sand beach. It is set in lush semi-tropical gardens bursting with colourful flowers and decked with pools, pagodas and fountains.

Once here, you don't need to move from the hotel grounds except to walk the few yards to the sea. The 250 stylishly furnished, airy rooms all have private terraces and terrific in-room amenities. Everything anyone could want in the way of recreation, sports and pampering is provided with friendly, efficient and unobtrusive service.

There are six bars and restaurants, each with its own ambience, serving an extensive choice of excellent food, plus a superb swimming pool and sports facilities, an impressive gym and a sensational spa with 17 treatment rooms offering a vast array of holistic Asian therapies, beauty treatments and different sorts of massage. The children can be kept happily entertained at the kids' club and there's a babysitting service so that you can enjoy the resort's evening entertainment or have a romantic dinner for two on the beach. Anyone looking for a self-indulgent, therapeutic break in beautiful natural surroundings and a secluded atmosphere will find it at the Rotana.

WHERE:
Al Aqah Beach, Fujairah

COST:
The room rates are reasonable but bear in mind that the sports amenities and spa will add to your bill.

BEST TIME OF YEAR:
It's an all-year-round resort, but go in March to May or from September to November to avoid the chilliest and hottest times of year.

DON'T MISS:
Fujairah Fort and Heritage Village; Fujairah Museum, stuffed with antiquities; Al Hayl Castle; Ain al Mahdab Gardens; the waterfalls of Wadi al Wurayah

THINGS TO DO:
Swimming; snorkelling; scuba diving; yachting; *dhow* trips; surfing; parasailing; deep-sea fishing; tennis; squash; beach volleyball; yoga; Tai Chi; spa therapies; hanging out on the beach; desert safaris; eating and drinking; sightseeing; shopping in nearby Dubai

YOU SHOULD KNOW:
The Rotana Resort is an accredited diving and water sports centre and operates its own shuttle bus service to transport guests to the main tourist attractions of Fujairah.

Burj al-Arab

WHERE:
Jumeirah Road, Dubai
COST:
Astronomical
BEST TIME OF YEAR:
Any time
DON'T MISS:
Being transported in an express lift for a cocktail 200 m (655 ft) up in the Skyview Bar, looking out on the futuristic skyline of Dubai; being pumped into the ground-floor aquarium by simulated submarine to savour the food in the hotel's Al Mahara gourmet fish restaurant; the hotel's private helicopter tour of Dubai; using one of the Burj's fleet of white Rollers to take you indoor skiing and shopping at the Mall of the Emirates; Deira Gold Souk, one of the largest gold markets in the world; Sheik Saeed Al Maktoum House, an architectural wonder and museum
THINGS TO DO:
Swimming and water sports on Jumeirah Beach; horse riding; polo; golf; tennis; hot-air ballooning; boat trips; desert excursions; eating and drinking; shopping in the malls and *souks*; enjoying Dubai's vibrant hotel nightlife
YOU SHOULD KNOW:
The Burj al-Arab has won the *World Travel Awards* World's Leading Hotel award. Dubai is a city of contrasts and extremes – note that it is important to obey the strict Muslim dress codes and alcohol laws in public places.

Arrange to be picked up from the airport in one of the hotel's white Rolls Royces or, if you prefer, climb aboard the hotel helicopter and land on the rooftop heliport. Whatever mode of transport you decide to use, get here you must – staying in the world's best hotel is an unmissable experience!

Designed to look like the billowing sail of an Arabian *dhow*, the Burj al-Arab stands as a brazen temple to mammon, epitomizing the sybaritic culture of Dubai. It soars 321 m (1,053 ft) into the sky from its own offshore artificial island, its Teflon-coated curves lit up at night in a choreographed rainbow of dancing colours. You can't help gawping in amazement when you enter the 180-m (600-ft) high atrium, an extravaganza of golden columns and lavish colours with fountains shooting cascades of water 32 m (100 ft) in the air. It is an unashamed Arabian Nights fantasy verging on the delusional.

The theme of decadent excess runs throughout the hotel. Even the most basic suite is an opulent duplex apartment decked in richly coloured satins, velvet and gold, with floor-to-ceiling windows, private dining room, hi-tech office, Hermes-stocked, Jacuzzi-fitted bathroom – and a round-the-clock personal butler to cater for your every whim. The Burj's ten restaurants and bars are an Epicurean dream come true, serving gourmet food and drink from every corner of the globe, and the hotel spa is a cavernous sky palace of plunge pools and mosaics.

Everything is extravagant at the Burj, including the bill. But the experience is so worth it. Save up the money, max out your credit card and join the Russian oligarchs in having the time of your life.

Palm Jumeirah

WHERE:
Dubai
COST:
Expensive
BEST TIME OF YEAR:
There is sunshine all year round, but December and March are especially favourable months when it is temperate but not too hot.
DON'T MISS:
A boat trip round the Palm Jumeirah man-made islands; swimming with dolphins at Dolphin Bay; the amazing Aquaventure water park; taking the world's fastest lift to the Observation Deck at The Burj Khalifa, the world's tallest building; Dubai Museum in the Al-Fahidi Fort, the oldest building in Dubai
THINGS TO DO:
Swimming; sailing; kayaking; windsurfing; waterskiing; fishing; boat cruises; tennis; volleyball; golf; desert excursions; sand surfing; designer shopping malls; restaurants, bars and nightclubs; seeing the sights of Dubai
YOU SHOULD KNOW:
Palm Jumeirah is one of the three Palm Islands, a land reclamation project which will ultimately add 520 km (320 mi) to Dubai's coastline. Palm Jumeirah is connected to the mainland by a 300-m (985-ft) bridge. Atlantis, The Palm was the first hotel to open here in 2008, and Palm Jumeirah is fast becoming one of the world's leading luxury resort islands.

The luxury resort of Palm Jumeirah is a Middle Eastern 21st-century nod to Venice, an ingenious man-made island archipelago just off Dubai's coast, created by land reclamation. From the air, the islands form the shape of a palm tree with a trunk and 16 fronds enclosed by a crescent-shaped breakwater. This mind-boggling feat of marine engineering has unselfconsciously been called the 'eighth wonder of the world'.

You can stay at Atlantis, a towering edifice on the Palm Jumeirah island tree. Everything is on a grand scale, with wonderful service and superb amenities. The hotel covers a 46-ha (114-ac) site with more than 1,500 luxury rooms either overlooking the Palm or the open sea, freshwater and saltwater pools, a gloriously peaceful spa retreat with 27 treatment rooms, 17 restaurants and bars, masses of entertainment to keep children and teenagers occupied, and 2 km (1.25 mi) of pristine sand beach.

If you prefer somewhere smaller and more secluded, One And Only is an attractive Spanish-Moorish residence with 90 rooms and four private villas on the very tip of the Palm's breakwater. In this chic boutique hotel, you can unwind in the intimate atmosphere of a tranquil beach resort while still being within spitting distance of the city-centre buzz. The rooms overlook the hotel's palm-fringed private beach, a mere 30-second stroll away; and there's a wonderful 50-m (164-ft) swimming pool in the garden, a relaxing spa and three gourmet restaurants.

In this thrilling, futuristic city of brash hedonism and frenetic shopping it can be a delight to trade in the urban hubbub for some chilling-out time in the exclusive offshore surroundings of amazing Palm Jumeirah.

ASIA

Banjara Camp

Because of their politically sensitive location, the twin regions of Kinnaur and Spiti in the far north of India have only been open to tourists for the past 20 or so years. One of the first enterprises to develop the visitor potential of the area's myriad attractions was Banjara Camp and Retreats. The basic concept was simple: choosing remote, unspoilt locations where travellers could have comfortable camping experiences in the midst of glorious natural settings.

The first of Banjara's camps was established at Sangla Valley, which would have to score highly as many people's ideal Himalayan valley, with the Baspa river surging and tumbling over its floor, flanked by pastures and wooded slopes and the whole ringed by

WHERE:
Baspa Valley, Himachal Pradesh
COST:
Budget
BEST TIME OF YEAR:
May to September
DON'T MISS:
The four-hour walk along the river to Rakcham village and its beautifully carved pagoda-style temple which combines Hindu and Buddhist deities
THINGS TO DO:
Trekking; guided nature walks; mountain biking; trout fishing; visiting local villages to see traditional weaving and woodcarving; jeep safaris; rock climbing; abseiling; wondering if you'll run into a yeti (you won't!)
YOU SHOULD KNOW:
Sangla Valley Camp is at 2,700 m (8,860 ft), so you need to come prepared for chilly temperatures at night.

towering, snow-capped mountains. The camp is laid out on a low plateau beside the river bank. There are 13 Swiss-style tents, each having an attached and tiled bathroom with hot and cold running water. Meals are taken in a communal tented area and the friendly and knowledgeable staff are on hand to lead tours of the area or to make suggestions for your own excursions. The emphasis is on creating the spirit of camp life without requiring too many sacrifices in terms of personal comfort. One of the special pleasures of a stay here is sitting round the evening campfire beneath the stars and swapping tales of the day's events.

If sleeping under canvas does not appeal under any circumstances, Banjara now offers the alternative option of a simple but comfortable room in their Retreat – a two-storey stone-and-wood house built in rustic style and adjacent to the campsite.

A Log Hut in Manali

High in the Himalayas, just below the 2,000-m (6,560-ft) snowline, the old hill station of Manali is surrounded by some of the most beautiful mountain scenery in the world. This northern end of the sacred Kullu Valley is a patchwork of lush meadows, tilled fields and fruit orchards enclosed by soaring mountains, their slopes swathed in rhododendrons, pines and tall cedar trees, dissected by swift whitewater rivers. Perched on rocky outcrops and hidden among the trees, ancient shrines and temples leave one in no doubt that this is the airy land of Hindu gods.

If you want to immerse yourself in all this awe-inspiring natural beauty, it is best to stay just outside busy Manali in one of the mountain log huts. These rustic hideaways are shrouded in greenery, hidden in a copse of tall cedar trees behind a temple. The fully serviced huts have two double bedrooms, each with a bathroom, living-cum-dining room and well-equipped kitchen with fridge and gas cooker. There is plenty of space for a family of four or two couples without anyone getting on top of anyone else. You can have all your meals brought to you, or shop in Manali market and cook your own, shamelessly leaving the washing up for the daily cleaner. And as sundown approaches you can sit on your porch in the glow of an open fire gazing at mesmerizing views of the snow-capped Himalayan peaks.

Backpackers, families, hippies, honeymooners and adventurers alike are all drawn here by the captivating landscapes and ancient cultural heritage. The soul-stirring beauty of the Himalayas is like nowhere else on earth. It has to be experienced to be believed.

WHERE:
Manali, Kullu, Himachal Pradesh
COST:
Budget
BEST TIME OF YEAR:
March and April are especially beautiful, when the fruit trees blossom. High season is from March until June, or from November to February for winter-sports enthusiasts. The monsoon season from July to September is best avoided.
DON'T MISS:
The Rahala Waterfalls and spectacular view from the Rohtang Pass; the dramatic gorge at the nearby village of Kothi; Hadimba Devi Temple;coffee and cookies as you watch a movie at Bob Dylan's Toasted and Roasted Coffee House in Old Manali town (but don't expect to meet Bob)
THINGS TO DO:
Trekking; horse riding; rock climbing; abseiling; paragliding; canyoning; whitewater rafting; trout fishing; skiing; heli-skiing; snowboarding; visiting temples; shopping for handicrafts and Tibetan curios in the bazaar; evenings in the lively cafés and restaurants of Old Manali
YOU SHOULD KNOW:
The Manali log huts are among many properties administered by Himachal Pradesh Tourism Development Corporation (HPTDC), a government agency which runs a long-distance bus service from major cities to the Kullu Valley, organizes local sightseeing tours and ensures a high standard of accommodation at reasonable rates.

Haveli Hari Ganga

WHERE:
Ramghat, Haridwar, Uttarakhand
COST:
Budget to reasonable (two sharing, young children free, supplement for older kids, worth paying extra for a river view)
BEST TIME OF YEAR:
Any (but beware monsoon rains between December and March)
DON'T MISS:
A speciality of the house is the sensational range of body-care programmes, with a dozen amazing massage treatments to choose from (yoga, steam rooms and a house astrologer too!). Take advantage of the private bathing *ghat* on the Ganges.
THINGS TO DO:
Marvel at the many stunning religious sites close to the Haveli, such as Hari Ki Pauri (a sacred *ghat*), the hill-top Mansa Devi Temple or *the* ancient temple of Maya Devi, the Adhisthatri deity of Haridwar. Take the wildlife safari day trip to Rajaji National Park to see wild elephants and much more. Explore Haridwar's bustling bazaar.
YOU SHOULD KNOW:
The most auspicious place in Haridwar for sacred bathing is the Brahma Kund (also known as Hari-ki-Pauri). Every night at about 18.00 there is worship (*arati*) of the Ganges (*Ganga*), consisting of a ritual offering of lamps to the Ganges, accompanied by the banging of ceremonial drums, music and hymns in praise of the holy river.

On the banks of the River Ganges in the Hindu pilgrimage town of Haridwar, where the sacred river emerges from the Himalayas onto the Indian plains, the Haveli Hari Ganga was built nearly a century ago by local rulers, inspired by this site of great religious significance. Their fine old building has been restored to blend innate old-world charm with modern facilities, and the interiors retain powerful echoes of the original spiritual motivation that determined the location, combined with lavish comforts and a palpable sense of the tranquillity that was also a part of the original Haveli's grand rationale.

The Haveli (a word used to describe a private mansion with historical significance, confirming this one's superior origins) was the personal residence of the Maharaja of Pilibhit, and today's visitors are stepping in illustrious footsteps (and then sleeping in illustrious beds). The public rooms were used by the royal family for entertaining, but only personal guests of the Maharaja with equal status would be invited to stay overnight. The place has been meticulously refurnished to restore the splendiferous original *decor*, with the subtle addition of modern essentials such air conditioning and all the other amenities now demanded by discerning travellers. The result is an unforgettable experience that harks back to the grandest era of the Raj, which can be enjoyed today. Needless to say, the level of traditional service required to complete this pampered picture should be incomparable – and so it is.

There's nothing better than sitting on the Haveli's terrace, overlooking the mighty Ganges, relaxing and watching the colourful tapestry of Indian life unfold, before repairing to the multi-cuisine restaurant for one of the most tempting menus in town.

Oberoi Udaivilas

WHERE:
Udaipur, Rajasthan
COST:
Budget to reasonable (veering towards expensive for a regal suite with private pool)
BEST TIME OF YEAR:
September to April
DON'T MISS:
Take a lavish picnic lunch on a private gondola on the scenic lake; dine *al fresco* at Chandni, the dining courtyard adjoining the hotel's three restaurants where guests can enjoy an open-air meal to the accompaniment of traditional music and dancing.

What could be better than staying in a classic Indian lakeside palace? Well, someone came up with the idea that the answer to that question is a new-build fake-old palace on the shores of Lake Pichola, across the water from the city of Udaipur, which is actually better than the real thing. It's an interesting concept and the result (in a great natural setting) is visually impressive. The Oberoi Udaivilas was constructed by local artisans in reasonably authentic Mewari style, and gleams proudly in the sunlight as if it has stood tall for generations. This may be fantasyland, somewhat divorced from the gritty reality of India's teeming city streets, but it certainly offers guests a romantic version of gracious Indian living that's hard (going on impossible) to resist.

This boutique hotel is incredibly luxurious, which is undoubtedly the proposition that keeps the place busy. It's plush to the point of overkill, with glitzily decorated guest rooms, large enough to house a Rajah's retinue, that have state-of-the-art bathrooms and tap water you can probably drink! There are nine or ten swimming pools (but who's counting?) and the spa is an out-station of Singapore's renowned Banyan Tree chain, so don't expect anything less than outrageous pampering. And of course there's right royal service, with attentive staff everywhere helpfully waiting to attend upon actual needs, or anticipating potential requirements before guests actually get around to articulating them. The cuisine is also first class with Thai, Mediterranean and other classic options vying for the dedicated gourmet's attention with Udaimahal's traditional Indian offerings.

Are there benefits to be had in building a brand-new palace instead of retrofitting an old one? For anyone keen to liberate their inner monarch at a surprisingly affordable price, the answer must surely be an imperious 'yes'.

THINGS TO DO:
Explore Udaipur, the magical city of majestic palaces and beautiful lakes; check out Gulab Bagh, a rose garden and library with a collection of ancient handwritten manuscripts and books, plus a garden zoo with tigers, leopards, many other animals and birds.

YOU SHOULD KNOW:
Two children up to eight years of age can stay in their parents' room without charge (and there are reduced room rates for additional youngsters). It is still possible to book a designated smoking room, although the hotel has recently gone 'smoke free'.

Devi Garh

WHERE:
Delwara, near Udaipur, Rajasthan
COST:
Reasonable (but don't hesitate to make an offer they probably won't refuse)
BEST TIME OF YEAR:
Any time is good but temperatures can soar to uncomfortable heights between May and August.
DON'T MISS:
The hotel's Kamal Court (one of five courtyards), an interesting take on the traditional lotus motif represented as a black marble water maze; the authentic flavours of *chaat* (wonderful savoury snacks), a quintessential aspect of Indian street life, prepared by Devi Garh's expert chefs instead of roadside vendors; fantastic sunsets observed from the hotel bar; a dip in the heated green-marble pool with its sublime views
THINGS TO DO:
Take a trip to Udaipur to see the splendid architectural sights and visit the City Palace Museum, which houses a large collection of stunning crystal among other fascinating exhibits; explore the colourful markets and visit the exquisite Jain temples in Eklingji; check out the local village of Delwara, which retains its traditional culture and time-honoured customs (then try a camel safari from the village into the Aravalli Hills to enjoy the scenic countryside).
YOU SHOULD KNOW:
Devi Garh is a bit of an up-and-down labyrinth, but there's a lift. The hotel offers a babysitting service. Garden Suites each have a private lobby and tented terrace overlooking a colourful flower garden.

The 18th-century Devi Garh palace-cum-fort stands four-square above the village of Delwara at the base of the rolling Aravalli Hills, guarding a pass into the Udaipur Valley. After decades of neglect, a full programme of renovation and rebuilding has created a characterful hotel. The historic qualities of this awesome structure are complemented by crisp new interiors, creating a felicitous conjunction of past, present and future. The hotel has 39 suites embellished with local marble and semi-precious stones, all equipped with the latest facilities to ensure that guests enjoy every comfort. For those who insist on the very best, the Devi Garh Suite even has its own swimming pool and Jacuzzi.

Fine food is an important part of Devi Garh's offering and, as with many top-flight hotel restaurants in the subcontinent, 'multi-cuisine' is the buzz phrase used to describe the choice of both Indian and international food (with fine wine, naturally). Wonderful views of the Aravalli Hills and surroundings can be enjoyed from the lofty eaterie, and it's also possible to request a private meal in a choice of romantic venues ranging from intimate venues where candlelight flickers in mirrored walls and music plays in the background to balmy corners of the landscaped grounds beside limpid water lit by the moon.

In addition to exemplary general service, there are tempting treatments available that both relax and invigorate. L'Occitane Spa offers wellness therapies based on a unique combination of traditional *ayurvedic* and thoroughly modern spa concepts, reflecting the hotel's desire to create a unique atmosphere from a happy marriage of traditional and modern, old and new. And of course all Indian luxury hotels are great value for money, compared with similar establishments elsewhere in the world.

Rambagh Palace

The world's most expensive wedding took place here, and its luxurious setting remains intact to this day. The Rambagh Palace hosted the two-week extravaganza back in the 1940s, as the Raj ended and India's princely families stepped down to allow democracy to take root. This amazing palace, just outside Jaipur, was then the luxurious home of the dashing local Maharaja. Known as the 'Jewel of Jaipur', this splendid building stands comparison with anything in the Pink City's amazing pantheon of extraordinary buildings.

The palace remained a royal residence until it was converted to a hotel and this architectural masterpiece has retained much traditional character, with elegant marbled hallways and lavish accommodation set off by the richest textiles, opulent furnishings and wonderful *objects d'art* that together recreate a fabulous bygone era when money was no object. Rambagh Palace has 79 rooms and stunning suites, all fully equipped with the full panoply of desirable modern conveniences.

The former ballroom is now the gilded Suvarna Mahal restaurant where guests feast on exotic Indian dishes and imbibe vintage wines to a background of classical music. The Verandah offers *al fresco* dining with great garden views, featuring international cuisine and Indian meals, while the Rajput Room is an informal all-day diner overlooking sweeping front lawns. The Jiva Grande Spa offers ancient Indian treatments blended with contemporary therapies, and you're sure to find something that engenders a right-royal sense of wellbeing. For the Rambagh Palace not only offers guests the finest Rajput hospitality, but also a taste of the extravagant living that was once the preserve of royalty. Is this one of India's finest hotels and a serious contender for international five-star honours? Yes indeed – it has actually been rated as the world's best hotel by *Condé Nast Traveler* magazine.

WHERE:
Bhawani Singh Road, near Jaipur, Rajasthan

COST:
Reasonable, indeed, for a serious slice of palace living

BEST TIME OF YEAR:
Any time – the reign in Rajasthan stays mainly on the plain

DON'T MISS:
A romantic evening meal by torchlight in a private tent within the 19-ha (47-ac) landscaped grounds, to the soothing accompaniment of a tinkling fountain; an evening cocktail in the atmospheric Polo Bar as the sun sets outside

THINGS TO DO:
An elephant ride in the grounds; a leisurely dip in the palatial indoor pool; that mandatory outing to explore Jaipur's visual delights

YOU SHOULD KNOW:
Every guest has the services of a personal butler who is on call throughout their stay. He will also help design shopping itineraries or arrange sightseeing excursions into the city or surrounding countryside. The fabulous Peacock Suite overlooks the Mughal Terrace and garden where Maharajas once celebrated the Holi festival of colour and lights.

WHERE:
Kacherawala, Kukas, near Jaipur, Rajasthan
COST:
Extremely reasonable
BEST TIME OF YEAR:
Go any time (but note that June to September are the hottest months, when it also rains a lot, and October to April is considered to be high season).
DON'T MISS:
The scenic terrace atop the ridge with a bird's-eye view of the entire valley (an ideal spot to simply lounge lazily, cooled by the breeze); peaceful meditation at the resort's Ganesh Abode, a quiet place surrounded by many statues of Lord Ganesh, the half-man, half-elephant Hindu God of luck and prosperity
THINGS TO DO:
Meet the people – visit the homes of warm and welcoming local villagers. Interact with the families and learn how they live and/or visit the school (supported by the resort, where you're actually able to spend time teaching if you wish). Take an elephant ride through lush vegetation in the foothills (see astonishing birdlife and occasional panthers), followed by an *al fresco* meal as the sun sets and villagers serenade you on traditional instruments. Thing not to do: don't get completely carried away by rewarding local possibilities and forget the big one – Jaipur and its wondrous sights.
YOU SHOULD KNOW:
The resort's boutique offers a wide selection of genuine Indian jewellery, luxurious silks and local handicrafts. Jaipur (let alone Jaipur combined with all that's on offer at The Tree of Life) requires a minimum stay of four nights (ask for an itinerary that meets your specific requirements).

Tree of Life Resort & Spa

The original walled town centre of Jaipur was beautifully planned and built in the 18th century according to the geometric principles of Hindu architectural theory, which makes it a much more orderly entity than most Indian cities. If you manage to properly explore but one place in all India, make it this one. And an ideal base for sallying forth to the fabled Pink City is the Tree of Life Resort & Spa in the nearby Aravalli Hills, in tranquil surroundings well away from the frenetic tourist-fuelled frenzy of Jaipur itself.

This collection of 14 luxury villas in beautiful gardens may seem at first glance like a case of Disneyland goes Indian, but the place is modelled on local style with modern twists and it does create a wonderfully authentic (to visitors at least) atmosphere. The spacious villas are beautifully appointed and the whole resort is designed to engender restful relaxation. The on-site facilities include a bell-shaped infinity pool with stunning views and there's a well-equipped gym for compulsive fitness freaks, while a spa oozing soothing treatments awaits those in need of sensual stimulation. The bar and CD/book library is the place to chill out of an evening, but the highlight for everyone is surely food.

Indian cuisine is infinitely varied, with regional dishes galore having their own flavour and enticing aromas, using techniques and recipes passed down from generation to generation. The resort's chefs are well versed in many of them, offering a huge variety of Indian dishes (with the accent on local specialities), and they can also turn a practised hand to the international menu if anyone is pining for a taste of home. It's even possible to visit the organic Eternal Garden with a chef and choose salads and vegetables for your next meal. Enjoy!

Chambal Safari Lodge

If anyone likes the idea of a most unusual and ecologically sound place to stay (with the Taj Mahal as a fallback), Chambal Safari Lodge should fit the bill (which, happily, won't be much). And in the unlikely event that the many rewarding activities offered by this haven in the unspoilt Chambal Valley pall, the Lodge is just 80 km (50 mi) south of Agra, so a day trip to see India's most famous building is an easyish option.

Chambal Safari Lodge (Mela Kothi) is situated at the centre of a long-established estate and offers relaxing cottage accommodation, plus rooms in the main building for those who like a touch of luxury. The natural charm of local dwellings combined with modern amenities has created comfortable, eco-friendly accommodation. Each of eight en-suite cottages with covered verandahs sits on a raised sandstone platform in woodland around the restored Mela Kothi lodge house. The twin-bedded rooms are spacious, while large windows admit fresh air and ample natural light. The Lodge serves authentic local cuisine with organic ingredients, prepared using traditionally tried-and-tested recipes.

With a little expert help, visitors can discover a magical world characterized by rugged landscapes and rare wildlife. The extensive grounds of the Lodge are home to numerous animals (such as palm civet cats, foxes, jungle hares and Indian striped hyenas) and birds (over 170 species). The Chambal natural sanctuary is rich in wildlife, including gharials, crocodiles, alligators and the endangered Gangetic Dolphin. And twitchers come to seek (and find) rare birds like the Indian Skimmer. If you love nature, and want to see rural India at its unspoilt best, this unpolluted land far from the chaos of city life will appeal mightily.

WHERE:
Uttar Pradesh
COST:
Super-reasonable (especially considering that full board is included)
BEST TIME OF YEAR:
October to May
DON'T MISS:
The guided evening wildlife walk with the resident naturalist
THINGS TO DO:
Explore the Sarus Crane Wetland Area with the help of a knowledgeable guide; an accompanied tour of Bateshwar's medieval temples, followed by a walk along the temple *ghats* and visit to *sadhu* (ascetics) caves; a camel safari through the ravines of the National Chambal Sanctuary to Fort Ater (with or without a guided tour of the Fort); a river safari and accompanied nature walk in the National Chambal Sanctuary
YOU SHOULD KNOW:
The Lodge is located on a rural electricity line and the supply can be unreliable. If the power fails, a generator operates for an hour in the morning and evening to power geysers that supply hot water in bathrooms. Candles and hurricane lanterns are provided in all the rooms. Welcome to the real India, folks!

A *Bhunga* in Gujarat

WHERE:
Kachchh region, Northern Gujarat
COST:
Budget
BEST TIME OF YEAR:
December to February (note that the resort is only open between October and March)
DON'T MISS:
Stunning handicrafts – embroidery and weaving in particular – have been produced for centuries by the women of these villages. There is also a tradition of fine leather working among the men of the Hindu Meghwal community.

Well off the beaten tourist track, the Shaam-e-Sarhad Village Resort is definitely a destination for the more adventurous traveller. Once here, though, you are unlikely to regret the conveniences you may have had to forego on the way, such as hot showers and reliable bus services. Shaam-e-Sarhad is situated in the village of Hodka in the immense Banni grasslands north of Bhuj. Owned and run by the village community itself, this resort is a model of good practice in terms of sustainable and responsible tourism in the developing world.

The idea is that guests live in low-impact conditions and gain a more authentic insight into the daily lives of the villagers than a day excursion from an air-conditioned western hotel could ever hope to offer. With training from enlightened industry professionals and the backing of a regional cooperative, the community has been able to take

on the management of the enterprise and to have the satisfaction of seeing profits being ploughed directly back into their village.

As well as eco-tents Shaam-e-Sarhad offers three *bhungas* to stay in. These traditional circular mud huts are a characteristic feature of the Kachchh landscape. You may be sleeping in a bed made from mud on a floor of baked earth, but this is no slumming experience.

The huts are colourfully decorated with exquisite examples of embroidered and mirror-work textiles made by local women and each has its own well-appointed bathroom with running solar-powered hot water. With their conical thatch roofs the *bhungas* of Banni have proved themselves to be remarkably durable, withstanding the major earthquake which devastated the region in 2001 more successfully than many a modern building.

THINGS TO DO:
Learning about Banni village life; shopping for traditional handicrafts (and knowing that the proceeds go direct to the makers); birdwatching in the Chhari Dhand wetlands; stargazing; listening to Kachchhi folk music

YOU SHOULD KNOW:
In accordance with the laws of a predominantly Muslim state, no alcohol is served at the resort. The food is vegetarian.

Oberoi Grand

WHERE:
Jawaharlal Nehru Road, Kolkata, West Bengal
COST:
Expensive (by Indian, though not international, standards)
BEST TIME OF YEAR:
Go any time, but summers (March to June) are best avoided if heat is a problem (temperatures peak in May).
DON'T MISS:
Getting out and about on foot – Kolkata may seem intimidating to some, but its vibrant street life is fascinating and the people are incredibly friendly; a stroll in the park – the huge Maidan is Kolkata's green lung and provides an ongoing pageant of city life
THINGS TO DO:
See the sights, including the Victoria Memorial (the Raj's answer to the Taj Mahal, an imposing edifice containing memorabilia such as Queen Victoria's piano), Kalighat (a temple dedicated to the goddess Kali), Raj Bhavan (the awesome former residence of the British Viceroy) and other fine examples of Raj architecture such as the Town Hall, Writers' Building (the old East India Company office) and St John's Church, the atmospheric South Park Street Cemetery or the Indian Museum (one of Asia's finest).
YOU SHOULD KNOW:
Most of the hotel is a no-smoking zone, but it's possible to book a 'smoking' bedroom and enjoy a leisurely cigar in the Chowringhee Bar.

It's time to embrace the 'Grande Dame of Chowringhee' and experience the stimulating delights of Kolkata, City of Joy. It all adds up to a stay in one of India's top luxury hotels, the aforementioned Grande Dame (aka the Oberoi Grand). This heritage hotel's wonderful neoclassical facade and grand portico were created when the Raj was at its height and the city was Calcutta, representing a fusion of dramatic Victorian architecture and charming Indian style. The hotel's colonial heritage is carefully respected and it offers a quietish haven where guests can escape from the frenetic city streets and relax in supreme comfort.

The Oberoi Grand sits proudly in the main business and shopping district of Kolkata, offering beautifully appointed guest accommodation ranging from deluxe rooms to luxury suites, all equipped with every modern facility and coming with nice touches like a basket of *ayurvedic* toiletries. Hotel dining is a real pleasure. The award-winning La Terrasse is an all-day restaurant offering a wide range of international cuisine, *à la carte* or from the breakfast or lunch buffets. Alternatively, Baan Thai is generally regarded as India's premier Thai restaurant. The Chowringhee Bar is the place to relax and discuss the day's events.

Apart from soothing slumber and fine food, the hotel's recreational dimension includes an outdoor swimming pool (with bar), a fitness centre and super spa where healing hands deliver treatments designed to refresh and rejuvenate. The 'Grande Dame' certainly has a lot to offer, but don't forget the City of Joy bit. If you can tear yourself away from the hotel's warm embrace, Kolkata awaits . . .

Taj Mahal Palace

You may say Mumbai and others still say Bombay, but top people have been saying 'book me into the Taj Mahal Palace' for over a century. This dome-topped Mumbai landmark was finished in 1903 and stands commandingly on the sea front overlooking the Gateway of India, that monumental arch built to commemorate the visit of King George V and Queen Mary in 1911. The Taj instantly became a favourite with travelling Maharajas, who felt the sumptuous interiors and extraordinary level of hospitality were well up to their demanding standards. Those standards have been maintained, more recently attracting countless celebrities and discerning guests who will settle for nothing less than one of India's (and the world's) finest hotels.

As that accolade would suggest, the 560 elegant rooms (including 44 suites) are superbly decorated and equipped, representing the happiest of marriages between old-world style and state-of-the-art facilities. The Palace's incredible interiors feature a treasure trove of historical furnishings and memorabilia and the grand staircase has to be seen to be believed. Welcoming staff members look after each guest personally and are happy to arrange meals, spa treatments, city outings, shopping trips, tours and just about anything legal Mumbai has to offer.

The food is as good as everything else, with a choice of restaurants and culinary bounty that ranges from the subcontinent's finest to international cuisine from the likes of France, Italy and Japan. The Palace also has excellent health and fitness facilities, including an outdoor pool and steam room. The Jiva Spa is a testament to the efficacy of traditional Indian *ayurveda* combined with modern techniques, ensuring that guests who are into pampering can be freshened and fortified. A hotel this good would be way beyond the reach of mere mortals almost anywhere else on the planet, but here it can be for you.

WHERE:
Apollo Bunder, Mumbai, Maharashtra
COST:
Reasonable (and you get a lot of love for the money)
BEST TIME OF YEAR:
December to February (to avoid summer heat and autumn monsoons)
DON'T MISS:
Take tea in the marvellous Palace Lounge, for nowhere better represents the refined beauty and traditional charm of this great hotel.
THINGS TO DO:
Revel in the sights and sounds of Mumbai, India's most populous (and frenetic) city; enjoy some serious floating luxury – the hotel has its own yacht with climate-controlled lounge and the attentive services of a personal butler. Cruises include a waterborne trip to Elephanta Caves, a Mumbai Harbour cruise, the spectacular Twilight Cruise and romantic overnight Arabian Nights Fantasy Cruise for couples.
YOU SHOULD KNOW:
Ask for a room in the original Palace rather than in the adjoining Tower, built in the 1970s on the site of a notorious sailors' dive called Green's Hotel – the accommodation in the Tower is well up to Taj standards, but there's no substitute for the extraordinary atmosphere of the real thing.

Otter Creek Tents at Elsewhere

WHERE:
Morjim, Anjuna, North Goa
COST:
Reasonable
BEST TIME OF YEAR:
December to the end of February; closed in the monsoon season from May to October
DON'T MISS:
A dolphin-spotting cruise with the local fishermen; watching otters playing in the creek; the Wednesday flea market in Anjuna
THINGS TO DO:
Swimming in the Indian Ocean; lazing on the beach; birdwatching; yoga; exploring the old Portuguese colonial towns of Goa; visiting churches
YOU SHOULD KNOW:
The minimum period of stay is one week. A car and knowledgeable driver can be provided on request to take you to see the sights, shop and eat out. Meals are provided at the restaurant shack on the estate.

Goa is renowned for miles of enchanting palm-fringed beaches, sparkling sea and permanent sunshine but, with more than two million visitors a year, this glorious stretch of coast has become increasingly crowded. However, it is still possible to come across romantic spots with breathing space and the Elsewhere Estate is one of the best.

This ancestral family home is a little slice of paradise. The present owner's great grandfather built himself a beach house on a sand spit, cut off from the mainland by a saltwater creek and fronting onto one of the most beautiful beaches of Goa. To get there, you follow an isolated sandy track and negotiate a rickety 60-m (200-ft) bamboo footbridge, to find yourself in a secluded sylvan haven of banyan and coconut trees.

Several old colonial buildings are scattered among the trees and three spacious tents, each pitched well apart, overlook Otter Creek. This is luxury with a capital L. You sleep in a muslin-draped four-poster bed, there is a fridge and minibar and an immaculate western-style en-suite bathroom with hot and cold running water. You have a private patio and your own bamboo jetty projecting over the limpid creek – the perfect platform for your morning yoga exercises.

A two-minute walk through the trees and across the dunes takes you onto a virtually deserted beach of pristine white sand, sloping gently down into the ocean. All nature's bounty is here – coconuts dangle over your head, colourful birds dart among the trees, otters swim in the creek and turtles hatch in the sand. Elsewhere calls itself Goa's 'best-kept secret'. It certainly feels like one of the most romantic places on earth – and now the secret's out.

Panchavatti

In the hinterland behind Goa's famed beaches, Panchavatti is a splendidly idiosyncratic hippy retreat, a private home that has been opened as an exclusive guesthouse. This is the place to come and recover after a surfeit of partying in the frenzied beach scene – a sanctuary to help you chill, relax and straighten out your head.

The lovely courtyard bungalow is set in a beautiful 8-ha (20-ac) tropical hillside garden, overlooking rolling countryside of lush paddy fields and a meandering river. You can laze in a stunning infinity pool that looks out from the edge of the hill top onto the panoramic landscape below, drift around the garden practising your yoga exercises or be tempted by the superbly prepared, nutritious food on offer. The wonderfully healthy communal meals are served on a beautiful colonnaded verandah which has staggering views over the surrounding countryside.

The owner has her own inimitable style. Everything in this exclusive hill-top haven is intimate and personal. Seven large, spotless guest rooms are decorated to create an atmosphere of relaxed tranquillity, the bathrooms casually curtained off with cotton saris. There are no locks on any of the doors, no phones and no TV. The two beautifully furnished living rooms are stuffed with the owner's collection of curios and art works, and you can retreat to the library to browse through an eclectic selection of books and CDs.

It's only half an hour from the beach but Panchavatti feels like a different world. You can purge yourself of excess in a blissful atmosphere of rural calm – an idyllic retreat in which to restore body and mind, concentrate on practising your *asanas*, and developing your spiritual side.

WHERE:
Corjuem, Aldona, Mapusa, North Goa
COST:
Reasonable
BEST TIME OF YEAR:
November to April
DON'T MISS:
Having an *ayurvedic* massage; seeing Aguada Fort, a 17th-century Portuguese coastal fort; a trip to Mapusa Friday market
THINGS TO DO:
Walking in the countryside; boat trips in Goa's backwaters; cycling; meditation; yoga; birdwatching; going to the beach
YOU SHOULD KNOW:
Inland Goa is completely different from the coast and is well worth exploring. It is still an agrarian economy and there is a sense of traditional rural life that has been lost on the coast through the massive annual influx of tourists.

A Nomadic Mansion at The Mandala

WHERE:
Mandrem, Pernem, North Goa
COST:
Reasonable
BEST TIME OF YEAR:
December to February
DON'T MISS:
The amazing banyan tree near Arambol; the picturesque Our Lady of the Rosary Church in Mandrem; Deshprabhu House in the nearby town of Pernem, the grandest Hindu mansion in Goa
THINGS TO DO:
Swimming; kayaking; yoga; meditation; dolphin-spotting; birdwatching; hitting the lively beach shacks and bars
YOU SHOULD KNOW:
As well as renting rooms, the Mandala is used as a space for retreats, workshops and training seminars. There are eight rooms and two suites in the main house and tents with shared bathroom facilities in the coconut grove.

On the banks of the meandering Avsem River, The Mandala is a tranquil retreat hotel run by a young British artist. His aim has been to establish a laid-back, creative space where guests can de-stress and regain inner balance in a mellow atmosphere of unpretentious comfort.

Five charming Nomadic Mansions look out over a tidal lake in the hotel's coconut grove, home to masses of exotic birds. These quirky two-storey 'mansions' are an ingenious cross between a Balinese bungalow and a Southern Indian houseboat, designed by a team of young artists who wanted to create an environmentally low-impact living space without sacrificing any comfort. Downstairs there is a living room, with sliding doors out onto a vine-covered patio, and a huge bathroom. Above, there is a wonderful master bedroom with a magnificent domed roof and a spacious balcony with a view of the lake. The living room converts into a second bedroom, so a single 'mansion' easily accommodates a family of four.

The retreat runs daily yoga sessions in a geodesic spirit dome in the grounds and there is an in-house massage service and a sacred garden spot for meditation exercises. The restaurant serves fresh seafood and vegetarian dishes, salads and health juices, using vegetables and herbs from the garden. The Mandala is completely secluded yet it is only 100 m (330 ft) from the road and a ten-minute taxi ride to the nightlife and beach markets of Arambol.

For anyone of an artistic or spiritual inclination, this quirky retreat is a wonderful place to recharge spiritual batteries, far from the madding throng yet near enough to the tourist attractions to have the best of both worlds.

Vivenda dos Palhacos

WHERE:
Majorda, South Goa
COST:
Reasonable
BEST TIME OF YEAR:
Go between December and February – the monsoon season from June to September is best avoided.
DON'T MISS:
The 16th-century church in Majorda; the wildlife at Chorao Bird Sanctuary; the night market at Margao; the magnificent Portuguese colonial mansion of Sat Banzam Gor in Margao

If you want to steer clear of the tourist hordes, the Vivenda dos Palhacos guesthouse in the little village of Majorda is a haven. In a quiet *cul-de-sac*, this beautiful 100-year-old Hindu-Portuguese colonial house has been lovingly renovated by a British brother-and-sister team whose family have lived in India for four generations. Here you can immerse yourself in traditional local culture, yet are still close to one of the world's most beautiful beaches – 26 km (16 mi) of fine, pure-white sand, shaded by palm groves.

As soon as you step inside the house you are back in the Raj – all polished dark-wood furniture, comfortable sofas and oriental antiques and art. There are seven completely individual, charmingly furnished

guest rooms, named after places that the owners have lived in and loved, all with air conditioning and en-suite bathrooms. Alternatively you can stay in the self-contained garden cottage or Rajasthani pavilion tent. The good-humoured owners are charming hosts who have the knack of making guests feel at home. On lazy days, when the beach feels like too much of a chore, you feel completely at ease hanging out in the house and garden, lazing on a sunlounger around the 12-m (39-ft) pool or in a secluded spot under the trees.

You stir in the mornings to the sounds of Indian daily village life – cocks crowing, children playing and dogs barking, and in the evenings you can sit around the enormous communal garden table in a convivial atmosphere of eating, drinking and socializing. Vivenda dos Palhacos has a unique ambience that makes a welcome change from soulless tourist hotels – a jewel in the Goan crown.

THINGS TO DO:
Swimming; scuba diving; waterskiing; fishing; birdwatching; cycling; horse riding on the beach; yoga; hanging out in the beach shacks; visiting the churches and temples of Old Goa; shopping for jewellery

YOU SHOULD KNOW:
The Vivenda dos Palhacos will arrange airport pick-up, sightseeing and shopping tours. If you don't want to walk to the beach, you can be driven in the hotel jeep or use one of the house bicycles. There are no TVs in the rooms but you can watch in the communal area.

Shanthi Guesthouse

WHERE:
Sanapur, Hampi, Karnataka
COST:
Lower end of budget (you may even feel guilty for not paying more)
BEST TIME OF YEAR:
January and February are the cooler winter months (but the Hampi area is an impressive water wonderland in the monsoon season from June until September).
DON'T MISS:
Hampi's greatest claim to fame is the amazing beehive Virupaksha Temple – and mighty impressive it is too (then check out the surrounding bazaar).
THINGS TO DO:
Hire the house taxi for sightseeing trips to interesting local places such as Badami, Aihole or Pattadakal.
YOU SHOULD KNOW:
Somewhat surprisingly, the Shanthi Guesthouse has internet access. The annual Vijayanagara Festival is organized in Hampi by the Government of Karnataka in November. The nearest train station is at Hosapete (Hospet), 13 km (8 mi) away, but there's public transport to Hampi and taxis are cheap.

Sitting sleepily on the banks of the Tungabhadra River and the very personification of rural India, the village of Hampi is located within the ruins of Vijayanagara, capital of the empire of the same name that thrived from the 14th to 17th centuries. Now an atmospheric World Heritage Site, Hampi contains impressive monuments belonging to the old city. This verdant corner of India is home to the Shanthi Guest House, a five-minute walk from the river after crossing by boat from the main part of Hampi.

A garland of hills, rocks, water and lush greenery surround the Shanthi Guesthouse (the name means 'peace' and seems entirely appropriate). This place is tailor-made for people who want to relax in serene surroundings and explore at their leisure, rather than cramming the sights into a morning before moving on. Shanthi's charming cottages with their verandahs and hard-to-resist hammocks are comfortable without being ostentatious. They're eco-friendly (which translated means 'open the windows because there's no air conditioning') and there are two succinctly titled options – the very affordable River View Rooms and the incredibly cheap Landscape View Rooms.

Shanthi is a great place to rest your weary head at the end of an active day's sightseeing if you've been exploring Hampi's fantastic art and architecture, and it's a good centre for mounting fascinating expeditions into the surrounding countryside. But then again, many guests are happy to just laze around the grounds doing absolutely nothing more strenuous that sunbathing, or perhaps turning an occasional book page, before adjourning to the River View Restaurant. This serves food in various styles – just tell the chef what makes your mouth water and await the arrival of a wholesome meal. And there really couldn't be anything better than sharing a table and good conversation with like-minded fellow guests as a fireball sun sinks into the mountains.

A Houseboat in Kerala

WHERE:
Kerala Backwaters, Kerala (the gateway to the Backwaters is the port city of Kochi, formerly Cochin)
COST:
Budget to reasonable (per person per night, excluding flights, depending on the choice of operator and number sharing the boat)

Kerala, at the southern tip of India, is on the romantic-sounding Malabar Coast of the Arabian Sea. But this particular escape has nothing to do with the sea, but involves a houseboat holiday – not the sort of static houseboat one might find in Kashmir, but one that cruises the bustling highways and byways of the Kerala Backwaters, a stunning network of canals, lakes and 44 rivers that criss-cross the coastal plain. This is a fascinating area with its own community that lives on and alongside the water – and that's the authentic waterborne world you will be exploring on your houseboat (or *kettuvallom* as it's known locally). With the advent of tourism these have been converted from former rice barges to various levels of finish, from comfortable to luxurious. Indeed, the venture has been so successful that new boats are being built by traditional artisans using *anjili* wood, bamboo and coconut fibre.

It's possible to book 'all-in' Backwater cruises (including flights) through an agent, or organize your own deal (there are plenty of houseboats to choose from, operating out of various centres). A reliable operator is the certified Lakes and Lagoons company, one of the first and best to provide cruises. They offer a typical service whereby guests are looked after by a guide/cook and two boatmen. This is low-impact tourism and a cruise can last for anything from a couple of days to three weeks. The ethnic food will be a highlight, consisting of traditional recipes cooked aboard using ingredients sourced from local markets. But the true joy of this unusual holiday is the beautiful green landscape of the Backwaters, perused in the most relaxing manner imaginable. It's an extraordinary experience.

BEST TIME OF YEAR:
Summer (that's June to August) must be avoided as the southwest monsoon can bring torrential downpours and cyclonic winds.

DON'T MISS:
Visit the dense forests and breathtaking lake of Periyar National Park and Wildlife Sanctuary (PNP) in the Idukki and Pathanamthitta Districts (you just might spot a tiger and could well see wild elephants among other prolific wildlife).

THINGS TO DO:
Birdwatching; a visit to one of the many vibrant markets in the Backwaters, such as Mannar or Alleppey; visiting a local village (or two) to see how the locals live

YOU SHOULD KNOW:
Houseboats can have anything from one to four bedrooms and it's possible to book your own boat or join a party on one of the larger craft.

Old Harbour Hotel

The former Portuguese, then Dutch, then English colonial settlement of Fort Kochi (Cochin) is a part of the city of Kochi and one of several waterside areas rich in history and culture towards the southwest of mainland Kochi, collectively known as Old Kochi. And that 'Old' is entirely valid in the case of the Old Harbour Hotel, for this fine building has been part of the local scene for three centuries. It was built in Dutch style with echoes of Portuguese influence, was the first hostelry in Old Cochin and has now been refurbished and reopened as a charming boutique hotel.

This grand old building has real character which has been preserved and enhanced by the renovation. The original facade and architectural elements of the interior remain intact, and sailors who stayed in years past would still recognize the place. But the 13 spacious rooms would have come as a pleasant surprise to those old sea-dogs, who would have known the names (each is called after a street in Old Cochin) but been astonished by the eclectic mix of modern design, atmospheric antiques, art and the latest conveniences. The rooms look into the peaceful central courtyard, with its soothing fountain, or at Fort Kochi's trademark Chinese fishing nets air-drying along the shore. There are also garden cottages with open-air showers and a private verandah. The lush outside space also features a swimming pool and large terrace and of course there is also every Indian hotel's 'must have', an *ayurvedic* spa.

Those who prefer being well-fed to wellness will not be disappointed, either. The restaurant offers the freshest and best. Organic vegetables are *de rigueur* and the meats are of the highest quality, while local seafood straight from the boat is a house speciality. The whole experience is an Indian delight.

WHERE:
Tower Road, Fort Kochi, Kochi, Kerala
COST:
Reasonable (with an off-season discount between April and September)
BEST TIME OF YEAR:
October to March
DON'T MISS:
The evening barbecue in the garden, featuring fresh locally caught seafood; live entertainment on the hotel's outside stage; sitting in the dappled shade of the giant mango tree as the sun reaches its zenith
THINGS TO DO:
Visit St Francis Church, originally a wooden structure from early Portuguese colonial days, rebuilt in 1516 (Vasco da Gama was once interred here); see the fascinating Indo-Portuguese Museum in the compound of the Bishop's House at Fort Kochi.
YOU SHOULD KNOW:
The hotel does not offer any rooms with special accessibility features.

Tranquil Plantation Hideaway

And now for something that really *is* authentic – a stay on a working plantation as house guests of the owners. And the fact that the name of that plantation is Tranquil tells its own tale. The verdant surroundings are serene and batteries recharge as though by magic, while there's something very special about unhurried main meals taken with the plantation's extended family and fellow guests. The fare consists of traditional Kerala recipes handed down over generations, classic Indian cuisine and some international favourites – accompanied by home-grown fruit and vegetables, bread warm from the oven, home-made relishes and wonderful preserves.

The Tranquil Plantation grows coffee, areca nut, cardamom and pepper, but don't be fooled by the working label. The accommodation is well up to speed comfort-wise, and also rather interesting. There are six rooms in an annexe that feels like an old-fashioned colonial bungalow, with its shady tiled verandah where rattan easy chairs overlook tropical gardens. For those who want a little extra, the deluxe room has oodles of space, his 'n' hers bathrooms and a private verandah, while the suite has a lounge and private garden in addition. All rooms have the amenities expected nowadays.

More adventurous guests may prefer the treehouse, perched amid greenery at a height of over 10 m (33 ft). But don't think kid's play area – this one has electricity, bedroom, bathroom with shower and a cool north-facing verandah with wonderful views across the estate. Approached by an inclined walkway, agility is not a prerequisite – but it is called Tranquilitree, proving that the British are not alone in adoring awful puns. Moving on (but still up), the ultimate family hideaway *is* a secure kids' play area (happily, health and safety have yet to reach epidemic proportions in India). The Tree Villa can sleep four and has two bathrooms, plus those vital verandahs on two sides.

WHERE:
Kuppamundi Coffee Estate, Sultan Battery, Wayland, Kerala
COST:
Reasonable (nudging expensive for the treehouses)
BEST TIME OF YEAR:
November to early March, post-monsoon months where there's an explosion of lush rainforest foliage and wildlife is at its most active
DON'T MISS:
A plunge in the swimming pool (or soak in the adjacent Jacuzzi); glorious walks around the estate; an *ayurvedic* massage session; yoga (or meditation) on the tree deck overlooking the pool; the coffee and areca nut harvests (from mid January to mid March, when the plantation hums with activity)
THINGS TO DO:
Make the uphill trek to the neolithic Edakkal Caves with their ancient rock etchings. Visit Muthanga Wildlife Sanctuary to try and spot bear, bison, deer, elephant, leopard, peacock – perhaps even that elusive tiger. Explore the town of Sultan Battery with its busy market and be sure to see the 9th-century Jain temple. Go birdwatching around the estate (with over 100 species to spot).
YOU SHOULD KNOW:
That wonderful cup of coffee served at the end of meals is made using Arabica/Robusta beans hand-picked from the estate, roasted and ground with accumulated expertise that makes Starbucks look like the new kid on the block. Talking of kids, this is a family-orientated establishment and children are not only welcomed, but welcomed with open arms (often literally).

A Fishing Hut in Surya Samudra

WHERE:
Pulinkudi, Kerala
COST:
Reasonable from April to November, expensive in the high season (December to March)
BEST TIME OF YEAR:
Any time
DON'T MISS:
A dip in the amazing swimming pool carved from living rock, complete with underwater sculptures; sunrise/sunset yoga sessions on a cliff-edge platform surrounded by water on three sides and cooled by sea breezes; watching local fishermen bringing in their catch (some of which you'll get to eat)

India is a land of stunning contrasts, between great wealth and grinding poverty, palaces and shocking slums, some of the world's most luxurious hotels and the simplest of rural retreats. At first glance, a fishing hut at Surya Samudra would seem to fall into the latter category but the truth of the matter is more complicated, because it does and it doesn't. The location is promising (a rocky promontory clad in palm trees on the fabled Malabar Coast that juts into the Arabian Sea, with splendid beaches on both sides) and the accommodation appears to be decidedly ethnic (old fishermen's huts with carved teak facades and domed wooden ceilings that overlook the water from a terraced hillside). But all is not as it seems.

This is not a backpackers' bolthole where the beachside living is

simple and accommodation primitive, but a carefully planned resort (if anyone doubts that, take note of Surya Samudra's Spa Niraamaya, which offers up-market *ayurvedic* treatments along with therapies such as massage and facials). No matter, it's a delightful spot with two quiet beaches and the authentic appearance of the huts (albeit with a little designer help) is augmented by good comfort levels within spacious interiors. Despite the illusion of simplicity, each has cleverly concealed air conditioning, satellite TV, wifi, telephone, minibar, tea- and coffee-making facilities, soundproofing, plunge pool and showers inside and out. For those who care not for 'authentic', there's a modern block with contemporary suites set back from the sea (equally well equipped and cheaper).

The resort has two restaurants (sea views, naturally) and although the cuisine is not inspired, it's tasty and wholesome. This is a decent beach resort that has made a real effort to appear different – and while the sun, sea and sand may be standard issue, that effort really does succeed.

THINGS TO DO:
Sip a cocktail as the sun sets over the sea; take a catamaran cruise; visit the bustling town of Kovalam; cross into Tamil Nadu to visit the 16th-century wooden palace of Padmanabapuram, seat of the Travancore princes; check out the nearby Keralan capital Trivandrum to see its huge Hindu Temple, centuries-old palace and assorted museums
YOU SHOULD KNOW:
There are facilities/activities for kids and children under six stay free, but noise is frowned on. Ask for one of the best locations when booking (a hut near the beach, for which you'll pay a little extra, is a worthwhile investment). Have a care when swimming in the sea – the surf can be fierce and currents strong (a red flag says 'no', a green flag says 'go').

Safari-Land Treehouses

It comes as something of a surprise in the densely populated subcontinent to find an area like the Nilgiri Hills, a relatively untamed wilderness in the far west of Tamil Nadu state. This mountain range forms part of the Nilgiri Biosphere Reserve which protects one of the largest remaining forest tracts in India. It is here you will find Mudumalai Wildlife Sanctuary and, at its heart, Safari-Land Farm and Guest House.

Mudumalai is a haven for many of South Asia's larger mammals, including the Asiatic elephant, the gaur (Indian bison) plus sambar and chital deer. The best way to get up close to the wildlife is by staying in one of Safari-Land's treehouses. Perched high up on timber platforms these wooden houses are cool, comfortable and hard to leave. Watching the sunset or the morning mist lift off the mountains from your private deck is a truly magical experience.

If you can tear yourself away from your elevated refuge there are plenty of treats waiting at ground level. The resort runs all sorts of guided treks into the lush green forests and to nearby mountain peaks. You can hire a jeep for your own safari but you do have to be accompanied by a guide. There are also trips to an elephant camp run by the sanctuary where elephants are bred in captivity and trained for work in the timber industry. And to answer the question that's been on the tip of your tongue: yes, tigers and leopards do roam these forests but you can count yourself exceptionally fortunate if you spot either of these rare and reclusive beasts.

WHERE:
Near Ooty (Udhagamandalam), western Tamil Nadu
COST:
Budget
BEST TIME OF YEAR:
Choose between September to December and March to May (during these months the undergrowth dies down and it becomes easier to see animals, especially at dawn when they are on the move).
DON'T MISS:
While you are in the area a trip on the legendary Blue Mountain Railway is not to be missed. This narrow-gauge steam railway, with its smart blue-and-cream livery, chugs 46 km (29 mi) from Mettupalayam up to Ooty, climbing nearly 2,000 m (6,560 ft) in the process.
THINGS TO DO:
Elephant rides; jeep and van safaris; guided jungle treks; birdwatching
YOU SHOULD KNOW:
The founder of Safari-Land is an Indian Nawab whose princely family used to own these lands and use them as a summer getaway.

Heritance Kandalama

WHERE:
Dambulla, north of Kandy
COST:
Reasonable
BEST TIME OF YEAR:
January to April
DON'T MISS:
The hotel can organize some unusual dining experiences, including a picnic breakfast afloat on the lake and dinner in a cave.
THINGS TO DO:
Swimming; nature walks; birdwatching; elephant rides; horse riding; cycling; boat rides on the lake; hot-air ballooning
YOU SHOULD KNOW:
The hotel is particularly proud of its track record in providing training and employment for young people from the local villages.

Few luxury hotels take their planetary responsibilities as seriously as the Heritance Kandalama. The impetus and sensibility were supplied by pioneering architect Geoffrey Bawa whose vision was to create a large man-made structure which would be re-absorbed over time into its natural surroundings. Designed in the shape of a bird with outstretched wings, the hotel extends for an entire kilometre (0.6 mi) along a rocky hillside overlooking Kandalama Reservoir. Looking at it today, you can see that several of the buildings are indeed almost completely concealed beneath a canopy of lush vegetation.

The whole thrust here is to provide a comfortable and relaxing experience for guests that is also low-impact and causes minimum disturbance to the local environment. So the air-conditioned rooms offer all the amenities you would expect, including wonderful vistas of the lake and the silhouette of distant Sigiriya Rock, yet behind the scenes the Heritance Kandalama boasts the country's most sophisticated waste-water recycling plant, while a recently installed biomass plant provides a renewable energy source which has cut the hotel's carbon emissions dramatically.

The hotel's 93-ha (230-ac) estate includes three restaurants and three outdoor swimming pools. Nothing but indigenous plants have been used in its landscaping and even the floral arrangements within feature only local plants and flowers. This is an excellent base for exploring the centre of the island, situated as it is in the middle of the so-called Cultural Triangle. You are a short distance from two World Heritage Sites, the Dambulla cave temple and the Lion Rock of Sigiriya with its remarkable frescoes of royal concubines, and the ancient cities of Anuradhapura and Polonnaruwa both make for an easy day trip.

Helga's Folly

Helga's Folly is a true original. How you respond to it is very much a matter of personal taste. For some this Aladdin's Cave of a hotel is outrageously over the top and inexcusably self-indulgent, but for a traveller jaded by the blandness and sterility of the typical international hotel this place will come not so much as a breath of fresh air as a lung-filling blast. Not that your host, Helga de Silva Blow Perera, cares about those who may be turned off by the extravagance on show – she has been in the hospitality business too long to mind about giving occasional offence, and anyway she has built up a sturdily loyal clientele over the years, including a fair sprinkling of celebrities.

Designed in the 1930s by her mother in Swiss-chalet style, the building was Helga's family home before opening its doors to paying guests. The red exterior is remarkable enough but gives little clue to the riot of colour and form to be found inside. Helga says she grew up 'in a world of colonial tea pots, Hollywood gossip and Marxist revolutions', and the hotel's interiors are expressions of this exotic childhood as well as of an artist's fantasy. The original Art Deco trappings have been lost beneath flamboyant murals, wax-encrusted candelabras, family portraits, ancient figure carvings and antiques of every shape and size, all reflecting the magpie mentality of their owner. No two guest rooms are alike in terms of furnishings and colour scheme. Some have air conditioning, some have four-poster beds, but all have exceptional views over Kandy, its lake, temple and surrounding mountains. Extraordinary indeed!

WHERE:
Kandy
COST:
Reasonable
BEST TIME OF YEAR:
April to September is good (but note that you will need to book well in advance if your visit is going to coincide with the Esela *perahera* Buddhist festival in July/August).
DON'T MISS:
A visit to the Agarsland tea estate, one of Sri Lanka's oldest plantations – owned by Helga's family, it supplies the tea served at the hotel
THINGS TO DO:
Exploring historic Kandy, last capital of the Sinhalese kings; visiting archaeological sites; seeing a cultural show (displays of local dances and folk culture); swimming; watching the monkeys swing through the trees – and sometimes visiting your balcony
YOU SHOULD KNOW:
Madame Helga was a hit single for the Stereophonics in 2003. The song was written by Kelly Jones as a tribute after a stay at the Folly.

Tree Tops Jungle Lodge

WHERE:
Buttala, near Yala National Park
COST:
Budget
BEST TIME OF YEAR:
June to October (but note that Yala National Park is closed each year from September 1 to October 16)
DON'T MISS:
Freshly made water buffalo yoghurt – delicious!
THINGS TO DO:
Jungle trekking; birdwatching; wildlife safaris in Yala; bullock cart rides; visiting Buddhist rock monuments and temples
YOU SHOULD KNOW:
Tree Tops recommends that you arrive before 15.00 to avoid a possibly awkward encounter with wild elephants on the access dirt track.

Unlike its celebrated namesake in East Africa, this lodge offers anything but luxury in the bush. Sri Lanka's Tree Tops, by contrast, aims to give its guests an experience of nature as untainted as possible by the trappings of the man-made world. The lodge is hidden away in an expanse of pristine jungle on the northern borders of Yala, the country's most famous national park.

There is a small collection of simple clay huts and treehouses, scattered around a communal area where meals are taken. The huts are built to traditional rural designs with plain mud walls and thatched roofs; only timber taken from fallen trees is used for the frames. The tree huts themselves are modelled on the structures used by Chena farmers to watch over their cultivated land while keeping safe from wild animals. There is no power or running water at the lodge so paraffin lamps provide your illumination at night while a freshwater well and bucket are available for your ablutions.

A stay at Tree Tops is not for everyone, but if you don't mind foregoing your creature comforts and are happy to rough it for a while, the pay-off can be enormous. The surrounding jungle is rich in wildlife, with over 160 bird species recorded, but the undisputed star is the elephant. Relaxing in a hammock on your verandah while one of these majestic animals forages obliviously in front of you should be reward enough but, if not, the friendly and attentive service from the staff, all of whom are recruited from local villages, and the tasty meals cooked over a wood fire, should seal the deal.

Lisu Home Stay

The Lisu are a traditional hill tribe living in the rugged mountains of northern Thailand, close to the Burmese (Myanmar) border. Descended from the indigenous semi-nomadic tribes of Tibet, they have migrated in the course of the past 300 years down through China, Burma and Laos, settling in their present home less than one hundred years ago. Like most ethnic minorities the world over the Lisu's traditional way of life is under threat from the influences of a globalized culture; in their case the particular pressures are to assimilate to modern Thai culture.

As a way of stemming the tide and promoting awareness of their own culture, the Lisu have in recent years started actively welcoming visitors into their homes. With support and guidance from like-minded outsiders they have developed a programme where guests live in a traditional bamboo or teak house in Nong Tong village and share the life of the community.

What the Lisu call 'cultural immersion' means that as a temporary resident you become part of village life, watching the tribespeople at work and play and participating in the daily round. You eat what the community eats – delicious home-cooked meals – and enjoy their natural, unforced hospitality. By way of deepening your immersion you are encouraged to sign up for a class during your stay to learn more about traditional skills. There are classes in weaving techniques, dancing, musical instrument-making, cooking and Lisu massage (very different from the Thai variety). Like many hill tribes of South East Asia the Lisu are renowned for their traditional dress, especially the elaborate headdresses and silver bodices worn by the women on special occasions.

WHERE:
Soppong, Mae Hong Son Province
COST:
Budget
BEST TIME OF YEAR:
November to June
DON'T MISS:
The Lisu are very fond of ceremonies, whether religious rituals or family celebrations, so you are almost bound to experience one during your stay.
THINGS TO DO:
Enjoying village life; watching and learning about village crafts; mountain trekking; visiting local markets; having a massage; guided nature walks to learn about medicinal plants and wild foods you can eat
YOU SHOULD KNOW:
You needn't worry about the language barrier as English-speaking interpreters are at your disposal.

WHERE:
Ko Phi Phi, near Phuket
COST:
Expensive
BEST TIME OF YEAR:
November to April
DON'T MISS:
The sunsets from the Coconut Bar, a short walk across the isthmus to the west coast of the island
THINGS TO DO:
Swimming; diving; snorkelling; walking; sea kayaking; rock climbing; longtail boat rides; massage; spa treatments; Thai cookery lessons
YOU SHOULD KNOW:
The resort has its own certified PADI dive centre which caters for all levels of experience and ability, including novice divers.

Phi Phi Island Village Beach Resort

Ko Phi Phi is an archipelago of six tropical islands dropped like pearls in the turquoise waters of the Andaman Sea, south of Phuket. Only Ko Phi Phi Don, the largest, is inhabited and it is there that you will find this exclusive resort. Ferries from the mainland put in at Ban Ton Sai, the islands' only significant settlement, from where it is a short boat ride around the coast to your destination (there are no roads or motorized vehicles on the islands).

The resort occupies the entire 800-m (2,625-ft) length of Loh Ba Gao Bay on the east coast of Ko Phi Phi Don. The stunning white sands are effectively the resort's private beach and one of the country's very finest. The bungalows and villas lie just back from the shoreline,

tucked discreetly away beneath gently swaying coconut palms and ensconced in tropical gardens. Wood and thatch are the predominant building materials in the guest accommodation but these are combined with all the mod cons you would expect, including air conditioning. You can choose between a beach-front bungalow or one of the large open-plan villas on the hillside, which come complete with private infinity pool and outdoor Jacuzzi.

Sheer limestone cliffs and dense forests are the defining features of these tropical islands but they tell only half the story. Beneath the waterline is a whole new world of delights which await your exploration. The islands are surrounded by coral fringing reefs teeming with marine life and many are easily accessible from the shallows of the beaches themselves. Afterwards, what better way to end a day's diving or snorkelling than with a Thai massage in the resort spa?

The Sukhothai

Even by the standards of an international metropolis Bangkok is well endowed with top-end hotels. The Sukhothai manages to stand out in this elite company, however, by virtue of an overall design concept which draws its inspiration from the ancient Thai kingdom of the same name. Under the inspirational leadership of King Ramkhamhaeng, the Sukhothai empire of the 13th century was the first seriously successful attempt to unify the Thai lands.

The art and architecture of this Buddhist kingdom are distinguished by the lotus-bud *chedi*, a religious tower capped with a tapered finial, and by sublimely graceful images of the walking and seated Buddha. Modern versions of these ancient artefacts are scattered throughout the hotel and its extensive gardens, while a whole row of red-brick *chedis* set in a lotus pond form a dazzling ensemble in the hotel's main internal courtyard. The guest rooms, meanwhile, evoke the glories of the country's medieval past in more subtle ways, with their refined use of teak floors and Thai silk wall hangings.

The Sukhothai likes to think of itself as a sanctuary in the hustle and bustle of one of Asia's most crowded cities, an oasis of tranquillity to still the beating heart of the overwrought traveller. Situated in the embassy district south of Lumphini Park, it is indeed a haven from which to sally forth into the frenetic commercialism of downtown Thanon Silom. While you won't want to miss out on the attractions of this fascinating city, facilities like the Sukhothai's award-winning Thai restaurant, set on an island in a lotus pond, and the garden spa, which harnesses the natural benefits of its green surroundings, will surely keep luring you back.

WHERE:
South Sathorn Road, Sathorn, Bangkok
COST:
Expensive
BEST TIME OF YEAR:
Any time (the city never sleeps)
DON'T MISS:
The hotel's Chocolate Buffet, served on weekend afternoons to the accompaniment of live Thai music, has become a Bangkok institution.
THINGS TO DO:
Sightseeing; shopping; nightlife; river trips; squash; tennis; jogging in Lumphini Park; spa treatments
YOU SHOULD KNOW:
The hotel offers a limousine service for those guests reluctant to trust themselves to the city's public transport system.

Four Seasons Tented Camp

WHERE:
Chiang Saen, Chiang Rai Province
COST:
Astronomical
BEST TIME OF YEAR:
November to June (but rates are lower during the 'Green Season' from April to September)
DON'T MISS:
If you want to extend your day with the elephants you can have dinner served beside their camp.
THINGS TO DO:
Elephant rides and tuition; river trips – on rafts and traditional longtail boats; jungle trekking; birdwatching; guided nature walks; swimming; craft workshops; cookery lessons
YOU SHOULD KNOW:
There is a minimum two-night stay requirement at the camp. Children under 12 are not allowed.

Deep in the bamboo jungle in the far north of Thailand, the Four Seasons hotel chain has established this luxury safari camp. If cost is no issue then this is as good as it gets for anyone who is looking for an immersion in untamed nature without compromising creature comforts. The commodious tents are elegantly fitted out with handcrafted furnishings and the open-plan design features a hand-hammered copper bathtub in the living area. Each tent sits on a timber platform and has an extensive deck; the higher-grade ones also have a wooden hot tub outside. Tents these may be, but with luxuries like king-size beds, air conditioning, wireless internet, fridges and coffee-makers you can be forgiven for forgetting you are in the middle of the jungle.

The Four Seasons camp is situated at the confluence of the Ruak and Mekong Rivers, at the point where three countries – Thailand, Burma (Myanmar) and Laos – meet. Known to the world as the Golden Triangle, this region is now emerging from the long shadow cast by its association with opium cultivation. Thanks to exhaustive programmes by the Thai government, the terraced fields you now see are more likely to be growing tea, coffee and fruit. Spectacular as the environment is, the undoubted highlight of a stay will be close encounters with elephants. On arrival you are given a traditional *mahout* outfit and after instruction in verbal commands and handling skills you can enjoy the thrill of an escorted jungle ride, driving your own elephant. And at the end of the day you can help out at the river during bath time for these gentle giants.

Soneva Kiri

Lying at the extreme southeastern limit of the country, the mainly undeveloped tropical island of Ko Kut is the second largest in the Ko Chang archipelago. The exclusive beach resort of Soneva Kiri spreads out around a sheltered white-sand beach on the west coast of the island. Its remote location in the Gulf of Thailand, together with easy access courtesy of a private plane service from Bangkok Airport, makes this resort a perfect getaway for some seriously indulgent R&R.

You can choose a villa on the beach front or on the hillside. Both come with a private infinity pool, split-level sunbathing terrace, master bedroom and separate living and dressing rooms. Rates include a personal butler, as well as air transfers and all meals and drinks. Even though this is a small resort you still have a range of dining options, with no fewer than three restaurants and other outlets such as an ice-cream parlour and a hut dedicated to all things chocolate. During your stay you should certainly take the short motorboat ride to sample the fare at Benz's restaurant where an acclaimed Thai chef cooks up locally caught seafood in idyllic surroundings. And at the end of the day you can kick back and enjoy a classic movie in the resort's open-air cinema.

It may take a lot to draw you away from the glorious beach and the resort amenities, including a state-of-the-art spa facility, but it would be a pity to leave Ko Kut without venturing into the pristine rainforest of its interior or visiting a traditional fishing village. The trek to Khlong Chao waterfall is particularly recommended.

WHERE:
Ko Kut, Gulf of Thailand
COST:
Astronomical
BEST TIME OF YEAR:
November to April
DON'T MISS:
For a very special dining experience try the Tree Pod in which you are winched high off the ground for an intimate meal in the trees, served by a flying waiter who arrives on a zipline.
THINGS TO DO:
Sunbathing; swimming; water sports; snorkelling; diving; sea kayaking; spa treatments; tennis; jungle trekking; birdwatching; stargazing; wine tasting
YOU SHOULD KNOW:
Soneva Kiri has recently opened its first Eco Villa, a prototype zero-emissions suite in which a range of environmental technologies are incorporated into a bio-climatically designed structure made from locally sourced building materials.

WHERE:
Khao Sok National Park, Suratthani Province
COST:
Budget
BEST TIME OF YEAR:
January to April
DON'T MISS:
Khao Sok is one of the few remaining habitats of the *Rafflesia kerrii*, an extraordinary parasite plant which emits a foul smell in order to attract flies for pollination. If you are lucky enough you may see one of these rare plants in bloom, resembling a large red bowl and with a diameter up to 75 cm (30 in), it is one of the world's largest flowers.

Tree Tops River Huts

Together with two neighbouring reserves, Khao Sok National Park forms the largest tract of virgin rainforest in southern Thailand. It is a very special environment as it is part of the oldest evergreen forest system in the world, dating back some 160 million years. You need to spend several days in the park to make the most of its many hidden delights and the best way to do that is to rent a holiday cottage at the Tree Tops complex.

Close to the park headquarters and visitor centre, Tree Tops is a friendly and unshowy place offering the best of Thai hospitality and service. The straightforward but characterful visitor accommodation blends easily into the surrounding forest. There is a choice of treehouses built on stilts or little stone cottages, some decorated with pebble-dash finishes which wouldn't look out of place in the Home Counties. Although fairly basic, the treehouses and cottages are all equipped with fans and air conditioning and have spotless modern bathrooms. However, you won't have come here to spend large amounts of time in your lodgings, but to be out and about exploring the amazing surroundings.

Khao Sok is home to elephants, bears, tigers, tapirs, gibbons, monkeys and more than 300 bird species, including spectacular hornbills. Your best chances of sighting the larger animals will be at dusk on a guided trek with a park ranger. While only the most skilled rock climbers can scale the heights of the dramatic limestone peaks which are such a feature of the park, there are also numerous waterfalls and cave systems which anyone can visit, as well as the large man-made lake of Cheow Lan.

THINGS TO DO:
Wildlife-watching; elephant trekking; guided nature walks; hiking; river and lake swimming; canoeing; tubing; visiting caves
YOU SHOULD KNOW:
Within the park boundaries you can also stay on one of the raft houses that float on Cheow Lan Lake.

Imperial Boat House Resort

You don't need to have sea legs or even river legs to sleep on a barge at the Imperial Boat House Resort on Ko Samui. The central feature of this beach resort is 34 old teakwood rice barges which have been carefully restored and converted into elegant guest suites. These traditional barges once plied their trade on the Chao Phraya River, transporting rice and other commodities from the fertile central plains down to Bangkok and the coast.

Now moored securely in tropical gardens just back from the beach, the barges present an unusual spectacle amid the resort's more conventional holiday accommodation. The boat suites feature separate living and dining areas and, below deck, a master bedroom with a sky-lit bathroom. They are equipped with everything you would expect from accommodation of this class, plus one or two facilities you don't always find, such as tea- and coffee-making facilities. And it goes without saying that you have your own sun deck, located in the vessel's prow.

The Imperial Boat House Resort is at Hat Choeng Mon on the northeastern tip of Ko Samui. The beach forms the southern end of Ao Thong Son, a sheltered bay with a small headland separating the sands from a rocky cove to the north. Choeng Mon is a perfect swimming beach, especially for little ones, and it is well situated for Hat Chaweng, the island's finest beach, and its principal nightlife spot, which is a short distance to the south (the resort runs regular shuttle buses). The island's airport is also an easy journey away, meaning that you need waste no time before stripping off and stretching out on those fabulous sands.

WHERE:
Hat Choeng Mon, Ko Samui
COST:
Reasonable
BEST TIME OF YEAR:
February to June (although you can also get fine, dry weather in September and October, when there are fewer crowds)
DON'T MISS:
The nautical theme is continued in the boat shape of one of the resort's two swimming pools.
THINGS TO DO:
Swimming; snorkelling; diving; canoeing; sailing; spa treatments; jungle trekking; elephant rides; seeing the Big Buddha at Hat Bangrak
YOU SHOULD KNOW:
The resort restaurant and bars all offer a Happy Hour from 18.00 to 19.00, when you can buy two drinks for the price of one.

Hintok River Camp

WHERE:
Hellfire Pass, Kanchanaburi Province
COST:
Reasonable
BEST TIME OF YEAR:
November to April
DON'T MISS:
Be sure to visit the outstanding Memorial Museum at Hellfire Pass, a joint project of the Australian and Thai Governments. The audio tour includes recorded memories of surviving POWs.
THINGS TO DO:
Jungle hikes; birdwatching; elephant trekking; bamboo rafting; canoeing; longtail boat rides; visiting a Mon tribal village
YOU SHOULD KNOW:
The best way to arrive at Hintok River Camp is by taking the train from Kanchanaburi to Nam Tok. This is the only section of the Thailand–Burma rail route in use today and yes, you *do* cross over that famous Bridge on the River Kwai.

This stylish safari camp sits on a small plateau on the east bank of the River Kwai. Although barely 200 km (125 mi) from Bangkok this feels like an entirely different world, a place to unwind and refresh the spirit. The camp is buried in the lush vegetation of the rainforest; from the opposite bank only the occasional flash of white canvas betrays its presence at all. The permanent canvas tents are large rectangular affairs mounted on timber platforms. The spacious interiors feature rustic wooden furniture, beds as comfortable as in any hotel, and a bathroom with shower and hot running water. Fans as well as air conditioning help ensure a good night's sleep. Meals are served in an attractive thatched-roof restaurant with an open terrace overlooking the river. And if the heat starts to get too much, a riverside plunge pool, fed by a natural spring, is perfect for a cooling dip.

It is hard to believe that the peace and natural beauty of this magical place hides one of the grimmest episodes of 20th-century history. Not far from the camp lies the aptly-named Hellfire Pass, a key section of the notorious Thailand–Burma Railway built by the occupying Japanese in 1942–43. Linking Bangkok and Rangoon, the 'Death Railway' was constructed by Allied prisoners of war and local forced labour in unimaginably harsh conditions, using little more than hand tools to break through some of the most challenging terrain on the planet. Today you can walk through the section at Hellfire Pass, a 500-m (1,640-ft) long, 26 m (85-ft) deep cutting through sheer rock, where some re-laid rail tracks provide a poignant reminder of the terrible suffering and loss of life.

Sandalwood Luxury Villas

WHERE:
Ko Samui
COST:
Expensive
BEST TIME OF YEAR:
November to April
DON'T MISS:
A visit to the market at the traditional fishing village of Hua Thanon
THINGS TO DO:
Swimming; snorkelling; diving; water sports; sea kayaking; hiking; elephant trekking; golf; cookery classes
YOU SHOULD KNOW:
A quaint but necessary house rule of the establishment is that Durian fruits are not permitted in the rooms – if you have ever smelt one you will know why!

This small and exclusive resort has a stunning location on the east coast of Ko Samui. Set on a hillside overlooking the sea, the resort's villas are positioned at different levels, giving them all spectacular and uninterrupted views of Hat Chaweng and Hat Lamai beaches.

The architectural inspiration for the villas is drawn from traditional Thai pavilions with their steep pitched roofs and the distinctive spikes of their gable ends. The refined interiors are a subtle blend of classic Thai motifs with contemporary style. Extensive use of marble and granite, together with floor-to-ceiling panoramic windows, give the rooms a deliciously cool feel throughout the day. There are just ten villas in all, sleeping two or four (one sleeps six). All are air conditioned and feature a private balcony or terrace, Jacuzzi and kitchen area. Some are built with two floors to make the most of the topography and three have their own private pools.

Set in landscaped tropical gardens where you will also find the resort's two infinity pools, the villas are linked by pretty stone paths. This is a relaxed and private environment, far removed from the bustle of beach life (although this is easily accessible using the resort's free shuttle service). The restaurant has an impressive reputation for serving authentic regional dishes with a modern twist, accompanied by some of the best views on the island. Sandalwood's spa is the ideal place to put the finishing touches to your sense of well-being – try the traditional Thai massage, which incorporates elements of yoga with pressure-point work, therapeutic stretching and reflexology to leave you feeling relaxed yet blissfully energized.

Four Rivers Floating Eco-Lodge

WHERE:
Tatai, Koh Kong province
COST:
Reasonable
BEST TIME OF YEAR:
November to April
DON'T MISS:
The sunsets are a highlight of a stay at Four Rivers, whether seen from the sun deck in front of your tent or on a Sunset Cruise on the river.
THINGS TO DO:
Swimming in the river; jungle trekking; guided nature walks; birdwatching; kayaking in the mangrove swamps; fishing; waterskiing; boat trips on the river
YOU SHOULD KNOW:
The eco-lodge is only accessible by boat so you should plan your arrival to coincide with one of the two free boat transfers offered each day (ten-minute ride). Alternatively, you can hire a boat taxi.

It has taken painful years and painstaking effort for Cambodia to recover from the collective trauma inflicted on the country by the brutal Khmer Rouge regime, but this small South East Asian nation is now re-emerging into the modern world and assuming its rightful place as a major holiday destination. Cambodia's late arrival on the scene has meant that much of its tourism infrastructure has been developed in tune with the keener environmental sensibilities of recent times. Nowhere is this trend better exemplified than at the Four Rivers Eco-Lodge, a charming development of 12 tented villas which literally float on raft-like platforms on the Tatai River in the southwest of the country. Sustainable, attainable luxury are the watchwords here. The safari-style tents are fully equipped with high-end facilities such as flat-screen TV, wifi internet and powered fans, yet they also exude an atmosphere of natural simplicity, thanks to the extensive use of rattan in the furnishings.

Arranged like a chevron in a bend of the river (the restaurant and central facilities are at the apex) the resort sits in glorious seclusion. The surrounding rainforest is a tropical Eden of birds of paradise, rare orchids and exotic perfumed plants. Although it has had to withstand poaching and illegal logging in the past, large parts of the jungle remain untouched, especially as it rises to the misty heights of the Cardamom Mountains. Your guide to these natural delights is likely as not a local villager who has been retrained from his previous job as a poacher to the more benign one of 'fostering the soft tread of an environmentally aware footprint'.

La Résidence Phou Vao

The ancient royal capital of Luang Prabang in the uplands of northern Laos has established itself relatively recently on the international tourist trail, thanks in no small measure to UNESCO's designation of the historic old town as a World Heritage Site. Before then it was one of South East Asia's better kept secrets, with *cognoscenti* and the occasional intrepid traveller coming back with tales of a fabled riverside town filled with glittering temples and genteel colonial architecture. The country's political and cultural isolation in the 1970s and 1980s spared Luang Prabang the more obvious excesses of 20th-century development so that today's visitor is treated to one of the best-preserved traditional towns in South East Asia.

La Résidence Phou Vao is a charming boutique hotel which perfectly captures the old-world mood of the former capital. Designed in a straightforward colonial style, the simple lines and muted colours speak of understated luxury, the spacious guest suites combining dark rosewood hues with grand marble bathrooms and rich wall fabrics. The hotel occupies a commanding site atop Phou Vao (Kite Hill) on the southern outskirts. The views are, as you would expect, magnificent – especially from the hotel's infinity pool which stops dramatically at the cliff edge. The old town is spread out in the valley below, dominated by the rock of Phu Si and the golden dome of Chomsi *wat*), against a stirring backdrop of mountain crags. If echoes of a colonial past are evoked in the mere creak of a floorboard, confirmation of the enduring legacy of the French, one-time rulers of Indochina, can be found here in the strong Gallic flavours which continue to infuse the delicious local cuisine.

WHERE:
Luang Prabang
COST:
Expensive
BEST TIME OF YEAR:
November to April
DON'T MISS:
At night La Résidence becomes a true land of enchantment, with dozens of lanterns hung in the trees and candles set adrift in jars on the water-lily pond.
THINGS TO DO:
Visiting the temples and other sights of historic Luang Prabang; swimming; spa treatments; Lao massage; cycling; cooking courses; boat trips
YOU SHOULD KNOW:
Making use of traditional herbal remedies, Lao massage is subtly different from the Thai version, but equally revitalizing.

Settha Palace

WHERE:
Pang Kham Street, Vientiane
COST:
Reasonable
BEST TIME OF YEAR:
November to April
DON'T MISS:
The hotel uses an old London taxi for its airport transfers.
THINGS TO DO:
Sightseeing; swimming; shopping; visiting the Lao National Museum; patronizing the Parisian-style cafés and bakeries
YOU SHOULD KNOW:
For a different kind of experience you could try your hand at the nearby Lao Bowling Centre – with boisterous locals and cheap beer, there's a great atmosphere beneath the bright lights.

Settha Palace is the grand old lady of Vientiane's hotels. Originally opened in 1932, it was appropriated by the state when the Communists took over in 1975 and turned into workers' housing. Shortly before the millennium, however, the original family who formerly ran the place was able to re-acquire it and they have since carried out a lavish but respectful restoration of the venerable building which has returned it to the days of its colonial glory.

This Vientiane landmark now stands proud once more amid lush landscaped gardens, a testament to a vanished age of gracious service and classical elegance. The service remains as courteous and discreet as ever and the French influence is still everywhere in evidence – from the upholstered furniture to the abundance of ceramic knobs, the wooden floorboards to the high ceilings of the guest rooms, complete with idly swishing wood-bladed fans and magnificent bathrooms in black and white Venetian marble.

The Gallic theme is naturally enough to the fore in the hotel's restaurant, La Belle Époque, where classic French dishes are ingeniously fused with a seasonally inspired Lao menu. To help you work up an appetite, a beautiful kidney-shaped swimming pool beckons, fringed by sweet-smelling frangipani. A central location – within easy walking distance of the river-front and the Lao capital's principal sights – reasonable rates and a relatively small scale (there are just 29 rooms) have made the Settha Palace a popular choice among discerning travellers. The sense of history here is palpable. If you enjoy musing on the past, you will want to join them too.

WHERE:
Dalat
COST:
Budget (but it is understandably popular so you will need to book well in advance)
BEST TIME OF YEAR:
Known as the City of Eternal Spring, Dalat has a pleasantly even temperature throughout the year. Even in the wet season (April to November) the deluge rarely begins before lunchtime, leaving mornings dry for sightseeing.
DON'T MISS:
Dalat's well-preserved townscape, with many reminders of the days when, under French rule, it was one of Asia's most fashionable hill resorts
THINGS TO DO:
Sightseeing; jogging around Xuan Huong Lake; chauffeured motorbike rides into the Central Highlands; visiting waterfalls; working on your fantasy novel
YOU SHOULD KNOW:
The Crazy House Hotel is the creation of Mrs Dang Viet Nga, an architect trained in Moscow who has a number of other public buildings to her name in the area. Having a father who was Ho Chi Minh's successor as the country's president has probably helped insulate Hang Nga, as she's generally known, from the worst effects of bureaucratic disapproval.

Hang Nga Guesthouse

Mention the mysterious orient and the images that come into most people's minds do not probably include a fairytale castle *à la* Disney, nor the kind of minatory lair encountered in a Grimm Brothers' tale. Yet those are the comparisons that are provoked almost inevitably when you first set eyes on this extraordinary building. Known universally as the Crazy House Hotel, it cuts a bizarre and determinedly incongruous figure amid the genteel suburban villas in this part of Dalat.

In architectural terms it has been described as a cross between Gaudi and the world of *Alice in Wonderland* and, indeed, the work of the eccentric Catalan master was a decisive influence on the building's creator. It is impossible to do justice to this phantasmagoria in mere words. Suffice it to say that you will look in vain for straight lines or right angles; here all is a riot of twisting organic shapes, dark recesses and unexpected openings. The exterior with its jagged profile and pitted surface resembles a giant hollowed-out tree. Inside, undulating walkways and cave-like spaces cry out to be explored by your inner child.

In the 20 years it has been open the guesthouse has become one of Dalat's most visited attractions. If this particular fantasy world does it for you, then you can opt for total immersion by staying in one of ten guest rooms, each named after an animal or bird with furnishings to match, including a large sculpture of the relevant creature. If you are of a nervous disposition, though, you might not take kindly to waking in the night to encounter a giant kangaroo staring at you with glowing red eyes!

Raffles Hotel

WHERE:
Beach Road, Singapore
COST:
Astronomical
BEST TIME OF YEAR:
Any time
DON'T MISS:
The Victorian Jubilee Theatre on the third floor; a bumboat cruise on the Singapore River to the riverside festival village of Clarke Quay; a tiffin curry in the Tiffin Room; treating the children (and yourself) to a Cold Marble Teppanyaki at the Raffles Creamery
THINGS TO DO:
Breathe in the heady scent of frangipani in the Palm Court; tennis; billiards; spa treatments; people-watching by the pool
YOU SHOULD KNOW:
The last wild tiger in Singapore was shot, killed and rendered extinct on the premises at Raffles.

Reputation is everything. Carrying with it a whiff of the tropics and a hint of scandal, Raffles in Singapore is unquestionably the most exotic of all the world's grand hotels. It's got form as well as luxury, some of it borrowed from its spiritual guide and actual founder of Singapore, Sir Stamford Raffles (a notorious charmer, intellectual and scientist who 'kept his head when all about were losing theirs'), and the rest made up of the distilled essence of all the *risqué* encounters and imperial confrontations that the place has witnessed since it opened in the late 19th century.

More than ever, Raffles looks the part today. New additions merge seamlessly with the original Victorian grandeur, but the graceful white arcades of the verandahs running round each floor of the period wings, the 4-m (13-ft) high ceilings of the central block and many other much-loved architectural features are reserved for the hotel's new arrangement of its oldest buildings into 103 suites. Of the six categories of suite even the cheapest is magnificent, overlooking a tranquil private courtyard to one side. But there is demand still for the Grand Hotel Suites, at the top of Raffles' sweeping grand staircase. Of course, with two bedrooms, three bathrooms, a parlour, private verandah and butler, these are also ten times more expensive. Who's counting? All the suites have Persian carpets on their dark teak floors, original art on their walls and extremely high-quality antiques and period furniture. This decor is a Raffles' hallmark.

Others include 18 restaurants, cafés and the Long Bar (where the Singapore Sling was invented), conference facilities for leaders of men, a shopping arcade to rival the Burlington, and the best service on the Straits. Takes you back, and forwards.

Wanderlust Hotel

The Wanderlust Hotel raises your spirits even from the outside. It's an unlikely, rectangular building, a disused 1920s school in the Little India district. Now smartly painted, strung with lights and with an Art Deco mosaic running up its centre above the door, it's intriguing. Inside, it's lunatic. With 29 rooms on four floors to dispose of, the owner (as hip as he must be courageous) offered a floor each to four award-winning design groups, and the freedom to express themselves in whatever way they saw fit. The result is breathtaking.

Asylum assigned 'Industrial Glam' to the lobby and restaurant; then there is 'Eccentricity' (:phunk Studio), 'Is It Just Black and White?' (DPA) and 'Creature Comforts' (fFurious) on the top. The artistic details are as exciting as the anarchic concepts – ten rooms are rendered in single, explosive neon colours, and another eight are inspired by origami and Pop Art. Loft rooms have themes like Bling, ASCII, Space, Tree and Typewriter. Clever lighting adds hugely to the dramatic theatre of each room.

It's not yet a gold mine, but the Wanderlust is already a success. Its quirks and whimsy bring visitors as to a gallery. Many end up staying, hoping to witness some detail of artistic evolution. Cocotte's French restaurant is another lure. Its distinctive industrial flair includes mismatched furniture icons by the likes of Tom Dixon and Frank Gehry. One of the communal tables (good for world travellers, the hotel's natural clientele) is crowned by a spider-like 'chandelier' of Anglepoise lamps. Cocotte herself believes the art and design that power the hotel are only meaningful if people come to eat her (delicious) food and get a good night's sleep, because that's what hotels are for.

WHERE:
Dickson Road, Little India, Singapore
COST:
Expensive
BEST TIME OF YEAR:
Any time
DON'T MISS:
The hotel peeking tour, including the Mono Deluxe Pop Art room in which an Eames chair is drawn on the wall; getting to grips with Singapore's amazing ethnic mix in Chinatown, Kampong Glam, and Little India; the 20 dioramas telling Singapore's history at the National Museum; the Night Safari at Singapore Zoo
THINGS TO DO:
Try Cocotte's 'sharing portions' with whoever is at the communal table (it is appreciated as good social politics); talk philosophy in the customized mosaic-tiled Jacuzzi (down the second-floor rainbow corridor to an outdoor deck).
YOU SHOULD KNOW:
All guests are given a book-like itinerary including everything about the Wanderlust, from its history to how to access your voicemail. It also includes bus and subway maps, and useful eating and shopping info with yet more maps. But it turns into a personalized diary of your journey by the inclusion of several blank but abstractly decorated pages where you can write your own thoughts and impressions.

Dragon Inn Floating Resort

WHERE:
Semporna, Sabah, Borneo
COST:
Budget or super-budget
BEST TIME OF YEAR:
Any time is good.
DON'T MISS:
The sundown return of the fishing fleet of *lepa* boats (a unique local design with an outrigger, a bit like a catamaran, traditional to the Bajau Laut); the bargains in the local Semporna market; the unbelievable value for money of freshly caught lobster and coral grouper
THINGS TO DO:
Book a different dive boat every day at the stand by the Dragon Inn entrance; keep your room while you travel light to a nearby island for a couple of days; swap local news and good stories in the bar with other travellers in slow transit; dive some more; join the others watching the day slowly taking place.
YOU SHOULD KNOW:
The Regatta *Lepa* each April celebrates the artistry and workmanship the Bajau put into their all-purpose boats. Their maritime heritage gets a boost from the parade along the coast of hundreds of brightly decorated *lepa*, draped in banners and trailing colourful streamers. Back on land, teams of lithe girls in fabulous traditional costumes contribute to the excitement with ancient Bajau dances.

It doesn't float and it's not really a resort, but the Dragon Inn is unquestionably a brilliant place to stay. It acts as a clearing house for travellers heading to the world-class dive sites in the offshore archipelago, and to the international brotherhood of island-hopping wanderers. It couldn't be more appropriate, because the whole, enormous complex looks like, and is built on, the highly traditional lines of the Bajau Laut, the Sea Gypsies of the region. Far out in the shallow Celebes and Sulu Seas, sailors pass small communities of houses built on stilts in the open sea, the dwindling remnants of a huge culture.

Nowadays, most Bajau have returned to the shore, but the Dragon Inn is a powerful reminder of their lifestyle. It, too, is built on stilts, jutting out from the shore over the waters close to Semporna's harbour. Like massive longhouses, their palm-thatched roofs twisted up and out at either end, the Dragon Inn's 70 rooms, two 'conference' halls, several aquaria (their fish unaware they themselves are the menu) and huge restaurant constitute a *Kampong Air* (water village) of its own. At the seaward end, with the best views and fewest smells, are the VIP rooms, comfortably furnished with cushioned rattan, a lovely balcony and a shower with floor slats widely spaced so the water runs straight down into the sea. Moving back towards the shore are family suites, singles, doubles, three 18-person longhouse 'units' and some dormitories.

It's all genuine. The Dragon Inn makes almost no concessions to cosseted Europeans, and it's as democratic a hotel as you'll find anywhere. It makes rich men of everyone. That's why many who pass through decide to stay instead. Dive by day. Dragon by night.

First World Hotel

It has all the subtlety of a five-year-old's coloured spinning top, but so big that it's mega-fun. The facade of the First World Hotel sets colour in motion, spinning waves of red, yellow, green, orange and blue across the surface of its twin 28-storey blocks, then eddying out across the roofs of the giant circular First World Plaza in front. Size is half the point. First World Hotel was launched as the biggest hotel in the world. Then its 6,118 rooms were outscored by the MGM Grand in Las Vegas and now it's only fourth – but still the biggest in Malaysia! Hotel and Plaza are symbiotic. The hotel is really just a dormitory for people who only come to spend a few days gambling and shopping in the huge adjacent malls. Their exuberant decoration is like a skittish monkey's red behind, except that the hotel and plaza seek to attract money instead of personal favours.

It works, because the hotel rooms are designed to help you decide to leave them as quickly as possible. Although perfectly functional, clean and well-maintained, the majority are both tiny and drab. The most popular (and inexpensive) three categories aren't even allowed a mini-fridge or TV (except for the hotel channel). Oh well, look outside – all that colour, noise, fun sounds and other people! It lures you back to the ground floor, spirits rising as you come through an attractively spacious Spanish-style lobby. At the front door a lush tropical rainforest marks the transition from hotel to plaza. The stimulus of nursery-level dayglo unfreezes your wallet. First World Hotel and Plaza know to spit you out only after you max out your cards. Willingly, and with a goofy smile.

WHERE:
Genting Highlands, Pahang
COST:
Reasonable (but check for multiple discounts which can reduce the bill to low-budget levels)
BEST TIME OF YEAR:
Any time
DON'T MISS:
The green, forested hills surrounding the complex (if only for a wistful glance); the indoor theme park (50 rides including the Venetian Experience where the gondoliers wear baseball caps); the Watersplash pool (indoor water games for children); the Sky Venture free-fall simulator
THINGS TO DO:
Cineplex; casino gaming; shopping (170 eating and shopping outlets); bowling; Ripley's Believe It Or Not museum
YOU SHOULD KNOW:
Expect a long wait to check in, and minimal service with a surly attitude; hotel rooms are unheated, and the mountains can be chilly at night.

Lankayan Island

WHERE:
Offshore from Sandakan (90 minutes by speedboat), Sabah, Borneo Island
COST:
Reasonable to mildly expensive
BEST TIME OF YEAR:
March to November (July to August for the very best diving)
DON'T MISS:
The gigantic whale sharks, regular visitors between March and May; the green and hawksbill turtles' nesting sites (you can watch the babies released back into the sea under the Lankayan protection programme); the three wrecks (an ocean-going poaching ship, now full of ghost pipefish, yellow pikes and huge groupers, the 'Mosquito Wreck', still full of WWII Japanese cargo, and the 'Pier Wreck', an artificial reef created by a fishing boat deliberately sunk off the pier for beginners to explore)
THINGS TO DO:
Admire the endless variety and colour of both healthy corals and the myriad fish that live among them; if that palls, take a day trip to see Orang-utangs; sailing; ocean kayaking
YOU SHOULD KNOW:
Next to the small resort shop (which sells film, batteries, toiletries, etc) there's a TV room set up for guests to review the day's video shots or other footage.

Lankayan Island is one of the lucky ones. It's idyllic, a teardrop of perfect tropical fantasy clad in thick vegetation topped with swaying casuarinas trees and pandan screwpines, and ringed with gold sand and ruffled turquoise waters. It's still officially uninhabited. Its good fortune was to be protected almost as soon as it was discovered to be one of the world's best dive sites. Inclusion in the Sugud Islands Marine Conservation Area (SIMCA) restricts the number of people allowed onto it to the 24 chalets of the existing dive resort, forbids boats from anchoring anywhere near it and minimizes their motorized activity, and completely bans fishing and motorized water sports. What's left is Nature, with all four elements zinging in harmony.

The chalets are set on low stilts along the edge of the beach. Built in the traditional style of Borneo (but with gleaming bathrooms), the steep wooden roofs trap breezes and overhang broad verandahs that project a metre or so onto the actual sand. An equally discreet and well-appointed, but far bigger, version by the jetty houses an excellent informal restaurant, a quiet upper-floor lounge, and a really pretty wooden terrace bar where people tell fishy tales in the warm twilight. When the water's high, you can look down through the floorboards at baby blacktip sharks wheeling in the phosphorescence.

Not everyone who comes is a diver (Lankayan is a wonderful place for kids to learn beach craft), but with roughly 30 prime sites catering to every level it would be criminal not to at least snorkel. Water clarity is excellent, and three totally different wrecks attract the brilliantly colourful 'macro fauna' (divespeak for big fish) for which Lankayan is justly famous.

Miniloc Island Resort

It can be tricky picking a holiday destination in Palawan, for this archipelago in the western Philippines has nearly 1,800 islands. And choosing that unspoilt location with crystal-clear waters, pristine beaches and a wealth of flora and fauna isn't helped by the fact that Palawan ('The Last Ecological Frontier of the Philippines') has these attributes in abundance. So here's a helping hand – look no further than resorts around El Nido or Taytay on the main island of Palawan. This spectacular area offers limestone cliffs soaring above marine sanctuaries rich in coral that teem with tropical fish, while on shore lush forests host countless exotic birds.

The Miniloc Island Resort should tick all the boxes. This charming hideaway close to El Nido is in a stunning cove off Bacuit Bay, surrounded by towering rock walls punctuated with clinging greenery. There are seven water cottages, built on stilts of local materials in traditional rustic style, standing in the limpid sea at the foot of those impressive cliffs. Five larger Seaview Rooms are also on stilts, while 13 Garden Cottages amid tropical foliage adjoin the beach. Three Cliff Cottages offer panoramic views, a dozen Beachside Rooms are right on the sand and ten Eco-rooms are solar-powered. Each sleeps two, three or four depending on size.

The resort is small enough to remain intimate, but large enough to support facilities like a clubhouse with restaurant and free wifi, a beach bar, boutique, marine sports centre, games area and spa *cabana*. Guests arrive at the resort's dock and everything they need for a great holiday is waiting. Although many feel the need to do no more than relax on the beach and enjoy messing about on (or under) the water, there are plenty of other tempting possibilities for those who like some action.

WHERE:
Miniloc Island, El Nido, Palawan
COST:
Expensive (but less so in low season, June to September)
BEST TIME OF YEAR:
October to May
DON'T MISS:
Get up close and personal with all or some of the five species of endangered sea turtles found in these waters; try a traditional Filipino *hilot* massage at the spa.
THINGS TO DO:
Snorkelling and diving; heading off by kayak to find a cave or private picnic beach (there are dozens to choose from within easy paddling distance); taking a sunset cruise around Bacuit Bay; a guided eco-tour; stargazing; making a coconut-fibre hat
YOU SHOULD KNOW:
The Cliff Cottages are reached by a narrow flight of stairs and are not therefore suitable for children. Room rates include boat transfer to the resort, all meals, use of snorkelling gear and non-motorized water-sports equipment (kayaks, hobie cats, windsurfing kit). There is a Kids' Activity Centre.

Alila Villas Soori

Blissful beach-front living, here you come! Alila Villas Soori is located on Bali's southwest coast in the Tabanan Regency – one of the island's most fertile and picturesque areas. The resort has gently sloping rice terraces behind and a wonderful black-sand beach lapped by the azure water of the Indian Ocean in front. Luxurious villas await those in search of panoramic ocean views, gentle sea breezes and tranquillity and there are opportunities, too, for the action-minded to have fun. Alila Villas Soori was constructed using the best contemporary eco-principles and sits comfortably in the landscape thanks to the use of local materials, but it also gives arriving guests a *frisson* of visual excitement generated by the cutting-edge Asian design by top Singapore architects.

There are 38 one-bedroom and six larger family/party villas (one with ten bedrooms), all carefully sited to take full advantage of the stunning natural setting and panoramic views. But great care has also been taken to ensure that every villa offers complete privacy. Each has its own pool and facilities that range from vanity units to LCD TV/DVDs and iPods. This really is as good as it gets, and the place has all the resort essentials that complement the superb beach-front accommodation – a large infinity pool; a spa with aqua ceiling, imaginatively located beneath the reflective water feature in reception; three eateries offering local and international cuisine; bar and boutique with branded gear, plus local arts and crafts.

For those who want more than the ultimate in beach holidays, the resort's helpful 'leisure concierges' are on hand to recommend (and arrange) numerous outings or activities tailored to the requirements of individual guests. But they'll need to be pretty persuasive to tempt you away from Alila Villas Soori's sybaritic delights.

WHERE:
Banjar Dukuh, Desa Kelating,
Kerambitan, Tabanan, Bali
COST:
Astronomical (but there are cheaper seasonal deals)
BEST TIME OF YEAR:
April to September are the dry months.
DON'T MISS:
The *al fresco* breakfast at the Cotto restaurant, offering a different tasting menu each day and majoring on local dishes and fun twists on western favourites; joining fellow guests over drinks in The Reading Room
THINGS TO DO:
Visit Tanah Lot Temple; see the famous Balinese dance school in nearby Abiantuwung; horse riding
YOU SHOULD KNOW:
An extreme Islamist bomb attack in 2002 killed 202 people in Bali's tourist district of Kutu, but the risk of a repeat atrocity is now regarded as very small.

COMO Shambhala Estate

Near Central Bali's Ubud, cultural centre of the island, the COMO Shambhala Estate is a luxurious well-being retreat that offers discerning guests an experience that is both relaxing and rejuvenating. Five residences are located around the extensive estate, which is in a horseshoe on the River Ayung. Each sits dramatically amid vibrant forest greenery and offers both rooms and suites, mostly one-bedroomed. These range from garden rooms through terrace and estate suites to amazing top-of-the-range COMO suites. Sizes and outlook vary, allowing for personal choice. The architecture is stunning and residences have pools, shaded pavilions and lounges. Retreat villas offer individuals and couples total privacy, plus the use of all facilities at the host residence.

The setting, accommodation and service might be very special in their own right, and are, but the true rationale of this magical enclave is the holistic retreat dimension. It's perfectly possible to book in simply to enjoy perfect tranquillity, but most guests do come for (or are seduced by) the wide range of wellness activities. This can be formal – as in the two-night Vitality Package or three-, five- or seven-night Holistic Wellness Programme – or involve picking and choosing from such energizing options as yoga, Pilates, Tai Chi, *Pranayama* (breath control), massage therapies, hydrotherapy, colonic irrigation, facial care, *ayurvedic* therapy or personal fitness training. In addition, many find true peace of mind in ceremonies such as the water-temple purification and traditional Balinese spiritual healing.

Nor is the temporal aspect ignored, albeit in the healthiest of contexts. The cuisine matches the estate's impeccable well-being standards, consisting of special Shambhala cuisine based on organic home-grown and locally sourced ingredients. It's prepared in an open kitchen, so you can see for yourself. Fancy lime-leaf, chilli and coconut curry with fern tips? That's just for starters!

WHERE:
Desa Melinggih Kelod, Payangan, Gianyar, Bali
COST:
Expensive to astronomical, depending on accommodation
BEST TIME OF YEAR:
Go any time for the wellness programmes, but the rainy season (December to March) can be very wet indeed.
DON'T MISS:
Leisurely Sunday brunch at the glow restaurant, while a *gamelan* orchestra plays and village girls perform their dance routines (and if you love the food, take a cookery class!)
THINGS TO DO:
Apart from almost limitless wellness possibilities, activities around the estate include jungle trekking, river swimming, rock climbing, tennis, biking, river rafting, guided challenges . . . or hey, simply relaxing. The estate also arranges local cultural visits.
YOU SHOULD KNOW:
All guests are assigned a personal assistant to help ensure a perfectly trouble-free stay. Families and parties of friends can book a residence for their private use (and children under 16 are only allowed in villas or residences booked in their entirety, to avoid disturbing other guests). COMO operates several resorts worldwide that apply similar principles.

Amankila

WHERE:
Candidasa, Bali
COST:
It's very expensive to astronomical (once essential extras are added).
BEST TIME OF YEAR:
April to October
DON'T MISS:
Traditional Balinese dancing by the pool, three nights a week, or the pleasing lilt of *rindik* music on the other nights
THINGS TO DO:
Treat yourself to an outing on *Aman XVI*, a sturdy Balinese fishing craft with sun deck used for private sunrise/sunset or lunch cruises, also snorkelling expeditions. Play a set of floodlit tennis. Make full use of the Beach Club's action facilities – including kayaking, hobbiecat sailing, boogie boarding and windsurfing. Enjoy lazy mountain biking (that's downhill all the way!).
YOU SHOULD KNOW:
The resort has a babysitting service and is child-friendly. Under 12s stay free of charge (there is a supplement for older kids). TVs and DVD players are not automatically supplied in the suites, but can be provided on request.

Against the stunning backdrop of Eastern Bali's dark volcanic mountains, Amankila is one of the most luxurious resorts in Indonesia – no mean achievement on an island that specializes in these top tourist havens. It is unobtrusively set among lush green foliage atop low basalt cliffs overlooking the Lombok Strait, above a black volcanic beach in the Candidasa area – a fine alternative to the crowded tourist hotspot of Kutu for those who value privacy and exclusivity.

There are 34 freestanding suites with thatched roofs set among coconut palms, each featuring a large bedroom with a great view from the wide window, canopied king-size bed, sound system with iPod dock and free wifi. Bathrooms have a window-side divan, soaking tub, separate shower and toilet rooms, coconut-shell dressing areas and double terrazzo vanities. Every outdoor terrace is furnished with daybed, table and rattan chairs – and the most expensive suites have a private pool and sun terrace. But a private pool is a self-indulgence rather than a necessity – there's a huge lap pool by the Beach Club coconut groves, and three-tier infinity pools that step down from reception towards the shore, with thatched *balé* pavilions and an ample supply of loungers.

The restaurant by the upper swimming pool offers local classics with a Western culinary twist, from a menu that includes good vegetarian options. You can eat on the terrace by the pool, enjoy snack meals in the Beach Club or order a private dinner in the romantic location of your choice. The open-air island bar beside the restaurant – a great place to chill – is capped with a thatched wooden roof and furnished in bamboo. There is, of course, a splendid spa, and the unobtrusive but dedicated service at Amankila is the icing on a wonderful holiday confection.

Hotel Tugu Bali

Canggu Beach in southwestern Bali is the island's trendiest surfing spot and also the place to find the incomparable Hotel Tugu Bali. For those in search of a romantic break, the place is just about perfect. And for those seeking the ultimate beach holiday the hotel is, to coin a phrase, just about perfect. The beach-side setting is stunning (with sunsets to drown in), staff are charming and attentive, the food is splendid with a choice of five in-house restaurants, and the icing on the romantic cake is the stunning collection of museum-quality Balinese antiquities that create an extraordinary ambiance throughout.

Delightful thatched suites are scattered among lush tropical gardens and lotus ponds, beside the Indian Ocean, with 22 rooms to choose from – 19 suites and three villas. Rooms open to balconies with sea views and private plunge pools. They feature satellite TV, CD/DVD player, minibar, English-language newspaper and free wifi. The hotel's recreational amenities include a palm-fringed pool adjacent to the beach, fitness facility, spa with six pavilions, snooker room and library with books, CDs and DVDs.

Breakfast is not included, but room rates do include private airport transfers, a welcome-to-our-house drink, complimentary massage, flowers, tropical fruit and mineral water in-room, plus scrumptious high tea at sunset that features local delicacies. These are the sort of touches that add to the stunning overall picture – and speaking of pictures, nothing better illustrates the hotel's deliciously idiosyncratic approach than the Walter Spies Pavilion, which is filled with the eponymous Dutch artist's own memorabilia in Art Deco surroundings. It's surreal, it's beautiful, it's (almost) too good to be true!

WHERE:
Jalan Pantai Batu Bolong, Canggu Beach, Badung Canggu, Bali
COST:
Reasonable
BEST TIME OF YEAR:
Any time is good, but take wet-weather gear if you opt for December through to March.
DON'T MISS:
Sample the sensational 12-course *rijstaffel* rice platter. Take a cookery class that starts with a dawn visit to the local market, or a Balinese dance lesson (or both!).
THINGS TO DO:
You won't want to stray far from the hotel's many attractions (not least the beach) but you should at least try the surfing or bodyboarding. Pay a visit to nearby Tanah Lot rock formation and pilgrimage temple. Imbibe the house cocktail, Canggu Romantic (vodka, fresh lime juice and a splash of ginger ale), served in the Keraton Bar where guests can socialize to the sound of soothing music, followed by a demon chaser in the form of a Guavatini (vodka, lime juice, guava juice with a liquid sugar topping).
YOU SHOULD KNOW:
Children are welcome (tots free, a small supplement for older kids, special children's western and Indonesian menus offered). Bring insect repellent – hungry mosquitoes can stray in from the surrounding paddy fields. This is an eco-friendly establishment that practises serious recycling.

A *Machiya* in Kyoto

WHERE:
Kyoto
COST:
Expensive (although if you shop around you should be able to find reasonably priced *machiya*, too)
BEST TIME OF YEAR:
Spring (March to May) and autumn (October to November)
DON'T MISS:
Some *machiya* still have their traditional tea rooms, while others retain the sliding paper doors which help to regulate humidity levels within the house.
THINGS TO DO:
Visiting the temples, palaces and gardens of the old imperial city; shopping for traditional handicrafts; cycling; jogging along the Kamo River; attending a tea ceremony; watching Noh drama
YOU SHOULD KNOW:
The *machiya* owes its classic long, thin form to the taxes levied on buildings in the Edo period according to the width of their street frontage. This has given rise to its nickname *unagi no nedoko* or 'bedroom of eels'.

Machiya are the traditional townhouses that were once a dominant feature of Kyoto's vernacular architecture. Although Japan's ancient capital and most historic city was famously spared destruction in World War II, it fared less well in the postwar years when the country's economic resurgence saw many *machiya* swept aside to make way for new development.

Fortunately, in recent years a more considered attitude to the past and the built environment has prevailed, with the result that many original *machiya* are now being rescued from demolition and restored to a range of new uses, including as bars, restaurants, galleries and accommodation. A number of historic townhouses in the centre of Kyoto have been converted into sophisticated holiday homes where modern amenities have been combined with elements of traditional Japanese living to give guests an unusual insight into a culture that can sometimes be hard to penetrate.

Because the classic *machiya* is built almost entirely of wood, it has been particularly susceptible to fires and earthquakes, so that most of the surviving ones are less than a hundred years old. Nevertheless, their distinctive form – a succession of rooms on a single long axis linked by a corridor stretching back the entire length of the building from a narrow street frontage – gives the *machiya* an other-worldly charm which is seriously seductive. As you bed down on your futon spread out on the *tatami* flooring, you can muse on the merchant whose home this once was and who will also have enjoyed the latticework doors, *mushiko* windows (narrow slits in the plaster walls), cedarwood bath and immaculate little courtyard garden.

Imperial Hotel

Tokyo's Imperial Hotel is not much to look at today, but this sober and undistinguished 1970s tower block conceals a far more colourful past. Overlooking leafy Hibiya Park (the country's first European-style park when it was laid out in 1903, complete with rose gardens and a bandstand), the Imperial was the Japanese capital's first hotel in Western style when it opened in 1890. The luxury establishment rapidly became a legendary address and *the* place to be seen for international travellers and Tokyo's fashionable set alike.

Its heyday came between the two world wars and coincided with the 1923 new building – an Art Deco masterpiece designed by celebrated US architect Frank Lloyd Wright, who took his inspiration from the palace architecture of the Mayan civilization of Central America. A world as exotic to Tokyo's population as Japan was to the West at the time was called forth in a symphony of green volcanic rock, yellow brick and terracotta grill work. Walls were adorned with casts of giant turtles and scarabs while ballrooms featured ornate ceilings covered in shimmering gold leaf.

Although Lloyd Wright's sumptuous creation famously withstood a huge earthquake on the very day of its opening and escaped damage during World War II, by the 1960s it had become structurally unsafe and was replaced by the present anodyne affair. Sadly, the only surviving traces of Wright's work are in the Old Imperial Bar, which incorporates some of the original brickwork. It may have lost some of its old glamour, but with its light, capacious rooms, central location, generously proportioned pool and no fewer than 13 different dining options, the Imperial remains a stylish option for a Tokyo stay.

WHERE:
Uchisaiwai-cho 1-chome, Chiyoda-ku, Tokyo
COST:
Expensive
BEST TIME OF YEAR:
Spring (March to May) and autumn (September to November)
DON'T MISS:
Take in a performance at the Takarazuka Theatre next door to the hotel – this all-female musical revue is a uniquely Japanese experience.
THINGS TO DO:
Sightseeing; strolling around the Higashi Gyoen, the East Garden of the Imperial Palace; picnicking in Hibiya Park; shopping in Ginza; sampling sushi and tempura
YOU SHOULD KNOW:
You can still see the original facade and main lobby of Frank Lloyd Wright's hotel at Meiji Mura near Nagoya, where they are on display in the open-air architectural museum.

Park Hyatt Hotel

For a bird's-eye view of one of the world's most vibrant and exciting cities you can do no better than check in at the Tokyo Park Hyatt. The hotel occupies the top 14 floors of the 52-storey Shinjuku Park Tower. It was designed by star Japanese architect Tange Kenz who was also responsible for the nearby behemoth that is the Tokyo Metropolitan Government Building (it looks like something out of Gotham City). The Park Hyatt tower by contrast is positively slimline, but it is height not girth that matters here and, not surprisingly, the hotel makes the most of its elevated setting. Floor-to-ceiling glass windows are a feature throughout the public areas as well as in many of the guest rooms so that your eyes are constantly drawn to the metropolitan panorama spread out around you and to the iconic profile of Mount Fuji on the horizon.

The guest rooms reinforce the atmosphere of peace and tranquillity with their gently subdued tones, original artworks and the use of materials such as green marble, granite and rare water-elm panelling from Hokkaido Island. The hotel also features the Club on the Park, a state-of-the-art spa and fitness centre, a library with over 2,000 titles and, on the top floor, the New York Grill where chefs in an open-plan kitchen compete for your attention with the breathtaking 360-degree views of the city below. Shinjuku is the beating heart of modern Tokyo and the Park Hyatt is perfectly located to catch the action while offering an ever-present haven in the sky from the frenetic life of the surrounding streets.

WHERE:
Nishi Shinjuku, Shinjuku-Ku, Tokyo
COST:
Expensive
BEST TIME OF YEAR:
Spring (March to May) and autumn (September to November) are good times to visit the Japanese capital. Winters can be sharp and humidity levels in summer uncomfortably high.
DON'T MISS:
Sip evening cocktails in the Peak Bar when the sky-lit indoor bamboo garden is transformed by 50 *washi* paper lanterns into an enchanted island, set above an ocean of twinkling city lights.

THINGS TO DO:
Sightseeing; shopping; swimming; shiatsu massage; spa treatments; cycling (complimentary bicycles available); watching Kabuki theatre; attending a tea ceremony; visiting the Meiji-jing Shinto shrine
YOU SHOULD KNOW:
The Park Hyatt has become known to a much wider audience thanks to its starring role in Sofia Coppola's acclaimed 2003 film *Lost in Translation*.

A *Ryokan* in Hakone

A stay in a traditional Japanese inn or *ryokan* will go a long way towards helping demystify a culture which, rich and fascinating as it is, can seem dauntingly alien. One of the best areas for your *ryokan* experience is Hakone, to the south of Mount Fuji. Much of this spectacular mountain and lakeland landscape is now protected by the national park which is renowned for the *onsen*, or natural hot springs, which bubble up through the earth's crust. Bathing in an *onsen* is a time-honoured and quintessential part of Japanese life. The spa resorts which have developed around the Hakone *onsen* offer a range of accommodation, including *ryokan*. These come in all shapes and sizes but, as this will probably be your only such experience, you might as well splash out on a top-end establishment. Two authentic examples are the Kansuiro and the Mikawaya, both of which have been welcoming guests to their historic wooden structures for more than a hundred years.

It pays to familiarize yourself with *ryokan* etiquette before a visit; knowing, for example, that the slippers you put on at the front door are not worn in the main room with its *tatami* (rice-straw mats) floor and that special slippers are worn for the toilet. The living room with its low table and traditional hanging scroll on one wall (joined nowadays by a TV and phone) is also your bedroom; in the evening, while you take a bath before dinner, your futon and quilt bedding is laid out on the *tatami* floor. Rates normally include breakfast and dinner, the latter a serious celebration of seasonal Japanese cuisine which is usually served in your room.

WHERE:
Hakone
COST:
It's expensive (but it is possible to find *ryokan* at all price levels).
BEST TIME OF YEAR:
Spring and autumn are especially popular with the Japanese, for the cherry blossom and the tree colours respectively, but it's an all-year-round destination.
DON'T MISS:
Soaking beneath the stars in the steaming mineral-rich waters of an outdoor hot-spring pool or *rotemburo*
THINGS TO DO:
Japanese-style living; bathing in hot springs; hiking; cruising on Ashino-ko lake; visiting Hakone Open-Air Sculpture Museum
YOU SHOULD KNOW:
Room rates depend on the number of people occupying them (most *ryokan* rooms sleep at least four). There are no room keys, so you are advised to leave your valuables with reception.

Hotel New Gyominso

WHERE:
Asakusa, Tokyo
COST:
Budget
BEST TIME OF YEAR:
Any time
DON'T MISS:
Unwinding in the hot 'Sky Bath', overlooking the Sumida River from the top floor (brilliant by night, especially during the summer Sumida Fireworks, and by day throughout the cherry blossom season); the monthly hotel *soba* party for which the hotel's president selects the buckwheat and himself kneads, rolls and cuts the noodles (how very Japanese!)
THINGS TO DO:
Visit Senso-ji temple, founded in 628, at the heart of Asakusa's historic district, including Kaminari-mon (Thunder Gate), Dempo-in Temple, the five-storied pagoda, and Nakamise-dori (the crowded small shops at the temple's approach); try a Denki-Bran (electric brandy) cocktail at the Kamiya Bar (the oldest western-style bar in Japan).
YOU SHOULD KNOW:
Asakusa is the heart of downtown Tokyo and the centre of *shitamachi*, the historical/nostalgic area that retains the closest feel to the 'old' city. Hotel New Gyominso is opposite Asakusa station (accessible direct from Narita airport), and therefore a great base from which to explore the inner city.

In the best traditions of Japanese hospitality, Hotel New Gyominso seeks to be all things to all people. Other places choose their market and set up accordingly. Hotel New Gyominso is almost alone in Tokyo in offering three kinds of hotel rooms – Japanese, Western, and capsule – under one roof. The Japanese rooms are similar to those in a *ryokan*, with *tatami* (woven straw mat) flooring, *shoji* sliding paper walls, a futon bed rolled out at night, and *yukata* cotton robes to relax in. But unlike traditional *ryokan*, these rooms also have fittings like kettles, TVs, hair dryers, refrigerators and telephones more routinely associated with 'business' hotels and all Western-style rooms. At the New Gyominso, Western style means a modest room with twin beds. They look like the sets for a Doris Day and Rock Hudson movie, but they do fulfil a need.

So, of course, do the serried ranks of capsule rooms. Whole floors consist of long corridors flanked by double stacks of horizontal cubicles into which you plunge head-first. Only the presence in each one of a TV with linked alarm clock, and a panic button, identifies them conclusively as habitations for humans, and their starkness is modified by the presence at the end of each corridor of a common room with basic kitchen facilities, and the bathing facilities essential to Japanese culture. Hotel New Gyominso is unusual in reserving separate capsule floors for men and women (capsule hotels are usually men only), and in providing gender-exclusive bathing. Capsule residents also share access (with those in more normal rooms) to the hotel's restaurant, sauna, rooftop 'Sky Bath', and 'karaoke pub'. All in all, the hotel encapsulates the authentic if all-embracing spirit of modern Japanese urban culture.

Alpha Resort Tomamu Ice Village

Shimukappu's microclimate makes it the coldest place in Hokkaido, Japan's northernmost island. Its super-low temperatures create a winter blanket of 'champagne' powder snow for which it is world famous. The Alpha Resort in Tomamu was built in the 1980s boom years to cash in, but no sooner had its twin skyscraper towers, wave-machine swimming pool and a host of upmarket facilities been completed than the economic downturn almost closed it. It survived by developing into a family resort as well as an off-piste dream destination. The Ice Village grew into its biggest single attraction.

The Ice Village is about art and fun, but it is underpinned by years of experiments in architectural engineering. Each winter a series of huge domes (15–30 m/50–100 ft in diameter) are created ('grown' is perhaps more accurate) by spraying water and snow onto a balloon and an arrangement of vinyl sheets. The technique leaves the ice translucent and receptive to hauntingly beautiful soft lighting (unlike snow igloos). The domes are not connected. Between them are wonderful ice sculptures, fields of ice candles and other installations that change every year. The domes themselves are glowing beacons, with functions ranging from the Information Dome, the Ice Glass Studio (where you go to make your own ice drinking glass), the Ice Café (where a highly amused bartender won't serve you unless you bring the glass you made), the Ice Tunnel (a stunning rainbow-bright installation of shape and colour to amaze your senses), an Ice Maze, a vast Ice Chapel bathed in serene, ethereal blue (and genuinely affecting), and the Ice Hotel (for two only) in which the double bed, bath, and full set of furniture are beautifully rendered with carved decorations. There may be gimmicks, but this Ice Village is an imaginative *tour de force*.

WHERE:
Shimukappu, in the Hidaka Mountains, Hokkaido

COST:
It's astronomical (the Ice Hotel is officially a 'hotel activity' and not a legitimate hotel room, so the law requires guests to pay for a regular hotel room as well; even the lowest option at the Alpha Resort adds 50 per cent to the Ice Hotel charges).

BEST TIME OF YEAR:
January to March/April

DON'T MISS:
The skiing – on powder or piste it really is wonderful, with whole areas reserved for children and families; any of the many winter festivals that may take place during your visit (for example the Tokachigawa Swan Festival in February); 'surfing' with the kids in the Olympic pool; the Emperor Penguin Walk at nearby Asahiyama zoo

THINGS TO DO:
Dog sledding; hot-air ballooning; 'tree-running' (on a rope runway); tubing; cat- or heli-skiing; Adventure Mountain family ski zone – 27 ha (67 ac) of games and skill-testing activities in what is effectively a winter sports amusement park

YOU SHOULD KNOW:
Tomamu is one of very few places in Japan where you are allowed to ski the backcountry – but you have to sign a disclaimer form at the Mountain Liberation Desk before you go.

Capsule Inn

WHERE:
Namba, Osaka
COST:
Budget
BEST TIME OF YEAR:
Capsule time is any time.
DON'T MISS:
Breakfast (included); getting full use from a range of toiletries that would do justice to a five-star establishment; playing *mah-jong* on an automatic table (at the Asahiplaza Shinsaibashi)
THINGS TO DO:
Party in one or more of the Asahiplaza Shinsaibashi's group rooms; try their all-night sauna and massage; take up the challenge of the game machines on most floors.
YOU SHOULD KNOW:
If circumstances really catch you out, the Asahiplaza Shinsaibashi can supply 'dress shirts, ties and underwear' for the morning after, and at the drop of a hat, too.

Osaka is Japan's second city and the world capital of capsule hotels. Call it the dogged pragmatism of people who work hard and recognize the logic of a bargain, but capsule living seems thoroughly practical to Osaka's citizens. The idea was born in the city. The Capsule Inn opened in 1979. Designed by Kisho Kurokawa as part of a widespread architectural enquiry into the most efficient use of space, each floor consists of 40 fibreglass pods stacked ten by two deep on both sides of a three metre hallway. Each pod has a locker where you swap luggage for a towel and a *yukata* (light kimono) and *obi* belt. Bathroom facilities are all shared, but since women were (relatively recently) allowed to use capsule hotels, floors have been divided by gender. Even so, women are still forbidden the use of the hotel's big, traditional bath and restricted to showers. Inside each capsule is a television with linked alarm clock, an uncertain temperature control and a reading light. Privacy is a bamboo curtain at the open end. Sleep often comes slowly because travellers arrive at all hours, and a major proportion of the rest of the clientele are folk whose partying has prevented them from getting home. Don't forget to take earplugs.

As Osaka's capsule hotels have multiplied, styles have evolved. The 441-berth Capsule Hotel Asahiplaza Shinsaibashi has rearranged its spaces to resemble a submarine. You get in sideways, more comfortably but with greater exposure. It has special four-berth rooms with an accompanying sitting area for people who want to play *mah-jong* (with automatic *mah-jong* tables for rent), and a selection of 'group' rooms for other celebrations. With restaurants, bars, saunas and free bathing, capsule hotels are now integrated into Osaka's culture.

Commune by the Great Wall Kempinski

Even with the wear and tear of more than a decade, the Commune by the Great Wall remains a magnificent tribute to artistic and political *rapprochement*. In 2001 China commissioned 11 villas and a clubhouse from 12 of Asia's most important architects. With names like See and Seen, Bamboo Wall, Cantilever, The Twins, Distorted Courtyard and Shared House, each villa draws on its designer's national culture, but also contributes to a shared Asian vision of architectural modernity.

China's extra contribution was to add context, by placing these buildings in an exquisite mountain enclave bounded on one side by the ultimate icon of Chinese history, the Great Wall. The houses were so successful that the four most popular were cloned, and by 2006 32 villas and ten 'contemporary chalets' between them offered 236 rooms and suites under their new name of Commune by the Great Wall Kempinski. You can still stay in the original four- to six-bedroom villas (at a price!), but with the commune dispersed along the valley, every building is arranged so that you wake up with the breathtaking sight of the Wall, right there, outside, almost touchable. In fact a private path leads to it from the property, and this particular stretch of unrestored Wall is exclusive to the hotel, so no crowds can interrupt your meditations on it or from it.

The Clubhouse offers respite from the villas' resolute minimalism. Besides the gourmet quality of its courtyard restaurant (be grateful – there's nothing else nearby), it has a fascinating library, cinema, art gallery, concert hall, sink-into comfortable lounge and bars. The Clubhouse is where the Commune's eye-popping design values come with the service to match – and you realize why this is one of China's best hotels.

WHERE:
The Great Wall, Badaling Highway (exit at Shuigan)
COST:
It's expensive (astronomical for one of the original, unmodified villas) but the Family Escape Package or Winter Package make a big difference.
BEST TIME OF YEAR:
Any time is a good time.
DON'T MISS:
Taking a picnic to the ruined watchtower; swimming in the pool with its unique vista; the Peacock Room of the Library (the walls are covered with peacock feathers); if you're with friends, rent your favourite villa for a 'Wall party'; the guided tour of all the original villas (a compendium of dazzling millennial architecture)
THINGS TO DO:
Take the (five-minute) shuttle to a restored section of the Wall, for comparison; explore the pamperings offered at the Spa (couples' rooms are a speciality).
YOU SHOULD KNOW:
Private helicopter hire is available from the airfield just five minutes away; if you hire an entire villa, you also get 24-hour butler service.

WHERE:
Central North 4th Ring Drive, Chaoyang District, Beijing
COST:
Very expensive to astronomical
BEST TIME OF YEAR:
Any time
DON'T MISS:
Ask the hotel concierge to get you tickets to any performances or exhibitions you want to see, and for privileged access to the best of Beijing – like the Summer Palace, built 1115 to 1234, and China's most serene gardens, set off by tiered pagodas. Also visit the 798 Art Space in Dashanzi (the city's newest hip neighbourhood, a Chinese 'loft district' of cafés, galleries, bookstores, artists, photographers and creatives).
THINGS TO DO:
Wallow in luxury – because you can; your 24-hour personal butler will see to that.

Pangu 7 Star Hotel

Towering above Beijing's 2008 Olympic Park, the Pangu Plaza is a five-building extravaganza representing a monumental dragon. The head is a stylized concrete-and-glass flourish atop a skyscraper and the dragon's tail, at the end of a 600-m (1,970-ft) corridor, is the Pangu 7 Star Hotel. Like the bright-blue 'Water Cube' Aquatic Centre and the 'Bird Nest' National Stadium which are its immediate neighbours, the complex is aligned on the dragon vein that historically links China's seat of power with the Forbidden City. The ultra-deluxe hotel is therefore a symbol combining China's most powerful ancient philosophy with its most intense aspirations to modernity. Inside, even the smallest detail is governed by carefully calculated auspicious *feng shui*, and guests are encouraged to enjoy layer upon layer of luxury as a respectful way of sharing in the good luck of the place.

The fusion of East and West is serious. Huge bedrooms have the decor and sensuous fabrics of an imperial palace. Dragons cavort on lampshades among auspicious clouds. Ancient Chinese culture is represented in every room by expert copies of the best pictures held in the Palace Museum. They hang above Western-style fireplaces or inlaid (in titanium-alloy frames, like the televisions embedded in the bath tub) into the Italian marble of bathrooms with imported spray fixtures that can transform each shower into a waterfall worthy of *South Pacific*. The hotel's Wenqi Chinese Deluxe restaurant has 26 private rooms furnished in the styles of Bali, France, Thailand, California, England and elsewhere. Other options include the Karma Lounge, the Auspicious Garden, and legendary Japanese Kaden Minokichi's first and only overseas outlet since its foundation in 1719. In this hotel, the seven stars are for the luxury of choice.

YOU SHOULD KNOW:
At Pangu 7 Star Hotel, Kaden Minokichi has just 38 covers in six private *tatami* rooms, and serves authentic *kaiseki* (Kyoto style) set menus ranging from $300 to $1,200 per person; Pangu Plaza was formerly known as Morgan Plaza, and Pangu 7 Star Hotel emphasizes its full name as a friendly challenge to Dubai's Burj al-Arab, the first hotel anywhere to claim seven stars.

Mao'er Hutong B&B

Mao'er Hutong is everything travellers hope to find in Beijing but seldom do. It has only four rooms to rent, but it is a palace of the traditional urban culture that the Chinese authorities have tried very hard to sweep away (most recently for the Beijing Olympics). '*Hutong* culture' is the name given to the teeming back alleys of Beijing. Behind the lifeless boulevards and concrete monotony of bureaucracy, the narrow *hutongs* form a maze crowded with workshops, sizzling food stalls, butchers, bakers and candle-stick makers, indiscriminately mixed with the homes of the common people.

Hutongs can also be individual courtyards opening off the lanes. Typically of five to ten houses sharing the central space, the courtyards are what is left of Beijing's 800-year-old social structure. Mao'er Hutong is one of 16, set eight parallel on either side of Nanluogu Xiang (known as 'Centipede Lane' because of the layout), built in the Yuan Dynasty (1271-1368) and still one of Beijing's most dynamic streets. It is the repository of a folk history as authentic – and important – as that of the Forbidden City, a mere street away, and whose red walls and golden roofs are easily visible above the grey walls of the *hutongs*.

Mao'er Hutong is one of Beijing's best preserved. The corner house belonged to Wan Rong, China's last empress, and the B&B itself is redolent of the famous artists and celebrities who have lived in the area. It's no luxury film-set. The four-posters, furniture and fittings are a patchwork of Chinese culture, clearly acquired over a long period. Impeccably maintained and very comfortable, Mao'er Hutong B&B is a living connection to ancient and modern Beijing. That's something to luxuriate in, not on.

WHERE:
Mao'er Hutong runs east to west between Nanluogu Xiang and Di'amnenwai Dajie, Jiaiodaokou Sub-district
COST:
Budget (except the gigantic three-room suite, which is very reasonable)
BEST TIME OF YEAR:
Any time (the rooms are both air conditioned and heated)
DON'T MISS:
Watch Beijing locals at work and play – along Nanluogu Xiang and its important side alleys (especially Lishi Hutong and Dongtangzi Hutong), at the bars around lovely Shichahai and Houhai Lakes, and the Drum Tower. The Forbidden City and Palace Museum are within walking distance.
THINGS TO DO:
Explore Mao'er Hutong – No 37 has a beautifully carved *chuihuamen* (side gate), No 35 (Empress Gate) a rock and bamboo garden, No 11 (Militarist's Mansion) belonged to a major late 19th-century warlord, and the Ke Yuan Garden is one of Beijing's best secrets (if you can get into it!).
YOU SHOULD KNOW:
There are rules to successful '*hutonging*'. Never open a closed door. Politeness at an open door will usually get you in for a look (and it's OK to push gently at an unoccupied open door). If a resident says '*zou!*' (go!), don't apologize or argue. Just do it.

Amanfayun

WHERE:
Fayung Nong, Xijujedao
Xihugenjungmingsheng District
COST:
Astronomical
BEST TIME OF YEAR:
Any time (the subtropical monsoon climate evens out year-round temperatures)
DON'T MISS:
The Six Harmonies Pagoda, octagonal and with 13 curling roofs, representing the six fundamental precepts of Buddhism; Qing He Fang Street in Hangzhou, much of which survives from the Southern Song dynasty (1127-1279), and full of speciality shops selling silks, brocades, parasols, Hangzhou's special fans, plus the exquisite teas for which the region is revered
THINGS TO DO:
Drink the finest of all green teas, *Longjin* (Dragon Well), grown all around Amanfayun; make the most of the five spa buildings; take a sunrise walk to the lake and its temples; cry for joy at the sheer beauty of it all (that's not a joke).
YOU SHOULD KNOW:
The Song Dynasty poet Su Dongpo (960-1027) compared West Lake to Xi Zi, the most beautiful woman in ancient China: 'Rippling water shimmering on a sunny day/Misty mountains shrouded the rain/Plain or gaily decked out like Xizi/West Lake is always alluring'. Marco Polo was also keen, but hoped it might be a business opportunity. That's an East-West contrast for you.

West Lake is the jewel of Hangzhou. It is set in the misty foothills of the Tianmu Mountains, its banks draped with weeping willows. Ancient Buddhist temples and tiered pagodas pierce the dense forests cloaking the hills, and around the lake stone bridges and moss-covered causeways lead visitors to the shrines and to the vantage points for the most picturesque vistas. New, fast trains bring them in by the thousand. Fine hotels have sprung up by the lake's edge to cater for them, and they are always crowded.

Amanfayun offers a chance to enjoy what is breathtaking about West Lake in the spirit of serenity in which its attractions evolved. Too far (3 km/2 mi) from the Lake for casual tourists, Amanfayun consists of 47 structures developed from a traditional Chinese village. Most of the original buildings have been retained and discreetly remodelled to astonishing levels of luxury and are accessed by Fayun Pathway, the original long village main street.

Roughly in the centre is Fayun Place, where two 19th-century courtyard houses have been merged into the reception area and informal facilities like the library, reading room, lounge, bar and cigar room. Like the huge guest rooms and suites, the furnishings are everywhere pale, unvarnished wood, set against the dark wood of the floors and overhead beams. The lack of bright colours makes the most of the fabulous greens of the woods, the hillside tea plantations and clacking bamboo groves, leaving scarlet and gold as a visual surprise to be enjoyed in the Buddhist ceremonies that weave from the temples. Amanfayun is certainly chic. It's also astonishingly sensitive to the deep meaning of West Lake's significance in Chinese Buddhism – probably a world first for a hotel chain.

Fairmont Peace Hotel

The Peace Hotel is the only hotel in China to be included on the World Hotel Association's list of historically famous hotels. It's been a Shanghai landmark since the early 20th century, when it epitomized Shanghai's most glamorous era and was adopted as the playground of the ultra-rich, the *uber*-powerful and the decadent international set.

A complete overhaul has restored its history as well as its glamour. Woven into its 270 rooms and suites are many of the original hotel's most prized architectural and stylistic features. They include the amazing sprung-timber dance floor of the 8th-floor Peace Hall, the original four (Chinese, English, Indian and American) of what are now the Nine Nations Suites (the new ones are styled to match), and the astonishing panelled splendour of the Presidential Suite, nothing less than the revitalized 1920s personal domain of Sir Victor Sassoon – financier, property developer, trader and (then) owner of the hotel. Its grandeur is immeasurably enhanced by its vistas along the Bund – Shanghai's smartest thoroughfare – and over the Huangpo River and Pudong skyline. Sophisticated and magnificent, Sassoon's penthouse sets the tone for the whole hotel.

The blend of Chinese and Western decor in the public rooms, brushed with the characteristic Art Deco of the 1930s, is among the finest anywhere of its kind. The 8th-floor Dragon Phoenix Chinese restaurant (as its name implies, reborn as part of the hotel's heritage) shows one extreme of the style. The Jasmine Lounge shows the subtleties of the other. A further four restaurants and the Cin Cin wine and cigar bar ring sympathetic changes in the same key of elegant comfort. You could easily get used to genuine opulence.

WHERE:
Nanjing Road East & The Bund, Shanghai
COST:
Expensive to (mostly) astronomical
BEST TIME OF YEAR:
Any time is good for a seriously luxurious stay.
DON'T MISS:
The hotel's Jazz Bar, epicentre of Shanghai's wild reputation in the 1930s and once again a magnet for some of the best touring musicians, great cocktails and pounding beats; the Sassoon Suite (ask the concierge for a glimpse); a night-time dip in the pool with the moon reflecting on the waters of the Huangpo
THINGS TO DO:
Helicopter sightseeing; desert tours; the beach – for swimming, scuba diving or other water sports; sailing; horse riding; making the effort to lift a finger to order some new treat from the impeccable service staff (or ask one of them to do it for you with a twitched eyebrow)
YOU SHOULD KNOW:
The Fairmont Peace Hotel regained its pride, luxury and romance from the same heritage hotel group that includes the Fairmont San Francisco, the Savoy in London, and New York's Plaza Hotel.

Sanya Nanshan Treehouse Resort and Beach Club

WHERE:
Nanshan Buddhist Culture Zone, Sanya, Hainan Province
COST:
Budget
BEST TIME OF YEAR:
Any time
DON'T MISS:
The 108-m (355-ft) tall bronze Guanyin Buddha (taller than the Statue of Liberty) standing in the sea and visible from three of the treehouses; the colossal Nanshan Temple (a short walk away), including the 3.8-m (12-ft) model of the Guanyin made from gold, diamonds and jade (the most valuable Buddha statue in the world); the Tang Dynasty relics in the 'Big and Small Caves' peppering the coastal cliffs
THINGS TO DO:
Chill, reflecting on the Zen sensibility that devised the aerial walkway connecting the treehouses to prevent the *Qi* (the flow of positive energy) escaping out to sea; carry the thought with you while exploring the many pleasures of the Sanya region.
YOU SHOULD KNOW:
The treehouse designer David Greenberg describes himself as an 'anti-architect' looking for radical ecological solutions. Prevented from putting his ideas fully into practice in Hawaii, he has worked in China ('unimpeded by bureaucratic red tape') for many years. He is widely respected there for letting nature guide his designs, consistent with his understanding of Taoism and Zen Buddhism.

There are only four treehouses. Your first sight of them instantly appeals to your inner romantic, adventurer and child. Very quickly these joyful responses are combined with deepening respect and admiration for the quality of thought underwriting their placing and actual construction. A second later, you jump down onto the sand dune below and rush down it into the warm waters of the South China Sea. Sanya is almost the southernmost point of China, in Hainan, and it's on the same latitude as Jamaica. This is a beach holiday.

The treehouses are Robinson Crusoe structures seemingly thrown together. In fact their haphazard shapes are determined by the beautiful tamarind trees that support them. The trees form a thick grove overlooking a huge sweep of empty beach, the edge of a 2,025-ha (5,000-ac) Buddhism Culture Park of temples, pagodas and botanical gardens. Apart from a barbecue pit and electric power, the treehouses have no facilities other than the space to dream, in sunshine and moonlight, to the music of whispering leaves and the sea.

Their proximity to the biggest Buddhist preaching site in the world is no coincidence. They are allowed to exist in solitude – in the middle of China's most popular tropical hotspot – because they are conceived on Buddhist principles, including that of not taking yourself too seriously. Humour is everywhere, from the Big Beach in the Sky Treehouse (sleeps six but you can only reach it via a rope suspension bridge) to the Beach Club (sleeps just two and please don't interrupt) and the mighty Hawaiian Hale Hotel Treehouse (sleeps 20 in seven spaces built over three levels), named for the designer's American origins. The treehouses represent his informed take on Zen. It's all just wonderful.

Mountain Retreat Inn

WHERE:
Feng Lou Cun Wei, Gaotian Zhen, Yangshuo, Guanxi Province
COST:
Budget to reasonable
BEST TIME OF YEAR:
September to June (July and August are very humid)
DON'T MISS:
Local song-and-dance troupes; cormorant fishing; bamboo river rafting from 600-year-old stone Yulong Bridge back to the hotel; gossiping with the staff

Yangshuo is a pretty resort town at the centre of one of China's most heart-stoppingly beautiful landscapes. As a major stopover on both Chinese and Western tourist trails it has become a cultural hybrid, attracting national and international hotel chains to promote (and profit from) its extraordinary and easily accessible natural charms.

The Mountain Retreat Inn is the polar opposite of standardization. It's a sublime local initiative that offers more original accommodation, at lower cost, and with considerably less environmental impact than anywhere else in the region apart from its own sister establishment. It brings together the disenfranchised from local villages. First, they cleared fallow rice terraces on the banks of the pristine Yulong River, well upstream of Yangshuo itself. They dug the well for their water, planted bougainvillea, bamboo, banana and fig trees plus 300 varieties of fruit and evergreens to surround the traditional rustic-looking eco-lodge as it emerged. Now they can offer 29 rooms of every denomination, most with a balcony and stunning views of the river and the forested limestone crags in the blue mist behind.

The collective experience of the staff in 'growing' the building, continually re-examining the best eco-practice in running it, and in supporting their own local culture, make the Inn beyond price to guests with ears to listen and eyes to see. For the curious who want to know more than just the dramatic, magical scenery, the hotel can be a unique opportunity for genuine cultural immersion. On one level, all the bathroom accessories are locally made and renewably packed. On another, you're welcome to volunteer a day of your time and maybe teach English in a village school, or take in a discussion about Yangshuo's eight local minorities. This hotel is the rarest of the rare, where beauty is far beyond skin deep, and there's no extra charge.

THINGS TO DO:
Explore Yangshuo town, especially the tourist centre of West Street (one half of the 'ladder' layout of the town's centre); take the advice of hotel staff on the best local walks/swimming holes/rock climbs/caves (they might even go with you if you ask).

YOU SHOULD KNOW:
The success of the Mountain Retreat Inn as a means of helping local people help themselves is emphatically demonstrated by the opening of the Yangshuo Village Inn and Farmhouse. It incorporates everything the team has learned so far, but with its own integrity and authenticity.

A bamboo raft on the Yulong River

Qixian (Seven Sages) Hostel

WHERE:
Courtyard 5, Qixianzhuang No 1, Beixin Street, Xi'an
COST:
Budget budget
BEST TIME OF YEAR:
Any time
DON'T MISS:
The Terracotta Warriors; the Tomb of Emperor Jingdi, the Muslim Quarter; the city walls; the pagodas
THINGS TO DO:
Skype your friends or family on the free wifi; play billiards and/or table-tennis; savour the tranquillity of the courtyard complex; settle into the library; hire a bike.
YOU SHOULD KNOW:
Although the restaurant and bar are above average, the Seven Sages could be the only youth hostel where they offer room service; the hostel is in a quiet, Chinese residential area, a fair distance from the city centre – on balance that's a big plus.

Xi'an is the city of the Terracotta Warriors, revered throughout the world as one of the most tangible relics of ancient China's glory. Xi'an prospered for a thousand years (under the name Chang'an) until a series of rebellions led to its virtual obliteration during the decline of the Tang dynasty in the 10th century. Today's modern city sprawls along the Wei River valley, but the wondrous historical relics beneath its industrialized chaos make it one of China's biggest visitor attractions. Naturally, the city is full of hotels catering to every market and tourist purse. Many of them suffer terribly from the cacophony of traffic and crowds. The Qixian (Seven Sages) Hostel is a wonderful exception.

It's a real find. Tucked against the city walls on a site going back to the 7th century, it's around the corner from the Shang De Gate and railway station. It's part of a classic Chinese row house, a continuous terrace divided into ten courtyards by a series of circular entrances. A banker built it at the end of the 19th century to house his business and various relatives and a museum in the adjoining courtyard tells how the hostel in courts 5 and 6 was formerly a Red Army command post, liaison office and reception centre for those fighting the Japanese. Now, the concrete has gone and the old house of bricks and tiles stands behind a courtyard brightened with green shrubs and tall trees, where backpackers, friends and whole families sit, talk and play. With simple but immaculate rooms of two, three and four beds, and single-sex dormitories for six (with TV, en suites and work tables in every one), there is something for everyone.

The Peninsula

WHERE:
Salisbury Road, Kowloon, Hong Kong
COST:
Astronomical
BEST TIME OF YEAR:
Any time
DON'T MISS:
A trip on the historic Star Ferry at night; the shops and boutiques of Nathan Road; the big-sky harbour view from the private, two-person spa treatment rooms
THINGS TO DO:
Take advantage of the R-R limousines and helicopter (any extra cost will be negligible within the final bill); arrange excursions, or theatre or restaurant bookings through the concierge (for privileged access and seating).

The Peninsula Hotel in Hong Kong, 'The Pen' as it is known to generations of high-fliers, remittance men, film stars, *taipans*, bonus busters and happily cynical, broken-veined *habitués* of the Foreign Correspondents' Club looking for a good story, was born into the elite of the world's grandest hotels. It's got class. It dominates Victoria Harbour in a way unmatched by any of the city's giant skyscrapers. Two giant arms reach out from the main tower block right behind the Star Ferry terminal, as though welcoming everyone crossing from Hong Kong island, and simultaneously releasing passengers from Kowloon side.

Its symbolism is as legendary as almost everything else about the hotel. It's integral to the city's culture, not just as part of the furniture. The Peninsula embodies an idea Hong Kong has about itself. Everyone knows its exorbitant luxury. Every day its helicopters

fly guests back and forth to the airport and its fleet of Rolls-Royces (and these days Mini Coopers, too) purr (zip) elegantly through the streets. It has the status of ultimate aspiration in a city where wealth is commonplace but style is harder to come by. The rooms and suites are, simply, better than anyone else's. So, generally, is the food, and the ideas about food, in its nine restaurants. It's in the details, and in the grand gestures too.

Preserving its aura in the face of constant competition isn't easy. In January 2012, The Peninsula began a two-year refurbishment of its 297 beautiful rooms and suites. The upgrade ratchets up any notion of sybaritic indulgence beyond existing scales. Voice commands for the bath, curtains, door lock, music system and everything else should help keep The Peninsula at the top for at least another generation.

YOU SHOULD KNOW:
Shopping around can get you a discount on a Peninsula room or suite during quiet months, although that's still astronomically expensive.

WHERE:
Hong Kong Disneyland, Lantau Island, Hong Kong
COST:
Expensive (but worth it just for the early and hassle-free access to Disneyland)
BEST TIME OF YEAR:
Any time
DON'T MISS:
The Mickey Maze (a maze of hedges tall enough to 'hide' small children, and shaped like a portrait of Mickey's head) in front of the hotel's main entrance; the indoor Roman swimming pool; the Ngong Ping 360 cable car across Lantau
THINGS TO DO:
Work your way through the six eating options available throughout the day, ranging from fast food to serious Beijing cuisine; try to avoid Disney themes for at least a few minutes in the bar called the Sorcerers' Lounge (who said it would be easy?).
YOU SHOULD KNOW:
Guests are offered room choices of garden view, sea view, sea view with balcony, fantasia (with Jacuzzi), Kingdom suite, or Presidential (Walt Disney Suite). Business conventions are offered ballroom choices of Snow White (includes Dreamer's garden), Sleeping Beauty or Cinderella. Even Walt Disney himself must look down and be bemused.

Hong Kong Disneyland Hotel

Disneyland's Hong Kong extravaganza is built on Lantau Island, far enough from the main city to satisfy visitors wanting to stay close to the theme park. Disney Corp's eye for the main chance created a cross between a turreted fairytale chateau and a vast, multi-storied car park with a Victorian twist. It belongs. In fact, inside and out it is touched with Disney's fairy dust. No guest could ever doubt his exact location and most would not wish to. The hotel is a joy for tens of thousands of families who adore Disney, as much for the happiness it appears to bring their children as for the hygienic *mores* it tries to propagate. The hotel encourages them all to star in their own, private version of Disney deluxe with touches like bedtime television stories, alarm calls from Mickey Mouse himself and (in case mummy and daddy get the heebie-jeebies too quickly) a complimentary minibar, if only on the first day.

It is a very accomplished hotel, its amenities honed by years of international practice. All 400 rooms and 13 suites share a chintzy, neo-Victorian decor which is both very comfortable and cosy in a storybook way that is highly unusual in China. They are also graded with the same demographic ruthlessness with which Disney calculates the amenities to accompany its park rides. It isn't cynical to suggest that the company knows what family wallets can stand and plans accordingly. It's good business, and that's why the hotel includes full conference facilities, including a full-sized ballroom. Business rep or Disney fan, the hotel wants to see you happy and enthusiastic. It has the means, and it's not afraid to use them.

Pousada de Sao Tiago

The massive stone ramparts of the Fortaleza da Barra were erected in 1629 to defend Portuguese Macau from other marauding Europeans and local pirates. The fort is anchored into the hills at the very tip of the Macau peninsular, a central feature in what is now the prestige residential *corniche* of leafy Praia Grande Bay. The addition of a chapel in 1740 gave the fort a name for its present incarnation, the Pousada de Sao Tiago (St James), but only recently has the Pousada attained its apotheosis as an exclusive, super-luxury boutique hotel of just 12 suites, developed within a historic complex of World Heritage significance. Just to reach reception you have to climb stone stairs and walkways through the 6-m (20-ft) thick walls, and do it again to reach your room.

All the suites look out over the harbour and most of them have balconies. Their decor is wilful colonialist, an updated Portuguese/Chinese fusion of imported mahogany furniture, marble bathrooms, hand-made (and frankly bizarre) chandeliers, sections of openwork Chinese screens and carefully placed antiques. It's a clever use of the surrounding history, and extremely comfortable. Even outside, sunbathing on the poolside lawn screened by century-old banyan trees, the Pousada is an enclave of tranquillity cut off from the languorous but noisy city. At a time when Macau's other important hotels are getting ever more frantic in association with the colossal and growing casino trade in Cotai district, the Pousada's restrained, neo-Old World style is at a premium. It may not be at the centre of the city or the action, but it's a perfect base for both. It represents the best of Macau.

WHERE:
Avenida da Republica, Praia Grande Bay, Macau

COST:
Expensive to astronomical

BEST TIME OF YEAR:
Any time is good (although some might prefer to avoid the July to September typhoon season).

DON'T MISS:
Eat well at the Pousada's Os Gatos Terrace and Bar (named after the title of a famous book whose author states 'Portuguese is the most refined, the most voluptuous, most succulent cuisine in the world'.

THINGS TO DO:
Check out The Venetian, the world's largest casino, on the reclaimed land of Cotai ('Las Vegas of the East'); shopping and theme park action at Fisherman's Wharf; the Macau Heritage Walk (including heritage buildings, the Sao Paolo Cathedral, Macao Museum and the Fort itself); the huge incense spirals like gigantic inverted lobster pots hanging from the A Ma Temple roof; climbing high to look down on the A Ma Temple's huddle of curling roofs and their colourful tiling patterns

YOU SHOULD KNOW:
The Pousada provides a complimentary service to and from the airport; every suite has a kitchen so that room service can be 'finished' at your own table.

Three Camel Lodge

WHERE:
Southern Gobi Desert
COST:
Expensive
BEST TIME OF YEAR:
May to September
DON'T MISS:
The Yol Valley, opening out of the Gobi Glacier in the ravine of fire and ice called Yolyn Am; the Flaming Cliffs at Bayanzag, most dramatic in the early morning and late evening (and a palaentological dream where the first clutch of dinosaur eggs was discovered in 1923); the singing dunes of Khongoryn Els; the Winter Palace of Bogd Khaan; the two-day Naadam Festival showcasing traditional sports of Mongolian warriors (wrestling, riding and archery, in July)

Three Camel Lodge is an oasis of luxury in the heart of the southern Gobi Desert. It is a real-world masterpiece of cultural sensitivity matching myriad aspirations to a single, gigantic achievement. Everybody wins.

The key is authenticity. Instead of dressing luxury amenities in a fantasy of local colour like most hotels in exotic places, the Lodge addresses the reality of Western expectations by adding a private bathroom with sink and toilet to each of their 20 *gers*. In every other way the *gers* are the traditional felt tents of Mongolia's nomadic herders, made by hand from layers of felt and canvas on a lattice frame put together without a single nail. There's a wood-burning stove and the beds and furniture are beautifully hand-painted. Their elegant simplicity is completed by a south-facing door (a nomadic tradition) which opens onto the sweep of the desert scrub and the Gobi-Altai Mountains.

You sleep sound. The centrepiece of the encampment is what looks like a Mongolian temple, with upturned roof and a broad verandah. This is Dani House, where guests and locals come together to swap mutual curiosity, music and dance – and where guests discover how deeply committed the Lodge is to the sustainable success of the local community. The locally produced organic food in the restaurant, the planting of 2,000 trees by children at their school in Dalanzadgad and the pioneering co-operative agreement with the town of Bulgan Sum and the Gurvansaikhan National Park (for a raft of local ecological and national conservation initiatives) are three of a hundred willing ways to give back to Mongolia what Three Camel Lodge and its guests receive by way of the Gobi's aesthetic blessing and spiritual nourishment.

THINGS TO DO:
Hang out in the Thirsty Camel, the naturally geo-cooled and fully stocked bar beneath the Lodge's Bulagtai Restaurant (named after the volcanic outcrop sheltering the *gers*); practice Bactrian (two-humped) camel riding under the tuition of (laughing) Mongolians – ready for the major excursions.

YOU SHOULD KNOW:
Three Camel Lodge truly is a two-way exchange. Lots of mime and big smiles will help win you friends – and some expert help identifying desert wildlife and birds.

Terelj Hotel

WHERE:
Gorkhi-Terelj National Park, about 75 km (47 mi) from Ulaan Baatar
COST:
Expensive to astronomical
BEST TIME OF YEAR:
Any time – but guests who love authentic wilderness will prefer April to October
DON'T MISS:
The dizzying descent to early 17th-century Gunjin Sum Temple; the hospitality of local nomads (if offered) who may suggest drinking milk vodka in their *gers*; boating on the Tuul River headwaters (flowing past the hotel); fine dining in the Morin Khuur restaurant
THINGS TO DO:
Karaoke Room (in Mongolian, Russian, Korean, Chinese, Japanese and English); art gallery (full of top-quality Mongolian antiques for sale 'as souvenirs'); fishing for *taimen*, Mongolia's native salmon; horse or camel riding; wildlife walks (brown bears, moose, wild boar, wolves and 250 bird species); winter ice-skating; indoor pool; spa; exploring the 70 whiskies in the super-plush Argali cocktail bar
YOU SHOULD KNOW:
The hotel is thoroughly, excellently and spookily OTT. Alternate dining tables are occupied by men in suits keeping their right hands free.

If you've ever wondered how oligarchs pass their down time, the Terelj Hotel will give you most of the answers. Otherwise it's hard to explain why a hotel so perfectly designed for very wealthy urbanites should exist in one of the most strictly protected national parks in Mongolia. Gorkhi-Terelj is part of the Khan Khentii wilderness stretching north from Ulaan Baatar. Its only inhabitants are a handful of nomads. Tourists may visit, briefly and only if accompanied, but they must stay in one of the *ger* camps or small hotels clustered inside the park's southern rim. The Terelj Hotel is another 40 km (25 mi) into the beautiful hills and forested valleys, a rich man's castle with Eden as a playground for all seasons.

The wall-to-wall luxury is stolidly masculine in style. The 52 rooms and suites are cushioned with velvet and Mongolian cashmere in stripes, checks and floral patterns (including elements of flock wallpaper, probably gilded). Make what you will of the unusual promise that 'solid mahogany doors offer privacy for the bedroom', but the furniture is certainly closer to Victorian than to Philippe Starck. Rooms are vast, with enclosed verandahs, large sitting areas with sofas and armchairs, and separate dining space as well as the ultra-comfortable beds. Suites verge on the irresponsibly presidential. Don't even ask about the actual Presidential suite. It may be occupied. Public rooms reinforce the general impression of a gentlemen's club (the name given at this hotel to what are actually boardroom-level conference facilities), and include a Cigar Lounge worthy of New York, two other lounge/bars and four restaurants, all but one fussy with crystal, samovars, oriental flagons and padded comforts. Why hike the gorgeous National Park when your staff can do it for you?

W Seoul

Unlike its prune-faced twin Pyonyang up north in the Democratic (really?) People's Republic, the capital of South Korea wears the broad smile that comes from presiding over a booming Tiger Economy. Officially known as the Seoul Special City, this lively mega-hub with 10 million inhabitants bestrides the Han River. Visitors can't help but be energized by the frenetic pace of life, and Seoul has wonderful buildings old and mostly new, beautiful parks and mountains, great food, entertainment in all its forms and lively night life.

This vast city and its sprawling conurbation has many thousands of places where visitors can stay, ranging from five-star hotels to simple pensions. Visitors are therefore spoilt for choice, but anyone who stays at the W Seoul – Walkerhill will have chosen well. This hotel is different, which certainly contributes to the experience, but the special attraction is a superb setting in parkland on the peaceful slopes of Mount Achasan, surrounded by greenery and overlooking the river, providing tranquil refuge after a sally into the hustling and bustling city.

Be prepared to be dazzled. The hotel has over 250 rooms, and the accent in each and every one is on vibrant and unexpected use of colour coupled with chic modern design. Selecting one of the options is tough. Should it be a Wonderful Room or Fabulous Room, Cool Corner Room or a Studio Suite, Mega Suite or Fantastic Suite, Wow Suite or Extreme Wow Suite? Decisions, decisions! Wherever you lay you head, you'll be lying on a signature W bed (round) and be able to look forward to bathing (right beside the window) with a river or mountain view. If there's one phrase that encapsulates the W Seoul's bold character it must surely be 'It's very . . . South Korea' (once experienced, never forgotten!).

WHERE:
Walkerhill-ro, Gwangjin-Gu, Seoul
COST:
Reasonable (with regular offers and deals to be done)
BEST TIME OF YEAR:
Winters can be very cold, so the best months are April to October (but note that there is a rainy season in July).
DON'T MISS:
A taste (or two) of fine *ginjo-shu* from Namu's *sake* cellars; a night-time tipple in the hotel's Woo Bar, one of Seoul's top watering holes, for a spectacular city light show; sharpening your golf swing on W's driving range, or playing a set of tennis; loafing around in the heated indoor pool; a serious pampering session at the AWAY Spa, or doing what it says on the tin in the SWEAT Fitness Centre
THINGS TO DO:
Visit one or more of the Seoul National Capital Area's four UNESCO World Heritage sites – Changdeokgung Palace, Hwaseong Fortress, Jongmyo Shrine and the Royal Tombs of the Joseon Dynasty. Explore the vast Namdaemun street market in the city centre. Sample power shopping Seoul style in the trendy Myeongdong area.
YOU SHOULD KNOW:
As well as being one of the largest cities on the planet, Seoul is also one of the safest – but it's also something of a giant warren where visitors can easily lose their bearings. The subway system is the way to get around – it's clean, comprehensive and efficient, with English signage.

AUSTRALASIA & THE PACIFIC ISLANDS

Kooljaman at Cape Leveque

WHERE:
Dampier Peninsula, Western Australia
COST:
From almost nothing (campground) all the way up (but not that far up) to very reasonable (en-suite cabin)
BEST TIME OF YEAR:
Whenever you arrive
DON'T MISS:
Take the eye-opening cruise on glass-bottomed *Oolard II* to see vibrant fish, coral and sea life around the reefs (and observe humpback whales between July and October); go on a cultural tour with a member of the Djarindjin community (parents will appreciate the culture and kids will love the spear making).
THINGS TO DO:
Fishing; self-guided wilderness walks; snorkelling and swimming (beautiful white-sand beaches, no saltwater crocs!); scenic flights over the Buccaneer Archipelago and its extraordinary horizontal waterfalls from the airstrip
YOU SHOULD KNOW:
Access is by 4x4 (it can be arranged and the bumpy effort is well worthwhile scenically) or by light plane to the private airstrip. This placc is really youngsters-run-wild-friendly, with accommodation suitable even for larger families. There's a good launching spot for those who bring their own boat.

Wilderness doesn't come much wilder than this, and wilderness living has surely never been more satisfying. Kooljaman at Cape Leveque is at the tip of the Dampier Peninsula, jutting into the Indian Ocean 220 km (137 mi) north of Broome. This welcoming camp is jointly owned by the One Arm Point Aboriginal and Djarindjin communities and can justly boast of its supportive connection with the local indigenous people. After the lighthouse was automated in the 1980s, the peninsula named Kooljaman by Bardi Aboriginals was developed as a low-impact project to be controlled by locals, restricted to a size that minimizes environmental impact. The link between Aboriginal people and their guests is hugely beneficial to both sides and gives Kooljaman a very special atmosphere.

The natural beauty of the unspoilt surroundings certainly also makes a spectacular contribution, ensuring that a visit to this wild place lingers in the memory for a long time. The accommodation is varied, but captures the spirit of the rugged Kimberley region. Choose between safari tents, mini-safari tents, dome tents, the bring-your-own-gear campground (camper vans allowed but strictly no caravans), basic log cabins, en-suite cabins and beach shelters. Self-catering is the order of the day, with a small general store on site and community shops in One Arm Point and Djarindjin within 20 km (12 mi). But lazy campers can order splendid meals, barbied to order and delivered by the somewhat informal Bush Butler or collected from the kitchen for subsequent sizzling. Breakfast baskets also make meal preparation easy, and there is a restaurant offering hearty seafood, salads, steak and pasta dishes.

This is not luxury 'glamping', but a seriously comfortable and well-considered opportunity to enjoy a wonderful wilderness experience that seems entirely unforced and natural. Be impressed!

Home Valley Station

This is very possibly as close as it's possible to get to gen-u-ine Aussie Outback life. Western Australia makes 'remote' look like the suburbs, so don't expect near neighbours when you pitch up at the working Home Valley Station, a modest 249,000-ha (615,290-ac) spread alongside the flat-topped mesas of the Cockburn Ranges, considered by aficionados of lonely places to equal Ayers Rock as a rugged spectacle (without the tourists). The macho way to journey in is thumping along the Gibb River Road stock route in a sturdy 4x4, although anyone who has a sensitive spine would be well advised to fly in to the Station airstrip.

There's a choice of accommodation (safari tents in the bush, Grass Castle suites along Bindoola Creek and creek-side Guesthouse rooms). Hearty food is served in the Dusty Bar & Grill, a large open-sided former stock shed still littered with cattle station bits and pieces, which operates as an outback pub complete with evening live music that competes with sport on the big-screen TV and lively conversation shouted above the din. It's not for everyone, but this is the authentic Outback experience and its very essence is bush brotherhood in the best traditions of remote rural living.

That doesn't mean there are *no* redeeming comforts. Beds are comfortable, there's air conditioning in the rooms, two pools, a varied menu, Station store and children's playground. And of course there's a spa (everywhere must have one), in this case wild-swimming holes under Bindoola Falls. But this remains a no-nonsense working station where guests are honestly welcomed as a valuable cash crop, but not pampered. And that – combined with a truly magnificent natural setting that offers wilderness panoramas, a creek, river, waterfalls and impressive sandstone or limestone rock formations – make staying here a rewarding experience.

WHERE:
East Kimberley, Western Australia
COST:
Budget (tents); reasonable (suites and guesthouse rooms) – but don't forget you've got to get there first and it's a long way from anywhere
BEST TIME OF YEAR:
April to November (closed to visitors in the hot, wet summer)
DON'T MISS:
Bindoola River Camp on the banks of the Pentecost River for wilderness tranquillity and amazing sunsets over the Cockburn Ranges; the mini-muster (anyone who can ride/learn to ride quickly on horseback – non-riders and kids in accompanying 4x4 vehicles)
THINGS TO DO:
Bush walks in Bindoola Gorge; fishing in the Pentecost River (beware of crocs); birdwatching (don't miss the resident barking owls); the scenic flight from Home Valley for a bird's-eye view of the stunning East Kimberley landscape; visiting locations used in the movie *Australia* with Nicole Kidman and Hugh Jackman
YOU SHOULD KNOW:
Owned by Australia's Indigenous Land Corporation, Home Valley was purchased in 1999 on behalf of the Balanggarra and Nyaliga Aboriginal peoples. If the seriously corrugated Gibb River Road (or Outback exploration) wrecks your 4x4, there's a workshop on Station. There are campgrounds for those who prefer to do their own thing.

Longitude 131

WHERE:
Uluru-Kata Tjuta National Park, Northern Territory
COST:
Astronomical (but Ayers Rock airport transfers, all meals, drinks, and an exceptional touring programme are included)
BEST TIME OF YEAR:
Catch it when you can (but May to August are the coolest months).

In 1873 surveyor William Gosse came upon an awesome red sandstone rock formation in the unmapped interior and obsequiously named it Ayers Rock in honour of South Australia's Chief Secretary, Sir Henry Ayers, little knowing or caring that it already had a name – Uluru – and was sacred to the local Anangu people. Nowadays this striking landmark is a must-see marvel for anyone willing to take on the Northern Territory's arid Outback by driving 450 km (280 mi) from the nearest settlement of any size, Alice Springs (okay, wimps can fly in).

Either way, the effort is more than justified and, once there, Longitude 131 is a suitably eco-sensitive place to stay. Just 15 luxuriously equipped tents stand at the end of a dirt road amid red-earth scrubland, each named after an Aussie explorer. Domed

luxuriously equipped tents stand at the end of a dirt road amid red-earth scrubland, each named after an Aussie explorer. Domed roofs and flowing fabric are more Arabian Nights than Australian Outback, but guests definitely don't have to experience the sort of privations suffered by early pioneers. Think the three Ss of scenery, solitude and serenity without wilderness angst, and relax in the knowledge that no expense has been spared when providing creature comforts, including in-tent air conditioning and a picture window with blinds that open at the flick of a switch to reveal 'The Rock'.

The Dune House Restaurant and bar provides a splendid base in which to socialize, with swimming pool and library. But there's more to a break at Longitude 101 than Uluru itself. For this is an opportunity to enjoy a programme exclusively reserved for guests, who experience amazing days of discovery in a living landscape which very few are privileged to explore, where expert guides bring ancient Aboriginal cultures and stunning flora and fauna to life. It's the perfect complement to that stunning sandstone monument.

DON'T MISS:
What you came to see – Uluru at sunrise and sunset, when this brooding monument is at its most mysterious; an *al fresco* dinner under the brilliant dome of the southern night sky

THINGS TO DO:
Chill out at Red Ochre Spa (Sails in the Desert Hotel, Ayers Rock Resort, where you can also visit the Aboriginal Mulgara Gallery). Take a camel ride (or opt for a Harley). Enjoy the desert helicopter tour.

YOU SHOULD KNOW:
Children under the age of 12 are not catered for. Most people opt for a two-day break at Longitude 101.

Lizard Island Resort

WHERE:
Near Cairns, Northern Queensland
COST:
Astronomical (but there are deals to be had)
BEST TIME OF YEAR:
Any time is tropical-paradise time (but note those umbrellas provided in the rooms – summers from December to March are not only very hot, but also very wet).
DON'T MISS:
The beach-dining experience (discuss and agree a seven-course degustation menu with the chef and choose matching wines, to be served in an exclusive waterside location); gourmet luncheon hampers for the ultimate beach picnic; the champagne sunset cruise
THINGS TO DO:
Nothing at all; diving the world-famous Cod Hole; night diving; snorkelling; exploring the bay on a glass-bottomed paddle ski, catamaran or motorized dinghy; tennis; big-game fishing (black marlin season is September to December); general fishing charters on the MV *Fascination*
YOU SHOULD KNOW:
The Lizard Island Resort is within the national park of the same name and shares the island only with a research station operated by the Australian Museum (tours available from the resort). The local Dingiil Aboriginals call this sacred-to-them island Jiigurru.

This island retreat – the most northerly resort on the Great Barrier Reef – is open to all, but enjoyed by only the few who can afford the tropical holiday of a lifetime. A beautiful and unspoilt waterside location is home to the Lizard Island Resort, consistent winner of top awards as a destination to die for (metaphorically speaking). Set beside dazzling white-sand beaches, the remote bolthole offers a luxurious experience of the highest order.

There's a choice of suites, villas or pavilions and if you can think of anything to enhance a dream-holiday guest room that isn't in yours, notify management. They'll be mortified because your accommodation should have *everything* – air conditioning, aromatherapy oil burner, books, bath robes, beach towels, Bose sound system with CD player/ iPod connection, ceiling fans, coffee- and tea-making facilities, hairdryer, iron and board, minibar, safe, stationery, telephone, umbrellas and work desk. Oh, no TV or wifi connectivity. But that's policy, people, for you don't come to a place like this to google or read emails. Choose between compact Anchor Bay Rooms (tropical-garden setting, private balcony, direct beach access, family size available), Anchor Bay Suites (spacious open-plan design, large verandah, private path to the beach), and Sunset Point Villas (total privacy on Sunset Ridge among eucalyptus bushland, deck with hammock, easy access to secluded beaches). Lottery winners always go for the Pavilion, perched high above the Coral Sea with a stunning panoramic view.

The main lodge in its idyllic setting houses the essential support systems – staff for whom nothing is too much trouble, the fine-dining Ospreys Restaurant, guest lounge with bar area, gym and (of course) the Azure Spa for ultimate skincare and rejuvenating relaxation. That's the canvas, so all you have to do is paint on the perfect holiday.

Bloomfield Lodge

Two World Heritage sites don't come closer than this. The Daintree Rainforest in Queensland's unspoilt Far North is right outside the door and the Great Barrier Reef is across the bay. You're staying at Bloomfield Lodge, an enchanting forest retreat for those who favour luxurious boutique accommodation and fine dining seasoned with memorable wilderness. The tone is set by a dramatic entrance that begins in Cairns and continues with a private charter flight up the Queensland coast, followed by a short Outback drive and boat trip down river and across Weary Bay to journey's end.

Guests are accommodated in one of 17 timber-built retreats in natural settings around the lodge with forest and sea views from each verandah. These personal havens have a traditional look and feature excellent facilities, including en-suite bathrooms. Apart from some serious relaxation and the many and varied activities available for the more actively inclined, the delicious and varied meals at Bloomfield Lodge are definite highlights of the day. The chefs work with fresh, local ingredients such as succulent North Queensland seafood, exotic game and juicy organic steaks to deliver a three-course evening feast, although a sumptuous barbecue buffet is a great alternative for those who want to go native. Breakfast consists of fresh fruit, juices, pastries and hot dishes cooked to order. Lunch is a set menu, or a lavish picnic for those taking an excursion. Meals are included in the price and served in the *al fresco* dining room overlooking the pool and gardens, where guests mingle over a glass of wine.

Is this the perfect sanctuary for anyone who *really* wants to get away from the stresses and strains of modern life? You bet it is, even though the stake money doesn't come cheap!

WHERE:
In the middle of nowhere, Northern Queensland

COST:
Astronomical and rightly so

BEST TIME OF YEAR:
Go any time (it's always hot, and the hottest period from late December to the end of March is also the wettest, while winter evenings from June to September are pleasantly cool).

DON'T MISS:
A long soak in the outdoor hot tub while enjoying the wonderful outlook over Weary Bay; sunbathing by the pool, punctuated by a refreshing dip whenever the mood takes you

THINGS TO DO:
Stroll along deserted beaches; take a guided walk and see some of Australia's most incredible plant, animal and marine life; cruise on the seriously impressive *Bloomfield Explorer*; dive the Great Barrier Reef without another boat to be seen; join the guided birdwatching; go sport fishing from *Paradise Kingfisher* (try for an iconic barramundi, but failing that there are around 1,500 other species in these waters).

YOU SHOULD KNOW:
Bloomfield Lodge has been voted by *Forbes* magazine as the World's Best Remote Hotel. Stay in Cairns overnight before travelling on, as flights for the Lodge leave at 09.00. No children under the age of ten are permitted, but older kids are welcome. There's no road, so bring personal essentials. Guests have to travel light as there is a stern baggage-weight restriction on the charter flight (but do include the camera and binoculars).

Gwinganna Lifestyle Retreat

Queensland's Gold Coast is a hugely popular tourist destination but those who choose to retreat (pun intended) into the verdant hinterland may have another agenda. The Gwinganna Lifestyle Retreat is the place to have a full body service that will leave you feeling like a million dollars, happily for a considerably smaller outlay. This is where you can re-energize your body and refuel your soul while learning techniques that will help you deal with the stresses and strains of the modern world.

The setting in the lush hills is life-affirming, with dramatic valley and distant sea views. There's a choice of programmes that ranges from two to seven days, during which time you will enjoy excellent facilities, delicious organic cuisine (with all special dietary requirements catered for), comfortable accommodation and constructive engagement with the Spa Sanctuary. The accommodation complements the whole experience, with guests choosing between five traditional Queensland heritage houses brought here and reassembled, restored Peel House (two bedrooms and lounge), Gwinganna House (a timber lodge), Orchard Suites and five wonderful villas.

Wellness programmes are many and varied, depending on personal requirements and time available, from simple weekend retreats featuring healthier living advice up to the full week-long special programme tailored to individual needs. These include such specialties as Women's Discovery, Men's Retreat, Organic Living, Nourishing Cuisine, Sleep Discovery and Combating Stress. All programmes include informative lectures, rewarding activities and sessions at the award-winning 33-room spa. Whatever your choice, be sure to take full advantage of your multi-faceted programme to ensure that you get the very most out of your stay, returning to the real world freshened and fortified . . . having learned lifestyle lessons that could stand you in good stead for a long time to come.

WHERE:
Tallebudgera Valley, Queensland
COST:
It's astronomical (but genuine eco-chic people won't begrudge a single penny).
BEST TIME OF YEAR:
Go any time (note that, thanks to its height, Gwinganna is usually a couple of degrees cooler than the coast).
DON'T MISS:
Soaking up the wonderful ocean views stretching from Moreton Bay to Coolangatta (*Gwinganna* translates as 'lookout' in the local Aboriginal language); simply enjoying the peace and quiet of this hidden forest location
THINGS TO DO:
Shop in the store for clothing, books and CDs, accessories, organic products and assorted useful incidentals (also serves as the reading lounge); use the Jacuzzi outside the dining room; play tennis; acquire medicinal herbs and supplements from the Wellness Centre; work out in the Mind Body Pavilion or well-equipped gym; take a sauna, followed by a plunge into the heated lap pool.
YOU SHOULD KNOW:
It's not for children. Courtesy transfers from Gold Coast airport are available. Pack good walking shoes or boots but don't bring (banned) alcohol, cigarettes or food. Mobile phone use is restricted to guest rooms.

Hinchinbrook Island Resort

Australia's largest island national park, Hinchinbrook Island is within the Great Barrier Reef Marine Park on Queensland's stunning coast. This unspoilt island extends to 40 sq km (15 sq mi) of heavily wooded wilderness, its rugged landscape punctuated by soaring peaks. Amid the wilderness, adventurous travellers can find but one haven to stay – the low-impact Hinchinbrook Island Resort.

Perhaps 'resort' is not the right word, for this place scarcely ruffles the natural environment, consisting as it does of just eight beach cabins and 15 treetop bungalows. The former have two bedrooms apiece, with bathroom, plus kitchenette and fridge on a covered verandah where you can lounge between dips in the sea, discussing the meaning of a cold tinnie. Bungalows have one or two bedrooms and are raised on stilts to provide good views from their rainforest locations, connected by a winding boardwalk. HQ has been designed to blend into the tropical background and is the place to eat, meet friends in the bar for a cocktail or hit the pool.

But that's as lively as this resort ever gets. This is a Robinson Crusoe island and if Girl Friday is there, too, it makes for a perfect wilderness break with sun, sea and sand thrown in. It's all very romantic, intimate, and totally refreshing. Fill the days snorkelling, hiking forest trails or fishing these prolific waters for sought-after sport fish. If all that sounds, well, a bit *energetic*, there's no shame in lounging in a hammock or browning on Orchid Beach. And when the time comes for some serious exercise, stroll to the restaurant and raise a finger to point at your choice of delicious meal, then watch the stunning sunset while you wait. Is this paradise on earth? If you're ever lucky enough to stay here, decide for yourself!

WHERE:
Hinchinbrook Island; from Cardwell, Queensland

COST:
Expensive

BEST TIME OF YEAR:
Any, but summer (December to March) is *hot* as in 'often scorching'

DON'T MISS:
Guided bush walks

THINGS TO DO:
A day-cruise of discovery in Hinchinbrook Island's teeming waters looking for dugong, turtles and crocodiles while learning from the informative commentary; swimming and snorkelling; wildlife-watching and birdwatching; exploring the mangrove everglades by canoe

YOU SHOULD KNOW:
Children are very welcome but, in keeping with the simple nature of the place, there is no child minding or kids' activities (use the huge natural playground). There is a TV/DVD in the guest lounge for compulsive viewers, but that's it. The associated Hinchinbrook Island Wilderness Lodge is available for group bookings only.

The Old Gaol

WHERE:
Margaret Street, Mount Gambier, South Australia
COST:
Budget
BEST TIME OF YEAR:
Whenever you happen to be passing
DON'T MISS:
Enjoying a good *craic* with fellow guests in the gaol's recreation room (actually the former chapel, now a comfortable lounge with TV, books and internet)
THINGS TO DO:
Exercise, obviously (there are three courtyards for leg-stretchers); consider your sins (if any) in the meditation garden; enjoy a cold one in the beer garden; catch a leisurely coffee in the café; work out what the Sports Bar does best; escape (perhaps reluctantly).
YOU SHOULD KNOW:
The 'custody sergeant' won't book anyone in after 21.00. Parolees can pitch up in their own camper vans and stay on the grounds for a nominal sum. Strictly no foreign bedding is allowed on the grounds or within.

It would be nice to discover *NED KELLY WAS HERE* scratched on the wall of your cell but sadly, although you *are* in gaol, it's not the right one. Ned and his gang rampaged through Victoria in the 1870s, and although this particular prison is of the right age (a handsome low building erected in 1866), it is in faraway South Australia. And to be honest it isn't even a prison any more, for The Old Gaol at Mount Gambier is now an affordable backpacker-style travellers' rest and key-jangling gaolers have morphed into welcoming hosts. And while you may still spend a night in the cells, there are also non-cellular rooms for those with a guilty conscience. Showers and toilets are communal, but there are plenty to go round.

Would-be inmates can take their pick from various dormitory rooms with a total capacity of 46, twins (authentic bunk beds), doubles (one big bed) plus one decent-sized family unit with private lounge and TV. The communal kitchens are available for use 24/7, so meals may be prepared, snacks grabbed and picnics packed at any time. Food and drink may be stored in the fridges (best labelled, to avoid a prison riot breaking out if ownership of that tempting cold chicken is unclear) and – as a thoughtful touch – tea, coffee and sugar are on the house.

The Old Gaol is midway between Adelaide and Melbourne, so it's a convenient stopover for travellers on their way through to The Great Ocean Road, Grampians and The Coonawarra Wine Region. But don't make the briefest of stops unless you're really in a hurry to be somewhere else. It's worth exploring Mount Gambier's enchanting Blue Lake and the surrounding landscape, while the city also has beautiful parks and gardens, caves and sinkholes.

Desert Cave Hotel

When in Coober Pedy do as the locals do – lay your weary head to rest in a hillside cave where nature's air conditioning provides a constant (and comfortable) temperature. The story's in the name. Is it in the desert? Yup, 850 km (530 mi) north of Adelaide on the Stuart Highway in arid country, where the first tree ever seen in town was made of welded scrap iron and thrives to this day. Is it a hotel? You can check in and they know about credit cards, so definitely. Are there caves? Indeed, although more conventional accommodation above ground may be had at the Desert Cave Hotel by those of claustrophobic bent (there are 30+ above-ground suites and just 19 'caves', but they're the ones to go for).

This boxy but not unattractive building was completed in the late 1980s and sits against a sandstone rock face, offering cool underground rooms inspired by the 'dugouts' (houses carved into the rock) favoured hereabouts, a fact that is perhaps unsurprising as most of the inhabitants are opal miners rather than builders. The award-winning four-star hotel's spacious subterranean rooms have high ceilings with a quiet, cool and airy atmosphere said to guarantee a great night's sleep. During waking hours guests can avail themselves of underground shops (opals a speciality) or the underground bar and gaming room (possibly the world's only cavern casino), while those in need of spiritual rather than temporal sustenance can nip along the street to the underground church.

Rooms have all mod cons, wifi is available throughout and main meals are prepared by top chefs and served in Umberto's Restaurant. The below-ground Crystal Café offers breakfast and lunch, plus snacks and coffee all day long. It's all very different, and that's what makes it special.

WHERE:
Hutchison Street, Coober Pedy, South Australia
COST:
Reasonable
BEST TIME OF YEAR:
Make it May to August unless you want to fry breakfast on the roof of your car.
DON'T MISS:
The hotel's opal and Outback interpretive centre; one (or more) of the fascinating tours (such as Sunset Ghosts and History, the Outback Mail Run or Painted Desert Tour)
THINGS TO DO:
Not a lot *per se*, Coober Pedy being the opal rather than entertainment capital of the world, but the surrounding landscape is spectacular in its own way and mining scars are almost surrealistic (some 250,000 shafts have been sunk over the years); a round of golf (best at night to avoid the heat) using a luminous ball and carrying your own square of artificial turf for teeing off (there's no grass hereabouts).
YOU SHOULD KNOW:
Local stone gathered from nearby Moon Plane (an important location in the apocalyptic movie *Mad Max Beyond Thunderdome*) was used to face the hotel. The name Coober Pedy comes from the local Aboriginal term *kupa-piti*, which means (those of a sensitive disposition look away now) 'white man's hole'.

Southern Ocean Lodge

WHERE:
Kangaroo Island, South Australia
COST:
Astronomical, and why not?
BEST TIME OF YEAR:
Go any time (although winters, between June and September, are mild and wet).
DON'T MISS:
The guided island excursions of various sorts that are included in the price
THINGS TO DO:
Wildlife-watching in 'Australia's Galapagos' – yes, there are kangaroos galore, but also look out for animals such as New Zealand fur seals, koalas and sea lions, along with abundant birdlife (especially the ospreys); cliff walks; photography (bring spare memory cards); bush walking; quad-bike safari; sea kayaking; fishing; visiting local artists in their studios
YOU SHOULD KNOW:
More than half of the island has never been cleared of vegetation and over a quarter is conserved in national parks, conservation parks and wilderness protection areas. Kangaroo Island has a full-time population of just over 4,000 souls, boosted by up to 150,000 visitors each year (but not many of them get as far as Southern Ocean Lodge).

Kangaroo Island off the South Australian mainland is the country's third largest. With a substantial percentage of its 4,500-sq-km (1,740-sq-mi) area permanently conserved, there's still a lot of untouched backcountry in which to get lost (metaphorically), while enjoying the stunning landscapes, rugged coastlines and abundant wildlife offered by this unique environment. And the way to see it wrapped with the most luxurious of trimmings is to head to the Southern Ocean Lodge above Hanson Bay on the southwest coast. This unique resort is strung out along a clifftop like modernist pearls above pounding surf, with commanding views across the sea to one side and a pristine landscape to the other.

Is there such a thing as iconic 21st-century wilderness chic? If there is, this is one place it's happening. Appropriately, there are 21 suites that combine mesmerizing locations with uncompromising creature comforts. With names like Osprey Pavilion, Ocean Family, Remarkable Suite and Ocean Retreat, it's not surprising that interiors feature such goodies as lavish emperor-size beds, walk-in wardrobes, sunken lounges, heated floors, climate control, internet access, dramatic glass-walled bathrooms packed with spa features, music systems, safes, telephones, complimentary bars plus outdoor terraces.

The lodge building offers fine dining with innovative menus that take full advantage of South Australia's reputation as the nation's culinary capital, where dedicated growers produce a bounty of premium produce, including great wines. The dining experience is a sensual delight that complements the Lodge's other luxurious resource, the Southern Spa. The dramatic outlook over a restless ocean that stretches all the way to Antarctica is counterpointed by the soothing range of therapies on offer. This is a place for those who really appreciate (and can afford) a wilderness sanctuary where the majesty of Nature is combined with the most lavish of personal comfort.

Tower Lodge

Two hours north of Sydney, the Hunter Valley is renowned as the centre of Australia's come-of-age wine industry. One man made a huge contribution to the ultimate success of the Valley's 70 wineries and has been described as 'the godfather of the Australian wine industry'. That man was the late Len Evans, an influential wine writer and founding director of the Australian Wine Bureau. He died in 2006 but left behind an extraordinary personal legacy – and it's one that can be enjoyed (and marvelled at!) by interested visitors to the wine-making region he loved.

Tower Lodge is an eclectic creation in the heart of the Hunter Valley, quite unlike any other boutique hotel in the world. The words 'extraordinary', 'exotic' (and even 'slightly bizarre') must surely spring to mind when first encountering its luxurious eccentricity. Spanish architecture meets Renaissance style, French antiques rub upholstery with Chinese old masters, huge mirrors reflect opulent fabrics, ornate chandeliers hang before massive fireplaces . . . and that's before mentioning angular purple walls, soaring ceilings, tinkling fountains and the cloistered courtyard with passageways that lead to ten impressive mega-rooms, plus two awesome suites. All the rooms have different (and striking) decor, but all have gleaming white-tiled bathrooms with green mosaics and a whirlpool bath for two. An opulent breakfast is served in the monumental dining room with its groaning side table, afternoon tea in the living room is a civilized ritual not to be missed and wonderful packed luncheons ('lunch' would seem an inadequate term) are made to order. Phew!

You'll never have stayed in a more in-your-face place (guests tend to be either delighted or slightly unnerved by its assertive character), but everyone has to agree that Tower Lodge is monumentally different . . . and mightily impressive.

WHERE:
Hunter Valley, New South Wales

COST:
Expensive (but less so midweek)

BEST TIME OF YEAR:
Any time is a good time (but January and February are the wettest months and the grapes are harvested in April).

DON'T MISS:
A gym workout (or working up a sweat in the sauna), followed by a plunge in the hotel pool (think Roman baths), followed by a session in the hotel's massage room; relaxing in the picturesque grounds; a tour of the attached winery plus a souvenir bottle (or two) from the fine cellar

THINGS TO DO:
Wineries (ride a bike and knock them off on two wheels, or rent a vintage car and tour in style) and fine dining (lots of choice); a round on the hotel's miniature 18-hole golf course; bush walking in Barrington Tops National Park; seeing the Hunter Valley from a hot-air balloon

YOU SHOULD KNOW:
There is no in-house restaurant but hotel staff will recommend a variety of first-class eateries – including the famed Roberts restaurant, which is a short walk away. Despite the funky decor, this place is not much frequented by the racy younger set. Tower Lodge is unsuitable for children under 16 years of age.

Tara Guest House Sydney

WHERE:
Edgeware Road, Enmore, New South Wales
COST:
Budget (two sharing a room, with a reasonable discount for a lone guest)
BEST TIME OF YEAR:
Any time is good (the climate is relentlessly warm and those who scorch might care to avoid the hottest months, January and February).
DON'T MISS:
Tara's free transfer service to and from the airport, ensuring a warm personal welcome to Sydney; the authentic world culinary tour – India, Portugal, Greece, Turkey, Italy, Thailand, Lebanon, Sweden . . . even Peru are all within restaurant range; nearby King Street's famous café culture
THINGS TO DO:
Head down to the bright lights and famous sights of central Sydney. Explore the Victorian Camperdown Cemetery in Newtown, now an important green space. Browse the local book stores (Newtown is known for them).
YOU SHOULD KNOW:
Book well in advance as Tara's *VACANCY* sign is rarely dusted off. Sydney's Enmore Theatre is just around the corner and is the place to catch popular live entertainment, especially shows for kids.

With a long history of sending its own backpackers off around the world, Sydney has a thriving bed-and-breakfast scene that caters for travellers who can't afford to exchange an arm (or leg) for accommodation at one of the city's posh hotels. One such establishment is the Tara Guest House in the Newtown area. This is not a 'new town' at all but a traditional inner suburb area close to the Central Business District and Sydney University. It offers a lively mixed community that attracts lots of young people and has numerous speciality shops, cafés, restaurants and pubs with live music. This is an excellent base from which to sally forth to explore the city and its environs (one bus takes you straight to the Circular Quay and Opera House).

Tara is not at the super-budget end of the cost spectrum but it does offer a very warm welcome, spacious rooms and delicious home-cooked tucker, all at a very reasonable price for this expensive city. The house's classic Victorian facade, behind a leafy front garden, promises gracious interiors and – after nearly a century as a doctor's home and surgery – a recent renovation has brought the house back to its original comfortable splendour, albeit with modern touches. There are only four rooms (one is a double suite, ideal for a family, that even has a piano for anyone who likes tinkling the ivories) – so the place has a pleasant family atmosphere.

The service is excellent, with nice touches like Egyptian cotton sheets, terry robes and an environmentally friendly pack of toiletries. There's free wifi throughout and breakfasts are not so much breakfasts as morning banquets (free-range eggs and free-trade coffee give a good idea of Tara's 'vibe'). A welcoming home from home in New South Wales wanted? This should do nicely!

Establishment Hotel

WHERE:
Bridge Lane, Sydney, New South Wales
COST:
Reasonable (Studio Room); expensive (Establishment Room); astronomical (penthouses)
BEST TIME OF YEAR:
Sydney is an any-time destination.
DON'T MISS:
Breakfast in the open-atrium Garden Bar; playing with the touch screen that controls just about everything in your room; socializing with the natives over a glass or two of real ale in the Establishment Bar, before working off the result in the hotel's small gym.

For a funky hotel that will make every guest want to brag about having stayed there, the Establishment's foyer has a surprisingly discreet entrance – tucked away off George Street in Sydney's bustling centre – although the trendy Establishment Bar on George Street itself is hard to miss. Don't expect water views, despite the fact that the iconic Harbour is only a few brisk strides away, because the watchwords here are 'urban' and 'chic'. Expectations engendered by the rather traditional nine-storey facade are swiftly (and delightfully) dashed by the dramatic modernity and spectacular level of personal service within.

Choose between a Studio Room (bedroom only), Establishment

Room (with extra lounging area) or one of two glitzy penthouses (if you're feeling flush). In all cases the bathrooms are literally brilliant, with lots of glass and mirrors to make preening a pleasure, and the general amenities are comprehensive. There's further refinement to perplex indecisive decision makers, as guests must also choose between Urban Scheme (lower floors) and Luxe Scheme (upper floors). What's the difference? The former are bright and breezy with high ceilings, black wooden flooring and bright splashes of colour, the latter are intended to be more womb-like and soothing. It really matters not, for the hotel will gain an A+ whatever you choose.

The wining and dining takes place on the George Street side of the building and is not confined to guests. The hotel has two upstairs restaurants that attract Sydney's serious diners in droves. The decor is crisp white linen meets modern design, with heritage features adding character. Alternatively, a serious snifter (cocktails a speciality) in the hotel's super-exclusive Hemmesphere Club (entry by hotel key, mix 'n' mingle with Sydney's finest) can be followed by a meal in the club's famous sushi restaurant, supposedly the city's best.

THINGS TO DO:
You don't need advice on what to see and do in Sydney!

YOU SHOULD KNOW:
If you see 'Balmain Bugs' on a menu it isn't bush tucker, but delicious local crayfish. Small children are not appreciated (although admitted) because the hotel is not really suitable for little ones, but over 16s are welcome. Be sure to book well in advance if you want to be around for the world-famous Sydney Harbour firework display on New Year's Eve.

Railway Square YHA

WHERE:
Lee Street, Sydney, New South Wales
COST:
Budget (and YHA members get a discount)
BEST TIME OF YEAR:
January to December
DON'T MISS:
Being seen in Scubar, the must-visit underground backpacker bar
THINGS TO DO:
Train spotting (only kidding); hitting the tapas bars in the Spanish Quarter (George and Liverpool Streets); exploring China Town (and its night markets on summer Fridays); bar-flying in bohemian Surry Hills, close to Central Station; seeing the sights and attempting the renowned Harbour Bridge Climb; taking the ferry to Watsons Bay and catching the spectacular sunset.
YOU SHOULD KNOW:
Railway Square YHA offers disabled access. A pick-up from the airport can be arranged for a modest fee. Breakfast is an extra.

There's no need to look too hard for Sydney's most unusual (and affordable) accommodation for young people and those who are young at heart. Right next to Central Station, Railway Square YHA wins hands down, offering a choice that ranges from a super-budget bed in an eight-person male or female dorm up to individual double rooms with private bath. But there's also a decision to make – should you opt for one of the funky red multi-share railway carriages on decommissioned Platform Zero or a comfortable crash pad in the stately restored and converted 1904 main building?

If it all sounds rather basic, that's actually the big idea for Railway Square YHA is a stop-over for those who want to experience this great city on the tightest of budgets. But 'basic' definitely doesn't equate with 'primitive'. The place has air conditioning, a café-restaurant, communal kitchen, barbecue area (naturally!), swimming pool with deck, hot tub/Jacuzzi, TV and video room, pool table, super-fast internet access, washing machines, secure lockers, 24/7 reception and information desk that can tell you all you need to know about sightseeing and having a turbo-charged time in Sydney. And of course the location means that most of the action is within walking distance.

Sounds good? It is but, although there's not much noise from the train station, boisterous sounds can persist into the small hours and start up again early in the morning. But this is not the place for you if your idea of good accommodation involves peace, quiet and privacy. This is a place to socialize, revel in the atmosphere of a lively young fellow-traveller community and have fun while hanging on to most of your Australian dollars.

Paperbark Camp

A two-hour drive south down the Pacific Highway from Sydney, and a world away from the big city, Paperbark Camp offers a unique bush-camping experience. This is an eco-friendly destination set in 40 ha (100 ac) of pristine forest, complete with creek, and based around The Gunyah (an Aboriginal term for 'meeting place'). This slightly haphazard (but architect-designed) building perched on stilts houses reception, a lounge, a restaurant and a kitchen, at the heart of the camp.

Accommodation consists of a dozen solar-powered 'standard' and four 'deluxe' tents, but don't think you need to go deluxe for luxury. The standards are super-comfortable, and even 'tent' is stretching the point – in truth, 'treehouse with solid roof, canvas sides and balconies' is nearer the mark. But however you look at them, these stilted tents among the foliage are both charming and practical. They are all close enough to base to provide reassurance for anyone spooked by the night-time bush (with solar lights marking the pathways), but sited to ensure individual privacy. All tents are en suite, although not quite in the normal sense – you step through the zippered rear to shower to one side (nice warm water!) with sink and toilet opposite. They are screened so you can look out at the forest when you're in action, but passing kangaroos can't infringe on your modesty. And when it comes to eating, the bush tucker is sensational. Expect wonderful local produce cooked in an imaginative fine-dining way, delivering goodies like citrus-crusted swordfish or seared kangaroo steaks.

Finally, some words of warning: this may be the perfect backwoods' experience but (in consequence) the dawn chorus is cacophonous and the mozzies are monstrous. Happily, ear plugs are offered to light sleepers who like lying in and super-effective mosquito repellent is provided. It is these thoughtful touches that make Paperbark Camp such a welcoming place.

WHERE:
Jervis Bay, New South Wales

COST:
It's reasonable to expensive, depending on choice of tent and time of year (Christmas and Easter periods attract a surcharge).

BEST TIME OF YEAR:
Any time is good except July and August, when Paperbark is closed. Autumn (March to May) is best for those who prefer a quieter time, while rain-averse adventurers should opt for November to April.

DON'T MISS:
The Wreck Bay Walkabout that includes a (genuine) bush-tucker tour and a talk round the camp fire on Aboriginal culture; a massage on your balcony amid the greenery and sounds of the bush

THINGS TO DO:
Dolphin-, penguin- and whale-spotting cruises in Jervis Bay (whales in May/June and October/November); wildlife-watching and birdwatching; hiking forest trails; mountain biking; horse riding; canoeing (river) and kayaking (sea); loafing on the beach; surfing at Caves Beach; exploring nearby Booderee National Park and the Botanic Gardens (beaches, bush and birdlife)

YOU SHOULD KNOW:
The sea is really only warm enough to frolic in comfortably between November and May. Don't forget to pack a good pair of binoculars for wildlife-watching purposes. It may seem like the back of beyond, but there's internet access. Perhaps surprisingly in view of its remote location, the camp can and does offer disabled access. It's not for tots but children over six are welcome.

Cradle Mountain Lodge

WHERE:
The northern edge of Cradle Mountain-Lake St Clair National Park, Tasmania
COST:
It's reasonable and you get a good discount for the highly recommended three-day stay.
BEST TIME OF YEAR:
Go any time (but note that Tasmania is generally colder than the rest of Australia and winter months from June to August are the coldest and wettest, often with heavy snowfalls on higher ground).
DON'T MISS:
A game of pool or darts in the Tavern; Christmas in July (yup, the Lodge drops into traditional Yuletide celebrations all month long, often accompanied by snow); the Tasmanian wine- and cheese-tasting session
THINGS TO DO:
If you've got what it takes, try the strenuous but rewarding climb to the summit of Cradle Mountain from the Dove Lake car park (allow six to seven hours). Try one of the spectacular wilderness walks. Take the night-viewing wildlife tour. There's fly fishing in season, canoeing (in summer) and tobogganing (in winter).
YOU SHOULD KNOW:
Children aged 12 and under stay free (and get a free breakfast). It's best to book the spa package in advance if you want it. Take warm clothes, waterproofs, stout walking shoes (or boots) and thick socks, camera and binoculars. A swimming costume is required if using the spa. Mobile phone access is patchy going on non-existent, but there is an internet kiosk and public phone.

Located in Tasmania's rainforest-clad Central Highlands, Cradle Mountain Lodge offers the wilderness experience *par excellence*. Tasmania delivers the spectacular wilderness, while the Lodge offers luxurious accommodation that lets you enjoy this thrilling landscape in style. Pencil Pine Cabins are the norm. Close to the Lodge, these snug refuges offer lake or bush-land views and come in two sizes suitable for couples and families, with simple but pleasing contemporary decor. Peaceful Spa Cabins are located in nearby bush and guests can choose between contemporary or rustic interiors. Both have verandahs with forest views and offer frequent sightings of local wildlife. All cabins have spacious bathrooms with spa baths, gas heaters or an open fire. The ultimate in wilderness luxury can be found in the spacious King Billy Suites, with their lounging area that has a double-sided log fire, oversize bathroom with spa and outside deck area that has a private hot tub.

The Lodge's Highland Restaurant is a renowned fine-dining venue, not least for the heaped mountain buffet breakfast and an innovative dinner menu (advance booking advised). The rustic Tavern & Bistro has a laid-back atmosphere and offers good company around the roaring log fire, along with informal meals. The Waldheim Alpine Spa combines nature's intelligence and skilled masseuses, while the dedicated therapeutic area known as The Sanctuary includes a steam room, sauna, large hot tub and cool plunge pool for an invigorating experience.

But the real star of the show is not the Lodge itself, however comfortable, but the stunning surroundings. It's easy to understand why everyone who stays here happily endorses the view that this is one of Australia's top wilderness destinations.

Kauri Cliffs

Tall, straight-growing kauri trees were greatly prized by mariners in the days of sail and were thus almost logged out. But there are still plenty of these ancient trees to be seen in the native forest that surrounds one of New Zealand's premier (wait for it, it's a mouthful) 'most awarded luxury boutique and spa resort hotels'. Hopefully no adjective was missed, for Kauri Cliffs really does try hard to deliver an incomparable break, helped mightily by its wonderful elevated setting with sweeping ocean views of Cape Brett, Cavalli Islands and the Pacific Ocean. But might there possibly be some chest-puffing going on here?

There's actually not much argument about positive delivery on the golfing side (a wonderfully scenic par-72 PGA Championship course in the Top 100 any keen clubmeister would be happy to take on and proud to tame), nor the pampering possibilities held out by the luxury spa (it nestles at the forest's edge, overlooking a ferny glen with winding stream, and offers the best holistic whole-body therapies and treatments known to woman, delivered by skilled practitioners using the finest indigenous natural ingredients). The 22 guest suites are pretty special, too. They are housed two-by-two in outlying cottages, surrounded by lush foliage. Eight cottages have deluxe suites and three cottages contain slightly smaller standard suites for mere mortals, but all are luxuriously appointed with splendid sea views. Neither does the impressive plantation-style lodge house disappoint. It has a spacious lounge, private day rooms, computer room and an elegant dining room with outdoor decks overlooking the Pacific, while fine cuisine matches the incomparable setting. Then there are a couple of pools (indoors and out) plus the 2,600-ha (6,425-ac) subtropical estate to provide you with a delightful private playground.

The verdict? No boasting here. Kauri Cliffs really is as good as it says on the box, and even non-golfers will enjoy a memorable stay.

WHERE:
Tablelands Road, Matauri Bay, Northland, North Island

COST:
Astronomical (but you get what you pay for)

BEST TIME OF YEAR:
High season (more expensive) is November to March.

DON'T MISS:
The sauna; finding the waterfall and three private beaches on the estate; horseback riding on deserted silver sand; the menu at the spa

THINGS TO DO:
Golf; super spa treatments; tennis; mountain biking; sailing; fishing; waterskiing, scuba diving; canoeing; sea kayaking

YOU SHOULD KNOW:
Gentlemen are required to wear jackets during cocktail hour and dinner (but casually dressed rogues straight from the beach can borrow one). There are a couple of rooms where the likes of bodyguards and chauffeurs can be parked. Children are welcome (under fives free) and there's a babysitting service.

Eagles Nest Retreat

WHERE:
Tapeka Road, Russell, Bay of Islands, Northland, North Island
COST:
Expensive to astronomical (off peak), astronomical (high season)
BEST TIME OF YEAR:
Go any time the bank manager isn't looking (May to October for the lowest rates; high season December to March).
DON'T MISS:
Although you can self-cater in your well-equipped kitchen (breakfast provisions delivered daily), treat yourself to one of those sensational private-chef-prepared meals served in the villa; take a sightseeing flight in the house chopper.
THINGS TO DO:
Stay around your villa to simply enjoy the stunning vistas and milk the luxurious lifestyle for every last drop. Sally forth into or onto the Bay of Plenty and take your pick of just about every water sport known to humankind. Jump on mountain bikes (provided) and go. Enjoy the dolphin-watching cruise.
YOU SHOULD KNOW:
Various superior services incur extra charges (for example, personal chef, chauffeur, massage therapists, personal trainer, business services). There's no central lodge at Eagles Nest. Children are welcome. Villas are supplied with eco-friendly products and the resort recycles all its bottles and paper.

The Bay of Islands is New Zealand's ultimate maritime playground and there couldn't be anywhere more dramatic than award-winning Eagles Nest Retreat from whence to enjoy the game. There are just five villas in a fabulous setting atop a dramatic peninsula that almost seems like an island. The views are almost unbelievable, and each villa is like a personal holiday home that any multi-millionaire would be proud to own. This is unashamed luxury piled lavishly on unashamed luxury.

The villas themselves have to be seen to be believed. Rahimoana (which translates from the Maori as 'Sun God over the Ocean') is decorated in soothing shades of white and light grey. With its copper aerofoil roof floating above towering glass walls, this is modern architecture at its most impressive. Four bedrooms and a vast living area, all with sensational views, flow out onto stone balconies, beyond which is your own estate with gardens, native bush, helipad, infinity pool, private beach and deep-water anchorage (billionaires please take note). There's also a gym, office, sauna, service area and wine cellar. Rahimoana may be the *crème de la crème*, but the other four aren't too shabby. They may not be quite so grandiose, but each is architect-designed to have a character all its own. Sacred Space, Eagles Spirit, The Eyrie and First Light have a varying number of guest rooms, but every one has living space galore and is comprehensively equipped.

Resident chefs using the finest ingredients, produced or caught locally whenever possible, ensure that the culinary standards reach the same height as everything else at Eagles Nest, as do the wines. Unobtrusive but attentive staff are waiting to cater for guests' every need (and whim), reinforcing that millionaire lifestyle feel to which you could so easily (and happily) become accustomed.

Treetops Lodge & Estate

Stand by for an indoor/outdoor experience second to none, enjoyed in a superb colonial-style lodge set amid 1,000 ha (2,470 ac) of unspoilt valleys and native forest in New Zealand's thermal region, Rotorua. Treetops Lodge & Estate offers stylish accommodation in the main building's Lodge Wing for families or groups of friends. With four en-suite bedrooms, kitchen and open-plan living area, it's easy for guests to maintain a homely atmosphere. For couples and those who prefer doing their own thing, there are villas tucked away in private spots within easy walking distance of the Lodge's central facilities. There's a choice of forest or lake view and each villa is beautifully furnished, featuring a bedroom, generous bathroom with spa bath, lounge with fireplace and a kitchenette. For most, this will prove unnecessary, for the cuisine at Treetops forms an integral part of the whole experience. The emphasis is on the very best local produce, complemented by the finest wines grown in New Zealand, and the head chef creates imaginative dishes that have the authentic flavour of New Zealand thanks to the use of traditional native herbs.

That's the 'indoor' bit. Good though that may be, it's by no means unique as luxury lodge living goes. But the 'outside' element really is extraordinary. The breathtaking terrain just cries out to be explored (on foot, mountain bike, horseback or from the relative comfort of a 4x4). Think native forest, a dramatic valley, 800-year-old trees, teeming wildlife, crystal-clear streams and trout-filled lakes. If that's not enough, the Rotorua region offers landscape drama galore for those who like to get out and about, and much more besides.

Inside or out, award-winning Treetops is a very special sanctuary that delivers an ultimate New Zealand experience.

WHERE:
Kearoa Road, Horohoro, Rotorua, North Island

COST:
It's expensive verging on astronomical, depending on season, party size and chosen accommodation.

BEST TIME OF YEAR:
Peak season is October to April.

DON'T MISS:
An intimate dinner for two in the Lodge's candle-lit library

THINGS TO DO:
World-class trout fishing on site (the chef will cook or smoke the catch for you); tramping the unspoilt estate (there are walking tracks of all lengths); 4x4 safaris; following the Maori Food Trail; driving to the Bay of Plenty (an hour away) for world-class beaches and stunning coastal vistas; wine tasting; heli-sightseeing; horse trekking

YOU SHOULD KNOW:
There's a special children's package, brilliantly designed to entertain, inform and amuse youngsters. Treetops Estate has one fabulous self-contained property that sleeps eight (Pheasant House, tucked away in the hills). The Rotorua region is New Zealand's Maori cultural centre, with many opportunities to experience this unique culture.

Huka Lodge

WHERE:
Huka Falls Road, Taupo, North Island
COST:
Astronomical
BEST TIME OF YEAR:
Go any time (it's a great base for winter skiing).
DON'T MISS:
Feeding the ducks on the lawn; an in-room spa treatment
THINGS TO DO:
Go fishing (no, they haven't forgotten the original rationale – there's access to over 20 rivers and trout streams); ask for a picnic hamper and explore the countryside; watch one of Lake Taupo's fabulous sunsets from the Western Bays area; check-out the water sports (the Lodge will book them for you).
YOU SHOULD KNOW:
Young children go free, but there's a bed supplement for older kids. Local airport transfers, breakfast and dinner are included in the price, but extras will add to the bill.

Once a fishing lodge, not always a fishing lodge. This characterful 1920s building on the banks of the Waikato River near the cascading Huka Falls was once just that, but nowadays serves as a boutique bolthole that will appeal mightily to anyone who loves the great outdoors and fine dining (oh, and you can still go fishing). Huka Lodge is a top retreat in Taupo in the heart of the North Island, home to the country's largest lake and rugged volcanic landscape.

The lodge has 18 breathtaking suites, although families and parties can opt for two-bedroomed Alan Pye Cottage (named after the founder) or the rather grander four-bedroomed Owner's Cottage in its spectacular location on a riverside promontory with a view downstream to the falls. This is a celebrity playground, and if celebrities march on their slim stomachs it's easy to understand why they like the place. The cuisine (directed by a Michelin-starred chef) is sublime and one of the main attractions. This is New Zealand food at its best, using the island's bounty to created modern dishes with a European twist. Dining is a major pleasure, not least because there's a choice of wonderful locations where you can eat, from main dining room to vaulted wine cellar, outside terrace to romantic riverbank. Facilities include three pools, a bar with a suitably old-fashioned clubby feel, a library and wifi throughout

Staying in this magical place is treat enough and you'll never be bored, but Huka Lodge also offers various 'specials' that can focus your energies. These include fishing packages (experts do their own thing, beginners try everything from fly-casting lessons to cooking the catch), romantic breaks, culinary and/or wine encounters, winter sports breaks and adventure options featuring the likes of horse trekking, golf and heli-safaris.

Wharekauhau Lodge

If it weren't for the name, rugged landscape and adjacent coast, this could be an Edwardian mansion in the genteel English Home Counties, complete with sweeping lawns and lake. As it is, elegant Wharekauhau Lodge is at the heart of a 2,200-ha (5,435-ac) working stock farm in South Island's Wairarapa wine region. Accommodation is limited to the number who can be fitted into the dining room at the main house for a communal meal, where a set menu consists of excellent home-cooked food, much of it produced on the estate, plus good local wine and lively conversation around shared tables.

The accommodation consists of 12 guest cottages (ten singles and two suitable for families) with the general facilities concentrated on the Lodge itself. These include a bar, book/DVD library with free wifi, recreation centre, Jacuzzi, heated indoor pool, gym, tennis court and the spa room. Each cottage stands alone and has high, beamed ceilings, skylights to admit as much natural light as possible (to save electricity, part of the Lodge's eco-friendly programme), a grand canopied bed and a comforting open gas fire in case you encounter some chilly evenings.

The estate is irresistible and it's hard not to dream of lottery jackpots and being the squire of such a place. Wharekauhau seems to have everything anyone could ever want from a country spread – ancient forests, peaceful lakes, rivers, rolling pastures and a wild and spectacular stretch of coast. But a word of warning: those of sensitive disposition may start to get the feeling they're being watched, and often it will be true. Those sheep just can't stop staring, But hey, that's rural New Zealand for you.

WHERE:
Western Lake Road, Palliser Bay, Featherston, South Island
COST:
Expensive
BEST TIME OF YEAR:
Any time
DON'T MISS:
The collective evening meal is great fun, but romantics might care to go private, dining *à deux* by candle light in front of a roaring fire. Another rewarding joint activity is a night-time soak beneath the stars in the hot tub outside your cottage. Those in need of pampering should definitely make the acquaintance of the Wharekauhau Day Spa.
THINGS TO DO:
Make full use of this wonderful estate by braving the ocean (or using the pool if the surf's up), exploring the varied terrain on foot, mountain bike or horseback, taking the farm tour, borrowing a quad bike; tasting the fruits of *pinot noir* in the many wineries in nearby Martinborough; clay pigeon shooting; a jet-boat ride on the Ruamahunga River
YOU SHOULD KNOW:
Take warm, windproof clothing and boots for daytime adventures around the estate plus something smart enough to ensure that you don't feel under-dressed during evening meals. If you're in a particular hurry to get to the Lodge, Wharekauhau is (surprisingly) just ten minutes from Wellington by helicopter.

Hapuku Lodge & Treehouses

WHERE:
Station Road (off State Highway 1), Kaikoura, South Island
COST:
It's reasonable to expensive, depending on choice of accommodation. (Breakfast is included, other meals are extra.)
BEST TIME OF YEAR:
Go any time, although winter is decidedly chilly (but roaring log fires help to ease the pain).
DON'T MISS:
In-room spa treatments if all that unaccustomed open-air activity results in stiff muscles; the thermal pools (and waterslides!) at Hanmer Springs
THINGS TO DO:
Watch whales and/or dolphins (bring binoculars, it's a top cephalopod location) and visit the seals; order a picnic and explore the grounds; check out Kaikoura Winery; surf on the beach at Mangamauna Bay.
YOU SHOULD KNOW:
Children are welcome, but only those over 12 may stay in the Lodge itself. As with many such establishments in New Zealand, the accommodation is but part of the estate's more traditional commercial activities, which in this case include olive oil production and deer farming.

Set between the rugged backdrop of the Kaikouru Seaward Mountains and wild Mangamauna Bay, Hapuku Lodge & Treehouses can certainly offer something a little different from the usual country boutique hotel. As the name suggests, the something different is a treehouse option. This is surely the one to go for, even though the accommodation in the lodge building is very good. The contemporary timber-clad treehouse rooms are set in a manuka grove away from the main house and the five lofty Upper Branch Rooms perched in the tree tops are very private and ideal for romantics, with picture windows and eye-popping views in all directions. Lower Branch Rooms are less expensive, while Family Tree Houses are a hybrid of the two. They're beautifully furnished with non-rustic comfort in mind, and that includes a double spa bath and separate shower.

Hapuku Lodge has a dozen well-equipped rooms, including four suites, and good facilities – delightful garden, bar with stone fireplace, DVD library, free wifi, guest computer, hot tub, sauna, pool house and swimming pool. Watching the chefs prepare your meal is a great appetizer and the airy alpine-style dining room has a wooden floor and window tables that make the most of the views. Dinner is superbly cooked local produce that comes in portion sizes designed to refuel you after an active day out.

And all this can be enjoyed in the comforting knowledge that the Lodge is suitably eco-friendly. Electricity comes from solar power, food is sourced locally from hunters, farmers and fishermen who use sustainable practices and an on-going tree-planting programme is helping to reforest this enchanting landscape.

Blanket Bay Hotel

Not too far from Queenstown (the world's adventure capital) but located in truly splendid alpine isolation on the banks of Lake Wakatipu, Blanket Bay Hotel is a super-desirable hideaway. Set against the dramatic backdrop of the snow-capped Humboldt Mountains, this small boutique hotel is based around a striking lodge built of local timber and stone that has as its centrepiece the soaring Great Room with vaulted timber ceiling and huge windows that almost seem to bring the shimmering lake and mountainscape indoors.

Accommodation is split between the main lodge and detached chalets, but all share breathtaking lake views and each has a private terrace or deck from which to enjoy them. The interiors are superb – think rich fabrics, expensive rugs, lots of polished wood, stone fireplaces and bathrooms that are a tribute to the art of stylish ablution (among other cleansing delights, we're talking steam showers here). There are five Lodge Rooms, three magnificent Lodge Suites and two chalets containing a total of four suites. The likes of air conditioning, free wifi, TV/sound systems and direct-dial telephones come as a given. The cuisine is suitably exquisite, completing the hotel's luxurious circle.

Even so, to sink back with a happy sigh into the Blanket Bay's enfolding arms would be a mistake. This may be one of the most soothing and comfortable bases on the planet, but the true excitement lies in a plethora of activities just begging to be tackled. Come at any time. Spring sees wildflowers exploding and lambs in the pastures, summer has hot days and long lazy evenings, autumn sees a wonderful foliage display and winter brings snow to this awesome landscape. But one thing's for sure. Whatever the season, your Blanket Bay experience will be uniquely rewarding.

WHERE:
Glenorchy Road, Glenorchy, Otago, South Island
COST:
It's expensive to astronomical (but with seasonal variations and deals to be done).
BEST TIME OF YEAR:
Arrive any time, according to the sort of sightseeing and activities you have in mind.
DON'T MISS:
An intimate dinner in the hotel's Wine Cave; a tasting visit to Amisfield Wines, which supplies may of Blanket Bay's finest tipples; a dip in (or lounge beside) the sheltered pool
THINGS TO DO:
The Milford Sound helicopter (or light aircraft) sightseeing flight; horse riding; hiking, perhaps tramping the famous Greenstone and Routeburn Tracks; jet boating on the Dart River (departing from the hotel's jetty); kayaking; heli-skiing and other snow sports in season; world-class trout fishing (heli-fishing takes you to near-virgin waters); wild swimming; sky diving; bungee jumping . . . for starters
YOU SHOULD KNOW:
Blanket Bay offers various tailored packages such as the Honeymoon Special, two-day Heli-ski Experience or Town & Country Alpine Escape (jointly with Blanket Bay and Eichardts Hotel in lively Queenstown).

Hangaroa Eco Village & Spa

WHERE:
Easter Island (Rapa Nui)
COST:
It's expensive (and that's before you include the air fare).
BEST TIME OF YEAR:
The island climate is always warm to hot, but June to October are the 'coolest' months (averaging around 21°C/70°F).
DON'T MISS:
A soak in one of two outdoor Jacuzzis; a session in the Manavai Spa's sand sauna, which uses traditional native cleansing techniques of body and spirit accomplished by covering the body with hot sand
THINGS TO DO:
Visit as many of the extant 887 *moai* as you can cram in (be sure not to miss the examples at Anakena Beach); hike the impressive volcanic terrain.
YOU SHOULD KNOW:
Not all the native Rapa Nui people are enamoured with Easter Island's increasing prominence as a tourist destination, and the siting of the Hangaroa Eco Village & Spa in particular, as they feel Chile's distant rule stifles local self-determination and over-rides property rights.

The astonishing moai *are the star attraction on Easter Island.*

Chile's distant island territory, a speck in the vastness of the Pacific Ocean, is said to be the most remote inhabited island on the planet – and it also happens to be one of the most fascinating places on earth. Everyone knows about Rapa Nui (Easter Island) and has seen pictures of its enigmatic *moai* (ancient stone heads), but few are lucky enough to explore this dramatic volcanic island and observe those amazing monuments for themselves.

The latest addition to the island's limited tourist facilities is the Hangaroa Eco Village & Spa. Built in a style that complements the island's rugged heritage, with circular buildings and low domed roofs with massive timber supports, this quirky establishment has a character all its own in the pantheon of spa hotels. The guiding philosophy is based on Kainga – deep respect for the motherland of Rapa Nui – which physically and spiritually nourishes the world that connects to it. Every aspect of the place, from its architecture to a genuinely warm welcome from the staff, invites guests to be part of an adventure that will let them appreciate this unique island and its culture, while helping preserve them for future generations of Rapa Nui people and visitors alike.

The guest rooms may have all the latest mod cons, but the design encompasses volcanic rock, cypress logs and adobe for a genuine 'Rapa Nui' feel. They come as singles, doubles or suites with climate control. Close to the main settlement of Hangaroa (and the airport), there are great sea views. The food is delicious and varied, a medley of local dishes with an international flavour based on what's available in local markets on the day. The pool and spa are well up to international standards, as is the visitor experience, but the *moai* remain the star attraction.

L'Escapade Island Resort

Close to the Pacific island of Grand Terre's principal town, Nouméa – but a world apart from it – is a rather different New Caledonian resort. Located on the island of Îlot MaÎtre, a marine reserve in the world's largest coral reef lagoon, it is apparent that L'Escapade is special from the moment you embark on the luxury cruiser *Coral Palms* for a 25-minute boat ride that ends at the resort's long wooden pier, where a golf buggy awaits to ferry the luggage ashore. But life on the ocean wave is soon resumed, as guests make their way to one of the bungalows that stand on stilts in the water at the lagoon's edge.

Each bungalow is reached along a walkway and has a living room with panoramic window and dining table for two overlooking the azure lagoon, large bedroom and luxurious bathroom. Outside is a generous verandah that has steps leading down to the crystal-clear water, where an astonishing variety of tropical fish may be seen. This is definitely romance central, and couples are sure to find the experience idyllic. Although kids cannot stay in these waterborne delights, families with children can instead opt for one of the cottages scattered throughout Îlot MaÎtre's lush gardens, which have up to four beds.

L'Escapade's Ouen Toro Restaurant boasts three dining rooms offering delicious French cuisine that will satisfy the most demanding of gourmets, and snacks are available at the two bars around the big swimming pool (with plenty of loungers upon which to enjoy drinks and snacks). Those wanting a *diner à deux* can have a table set up by the water and enjoy eating a splendid meal in one of the most romantic spots in all New Caledonia.

WHERE:
Îlot MaÎtre, Nouméa
COST:
Reasonable (per person, cottage), expensive (per person, on the water)
BEST TIME OF YEAR:
Go any time. Temperatures remain high all year, with July and August the coolest months and September and October the driest.
DON'T MISS:
A high-speed circumnavigation of the island in a banana boat, towed by a jet ski; the lively weekend buffet that brings out Nouméa residents for a day of good food and partying in the sun
THINGS TO DO:
Lazy options – sunbathing on the verandah/private white-sand beach, a drink at the swim-up bar beside the pool; action options – snorkelling in the lagoon to see the mind-blowing reef (equipment provided), jet-skiing, kayaking, a windsurfing lesson; a return trip on *Coral Palms* to check out bustling Nouméa (a working town that's not the least bit touristy).
YOU SHOULD KNOW:
If the romantic atmosphere of L'Escapade really gets to you, the resort has a wedding chapel (but do mention to your would-be companion for life that wedding ceremonies in New Caledonia are not actually legally binding on non-islanders). But couples who have already tied the knot often choose to re-affirm their vows in this magical spot.

WHERE:
Moto Tautau, Taha'a, Leeward Group, Society Islands
COST:
Astronomical (but there are deals)
BEST TIME OF YEAR:
This is an all-year-round destination.
DON'T MISS:
The Polynesian buffet at Le Vanille Restaurant, complete with local live music; the sensational sightseeing helicopter ride to Bora Bora; a good helping of *poisson cru*; a piece of Tahitian pearl jewellery from the resort's boutique as a lasting souvenir.
THINGS TO DO:
The number-one priority is to relax and enjoy; take a dip in the pool (if you don't fancy mixing it with the shoals of bright tropical fish in the lagoon); visit the fitness centre (but no need to overdo it); play a set of tennis; go scuba diving and snorkelling; catch up with the world from the internet centre (if you ever get around to it).
YOU SHOULD KNOW:
A babysitting service is available for families with little ones. Honeymooners (and those who arrive on their own yacht) get a handsome discount.

Le Taha'a Island Resort and Spa

Tahiti and her islands (aka French Polynesia) have long been regarded as the ultimate destination for travellers in search of a South Sea island paradise – and definitely don't disappoint those seeking exotic holidays today. In fact, French Polynesia consists of 118 islands scattered over an area as large as Europe, and the luxurious Le Taha'a Island Resort and Spa is on Taha'a. The old Polynesian way of life still thrives here, but nowadays tourism plays an important role everywhere the sun shines and this island is no exception.

This tropical jewel has lush mountains and valleys and the five-star resort is situated on secluded Moto Tautau islet. But while Le Taha'a Island Resort and Spa makes an important contribution to the local economy, it remains the ultimate Tahitian hideaway, a place that's in harmony with the pristine environment and island culture. After a short boat transfer, guests arrive at a collection of 45 over-water suites curving into the turquoise lagoon. The resort's facilities are on dry land, cleverly woven into stunning natural vegetation along with 12 beach villas. The construction materials are natural and local, ensuring harmony with stunning surroundings.

Here visitors live the outdoor tropical life, with a little help from the lap of luxury. The experience is enhanced by three excellent restaurants – Le Vanille for regular meals, La Plage for delicious *al fresco* beachside snacking and the Ohiri for fine dining. Meals can also be taken in suites or in romantic private settings ashore, and few can resist the room service delivered by ukulele-playing locals in a canoe, along with a garland of flowers. The spa offers a full range of treatments (many including generous use of *monoi*, the sacred traditional Polynesian oil that is blended from coconuts and flowers). For those lucky enough to enjoy the Taha'a experience, it's pure South Sea magic.

Bora Bora Lagoon Resort & Spa

WHERE:
Bora Bora, Leeward Group, Society Islands
COST:
Reasonable to expensive (per person, per night)
BEST TIME OF YEAR:
Go any time. (It's always hot but it's driest in May and June for those who don't like warm rain.)
DON'T MISS:
The tropical fish show, as viewed through the glass-topped coffee table in each bungalow (it has a sliding top so you can tempt reluctant stars with a free lunch); a romantic sunset cruise on the lagoon; a boat trip from the resort that allows you to explore Bora Bora's main village of Vaitape

Close to Taha'a Island is one of French Polynesia's most iconic destinations, beloved of honeymooners and famous international centre of stunning aqua-centric resorts. The five-star Bora Bora Lagoon Resort & Spa is one of the island's most luxurious, occupying a *motu* (islet) in the lagoon. In common with most of the island's resorts, the accommodation mostly consists of over-water bungalows on stilts, neatly thatched with pandanus leaves and connected by walkways, set against the dramatic background of the island's green-clad twin volcanic peaks, Mounts Pahia and Otemanu. The interiors have polished wooden floors, beamed ceilings, electric ceiling fans, satellite TVs, bathrooms with separate showers and an outside *lanai* (roofed verandah) with loungers and a post-dip freshwater shower.

But landlubbers can enjoy suites and villas ashore, also built in traditional style and equipped with all mod cons, with the ability to jump straight into the lagoon replaced by plunge pools set in private sun decks.

A major selling point is the peace and tranquillity of this private island resort, reached by launch from the airport (a former American World War II base) or main island. There are no roads, no other occupants, lush tropical vegetation (including those mandatory coconut palms), pristine beaches all round and fabulous coral reefs beyond. There's a swimming pool, tennis courts, fitness room, the Otemanu fine-dining restaurant, Café Fair for casual light meals, bars . . . and the South Pacific's only treetop spa, high in the branches of two ancient banyan trees. Using only local plant and flower ingredients, the signature Maru Spa products and treatments make this an essential part of the resort experience. Canny couples would do well to claim they're just married in order to enjoy the Honeymoon Bliss session for newly-weds only. Enjoy!

THINGS TO DO:
Try doing absolutely nothing, Those who find that totally committed relaxation starts to pall can enjoy the usual diversions – fishing, snorkelling, scuba diving, outrigger canoeing, kayaking, parasailing, windsurfing, jet-skiing (they're tough challenges, but someone has to take them on). Bolder souls might care to try the shark-feeding trip (as observers only, naturally).

YOU SHOULD KNOW:
The local languages are Tahitian and French, but English is widely spoken in this tourist-savvy island. The resort has a dedicated desk that will arrange just about any feasible activity.

WHERE:
Yasawa Island, Republic of Fiji
COST:
It's expensive to astronomical (but almost everything is included and there are deals to be had, including special family packages).
BEST TIME OF YEAR:
The warmest season is from November to April and the cooler season from May to October (but 'cooler' is a relative term, as the climate is very pleasant all year round).
DON'T MISS:
Seeing giant manta rays (between May and October); having a lavish picnic on one of the island's eleven deserted beaches
THINGS TO DO:
Various diving courses and guided dives (extra charge, but equipment included); snorkelling; hand-line fishing, kayaking, catamaran sailing, windsurfing, big-game fishing (blue marlin from April to December, sailfish from July to September, yellow-fin tuna from December to May); a visit to the Blue Lagoon Caves beneath the dramatic volcanic peak at the southern end of Yasawa Island, linked to the sea by underwater passages
YOU SHOULD KNOW:
Children aged two and under go free, but older kids attract a supplement. Many married couples are tempted to renew their vows in this idyllic spot, serenaded by a choir of local singers, but it only comes free to those who stay six nights or more.

Yasawa Island Resort & Spa

The tropical islands of Fiji (over 300 of them) are volcanic, with tall peaks and heavy forest cover. Tourism is an important plank of Fiji's economy and has led to considerable development. For those seeking to get away from the main tourist centres, the Yasawa Island Resort & Spa is ideal. This dream destination is located on one of the most remote and unspoilt of Fiji's islands, with just 18 luxurious holiday cottages hidden among palm trees, just yards from a pristine beach. Each *bure* (it means 'sanctuary' in Fijian) is thatched in local style, but contains every modern facility, plus private sun deck, outdoor shower for returning swimmers, beach hut –and super-tempting hammocks in perfect working order!

The resort has a main complex featuring an *al fresco* restaurant with beach and ocean views, and a private dining room for intimate occasions, plus Manasa's Bar beside the pool with cocktails and complimentary wifi for those who must stay in touch. The Baravi Spa faces a sweep of white sand and has an ocean-view massage deck. The spa's signature massage, the Baravi Rhythm, is performed by two therapists, working to the sound of waves. Active guests can play tennis or join the beach volleyball game.

Part of the Yasawa experience is about the place, using the island's hiking trails to explore the bays and headlands of this small but scenic isle. There are traditional villages such as Bukama nearby, where the chief will give permission for guests to visit and be welcomed with a song (the Fijians are great singers) by local children. The resort often stages a *lovo* (feast) or *meke* (local dance ceremony), while village choirs frequently visit to perform. It's this authenticity that makes the Yasawa Island Resort & Spa so special.

Turtle Island

Ever fancied making like a star in one of those tropical paradise movies (and doing your bit for ecotourism at the same time)? That's the double whammy offered by the super-exclusive Turtle Island resort. This is the place to find the Blue Lagoon that appeared in the 1980 film of the same name, featuring young lovers Brooke Shields and Christopher Atkins. As for ecotourism, Turtle Island was once an uninhabited 200-ha (500-ac) islet called Nanuya Levu where feral goats had stripped most of the natural vegetation. It was purchased by an American in the 1970s, who cleared the goats, preserved mangrove and coconut groves and subsequently planted half a million trees. He renamed his new home Turtle Island and the rest is, as they say, history.

Today's visitors enjoy one of the South Pacific's most exclusive resorts, a vision of lush greenery, pristine beaches and intense blue waters. Just 14 couples at a time occupy spacious *bures* built by native craftsmen using authentic materials. This is sustainable tourism at its best, providing employment for many Fijians (the Turtle Island Family) with revenues devoted to worthwhile causes such as educating children from surrounding villages at the island's school, operating a clinic and running release programmes for endangered turtles.

So what's to know? The setting around that famous Blue Lagoon is magical. Service is incomparable. Luxurious accommodation is sensational (each *bure* has sleeping and dressing areas, bar, double shower, bath, outdoor shower, verandah . . . and private beach). The food is wonderful and every night there is a dinner party at one of several amazing locations around the island, featuring exquisite cuisine and fine wines. The resort's friendly staff are dedicated to creating the ultimate romantic getaway. And anyone lucky enough to stay on Turtle Island will know just how well they succeed in living up to the resort's proud 'Once Discovered, Never Forgotten' claim.

WHERE:
Turtle Island, Yasawa Islands, Republic of Fiji
COST:
Something this special doesn't come cheap so, yes, if you have to ask the price you most certainly can't afford it.
BEST TIME OF YEAR:
This is a year-round destination.
DON'T MISS:
Lomi-lomi massages and the other sensuous spa treatments; a dawn horseback ride on your private beach
THINGS TO DO:
Togetherness (this is no place for loners); big-game fishing; world-class diving; snorkelling; practically anything practicable that takes your fancy, which helpful staff will always be happy to arrange
YOU SHOULD KNOW:
Although the resort is primarily for couples, there are special periods set aside to welcome families, often extended families, when every little one has a nanny and older children are given a wonderful time by local buddies. Romantic honeymoons and grand Fijian-style beach weddings are a speciality of the island (and what weddings they are!). You arrive by seaplane, so luggage should be kept to a minimum (dress is informal and there is a daily laundry service).

WHERE:
Likuliku Bay, Malolo Island, Mamanuca Archipelago
COST:
Astronomical is almost an understatement.
BEST TIME OF YEAR:
If you like it hot, hit the summer months (December to March).
DON'T MISS:
A guided tour of the ancient sites of Likuliku, including the old village of Yaro and Potters Cave, Vatu Tagi weeping rock, Vatu Tabu sacred wishing rock and Yadra Vula – a significant site of early Fijian habitation; the fizzing Jacuzzi areas in the main pool
THINGS TO DO:
Relax and enjoy the resort's sensual pleasures; explore the island's bush trails and pristine shore; snorkelling (in the lagoon, or be taken by boat to special places); scuba diving in one of the world's very best dive destinations (start the online dive course in advance and get a flyer if you're beginners); big-game fishing in season; windsurfing; visit the local village to experience the traditional Fijian way of life
YOU SHOULD KNOW:
Be careful when ordering lunch (only kidding!) – but in 1840 two members of the United States Exploring Expedition were killed by natives as they attempted to negotiate for food on Malolo. In an early retaliatory triumph for US foreign policy, two villages and their crops were destroyed. That said, worry you not – *likuliku* means 'calm waters' in Fijian.

Likuliku Lagoon Resort

Yes, yet another South Sea holiday destination with 'lagoon' and 'resort' in the title – hardly a surprise, because that's what this part of the world does so well. The Likuliku Lagoon Resort (named in a list of the World's Top 20 Greatest Escapes) only takes couples, ideally those bent on romance. Set around (and in) a delightful horseshoe bay on Malolo Island, it's Fiji's only resort with overwater *bure* accommodation on stilts, complemented by on-shore options. The whole resort is constructed in traditional materials and the main building looks like an ancient Fijian canoe house, but getting there is thoroughly 21st century (by fast catamaran, private speedboat, seaplane or helicopter).

Each of ten overwater *bures* has a guest room, bathing pavilion and large deck with ladder down to the water. Close to the beach, a combination of 18 garden and beach-front *bures* awaits. These have a private courtyard, outdoor shower, spacious deck, daybed retreat and personal plunge pool. All *bures* feature beautiful interiors and have air conditioning, phone, complimentary wifi, TV/ DVD player, music systems and king-size bed. The Fijiana Restaurant has wonderful views over the lagoon, gardens and an infinity pool, offering an intimate dining experience for visiting couples to savour.

After all that, the Tatadra Spa needs to be impressive, and is. The clue is in the name, which means 'House of Dreams', and this tranquil enclave nestles among the foliage with great lagoon views and is cooled by sea breezes. The natural beauty and body treatments are many and varied, but all are in tune with the unique surroundings. It all adds up to a very special romantic break in stunning surroundings, to be remembered for a lifetime.

Wakaya Club & Spa

The creator of the Wakaya Club & Spa has a pearl of wisdom that encapsulates the philosophy behind this island resort: The more the world changes, the more we gravitate to places that don't. Wakaya Island is indeed one such, located in the Koro Sea to the east of Fiji's main island, Viti Levu. It extends to 900 ha (2,200 ac), has an unspoilt ecosystem and is surrounded by a coral reef that encloses those signature South Pacific turquoise lagoons, along with awesome cliffs and pristine white-sand beaches. Expect to arrive in style thanks to Air Wakaya's one aircraft, the resort's own Grand Cessna Caravan.

Well-heeled visitors are spoilt for choice when it comes to exclusive island resorts in Fiji, but choosing this one won't induce a moment's regret – quite the opposite! Canadian mega-entrepreneur David Gilmour discovered Wakaya in the 1970s and liked the place so much that he bought it, later deciding to share his private island paradise with a few guests. The resulting Wakaya Club & Spa is a sustainable development that contributes mightily to the local economy – an ecologically sound venture that marries the warmth and genuine hospitality of the Fijian people with a stunning environment that virtually guarantees spiritual renewal.

The accommodation consists of just ten ocean-view *bures*, each a luxurious hideaway close to the water with every comfort (but mercifully no television). Expect exceptional Pacific Rim fare, including produce from the island's organic gardens and locally reared meat. Seafood comes from the Koro Sea – lobster, shrimp, mangrove crab and fish such as tuna. The heightened sense of well-being engendered by a stay at this hideaway retreat is reinforced by the Breeze Spa for couples, offering sensational massages and natural treatments. Let's give David Gilmour the last word on his inspired creation: 'Where those who have it all go to get away from it all'.

WHERE:
Wakaya Island, Lomaiviti Group, Republic of Fiji
COST:
It's astronomical (but it's all-inclusive and there are deals).
BEST TIME OF YEAR:
Any time
DON'T MISS:
The especially healthy (but tempting) spa menu; a beach picnic; the Sunday service at Wakaya village church (and can those Fijians sing!); the native dance pageant; cookery demonstration and coconut-oil pressing
THINGS TO DO:
Nature walks; birdwatching; games (golf, tennis or croquet with tuition available for beginners, boules, billiards, beach volleyball); a workout in the fitness *bure*; scuba diving and snorkelling; sea kayaking; paddle boarding; fishing
YOU SHOULD KNOW:
There is no minimum length of stay but at least four days is highly recommended in order to fully appreciate everything that's on offer, and really experience the energizing 'Wakaya effect'.

Princeville at Hanalei

WHERE:
Kuhio Highway, Princeville, Hanalei, Kauai
COST:
It's expensive (but be sure to look for a deal).
BEST TIME OF YEAR:
The climate is uniformly hot all year round, but there's a lot of rain on the island (November to March are the wettest months).
DON'T MISS:
A gastro-tour of the many eateries in the resort, from fine-dining restaurants to outdoor grills (Thursday's Malani Dinner Show encompasses a splendid buffet and lively Hawaiian-style song and dance show); a waffle cone of the locally made Lappert's Ice Cream (the Kaui Pie is very special)
THINGS TO DO:
An outing to nearby Waimea Canyon, one of the world's most spectacular, known as The Grand Canyon of the Pacific; a round (or two) on one of the resort's two championship golf courses; shopping (at the huge selection of trendy stores, for everything from shell jewellery to handmade soaps and lotions)
YOU SHOULD KNOW:
You won't be lonely – well over a million visitors flock to Kauai each year (mostly Americans) and tourism is the island's most important industry by far.

Known as The Garden Isle (you'll understand why as soon as you arrive), Kauai is the fourth-largest Hawaiian island and is indeed a lush tropical paradise with fertile land that will grow just about anything. Up on the north coast is Princeville at Hanalei, a luxurious resort that sits serenely amid greenery against the dramatic backdrop of dark volcanic peaks. This is the American Holiday Dream made real. Princeville has a perfect setting overlooking picturesque Hanalei Bay, atop towering sea cliffs that make up this spectacular coastline. And despite its development as a premier resort, great care has been taken to preserve the tranquillity and beauty of this former cattle ranch and sugar plantation (named way back in 1860 in honour of Hawaii's Crown Prince Albert).

In addition to holiday homes (some of which are available for rent) there are two luxury hotels on site, cannily sited overlooking one of the world's most beautiful bays to take advantage of sea views that have to be seen to be believed. Visitors can choose between the St Regis Princeville and the Westin Princeville. The St Regis offers spacious rooms, some with terraces, plus popular junior suites. The Westin Princeville has self-catering one- and two-bedroom villas, the latter ideal for families. In both cases the in-room and general facilities are first class (and each has a splendid spa).

The resort as a whole offers numerous leisure possibilities for young and old alike, but the thing that absolutely guarantees a fabulous family holiday to thrill the kids is the Princeville Ranch. This working cattle ranch overlooks the Pacific Ocean, with great mountain views, lush valleys, waterfalls, streams and forested areas, all adding up to a wonderful natural playground, with activities ranging from ziplining to jungle adventures.

Hana Lani Treehouses

Where better to conclude this travel adventure in words and pictures than Hawaii – one of the world's top holiday destinations? But let the journey end with a visit to a place that captures the true spirit of responsible modern tourism. The Hawaiian islands have countless hotels and resorts, offering wonderful locations and a memorable experience for those who like their holidays wrapped in luxury. But increasing numbers of people are seeking another way, looking for and finding holidays conducted along eco-friendly lines. These travellers take satisfaction from knowing that their simple, sustainable choice is not only personally rewarding, but also kind to the suffering planet.

One such place is Hana Lani Treehouses on Maui. Hana Lani Farms occupy just 8 ha (20 ac) of this tropical island with its diverse landscapes and contrasting microclimates. It is a conscious experiment in sustainable rural economics as the flower farm, organic vegetable garden, glasshouses for herbs and orchids, plus commercial bamboo plantation, are supported by (and complementary to) ecotourism.

The bed-and-breakfast house, which is surrounded by verdant foliage, can accommodate couples, families or groups. It sleeps eight, has electricity and a fully fitted kitchen. It's reached by 4x4 vehicle or a brisk five-minute uphill walk. But the really special accommodation is the pair of delightfully rustic treehouses in real jungle. Treetops sleeps two (three at a pinch), has sea views from the elevated master bedroom and a ground-level kitchen/dining area. The secluded Tree Pavilion sleeps five and also has a sensational sea view, along with a kitchen/dining area. This is indeed simple (but not primitive) living. There's no electricity, but kitchens have propane cookers and each treehouse has a toilet and shower. The setting is truly fabulous, and this is as good as ecotourism gets. Is it the way of the future? Anyone who stays at Hana Lani Treehouses must surely think so. Aloha!

WHERE:
Near Hana, Maui
COST:
Reasonable (per person, per night)
BEST TIME OF YEAR:
The climate is warm all year round (but expect rain at any time, albeit often no more than a short shower).
DON'T MISS:
Hana's stunning red-sand beach, protected from surging surf by shark-tooth rocks
THINGS TO DO:
Experience the authentic rural-living adventure – open-air showers, cooking in the fire pit, exploring the farm and checking out the sleepy village of Hana; take 4x4 excursions to the island attractions, including the three nearby forest reserves – Koolau, Hana and Kahikinui.
YOU SHOULD KNOW:
Hana is a remote village on Maui's undeveloped east coast and the journey from the airport takes two hours. Bring your own food. If you like the Hana Lani experience and fancy repeating it elsewhere, the sustainable approach based on the Hawaiian model has been exported to China, where treehouses at the larger Sanya Nanshan Treehouse Resort and Beach Club overlook the South China Sea in a wonderfully unspoilt natural setting.

INDEX – Places by name

INDEX – Regions and countries

The publisher would like to thank all the venues that kindly supplied photographs for use in this book. All photographs supplied courtesy of the venues, except for the following:

Alamy/Adam Alexander 448; /Adam Eastland 354; / AfriPics.com 176; /Aivar Mikko 460; /AlamyCelebrity 22, 253; /Andreas von Einsiedel 334; /Andrej Crcek 6 centre below, 398; /Andrew Doggett 190-191, 238; /Andrew Lloyd 202; /Arctic Images/Ragnar Th Sigurdsson 274; /Ariadne Van Zandbergen 180; / AsiaTravelCollection 5 centre below, 489 below; / BL Images Ltd. 218; /blickwinkel/McPHOTO/ZAD 156; /Caroline Sylger Jones 155, 443; /Chris Howes/ Wild Places Photography 280; /Christine Osborne Pictures 150; /Christopher Nicholson 206; /Clive Tully 230; /Colau 379; /Colin Leslie 237; /Collectiva 299; /CuboImages slr/Caterina Bruzzone 349; / CuboImages slr/Michele Bella 399; /Dan Leeth 59; / Danita Delimont/Lisa S. Engelbrecht 400; /Dave G. Houser 523; /David Martyn Hughes 217; /David Noton Photography 81; /David Pearson 427 above; / David Wall 513; /David Zaitz 71; /dbimages/Jeremy Graham 26; /Design Pics Inc. - RM Content/Keith Levit/ Destinations 475; /Design Pics Inc. - RM Content/ / Directphoto.org 303; /Directphoto.org 304; /Don Brownlow 226; /Don Smetzer 48; /doughoughton 240; /Douglas Lander 342; /Douglas Peebles Photography 502 right, 534, 536; /Ei Katsumata 428 right, 480; / Etcheverry Images 107; /Eye Ubiquitous/Stephen Rafferty 247; /F1online digitale Bildagentur GmbH/ URF 424; /Frank De Luyck 273; /Friedrich von Hörsten 470; /Gareth Byrne 252; /Gary Corbett 28; /GFC Collection 181; /Gianni Muratore 7 below, 528-529; / Glyn Genin 250; /greenwales 234; /Greg Vaughn 502 centre, 525; /Hemis/Alain Felix 309; /Hemis/Bertrand Rieger 232, 246; /Hemis/Domenico Tondini 144; / Hemis/Francis Cormon 310; /Hemis/Franco Barbagallo 133; /Hemis/John Frumm 151, 485; /Hemis/Ludovic Maisant 271, 277, 355; /Hemis/Marc Dozier 164; / Hemis/Peter Bruce 288; /Hercules Milas 412; /Horizon International Images Limited 70; /Howard Davies 258; / Ian Trower 474; /ilpo musto 194; /imagebroker/Martin Moxter 290; /imagebroker/Martin Siepmann 295; / ImagesEurope 331; /IML Image Group Ltd. 7 centre, 80; /Ingolf Pompe17 456; /Ingolf Pompe62 203; / INTERFOTO 123; /J Marshall - Tribaleye Images 481 above; /Jack Sullivan 207; /Jason O. Watson 69; /John Baran 382; /John Warburton-Lee Photography/Allan White 493; /John Warburton-Lee Photography/Calum Stirling 88; /John Warburton-Lee Photography/Nick Laing 407; /Johner Images/Eddie Granlund 263; /Jon Arnold Images Ltd./Walter Bibikow 46, 187; /JTB Photo Communications, Inc. 483; /Julio Etchart 128; /June Hoyle 231; /LatitudeStock/Dennis Stone 375; /Laurie Strachan 471; /Les Gibbon 242; /Liam White 356; / LOOK Die Bildagentur der Fotografen GmbH/Don Fuchs 503 right, 511; /LOOK Die Bildagentur der Fotografen GmbH/Elan Fleisher 32; /LOOK Die Bildagentur der Fotografen GmbH/Franz Marc Frei 138 left, 161; /LOOK Die Bildagentur der Fotografen GmbH/Ingolf Pompe 300; /LOOK Die Bildagentur der Fotografen GmbH/ Walter Schiesswohl 291; /Manor Photography/Robert Slade 235; /Marcos Veiga 365; /MARKA/Raffaele Meucci 160; /mediasculp 278; /Melvyn Longhurst 120; /Mike Kipling Photography 224; /nagelestock. com 243; /Nature Picture Library/Jose B. Ruiz 377; /Niall Ferguson 392; /Nicholas Bird 396; /Oleksiy Maksymenko Photography 14; /Palle Porila 270; / Panorama Media (Beijing) Ltd. 496; /Patrick Batchelder 406; /Paul Bernhardt 229; /Peter Fields 2-3 centre, 472; /Peter Schickert 380; /Petr Svarc 338; /Phil Seale 239; /philipus 426-427 below; /Planetpix 42; /Prisma Bildagentur AG/Christian Heeb 84; /Prisma Bildagentur AG/Frank Chmura 403; / Prisma Bildagentur AG/Jürgen Held 289; /Renato Granieri 264, 362; /Richard Broadwell 72; /Rob Crandall 101; /Robert Fried 95, 489 above; /Robert Harding Picture Library Ltd./Christian Kober 486, 486 below; /Robert Harding Picture Library Ltd./Gavin Hellier 5 centre above, 425; /Robert Machin 82; / Robert Morris 222; /Ron Niebrugge 538; /Russell Kord 76; /SAGAPHOTO.COM/Patrick Forget 317; /Skyscan Photolibrary 233; /Stan Kujawa 214; /Stock Connection Blue/Dallas and John Heaton 468; /Superstock/George Oze 73; /Susan Pease 25; /TidalStock/Ryan Cardone 7 above; /Tips Images/Tips Italia Srl a socio unico/ Andrea Pistolesi 429 right, 473; /Tracey Whitefoot 12; / Travel Division Images 518; /travelstock44 393; /vario images/Ulrich Baumgarten 186; /Vittorio Sciosia 352; / Westend61 GmbH/Hagge-Puchta 139 left, 174, 175 above, 175 below; /Wolfgang Kaehler 170, 465.

Atelier Für Sonderaufgaben 298.

Denis Beauvais 21.

Corbis/First Light/Roderick Chen 10; /First Light/Yves Marcoux 11; /Holger Leue 390; /Kenneth Johansson 68; /National Geographic Society/Richard Nowitz 153; / Richard T. Nowitz 5 below, 24.

Catharina Hård 266 above.

Skogens Konung 261.

Bosse Lind 266 below.

Roberto Patti 158-159.

Dave Quinn 20.

Richard Tamblyn 199.